ANTHROPOLOGICAL PAPERS

MUSEUM OF ANTHROPOLOGY, UNIVERSITY OF MICHIGAN
NO. 65

MEADOWOOD PHASE SETTLEMENT PATTERN IN THE NIAGARA FRONTIER REGION OF WESTERN NEW YORK STATE

by
JOSEPH E. GRANGER, JR.

ANN ARBOR, MICHIGAN
1978

DEDICATED
TO THE MEMORY OF
MARIAN E. WHITE

Printed in the
United States of America

TABLE OF CONTENTS

LIST OF FIGURES v
LIST OF PLATES vi
LIST OF MAPS vii
LIST OF TABLES viii
PREFACE xi

I. INTRODUCTION 1
Methods of Analysis 1

II. HISTORICAL REVIEW AND GENERAL DESCRIPTION OF MEADOWOOD PHASE CULTURE 21
The Point Peninsula Focus, Vine Valley Aspect, Woodland Pattern 22
The Early Woodland Period 23
Meadowood Phase of New York State 25
Chronological and Geographical Relationships of Meadowood Phase 33

III. THE NATURAL ENVIRONMENT OF THE STUDY AREA 43
Flora and Fauna 45
Climate: Palynology and Other Evidence 49
Meadowood Sites: Locations and Natural Associations 51

IV. THE SINKING PONDS SITE 71
Introduction 71
Physiography and Geology 72
Excavations 76
Features 93
Artifacts 111
Natural Resources 139
Intrasite Activities and Chronology 144

V. THE RIVERHAVEN COMPLEX 157
Introduction 157
Physiography and Geology 159
Spicer Creek 1, 2 and Riverhaven 4 Sites 165
Riverhaven 2 Site 177
Natural Resources of the Riverhaven Complex 229
Riverhaven Complex: Intrasite Activities 242
Riverhaven Complex: Chronology 253

VI. SINKING PONDS, RIVERHAVEN 2 AND AFFILIATED SITES AS SETTLEMENT TYPES 255
Sinking Ponds and Associated Loci as Settlement Types 255
Riverhaven Complex Sites as Settlement Types 261
Summary of Settlement Types 264

VII. THE SYSTEMICS OF MEADOWOOD PHASE SETTLEMENT PATTERN: INTERPRETATION AND SPECULATION ... 267
The System of Procurement ... 270
The System of Processing ... 274
The System of Manufacture ... 276
The System of Storage ... 280
The Ceremony and Exchange System ... 282
The Habitation System or Settlement Pattern ... 288
Summary ... 294

APPENDIXES ... 299
Appendix A: Artifact Attributes ... 299
Appendix B: Flint Detritus Analysis ... 355
Appendix C: Faunal Relationships ... 361

REFERENCES CITED ... 375

PLATES ... 386

LIST OF FIGURES

1.1 Activity—artifact relationships 12
1.2 Development of Meadowood flint tool types 18
2.1 Relevant radiocarbon dates 34
2.2 Distribution of Some Late Archaic—Early Woodland projectile points 40
3.1 Standard faunal curve of usable meat 69
3.2 Comparison of utilization of fauna for usable meat 69
4.1 Comparison of percentages of excavated square feet, features, feature associated artifacts, and non-feature associated artifacts 80
4.2 Distribution of flint detritus percentages by sampling tracts 82
4.3 Distribution of fire-cracked rock percentages by sampling tracts 83
4.4 Non-feature associated artifacts by 1 tenth levels 91
4.5 Artifacts versus flint detritus in units by levels 92
4.6 Distribution of percentages of artifacts, flint detritus, and fire-cracked rock in features 97
4.7 Plans and profiles of rock heap features at Sinking Ponds 98
4.8 Plans and profiles of other features at Sinking Ponds site 102
4.9 Plans and profiles of composite features at Sinking Ponds site 107
4.10 Diagram of cultural material distribution in Feature 2 108
4.11 Artifact—category relationships 113
4.12 Ceremonial artifacts 119
4.13 Utilized flakes in feature types 125
4.14 Feature relationships at Sinking Ponds site 145
5.1 Feature type distribution at Spicer Creek sites 1 and 2 169
5.2 Feature plans and profiles at Spicer Creek 1, 2 and Riverhaven 4 170
5.3 Spicer Creek artifact—category relationships 176
5.4 Plans and profiles of features at Riverhaven 2 185
5.5 Distribution of feature types at Riverhaven 2 192
5.6 Riverhaven 2 artifact frequency distribution in features of Locus 1 193
5.7 Artifacts by 0.5 foot arbitrary levels 195
5.8 Riverhaven 2 reconstructed profile at 8 North 199
5.9 Riverhaven 2 reconstructed profiles at 4 West and 8 West 200
5.10 Distribution of artifact percentages of N for units, exclusive of features, features, and totals in each locus 203
5.11 Riverhaven 2 distribution of percentages of artifacts in features 206
5.12 Riverhaven 2 artifact—category relationships 209
5.13 Riverhaven 2 faunal sample 232
5.14 Riverhaven 2 comparison of faunal sample, minimum individuals and usable meat 233
5.15 Riverhaven 2 faunal sample compared to standard usable meat curve 237
5.16 Riverhaven 2 feature relationships 245
7.1 Chert inclusion comparison 273
7.2 Comparison of activities at Sinking Ponds, Riverhaven 2 and Spicer Creek 1-2 . 279
7.3 Meadowood settlement pattern in the Niagara Frontier 290
7.4 Distribution and relationships of Meadowood Components as settlement types 292
B.1 Comparison of qualitative attributes of flint detritus 358
B.2 Distributions of ranges of quantitative attributes of the selected sample of flint detritus 359
C.1 Mammals by eating habits, density, and usable meat 365

LIST OF PLATES

1. Sinking Ponds site: overall site view. 386
2. Sinking Ponds site: Feature 2. 386
3. Sinking Ponds site: Meadowood sidenotched projectile points. 387
4. Sinking Ponds site: cornernotched and stemmed projectile points. 387
5. Sinking Ponds site: blanks. 388
6. Sinking Ponds site: drills and longitudinal knife/scrapers. 388
7. Sinking Ponds site: uniface scrapers. 389
8. Sinking Ponds site: biface scrapers. 389
9. Sinking Ponds site: pitted stones, netsinkers, and mano abrading stones. 390
10. Sinking Ponds site: adzes and abrading stones. 390
11. Sinking Ponds site: pipe, bead, birdstone, and gorgets. 391
12. Sinking Ponds site: clay and steatite vessels. 391
13. Riverhaven 2 site: overall view of Kochan's excavations. 392
14. Riverhaven 2 site: Feature 3 profile. 392
15. Riverhaven 2 site: sidenotched projectile points. 393
16. Riverhaven 2 site: sidenotched projectile points (Meadowood variants). 393
17. Riverhaven 2 site: miscellaneous projectile points. 394
18. Riverhaven 2 site: primary blanks. 394
19. Riverhaven 2 site: secondary blanks. 395
20. Riverhaven 2 site: tertiary blanks. 395
21. Riverhaven 2 site: quaternary blanks ("mortuary cache blades"). 396
22. Riverhaven 2 site: longitudinal knife scrapers. 396
23. Riverhaven 2 site: biface side-scrapers. 397
24. Riverhaven 2 site: end scrapers. 397
25. Riverhaven 2 site: circumferential and spokeshave scrapers. 398
26. Riverhaven 2 site: uniface side-scrapers and utilized flake scrapers. 398
27. Riverhaven 2 site: drills. 399
28. Riverhaven 2 site: adzes. 399
29. Riverhaven 2 site: grooved abrading stones. 400
30. Riverhaven 2 site: hammerstones and pitted stones (anvilstones). 400
31. Riverhaven 2 site: netsinkers. 401
32. Riverhaven 2 site: birdstones, pipe, and gorget. 401
33. Riverhaven 2 site: bone and tooth artifacts. 402
34. Riverhaven 2 site: antler and tooth artifacts. 402
35. Riverhaven 2 site: clay pottery. 403

LIST OF MAPS

3.1 Meadowood phase sites in Western New York 43
3.2 Meadowood phase and associated sites in New York State 44
3.3 Early Woodland sites outside New York State 45
3.4 Biotic divisions of the study area 46
3.5 Regional physiographic provinces of New York State 52
3.6 Hunter and Muskalonge Lakes 58
3.7 Waterport South 58
3.8 Scaccia and McCauley complex 58
3.9 Wray 58
3.10 Nahrwold 2 60
3.11 Eaton and Nine Mile Swamp 60
3.12 Vinette, Oberlander 2, and Pickins 60
3.13 Morrow 62
3.14 Winters 62
4.1 Sinking Ponds site and locality 73
4.2 Sinking Ponds site and its original physiographic association 75
4.3 Sinking Ponds sampling tracts 77
4.4 Detail of sampling tracts 3, 4, 5, 6 and 7 85
4.5 Distribution of hearths, rock heaps, storage pits and cache pits at Sinking Ponds 94
5.1 Riverhaven site complex, Grand Island, New York 158
5.2 Kochan excavation at Riverhaven 2 160
5.3 Spicer Creek sites 1 and 2 161
5.4 Original water features on northeast Grand Island 164
5.5 Spicer Creek excavation areas 166
5.6 Riverhaven 2 excavations and profiles 181
5.7 Riverhaven 2 areas investigated 202
6.1 Aerial photograph of Sinking Ponds and vicinity 256
6.2 Sinking Ponds and related sites in the East Aurora area—drainage pattern association 258
6.3 Riverhaven site complex—Grand Island area—drainage pattern association 262
7.1 Niagara Frontier local band areas 271

LIST OF TABLES

1.1 Summary of Meadowood traits as outlined in Ritchie (1969) 5
2.1 Collections of Meadowood cache blades and related materials or features from sites reported but not described in detail 27
2.2 Meadowood sites with in situ remains 28
2.3 Postulated material inventory of Meadowood phase 31
2.4 Compilation of Meadowood burial statistics 32
2.5 Settlement Data on phases associated with Meadowood phase 36
3.1 Distribution of Meadowood phase components 64
3.2 Distribution of Meadowood site associations 66
3.3 Summary faunal comparison at Riverhaven 2, Scaccia, Lamoka Lake, and Kipp Island sites 67
4.1 Sinking Ponds sampling tracts, square feet excavated, features, artifacts, flint detritus and fire-cracked rock 79
4.2 Sinking Ponds artifact fragment distribution by feature, 5-foot squares exclusive of features, and sampling tract 79
4.3 Distribution of flint detritus categories in sampling tracts 81
4.4 Fire-cracked rock distribution by sampling tract 81
4.5 Non-feature associated artifacts by tenths and level 91
4.6 Distribution of non-feature associated flint detritus by level 92
4.7 Distribution of feature types by sampling tract 93
4.8 Distribution of artifact classes in feature types 95
4.9 Distribution of flint detritus by feature type 96
4.10 Feature distribution of artifact types 99
4.11 Cultural material distribution in Feature 2 (possible house) 109
4.12 Distribution of artifact types in functional categories 112
4.13 Distribution of functional categories of artifacts 114
4.14 Distribution of artifacts of procurement 114
4.15 Distribution of artifacts of processing 120
4.16 Distribution of ventral and dorsal wear flaking on utilized flakes 123
4.17 Distribution of artifacts of manufacture 129
4.18 Distribution of blank fragmentation 130
4.19 Distribution of ceremonial and storage artifacts 135
4.20 Material of lithic artifacts compared to local lithic pebble availability at the Sinking Ponds site 140
4.21 Distribution of cultural material related to procurement 147
4.22 Distribution of cultural material related to processing 148
4.23 Distribution of cultural material related to manufacture 150
4.24 Distribution of cultural material related to storage 152
4.25 Distribution of cultural material related to ceremonial activities 153
4.26 Distribution of cultural material related to habitation activities 153
5.1 Spicer Creek 1,2 and Riverhaven 4 square feet investigated, features, artifacts, flint detritus and fire-cracked rock 168
5.2 Features at Spicer Creek 1,2 and Riverhaven 4 171
5.3 Spicer Creek 1,2, flint detritus by feature types 171
5.4 Spicer Creek 1,2 and Riverhaven 4, feature distribution of artifact types . 171
5.5 Distribution of artifact types in functional categories at Spicer Creek 1,2 and Riverhaven 4 175
5.6 Distribution of functional categories of artifacts, Spicer Creek 1,2 and Riverhaven 4 178

5.7	Distribution of artifacts of processing at Spicer Creek 1,2 and Riverhaven 4	178
5.8	Distribution of artifacts of manufacture from Spicer Creek 1,2	179
5.9	Distribution of quaternary blanks and fragments, Spicer Creek 1,2	179
5.10	Riverhaven 2 excavated areas, square feet excavated, features, artifacts, and flint detritus	183
5.11	Riverhaven 2 vertical distribution of artifactual material by those assigned to features and those exclusive of features	194
5.12	Riverhaven 2 natural stratigraphy of the 562 foot contour bench	197
5.13	Flint detritus by area investigated	201
5.14	Feature associations of artifact types, Riverhaven 2	207
5.15	Distribution of artifact types in functional categories, Riverhaven 2	208
5.16	Distribution of artifacts of procurement, Riverhaven 2	210
5.17	Distribution of artifacts of processing, Riverhaven 2	215
5.18	Bifacial scrapers, Riverhaven 2	216
5.19	Distribution of artifacts of manufacture, Riverhaven 2	220
5.20	Distribution of blanks and fragments at Riverhaven 2	224
5.21	Riverhaven 2 compiled faunal analysis	231
5.22	Riverhaven 2 fauna by shoreland or upland association	235
5.23	Summary of lithic materials, Riverhaven 2	238
5.24	Rock material frequencies in features at Riverhaven 2,4 and Spicer Creek 1, 2	240
5.25	Distribution of cultural materials related to manufacture, Spicer Creek 1, 2 and Riverhaven 4	244
5.26	Distribution of cultural materials related to procurement, Riverhaven 2	247
5.27	Distribution of cultural materials related to processing, Riverhaven 2	248
5.28	Distribution of cultural materials related to manufacture, Riverhaven 2	248
5.29	Distribution of cultural materials related to storage, Riverhaven 2	251
7.1	Distribution of cultural materials related to procurement	272
7.2	Distribution of cultural materials related to processing	275
7.3	Distribution of cultural materials related to manufacture	277
7.4	Correlation coefficients for "cache blade" attributes at Meadowood sites	278
7.5	Distribution of cultural materials related to storage	281
7.6	Distribution of quaternary blanks and subsidiary products outside principal area of Meadowood phase occupation	286
A.1*a*	Sidenotched projectile point attributes	300
A.1*b*	Sidenotched projectile points—table of variable attribute frequency	301
A.2*a*	Cornernotched projectile point attributes	307
A.2*b*	Cornernotched projectile points—table of variable attribute frequency	307
A.3*a*	Stemmed projectile point attributes	310
A.3*b*	Stemmed projectile points—table of variable attribute frequency	311
A.4*a*	Quaternary blade attributes	315
A.4*b*	Quaternary blades—table of attributes	316
A.5*a*	Quaternary blade base attributes	325
A.5*b*	Quaternary blade base fragments—table of attributes	325
A.6*a*	Quaternary blade tip attributes	327
A.6*b*	Quaternary blade tip fragments—table of attributes	327
A.7*a*	Tertiary blade attributes	328
A.7*b*	Tertiary blade widths—table of attributes	329
A.8*a*	Tertiary blade base attributes	331

A.8*b* Tertiary blade base fragments 332
A.9*a* Tertiary blade tip attributes 334
A.9*b* Tertiary blade tips—table of attributes 334
A.10*a* Longitudinal knife attributes 335
A.10*b* Longitudinal knives—table of attributes 336
A.11*a* Unifacial scraper attributes 339
A.11*b* Unifacial scrapers—table of variable attribute frequency 339
A.12*a* Bifacial scraper attributes 341
A.12*b* Bifacial scrapers—table of attributes 341
A.13*a* Drill attributes 343
A.13*b* Drills 343
A.14*a* Primary blank attributes 345
A.14*b* Primary blanks 345
A.15*a* Secondary blank attributes 346
A.15*b* Secondary blanks 347
A.16*a* Netsinker attributes 348
A.16*b* Netsinkers—table of attributes 349
A.17*a* Hammer-anvilstone attributes 350
A.17*b* Hammer-anvilstones—table of attributes 350
A.18*a* Abrading stone attributes 351
A.18*b* Abrading stones—table of attributes 352
B.1 Qualitative attributes of the selected sample of flint detritus 357
B.2 Quantitative attributes of the selected sample of flint detritus 360
C.1 Habitat, habits, density, and meat value of Niagara Frontier mammals 363
C.2 Habitat, habits, and food of Niagara Frontier land birds 366
C.3 Habitat, habits, and food of Niagara Frontier aquatic birds 367
C.4 Habitat, habits, food, and capture methods of Niagara Frontier fishes 369
C.5 Habitat, habits, and food of Niagara Frontier turtles and frogs 373

PREFACE

Archaeological manifestations of Meadowood phase have been systematically investigated since 1944 but much of these data have been concerned with burial and mortuary practice. This study presents an analysis of another aspect of Meadowood phase data which is becoming increasingly available. Since 1965 several components of Meadowood affiliation have been discovered and excavated, yielding material principally concerned with habitation, subsistence and tool technology. In this work we have attempted to use a functional interpretation of artifacts, structures, and other cultural remains in order to define the sum of activities on two excavated sites. The author has also sought to suggest the settlement pattern of Meadowood phase by comparing materials from the Niagara Frontier with other excavated and reported Meadowood sites in New York State.

The Sinking Ponds site was excavated by the author as part of a project which sought information about preceramic cultures in Erie County, New York, a major segment of the Niagara Frontier region. This investigation was accomplished as a research project directed by Dr. Marian E. White. The Riverhaven 2 site was excavated by Mr. Edward Kochan, a dedicated and highly skilled nonprofessional archaeologist, as part of his extensive survey of Grand Island, New York for in situ archaeological materials. Unfortunately, he was transferred to another area of the country before his researches were completed but he made available his collections, notes, and other materials to the Department of Anthropology of the State University of New York at Buffalo.

With the wealth of material produced by the three seasons of work at Sinking Ponds and the large collection from Riverhaven 2, it was decided that a study of Meadowood phase in the Niagara Frontier be accomplished. Mr. David W. Taggart and the author were working on lithic technology and its relation to functional tool groupings at sites of the Late Archaic and Early Woodland periods in Michigan and New York. Several short-term explorations of the Riverhaven area provided more data on lithic technology and settlement. Although it was thought initially that artifact variability in the Meadowood phase suggested regional diversity of settlement and subsistence patterns, it was found that settlement and subsistence variability were probably seasonal and that instead of variability between groups there was consistency among all groups occupying the region close to the lower Great Lakes during this period. Thus, any variability observed seemed to be due to seasonal activity.

Within the last five years much additional evidence about the artifactual and structural aspects of Meadowood phase culture has been gathered through the emergency salvage work at Grand Island. Due to the efforts of the River Oaks Corporation, Ms. Karen Noonan, Mr. Gordon Schmahl, Mr. James C. Donahue and others, to use the most scientific methods possible under these circumstances, the data gathered are reliable. Dr. William Englebrecht and the author conducted additional excavations at Riverhaven 2.

This work represents a revised version of the author's dissertation and it is hoped that with the addition of major new work by Dr. William A. Ritchie and Dr. Robert E. Funk that many otherwise speculative propositions are now more securely identified and set upon the road to explanation. The study of the faunal material from all Riverhaven 2 excavations has been undertaken by Dr. Donald Grayson. His approach has been innovative and has produced theoretical as well as descriptive results. This study has consequently benefited.

A word must be added about measurement. The excavations at the sites mentioned herein were done in some cases by the engineer's scale using tenths and hundredths of feet and in other cases, the English measurement system. Measurements in the text have been converted to metric scale, but we have left the map, table, and figure measurements largely in English scale. This inconvenience to the reader is regretted.

The list of those to whom the author owes a debt of gratitude for their cooperation and interest is long, but a few must be singled out for special thanks. Mr. Gordon Schmahl was responsible for helping a neophyte archaeologist conduct his first project in Erie County, and the leaders and people of the Village of East Aurora made the experience at Sinking Ponds a pleasant and productive one. Mr. Andrew Kuster, now deceased, spent several sessions describing his collection and his knowledge of the locations of sites in the vicinity of East Aurora. David A. Taggart patiently allowed the author to test hypotheses on his knowledge of Late Archaic materials and responded with helpful advice and criticism. He also showed an interest in demonstrating how to accomplish a definition of settlement pattern without houses in the field by assisting the writer in a reexamination of Riverhaven 2 and in the laboratory by his teaching and discussion of techniques.

The authorship of this study must be credited to those who have with more than a great deal of patience listened to and argued with the author about Meadowood phase ad nauseum. This was half the process of the writing.

Dr. Orrin Shane patiently gave of his time to read and comment on a draft of this work. His association with this project goes back to his analysis of soil samples from Sinking Ponds in 1966. His interest and effort has been greatly appreciated.

Several students who worked on this project as assistants to the writer should be singled out for their yeoman efforts at compiling statistics, recording, and preparing countless computer turnarounds. To Nancy Reeves, Anne Tobbe Bader and Terry Weis, a great debt of gratitude is owed. The photographic work herein was accomplished by Jeffrey Tallent, another student who patiently reworked the plates until they were as close to our specifications as possible.

Finally I would like to express my deep appreciation to Dr. Marian E. White. It was she who gave me my field and laboratory technique and my interest in New York State archaeology. More than that, her interest and support enabled me to complete this work. Without her sustained encouragement and advice, not all of it taken, it might still be unwritten.

Subsequent to the submission of this manuscript for publication and prior to the last editorial revision Marian E. White passed away. She, therefore will not be able to review the completed work. Because of her great contribution in time and effort and as a memorial to a friend and colleague whose interest was a sustaining force, I am dedicating this work to her.

CHAPTER 1

INTRODUCTION

This study will examine the Meadowood phase of the Early Woodland period in New York State. Meadowood phase will be defined and described and the Early Woodland adaptive milieu explored. We will deal with several sites of Meadowood phase in the western New York State's Niagara Frontier region in order to determine settlement pattern, settlement system and settlement type. Furthermore, the activity variation within two Meadowood phase sites, Sinking Ponds and Riverhaven 2 will be analyzed. Detailed in situ comparisons of habitation residues on the Sinking Ponds and Riverhaven 2 sites should allow the recognition of a series of activities which may shed some light upon Meadowood phase adaptive articulations with the environment. With respect to these sites the following three hypotheses will be examined. First, the Sinking Ponds site and Riverhaven 2 site represent contemporary sites but different settlement types as indicated by activities carried out on each, and these activities can be isolated within the excavated assemblages. Second, these sites show seasonal variation in exploitation pattern and were occupied at different times of the year by segments of a regional group. And third, the seasonal settlement pattern was that of a group which occupied a base camp during late autumn, winter and early spring and which fissioned into smaller groups to perform extractive activities at separate locations during late spring, summer, and early fall, a pattern which differs little from the Late Archaic seasonal round in the Lake Forest area.

METHODS OF ANALYSIS

Definitions

Settlement Pattern, Settlement System and Settlement Types

We shall assume in this study that the term *settlement pattern* refers to the geographic distribution of contemporary sites of a particular culture within a designated area and the way the physiography, biomass and other cultures of that area condition that arrangement. These sites are connected by a series of functional interrelationships which are the network of that culture's adaptation to its surroundings. This is hereafter referred to as the *settlement system* (Winters 1969:110). Struever suggests:

> To reconstruct a settlement system, it is necessary to work within a regional universe. The problem is to identify the variability in functional types of artifacts, features, and food remains, and, thereby, define one or more *settlement types,* which, together, comprise the total settlement system. In sum, exploitative maintenance activities are differentially distributed within the geographic area encompassed by a culture, and, therefore, no site can be expected to reflect more than a fraction of these activities. [Italics mine.] (1971:11)

Settlement types are classifications of sites which show an aggregate of activities which vary from site to site and they are determined by the presence, absence, quantity and quality of the activities represented on contemporary sites. The distribution of this aggregate of activities and the reasons for such an arrangement defines the adaptive system represented by settlement types.

> Sites in which a particular configuration of exploitive and maintenance activities were carried out will disclose a similar structure of material elements; all such sites are representative of a single settlement type. If focus shifts to a regional universe the structure of an extinct settlement should be reflected in the kind, number and distribution of settlement types.
>
> An underlying assumption here is that the biophysical environment is itself structure and that as an adaptive system, a culture articulates with this environment through a highly complex set of patterned relationships.
>
> Aspects of biophysical environment include topography, water sources, animal life, vegetation etc. (which define the *total adaptive milieu*). Each may be expected to have a highly variable distribution within the total geographic area encompassed by a single settlement system. (Struever 1968:136)

Activity Areas

The inventory of material culture produced and derived from each type of limited activity site should be structured in terms of the adaptive part of the system it represents and when correlated provide information on the "total adaptive milieu" (Struever 1968:136). Further:

> Within a site, such structure (of material culture) might manifest itself in the definition of *activity areas*. Each will have a formal definition based on correlations of material cultural elements. One type of activity area might be defined in terms of one or more *tool kits,* or *activity sets,* themselves defined on the basis of the spatial clustering of certain artifact types, kinds of life maintenance by-products, and structural feature types. [Parentheses and Italics mine.] (Struever 1968:135)

Only as various representatives of settlement types are excavated systematically can the settlement system be understood. Thus such variables as site size, intensity, stability and season of occupation may be used to understand those factors which condition the presence or absence of certain activities on a site. Sampling error is possible, but given a reasonable amount of site survey from a region such as the Niagara Frontier certain patterns of association of coeval but variable sites should emerge. When two or more sites have been excavated, they can be compared to see whether they are representatives of the same or different settlement types. This is attempted below.

Procedure

Defining settlement pattern for Meadowood phase is of paramount importance before specific statements concerning its articulations with other entities in time or space are attempted. Systematically analyzing the sites Riverhaven 2 and Sinking Ponds and identifying their roles as representatives of different settlement types in a settlement system, as outlined above, are the focus of this study. Once the system of settlement is delineated, comparisons with other sites can later be made and further hypotheses advanced for the role of mortuary ceremonialism and its operation in the whole cultural system. A site defined as a "ceremonial site" (Ritchie 1956, 1969; Ritchie and Funk 1973:346) also presents a number of articulations with the total adaptive milieu. As the hypotheses presented above for explanation of Meadowood habitation and adaptive processes are tested, a basis for later statements concerning the religious or ideological system of Meadowood culture will be established.

Types of Evidence

Preservation of evidence is a problem which must be confronted when attempting to define activities within archaeological sites. In Michigan, D. W. Taggart was faced with interpreting two Late Archaic sites, Feheeley and Schmidt; where no definite structural residence evidence, i.e., houses or house patterns were disclosed, he found that the kinds of information relating to site structure "including density of occupation, site size, kinds of pit structures, food remains and functional classes of artifacts analyzed quantitatively," disclosed both activity patterns and two different settlement types (Taggart 1967:153, 167). We have categorized available preserved cultural materials into three types: structural, nonartifactual, and artifactual. These broad categories will be referred to in combination as organizing the evidence which defines activity and its form. Table 1.1 shows all the information summarized by William A. Ritchie (1969:180-201) for Meadowood phase arranged in the above categories of evidence. We have added a column for any inferences which are associated with his divisions based upon function. Presentation in this tabular form of the recovered evidence applicable to Meadowood phase has helped to organize the cultural inventory for delineation of specific activities.

Structural Evidence. This form of evidence consists of features, or combinations of features, such as a house which might be demonstrated to be a combination or *composite* feature by the association of post molds, pits and hearths. Types of features recognized in this study are rock heaps, hearths, storage or refuse pits, pits containing raw materials or products of manufacture in caches, post molds and composite features.

Nonartifactual Evidence. Preservation of certain forms of nonartifactual evidence is often quite poor. While fire-cracked rock and flint detritus are well preserved in the Sinking Ponds and Riverhaven 2 sites, organic remains are less well represented. At Sinking Ponds no organic remains were preserved in the highly acid soil, while at Riverhaven 2 there was excellent preservation of faunal remains. Although floral remains were recovered at Riverhaven 2 by flotation they were not charred and context was suspect (David Starbuck 1971: personal communication).

Artifactual Evidence. A first step in the analysis of Early Woodland settlement pattern in the Niagara Frontier is the definition of artifact categories which reflect activities within the site. In addition, analysis of categories of tool function is necessary to the definition of activity areas.

Winters, in his studies of the Late Archaic Riverton Culture of Illinois, has created functional classes of artifacts. He makes a distinction between the individual artifact and the functional artifact class which may show utilization consistent with context (1969:30-31). Frequent observations of associated artifacts may be one basis for defining functional classes, albeit with a degree of subjective decision making. In all such decisions we recognize two attribute levels that Winters has suggested: (1) *Primary Attributes:* techniques of manufacture, morphology and use. (2) *Secondary Attributes:* provenience and associations.

Adequate description is essential for comparative purposes and basic to any report. This is presented here (see Appendix A), but, as

TABLE 1.1
SUMMARY OF MEADOWOOD TRAITS AS OUTLINED IN RITCHIE (1969)

Artifactual	Nonartifactual	Structural	Inference
		Geography	
		Near water — rivers or lakes	Hardwood forests
		Burials on knolls	Cool and moist climate
		Lived on level areas	
		Close to flint quarry	
		Distribution — north, central and western New York	
		Subsistence	
Fishnets	Flora	Baking pits	Bolas
	Chenopodium seeds		
Baskets	Hickory nuts	Storage pits — basin-shaped	Hunting
	Acorns		
Net sinkers	Grape seeds	Refuse deposits	Gathering
	Virburnum seeds		
Projectile points	Beechnuts	Hearths	Fishing
	Charcoal		
Flint — sidenotched			
	Fauna		
Bone projectile points	Dogs		
Barbed	Fish and animal bones		
Unbarbed	Whitetail deer		
	Gray squirrel		

TABLE 1.1 (Continued)

Artifactual	Nonartifactual	Structural	Inference
Subsistence (Continued)			
Antler club spike	Woodchuck		
	Muskrat		
Flat bone dagger	Beaver		
	Porcupine		
Steatite vessels	Rabbit		
	Raccoon		
Fire making kits	Black bear		
	Turkey		
Muller	Blue or Snow goose		
	Duck		
Grinding stone	Turtle		
	Bullfrog		
Choppers	Catfish		
	Sucker		
Birdstones	Perch		
	Sunfish		
Barbed bone harpoon			
	Other		
	Fire-cracked rock		
Technology			
Adzes	Paintstone		Workshops
plano convex			
copper			Skin working
ground stone			
Hafted beaver incisors			Pottery on baskets
Awls			Polished teeth wood working tools
bone			
copper			

TABLE 1.1 (Continued)

Artifactual	Nonartifactual	Structural	Inference
Technology (Continued)			
Hammerstones			
Anvilstones pitted			
Sinewstones			
Abrading stones			
Bone needles			
Drills (perforators)			
Scrapers			
Flaking tools bone antler copper			
Knives longitudinal broad blade with re- touched edges prismatic blade with or without marginal retouching			
Twine			
Cores			

TABLE 1.1 (Continued)

Artifactual	Nonartifactual	Structural	Inference
Technology (Continued)			
Blanks			
Polished celts			
Strike-a-lights			
Grit tempered pottery			
Vinette I pottery			
Social			
		Living sites separate from cemeteries	Band organization
			30-50 people
		Mortuary sites	Trade goods
			High male status
			Habitation area
			Fishing station
Ceremonial			
Gorgets	Pigments	Cremation	Food in graves
Striped slate	Graphite	Individual	
Trapezoidal	Limonite	Group	Renewal of life belief
Rectangular — with and without keel	Hematite	Dog	Cremated or killed artifacts
Dumbbell shape	Hide shrouds	Flexed burials	
Rhomboidal			
Rectangular — excurvate edge	Red ochre on burials	Charnal houses	

TABLE 1.1 (Continued)

Artifactual	Nonartifactual	Structural	Inference
Ceremonial (Continued)			
2 or more holes	Galena cubes	Crematoria — rock heaps	
Beads — Necklace Rolled copper Spheroid Tubular copper Birdbone tube Rectangular — marine shell Discoidal white and purple shell		Mound-like burial sites Burial groupings Cemeteries on knolls Graves face east Container artifact clusters	
Pipes — tubular pottery		Bark lined graves	
Fire making kits pyrite flint — strike-a-light birchbark		Burials without grave goods with grave goods	
Birdstones		No pottery in graves	
Baskets			
Birdbone whistle			
Slate pendant			

TABLE 1.1 (Continued)

Artifactual	Nonartifactual	Structural	Inference
		Ceremonial (Continued)	
Fishnets			
Meadowood projectile points — thin			
Chalcedony knife			
Copper hafted flaker			
Phallic symbol — hammerstone			
		Trade	
Steatite pots	Copper		Atlantic coast
Striped slate gorgets	Jasper		Upper Great Lakes
Chalcedony knives	Marine shells		Eastern Pennsylvania
Birdstones — striped slate	Graphite		Indiana
Turkey tail points	Galena cubes		Quebec

Winters notes, description must also include the selection of primary attributes which are functionally informative. For example, metric attributes of projective points do not suggest the functional inferences that edge wear does. Secondary attributes of context are equally essential and therefore much attention was paid to the *precise* location and association in excavation and analysis. This form of analysis is seen in the valuable work of those archaeologists who have, through their studies, actually demonstrated functional context for artifact classes (Binford 1963*a*). Although care must be exercised in using ethnographic information, certainly if function has been demonstrated for materials which are from the broad geographic area under study and which are temporally close, it can be adopted (Taggart 1967; Fitting 1970:43, 1972:191-224).

Winters defines utilitarian artifact classes as those which are general enough not to imply a specific use. These do, however, suggest a general category of uses which can be subdivided should the need arise (1969:30). A problem with such a categorization is the possibility that some artifacts may have served multiple functions. Not much can be done about this source of error except to recognize it and attempt to make the most reasonable decision, based upon secondary attributes of context; for example, a cache of blades is functionally different from a single blade. The decision can also be based upon the last obvious use, such as a projectile point that has been reworked into a drill. This last use should be reflected in primary attributes if description is detailed enough.

Functional Categories of Artifacts

We will divide the assemblages into several broad categories in order to deal functionally with the artifacts, features and nonartifactual evidence excavated from the Riverhaven 2 and Sinking Ponds sites. These activity categories presented in Figure 1.1 are:

1. Procurement
2. Processing
3. Storage
4. Manufacture
5. Ceremonial
6. Habitation

Procurement defines activities which extract subsistence, by any method, since agriculture or horticulture have not been evidenced (Ritchie 1969:171; Ritchie and Funk 1973:346-69). Figure 1.1 presents

FIGURE 1.1
ACTIVITY-ARTIFACT RELATIONSHIPS

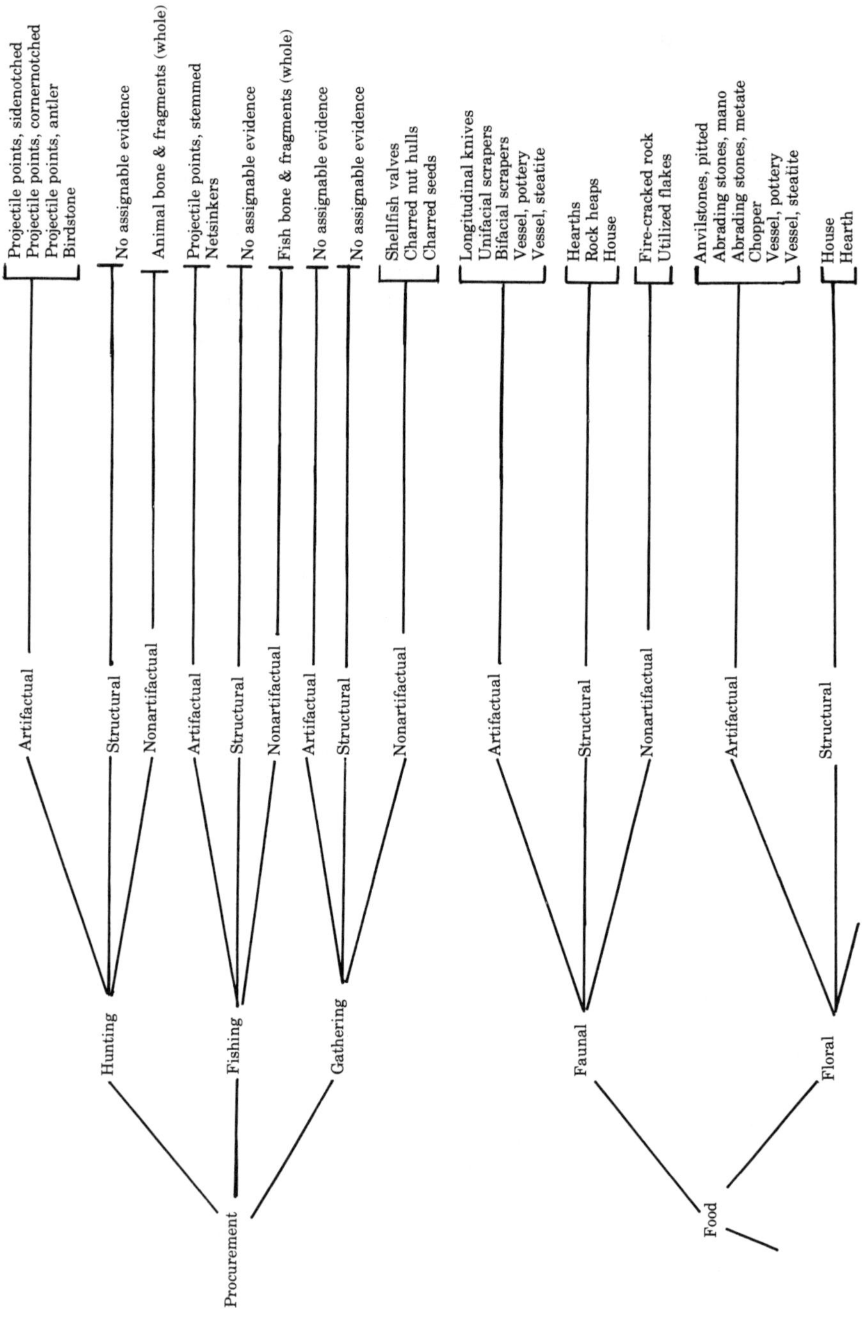

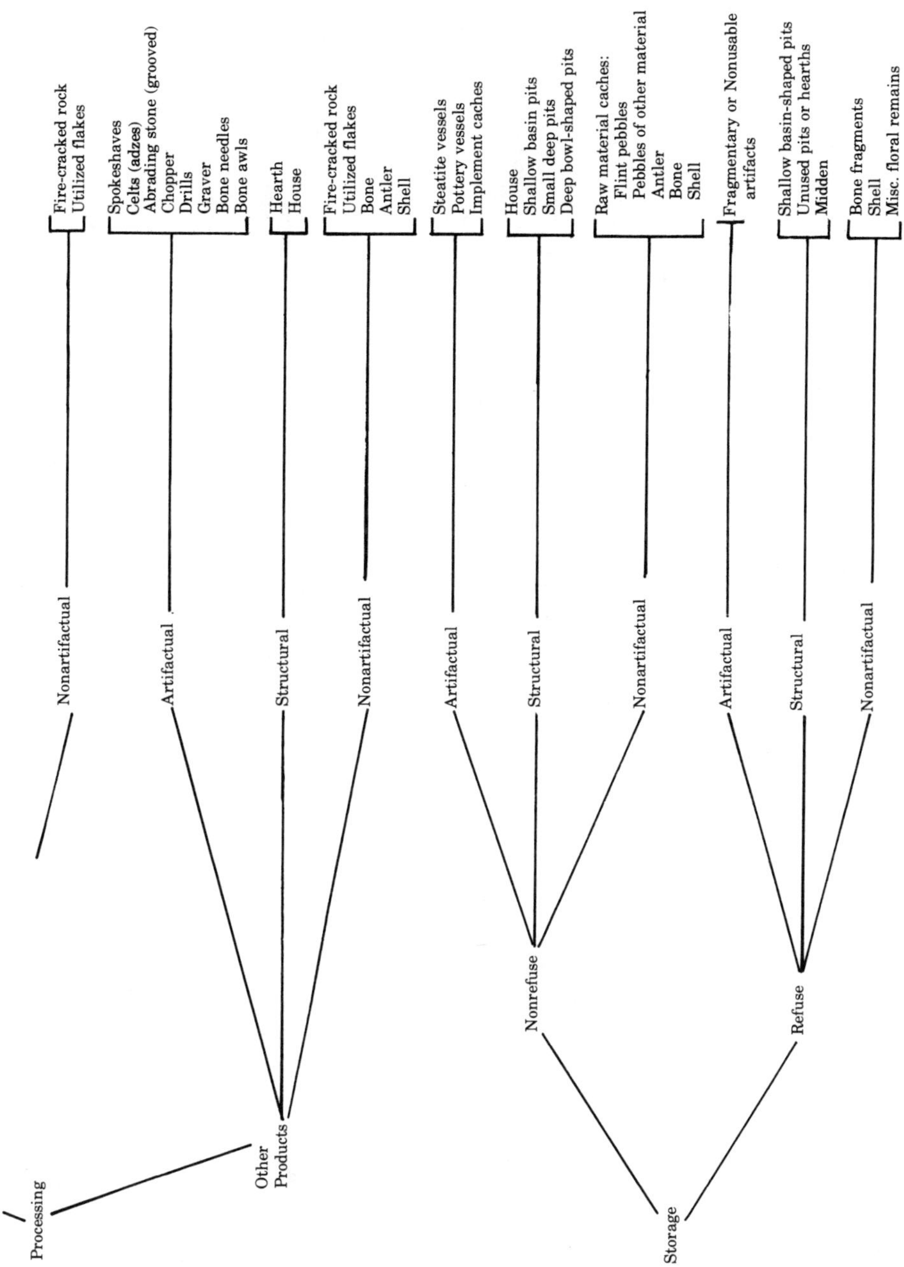
Processing
Other Products
Nonartifactual
Fire-cracked rock
Utilized flakes
Artifactual
Spokeshaves
Celts (adzes)
Abrading stone (grooved)
Chopper
Drills
Graver
Bone needles
Bone awls
Structural
Hearth
House
Nonartifactual
Fire-cracked rock
Utilized flakes
Bone
Antler
Shell
Storage
Nonrefuse
Artifactual
Steatite vessels
Pottery vessels
Implement caches
Structural
House
Shallow basin pits
Small deep pits
Deep bowl-shaped pits
Nonartifactual
Raw material caches:
Flint pebbles
Pebbles of other material
Antler
Bone
Shell
Refuse
Artifactual
Fragmentary or Nonusable artifacts
Structural
Shallow basin-shaped pits
Unused pits or hearths
Midden
Nonartifactual
Bone fragments
Shell
Misc. floral remains

FIGURE 1.1 (Continued)
ACTIVITY-ARTIFACT RELATIONSHIPS

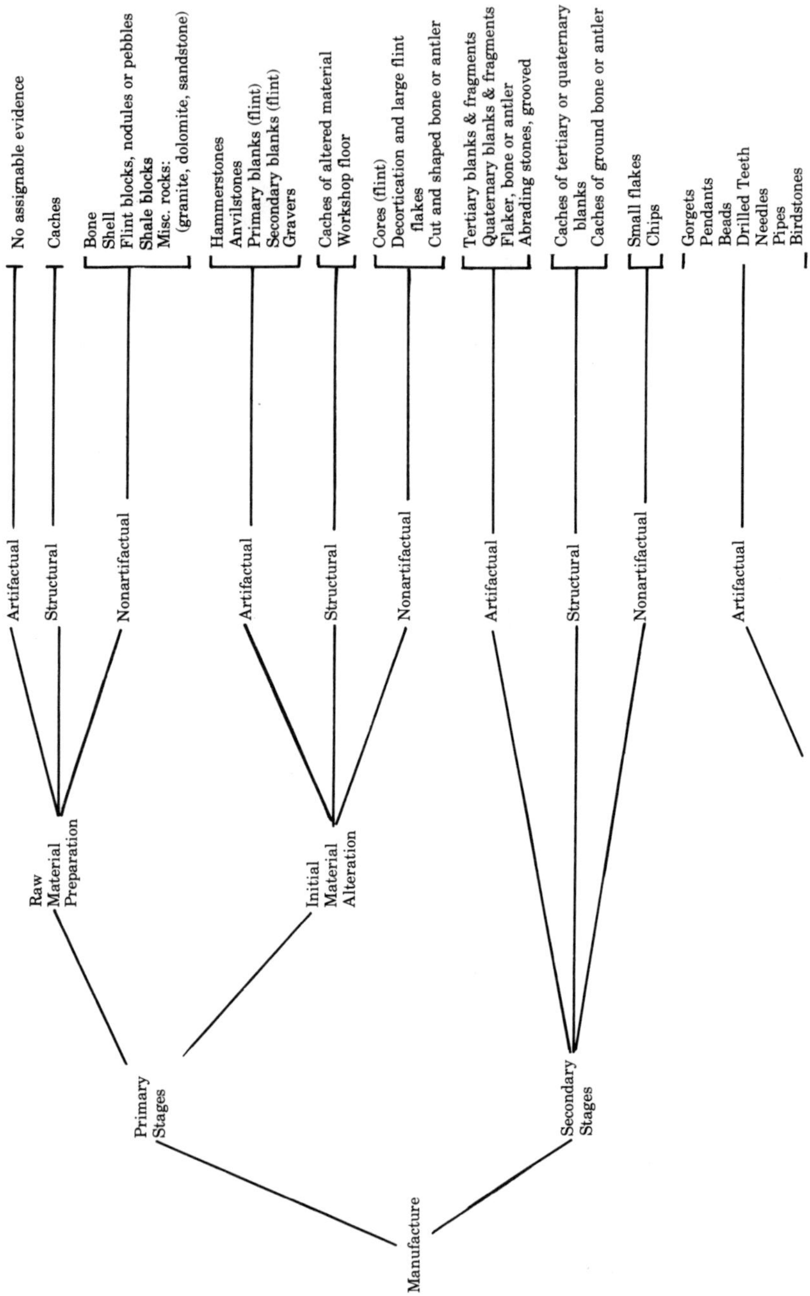

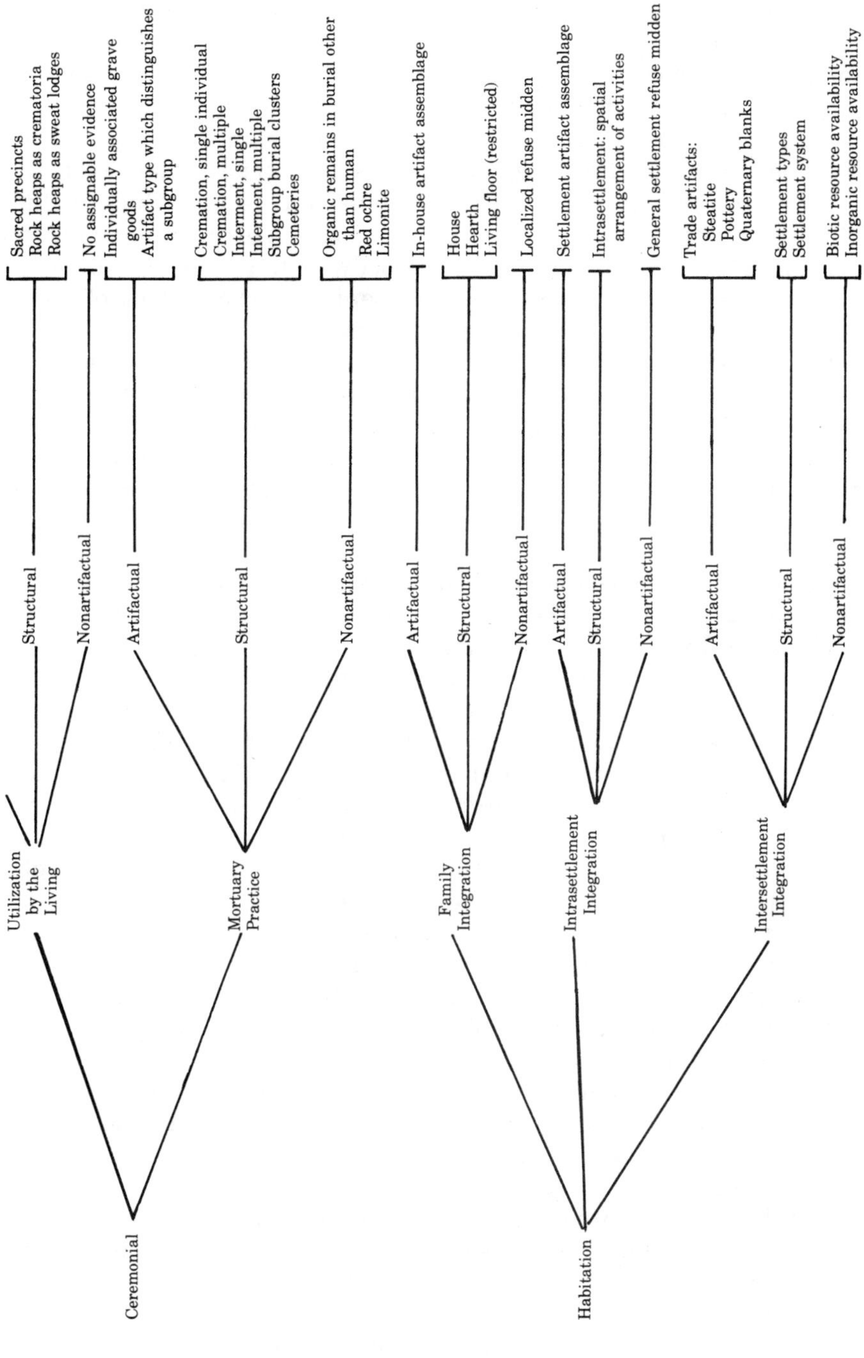

Fig. 1.1 Activity-artifact relationships.

our conception of those subgroupings within procurement which account for the types of subsistence extraction which have been suggested for Meadowood culture. We have indicated the forms of evidence that *may* demonstrate our subdivisions. We are aware that the categories are not totally mutually exclusive, and that, for instance, a birdstone may well have also functioned as an ornament or social status symbol.

Processing represents a fairly extensive category which includes Winters' categories of general utility tools, domestic implements, fabricating and processing tools, and woodworking tools (1969:30). The width of this category (Fig. 1.1) represents indecision, lack of specific analogies or historic parallels, and the recognition that some tools and structures represent alteration of biotic resources for cultural use. However, the specific type of alteration may be unclear; for instance, what does a drill drill or an adze shape? Our assessment of the activity suggests that it may be divided into food and other products formed from processing organic resources. The "other products" subgroup overlaps most notably with manufacturing. The manufacture category deals mostly with nonorganic materials such as chert, since lithic tools represent such a major segment of the assemblage. Where a sequence of manufacture is clearly indicated for tools of organic origin it has been included in the manufacture activity.

Storage activity (Fig. 1.1) may be subdivided into nonrefuse and refuse, since both imply placement of cultural materials in areas, the spatial dimension of which may be discovered. These refuse categories are generalized storage in that they represent a final stage of placing unwanted living residue in order to be rid of it. Schiffer suggests that refuse is either primary or secondary, depending on whether or not it is in or out of the location where the activity which produced it took place (1972:161-63). This, we believe, represents an inferential problem which cannot be solved at this point. However, we can suggest that those artifacts or other materials which are set apart by deliberate action constitute nonrefuse storage. This storage may be short-term or long-term, but to show which is difficult. Taggart (1967:160-62) has shown that storage tends to covary with occupational intensity; that is, long-term storage occurs in sites occupied for longer periods of the year. We shall use this proposition in dealing with our analysis of storage activities and recognize its inferential nature.

Manufacture activity (Fig. 1.1) refers to the process of working natural resources into tools and is apparent when materials that are used or produced during the sequence of tool making are found in an assemblage. Primary manufacture activity represents the first stages of tool development, while secondary manufacture represents the latter stages of production as well as the finished tools.

Using several recent studies (Granger n.d.; White, Binford and Papworth 1963; Taggart 1967) an ordered sequence of Meadowood flint tool types is proposed (Fig. 1.2). This chert tool sequence begins with either of the two forms of basic raw material: the locally available pebble or the tabular block. These are modified by percussive techniques in Stage 1 (A or B) to form a primary blank. Decortication occurs and large longitudinal flakes are produced. By-products of the transition toward a secondary blank and earlier preforms are generally flakes with conspicuous bulbs of percussion, striking platforms, and bulbar scars which lack the faceted platforms and lipping seen in the chips produced by subsequent stages (App. B). Functional tools such as utilized flakes, unifacial scrapers, various utilized cores, and gravers are formed on these fortuitous by-products.

In Stage II, orientation of the residual striking platform to the proximal end of the tool is noted. It becomes successively smaller during the development of the tertiary blank, with basal and lateral pressure flaking producing smaller expanding chips from the lateral portions and small expanding flakes from the proximal or basal portion which retain segments of the platform. By-products of Stages III and IV appear to have been utilized for subsidiary tools such as longitudinal knife-scrapers, strike-a-lites, or scrapers which are either unifacial or with some bifacial working. Edge wear is the only additional modification seen in association with the primary flaking prior to the tertiary blank. Subsequently, secondary edge modification removes all traces of the striking platform and refines the symmetry of the blank. Fragments produced are transformed into functional by-products as well as specifically derived items such as the bifacial unilaterally excurvate longitudinal knife and the drill formed after massive lateral reworking by secondary pressure flaking toward the low medial ridge. The quaternary blank is the "cache blade" described as characteristic of the Meadowood phase. The projectile point is produced in Stage V by addition of side notches laterally at the proximal end and some tertiary nibble flaking to produce on some items a moderately serrated edge. Also at this point fortuitous by-products are again further modified for use as other tools.

Ceremonial activity (Fig. 1.1) may be represented by meaningful symbolic activities performed by and for the living and those mortuary rites which are performed in association with the dead. Much of the definition of Meadowood phase has been derived from assemblages associated with the dead. We will attempt to show that mortuary assemblages show a differential distribution from those of habitation and subsistance but represent a binding social force.

Habitation activity (Fig. 1.1) includes aggregates of structures and

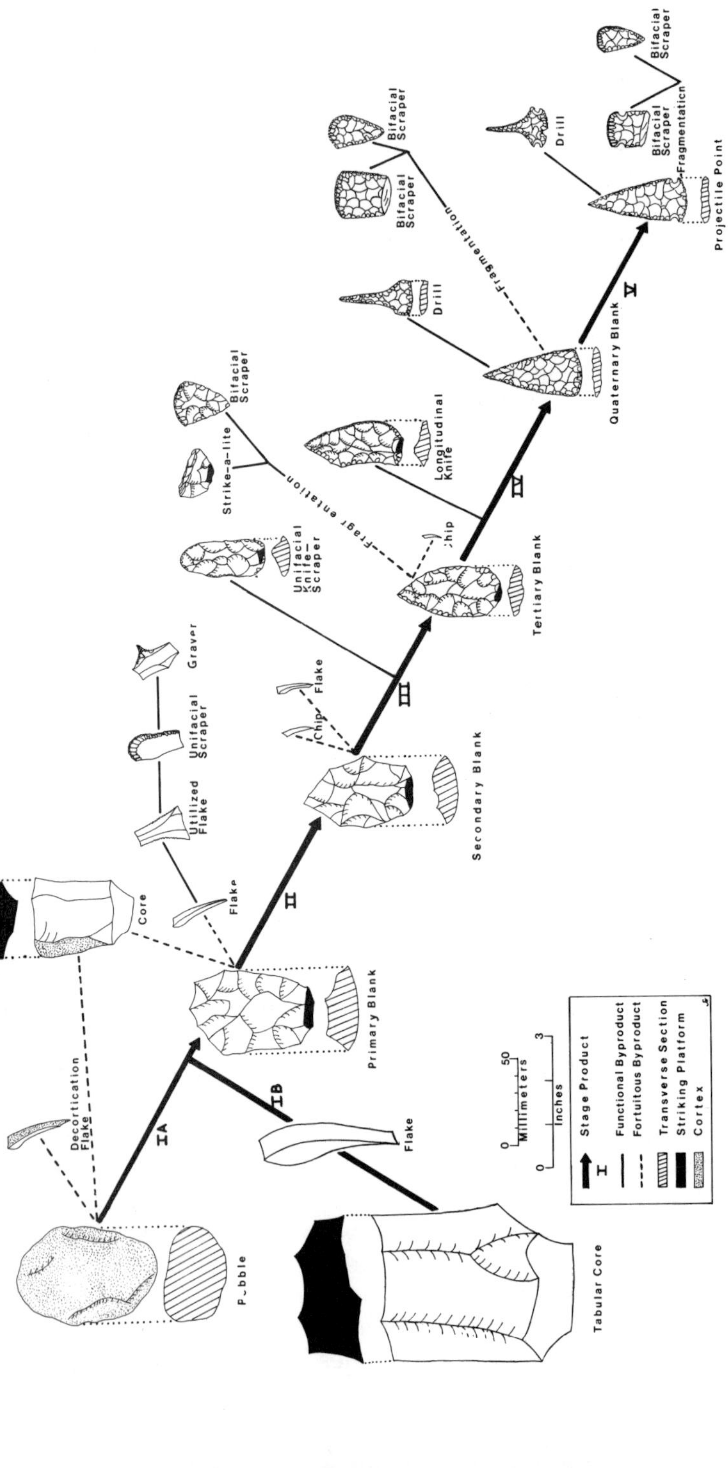

Fig. 1.2 Development of Meadowood flint tool types.

artifacts; for example, houses are aggregates of features and may contain accumulations of domestic artifacts. It is, therefore, an activity concomitant with the integration of the social group and reflects the organization of the family, the composition of intrasettlement groups, and the relations such as trade between settlements or groups. A midden concentrated in a single area may illustrate clustering of the various elements that make up a settlement whereas house-associated middens may show, at least minimally, separateness of subgroups. We shall test some of the propositions suggested by our subdivision of the activity in attempting to portray the settlement pattern for Meadowood phase in the Niagara Frontier region.

Before discussing the Sinking Ponds and the Riverhaven 2 sites we will attempt to gather what is known of the Meadowood phase together in Chapter 2 and relate this information to our study in Chapter 3 by discussing the physiography and biotic associations which form the adaptive milieu. Then using the assemblages excavated in the Niagara Frontier, we will try to achieve a basic explanation of the adaptive processes which conditioned the Meadowood settlement pattern and settlement system.

CHAPTER II

HISTORICAL REVIEW AND GENERAL DESCRIPTION OF MEADOWOOD PHASE CULTURE

When William A. Ritchie defined the archaeological manifestation now known as the Meadowood phase of the Early Woodland stage, his definition was based on nearly fifty years of refinement of the New York State cultural sequence.

Possibly the most enduring problem in the entire prehistoric New York sequence was definition of the Early and Middle segments of the Woodland stage or period (Ritchie 1969:Fig. 1).

The primary difficulty in the years before 1965 was dividing this stage into meaningful cultural expressions which demonstrated continuity in time and space. While formal trait complexes were distinguished, assignment of the observed assemblages was not easily accomplished. This situation developed because of two factors: (1) Few stratified multi-component sites with isolatable components had been discovered. (2) There was no suitable dating method prior to 1950 and, subsequently, errors appeared in radiocarbon dating prior to 1965. The result was that until absolute temporal assignment could be made, the archaeological sequence of New York State was unknowingly compressed. This truncated sequence was derived from the work of archaeologists in the early part of the twentieth century. At this time the prevailing thought on aboriginal time depth was that all Indian occupations were relatively recent and tribally affiliated.

During the period from 1920 to 1944, Parker's tripartate sequence Iroquois—Algonkian—Eskimo, was revised and refined. (1922:39-162). First, the Algonkian period was subdivided into three parts, the earlier segments consisting of groups who occupied small campsites clustered near water and generally on terraces or hills. These people had hunting—gathering—fishing subsistence practices. Later populations became more sedentary and practiced agriculture. Ritchie (1932*a*:406-15) broadened and redefined the Algonkian period to accommodate new data acquired from his excavations in central New York. He was able to demonstrate an essentially continuous developmental sequence for central New York State and establish that the Coastal Algonkian sequence must be considered apart from that of the Interior manifestations due to significant environmental differences.

THE POINT PENINSULA FOCUS, VINE VALLEY ASPECT, WOODLAND PATTERN

In 1936 Ritchie reclassified the Archaic as a separate period, and used a pre-ceramic—ceramic distinction as an arbitrary boundary between the Archaic period and Early Woodland (Byers 1959:229). In 1938 and 1940 Ritchie investigated several sites near Brewerton, on Oneida Lake. At one, Oberlander 2, evidence for a distinct mortuary complex was found with large frequencies of grave goods associated with a crude interior-exterior cordmarked pottery, which came to be called Vinette I. From these data, the Vine Valley aspect was described with two foci, Point Peninsula and Middlesex, and was placed intermediate between the Laurentian aspect of the Archaic pattern and the Owasco aspect of the Woodland pattern.

A Point Peninsula focus zone overlay the Laurentian Archaic occupations in the Robinson and Wickham sites at Brewerton, New York. This focus, named for a site on Lake Ontario, contained most of the artifactual traits we now recognize as belonging to both Early and Middle Woodland. From stratigraphic evidence, it was placed earlier than Owasco and later than Laurentian. Point Peninsula mortuary ceremonialism was considered to have had direct affinities with cultures to the south and west.

The use of pottery types as temporal indicators was introduced into New York from the Middle West by MacNeish ten years after its use in that area and the Southeast. This led to an attempt at seriation of components within the Point Peninsula focus based upon such determinations. The series of types described by Ritchie and MacNeish included Vinette I (1949:97). This type, defined for the first time, was found to be similar to the Adena type, Fayette Thick, and the Red Ochre type, Marion Thick. A definite association with the mortuary complexes outside New York was made on the then fairly secure archaeological basis of typological similarity.

These observations on pottery seriation made possible a new synthesis of chronological development in New York State (Ritchie 1951:130-36). Radiocarbon dates were obtained to shed light on two problem areas of the sequence, Early Woodland and Archaic. The periods Archaic, Early and Middle Woodland were each given tripartite divisions, I, II, and III. The Vine Valley aspect was segmented in the same manner as before but spread over a longer temporal span, Early Woodland II to Middle Woodland III, and the point Peninsula foci were numbered sequentially 1-4 within the Vine Valley aspect.

The components of Early Woodland II were arranged as follows:

Vine Valley Aspect (Interior)	Point Peninsula I Focus	Cuylerville Fall Brook Oberlander 2 Vinette I

Oberlander 2 was dated by an average of two radiocarbon readings on Burial Pit No. 6 (2817 ± 270 B.P. and 3080 ± 200 B.P.) at 2948 ± 170 B.P. (C-192) or 998 B.C. (ibid.:133). The secure temporal placement of this cemetery with cremations and ceremonial artifact inclusion was used to cross-date a nearby site, Vinette, where the Vinette I pottery of the lower level graded into a series of Middle Woodland types in the upper levels of a thick restricted midden.

In a contemporaneous article MacNeish made a clear distinction between Point Peninsula I and Middlesex, clearly relying heavily on Ritchie's trait definitions. He postulated that either a westward or eastward migration had established the Adena-like Middlesex and he added a further "migration from the north or west to account for a 'proto Iroquois' " Point Peninsula I (MacNeish 1952:48-49).

THE EARLY WOODLAND PERIOD

Two new sites excavated in 1953 and 1954, the Muskelonge Lake site and Hunter site on Red Lake, produced mortuary data which led back to Oberlander 2, Wray, Pickens, and other sites with excavated burial data. Such studies produced the term "Early Woodland Burial Cult." In retrospect, interpretation of this complex was seriously flawed by an erroneous radiocarbon date. This date was 2500 B.C. ± 260 (See below) from the Hunter Site. The 998 B.C. date at Oberlander 2, Burial 6, (Ritchie 1951:133) and the lack of early dates in the Ohio Valley led Ritchie to conclude that the Burial Cult appeared earlier in the Northeast.

The first approximation of a settlement pattern approach to Early Woodland added little to the carefully defined structure of the Burial Cult. In fact, the cult was used to explain not only the settlement pattern but broad portions of the cultural pattern:

> . . . No appreciable modification in the way of life of the northeastern groups is implied by the archaeological data for the earlier part of the Woodland period . . . With the appearance of an Early Woodland burial cult, however, there occur the first tangible inklings of social differentiation . . . Broadly conceived, *ceremonial centers* made their appearance at first as *small cemeteries on sacred burial precincts,* set apart from habitation quarters . . . Because these cemeteries contain a variable proportion of more carefully prepared graves with richer offerings it seems logical to assume some sort of social hierarchy. The use of *symbolic ritualistic objects and substances,* like red ochre, suggests religio-ceremonialism under shamanistic or priestly control, a primitive church operating as an integrative social force. (Ritchie 1956*a*:76) [Italics mine.]

The only substantive settlement data presented or known for the Early Woodland of central New York at this time were: (1) Cemeteries were separate from habitation areas. (2) Pottery may have indicated sedentariness and hence horticulture. (3) Thicker refuse accumulations suggested greater population. Even though the scanty evidence favored a broadly based continuity of subsistence–settlement patterns from the Late Archaic (Ritchie 1956*a*: 75), the Early Woodland cultural adaptation was believed to have been carried to the area by "an independent tradition of obscure pedigree which exerted itself variously upon the resident Archaic Cultures" (Ritchie 1956*b*:10).

In 1959 Ritchie published a clarification of the Orient complex of coastal New York. Relatively little settlement data was added but detailed local burial data were well delineated. The dating of the Orient complex at 1000 B.C. suggested a trait linkage between the coastal Late Archaic, Transitional, and Early Woodland (Ritchie 1959:74), but the Orient complex stood essentially separate from the manifestations of interior Early Woodland because it appeared to be well connected with cultures that preceded and followed it in the coastal area (ibid.:76). A basic change in evidence which altered the chronology of the Early Woodland period was the revision of the radiocarbon date for the Hunter (Red Lake) site. The date was originally reported as 2448 B.C. ± 260 but it was altered to 841 B.C. ± 68 (Y-981). It thus became coeval with the date at Oberlander 2 of 998 B.C. ± 170 (C-192) (Ritchie 1961:583-84). New C-14 dates on a related burial component, Morrow, in central New York, were reported as 563 B.C. ± 250 (M-640) and 630 B.C. ± 100 (Y-1171). The temporal boundaries for the Early Woodland in central New York were then established as 500 B.C. to 1000 B.C. New evidence was being developed which would make possible intensive studies of regional insitu development of Early Woodland culture, for as Dragoo states:

> . . . New and unequivocal evidence . . . is coming from a single period-habitation site of this culture (Early Point Peninsula), Riverhaven No. 2 now under investigation on the Niagara River in western New York. [Parentheses mine.] (1963:583)

MEADOWOOD PHASE OF NEW YORK STATE

In 1965 Ritchie presented the now classic redefinition and description of all cultures in New York State. The revised culture sequence was presented for five subareas based upon the cardinal points of the compass plus a central subarea. The basic organization of the *Archaeology of New York State* was made consistent with theoretical positions taken by Willey and Phillips (1958). The sequential ordering of data was applied over each subarea and broken down into stages, cultures, phases, and components. Significantly these subarea comparisons made more meaningful distinctions within substages in Early Woodland by eliminating the necessity to derive by migration or diffusion minor differences noted between contemporary units. Yet overall relationships were still thought to have been products of diffusion.

Settlement pattern data was organized by use of the scheme suggested by Beardsley et al. (1956:132-57), and components were evaluated along lines more closely attuned to their functional role in the culture. Subsistence activity, ceremonial activity, and secondary functional activities were recognized. Evaluations of each phase and culture accounted for lack of data.

Point Peninsula I was redefined as 2 phases, the Meadowood and Middlesex phases. The Point Peninsula culture of the Middle and Late Woodland substage was subdivided into phase names, replacing the numerical taxonomy. Piffard focus was dropped and subsumed within the Susquehanna culture of the Transitional stage. Middlesex was assigned to the Adena culture and placed later than Meadowood (Ritchie 1965*a*:xxx-xxxi). Meadowood phase, securely placed by four radiocarbon dates, was inserted slightly later than Orient phase, now assigned to the Transitional stage. Neither the Meadowood nor the Orient phase was assigned to a culture or tradition (ibid.).

At this time several other investigators suggested relationships for Meadowood phase which substantially differed from Ritchie's interpretations. Briefly, they assigned sites of this phase to the Late or Terminal Archaic, arguing that they differed little from sites observed to the west in Michigan, northern Ohio and Illinois (Griffin 1965:664, 1961:147-55; Jennings 1968:185-86; Fitting and Brose 1970:45-46). This alternative view was stated succinctly by Papworth within an environmental paradigm when he defined the Lake Forest Archaic cultural tradition:

> . . . We offer here a definition of a shared environment which encompasses the archaeological remains of these culturally related peoples. This environment is called the Lake Forest region by several ecologists . . . The people of the Lake Forest shared common burial practices reflecting widespread beliefs. In addition to these

> supernatural beliefs these Archaic peoples shared many tool types and materials . . . Regional variety among artifacts of the Lake Forest Archaic period suggests that the cultures in the area at that time were *not* united in a single tightly homogeneous society. Rather there appear to have been several culturally distinct centers participating in a broader cultural milieu . . . New York State contains Point Peninsula (Meadowood) artifacts linking it to the Lake Forest as the easternmost area of common adaption. [Parentheses mine.] (Papworth 1967:abs.)

Subsequent revision of his treatment of the archaeology of New York State by Ritchie (1969) added more components to the Meadowood Phase but left unchanged the internal or external descriptions of the units in the sequence and the assignment to the Early Woodland (ibid.:180-201). His burial cult model was also left unmodified.

Reported sites of Meadowood phase fall into two broad categories: those with in situ features and artifacts investigated by excavation, and those from which materials are reported. Table 2.1 lists the ten sites of the latter type and the materials assigned to each, while Table 2.2 lists the 21 of the former type and their general in situ remains (Ritchie 1955*a*:68-69, 1969:180-90). The sites with in situ data show that six have yielded primarily burials or ceremonial data while 15 provided settlement or habitation information (Ritchie 1944, 1955*a*, 1969; Funk n.d.; White n.d.; Vanderlaan 1966; Rhodes n.d.; Funk and Rippeteau 1973).

Information on habitation sites is very sketchy at present. Only two sites have been reported fairly extensively, Vinette and Scaccia (Ritchie 1944; Ritchie and Funk 1973). Several of the others, such as Dennis 4 and Nahrwold 2, are only outlined in print and remain essentially unanalyzed at present. Riverhaven 2, Sinking Ponds, and Spicer Creek 1-2 are reported in detail in Chapters 4 and 5.

A brief summary of Ritchie's 1969 interpretation is that these sites represent the inception of a "more stable pattern of living" than in the preceding Late Archaic (Ritchie 1969:181). This interpretation was qualified however:

> . . . The small size of Meadowood sites bears testimony to a diminutive population probably no larger than the little bands of some thirty to fifty people which we have postulated for their Archaic predecessors. (Ritchie 1969:190)

Evidence for this interpretation came from the finding of U-shaped pits (Ritchie 1969:xxiii, 181, 188, 190) with an attributed storage function, fire hearths, loose concentrations of fire-cracked rock, scatters of fire-shattered rock and large and fairly deep midden deposits such as Riverhaven 2. Caches of seeds of goosefoot and smartweed, charred nuts and basketry, on the other hand, argue for a mobile foraging group not too different from the pattern evident in the Archaic (Jennings

TABLE 2.1
COLLECTIONS OF MEADOWOOD CACHE BLADES AND RELATED MATERIALS OR FEATURES FROM SITES REPORTED BUT NOT DESCRIBED IN DETAIL

N. Y. Physiographic Province	County	Reported Component	Date	Cache Blade No.	Other Associations
Great Lakes Lowland	Onondaga	Jacks Reef (?)	1890	100+	Red Ochre, Limonite
Great Lakes Lowland	Monroe	Point Pleasant (Irondequoit Bay)	1880-86	150	Red Ochre
Great Lakes Lowland	Erie	Buffalo G	1890	18	3 Meadowood Points 2 Stemmed Points Beveled Adze Misc. Tools, Flint Red Ochre
Great Lakes Lowland	Erie	Larkin	1924	9	2 Meadowood Points Birdstone Scrapers Deep Storage Pit
Great Lakes Lowland	Cayuga	Montezuma Marsh	1952	None	Red Ochre
Glaciated Allegheny Plateau	Seneca	Canoga	1940	100+	None Reported
Glaciated Allegheny Plateau	Yates	Yates (?)	1930	400	None Reported
Mohawk Lowland	Montgomery	Tribes Hill	1950	21	Red Ochre (?)
Coastal Lowland	Long Island	East Northport	1955	263	None Reported
St. Lawrence-Champlain Lowland	St. Lawrence	Rockaway Point	1954	None	Rock Feature Crematory Red Ochre

SOURCES: Ritchie 1955; Granger n.d.

TABLE 2.2
MEADOWOOD SITES WITH IN SITU REMAINS

Site	County	Type of Data	Radiocarbon Date
Muskalonge Lake	Jefferson	Burials, Crematoria, Hearths	None
Hunter	Jefferson	Burials, Crematoria	841B.C.±68(I-981)
Oberlander 2	Oswego	Burials	998B.C.±170(C-192)
Wray	Monroe	Burials	None
Pickens	Onondaga	Burials	None
Scaccia	Livingston	Midden, Features (Burial Pits, Hearths)	870B.C.±60(Y-1654)
Morrow	Ontario	Burials, Features (Pits)	663B.C.±250(M-640) 630B.C.±100(Y-1171)
Vinette	Oswego	Midden, Features (Pits)	None
South Waterport	Orleans	Features (Pits)	None
McCauley Complex	Livingston	Caches, Features, Midden (?)	None
Nahrwold 2	Schoharie	Features, Midden	760B.C.±80(Y-1651)
Dennis 4	Albany	Features, Midden	None
Fortin	Delaware	Feature (Hearth), Midden	1230B.C.±95(I-6740)
Sinking Ponds	Erie	Features, Midden	None
Riverhaven 2	Erie	Features, Midden	None
Spicer Creek 1, 2	Erie	Features (Pits, Hearths)	None
Petrie	Erie	Features (Pits)	None
Allen	Erie	Features (Pits)	None
Winters	Erie	Features (Pits)	None
Eaton	Oneida	Features, Midden	None
Nine Mile Swamp	Oneida	Features, Midden	None

1968:186). Although studies of feature-associated fauna, deer, fish and other animals clearly tie the people to an environmental setting they remain equivocal on the point of sedentarization. The question of the degree to which Meadowood settlement differs from the Late Archaic settlement at Lamoka Lake is also unresolved.

Recently Ritchie and Funk have presented a detailed exposition of Meadowood phase settlement in which they described it as consisting of camps and cemeteries. Camps are apparently defined by small size, low density homogeneous activities, and a low intensity of occupation. They suggest that Meadowood habitation sites are all considerably less than one acre in size, excepting Scaccia (1973:346-47). Using the Scaccia data as a basis for their interpretation, they hypothesize that it was occupied by small bands as a central base camp, while the Vinette, Morrow, Nahrwold 2, Sinking Ponds, and Riverhaven 2 sites "were seasonally utilized fishing camps with smaller resident groups." Further hypotheses which they present are: (1) Due to the lack of "back country" sites of Meadowood affiliation "seasonal rounds were *not* an aspect of the settlement pattern." (2) Creekside or lakeside sites were not occupied throughout the year. (3) The special micro-environment of valley peripheries near small streams was used in fall and winter but that near major waterways was used in all seasons. (4) Meadowood economy was strongly oriented toward riverine or lacustrine resources. (5) Storage pits similar in form and function to those of Lamoka may have indicated intensive use of acorns and other plant foods but do not substantiate in their content agriculture by the presence of cultigens. (6) Cemeteries are usually located some distance from the camps, but some brief habitation may occur during burial rites.

They summarize Meadowood settlement as having:

> . . . greater stability than in earlier times, with the settlement pattern approaching a semi-sedentary character. (Ritchie and Funk 1973:348)

In Table 2.5 we will present the settlement data currently known from this phase, from contemporary phases, and from later phases in New York State (Ritchie and Funk 1973). The similar settlement types of post-Lamoka are especially consistent with some of those in the Saginaw Bay area of Michigan and the environmental adaptations also appear quite close (Fitting 1970).

Fitting has suggested a broadly representative settlement system within the Lower Great Lakes area:

> . . . The Early Woodland settlement system appears to be the same as that of the Late Archaic, with winter population concentrations and summer population dispersion.

> In the Great Lakes area . . . ceramics seem to have little importance in altering the basic settlement system (1969:368).

This model, derived from Michigan site studies (Taggart 1967; Fitting 1972), may account for the resemblance between Meadowood, Transitional, and Lamoka settlement patterns. In any case, it provides a basic hypothesis for further study.

The technological inventory of the Meadowood phase as defined by Ritchie (1969:180-201) is summarized by material in Table 2.3. Ornamental ceremonial materials and trade are initially defined in this description of the material culture of the phase. Generally Ritchie based his interpretations of the cultural inventory on a cluster of material traits within a particular range of time and space, in this case the Meadowood phase. The most diagnostic artifact of this phase is the distinctive thin, sidenotched point named after Meadowood, an estate owned by one of the codiscoverers of the type site, which is now called the Wray site (Ritchie 1969:180).

Meadowood mortuary ceremonialism and the conception of an Early Woodland Burial Cult have long dominated discussion of the Meadowood phase culture. Later accounts (Ritchie 1965, 1969; Ritchie and Funk 1973) have presented a more complete cultural inventory but one which is still heavily dominated by inferences about spiritual activities. In the descriptions and syntheses of this period there appears a dichotomy between ritual and secular activities, but the former are clearly distinguished and the latter less well defined. The question of balance is a disturbing one, and the data collected from 1944 to 1973 have not answered this question. On frequency alone, the overwhelming number of artifacts are *mortuary* associated, but descriptions of mortuary practice, no matter how detailed, only inform us of that portion of Meadowood culture presented by the assemblage of mortuary data sampled. We hear, for example, more of how the burials at Oberlander 2 fit into or differ from modal trends in the proposed "Burial Cult" than of how they reflect the articulations between the Oberlander 2 and Vinette sites (Ritchie 1969:181-90). However, Ritchie stated, while referring to Vinette:

> . . . Clearly it was an extensive and important settlement on the rifts of the now canalized river, and there is every reason to conclude, from the typological identity of the artifacts, that the cemetery of cremated burials on the nearby knoll, just described (Oberlander site, number 2), is the burial place of the inhabitants of this shore village. (Ritchie 1944:160)

Later he contrasted Oberlander 2 with the Indian River sites, Muskelonge Lake and Hunter, with reference to presence or absence of red

TABLE 2.3
POSTULATED MATERIAL INVENTORY OF MEADOWOOD PHASE

Subsistence	Ornamental or Ceremonial	Indeterminate/Trade
	Lithic	
"Meadowood" Projectile Points Quarry Blanks Fire Kit (Pyrites & Strike-a-Lites) Triangular End Scrapers Expanded Base Drills	Cache Blades Turkey Tail Points	Birdstone, bar Birdstone, popeye Exotic Cherts
Plano-Convex Adze Muller (Grinding Stone) Side Scrapers, Flake Rectanguloid Celts Hafted Beaver Incisors Knives — varieties Choppers Hammerstones Bola Stones (?) Netsinkers Abrading Stone Sinewstone	Trapezoidal Gorget Rectanguloid Gorget Bar Gorget Rhomboidal Gorget Quartz Crystals, unworked Hematite } Paintstones Limonite } Paintstones Graphite } Paintstones	Steatite Bowls
	Metal	
Copper Flaker Copper Awl	Copper Beads	Copper
	Bone	
Awls Harpoons Needles (Antler) Flaking Tools Projectile Point Dagger	Bone Whistle Shell Beads Birdbone Beads	
	Pottery	
Vinette I Pots	Tubular Pipes	None
	Other	
Nets Baskets Cordage	None	None

SOURCE: Ritchie 1969:180-201.

TABLE 2.4
COMPILATION OF MEADOWOOD BURIAL STATISTICS

Sites	Cremations, No Grave Goods	Cremations, Grave Goods	Inhumation—Single, No Grave Goods	Inhumation—Single, Grave Goods	Inhumation Multiple No Grave Goods	Inhumation Multiple Grave Goods	Individuals Identified	Minimum Burials — N	Total Burial Features	Crematoria	Other Features	Total Features (N_1)
Muskalonge Lake 1	0	6 (2)	2	1	0	0	5	9	8	6	4	18
Hunter[1]	0	9 (7)	0	1	0	3 (5)	13	15	3	14	6	23
Morrow[2]	8 (5)	16 (8)	15	6	0	0	34	45	44	0	6	50
Oberlander 2[3]	6	16	0	0	0	0	22	22	22	0	0	22
Wray[3]	0	0	2	5	1 (4)	2 (4)	8	16	10	0	0	10
Subtotal	14	47	19	13	1	5	82	107	87		16	123
Percent of Feature Subtotal									70.7	16.3	13	100
Scaccia[4]	0	0	0	0	1 (2)		2	2	1	0	76	77
Total	14	47	19	13	2	5	84	109	88	20	92	200
Percent of Feature N_1									44	10	46	100

NOTE: Parentheses indicate identified individuals.

[1]Ritchie 1955
[2]White n.d.
[3]Ritchie 1944
[4]Funk n.d.

ochre and other traits, but made no reference to the distribution of artifacts which occur as secular items at Vinette or ritual items at Oberlander 2 (Ritchie 1955:68-70). Similarly, no structural comparisons were made between sites in more immediate proximity. Ritchie and Funk are, however, impressed with the degree of stability that such a pattern of camps and cemeteries seems to suggest (1973:349).

The simple burial pattern frequencies for Meadowood mortuary sites are presented in Table 2.4. Much of this evidence has been gleaned from Ritchie (1944, 1955, 1969) and White (n.d.), for in no single place have all the data been correlated in statistical tables. Ritchie indicated that the modes of cremation, flexed inhumation, bundle inhumation, and combinations of the three were typical, but even though no significant pattern of emphasis occurs overall (1969:197) significant social differentiation and stratification may have been present based upon age, sex, or role such as that of a shaman or leader (Ritchie and Funk 1973:349). There are suggestions that local cultural groups exercised dissimilar burial preferences in their separate regions; for example, the Indian River site shows an emphasis upon total cremation in crematoria with secondary burial, as opposed to the lack of cremation at Wray on the Genesee River or the failure to include red ochre in graves at Oberlander 2 on Oneida Lake (Ritchie 1955:11-33). Papworth argues that:

> . . . What we are trying to stress here is that each of these centers of participation (i.e. Meadowood) in the Late Archaic of the Northeast were probably the result of stable *local populations,* which interacted with one another, spreading certain elements such as burial ceremonialism among all of them and as is characteristic of stable populations, *preserving certain autonomous characteristics*. [Italics and parentheses mine] (1967:252)

CHRONOLOGICAL AND GEOGRAPHICAL RELATIONSHIPS OF MEADOWOOD PHASE

We have discussed in the sections above the dating of the Meadowood phase sites known before 1965. Recently, however, several new components have come to light and have been radiocarbon dated. These dates are presented in Figure 2.1 along with dates from some contemporary sites as well as some earlier and later sites which may be related geographically or typologically to Meadowood phase.

These new components considerably extend the known temporal and spatial range of Meadowood phase. The Fortin 2 site in the Susquehanna River Valley yielded a date from a hearth associated with Meadowood phase materials, cache blades, and two projectile points, of

FIGURE 2.1
RELEVANT RADIOCARBON DATES

	Michigan-Ontario-Ohio (Lakes Erie-Ontario)	New York (Lakes Erie-Ontario)	Susquehanna-Delaware Drainage Area	Coastal Mid-Atlantic and New England Area
	Leimbach (EW) 520± 210(OWU185)			
500—	Schultz (EW) 530±150(M-1524)	Morrow(M)563±250(M-640)		
	Schultz(EW) 540±180(M-1525)	Morrow(M) 630±100(Y-1171)		
	Green Point(LA) 530±120(M-1432)		Rosencrans(MA)610±120(?)	
		Nahrwold 2(M) 760±80(Y-1651)	Faucett(M)750±100(Y-2475)	Jamesport 763 ±220(W-543)
		Hunter(M) 841±68(Y-981)		
		Scaccia(M) 870±60(Y-1654)	Faucett(O)810±100(Y-2477)	
				Orient 2(O)944± 250(M-494)
				Stony Brook 2(O)944±250 (M-587)
		Oberlander 2(M)998±170 (C-192)		Stony Brook 2(O)974±250 (M-588)
1000—				
				Sugar Loaf Hill (O) 1043±300(M-586)
	Andrews(LA)1220±150(M-659)		Miller Field (O) 1220±120(Y-2589)	
		O'Neil 2(FI)1250±100(Y-1274)	Fortin 2(M)1230±95 (I-6740)	
			Camelot 2(O)1290±95 (I-6744)	
			Zimmerman(O)1280±120 (Y-2343)	
1500—			Camelot 1(FI)1475±95 (I-6641)	
			Kuhr I(FI)1550±105 (I-6751)	
	Feheeley(LA)1980±150 (M-1139)	Cole Gravel Pit(LA) 1922±120(Y-2346)		
2000—		Cole Gravel Pit(LA) 2112±160		

NOTE: References are in text.

Legend: EW Early Woodland; M Meadowood phase; FI Frost Island; O Orient phase; MA Middlesex-Adena phase; LA Late Archaic

All dates are B.C.

Fig. 2.1 Relevant radiocarbon dates.

1230 B.C. ± 95 (I-6740) (Funk and Rippeteau 1973:16).

Further to the southeast the Faucett site in the Delaware River Valley yielded a date of 750 B.C. ± 100 (Y-2476) (Kinsey 1973:190-91, 1974:44) from a more extensive level which yielded Meadowood cache blades, projectile points of Onondaga chert, and miscellaneous other artifacts, including a gorget and some Vinette 1 pottery. Kinsey demonstrated that:

> The Meadowood occupation is extensive but not intensive . . . which apparently was an encampment of brief duration, possibly no longer than several days or at most a couple of weeks. (1974:42)

He states that at the nearby Zimmerman site, intensive use of a small area on the floodplain was noted. The general impression based upon cultural deposits at both sites is that Meadowood occupation was transitory, occurred during warmer months, and showed clear interactions with a more indigenous Late Orient phase occupation. His suggestion that the Meadowood tool kit was imported for the most part is based upon low flint detritus counts and the almost ubiquitous use of Onondaga chert for those items produced of chert (Kinsey 1974:88-89).

Ritchie has noted (1969:200-201) that there are significant relationships between the Meadowood ceremonial complex and Red Ochre sites, especially in Michigan. He states that the Andrews site, clearly a cemetery, dated at 1220 B.C. ± 150 (M-659) (Fitting 1970:84), shows close parallels to the Indian River sites (Ritchie 1969:201), which are also heavily mortuary in nature.

Fitting (1970:68-95) ordered Late Archaic and Early Woodland sites in the Saginaw Valley into a reasonably secure sequence of adaptations to the local environment, and Papworth (1967) discussed the unitary nature of contemporary ceremonial complexes within the Lake Forest area. Meadowood Phase appears to be contemporary with a later portion of these developments in the Saginaw Bay Area and there are some Late Archaic sites in New York which show resemblances to those of the Late and Terminal Archaic in the Michigan sequence; for example, the Cole Gravel Pit and the Feheeley site. The relationship of these earlier sites in Michigan to Meadowood phase are, however, presently unclear, but we have presented what settlement data is currently known from this phase and from contemporary and later phases in New York State in Table 2.5 (Ritchie and Funk 1973). The settlement types in Lamoka conform especially with those of the Saginaw Late Archaic as do the general subsistance practices (Fitting 1970).

The Leimbach site in northern Ohio is synchronous in time with the Meadowood phase but appears to relate more closely to the Early Wood-

TABLE 2.5
SETTLEMENT DATA ON PHASES ASSOCIATED CHRONOLOGICALLY AND GEOGRAPHICALLY WITH MEADOWOOD PHASE IN NEW YORK STATE

Phase Date and General Location	Settlement Types	Demography and Social Organization	Seasonal Environmental Associations	Subsistence Activities	Remarks
LAMOKA 2500-1900 B.C. (Central, Western and Southern N.Y. to North Pa.)	Large Central Base Camps: Lamoka Lake Geneva Cole Gravel Pit	150-200 persons band-kinship organization	Year-round near large lake outlets streams or marshes	Fishing-major emphasis Hunting Acorn gathering and storage	Houses-Rectanguloid ca. 15′x10′ in size Intense occupation Deep middens
	Small Temporary Camps: Scottsville DiSanto Lawson Avon Ross Gucker	25-75 persons Lineage or family?	Season unknown, perhaps summer Recurrent occupation Streams, lakes and marshes large and small	Fishing Fowling	Occupation debris not dense
FROST ISLAND 1400-1000 B.C. (Central N.Y.)	Small Temporary Camps: O'Neil 2 Zimmerman (Pa.) Hickory Hill Marsh	25-50 persons Small bands	Season unknown Most occupations on navigable waterways	Hunting and Fishing emphasis unknown Data on storage lacking	No data on dwellings Possibly used canoe extensively
ORIENT 1100-500 B.C. (Eastern, Coastal N.Y., N.J. and Pa.)	Small Coastal Camps: Stony Brook(a) Muskeeta Cove Baxter Faucett (Pa.)	25-75 persons Patrilocal bands?	Season unknown Coastal estuaries and marshes Protection from north and west winds	Marine shellfish major emphasis Hunting Vegetal foods	Earth ovens No data on habitation or storage Stone platforms

Phase Date and General Location	Settlement Types	Demography and Social Organization	Seasonal Environmental Associations	Subsistence Activities	Remarks
	Inland Camps:	Unknown	Winter occupation?	Hunting?	Little data
	Cemeteries: Orient 1-2 Jamesport Sugarloaf Hill	Contain only small percentage of population Ossuaries Special treatment of high status persons by cremation	Close to seashore		Sacred precincts located well apart from habitation sites
CANOE POINT ca. 500-250 A.D. Central and North N.Y.	Small Temporary Camps: Grindstone Island O'Neil 3 Wickham 1 Vinette 2 Cottage East Sugar Is. (C)		Season unknown Summer? River and marshes Back-country sites reported	Hunting Fishing-major emphasis some sites Vegetal food gathered	
(SAUGEEN)	Large Temporary Camps: + 1 acre Donaldson (C)	100-150 persons Two or more bands	Spring-summer major stream	Fishing and shellfish emphasized Wild rice harvested	Houses rectanguloid ca. 19′x13′ Few storage pits Earth ovens
	Cemetery: Donaldson(C)	Small	Near large temporary camp		Inhumations flexed

land developments in the Ohio Valley (Fitting and Brose 1970:36). Other sites which appear to be related typologically to Meadowood phase but which are not yet securely dated are the Stroebel and Hodges sites in Michigan (Fitting 1970:68-95; Binford 1963*b*).

Several phases common to New York State are also shown (Table 2.5). One of these is the earlier Frost Island phase of the Susquehanna tradition in which Vinette I pottery is represented in central New York at approximately 1500 B.C. (Ritchie 1969:156-64). Frost Island phase settlement pattern is not well developed in central New York and although its associations with Susquehanna tradition sites on the coast have been documented, there is little information beyond a vague similarity in settlement location (Ritchie and Funk 1973:345-46).

The Orient phase of the Transitional stage is a contemporary coastal manifestation which displays steatite ware, complex mortuary ceremonialism, and close affiliations to other sites on the mid-Atlantic and New England coast. Its direct associations with Meadowood phase are not well known nor is its settlement pattern, which is only now becoming more distinct (see Table 2.5).

The Meadowood articulation with temporally later cultural groups such as those of the Early Point Peninsula, Canoe Point phase (Ritchie 1969:302-13; Ritchie and Funk 1973:349-51) has not yet been defined. However, data available from the Schultz site in the Saginaw Bay area of Michigan, which has components contemporary with and later than Meadowood phase, suggest that no major settlement shifts, but instead only minor alterations in artifacts and activities were taking place. (Fitting 1972). It is most likely there was increasing dependence upon the fruits of a more intense horticultural expression, however, as Ritchie and Funk note:

> The overall impression given by Early Point Peninsula sites is impoverishment in material culture and in religico-ceremonial life. Populations were evidently rather small and probably organized in bands of canoe travelers who spent most of their time fishing and hunting (1973:351).

Clarification of the network of relationships in the Lake Forest area has depended upon increasing amounts of information becoming available for similar adaptive modes in similiar but geographically disparate regions. Thus understanding the central New York cultural sequence in Late Archaic and Early Woodland times has aided in developing the Michigan Saginaw Bay sequences for those periods. Recent work in southern Ontario such as the combination of Early Point Peninsula, Canoe Point, and Saugeen into a single phase has had a significant bearing on development of concepts of settlement archaeology in the Lake Forest area (Ritchie and Funk 1973:349-50). Meadowood phase associations in Canada are not yet known as well as seems necessary to define eastern Lake Forest area cultural processes. Wright (1972*b*:39-43) notes traits such as gorgets, birdstones, and Meadowood projectile points throughout southern Ontario but the only fully known habitation component is at Batiscan in Quebec. Although clearly contemporary with Meadowood phase, Batiscan has elements which make assessment difficult, such as Adena-type projectile points and several other exotic artifact categories. Other Meadowood habitation sites are known to be small campsites but these remain essentially unreported with the exception of a survey report on site BkGr-1 on Rosebary Lake, Ontario (Hurley and Kenyon 1970:64-66).

There has been much controversy over the early date for Saugeen (Fig. 2.1) from the Donaldson site which clearly has a pottery series which appears to be later than the early Vinette 1 wares; however, similarity in adaptation, location, size, dwellings, and activities suggest its relationship to post-Meadowood phase times and to the Saginaw Bay Early Woodland in Michigan (Wright and Anderson 1963). Other Canoe Point phase sites such as Brock Street (Kenyon and Cameron 1961) also show this affiliation.

A continuing source of difficulty in connecting obvious similarities between the Archaic and Woodland adaptations and inventories in New York and eastern Michigan has been the lack of information on Late Archaic adaptations to the Lake Forest environment in southern Ontario. Wright suggests two variants, an eastern and a western, of Laurentian in Ontario during the Late Archaic, divided by a line which would run through Toronto (1972:31). The western variant, "an Archaic of obscure tradition," apparently encompasses the Iverhuron site (Kenyon 1957) and the Knechtel I site (Wright 1972:31). The settlement pattern of summer agglomeration and winter dispersal proffered for this expression is, however, more closely affiliated with subarctic groups than with those of the Lake Forest Late Archaic (Wright 1972; Fitting 1970).

Examination of the settlement patterns of chronologically and geographically associated cultural groups from 2000 B.C. to 0 A.D. in the Lake Forest area shows that there is first a significant dearth of information and second a clear impression of similarity in the available data. Artifactually there is a great degree of uniformity (Papworth 1967, Fitting 1971, Ritchie 1969). Figure 2.2 presents information on projectile points of the Lake Forest area which appear to be related and which

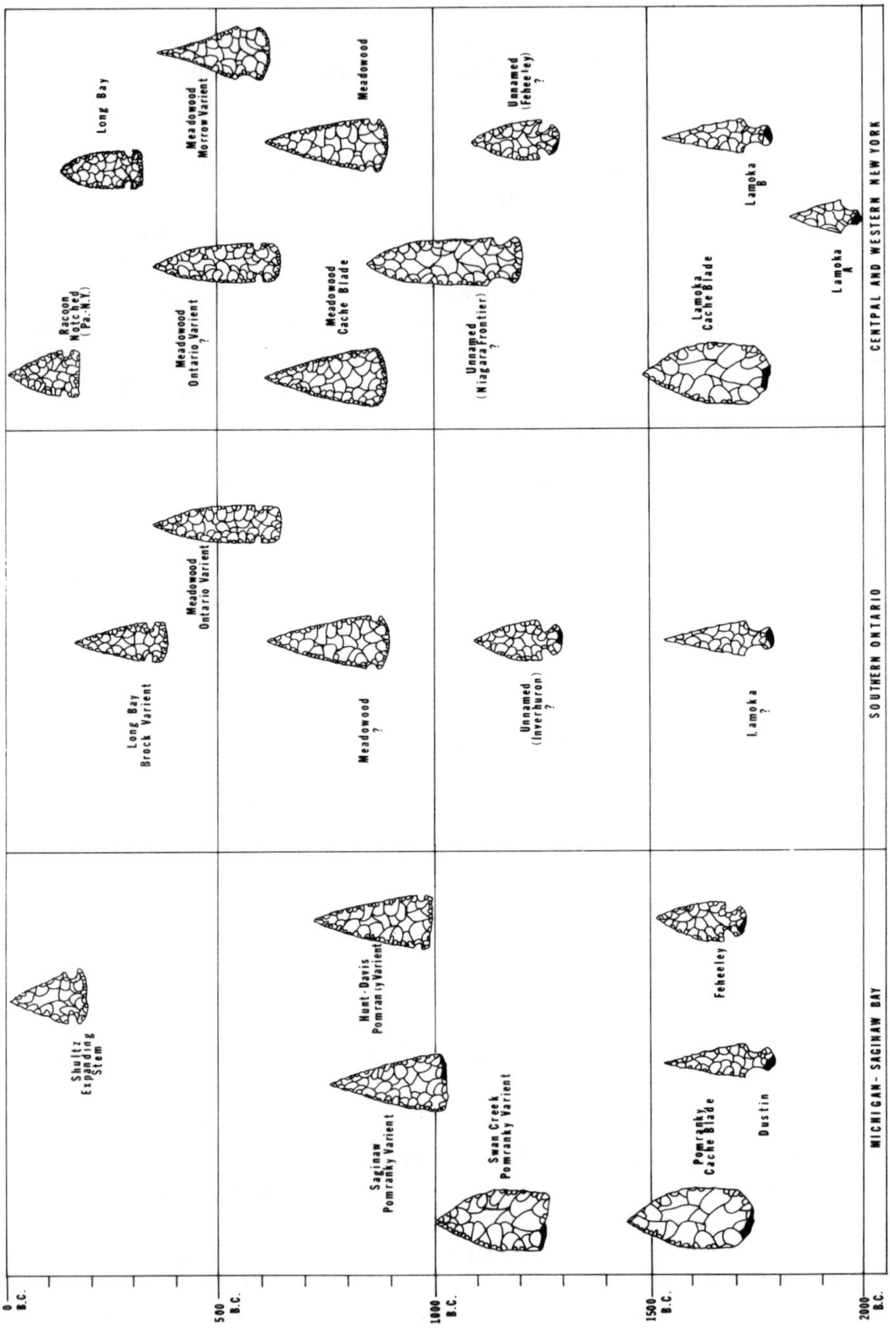

Fig. 2.2 Distribution of some Late Archaic—Early Woodland projectile points.

have been found on the sites which we have described above. These projectile points are derived from technologies which manifest like traits such as end-struck flakes and production of laterally trimmed relatively thin points (except for the earlier ones such as Lamoka and Dustin where medial thickness is present). A gradual transition from stemmed to cornernotched and sidenotched forms is evident and seems to be dependent on broadening of the blade and basal elements (Binford 1963*a*). While genetic sequences of projectile points are subject to error, it may be argued that within the Lake Forest Area there appears to be chronologic and geographic continuity in at least one artifact category intimately related to subsistence activity. It remains to be demonstrated by further evidence whether this continuity in artifact morphology is related to parallel adaptive change in this area of environmental likeness.

Meadowood phase stands at a point in definition where it has become necessary to reexamine the data in New York State carefully in order to assess the interpretive changes necessitated by the recent addition of information. The most persistent gap in the long history of interpretation of the phase is not lack of sites but lack of information on their spatial and environmental associations, i.e., Meadowood settlement pattern. The settlement system, while not represented by a great amount of excavated data, may be deduced by careful analysis of settlement data in the context of a restricted region such as the Niagara Frontier. In this way we may determine the stability of the cultural adaption and the network of associations between various groups. New approaches can organize already known facts into a form which frees the investigation from the circularity of trait tracing. In the next chapter we will attempt to examine as precisely as possible the environmental circumstances of Meadowood settlement and their consequences for cultural adaptation over the broad distribution of Meadowood sites and particularly for Meadowood phase sites within the Niagara Frontier.

CHAPTER III

THE NATURAL ENVIRONMENT OF THE STUDY AREA

The Niagara Frontier, for the purposes of this study, is defined as that area in western New York within an approximate radius of fifty miles from the present city of Buffalo, New York (Zenkert 1934:24 and map). The area contains portions of the glaciated Allegheny Plateau to the south and Erie–Ontario Lowland to the north. Generally the elevation ranges from 75 meters (246 feet) at Lake Ontario to 365 meters

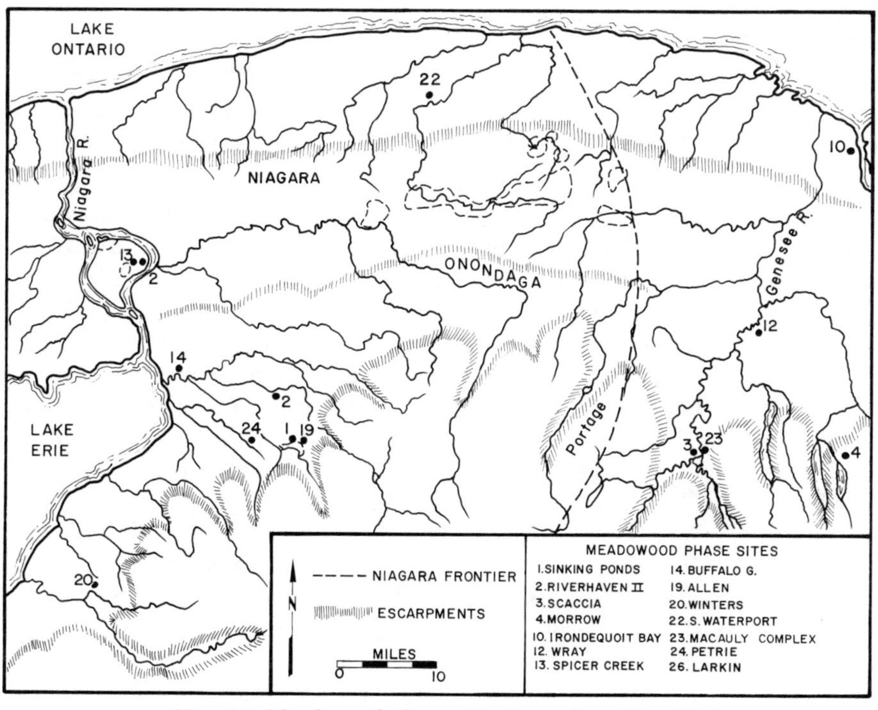

Map 3.1 Meadowood phase sites in western New York.

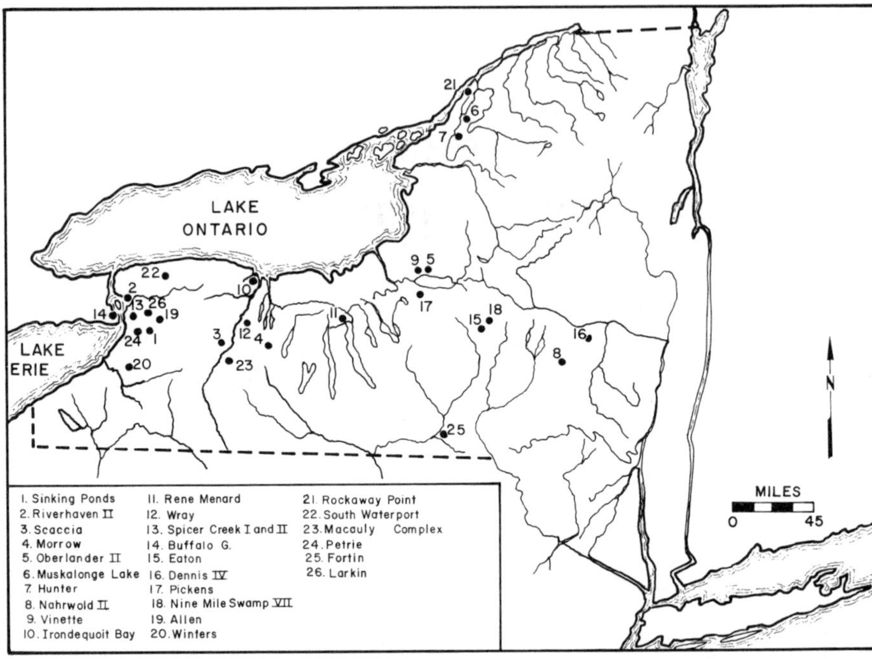

Map 3.2 Meadowood phase and associated sites in New York State.

(1200 feet) in the Plateau (ibid.:25). The primary drainage for the area is the St. Lawrence River system with most of the streams draining northward, or westward into Lake Ontario, Lake Erie, and the Niagara River (Map 3.1). Streams to the south drain into the Allegheny River and then through the Ohio and Mississippi valleys to the Gulf of Mexico. The divide generally follows the crest of the Portage Escarpment (Zenkert 1934:36). The subsurficial geology of the area consists of Silurian, Devonian, and Carboniferous period sedimentary rocks, limestones, sandstones, shales and conglomerates (ibid.:28), modified by glaciation (Kindle and Taylor 1913; Von Engeln 1914). Rainfall ranges between 30 and 40 inches per year with the snowfall on the Lake Plain often averaging 60-80 inches. The growing season ranges between 165 and 170 days per year (Zenkert 1934:38-44). Seven sites of Meadowood phase affiliation have been recorded in this area. These are illustrated by Map 3.1 and Map 3.2.

Also essential to the understanding of archaeological expressions in the Niagara Frontier Region of New York State is a brief general

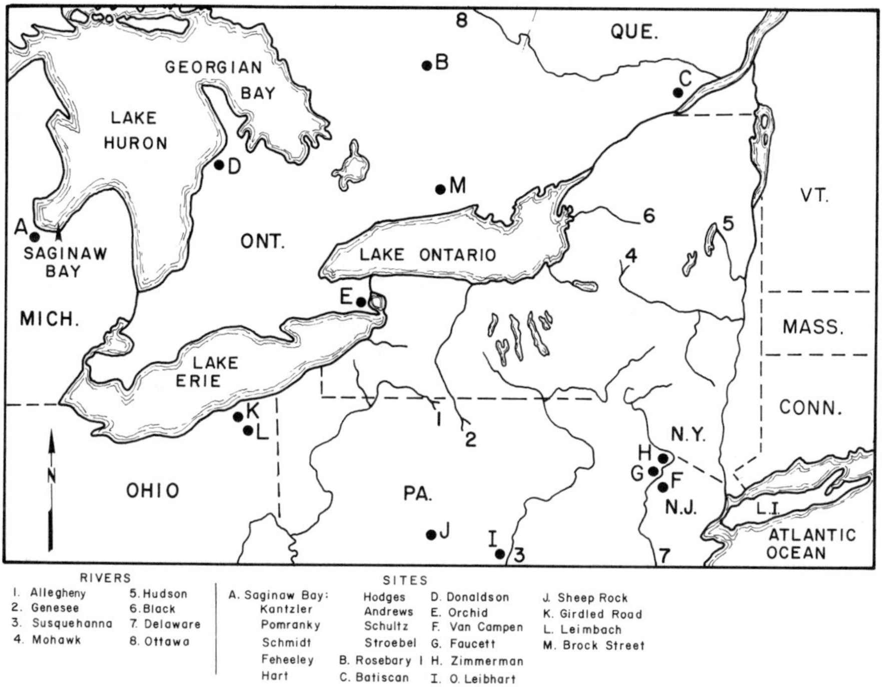

Map 3.3 Early Woodland sites outside New York State.

description of other areas in which contemporary and culturally affiliated sites occur. The general area of distribution is centered around upper New York and on the southern periphery of the lower Great Lakes, Erie and Ontario (Map 3.3). Southeastern Ontario, Michigan's Saginaw Bay area, and portions of the Susquehanna and Delaware River drainages have disclosed sites with some affinity to Meadowood phase culture (Map 3.3). Description of the general area in biologic and physiographic terms will provide an overall frame of reference for examination of the specific environmental associations of the sites in the Niagara Frontier.

FLORA AND FAUNA

The most useful biotic division is that suggested by Dice. He divides the study area between the Canadian and Carolinian Biotic Provinces (1943: Map 3.1 and Map 3.4). Another concept of biotic division is that proposed by Potzger as the Lake Forest Formation. Papworth found that:

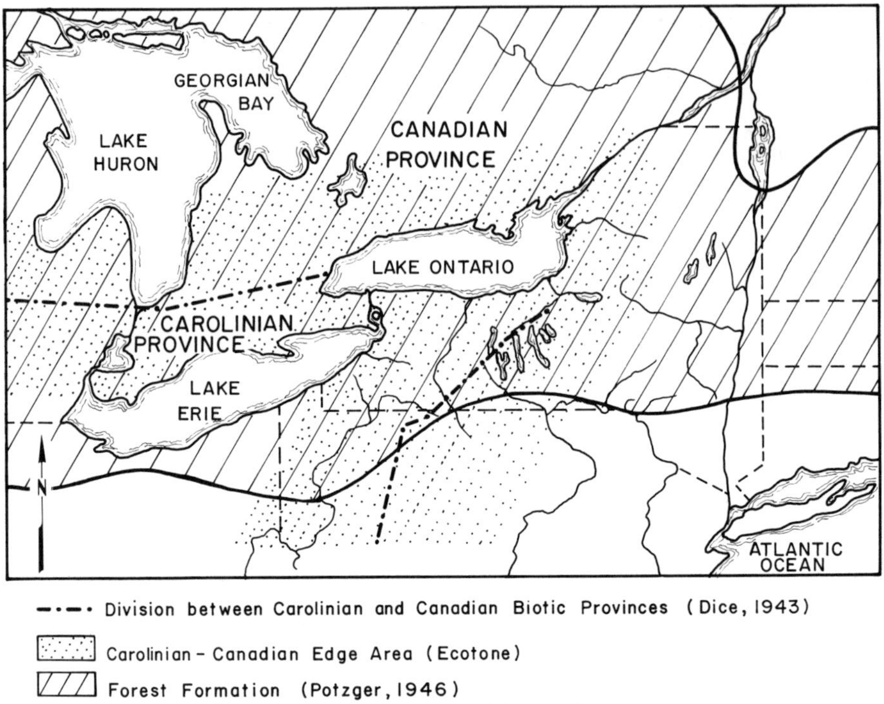

Map 3.4 Biotic divisions of the study area.

> . . . Burial ceremonialism (Late Archaic) links cultural manifestations across a wide area which approximates today a natural area, defined by soils and vegetation known as the Lake Forest Region. [Parenthesis mine.] (1967:234).

Potzger defines this region as follows:

> It requires but small acquaintance with the Lake Forest to recognize that its vegetational complex differs from that of forest formations to the north and to the south of it . . . it possesses an atmosphere all its own. Its early history is linked with frontiers of continental ice caps, and its development was associated with a pole-ward march of forests when moderating climate transformed ice masses of millennia of accumulations into rushing streams and countless lakes and ponds.
>
> This is preeminently a lake formation, being centered on the Great Lakes and recurring to the eastward in New York and New England, where larger lakes and rivers produced similar conditions. (Potzger 1946:227)

The flora of these areas is chestnut, oak, and poplar, of the more southerly Oak-Southern Forest type, intergraded with a more northerly birch, beech, maple and hemlock forest (Shantz and Zon 1924:Map 4; Braun 1950:321; Shelford 1963:Map 3). Internal relations are complex, due to several forest successions and remnant communities (Braun

1950:527; Potzger 1946:233), but generally it is characterized by distinctive soils such as alluvial deposits, glacial till, and an unstable, mixed hardwood–conifer community (Potzger 1946:215; Braun 1950:527). These communities are located in a loose boundary between the two biotic provinces, the Carolinian and the Canadian (Dice 1943:Map 1).

The "edge effect" or overlapping of gradients in floral and faunal communities creates ecotones or edge areas (Odum 1971:158). This situation occurs within the Lake Forest area and is a cause of the complexity in forest and animal types observed in the study area. We can think of the Lake Forest region as a transition between biotic provinces, north and south. Map 3.4 shows the transitional and complex nature of the area under consideration by associating the biotic provinces, edge area, and Lake Forest formation.

Zenkert (1934:45-48) defined the relationships of dominant maple–beech forests and relict boreal communities in the Niagara Frontier. He suggests that:

> . . . Such large inland bodies of water as the Great Lakes have a moderating and equalizing influence on the climate of adjacent tracts of land making it possible for more southern plants to extend their range northward. In the Niagara Frontier Region the lower levels of its northern portion, the tempering effects of the Lower Great Lakes and the higher elevations of the southern plateau land have interacted to produce the rather interesting phenomenon of a reversal in the zonation of vegetation, southern plants thriving to the north in the Erie-Ontario Lowlands, with northern forms abiding southward in the Allegheny uplands. (Zenkert 1934:23)

Both Shelford (1963:45-48) and Zenkert (1934:46-48) state that much of the floral diversity is caused by immediate location in bogs, on sand ridges, or on rocky outcrops. The beech dominant favored the marshy wet ground while an oak–maple association favored the sandy ridges. Shelford notes a significant admixture of hemlocks with the maple–beech forests in western New York, especially in ravines and on north slopes. Zenkert suggests causative factors such as:

> . . . The freshness and richness of the comingled soil deposits, the shore lines of lakes, large and small, and the morainic hills and ridges alternating with marshy depressions — this diversity of substratum and habitat induced a general migration of vegetation back northward and . . . not a few components of sub-arctic flora [hemlocks] found a congenial environment. (1934:33)

The reconstructed precontact floral associations of Erie County, a large part of the Niagara Frontier, were described by H. Perry Smith in 1884 as follows:

> In the southern part of the county the valleys were covered with beech and maple, the hills with oak and elm and occasional bodies of pine, and a little farther north with large quantities of hemlock. In the center the pine increased in quantity,

> the land largely occupied by towering pines of the finest quality. In the northern section hardwood trees again predominated, the low ground north of the limestone ledge being thickly covered. Birch appeared in large quantities on the Tonawanda. Throughout the county the various species were more or less intermingled, and numerous other kinds were found in smaller quantities. (Zenkert 1934:54)

Seasonally a wide variety of plants becomes available in the Niagara Frontier region. During the autumn vast quantities of acorns, hickory nuts, beech nuts, and walnuts, become available in lowland and upland areas to support humans and mast-consuming herbivores. During the spring and summer months many usable plants such as *Chenepodium* or goosefoot, *Polygonum* or smartweed and *Amaranthus* were present. Grapes, berries, and other fruits were distributed in the marshes and on the higher elevations in spring, summer and fall.

The fauna available in the general study area are presented in tabular form in Appendix C by habitat, habits, foods consumed, density, and in some cases, means of capture (Burt 1957; Burt and Grosenweiler 1964; Cleland 1966; De Vos 1964; Rostlund 1952; Shelford 1963; Taylor 1956; White 1953; Linduska 1964; Collins 1959; Hawkinson 1924; Hamilton 1943; Cahalane 1947; Stewart 1961).

Many species of animal inhabited several provinces : bear, wolf, woodchuck, beaver, elk, etc., while some were characteristic of only one but with minor overlaps. The Carolinian province was heavily populated by whitetail deer, turkey, passenger pigeon, raccoon, gray fox, gray squirrel, and numerous other bird and mammal species. Shelford (1963:45-47) reports that the general study area was located within an elk–deer association forming a faciation with maple–beech forests, but the elk, which was not frequent even during prehistoric times, became extinct in the study area during the mid-nineteenth century (De Vos 1964:211). Shelford characterizes the whitetail deer as still a major permanent dominant; that is, a controlling species which influences the forest which it inhabits (1963:15-16, 30-33). The deer crosses all zones of the forest and

> . . . is not a year around dweller in dense forest but frequents openings, edges and burned areas. Large populations of deer occur in closed climax stands only in winter. (Shelford 1963: 33)

Consequent with large deer populations was the presence of such predators as wolf, bear, cougar and lynx, now largely extinct in the area. Table C.1 and Figure C.2 in Appendix C show the numbers of these carnivores in relationship to the herbivores in the study area.

The area also benefited from a number of more northerly mammalian fauna, such as the elk and caribou, penetrating southward and some southerly species such as the raccoon extending their ranges northward due to the moderating climatic effects of the lower Great Lakes (see App. C, Table C.1); (Cleland 1966:27; De Vos 1964:225-26).

Large populations of turkey and passenger pigeon also existed in the lower Great Lakes area (App. C, Table C.2). The latter are now extinct while the range of the former is highly restricted. These birds were available during spring and fall, with the turkey also available in the winter.

Large numbers of aquatic birds were seasonal migrants in these areas. The watered bogs and marshes in the Niagara Frontier (Zenkert 1934:33) formed major stopover points on the inland branch of the Atlantic Flyway (Linduska 1964:167-83; Axtell 1956; see also App. C, Table C.3). Numerous species of reptiles and amphibians also occupied these bogs and formed a large subsistence resource for waterfowl and man (App. C, Table C.5).

The larger streams of the Erie–Ontario Lowland are of the meandering type on a more or less level plain with only minor irregularities (Zenkert 1934:36). These streams, together with the shallow lakes and bogs, formed what Rostlund (1952:74) describes as an inland fishery with rather low productivity except in spring and summer. Table C.4, Appendix C, shows the species of fish available, but Rostlund suggests that shallow water varieties (catfish, burbot, drumfish, and suckers) were the most available and commonly utilized (1952:46-48). In the slower streams like the Buffalo River and in backwaters of the swifter streams such as the Niagara River, numerous varieties of freshwater mussels were available in the summer and fall during low water (Clarke and Berg 1959).

The Niagara Frontier region and the entire study area had a diverse and rich floral biota which supported a variety of fauna overlapping two biotic provinces, the Canadian and the Carolinian, in what is known as the Lake Forest Formation. This situation produced an area in which food resources were plentiful and easily hunted, fished, or gathered.

CLIMATE: PALYNOLOGY AND OTHER EVIDENCE

Several biogeographers have been able to present reconstruction of climate and forest succession for the northeastern states. There is evidence for a warm climax period known as the Hypsithermal in the Northeast and a shorter period, the Xerothermic in the Midwest (Deevey and Flint 1957:182; Cox 1965:6).

Over the area of our inquiry there is little valid data for temperature beyond growing season, which depends on frostfree days (Cline

1970:5). Most of the area today has a growing season of 100 to 150 days, extending concentrically from Lake Ontario, while 180-day seasons occur only in a small area southeast of Lake Ontario. Elsewhere the highest number of days is 165 grading to 150 as higher elevations are reached.

A general rule of thumb in understanding the climates of upper New York State is proposed by Cline:

> . . . The lowland areas are generally warmer than the adjacent highlands and temperatures are generally higher in the south than at equal elevations in the north. Near Lakes Erie and Ontario . . . the climate is somewhat modified (warmer) by the nearness of large bodies of water. [Parentheses mine.] (Cline 1970:5)

It seems reasonable that since essentially the same geographic conditions affected climate in the past, at circa 3000 years, that the above axiom should be kept in mind as we explore other evidence relating to climatic reconstruction.

Rainfall patterns show that broad areas encompassing most of the Niagara Frontier Region are in the 30 to 40 inch zone while a 30 to 50 inch zone encompasses most of adjacent upper New York (ibid. 6).

Climatic reconstruction for the area has been facilitated by a research project conducted by palynologists Donald D. Cox and Donald M. Lewis in the Crusoe Lake Area of the Montezuma Marsh in central New York. They state:

> . . . Beginning about 3000 B.C. and extending to about 2000 years ago (0 A.D.) was an interval of time during which there was less available moisture than either the period preceding or following it. Based on the pollen record, the most noticeable change in the forests of central New York State was a decrease in the amount of hemlock. Beech probably replaced much of the hemlock on the more moist sites (lowland swamps and lake periphery) with oak and hickory abundant on the drier locations. [Parentheses mine.] (Cox and Lewis 1965:21)

The effects of this drying period were marked by ecological shifts. An increase in mast producing oak, beech, and hickory trees, most likely caused an increase in deer and other mast eating populations, while the lake eutrophication and extinction cycle advanced. Local fish populations probably became more accessible to exploitation due to the advancing shallowness of lakes. Northward shifts of warm temperate zone mammals occurred and also of more climatically sensitive amphibians and reptiles (Smith 1965:634; Cleland 1966:26-27). Waterfowl flyway patterns remained fairly unaltered. An inland branch of the Atlantic Flyway passes over central and western New York, and here there were probably minor alterations in lake, bog, and marsh utilization (Linduska 1964:167-70).

The consequences of the climatic change from a cooler, moist period to a warmer, dry period appears to have had no particular environmental and cultural implication beyond an increase in some resources, a decrease in others, and minor shifts in exploitation patterns. Water resources may have become productive in the short run, but as the shallow lakes became marshes, exploitation may have begun to shift toward heavier reliance on the upland mast eating animals. Nut collecting and utilization probably became a more intensively developed pattern, but it was not a new pattern due to the increased availability of beech nuts and hickory nuts as well as acorns.

Grayson compared faunal inventories for 12 archaeological sites which span the post-Paleo-Indian time period and suggested that mammalian utilization depended largely upon the frequency of specific animals in the deciduous forest rather than any focal cultural emphasis (1974:32-33). In this light, deer hunting may have been more strongly emphasized during the period 3000–2000 B.P.

MEADOWOOD SITES: LOCATIONS AND NATURAL ASSOCIATIONS

Physiography and Geomorphology

The area of Meadowood phase distribution includes all of the physiographic areas of New York State (Cline 1966:4). In all, 26 components of Meadowood phase are now known however incompletely (Map 3.2). The major physiographic divisions of the area are generally defined as the Ridge and Valley in the eastern sections of New York, the Appalachian Plateau also in the east and in the south–central portions of the area, and the Central Lowland Province in central and western lake-associated areas (Thornbury 1965). These geomorphic structural areas and their local divisions in New York State have defined a diverse series of topographic zones, yet within these zones there exist structures caused by glaciation which have tended to level sharp distinctions in local topography (Map 3.5). These are areas where change has been recent, after 13,000 B.P. The geomorphically recent nature of some of the topography associated with glacial remnants has provided loci for man's occupation which may well have been markedly different than those we see today. In order to examine these changes and different features it is necessary to briefly define the underlying structures and the glacial changes in the provinces in which Meadowood sites are found.

The Adirondack Upland is a mountainous area of folded and worn igneous Precambrian rock with overlays of glacial till. Structurally the area is ridge and valley but with a radial drainage pattern of outflowing streams to the north, south, east and west (Thornbury 1970:120). Two Meadowood phase sites, Muskalonge Lake and Hunter, are located in

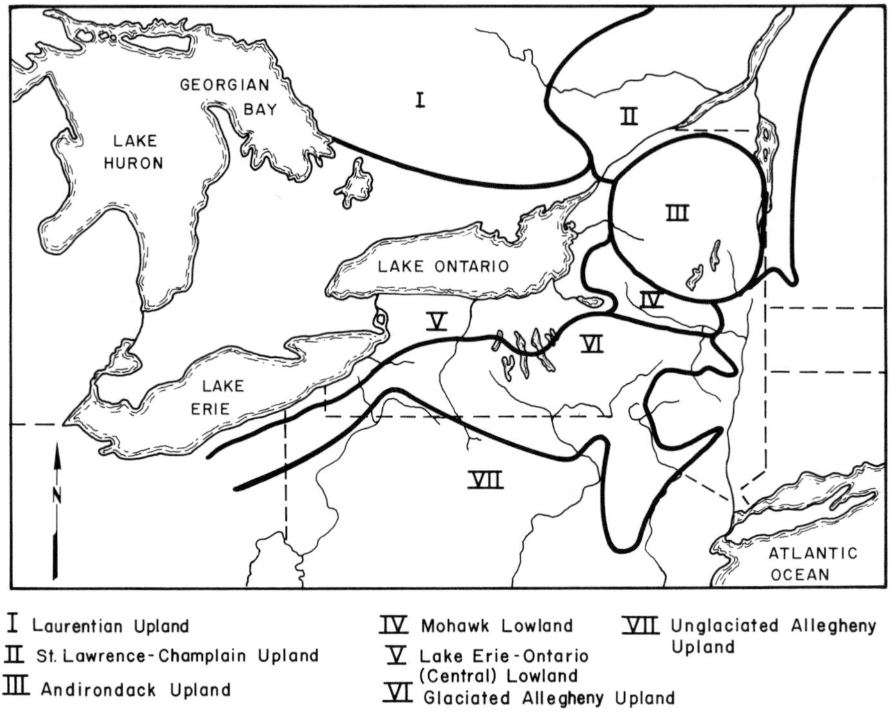

Map 3.5 Regional physiographic provinces of New York State.

the Adirondack Upland, in a major stream valley, that of the Indian River.

The Mohawk Valley Section (Map 3.5) is formed upon a base of Ordovician shales with numerous uplift benches to the north and south. Drainage is longitudinal, extending to the Hudson River Valley, which it joins perpendicularly from the west. Two sites, Dennis 4 and Nahrwold 2, are located within this valley.

The glaciated Allegheny Upland Section (Map 3.5) covers much of central, western, and southern New York State. It intersects with the unglaciated Allegheny Upland in a very indistinct boundary close to the New York–Pennsylvania line and was caused by extensive early Pleistocene glacial scouring. It is generally the highest area in elevation. Eight Meadowood sites cluster at the northern edge of this section: Sinking Ponds, Allen, Petrie, Scaccia, MacCauley Complex, and Morrow (Map 3.2) in the central and western portions and Eaton and Nine Mile Swamp 7 in the east. The original topography has been intensively altered by glaciation, subsequent stages of which even altered previous glacial actions. This leaves topographic expression to the latest Wisconsin ice advances. Several substage tills or end moraines have been recognized in this province (Fairchilde 1932:627-62). These run in an east–west direction in the plateau. Although the steepness and elevations of the terrain have promoted erosion, which results in problems of identification, moraines such as the Late Wisconsin Valley Heads Moraine, found at the southern tips of the Finger Lakes, are typical (Flint 1971:574-76). Fairchilde recognized "moraine belts" which can be traced southward from Lake Ontario (Flint 1971:633; Hough 1958:94). These "belts" illustrate an important point: major topographic zones proceed in a southerly direction away from Lake Ontario. This is somewhat altered to the west where marine sediments are more extensive, and where the Lake Erie Plain is obliquely situated northeast-southwest and is more severely constricted by the Allegheny Plateau. Glaciation scoured deep valleys, the Finger Lakes, and deposited patches of moraine at their southern ends which acted as huge dams. A system of "through valleys" or abandoned drainage channels was created (Thornbury, 1965:133). These lead south, cutting off from the west the Susquehanna River drainage system in which the Meadowood component Fortin 2 is located. Streams flow south off the moraines in the north into this major drainage system. This divide, or watershed, is very narrow and is all that separates the drainage systems of the Genesee, Oswego, and Seneca rivers, in the north from the major riverine system, Susquehanna, Delaware, Allegheny, flowing to the southeast or southwest.

Communication by way of these valleys is possible from the Susquehanna River to the lower portions of the Finger Lakes, which because of the moraine belt, drain to the north. Stream channels such as the Genesee River illustrate the effects of a through valley which captured a portion of the Susquehanna system's southeasterly flow into a northward flow. The east side of the valley of the Genesee has a series of hanging valleys with a trellis stream structure modified by the meandering of the river in a valley filled with glacial till. This pattern has left many perpendicular ridge protrusions, often used by man for settlement, into the valley, with each separated by streams on the east. The other side of the valley, on the west, has a series of open through valleys in which water has been cut off, forming marshes and small lakes drained by stream tributaries of the Genesee such as Beards Creek. The main valley itself has retained a portion of the older deeper valley structure, and subsequent to the glacial deposition of till on the main floor it has developed a peneplain, with oxbow lakes and marshes created by infusion of water from the upper plateau to the south.

The important features here are the high–low, north–south horizontal linear developments created by the glacial moraine belts. New drainage patterns at lower elevations in glacially-filled valleys developed overburdened hydrologic systems which formed marshes in postglacial times, such as the Montezuma Marsh in the Erie–Ontario Lowland Province. These shallow lakes or marshes existed prior to and during the time of Meadowood settlement.

The Erie–Ontario Lowland Province is located in the north central sector of the state and encompasses much of the Niagara Frontier to the west. It is characterized by lake sediments underlain by glacial till. The bedrock is Ordovician, Silurian, and Devonian and consists of shales, sandstones, dolomites, and limestones with spectacular chert inclusions which are seen in uplifted escarpments such as the Onondaga and Niagara escarpments. This section takes its name from Lakes Erie and Ontario, the successive stages of which form the most prominent part in the area's physiographic history. Numerous lakes and marshes formed behind glacial end moraines (Thornbury 1965:232). Drumlins, eskers, and kames interrupt and derange the drainage pattern, while kettles provide basins for shallow lakes and marshes. The most recent glaciation, the Port Huron Stadial Episode, is responsible for most of the visible topography.

On the plain to the west, the Niagara River was a swift-flowing outlet draining early Lake Erie into Lake Iroquois, an earlier and expanded Lake Ontario. Cutting by this river, which carried large loads of sediment from the marine laid bed of former Lake Tonawanda, created the Niagara Gorge (Kindle and Taylor 1913:64; Buhler and Tesmer 1963:15; D'Agostino 1958). Much alluvium was deposited around higher indurated limestone bedrock in the upper river, creating islands and expanding existing structures such as Grand Island (Heubusch 1967:1-10; Kindle and Taylor 1913:16). In the Niagara Frontier, the drainage of the Buffalo River is a clear example of stream piracy which affected man's utilization of the local topography. Cazenovia Creek captured much of the southern drainage of Buffalo Creek in post-Lake Warren times, circa 11,000 B.P., creating cutoff drainage areas where small lakes or marshes were formed in relict glacial kettles such as Sinking Ponds. Beach lines express stages of Lake Erie in this western zone but become unclear further to the east (Buhler and Tesmer 1963:11). Immediately to the east the last evident beaches are those of the post-Valders Lake Iroquois (Hough 1963:95-97), and in the north along the Niagara Escarpment, the beaches of Lake Tonawanda have also been defined (D'Agostino 1958).

These events have formed a topography which is level close to the presently outlined lakes and more dissected and rolling inland where the terrain grades up to the portion of the Allegheny Plateau which was beyond marine inundation. A drainage history including piracy and channel abandonment formed numerous dead end areas in this higher portion of the lowland. Moraines acted as dams and eskers, and kames canalized the stream flow, often in wholly new directions (Buhler and Tesmer 1963:9-10). Oak Orchard Swamp, a remnant of Lake Tonawanda, is one example of this form of change. This physiographic province is the most heavily occupied by Meadowood phase culture. Thirteen Meadowood sites are located in the Central Lowland on the Erie–Ontario plain. These are Oberlander 2, Vinette, Irondequoit Bay, Rene Menard 1, Wray, Riverhaven 2, Spicer Creek 1 and 2, Buffalo G, Pickins, Winters, Rockaway Point, South Waterport, Frank and Larkin.

There is a single thread which connects all the areas—glaciation. Glacial events produced a leveling influence, creating local areas of similar topography. We believe that the distribution of sites of Meadowood affiliation with one distinct kind of local area found in all physiographic provinces is hardly fortuitous. As we shall see below, the Meadowood sites of the Niagara Frontier and elsewhere are located near streams or marshes, which were possible desiccated fossil lakes or deep water lakes. For this reason, the geomorphic processes which developed streams, lakes and marshes, expecially in the Niagara Frontier, will be described more fully.

Since we are dealing with streams in glacial contexts, two examples — one outside the immediate area but important to the Niagara Frontier will be used — the Genesee and Niagara Rivers. These two streams illustrate differing fluvial forms; one is a swiftly flowing, heavy load carrying kind, and the other is a meandering, slow flowing low load supporting type.

The Niagara River is a swift flowing stream which exits from Lake Erie through a narrow, scoured channel, divides around Grand Island, and then drops into a gorge cut seven miles into the Niagara Escarpment. The gradient of the river is steep with much of the fall concentrated in the Niagara Falls, 167 feet. In its upper reaches and also below the gorge, the river flows at 15-20 miles per hour, which allows it to scour rapidly and carry a relatively large load. Much of the load of the upper river is deposited at the north end and on the eastern periphery of Grand Island particularly where the east channel makes a sharp turn to join the west channel. The velocity of the Niagara did not allow formation of meanders and oxbow lakes, but the aggradation levees formed on the north end of the island trapped shallow water features. Burnt Ship Swamp is a contemporary example of this type of feature (Kindle and Taylor 1913:27;Leet and Judson 1971:180-85).

The Genesee River is a contrast to the Niagara because throughout most of its length the velocity and gradient are low (excepting the Letchworth Gorge), until it reaches Rochester where it drops over the Niagara Escarpment at Genesee Falls. It meanders in a broad, glacially scoured valley filled by till where its course winds and loops back upon itself. Evidences of this situation are the numerous hanging valleys on the valley's east side at Geneseo (Leet and Judson 1971:187-92). In the process of meandering the Genesee cuts off these loops and aggrades closures which form oxbow lakes where its channels move back and forth across the valley floor. Since the load capacity of this river is low, except in spring flood stage, it does not aggrade rapidly nor does it cut rapidly (Leet and Judson 1971:183-85).

Lakes are formed by accumulation of water in natural depressions, and as soon as a lake is formed, the processes of erosion, sedimentation, and vegetation growth begin to cause its extinction and the eventual formation of dry land (Leet and Judson 1971:317). We mentioned above that glaciation had an unusual effect in the areas under discussion; by far the most numerous types of lakes are those which fill depressions behind morainal dams or in glacial kettles. Honeoye Lake, which is outside the study area but close to it, is an example of the former while the Sinking Ponds fossil lake is an example of the latter.

Honeoye Lake fills the stream valley of Honeoye Creek. The glacial origin of the valley is indicated by its steep sides, hanging valleys, and trellis drainage structure. This lake was formed after the Valley Heads moraine blocked the valley (Hough 1963:97-99). Since it was filled, the northern periphery has partially dried, creating a considerable swamp at its north outlet, although the more deeply-scoured portions of the valley lake are unaffected.

Fossil lakes such as the one near the Sinking Ponds site form in smaller pocket depressions of moraines which are left by melting blocks of ice or in low areas blocked by subsequent moraines which cut off a pre-existing drainage pattern. This lake, or more properly, this series of connected kettle ponds, occurs in a low valley formed by several eskers and old beach strands of Lake Warren. It was created when Cazenovia Creek captured much of the southwestern portion of the Buffalo Creek drainage below the Portage Escarpment when a subsequent moraine cut off the area. This obstacle created a broad and shallow lake, now almost totally extinct except for deeper portions in two of the kettles

(Blackmon n.d.: 23-31). Previous to the intrusive esker on the east edge of this complex of kettle ponds the area drained east to Buffalo Creek (Blackmon n.d.:32).

Eutrophication of lakes, or loss of oxygen caused by overuse by plant life, results in sedimentary enrichment and filling of lake bottoms, a prime cause of marsh formation. We have noted above several other causes. Often shallow lakes are filled by sediment before the plant-eutrophication cycle can begin (Deevey 1958:840-48). A marsh can be defined as any soft wet spongy ground periodically covered or saturated by fresh water, and such marshes are quite common on the lowland plain particularly close to the Niagara, Onondaga and Portage escarpments.

Uplands and lowlands, with their minor but significant differences in topography, have variations in climate, temperature, and soils which act as selective pressures on floral, faunal, and cultural communities (Cline 1970:4). It is noteworthy that when the biotic provinces are placed in juxtaposition with upland and lowland zones, an edge area between Carolinian and Canadian provinces occurs in the central portion of upper New York State or in that area of broadest lowland expression; whereas in the east, the area of least lowland breadth is in the Canadian province, and the Niagara Frontier Region in the west, an area of less constricted lowland, is wholly in the Carolinian province.

Site Location Descriptions

Table 3.1 lists all sites known to have produced Meadowood artifacts, settlement remains, or burials. The sites have been arranged in the table by upland, lowland, and physiographic province association as we have discussed above. We will begin our examination of the association of cultural and natural phenomena by establishing a general twofold site division of known Meadowood phase sites. Sites have been classified by the broad general functions of habitation and burial. A site is classified as a habitation locus if a major portion of the data used to affiliate it to Meadowood culture is derived from activities other than grave inclusions. Sixteen such sites are suggested (Table 3.1). Burial stations are sites that are defined as Meadowood primarily from artifact associations with inhumations or cremations. Ten such stations are recorded (Table 3.1). Below we will examine fourteen sites—seven habitation and seven burial—for which information on settlement is available in enough detail to be useful.

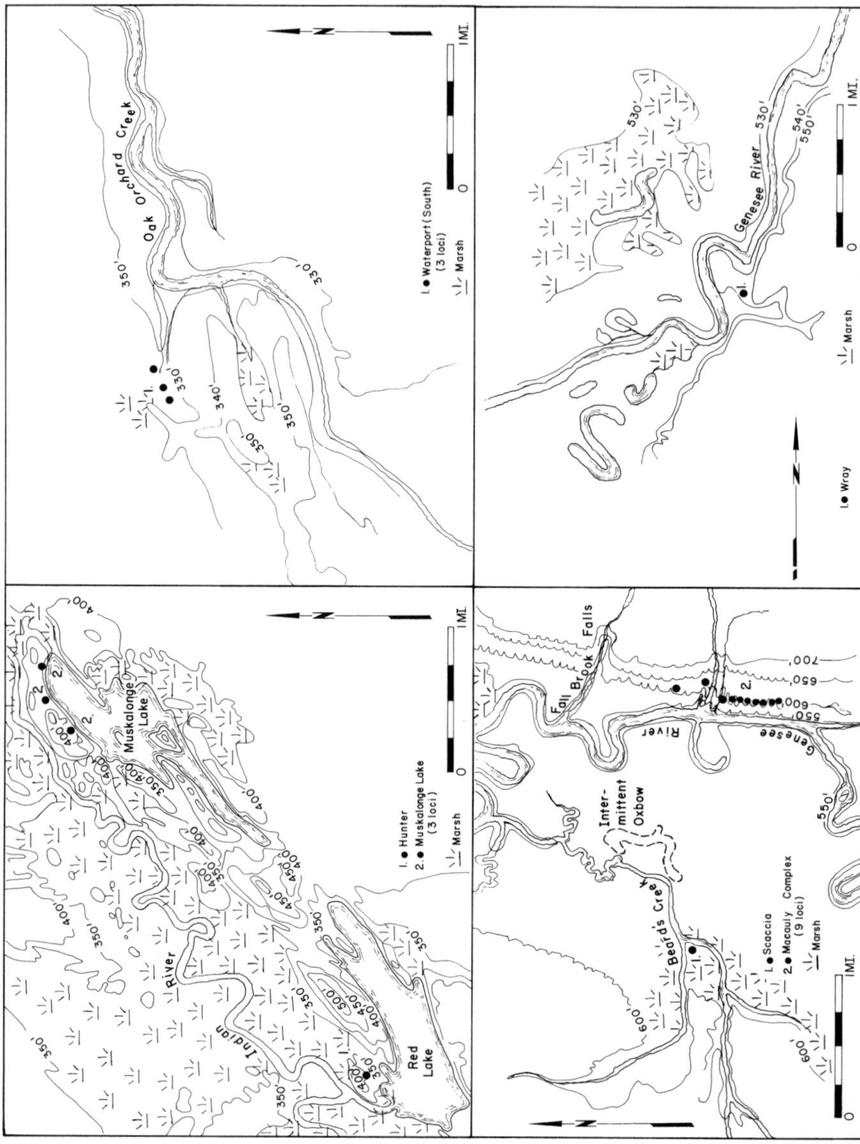

Map 3.6 Hunter and Muskalonge Lakes. Map 3.7 Waterport South. Map 3.8 Scaccia and MacCauley complex. Map 3.9 Wray.

Hunter and Muskalonge Lake (Ritchie 1955) (Map 3.6)

The burial stations are located in the vicinity of the Indian River, which meanders through a lowland of marshes and extant lakes (Ritchie 1955:9). Both sites lie below 155 m (500 ft) elevation and occupy ridges—terraces adjacent and parallel to both the Indian River floodplain and the longitudinal remnant of Muskalonge and Red Lakes. The ridge near Muskalonge Lake has several prominent sand knolls which were cultural loci. Both sites are known primarily from grave lots associated with burial pits containing cremations and several inhumations. Several crematoria were located in swales between sand knolls. The sites are associated with a broad riverine marsh.

South Waterport (Vanderlaan 1966:8-11) (Map 3.7)

The South Waterport habitation sites are located on three small knolls on the V-shaped confluence of a small intermittent stream with Oak Orchard Creek, which is a large meandering stream flowing toward Lake Ontario. There are several small upland marshes caused by springs and poor drainage. East of the site a steep hillside drops down 27.5 m (80 ft) to Oak Orchard Creek (Vanderlaan 1966:8-11).

Scaccia and MacCauley Complex (Ritchie and Funk 1973:99-116; Ritchie 1969:xxii-xxiv; Rhodes, n.d.) (Map 3.8)

The MacCauley Complex is a series of loci which have produced Meadowood materials and a single grave lot. These locations are ridges perpendicular to the east side of the Genesee River valley formed by the hanging valley drainage pattern characteristic of Fall Brook. Most of the perpendicular ridges display a steep drop of 15.5-18.5 m (50-60 ft) to the floor of the floodplain and the river. Little more has been reported on this complex multi-component series of loci.

The Scaccia site is located 2.41 km (1.5 mi) to the west of the Genesee River and MacCauley Complex on a perpendicular ridge extending out into the confluent floodplains of Beards Creek and the Genesee River. This ridge is steep-sided on the north, south, and east, rising 9.3 m (30 ft) above an oxbow marsh created by levee cutoffs (Ritchie and Funk 1973:99). The surface of the hogback is relatively level. Although several burials were disclosed most of the data was derived from a total of 75 pits filled with refuse materials (ibid.:5). A large faunal sample from the site was analyzed and reported (ibid.:114).

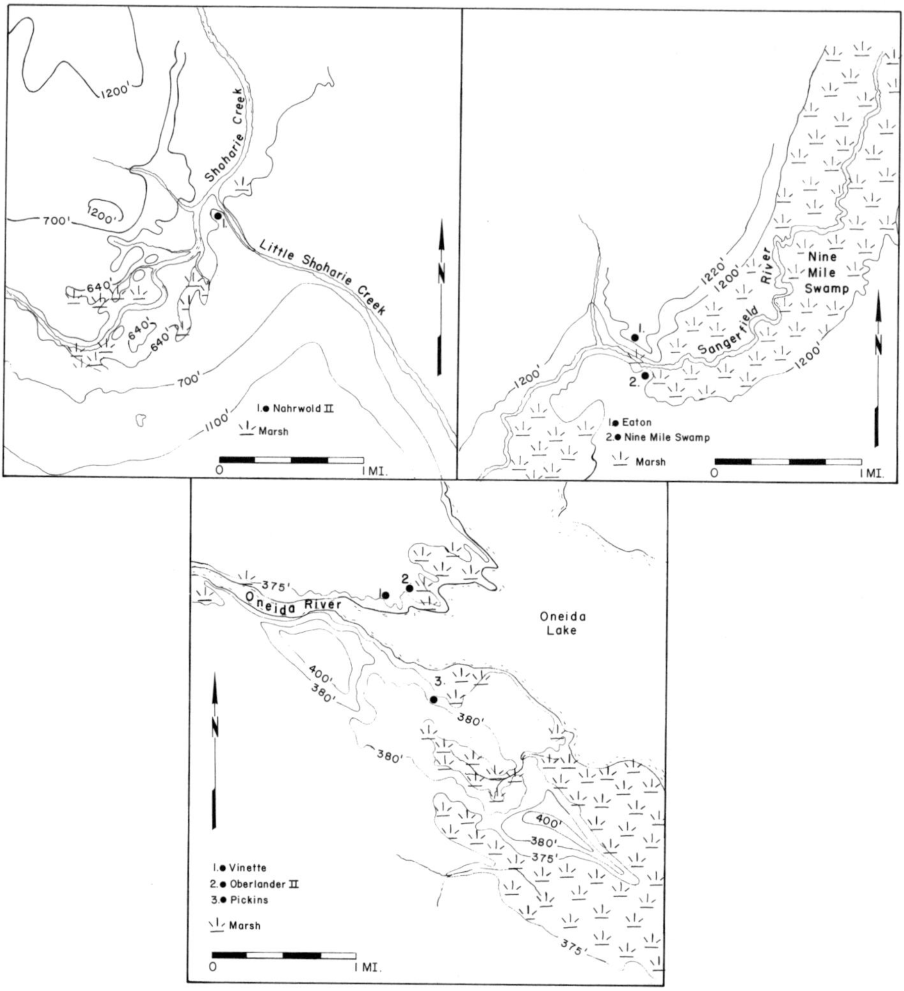

Map 3.10 Nahrwold 2. Map 3.11 Eaton and Nine Mile Swamp.
Map 3.12 Vinette, Oberlander 2, and Pickins.

Wray (Ritchie 1944:125-26) (Map 3.9)

Ten grave lots produced the only evidence from this site which was located on a sand ridge perpendicular to the Genesee River at West Rush, New York (Ritchie 1944:125). The ridge rises steeply to 12.2 m (40 ft) above the river. A large marsh in an old oxbow is situated less than a mile west across the Genesee River.

Nahrwold 2 (Ritchie 1969:xxiii and xxvi) (Map 3.10)

This site represented a second component at the Nahrwold site which produced a few features and a small amount of occupational debris attributable to Meadowood Phase. Some calcined bone samples were recovered and found to be attributable largely to the whitetail deer (Ritchie 1969:xxiii).

The site was located on a high sand terrace bordering the floodplain of Schoharie Creek in a shape confluent with the Little Schoharie Creek. The parallel terrace cut by this latter stream rises 7.5 m (25 ft) above the floodplain of Schoharie Creek, 320 m (.2 mi) to the west. Several small marshes caused by springs occur at the base of the steep terraces where drainage was cut off by Schoharie Creek levees.

Eaton and Nine Mile Swamp 7 (Whitney 1967, 1970) (Map 3.11)

These sites are actually two loci within what Whitney describes as the Nine Mile Swamp complex. Both sites give evidence of artifacts and occupational debris but no burials. The loci are located on low perpendicular sand ridges which lie to the north and south of the Sangerfield River and constrict the southern portion of the Nine Mile Swamp, a large marsh or remnant of a fossil lake (Whitney 1967:Pl. VI, 1970:Pl. I). The Eaton site lies approximately 6.2 m (20 ft) above the river while Nine Mile Swamp 7 is closer to 3.1 m (10 ft) above the stream.

Vinette, Oberlander 2 and Pickens (Ritchie 1944:150-66, 1969:180-201) (Map 3.12)

The Pickens site lies on a gravel knoll on a terrace above a marsh on the south side of the Oneida River where it enters Oneida Lake. Within a mile of the site are several marshy remnant portions of a once expanded lake border. Ritchie classifies this site as a cemetery although only traces of cremations were left after the site had been despoiled (Ritchie 1944:150).

The Oberlander 2 and Vinette sites are situated to the north of the Oneida River on the second terrace. Oberlander 2 is contained on the

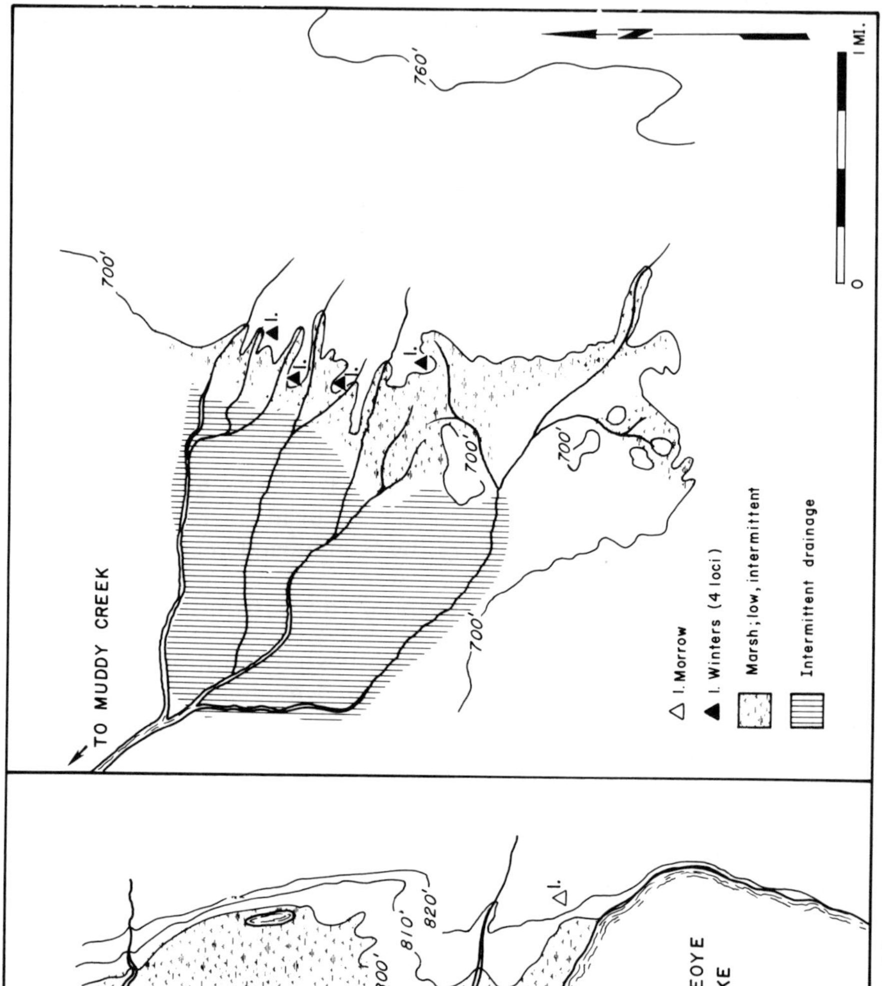

Map 3.14 Winters.

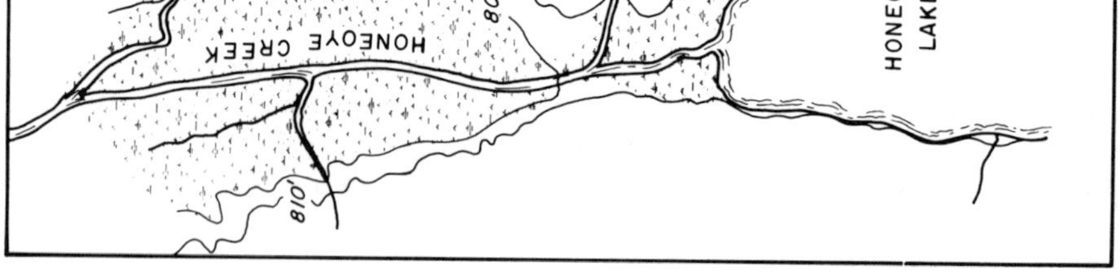

Map 3.13 Morrow.

level top of a small knoll on the terrace. Twenty-two burials were excavated with grave lots consisting of Meadowood phase artifacts (Ritchie 1969:180-81). Some grave lots evidenced "burned dog, deer and fish remains" (ibid:118).

Three hundred and ten m (1000 ft) away on the low, level second terrace was the Vinette site whose lower component gave evidence of Meadowood phase habitation in the form of midden debris and associated features (Ritchie 1944:160). Fragments of preserved calcined bone were analyzed, showing utilization of deer, bear, beaver, turkey, common bullhead, and various turtles (Ritchie 1969:188).

Morrow (Ritchie 1969:180-201; White 1956) (Map 3.13)

The Morrow site disclosed number of burial pits with cremations and grave lots of Meadowood affiliation during a soil stripping operation. Indisputable evidence for fish utilization was found in the form of a carbonized fishnet made of "Indian hemp fiber, twisted into a cord of small diameter, which was woven into a net with about a two-inch mesh" (White 1956). The site was situated on a parallel ridge above the north end of Honeoye Lake where Honeoye Creek debouches out into an extensive marsh which at one time was a northward extension of Honeoye Lake (Von Engeln 1961:39-40). The location of the grouped burial pits was a sloping but nearly level portion of the ridge (Ritchie 1969:181), approximately 13.7 m (45 ft) above the current shore line of the lake. To the east, the terrain again rises sharply to an elevation of 496-527 m (1600-1700 ft) (White 1956:2).

Winters (UB-145; Notes, Department of Anthropology, SUNY at Buffalo) (Map 3.14)

Four sites with occupation debris, features, and artifacts of Meadowood type were discovered on several perpendicular ridges formed by intermittent streams flowing toward Muddy Creek on the Lake Erie Plain. A marsh was formed at the base of these ridges by the intermittent, poor drainage. The ridges rose to a height of approximately 8 m (25 ft) above the marshy ground which was dry during a portion of the year. In a surface collection from the sites made by Winters, several fragments of dear phalanges and bear canines were noted.

TABLE 3.1
DISTRIBUTION OF MEADOWOOD PHASE COMPONENTS

	Physiographic Areas (Cline 1966)	Component	Type*	County	Elevation	No.
UPLAND	Glaciated Allegheny Upland	Sinking Ponds[6]	H	Erie	930′	
		Scaccia[2, 9]	H	Livingston	600′	
		Morrow[2, 10]	B	Ontario	820′	
		Fortin[2]	H	Delaware	1,500′	
		Allen[12]	H	Erie	920′	
		McCauley Complex[7, 12]	H	Livingston	600′	
		Petrie[12]	H	Erie	845′	
		Eaton[4]	H	Madison	1,220′	
		Nine Mile Swamp 7[5]	H	Madison	1,200′	9
	Adirondack Upland	Muskalonge Lake[3]	B	Jefferson	400′	
		Hunter[3]	B	Jefferson	398′	2
LOWLAND	Erie–Ontario Lowland	Riverhaven 2[2]	H	Erie	573′	
		Oberlander 2	B	Oswego	378′	
		Vinette[1]	H	Oswego	378′	
		Irondequoit Bay[3]	B	Monroe	269′	
		Rene Menard[2]	B	Cayuga	506′	
		Wray[1]	B	Monroe	540′	
		Spicer Creek 1 & 2	H	Erie	580′	
		Buffalo "G"[12]	B	Erie	580′	
		Pickens[1]	B	Onondaga	376′	
		South Waterport[8]	H	Orleans	335′	
		Larkin[12]	H	Erie	830′	
		Winters[12]	H	Erie	706′	
		Rockaway Point[3]	B	St. Lawrence	259′	13
	Mohawk Valley Lowland	Nahrwold 2[2]	H	Schoharie	648′	
		Dennis 4[9]	H	Albany	965′	2
	Total					26

[1]Ritchie 1944
[2]Ritchie 1969
[3]Ritchie 1955
[4]Whitney 1967
[5]Whitney 1970
[6]Granger 1966
[7]Rhodes n.d.
[8]Vanderlaan 1966
[9]Funk n.d.
[10]White n.d.
[11]Funk & Rippeteau 1973
[12]SUNYAB Anthropology Department Files

*H-Habitation
B-Burial

Association of Sites

Table 3.2 is a detailed breakdown of 26 Meadowood sites by elevation, fluvial association, lacustrine association, and marsh association. After such distributions were established, comparative associations were tested using Fisher's Two-Tailed Exact Probability Test.

We found that Meadowood sites could not be precisely examined by physiographic province (Table 3.1) because of variation in elevations within these areas. However, using elevation above and below 186 m (600 ft) it can be seen that most habitation sites, 46.2% of the total, cluster above 186 m while burial sites, 34.6% of the total sites, cluster below 186 m. The probability that this distribution occurred by chance is less than 1 in 1000. The uppermost elevation recorded for these sites is 465 m (1500 ft) and only three, or 11.5% of the total, occur above 310 m (1000 ft).

When the fluvial associations were tested, it was found that habitation sites, 38.5% of the total, tended to cluster on perpendicular ridges above streams, while burial sites, 34.6% of the total, clustered on parallel ridges or terraces. This distribution was significant at the .01 level (Table 3.2). Another significant association was the clustering of habitation sites with narrow, small streams, and burial sites with wider, larger, and possibly navigable streams. This distribution may have occurred by chance 3 times out of 100 (Table 3.2).

The distribution of sites on parallel and perpendicular ridges was repeated in the same way when lacustrine associations were tested with a smaller number of sites—16 (Table 3.2). The null hypothesis that there was no significant association of sites was rejected at the .01 level. The most striking association appears to be be the almost perfect correlation of lake-associated habitation sites with marshy fossil remnant lakes and lake-associated burial sites with existing deep water lakes (Table 3.2). While sampling error is clearly possible, a suggested explanation is that burial sites may have been located in areas where water transport was readily possible.

When the distribution of lake type was compared with elevation, a significant result showed the existing lake-associated sites to be below 155 m (500 ft) and those associated with fossil lakes or the retracted periphery of existing lakes to be above 155 m in elevation. The null hypothesis of no association was rejected at the .02 level. The situation outlined by Zenkert (1934:33 and quoted above) relating to lake isolation and bog formation appears to have been a fairly widespread phenomenon throughout the area of Meadowood site distribution. Fifty percent of lake-associated sites were on perpendicular ridges extending

TABLE 3.2
DISTRIBUTION OF MEADOWOOD SITE ASSOCIATIONS

		Elevation (N=26)		Fluvial Ass'n. Phys. (N=26)		Fluvial Type (N=26)		Lake Phys. Ass'n. (N=16)		Lake Type (N=16)		Marsh Ass'n. (N=20)	
		Above 599 Feet	Below 599 Feet	Parallel	Perpen-dicular	Narrow	Wide	Parallel	Perpen-dicular	Fossil	Extant	Parallel	Perpen-dicular
HABITATION	Sinking Ponds	930			+	+			+	+			+
	Riverhaven 2		573	+			+	+		+		+	
	Scaccia	600			+	+			+	+			+
	Nahrwold 2	648			+	+							+
	Vinette		378	+			+		+		+	+	
	Spicer Creek 1-2		580	+		+		+		+			+
	Eaton	1220			+	+			+	+			+
	Dennis 4	965		+		+							+
	Nine Mile Swamp 7	1200			+	+			+	+			+
	Allen	920			+	+			+	+			+
	Winters	706			+	+							+
	South Waterport		335		+		+						+
	MacCauley Complex	600			+		+						
	Petrie	845			+	+			+	+			+
	Fortin	1500		+			+						
	Larkin	830		+			+						
	Subtotal	12 (46.2%)	4 (15.4%)	6 (23.1%)	10 (38.5%)	10 (38.5%)	6 (23.1%)	2 (12.5%)	7 (43.7%)	8 (50%)	1 (6.3%)	2 (10%)	11 (55%)
BURIAL	Morrow	820		+		+		+			+	+	
	Oberlander 2		378	+			+		+		+	+	
	Muskalonge Lake		400	+			+	+			+	+	
	Hunter (Red Lake)		398	+			+	+			+	+	
	Irondequoit Bay		269	+		+		+			+		
	Rene Menard 2		506		+		+						+
	Wray		540	+			+					+	
	Buffalo G		580	+			+	+			+		
	Pickins		376	+			+	+			+	+	
	Rockaway Point		259	+			+						
	Subtotal	1 (3.8%)	9 (34.6%)	9 (34.6%)	1 (3.8%)	2 (7.7%)	8 (30.7%)	6 (37.5%)	1 (6.3%)	0	7 (43.7%)	6 (30%)	1 (5%)
	Column Total	13	13	15	11	12	14 (100%)	8	8	8	8	8	12
	% of N	50	50	57.7	42.3	46.2	53.8	50	50	50	50	40	60
		Fisher's Exact Probability .00174		Fisher's Exact Probability .01036		Fisher's Exact Probability .03731		Fisher's Exact Probability .01958		Fisher's Exact Probability .00069		Fisher's Exact Probability .00433	

to the periphery of the lake or marsh.

When the physiographic association of marsh-associated sites was tested, the distribution repeated and confirmed for the third time the perpendicular ridge affiliation of habitation sites and the parallel ridge or terrace affiliation of burial sites, showing that such a distribution would occur by chance only 4 times in 1000.

It is clear that a study of location alone does not inform us about the exploitation of biotic resources or even if the inhabitants of sites were utilizing those physiographic features that we would consider most prominent, those located nearest the area of occupation. In the brief description of available information on sites, evidence was presented, wherever possible, for the types of faunal materials being exploited. Only Nahrwold 2, Oberlander 2, Vinette, Morrow, and Winters sites had such data, but it was not available in a usable quantitative form.

A further attempt was made to adduce any quantitative data for faunal samples from Meadowood sites and those which were temporally earlier from sites of the Late Archaic or the later Early Point Peninsula sites in New York. Such data was available in usable form from only five sites: Riverhaven 2, Scaccia (Ritchie and Funk 1973:114), Lamoka Lake (Ritchie 1932; Guilday in Ritchie 1969:54-59), Cole Gravel Pit (Brown, Kelley, Penman, and Sparling 1973:24-40), and the Kipp Island site (Guilday in Ritchie 1969:242-43). The data for these five sites is presented in a form which divides water-related or shoreline fauna from fauna which exploit dry land, or upland resources, a majority of the time (App. C). This data is then summarized in Table 3.3 by faunal type—mammal, bird, etc.—and subtype, herbivorous, carnivorous, or om-

TABLE 3.3
SUMMARY FAUNAL COMPARISON
LAMOKA LAKE, RIVERHAVEN 2, SCACCIA AND KIPP ISLAND

		Lamoka Lake				Riverhaven 2				Scaccia				Kipp Island			
		MNI		U.M.		MNI		U.M.		MNI		U.M.		MNI		U.M.	
		#	%	#	%	#	%	#	%	#	%	#	%	#	%	#	%
UPLAND	Herbi-Mam	110	47	7793	83	14	24	1550	70	8	30	418	44	28	5	2560.5	59
	Carni-Mam	17	7	121	1	2	3	34	2	1	5	30	3	4	1	79	2
	Omni-Mam	8	3	804	9	2	3	420	19	2	9	420	45	4	1	635	14
	Bird	51	22	111	1	4	7	34	2	1	5	9	1	1	0+	8.5	.1
	Subtotal	186	79	8829	94	22	37	2038	92	12	55	877	93	37	7	3283	75.1
SHORELINE	Herbi-Mam	9	4	450	5	5	8	47	2	2	9	41	4	14	3	137.5	3
	Carni-Mam	2	.8	20	.2	0	0	0	0	0	0	0	0	3	.8	32.5	.6
	Omni-Mam	3	.1	20	.2	8	14	72	3	1	5	9	1	2	.4	35	.6
	Bird	3	.1	5	.1	7	12	20	1	2	9	7	1	2	.4	7.7	.1
	Reptile	16	7	10	.1	1	2	3	0+	3	14	4	0+	15	3.2	34.3	.1
	Fish	17	7	26	.3	16	27	30	1	2	9	5	1	425	85.2	903	20
	Subtotal	50	21	531	6	39	63	172	8	10	45	66	7	461	93	1150	24.9
	N	236	100	9360	100	59	100	2211	100	22	100	943	100	498	100	4431	100

nivorous mammal. White (1953) suggests usable meat figures for various species of animal. Using his figures we have created a faunal standard of usable meat by estimating the usable meat produced by one representative of each species seen at any of the five sites. We then tested the data from each site against this standard, recognizing possible error.

Exploitation of fauna by usable meat available at each of the sites was compared (Fig. 3.1), but each replicated the standard curve (Fig. 3.2). Chi-square test comparisons between each site for shoreline or upland exploitation show a null hypothesis that there was no focus on upland fauna exploitation, which was rejected at the .01 level on tests between all sites. However, when the number of individuals taken are considered, a different situation is observed. There appears to be greatest emphasis on shoreline species at Riverhaven 2 and when tested against Lamoka Lake, the null hypothesis that there is no differential exploitation is rejected at the .001 level, as it is when tested against Scaccia, but less significantly at the .02 level. Tests between Lamoka Lake and Kipp Island are significant at the .001 level indicating, not only differential exploitation but opposite emphases. This situation is less strong between Kipp Island and the other sites but is so pronounced that it is reflected in the usable meat percentages which fall below 90% upland emphasis to 75% upland emphasis. We might suggest that Cleland's definition of diffuse economy (1966:44) appears to fit the range of species exploited. However, there does appear to be an emphasis on large upland meat producers, herbivorous and omnivorous mammals, from the figures for usable meat. Despite the indication that proximity to productive shore situations conditions the character of the sample of individuals represented on Meadowood sites, it does not substantially affect the emphasis on large meat producing mammals.

We further suggest that the later Canoe Point phase site, Kipp Island, may give an indication of stability with a focus on exploitation of deer and restricted use of fish—only those of the *Ictalurus* genus (App. C).

Although we have attempted to acquire more information on subsistence from the Sinking Ponds site and the Riverhaven 2 site, our efforts have met with differing degrees of success. In the next chapter we will attempt to reconstruct the environmental situation at Sinking Ponds, but due to the lack of preservation of faunal remains we will be unable to deal directly with the occupants' exploitation of it as revealed by faunal material. We shall resort to alternative methods to achieve workable data for comparison with the more directly available information from Riverhaven 2. Recently an intensive study of the faunal

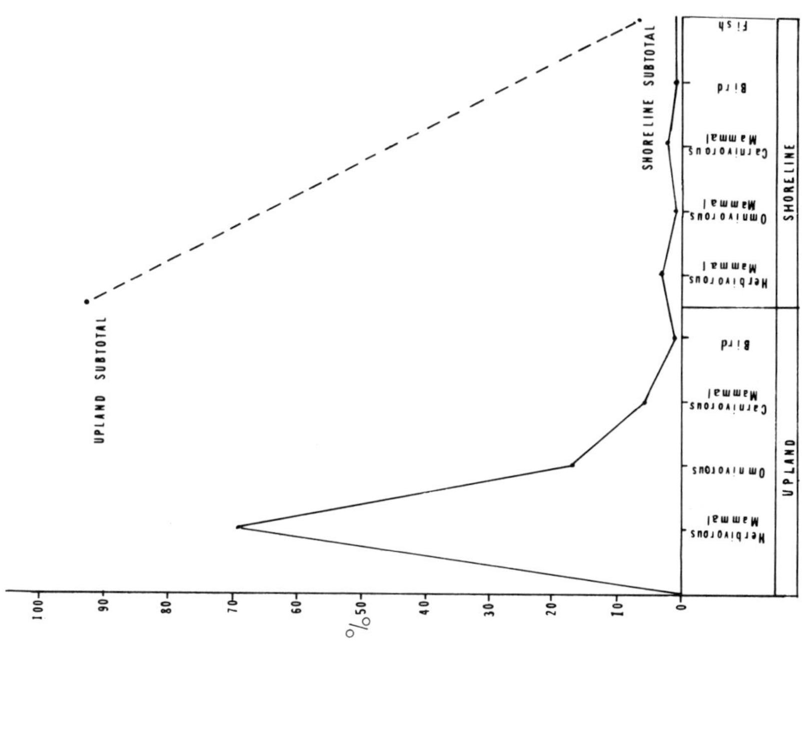

Fig. 3.1 Standard faunal curve of usable meat.

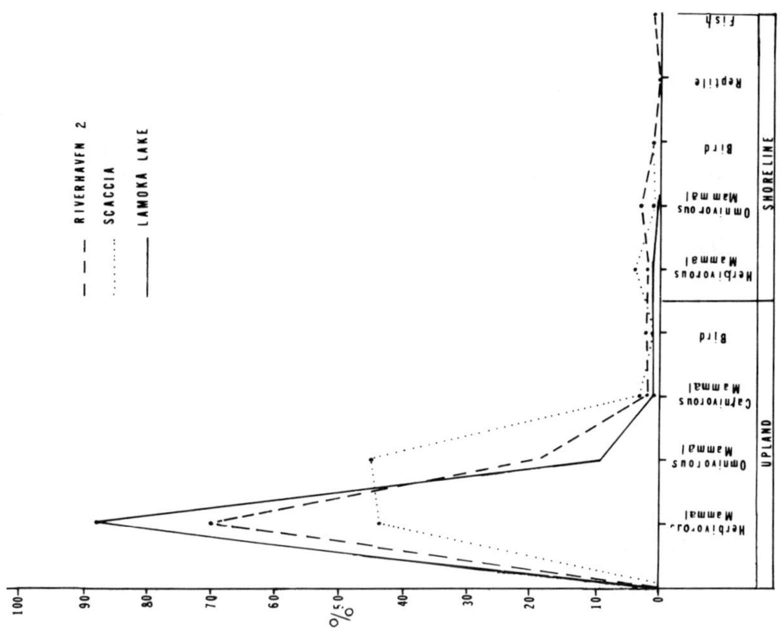

Fig. 3.2 Comparison of utilization of fauna for usable meat.

remains from Riverhaven 2 was made, using samples from the excavations reported here and a larger, more controlled sample excavated by the author in 1971 (Grayson 1974:28-29). The samples were not significantly different from one another as to percentage of species represented, or number of individuals or amount of usable meat. However, until the formal analysis of the total sample is available, comparisons will be made with the present, apparently representative collection (Grayson 1974:24-29).

CHAPTER IV

THE SINKING PONDS SITE

INTRODUCTION

Investigation of the Sinking Ponds site began in 1964 and continued for portions of three field seasons until 1967. The site was initially selected because of its abundance of artifactual materials which appeared to be eroding out of a previously undisturbed occupational deposit. Preliminary examination of these artifacts suggested that the site was affiliated with the Early Woodland Meadowood culture.

Cultural materials were then sought by intensive surface hunting. It was found that artifacts and flint detritus were distributed over an area of approximately 70.2 m (230 ft) north-south by 54.9 m (80 ft) east-west. This distribution was most abundant on erosion surfaces of slopes and at the brink of the ridges and hogbacks. Shovel tests showed that there were in situ cultural materials of the same types as those on the uneroded portions of the 3850 m² (41,400 sq ft). Early testing revealed that the site was shallow and consisted of one homogeneous deposit within which features could be recognized. No burials were reported or found during these tests or subsequent excavations. Although sheet erosion and lack of topsoil formation in the forest cover left the shallow deposits at Sinking Ponds exposed, there seemed to be an intact living floor used intensively but for no extremely long periods of time. Rock features could be traced on the original ground surface and it was later proved that they were in situ.

The Sinking Ponds site produced a total of 1137 artifact fragments representing 453 artifacts. In the following tables counts of either artifact fragments or of artifacts represented by fragments are used. The majority of these cultural materials were in situ and can be analyzed as a systematic representation of the activities performed there.

PHYSIOGRAPHY AND GEOLOGY

The Sinking Ponds site (Dep-7-4 and UB262) is located in the Sinking Ponds Wildlife Sanctuary. This sanctuary occupies the northeastern perimeter of the incorporated Village of East Aurora, approximately 152.5 m (500 ft) northeast of the village water pumping station. The site is located in Lot 16 of Aurora Township in Erie County. Excavations were undertaken on the fairly level summit of a ridge or hogback which extends westward, perpendicular to an eskerine ridge formation bordering several low ponds and fossil lakes (Map 4.1 and Pl. 1). The elevation of the site was 282-325 m (925-930 ft). The occupation area was bounded by steep slopes which fell to the 275 m (900 ft) level in the basin to the west.

Physiography

The perpendicular hogback ridge upon which the site is located has a narrow fingerlike extension which runs to the southwest, creating a natural levee between adjacent ponds—one extant, the other fossil except in very wet years. The most prominent feature of the area's physiography is the glacial topography which nestles close under the Portage Escarpment. The area is bounded to the east by the Buffalo Creek drainage system and to the west by the Cazenovia Creek drainage system. In the natural depressions and basins, ponds and low marshy tracts are maintained by seepage and springs. Drainage into the area from the surrounding uplands is excellent but outlet is poor and confined to Pond Creek which flows northwest to Cazenovia Creek.

The ridges surrounding this basin are glacial in origin and have steep banks, 6.1-12.2 m (20-40 ft) in height. Soil retention is poor and a talus bank is uniformly present at the foot of the ridge. Generally this line of ridge sustains an elevation 6.1-18.3 m (20-60 ft) higher than the floor of the swampy depression. The area's mean annual rainfall is 76.2-101.6 cm (30-40 in) (Cline 1970:4).

Adjacent to the occupation site is the largest standing body of water in the immediate area. This pond is 152.5 m (500 ft) by 61 m (200 ft) with a mean depth of standing water of 1-1.9 m (3-5 ft). No stream serves as an inlet, and the pond is maintained by melt waters and springs. Likewise, two small shallow subsidiary ponds to the northwest are fed only by rain and melt waters and are in the final stages of eutrophication.

Tracing the flow of Pond Creek within the low areas is difficult, compounded now by new structures and historic filling for a railroad,

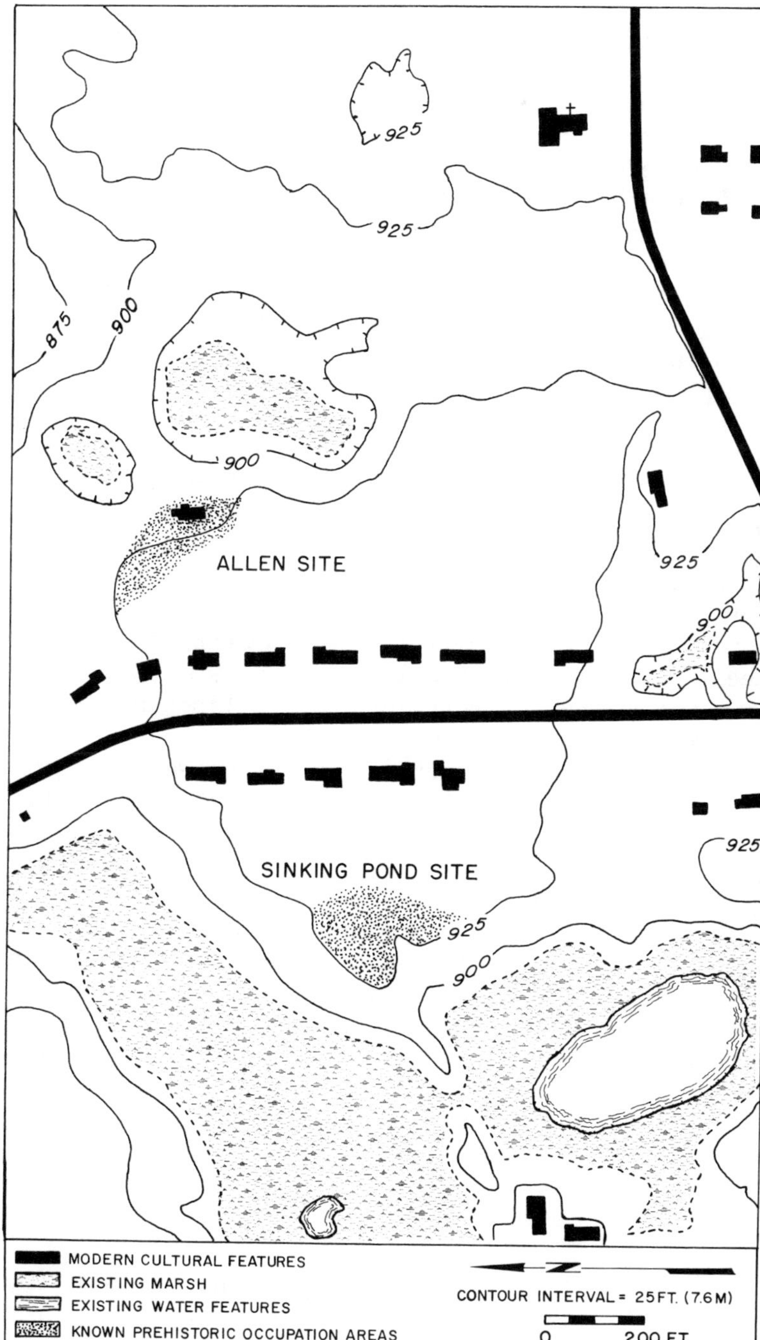

Map 4.1 Sinking Ponds site and locality.

houses, and roads. Its erratic, meandering course is such that it has done little cutting, and it is often dry at the outlet. It serves primarily to take off overflow during wet seasons.

The dominant soil type in the area is the podzolic Palmyra series. These soils are found primarily as old lake beaches and glacial kames. On the ridges there tends to be development of 7.6 cm (0.25 ft) and 16.8 cm (0.55 ft) of grey-brown sandy humus with a podzolic, A-2 horizon of 3.1-9.2 cm (0.10-0.30 ft) intermittently. A red-orange sandy gravel subsoil of 30.5-61 cm (1.0-2.0 ft) underlies these as a B horizon. The C horizon is generally a pink, compacted glacial till. Erosion is prevalent on the steep slopes carrying sandy soil to the low areas where humic buildup is greater, 30.5-36.6 cm (1.0-1.2 ft), due to greater perennial vegetation decay. On the higher elevations leaching is highly operant due to the porous nature of the soil (U.S. Soil Conservation Service, East Aurora, March 1974: personal communication). Acidic water percolating through the humus has removed most organic elements. Blackmon (n.d.:27) reports that leaching is consistent to a depth of 58.4-101.6 cm (23-40 in) in tests conducted over the site area and adjacent ridges. Soil pH ranges from 4.2 to 4.4 in all horizons. Development of the basic A-2 horizon is thought to be contiguous with the invasion of deciduous forest but the high acid conditions were previously instituted by coniferous forests with their low humic buildup (ibid. and Linda and Orrin Shane 1966: personal communication).

The ridges on the eastern periphery maintain a secondary growth of deciduous trees (maple, elm, oak) with some imported conifers. Previous to this second growth, the ridge tops were denuded meadows maintained for pasturage. Below, the 274.5 m (900 ft) contour marsh flora consisting of perennial vegetation and low brush leads to an increase in soil buildup and extinction of water features. While soil buildup is high in the depressed areas it is quite low on ridge tops. Another factor which is significant in soil formation at Sinking Ponds is sheet erosion. This erosion is differential in the sense that some gradual slopes suffer less than others, depending upon the amount of vegetative protection. Predictably, low humic formation, leaching and erosion have held the topsoil depths on the ridge constant or on a slight decrease. In adjacent areas the importation of sod and loam has slowed the degradation of topsoil to almost zero.

Geology

The East Aurora area is underlain by sedimentary rock. The local bedrock consists of Silurian, Devonian, and Carboniferous limestones, shales, conglomerates, and sandstones. The bedrock is presently re-

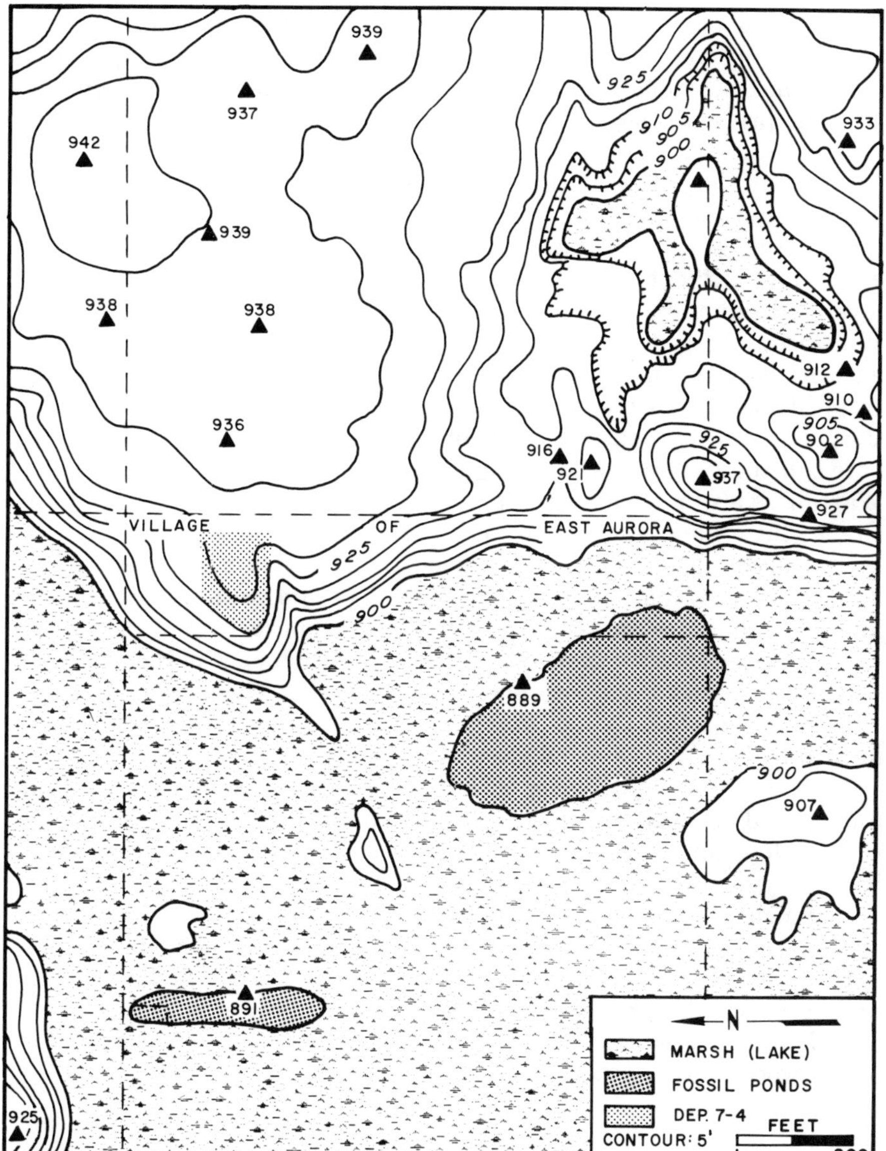

Map 4.2 Sinking Ponds site and its original physiographic association.

flected in pebbles of the glacial till scoured from the surrounding areas. Shales dominate the pebbles with lesser quantities of limestones, sandstones, siltstones, chert, igneous rock, and quartzite represented.

The present topography is the result of the Cary Advance of the Wisconsin Epoch. The Hamburg–Marilla moraine which was left during the late Cary, 14,000 B.P., formed the present drainage patterns and ridge system consisting of glacial kames and eskerine formations. The terminal moraine cut off drainage in the valley of Buffalo Creek, impounding a body of standing water at the 289.75-274.5 m (950-900 ft) level (Blackmon n.d.:50-53). This body of water was coeval with Lake Whittesey. Deposits of glacial till in the standing waters left the area with a rounded and subdued appearance (ibid.: 3). Melting of large trapped blocks of ice created kettleholes, of which the largest remnant is the pond adjacent to the site (ibid.: 60-63). Gradually as an outlet formed between the eskers to the north of the area, waters lowered to Lake Warren levels and drained off to the Cazenovia Creek Valley. Buffalo Creek, cut off and abandoned in the East Aurora area, formed a new system to the east of the morainal deposits. The body of water left at the 274.5 m (900 ft) contour in the abandoned stream valley was irregular and had numerous embayments while ponds characterized the topography (Map 4.2). With time and further deposition most of the standing water has been forced into ever smaller ponds. Blackmon (n.d.:96), however, states that this so-called lake impounded by the natural levees formed by moraines and eskers was probably of long duration.

The relative shallowness of the lake is illustrated by the elevation differential between the present water standing at 271.5 m (890 ft) and the 900-foot contour. Depths ranging between 0 and 10 ft would have been subjected to decrease over time.

During primary occupation, ca. 3000 B.P., the Sinking Ponds site was situated in a lacustrine environment with numerous marshy areas within a directly adjacent basin. Poor drainage below 274.5 m (900 ft) probably served to retain large tracts of shallow water with numerous islands and embayments which provided the physiographic setting for Meadowood culture's exploitive orientation.

EXCAVATIONS

Preliminary determinations indicated that approximately 3850 m^2 (41,400 sq ft) contained cultural materials. The productivity of this area was differential for some of the reasons discussed above. Generally slopes and ridge or hogback edges seemed to have the most abundant surface materials and lowest depth of humus formations. On the more

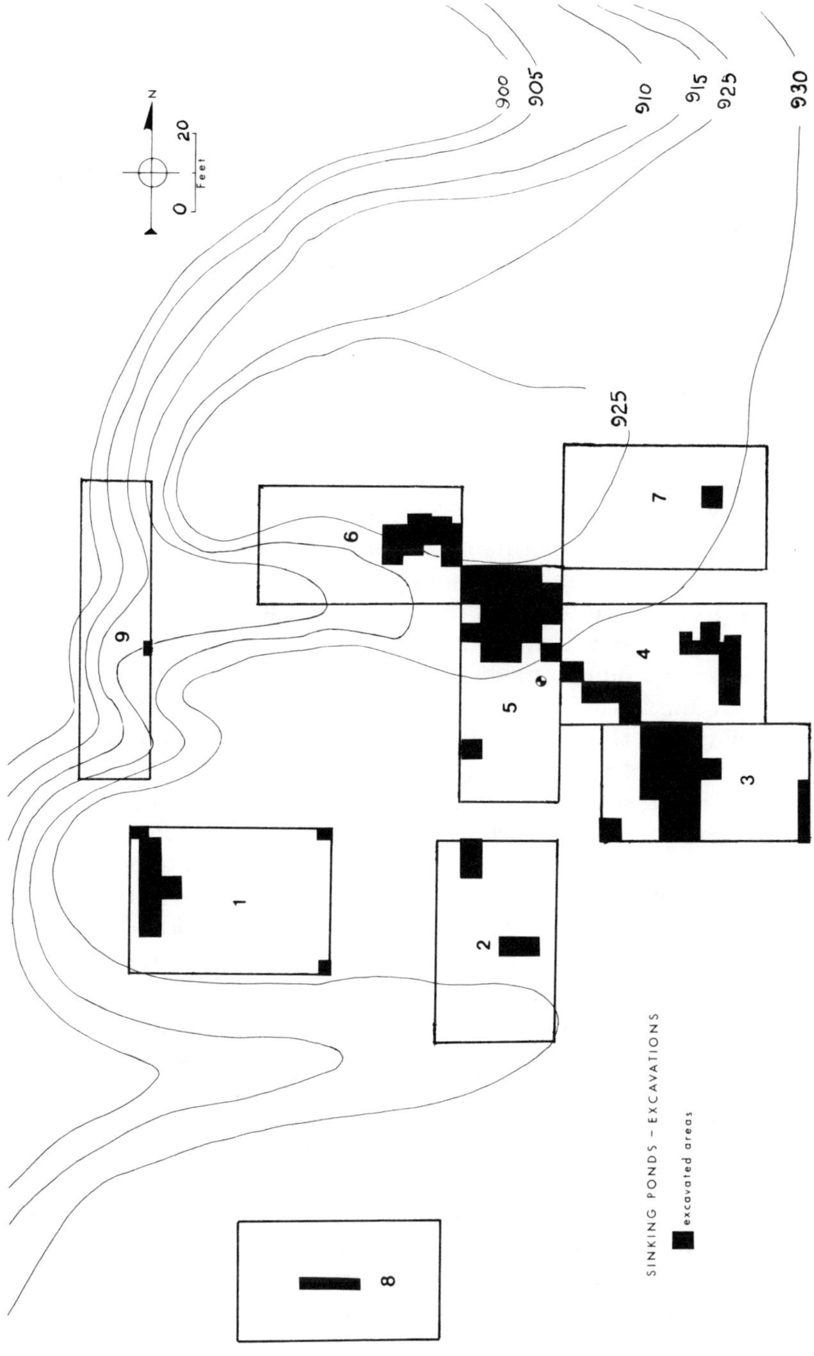

Map 4.3 Sinking Ponds sampling tracts.

even terrain the surface was more stable, topsoil depth was relatively constant, and less evidence was found on the surface.

Excavations were begun with surface hunting and small test pits in 1964, limited tract testing in 1965, and full sampling tract excavation in 1966, which continued into 1967. A datum point was established at a metal survey stake on the 305.3 m (1000.9 ft) property line of the Village of East Aurora Water Works District. A 24.4 m (80 ft), 90 degree offset was made to the west and a O-North, O-West site datum established. The base line was extended to the north and south and a transverse line established along the westward running subsidiary perpendicular ridge. From there, a grid system was begun so that selected areas could be investigated. During the testing phase of 1965, units were progressively selected to test the distributions along the main portion of the hogback. Since two small pit tests had revealed a low frequency of materials in the central portion of the ridge, a large test was begun at the end of the portion most closely adjacent to a slope where numerous surface finds had been made, Sampling Tract 9. Progressive testing moved toward the juncture of the hogback with the main ridge line and then on to the main north-south ridge line. Preliminary conclusions drawn from these tests led to the concentration of excavations on the main ridge line, roughly 9.2 m (30 ft) to either side of the base line.

The perpendicular ridge appeared to be so heavily sheet-eroded and so unproductive of in situ artifacts that it did not justify further investigation at that time. Excavations east of the base line were quite different in terms of productivity and in situ information. The other knolls and dips in terrain were left for further investigation.

Subsequent to the 1965 season, an excavation plan was worked out to sample the site in a systematic fashion. The site was divided into tracts of 130.5 m^2 (1500 sq ft). The shape of these tracts was then adjusted to fit the terrain or to take into account other circumstances. Each tract was then divided into 1.5 m (5 ft) squares (Rootenberg 1964:182-85). Eleven sampling tracts were defined enclosing a total of 1534.5 m^2 (16,500 sq ft), representing 40% of the 3850 m^2 (41,400 sq ft) site area (Map 4.3). A total of 39 features was disclosed and 163 m^2 (1752 sq ft) were excavated, sampling 13% of the undisturbed, noneroded, nonsloping portions of the site, which totaled approximately 1302 m^2 (14,000 sq ft) (Table 4.1). No one tract was given more weight than others in terms of priority for excavation. With the physiographic features of the site included, modifications of the strategy were made. Contiguous 1.5 m squares (5 ft squares) were opened to test for settlement remains and some emphasis was placed on tracts such as 3, 4, 5, 6, 7 where undisturbed deposits were most abundant. Each tract was not

TABLE 4.1
SINKING PONDS SAMPLING TRACTS: SQUARE FEET EXCAVATED, FEATURES, ARTIFACTS, FLINT DETRITUS AND FIRE-CRACKED ROCK

Sampling Tracts

	1		2		3		4		5		6		7		8		9		10		11		N	
	#	%	#	%	#	%	#	%	#	%	#	%	#	%	#	%	#	%	#	%	#	%	#	%
Square Feet Excavated	162	9.3	100	5.7	483	27.6	275	15.7	525	30.0	137	7.8	25	1.4	33	1.9	6	0.3	6	0.3	0	0	1,752	100
Features	1	2.6	0	0	6	15.4	4	10.2	19	48.7	8	20.5	1	2.6	0	0	0	0	0	0	0	0	39	100
Artifacts	11	1	5	0.4	692	60.9	31	2.7	323	28.4	42	3.7	6	0.6	27	2.4	0	0	0	0	0	0	1,139	100
Flint Detritus	1621	5.8	813	2.9	9809	35.4	2996	10.9	8657	31.3	1894	6.8	872	3.2	131	0.5	872	3.2	0	0	0	0	27,665	100
Fire-Cracked Rock	0	0	0	0	26	4.8	44	8.1	420	77.4	40	7.4	6	1.1	7	1.2	0	0	0	0	0	0	543	100

TABLE 4.2
SINKING POND ARTIFACT FRAGMENT DISTRIBUTION BY FEATURE, 5 FOOT SQUARES EXCLUSIVE OF FEATURES, AND SAMPLING TRACT

	Sampling Tract																							
	1		2		3		4		5		6		7		8		9		10		11		N	
	#	%	#	%	#	%	#	%	#	%	#	%	#	%	#	%	#	%	#	%	#	%	#	%
Artifacts Associated with																								
Features	1	0.1	0	0	665	58.5	23	2.0	225	19.8	39	3.4	6	0.5	0	0	0	0	0	0	0	0	959	84
5 Foot Squares	10	0.9	5	0.4	27	2.4	8	0.7	98	8.6	3	0.3	0	0	0	0	0	0	0	0	0	0	151	13.6
Tract Surface	0	0	0	0	0	0	0	0	0	0	0	0	0	0	27	2.4	0	0	0	0	0	0	27	2.4
N	11	1	5	0.4	692	60.9	31	2.7	323	28.4	42	3.7	6	0.6	27	2.4	0	0	0	0	0	0	1139	100

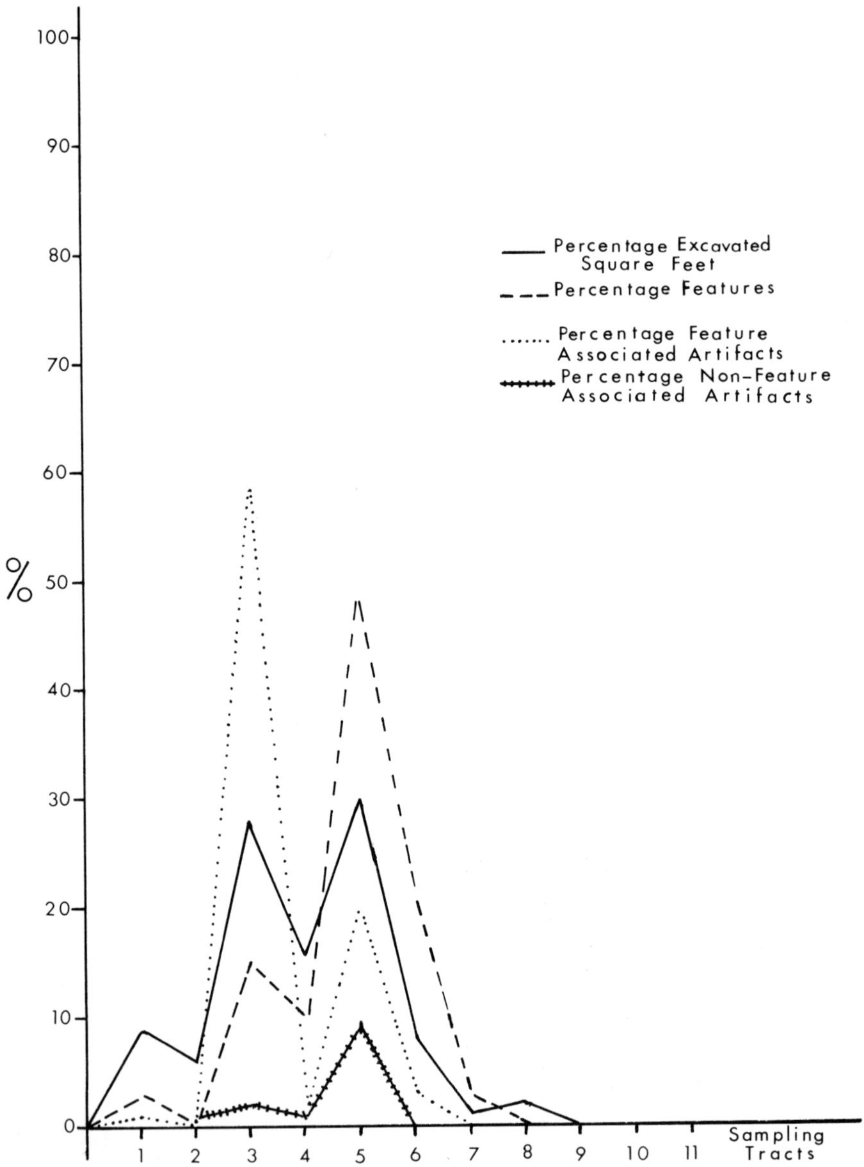

Fig. 4.1 Comparison of percentages of excavated square feet, features, feature associated artifacts, and non-feature associated artifacts.

TABLE 4.3
DISTRIBUTION OF FLINT DETRITUS CATEGORIES IN SAMPLING TRACTS

	Sampling Tracts																							
	1		2		3		4		5		6		7		8		9		10		11		N	
	#	%	#	%	#	%	#	%	#	%	#	%	#	%	#	%	#	%	#	%	#	%	#	%
Utilized Flakes	30	4.5	12	1.8	217	32.2	72	10.7	248	36.9	74	11.0	3	0.4	1	0.1	16	2.4	0	0	0	0	673	100
Non-Utilized Flakes	533	5.1	160	1.5	2906	28.0	1225	11.9	3978	38.4	779	7.5	321	3.2	58	0.6	397	3.8	0	0	0	0	10,367	100
Chips	1058	6.5	620	3.8	6611	40.9	1668	10.3	4174	25.8	970	6.2	536	3.3	72	0.4	459	2.8	0	0	0	0	16,168	100
Cores	0	0	21	4.8	67	15.2	31	7.0	257	58.1	54	12.2	12	2.7	0	0	0	0	0	0	0	0	442	100
Flint Pebbles	0	0	0	0	8	32	0	0	0	0	17	68	0	0	0	0	0	0	0	0	0	0	25	100
N	1621	5.8	813	2.9	9809	35.4	2996	10.9	8657	31.3	1894	6.8	872	3.2	131	0.5	872	3.2					27,665	100

TABLE 4.4
FIRE-CRACKED ROCK DISTRIBUTION BY SAMPLING TRACT

	Item	3		4		5		6		7		8		N	
		#	%	#	%	#	%	#	%	#	%	#	%	#	%
Non-Feature Unit	Fire-cracked rock weight	0	0	14	19.4	51	70.8	0	0	0	0	7	9.8	72	100
Features	Fire-cracked rock weight	26	5.5	30	6.4	369	78.3	40	8.5	6	1.3	0	0	471	100
		26	4.8	44	8.1	420	77.4	40	7.4	6	1.1	7	1.2	543	100

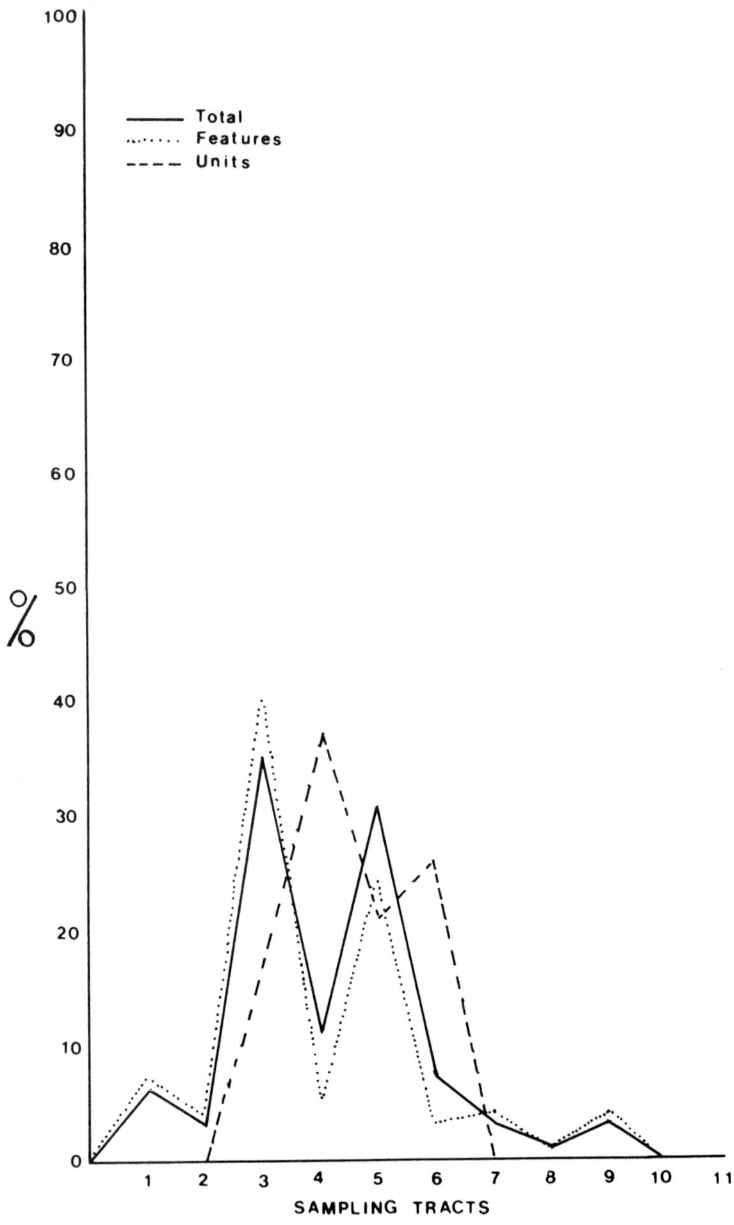

Fig. 4.2 Distribution of flint detritus percentages by sampling tracts.

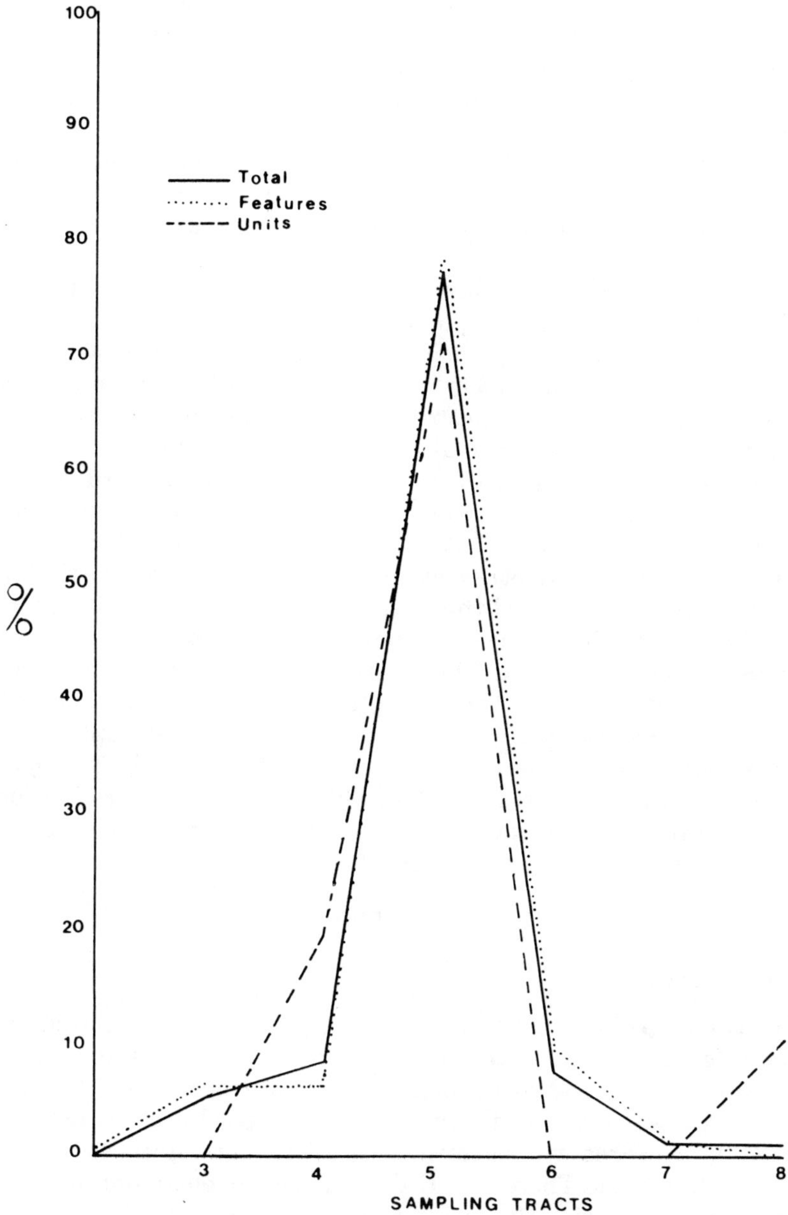

Fig. 4.3 Distribution of fire-cracked rock percentages by sampling tracts.

necessarily explored by excavation, and tracts 9, 10, and 11 were carefully and extensively surface collected once deposition and erosion rate had been checked by shovel test. In tracts where mixing of materials at the bottom of slopes or depressions occurred, only a cursory surface hunt was conducted.

All artifacts below 3 cm (0.1 ft) were measured horizontally and vertically with all nonartifactual evidence saved to a screen mesh of 7 mm (.25 in). Fire-cracked rock was weighed for each unit and feature excavated.

Artifact associations are illustrated in Table 4.2. Tracts with features showed a much greater frequency of artifacts (Fig. 4.1) than those without features. These frequencies do, however, coincide with the number of square feet excavated in Sampling Tract 5. In Sampling Tract 3, which has a relatively low feature frequency, the feature-associated artifacts stand out and demonstrate a clustering observed in the field (Fig. 4.1). We believe this clustering to be due to high sherd counts grouped within a composite feature. Flint detritus is categorized for each sampling tract in Table 4.3. Although the figures coincide with the number of square meters (feet) excavated (Table 4.1), we can see that in Sampling Tract 3 they exceed this ratio. In Sampling Tract 5, figures similar to Sampling Tract 3 are seen but represent a larger number of square meters (feet) excavated. This distribution appears to covary with the number of features present in a sampling tract for all tracts except 5 and 3. Figure 4.2 shows the distribution of flint detritus graphically.

Fire-cracked rock is heavily represented on the site with the majority associated with features (Table 4.4). This heavy feature association of 87% of the fire-cracked rock may be seen in Figure 4.3 where the feature curve almost exactly parallels the total curve.

Description of Sampling Tracts

Sampling Tract 1

This tract was located on the western extremity of the subsidiary hogback ridge. Six 1.5 m (5 ft) squares and one test pit were excavated for a total of 15 m^2 (162 sq ft), or 10.8% of the tract area. Although erosion surface was close by, there remained a topsoil cover of 6-11 cm (0.20-0.35 ft). The area was selected because of its proximity to numerous surface materials. There was little podzolic development over the orange subsoil, indicating that erosion, not leaching, had operated over this portion of the ridge. This point of the ridge was more exposed than any other surfaces in the site.

A probable feature, Feature 1, was investigated, and although it

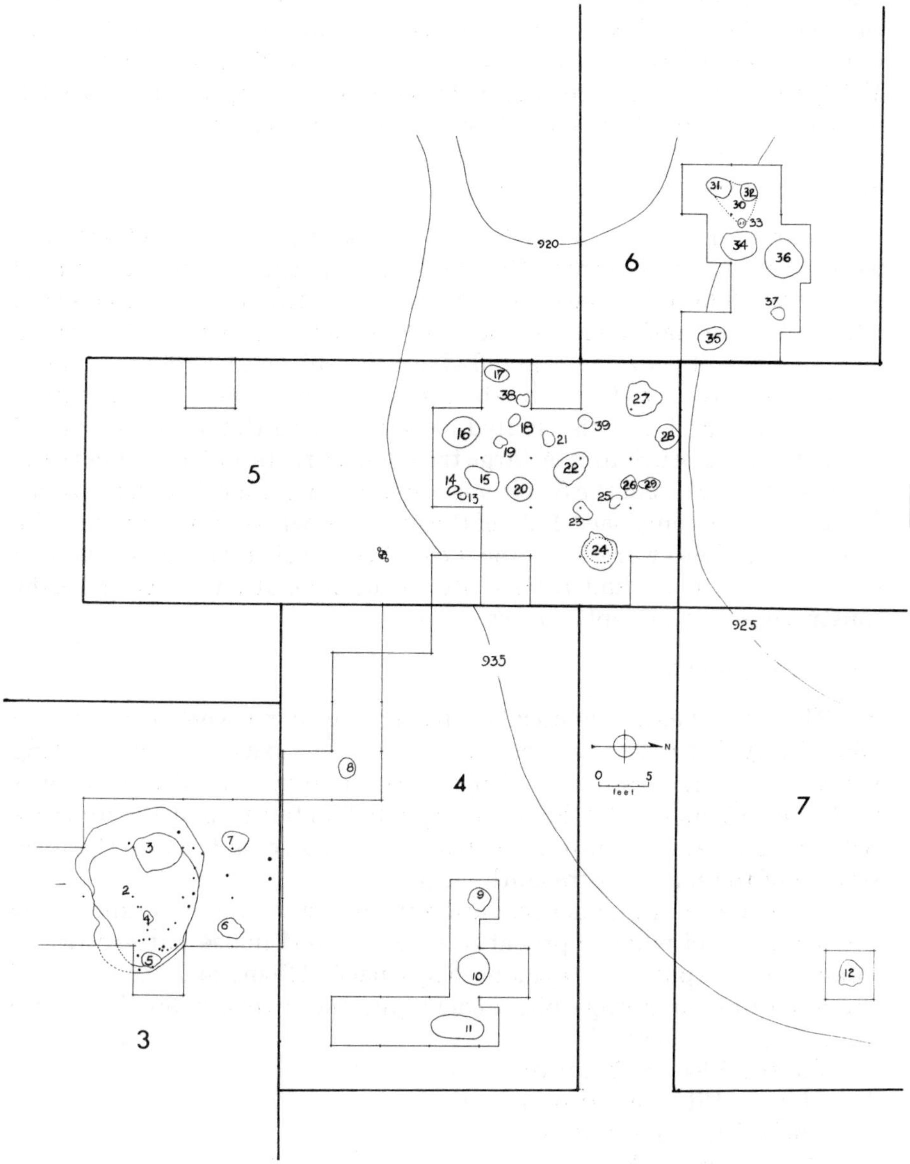

Map 4.4 Detail of sampling tracts 3, 4, 5, 6 and 7.

may have been a treefall, it is included in the list of features as a possible storage or refuse pit. One artifact was found on the surface of this feature, but it was otherwise sterile. Eleven artifacts, 1% of N, the total number in Feature 1, were found, with more than half in Level I. There was no fire-cracked rock, but flint detritus was represented by 1621 items (Table 4.2) distributed heavily on the surface and in Level I. Thirty utilized flakes formed 2% of this sample and represent 5% of such implements found. Cores are, however, unrepresented.

Sampling Tract 2

Four 1.5 m (5 ft) squares 9.3 m² (100 sq ft), 6.7% of the tract area were excavated in this tract. Erosion surface in the tract was estimated at 27.9 m² (300 sq ft) concentrated where the tract fell off into a small rill. Humus formation on the uneroded portions was 9-14 cm (0.30-0.45 ft) and a lack of podzol was noted above the subsoil. One feature, later determined to be a rodent disturbance, was investigated. Five artifacts, 0.4% of N, were found distributed in Levels I and II. Sampling Tract 2 showed much disturbance by large trees whose roots forced flint detritus to the surface. Most of the 813 items of detritus were surface indications. Utilized flakes comprised 1.5% of the detritus, while approximately 3% were cores. These were 1.8% and 4.8% of their respective categories on the site. This tract had little cultural manifestation which could be construed as settlement pattern.

Sampling Tract 3

This tract was given much attention in the early work on the site in 1965. Forty-five square meters (483 sq ft) were excavated, accounting for 32.2% of the tract area. The depth of humus in this tract was uniformly 15 cm (0.5 ft). Podzolic deposits had built up at the juncture with the glacial till subsoil. The tract was wholly confined to the level terrain of the main north-south ridge.

Intensive contiguous excavation in this tract was necessitated by the discovery of what is probably a Meadowood house pattern (Pl. 2) (Map 4.4). This pattern is evidenced by a packed floor, 24 postmolds, and three features: a storage pit, a cache pit, and a rock heap. These are numbered as follows:

Packed Floor = Feature 2
Storage Pit = Feature 3
Cache Pit = Feature 4
Rock Heap = Feature 4
Postmolds = 1-5, 7, 8, 10-20, 22-27

These will be discussed in more detail below in the discussion of Feature

2. Two other features, a hearth and rock heap, were also discovered. Three postmolds were also seen outside the possible house. More artifacts (692) were found in this unit than anywhere else on the site; these comprised 60.8% of the total, with 96.1%, or 665, occuring within the presumed house pattern or clustered in subfeatures of the house. The distribution of these artifacts will be discussed in more detail in the explanation of Feature 2 which also contained 99.7% of the clay pottery sample, which totaled 592 sherds.

Heavy concentrations of flint detritus were seen in this tract. Flint detritus included 9808 items, 35.4% of the total sample, and the most numerous items were chips, 6611 or 67.4% of the detritus in the tract. Significantly this tract had few cores, 0.7%, and utilized flakes constituted only 2.2% of the tract sample. However, the tract had 30.3% of all blanks excavated from the site. One hundred percent of the fire-cracked rock (118 kg or 26 lb) from this tract was feature associated.

Sampling Tract 4

This tract lay directly adjacent to and north of Tract 3. It was also situated on the main ridge but included a portion of the ridge which dipped into a shallow sheltered depression approximately 1.5 m (5 ft) below the highest elevation of the main ridge. Eleven 1.5 m (5 ft) squares were excavated for a total of 25.6 m² (275 sq ft), or 18.3% of the tract. Erosion surface was estimated at 14.5 m² (150 sq ft), or 10% of the tract. In the excavated units there was little podzolic buildup except under features, and topsoil was 15-117 cm (0.5-0.55 ft) in depth.

Four features—a storage pit, cache pit, rock heap and hearth—were excavated and determined to be of cultural affiliation. The storage and cache pits and rock heap seemed to have the same lineal alignment within approximately the same distance as the features comprising the probable house pattern in Tract 3 (see Map 4.4). No postmolds were seen but the muddy conditions prevalent when this area was excavated may have obscured them. Thirty-one artifacts were recorded with 23, or 74.2%, feature associated (Table 4.2). Flint detritus was evenly distributed in the units exclusive of features but clustered heavily around the cache pit in the features. Nonutilized flakes and chips dominated the detritus. Twenty kg (44 lb) of fire-cracked rock were confined to the rock heaps and immediate vicinity, and 68.2% of it was feature associated.

Sampling Tract 5

Sampling Tract 5 encompassed most of the 1966 excavations and revealed a surprisingly large cluster of features. In all, 21 1.5 m (5 ft) squares or 48.8 m² (525 sq ft) were excavated. This represented 35% of the tract and 30% of the total excavations. Only 5.3% of the area (7.4 m^2 or 80 sq ft) was erosion surface. One square which was placed to sample the higher south end of the tract on the hogback was totally sterile. The excavation was concentrated in the northern portions due to the large number of features, 19, which comprised nearly half, or 48.7%, of the 39 discovered at Sinking Ponds. The northern section of the tract was located in a minor depression in the main ridge, and was surrounded on three sides with level terrain averaging a height of 1.5 m (5 ft). To the west this depression fell more gently through a rill to the marsh below (Map 4.3). The most heavily excavated area was at the upper end of this rill in the low, level, protected area. This area's bowl like nature precluded erosion to the extent seen on the higher perpendicular ridge but encouraged heavy leaching leading to the heaviest podzolic formation on the site. Humus was fairly uniform at 11 to 14 cm (0.35-0.45 ft) in depth and A_2 podzol formed over much of the excavated area. Features with organic content bore evidence of the leaching in that all lower portions were the white, powdery A_2 podzol.

The subsoil was orange glacial till over a compact pink till. Nine rock heaps and six hearths comprised 60% and 67% of the features of each type at this site. The rock features formed a rough semicircular pattern within which hearths clustered. Four other features were subsidiary and close to the rock heaps. Of the artifacts in the tract, 69.7% were associated with features while the remainder were in close proximity to the cluster of features. In this tract, almost exclusive distributions were recorded for netsinkers, 96.9% of the sample, and steatite vessel sherds, 100% of the sample. Large amounts of flint detritus were scattered over the area, 8657 items, or 31.3% of the total sample, but the majority, 88.6%, were associated with squares only. This tract also displayed the largest amount of fire-cracked rock, 77.4% of the total sample (246.3 kg or 543 lb). In this tract, 87.9% of this rock was feature associated.

Sampling Tract 6

The 1967 excavations sampled this tract as well as Tracts 3 and 7. The location of this tract encompassing the portions of a subsidiary knoll on the main ridge immediately adjacent to Sampling Tract 3 was deliberate in order to test any extension of the settlement pattern so abundant in the north section of Tract 5. Excavation covered 12.7 m^2 (137 sq ft), 9.1% of the tract. Humus depth was 12-14 cm (0.40-0.45 ft). Again in this area podzolic formations were low, occurring only under features, but erosion of the surface area was high, 83.7 m^2 (900 sq ft), or 60% of the tract. Eight features, or 21%, of the total were investigated.

Three rock heaps extended and completed the semicircular formation of features alluded to above in the description of Tract 5. Other features include one hearth, one storage pit, two manufacture cache pits, and a composite feature, possibly a workshop floor. Forty-two artifacts, the largest number of which were manufacture debris, comprised 76.2% of the sample and were associated in the features or close to them. In comparison with other tracts flint detritus was low at 6.8% of the total sample. The flint detritus associated with the two manufacture or cache pits was almost double that found in the excavations outside features. Decortication flakes were abundant in this sample, 314 or 16.6% of the detritus sample in this unit. This figure, however, represents 100% of such flakes on the site. All fire-cracked rock found, 18.1 kg (40 lb), was confined to features.

Sampling Tract 7

This tract was emplaced to provide coverage of the eastward extension of the depression described above for Sampling Tract 5. The topsoil reached a depth of 12-15 cm (0.40-0.50 ft). Podzolic formation was as high as it was in Tract 5. Only one square was excavated here, but this unit exposed a storage pit in dead center. The pit contained all of the artifacts recorded in the tract and all of the fire-cracked rock. All of the flint detritus was contained in the portion of topsoil just above the feature. Although little area was excavated, the location of the feature in relation to Tracts 3 and 4 suggests, at least, the possibility of another house pattern located in this tract. Erosion surfaces in the tract totaled less than 10% of it.

Sampling Tract 8

Attempts to determine the southern limits of the site led to the placement of a tract on a second smaller subsidiary perpendicular ridge south of the large one tested by Tracts 1, 2 and 5. One and one-third squares were excavated and although some flint detritus (131 items or 0.5% of the total sample) and fire-cracked rock were found, explorations went no further. The general sterility of the tract approximated Sampling Tract 2 and it was concluded that there was a tapering off of materials to the south of Tract 2. Topsoil depth in the excavations was 12 cm (0.40 ft) with little evidence of erosion.

Sampling Tract 9

The Sinking Ponds site was discovered in what later became Sampling Tract 9. It is primarily a surface tract consisting mostly of slopes with little or no topsoil, less than 6 cm (0.20 ft), due to erosion over the entire tract. One test of .6 m² (6 sq ft) that was put in to sample the soil stratification showed:

Dark Sandy Humus	5 cm (0-0.15 ft)
Orange Glacial Till	6-25 cm (0.16-0.8 ft)
Pink Compact Till	26 cm (0.81 ft - unknown)

The test was sterile. During all seasons this tract was continually surface surveyed with all materials retained. Twenty-seven artifacts covering almost all classes found on the site were recorded and these resulted in 62.4% of the total sample. Flint detritus was 3.2% of the total and was fairly abundant; however, no fire-cracked rock was found.

Sampling Tract 10

Much of the rationale for locating Sampling Tract 10 related to the need to organize some observations made on the southern portions of the site. A large rill or depression projects eastward into the main ridge and separates two subsidiary perpendicular ridges. In this depression there has accumulated much slope wash which is sterile on the surface. Shovel tests also were sterile. The erosion slopes, roughly 75% of the tract, were also sterile. Topsoil was less than 6 cm (0.2 ft) on the slopes and up to 25-27 cm (0.8-0.9 ft) in the accumulation areas.

Sampling Tract 11

Tract 11 represents a situation where significant sampling had occurred prior to this investigation. It was learned that a collector had intensively hunted the northern edge of the first subsidiary ridge over a period of 10-20 years (A.S. Kuster: personal communication). He pointed out almost the exact confines of Tract 11 as his "favorite pick-up spot." Tract 11 is 90% erosion surface. It is also sampled surface and was nonrandomly stripped of its artifactual content by intensive surface collecting by several persons, both known and unknown to the investigators. Because of the lack of control over artifacts from this tract, no further work was done here and the sample from it that is in the Kuster collection was not included in this work although it has been acquired for future study.

Vertical Distribution of Cultural Material

There was no cultural stratigraphy at Sinking Ponds. The site area had been affected historically by only animal pasturage, but physiographic and environmental conditions outlined above prevented topsoil

TABLE 4.5
NON-FEATURE ASSOCIATED ARTIFACTS BY TENTHS AND LEVEL

	Surface	Level I						Level II					
	N	0-1	1-2	2-3	3-4	4-5	N	5-6	6-7	7-8	8-9	N	Total N
#	28	7	10	19	34	57	127	16	3	3	1	23	178
%	15.7	3.9	5.6	10.7	19.1	32		9	1.7	1.7	0.6		100
N%	15.7						71.4					12.9	100

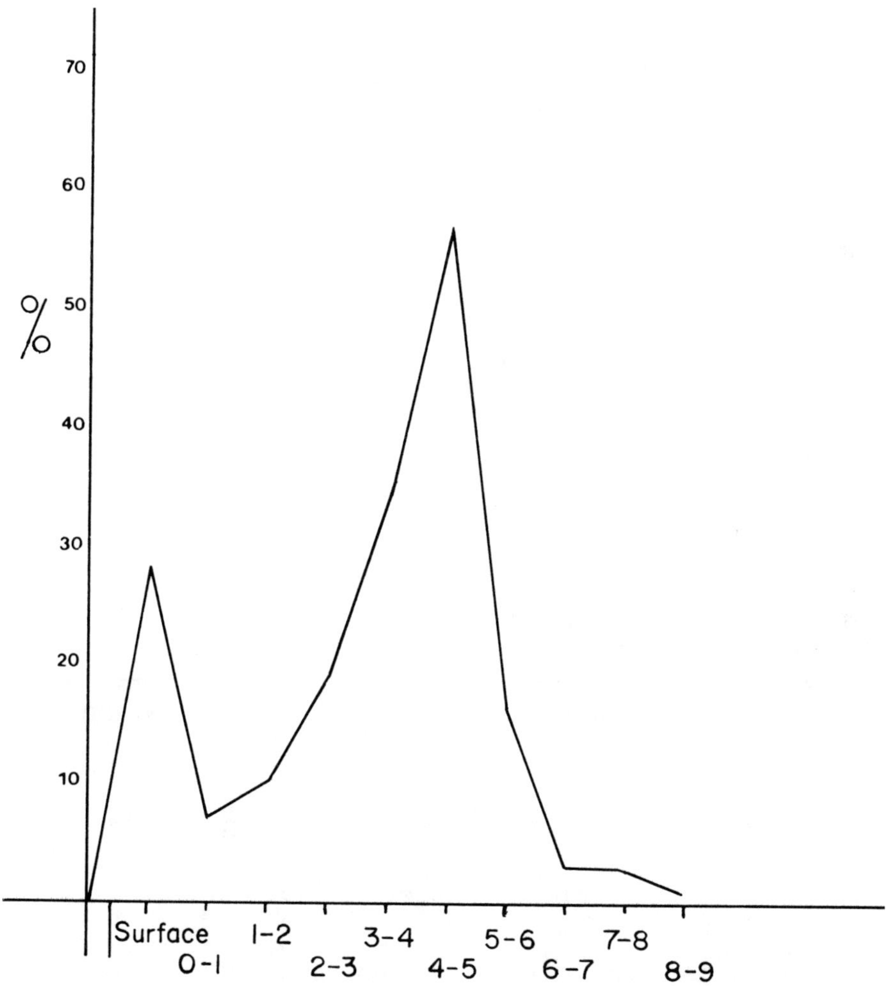

Fig. 4.4 Non-feature associated artifacts by 1 tenth levels.

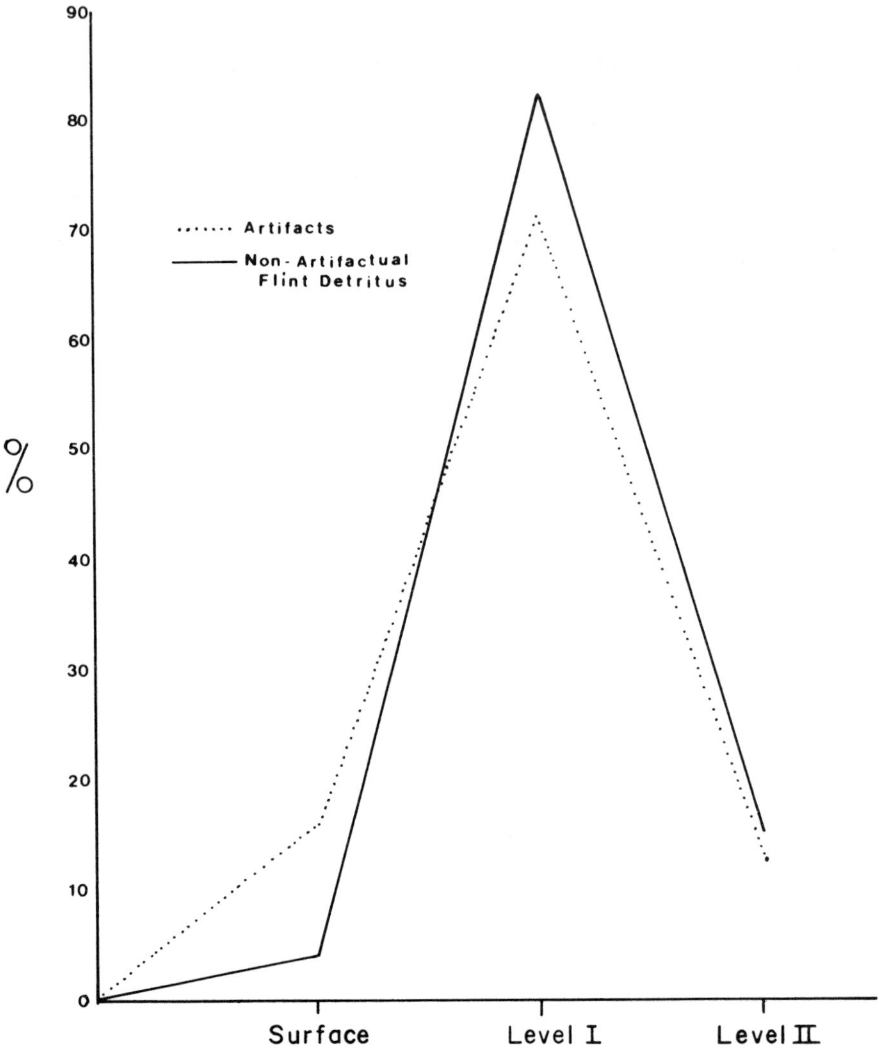

Fig. 4.5 Artifacts versus flint detritus in units by levels.

TABLE 4.6
DISTRIBUTION OF NON-FEATURE ASSOCIATED FLINT DETRITUS BY LEVEL

Item	Surface		Level I		Level II		N	
	#	%	#	%	#	%	#	%
Utilized Flakes	16	4.0	329	82.7	53	13.3	398	100
Nonutilized Flakes	397	4.6	7,108	81.7	1,199	13.7	8,704	100
Chips	459	3.4	10,790	80.8	2,123	15.8	13,372	100
Cores	0	0	309	86.1	50	13.9	359	100
Total Flint Detritus	872	3.5	18,536	81.5	3,425	15.0	22,833	100

TABLE 4.7
DISTRIBUTION OF FEATURE TYPES BY SAMPLING TRACT

	Sampling Tracts													
	1		2		3		4		5		6		N	
Features	#	%	#	%	#	%	#	%	#	%	#	%	#	%
Rock Heaps	0	0	2	13.3	1	6.7	9	60.0	3	20.0	0	0	15	100
Hearths	0	0	1	11.1	1	11.1	6	66.7	1	11.1	0	0	9	100
Storage Pits	1	14.3	1	14.3	1	14.3	2	28.5	1	14.3	1	14.3	7	100
Manufacture Pits	0	0	1	16.7	1	16.7	2	33.3	2	33.3	0		6	100
Composite Features	0	0	1	50	0	0	0	0	1	50	0		2	100
N	1	2.6	6	15.4	4	10.2	19	48.7	8	20.5	1	2.6	39	100

formation. All cultural materials of the site were contained in the first foot of soil. The A_1 horizon ranged from 11 cm (0.35 ft) in the moderately eroded areas to 15 cm (0.5 ft) in the uneroded places. The B soil horizon underlay the humus with many patches of A_2 horizon, especially in depressions subject to heavy leaching. Cultural materials were most abundant in the zone lying at the juncture of the A_1 horizon with the B horizon.

Table 4.5 shows the distribution of nonfeature-associated artifacts in levels by tenths of feet and Figure 4.4 portrays this distribution graphically. Here we can see a major cluster between 9 cm (0.3 ft) and 18 cm (0.6 ft) which coincided with the natural soil juncture observed above. A single sample chi-square test of this distribution shows that it could occur in less than one case out of 1000 by chance.

This distribution assigned to levels of 15 cm (0.5 ft) was tested against the flint detritus whose provenience was kept by these arbitrary designations. Here Level 1 dominates the graph (Fig. 4.5). It is clear from the provenienced artifact distribution that concentration in the lower portions of Level 1 is probably obscured by the arbitrary level designation. The distribution of categories of flint detritus outside features by level is shown in Table 4.6.

FEATURES

Thirty-nine culturally affiliated features and 27 postmolds were investigated at the Sinking Ponds site. General descriptive categories which in some cases have functional connotations are shown in Table 4.7. The spatial distribution of features can be seen in Maps 4.4 and 4.5 and in Table 4.7.

Rock heap is a term which describes exactly the form of one type of feature. Generally a rock heap is a shallow depression filled with broken

Map 4.5 Distribution of hearths, rock heaps, storage pits and cache pits at Sinking Ponds.

fire-cracked rock heaped up above the occupation surface.

Hearths are shallow stone-lined pits with indications of fire-reddening on the stones and flecks of charcoal in the pit fill. Their appearance suggests that other rocks may have been heated in them and removed. *Storage pits* on this site were shallow basinlike depressions filled with general refuse subsequent to their possible storage function. *Manufacture pits* were generally deeper with more vertical sides and usually associated with caches of blanks, flint detritus, hammerstone, and other items of lithic manufacture. Flint chips and flakes formed an almost solid lens in each of these features. Pits determined to be caches were small depressions containing a single artifact type, for example, netsinkers.

Composite features are made up of a packed floor or other manifestation within which several features of different types are associated, for example, pits and postmolds which form a house pattern. The house pattern with all of its component features is a composite feature. Only two composite features were seen in the ground but the possibility of others exists.

The feature numbering system used in the field was modified to a sequential order progressing from tract to tract with two exceptions, Features 38 and 39.

TABLE 4.8
DISTRIBUTION OF ARTIFACT CLASSES IN FEATURE TYPES

	Feature Type											
	Rock Heap		Hearth		Storage		Manufacture		Composite		N	
Artifact Class	#	%	#	%	#	%	#	%	#	%	#	%
Flint	69	32.7	28	13.3	22	10.4	50	23.7	42	19.9	211	100
Other lithic exclusive of steatite	70	70.7	11	11.1	3	3.0	12	12.2	3	3.0	99	100
Pottery	2	0.3	0	0	88	14.9	0	0	502	84.8	592	100
Steatite	49		8		0		0		0		57	100
N	190	19.8	47	4.9	113	11.8	62	6.5	547	57.0	959	100

Table 4.8 shows the associations of artifact classes with features, in order to illustrate the range of cultural materials included in each feature. In other tables, artifacts are grouped with flint nonartifacts and fire-cracked rock by their functional categories—procurement, processing, storage, manufacture, and ceremonial—discussed in chapter one.

Features contained the bulk of fire-cracked rock encountered. Rock heaps contained 142.9 kg (315 lb) or 60%, storage pits 2.7 kg (6 lb) or 1%,

TABLE 4.9
DISTRIBUTION OF FLINT DETRITUS BY FEATURE TYPE

	Composite	Rock Heaps	Hearths	Storage	Manufacture	Total
Utilized Flakes	55	60	51	8	101	275
Nonutilized Flakes	183	135	92	33	1,210	1,653
Chips	402	217	113	42	2,022	2,796
Cores	0	23	9	0	51	83
Flint Pebbles	0	0	0	0	25	25
Totals	640	435	265	83	3409	4803

hearths 39.4 kg (87 lb) or 17%, and manufacture pits 10% or 23.5 kg (2 lb). Flint detritus distributions are shown in Table 4.9. Here we note that the manufacture pits contain the majority of all categories. Figure 4.6 represents a graphic plot of artifacts, flint detritus, and fire-cracked rock. It shows the clustering suggested by functional categorization. Thus rock heaps have the most fire-broken rock and manufacture pits the largest percentage of flint detritus. Storage pits generally have the lowest percentage of each class, perhaps indicative of a generalized refuse situation. While hearths have a high percentage of fire-cracked rock and artifacts, the flint detritus frequency is low, suggesting hearths were not involved in the immediate manufacturing process. Composite features had the lowest rock frequency of all, indicating an obvious localization of rock into small subsidiary components.

Description of Individual Features

The features are described individually within category groupings. Plans and profiles of each are illustrated in Figures 4.7 and 4.8. Artifacts located in each feature are shown in Table 4.10. Unless there is an especially noteworthy association of particular items, artifacts will not be discussed under each individual feature.

Rock Heaps (Fig. 4.7)

Feature 5. This feature was a small rock heap located within the composite feature, 2. It was 61 cm (2.0 ft) by 52 cm (1.7 ft) and 27 cm (0.9 ft) in depth. It consisted of a heap of fire-broken rocks underlain by a podzolic formation. Three artifacts were found (Table 4.10). Weight of fire-cracked rock was not recorded.

Feature 6. A partial disturbance of one end by tree roots and rodent activity characterized this rock heap of 88 cm (2.9 ft) by 70 cm (2.3 ft). The depth was 24 cm (0.8 ft) but broken rocks projected up

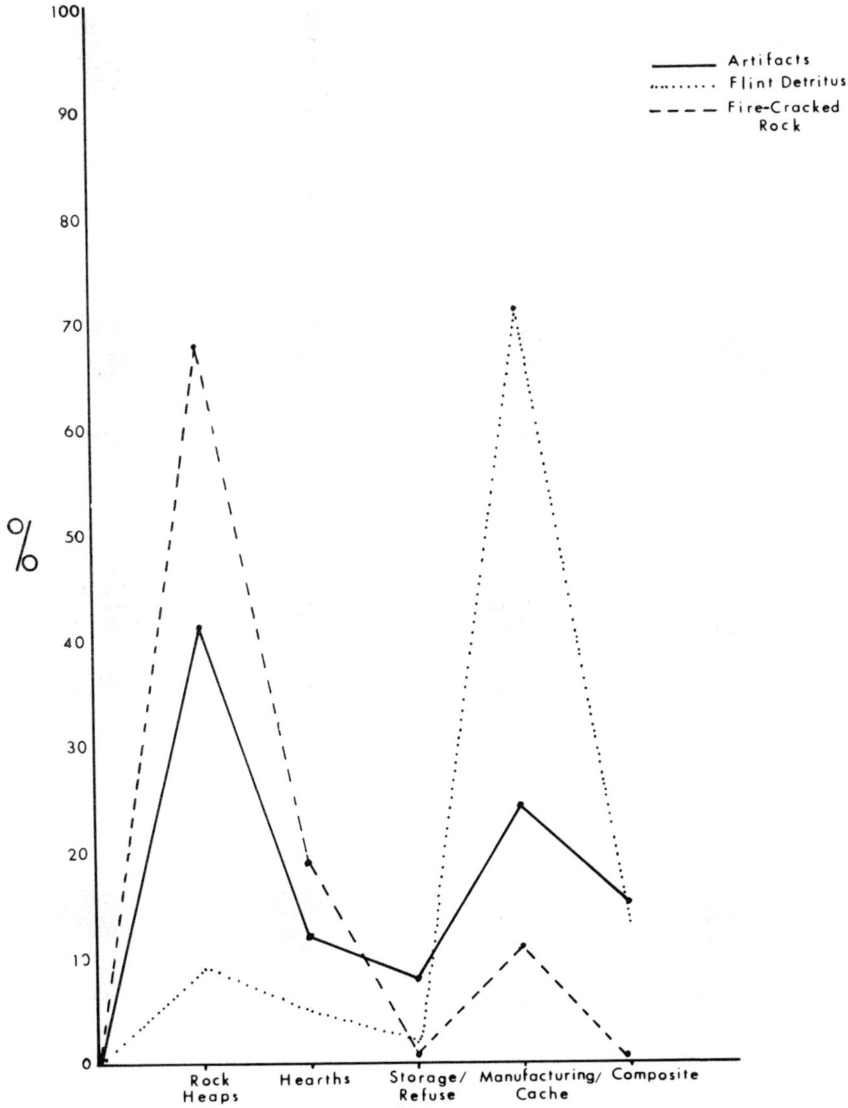

Fig. 4.6 Distribution of percentages of artifacts, flint detritus, and fire-cracked rock in features.

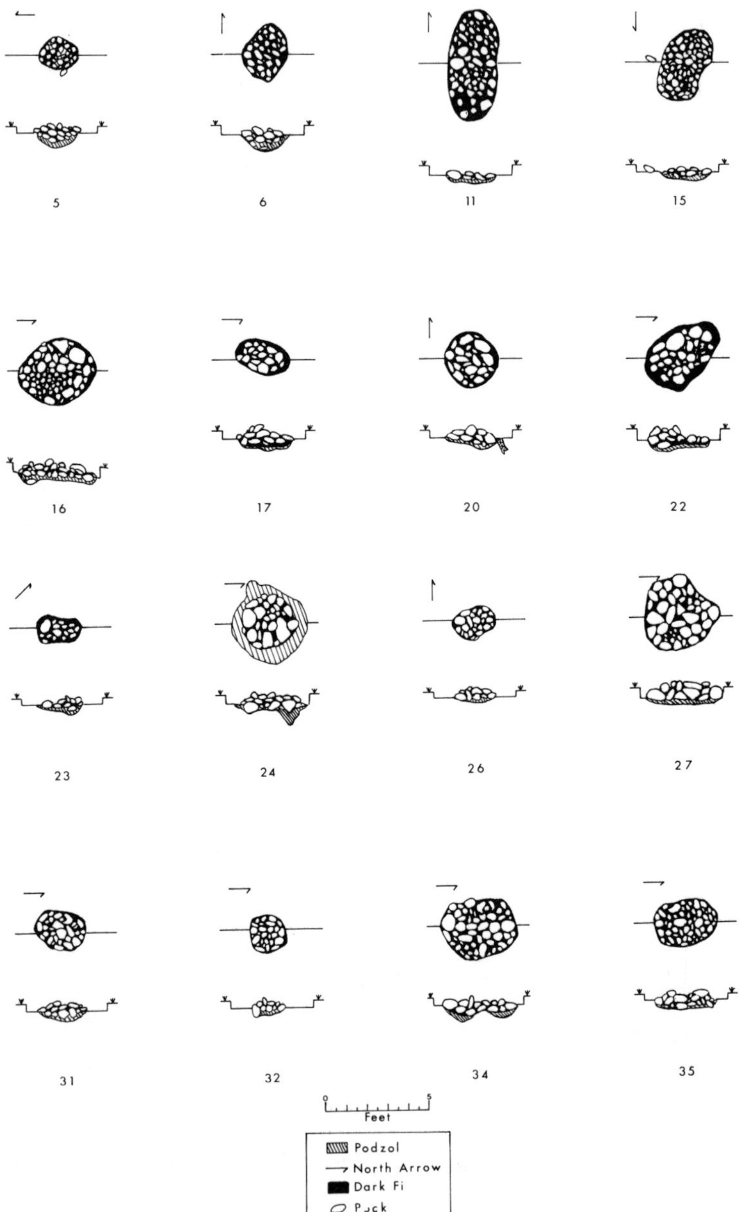

Fig. 4.7 Plans and profiles of rock heap features at Sinking Ponds.

TABLE 4.10
FEATURE DISTRIBUTION OF ARTIFACT TYPES

Artifact Type	Features*																													
	1	2	3	4	5	7	9	10	11	12	15	16	17	18	19	20	21	22	23	24	25	26	27	28	29	32	34	36	37	38	39
Sidenotched Proj. Pt.		4	1							1	1	2	1				1	1		1					1			3			
Stemmed Proj. Pt.			1																									2			
Cornernotched Proj. Pt.					1									1						3											1
Quaternary Blanks		9	4		1	4	8		3	4	1	2		3			2	1		5			1				1	13	2		
Tertiary Blanks	1	11	4	2			5	3	1		1	1		1								2	3					4	3		1
Secondary Blanks		3	1												1			1	2							1					1
Primary Blanks		1	1				1												2				1					2	1		
Longitudinal Knives		1		1							1											3						1			
Unifacial Scrapers		4				1						2	1			2		3		1			1					2			
Bifacial Scrapers		6			1						1		1																		1
Drills		3		1							1	1																2			
Mano Abrading Stn.															1	1															
Groove Abrading Stn.		1		1			1												2												
Pitted Anvil Stn.		1										1						3	1			1								1	
Chopper										1																	1				
Hammerstones									1		1	2	1					4		2		1	1					1			
Netsinkers						2					12	7			1	3		6	3	13	17	2			3					3	
Celts						1														1											
Gorgets			1																	1											
Birdstone																									1						
Bead			1																												
Pipe		1																													
Pottery Vessels		502	87																				2								
Steatite Vessels											30		1			1	2	4	2	7		1	2								6
Totals (N = 959)	1	547	102	5	3	8	15	3	5	6	49	18	5	5	3	7	5	23	12	34	17	10	11	6	6	1	2	30	6	4	10

*Features 8, 13, and 14 were devoid of artifacts and have been omitted.

toward the surface an additional 15 cm (0.5 ft). There was a podzolic underlayer of 12-15 cm (0.4-0.5 ft). Fire-cracked rock was not saved or recorded.

Feature 11. This shallow bathtub-shaped feature produced three quaternary blanks, one tertiary blank, and a hammerstone. Its dimensions were 168 cm (5.5 ft) by 73 cm (2.4 ft). Depth was 12 cm (0.4 ft), with rocks protruding toward the surface. The north end was rodent disturbed. Fire-cracked rock was not recorded.

Feature 15. The feature was shallow, 12 cm (0.4 ft), but the rocks added an additional 9 cm (0.3 ft) of height. A podzol zone of 3 cm (0.1 ft) occurred below the rocks. Dimensions were 104 cm (3.4 ft) by 79 cm (2.6 ft) in a rough kidney shape. Two utilized flakes were found with 49 artifacts (Table 4.10). This square produced 15.4 kg (34 lb) of fire-cracked rock.

Feature 16. This large circular feature yielded 18 artifacts, and four utilized flakes (Table 4.10). The feature was roughly 107 cm (3.5 ft) in diameter and 9 cm (0.3 ft) in depth with two deeper lobes in the north and south ends. Podzol of 3-6 cm (0.1-0.2 ft) in depth lay under the rocks which projected above the surface and could be discerned as a small pile of 10 cm (0.35 ft) height on the surface. Twenty-eight and six-tenths kilograms (63.1 lb) of fire-cracked rock were recorded.

Feature 17. This rock heap was a small oval pile 64 x 59 cm (2.1 x 1.9 ft), consisting of 7.7 kg (17 lb) of fire-cracked and broken rock. The depth was 18 cm (0.6 ft) but rocks projected 15 cm (0.5 ft) above the surface. Podzol deposits underlay the feature which was otherwise filled with dark soil.

Feature 20. This circular feature was 88 cm (2.9 ft) in diameter and had some rodent disturbance on the eastern edge. Depth was 12 cm (0.4 ft) with a podzol underlining. Fire-cracked rock consisted of 8.2 kg (18 lb). Many of the rocks were large, flat pebbles. A large reworked basal steatite sherd found here could be joined to a smaller sherd found in Feature 18. A utilized flake was found in direct association (Table 4.10) with the basal sherd.

Feature 23. The constricted oval shape of this feature displayed a concentration of 7.5 kg (16.5 lb) of rock in the eastern portion. It was approximately 70 x 50 cm (2.3 x 1.9 ft) with a maximum depth of 15 cm (0.5 ft) in the eastern portion. Rocks protruded on the surface and a podzol underlayer was present. Twelve artifacts were found in the feature with seven utilized flakes (Table 4.10).

Feature 24. This feature was a 107 cm (3.5 ft) circular rock heap surrounded by a band of podzol soil 30-15 cm (1.0-0.5 ft) in width. To the west a tree root disturbance formed an extension. Rodent disturbance as well formed a deep pocket on the northern edge. The general depth below subsoil juncture was 12 cm (0.4 ft). Fire-cracked rock, 19.3 kg (42.5 lb), extended to the surface and consisted of several large rocks and small fragments. Fourteen utilized flakes and 34 artifacts made up the contents of the feature (Table 4.10).

Feature 26. This feature was roughly circular with a diameter of 60 cm (2 ft) and contained 7.7 kg (17 lb) of fractured rock. The depth was 9 cm (0.3 ft) with a podzolic underlayer. Rock extended to the surface. Twelve utilized flakes and ten artifacts were found in the central portion of the heap (Table 4.10).

Feature 27. Forty-eight pounds (21.7 kg) of large, flat, cracked and fractured rocks formed this feature whose depth was confined to the podzolic soil underlayer of 6 cm (0.2 ft). Rock extended approximately 10 cm (0.35 ft) above the ground surface. Eleven artifacts were found (Table 4.10).

Feature 31. This feature was completely sterile. It was circular, 76 cm (2.5 ft) in diameter, with much fire-cracked rock extending to the surface. Depth below the subsoil juncture was 17 cm (0.57 ft). Fire-cracked rock weight is unknown.

Feature 34. The oval shape of this feature contained much fragmented and reddened rock, 7.7 kg (17 lb). Dimensions were 146 x 92 cm (4.8 x 3.0 ft) with an average depth of 12 cm (0.4 ft). North and south in the feature were two deeper lobes, each with a podzolic zone extending to approximately 23 cm (0.75) ft). Two artifacts and five utilized flakes were recorded (Table 4.10).

Feature 35. Feature 35 was another sterile feature of this type. There were three large rocks extending to the surface along with numerous small fragments of broken stone. Fire-cracked rock weight is unknown. This oval feature's dimensions are 92 x 76 cm (3.0 x 2.5 ft) and the depth below juncture was 12 cm (0.4 ft).

Hearths (Figure 4.8)

Feature 7. This feature was roughly circular and 72 cm (2.35 ft) in diameter. This deep pit went to 46 cm (1.5 ft) below juncture. Grading down from 12 cm (0.4 ft) to 30 cm (1.0 ft) was a lining of 11.8 kg (26 lb) of fire-reddened stone. Below was 27 cm (0.9 ft) of podzolic deposit. Charcoal flecks were abundant above the stone and absent in the podzolic soil. Eight artifacts, which were found above the stone, were recovered (Table 4.10), as well as nine utilized flakes.

Feature 8. The diameter of this round hearth was 72 cm (2.35 ft) and it consisted of 3.6 kg (8 lb) of reddened rocks at the periphery of a dark charcoal flecked soil. A podzolic underlayer was under the rocks. Artifacts included five items (Table 4.10) and 12 utilized flakes. The

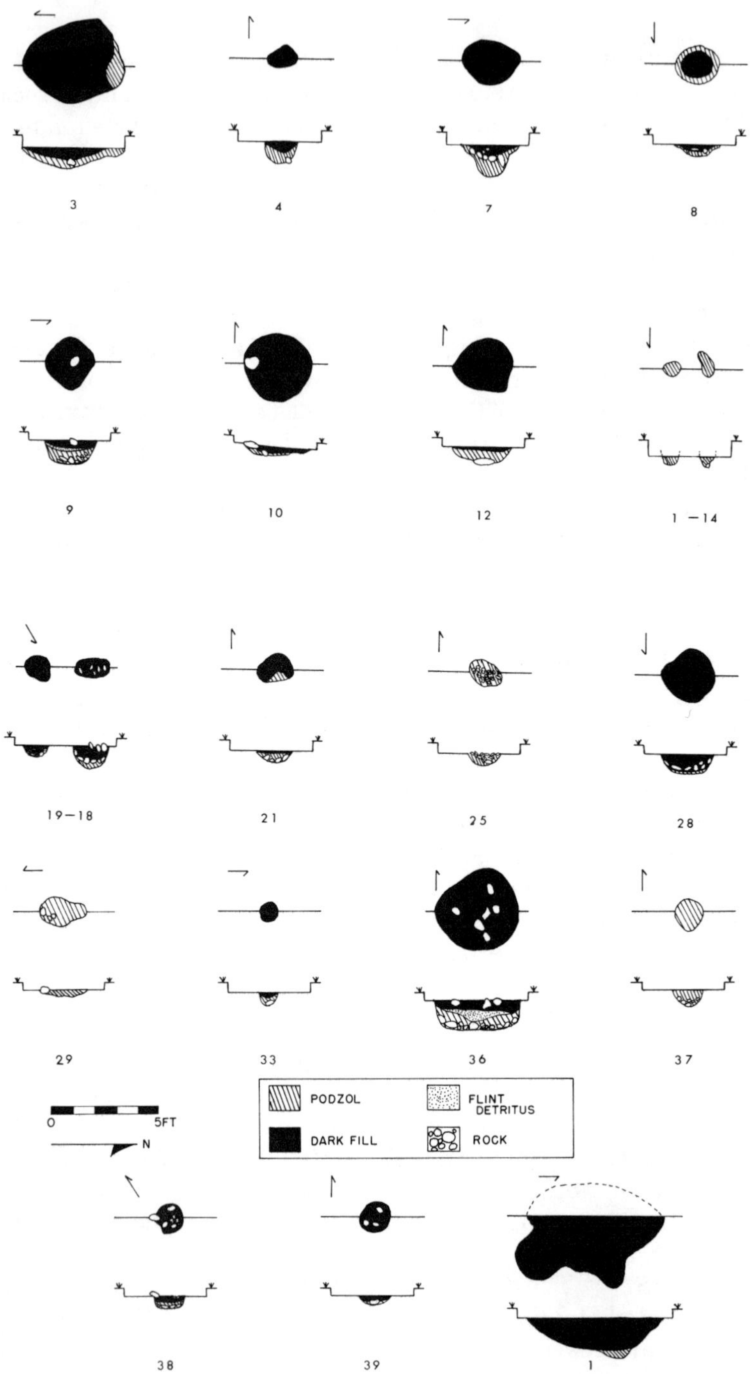

Fig. 4.8 Plans and profiles of other features at Sinking Ponds site.

steatite sherd joins one from Feature 20, suggesting the contemporaneity of these two features. Several unbroken stones were found at the top of the feature as if placed there for heating.

Feature 19. This small fire pit was also lined with 5.4 kg (12 lb) of small, fire-reddened stones and filled with charcoal-flecked humic soil. The diameter was approximately 37 cm (1.2 ft) and depth 15 cm (0.5 ft) below juncture. Three artifacts were recorded (Table 4.10).

Feature 21. This feature was small (55 cm or 1.8 ft) in diameter, 15 cm (0.5 ft) deep, and lined with fire-reddened rock. Podzolic soil is present above the rock lining and charcoal flecks are seen. Four utilized flakes and five artifacts were recovered from the pit fill (Table 4.10). Rock weight is unknown.

Feature 28. This was a large fire pit with a lining of 7.3 kg (16 lb) of fire-cracked and reddened stone. The diameter was 84 cm (2.75 ft) and depth was 26 cm (0.85 ft). A podzol zone 30 cm (0.1 ft) lay under the rock lining, above which was charcoal-stained dark soil. Six artifacts were recovered (Table 4.10).

Feature 37. The diameter of this small round hearth was 46 cm (1.50 ft). It was almost completely podzolic, 24 cm (0.80 ft) below juncture. Charcoal staining was observed, especially around rocks, but no large flecks were left. Very small fire-reddened rocks lined the bottom of the pit. Six artifacts were clustered just above the stones (Table 4.10).

Feature 38. The diameter of this feature is 47 cm (1.55 ft) with a depth below juncture of 15 cm (0.50 ft). A rock liner is present in podzolic deposits underlying a dark charcoal-stained organic pit fill. Four artifacts were found on the surface of the pit at juncture (Table 4.10). Fire-cracked rock weight is unknown.

Feature 39. This feature was quite similar to Feature 38 except that there was an incomplete stone liner. The rock weighed 4.5 kg (10 lb) with several large fire-reddened stones near the top of the feature accounting for most of the weight. The depth was 15 cm (0.5 ft) and diameter 46 cm (1.50 ft). Four artifacts were found with six steatite body sherds (Table 4.10). Three of the larger steatite sherds made up a portion of the stone liner.

Storage Pits (Fig. 4.8)

Feature 3. The pit, which was a part of the house floor known as Feature 2, a composite feature, was a large oval feature approximately 153 x 122 x 30 cm (5.0 x 4.0 x 1.0 ft) in depth. The outline of the pit was obscured by a podzol underzone of 15-21 cm (0.5-0.7 ft) in depth. Several large rocks were contained in the dark humic fill just above the podzol.

There was a large assemblage of cultural materials (Table 4.10). Eight utilized flakes were also recovered.

Feature 10. The pit was circular, 107 cm (3.5 ft) in diameter, and shallow in profile, 17 cm (0.55 ft). A narrow band of podzol underlay the dark humic contents. The pit contained three artifacts and 16 utilized flakes (Table 4.10). Several pebbles were encountered but no fire-cracked rock was present. This feature may have been a portion of a possible house pattern, similar to Feature 2 of the composite category (Map 4.5).

Feature 12. This roughly circular feature, 85 cm (2.8 ft) in diameter, had evidence of some rodent disturbance in its southeast quadrant. A large 2.7 kg (6 lb) heat-cracked rock formed the bottom of the pit at a depth of 24 cm (0.8 ft). A fairly thick podzolic formation of 23-24 cm (0.75-0.8 ft) underlay a shallow, dark fill that was 3-6 cm (0.1-0.2 ft) thick. Six artifacts were found above the rock (Table 4.10).

Features 13 and 14. These small deep pits were less than 30 cm (1.0 ft) in diameter and were recorded primarily because of their great depth of podzolic soil: 18-23 cm (0.6-0.75 ft). Although both features were sterile, Feature 14 had a sandstone pebble in the bottom of the pit. Generally, each of these features was symmetrical in plan and profile.

Feature 33. This pit was quite similar in size to Features 13 and 14, especially the latter. A large stone was noted at the bottom. The pit was sterile with an underzone of podzol below a dark organic pit fill.

Manufacture Pits (Fig. 4.8)

Feature 4. This feature is a portion of the possible house pattern, Feature 2, discussed below. Generally this was a deep, symmetrical pit approximately 30 cm (1.0 ft) in diameter with a dark organic upper portion of 18 cm (0.6 ft) and podzolic lower portion of 21 cm (0.7 ft), combining into a total depth of 40 cm (1.3 ft). Flint pebbles that were found in the pit comprised 32% of the total sample of such items. One was quite a large pebble which weighed 1 kg (2.3 lb) (Fig. 4.8). All of the flint pebbles were found in the podzolic portion, while the artifacts were found clustered above in the dark soil portion. Five other artifacts and six utilized flakes were also recovered (Table 4.10).

Feature 9. Feature 9 was roughly circular with a diameter of 76 cm (2.5 ft). The profile showed a deep pit with fairly vertical sides, a depth of organic soil to 14 cm (0.45 ft) below juncture, and podzolic formation below it to 34 cm (1.1 ft). A cluster of fire-cracked and reddened pebbles occurred on the bottom of the feature and tended to be more numerous in the northern hemisphere. A very large number of flakes and chips formed a pavement base at 18-23 cm (0.6-0.75 ft), between organic and podzolic soils. Three cores were found with the fire-cracked rock. Eight quaternary blanks — three whole, five tertiary — and a primary blank generally associated with the podzolic portions, showed up in the pit fill (Table 4.10). An abrading stone was found in the humic portion, and 28 utilized flakes were localized in a small pocket on the northern edge.

Feature 25. This small oval bowllike depression, 30 x 47 cm (1.0 x 1.55 ft), is the only *pure* cache pit seen on the site. This feature was completely filled with a white podzolic deposit to 18 cm (0.6 ft) below juncture and in addition, 17 cached netsinkers. The obvious possibility is that these represent a net dropped or deliberately cached. The podzolic deposit reinforces this hypothesis since destructive decomposition by leaching would have been rapid, completely disintegrating the loose organic net.

Feature 29. This problematic pit was a shallow podzolic deposit of 10 cm (0.35 ft), in an irregular circular form with a southward extension, totaling a length of 69 cm (2.25 ft). An inordinately large number of flint chips and flakes were scattered throughout, with some fire-cracked rock near the surface. Nine cores were clustered with the fire-cracked rock in the northern portion, along with a fragmentary birdstone. Five other artifacts were scattered in the fill (Table 4.10). Twenty-five utilized flakes clustered in the southern extension.

Feature 32 (Fig. 4.8). Although this feature has the form of a rock heap, the circular depression, 82 cm (2.7 ft) in diameter, was filled with 17 flint pebbles, some of which had been trimmed of cortex or fossil inclusions. Ten pounds (4.5 kg) of other sandstone rock were also noted. A secondary blank which was a completely retouched, trimmed pebble completed the artifact inventory. As in Features 9 and 29 a small cache of utilized flakes lay in the podzol underlayer in the center of the feature. The depth was 14 cm (0.45 ft) below juncture in the southern portion.

Feature 36. The three-foot diameter of this feature made it the largest pit. Its vertical walls extended below juncture to 43 cm (1.4 ft). The interior of the pit showed a complex arrangement (Fig. 4.8). On the bottom were a number of rocks and pebbles, some fire-cracked. Among these rocks was a hammerstone. Above it was a podzolic zone succeeded by a heavy concentration of flint flakes and chips. Above them a dark organic zone occurred in which were projectile points, one Meadowood and the other stemmed, a drill, a unifacial scraper, a longitudinal knife, and 13 utilized flakes. Below, in the flint concentration, 17 cores were clustered in the central portion of the pit.

Composite Features (Fig. 4.9)

Feature 2 (Pl. 2). This feature was a compacted floor first appearing at 10 cm (0.35 ft) and extending to 17 cm (0.55 ft). Its overall form was roughly oval with a length of 4.73 m (15.5 ft) and a width of 3.97 m (13.0 ft). The area encompassed Features 3, 4, and 5, as well as 24 postmolds which were recognized after very careful cross checking of notes, plans, profiles, and photographs. Also identified as postmolds, but later eliminated, were 12 rodent disturbances and one large root-disturbed area.

Over much of this floor were strewn pottery sherds, flint chips, and artifacts. Close examination of the artifact distributions, however, leads to some interesting results. Ten fragmentary tertiary blanks and one whole one were distributed close to Feature 4 in an area designated as Flint Area I (Fig. 4.10, Table 4.11). A primary blank, 3 secondary blanks, and 9 quaternary blank fragments were also found in this area, which had 129 chips but only 37 flakes. Adjacent to Feature 4 in the north was Fire-cracked Rock Area V (Figure 4.10). Approximately 9.1 kg (20 lb) of this material was loosely scattered about on the floor. Included in this cluster were 2 Meadowood projectile points, 4 bifacial scrapers, 3 unifacial scrapers, a pitted anvilstone, a longitudinal knife, and a drill. In the Flint Detritus Areas (Fig. 4.10, Table 4.11) were 40 utilized flakes and 62 nonutilized flakes, but only 26 chips. Artifacts in this area included 2 drills, a Meadowood point, 2 bifacial scrapers, a unifacial scraper, and a grooved abrading stone. In Flint Detritus Area II (Fig. 4.10, Table 4.11) were found 84 flint flakes, 247 chips, and 5 utilized flakes. The only artifact found here was one fragmentary Meadowood projectile point. In Pottery Area IV (Fig. 4.10, Table 4.11) were found 323 body sherds, most of which were extremely small. All of the pottery was worn as if by abrasion and five small rim sherds with this abraded appearance were recovered. No other artifacts appeared in this area, but just south of the area a pipe fragment was recovered. All of these areas seem to relate well to various activities which might reasonably be expected in a house.

Feature 4 was a cache pit for flint pebbles and some tertiary blanks. Close to it, Area I shows an unusual number of items in all stages of manufacture. This is borne out by the relatively large frequency of chips to flakes (Table 4.11). Flint Area III seems clearly related to by-product usage with flakes of all types predominating over chips, 102 to 26 (Table

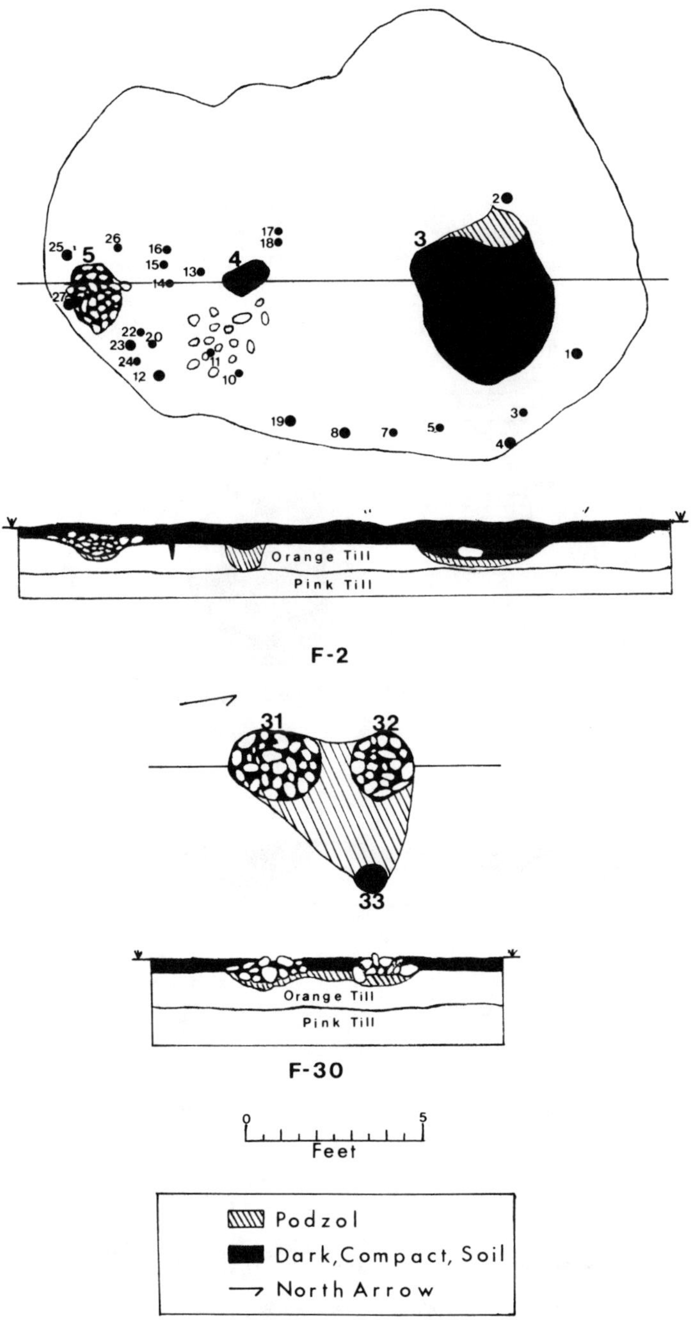

Fig. 4.9 Plans and profiles of composite features at Sinking Ponds site.

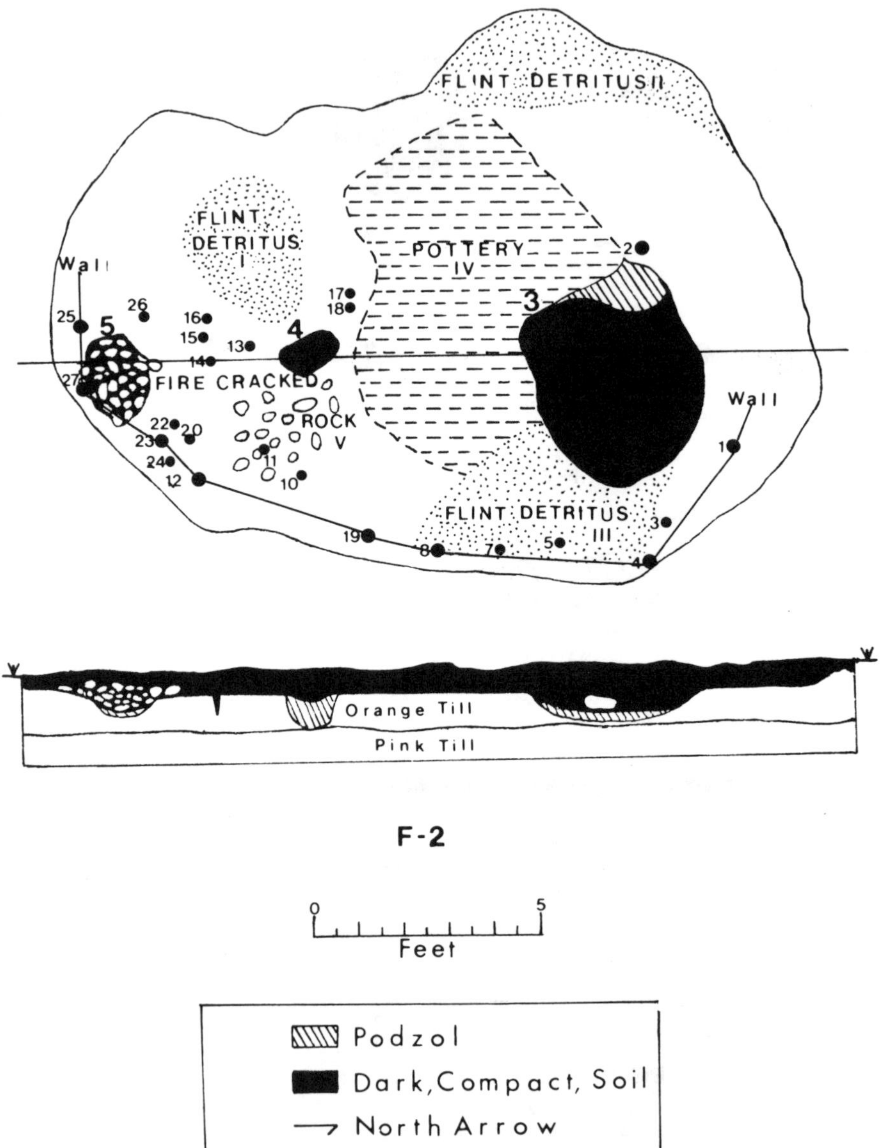

Fig. 4.10 Diagram of cultural material distribution in Feature 2.

TABLE 4.11
CULTURAL MATERIAL DISTRIBUTION IN FEATURE 2 (POSSIBLE HOUSE)

Artifact Type	Features			Feature 2 "Floor"						Total	
	Fea. 3	Fea. 4	Fea. 5	Area I	Area II	Area III	Area IV	Area V	Other Areas		
	#	#	#	#	#	#	#	#	#	#	%
Sidenotched Projectile Point	1				1	1		2		5	0.8
Cornernotched Projectile Point			1							1	0.2
Stemmed Projectile Point	1									1	0.2
Quaternary Blank	4		1	9						14	2.1
Tertiary Blank	4	2		11						17	2.6
Secondary Blank	1			3						4	0.6
Primary Blank	1			1						2	0.3
Longitudinal Knife		1						1		2	0.3
Bifacial Scrapers			1			2		4		7	1.1
Unifacial Scrapers						1		3		4	0.6
Drill	1	1				2		1		5	0.8
Pitted Anvilstone								1		1	0.2
Grooved Abrading Stone		1				1				2	0.3
Gorget	1									1	0.2
Bead	1									1	0.2
Pipe									1	1	0.2
Pottery-Rim							5			5	0.8
Pottery-Body	88						497			585	88.9
Artifact N	103	5	3	24	1	7	502	12	1	658	100
Nonartifactual Material											
Utilized Flakes	8	6			5	40				59	8.2
Nonutilized Flakes	18	11		37	84	62				212	29.5
Chips	24	14		129	247	26				440	61.2
Pebbles		8								8	1.1
Nonartifact N	50	39	0	166	336	128	0	0	0	719	100

4.11). The 40 utilized flakes were tested for wear and fragmentation, and 28, or 70%, showed heavy wear while 7, or 17.5%, showed lighter wear. Five, or 12.5%, were fractured. Scrapers, the utilized flakes, and an abrading stone suggest that this area was the scene of some bone working although there is no direct evidence for this. The fire-cracked rock scatter, Area V, has a larger number of more finely worked scrapers, with an end or transverse form predominating. The scrapers and drill also suggest some form of processing activity, and pigment adhering to the pitted stone in which a depression was ground (rather than pecked) supports the possibility of some form of processing. However, the relatively low yield of artifacts implies a lack of intensity of processing of any one type of material.

Features 3, 4, and 5 form a line of approximately 4.6 m (15 ft). Each of these features represents two differing types of activity. The identification of Number 5 as a rock heap is obvious, but quite possibly this feature doubled as a hearth. Although no charcoal was found, this might be due to soil leaching. Artifactually, the heap was not instructive beyond producing, in association with a bifacial scraper and quaternary blank, a corner-notched point that had been reworked to an end scraper. The storage pit, Feature 3, produced some data on function. The general distribution of material shows no specific activity and supports the conclusion that the pit was filled with refuse.

The pottery confirms the accumulation of rubbish in the pits. Sherds found in the pit were unabraded and showed less wear. Usually the sherds were larger than those outside, and several displayed a charred deposit on the interior surface. Further evidence that this feature was a refuse pit were the eight utilized flakes found. Three of these were fractured in use and four were so worn that they were probably discards.

The wall of the structure appears to be outlined by large postmolds, 10 cm (0.35 ft) in diameter, spaced 61-92 cm (2-3 ft) apart (Nos. 25, 27, 23, 12, 19, 8, 4 and 11). Smaller posts (Nos. 7, 5, 3, 11, 20, 22 and 24) may provide structural support, while others represent interior structures. Molds 13-18 clustered about Feature 4 and Area I may represent a rack or bench of some kind (Fig. 4.10). Possibly the double postmolds (15-16 and 17-18) represent, with the large postmold (2) near Feature 3, a form of central support.

Feature 30 (Fig. 4.9). This was another floor composed of compacted podzolic soil in the form of a triangle, 162 x 143 cm (5.3 x 4.7 ft). The podzolic soil formed the intervening space between Features 31, 32, and 33. The floor was sterile of artifacts as were Features 31, a rock heap, and Feature 33, a small refuse pit containing one stone. Feature 32, a manufacture pit, contained 17 flint pebbles, 22 cores, 216 nonutilized flakes and 214 chips. Twenty-nine utilized flakes were clustered in the center of the feature. It may well be that Feature 30 is a depression filled with organic soil now podzolized by leaching. However, its conformity to the three features outlined above suggests that it is related, possibly as a workshop floor where a flint knapper plied his activity. It is noteworthy that there was manufacturing debris from all stages but no artifacts beyond a fragmentary secondary blank which could not be modified further because of a large fossil inclusion.

ARTIFACTS

A total of 1137 cataloged artifacts were recovered from the excavation at Sinking Ponds; 959 were feature related and 178 were found elsewhere in the sampling tracts. Stratigraphically the distribution of those found outside features was:

Surface	28	(15.7%)
Level I	127	(71.3%)
Level II	23	(13.0%)

Laboratory examination significantly reduced the total number of artifacts by forming whole vessels of several sherds and by repairing lithic fragments. Thus, the working total of artifacts became 453, with 317 in features and 136 in units. This total became the figure which has been used for subsequent calculations, except where noted.

In some cases, discussion of one artifact type may consist of more prose description than another. This is because many artifact types have been described by attribute, with frequencies and percentages within these attributes set out in tabular form in Appendix A. Tables have also been compiled showing those attributes which vary and those which are constant. Collections from all sites studied are included for comparison.

In Chapter 1 we discussed the assignment of artifacts, nonartifacts, and structures, to general functional categories. Table 4.12 assigns artifacts to the general functional categories for Sinking Ponds, and Figure 4.11 illustrates the percentage distribution in these functional categories. The assignment of artifacts to these categories was done with the intention of ordering this data to define activity areas, and these attributions are discussed in more detail below. Figure 4.11 is designed to illustrate the major frequencies of artifacts within functional categories; for example, netsinkers in procurement, unifacial scrapers in processing, quaternary blanks in manufacture, and pottery vessels in storage. Also portrayed in the graph are the relative frequencies of each category. Manufacture was the most productive of artifacts at nearly 50%. Artifact type frequencies based on the total sample are

TABLE 4.12
DISTRIBUTION OF ARTIFACT TYPES IN FUNCTIONAL CATEGORIES

Artifact	N	% of Total N	% of Subtotal N's	
Sidenotched Projectile Point	21	5	15	
Cornernotched Projectile Point	9	2	7	
Stemmed Projectile Point	10	2	8	Procurement
Birdstone	1	0+	1	
Netsinker	97	21	70	
Subtotal	138	30	100	
Longitudinal Knife	9	2	11	
Unifacial Scraper	26	6	32	
Bifacial Scraper	15	4	19	Processing
Drill	13	3	16	
Mano Abrading Stone	3	1	4	
Chopper	2	0+	3	
Pitted Anvilstone	12	3	15	
Subtotal	81	26	100	
Primary Blank	12	3	5	
Secondary Blank	20	5	9	
Tertiary Blank	61	14	27	
Quaternary Blank	105	23	47	Manufacture
Hammerstone	19	5	8	
Grooved Abrading Stone	8	2	4	
Subtotal	225	50	100	
Gorget	2	0+	50	
Bead	1	0+	25	Ceremonial
Pipe	1	0+	25	
Subtotal	4	1	100	
Steatite Vessel	2	0+	40	
Pottery Vessel	3	1	60	Storage
Subtotal	5	1	100	
Total N	453	100		

also portrayed, although this distribution generally follows that of individual categories. This distribution is further broken down to show the relationship of artifacts to levels and structures by functional category (Table 4.13).

It is significant at the level of one case out of 1000 occurring by chance that the highest percentage of artifacts in those categories represented in levels are clustered in Level I, albeit at the juncture with Level II. An occupation floor between 9 and 18 cm (0.3 and 0.6 ft) has been suggested. The cluster of artifacts above 15 cm (0.5 ft) suggests its greatest density to be at between 9 and 15 cm (0.3 and 0.5 ft), quite probably at 10-12 cm (0.35-0.4 ft).

All functional categories of artifacts were heavily represented in features although artifacts of procurement were most heavily rep-

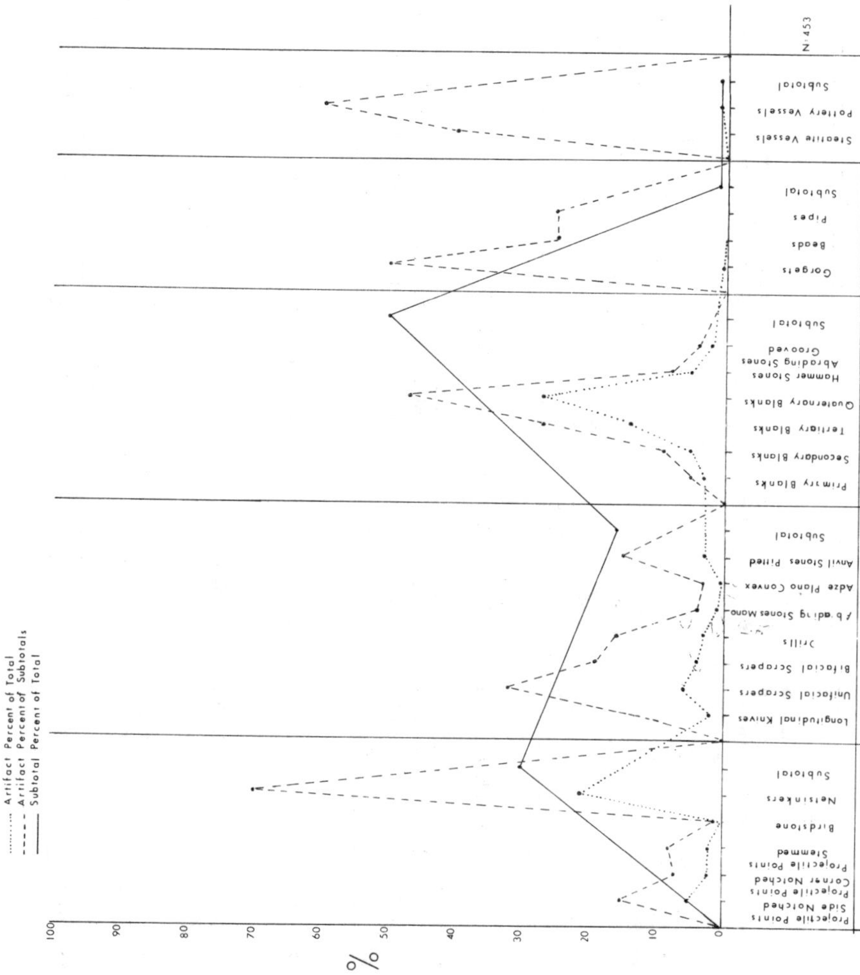

Fig. 4.11 Artifact-category relationships.

TABLE 4.13
DISTRIBUTION OF FUNCTIONAL CATEGORIES OF ARTIFACTS

	Surface		Level I		Level II		Non-Feature Subtotal Units		Rock Heap		Hearth		Mfg/ Cache		Storage/ Refuse		Com-posite		Subtotal Features		Total	
	#	%	#	%	#	%	#	%	#	%	#	%	#	%	#	%	#	%	#	%	#	%
Procurement	5	3.6	33	23.9	0	0	38	27.5	56	40.6	10	7.2	27	19.6	3	2.2	4	2.9	100	72.5	138	100
Processing	5	6.2	14	17.3	6	7.4	25	30.9	27	33.3	5	6.2	7	8.6	2	2.5	15	18.5	56	69.1	81	100
Manufacture	17	7.6	50	22.2	6	2.7	73	32.4	45	20	24	10.7	39	17.3	18	8	26	11.6	152	67.5	225	100
Ceremonial	0	0	0	0	0	0	0	0	1	25	0	0	0	0	2	50	1	25	4	100	4	100
Storage	0	0	0	0	0	0	0	0	3	60	0	0	0	0	0	0	2	40	5	100	5	100
N	27	6	97	21.4	12	2.6	136	30	132	29.1	39	8.6	73	16.2	25	5.5	48	10.6	317	70	453	100

TABLE 4.14
DISTRIBUTION OF ARTIFACTS OF PROCUREMENT

	Surface		Level I		Level II		Subtotal Units		Rock Heap		Hearth		Mfg./ Cache		Storage/ Refuse		Composite		Subtotal Features		Total	
	#	%	#	%	#	%	#	%	#	%	#	%	#	%	#	%	#	%	#	%	#	%
Projectile Points: Sidenotched	2	9.5	2	9.5			4	19	6	28.7	1	4.8	4	19	2	9.5	4	19	17	81	21	100
Projectile Points: Cornernotched			3	33.3			3	33.3	4	44.4	2	22.2							6	66.8	9	100
Projectile Points: Stemmed	3	30	3	30			6	60			1	10	2	20	1	10			4	40	10	100
Netsinkers			25	25.8			25	25.8	46	47.4	6	6.2	20	20.6					72	74.2	97	100
Birdstone													1	100					1	100	1	100
N	5	3.6	33	23.9			38	27.5	56	40.6	10	7.2	27	19.6	3	2.2	4	2.9	100	72.5	100	100

resented in rock heaps as were artifacts of processing (Table 4.13). Manufactured artifacts appear most often in manufacture pits and rock heaps. Storage and ceremonial artifacts also are split between rock heaps and composite features but the number of such artifacts is so small that not much can be inferred (Table 4.13). Generally, individual categories of artifacts show a fairly random distribution and do not readily separate into distinct activity clusters.

Artifacts of Procurement

This grouping of artifacts includes 40 projectile points, 97 netsinkers, and a birdstone. Their assignment to this category rests upon their functional relationship to the direct procurement of food, i.e. hunting or fishing. The most frequent occurrence of these artifacts (72.5%, 40.6%) was in the rock heaps alone (Table 4.14). The next highest frequencies in the manufacture pits may simply be those items which were discarded before they performed their appointed function. Although there is a risk in using single artifacts as indications of strength of association, the 2:1 distribution of the 97 netsinkers to 40 projectile points in this category may reflect emphasis in the type of procurement activities, i.e., fishing. The netsinkers considered above are most heavily represented in rock heaps at 47.4%, with less in the manufacture pits or caches where most are accounted for in a single feature, perhaps associated with net making or repair. The birdstone has been included in this category rather than ceremonial, based upon its functional rather than aesthetic qualities (Mau 1963:10-11).

Projectile Points, Sidenotched (Pl. 3)

A sample of 21 sidenotched projectile points was recovered. Morphologically and metrically these points fit the classification of Meadowood Point (Table A.1*b*, App. A;Ritchie 1961:35, 89). Twelve were either whole or reconstructable. Thickness clusters between 4 mm and 6 mm, the mean length is 50 mm, and the mean width, 26 mm. A Fisher's Exact probability of 0.017 showed that a correlation of width which was close to 50% of the length would occur by chance less than one case in 100. Other correlations such as base height to width and length were less significant. Although most of the bases are sub-convex, 66.7%, the height of sidenotches above the base appears to be variable but is usually within one centimeter above the base (Table A.1*b*, App. A).

The distribution of these points on the site shows heavy occurrence in features, 81%, but a random distribution by feature type and by depth in units (Table 4.14). A projectile point with fire pocking did, however, come from a feature classified as a hearth, Feature 21. Three fragmentary bases were recovered in association with three fragmentary stemmed points in Feature 36, a manufacture cache pit, suggesting that both types of points may have been manufactured simultaneously. Materially these points were indistinguishable. Matrix percentage in the Onondaga flint for the Meadowood points, blades, blade fragments, and stemmed points in this pit was within 20-40%, while the range of matrix inclusion on the site was from 0-100%. This suggests that both types of point in this particular feature were manufactured from a higher quality of chert than was generally available at the site. No wear was observed on these fragments. Two points found in context with storage pits were whole as were three of the four found in association with the composite feature, Feature 2. Two of these exhibited lateral and basal wear.

The majority of this type of projectile point on the Sinking Ponds site, 14 or 66.7%, were incomplete, exhibiting either distal or proximal breakage, or poor lateral symmetry on the blade. The two points upon which edge, basal, or sidenotch wear was observed were both located in what may have been a house.

The flaking techniques seen on these points show progressive refinement by secondary and tertiary pressure flaking of an end-struck flake with a remnant striking platform on the base. The base, haft element, and lateral portions of the blade were finished by tertiary flaking, obscuring the striking platform and showing a slight reverse bevel on each side of the blade.

Projectile Points, Cornernotched (Pl. 4*a-g*)

Nine examples, four complete, of this type of projectile point were found. Although the term "cornernotched haft element" is used to describe this group, these points only moderately fit the description of the proximal point of juncture being coincident to the base (Binford 1963*a*:212). The majority of bases are straight to subconvex, with the corner notches proceeding distally from the ears at the point of juncture. The bases, with two exceptions, show scarring, reworking and uneven rethinning. Nonsymmetrical outlines suggest the strong possibility that these are reworked Meadowood points. Two of the points resemble the Brewerton Eared notched variety, while four exhibit affinities to the Brewerton sidenotched variety, except in thickness and flaking (Ritchie 1971:Pl.5,7). Several factors, however, made such a placement unlikely. Three appear to be as thin and well worked as Meadowood cornernotched (Table A.3*b*), while the others display a greater degree of thickness with cruder overall flaking. Blade shape reflects a moderate Meadowood association (Table A.3*b*, App. A).

The majority of these points were concentrated in the features of Sampling Tract 5, where four occurred in rock heaps and two in hearths. A Fisher's Exact Test of the distribution of these points compared to other points for association with units or features in a 2 x 2 table, showed that there was a nonrandom distribution.

One fragmentary projectile point of this type was of rhyolite and may represent an import of a broad-blade type from the east. No typological assignment of this point is possible at present.

Projectile Points (Pl. 4*h-n*)

Ten stemmed points were distributed randomly over the site. Although no clustering of this sample was observed, there was generally no difference between its occurrence and that of any other point type on the site (Table 4.14). In two cases—Features 3 and 36—evidence was quite clear that these points were directly associated with Meadowood points in a homogeneous cultural context. Correlations between all five points were made with pit structure, material of manufacture, and attributes of blade shape, flaking, and size. Only insignificant differences were noted. In our opinion, the stemmed points were coeval with the sidenotched points.

These points resemble most closely Ritchie's Lamoka, subtype B, which he relates most closely to Dustin Points (Ritchie 1971:29-30, 83-85). Their most prominent feature is the lobate-basal portion with broad sidenotches extending distally, forming "stems." In the Sinking Ponds sample, two points exhibit fragmentary bases, but with the exception of a surface find, they were more akin to Lamoka A with its rhomboidal cross section. All the points show the sidenotch–stem combination and overlay the lower length range of the sidenotch points. Bases of five of these points showed remnants of a basal striking platform. Since a finished stem is not a prerequisite for socket hafting, the striking platform was retained. Seven of these points show weak shoulder development at the distal point of juncture. Further attribute observations are shown in Table A.2*b*, Appendix A, where comparative data on other points of this type associated with Meadowood complexes are available.

Netsinkers (App. 1, Table A.16*b*; Pl. 9*c-e*)

The netsinkers were a fairly uniform group of artifacts both in shape and function. Of the 97 recovered, 99% were of sandstone on double notched biplano glacial pebbles. Several, 13, showed the utilization of a natural notch in opposition to a man-made notch. In the main, the netsinkers were similar in plan and execution to those illustrated in Ritchie (1969:Pl. 12, 10), but assigned to the Lamoka phase or (ibid.: Pl. 53, 7) the Frost Island phase. It is significant that there was a lack of endnotched round pebbles (ibid.: Pl. 66) although the material for such sinkers was abundantly available. The thickness of 84, 87%, of the netsinkers ranged between 11 and 30 mm and indicated an emphasis on flat pebbles. A flat pebble with the line attached perpendicular to the broad surface would act as a drogue anchor in mud, possibly to hold a net edge to a muddy pond bottom, whereas such a pebble would impede a drag net. Most of the variation occurs in the weight (Table A.16*b*, App. A). The range was between 70 and 200 g, with 67, 69%, below 100 g, perhaps reflecting the calmness of the embayed waters where fishing took place and also the method employed (Table A.16*b*, App. A). The weight range was probably not a major factor in the use of these objects if they were used on stationary nets in a weir arrangement.

The majority of netsinkers, 72 or 74.2%, were feature associated (Table 4.14), with 46 or 47.4% in rock heaps. A cache with 17 netsinkers of various sizes, all under 100 g in weight, appears to have marked either a manufacture or repair station for nets.

Although this distribution might also suggest the number of netsinkers attached to a single net or segment of a weir we have no way of determining the spatial placement or the mean weight per net. All netsinkers were of local materials except for a small netsinker of greenish-gray flint, identified as Deepskill chert. This feature-associated netsinker may have been a trade item. It was not, however, markedly dissimilar from those locally produced.

Birdstone (Pl. 11*b*)

A single birdstone fragment was recovered from Feature 29, a cache pit (Table 4.14). This birdstone is made of a dark green indurated shale and is minus a head and tail (Fig. 4.12). Two drilled biconical oblique holes are placed at either end of the base. The basal width is 24.5 mm and basal length is 54 mm. Height of the back above the base is 19 mm. The stone shows wear, and on one side striations suggest a forward and backward motion. Otherwise the birdstone was finely ground and polished. The angle of the neck scar inclines toward the base at approximately 20°. This suggests that the head was forcefully detached. The tail scar indicates that the tail was battered off.

We suggest that the birdstone functioned as an atlatl weight after Mau (1963:10-11). He states that this type of weight might lend a

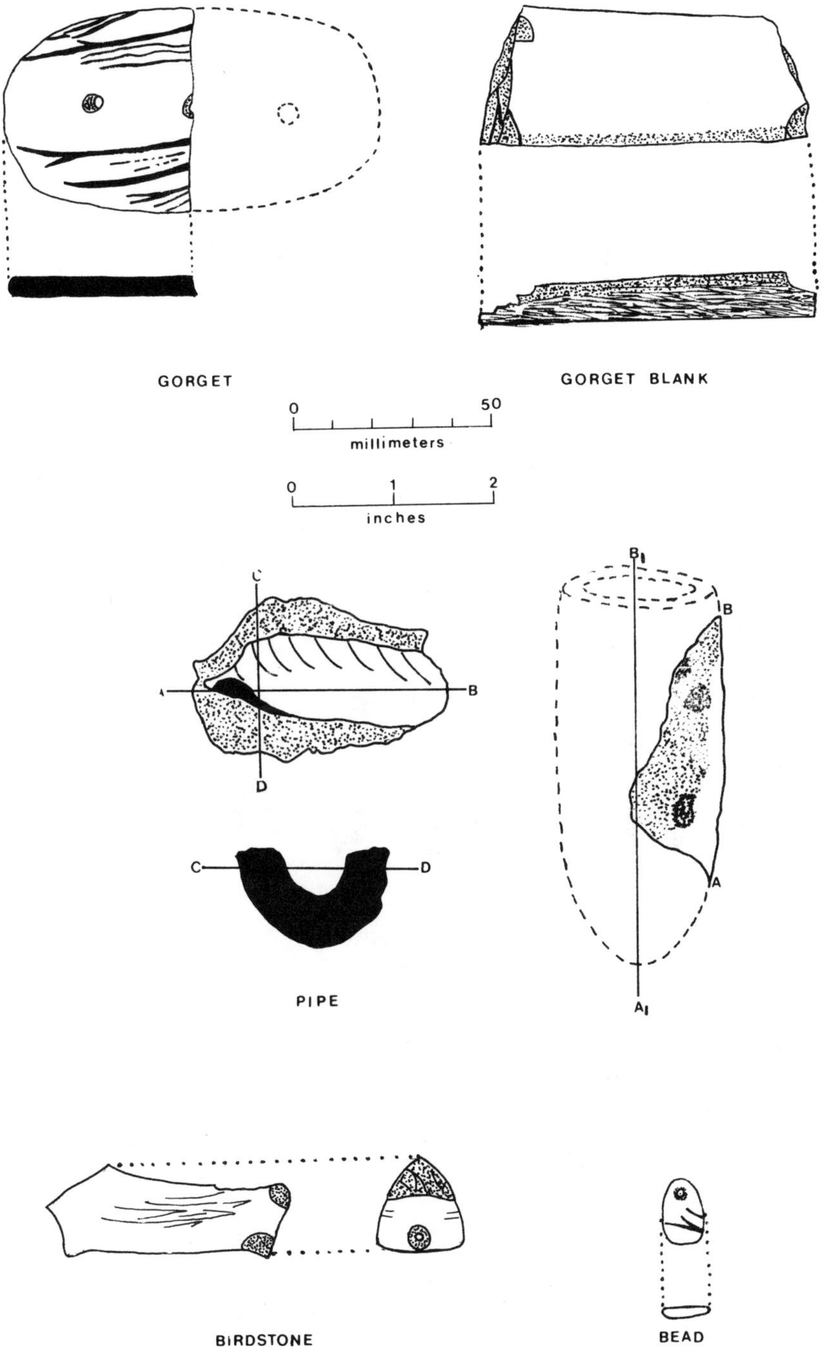

Fig. 4.12 Ceremonial artifacts.

TABLE 4.15
DISTRIBUTION OF ARTIFACTS OF PROCESSING

	Surface		Level I		Level II		Non-Feature Subtotal Units		Rock Heap		Hearth		Mfg./ Cache		Storage/ Refuse		Composite		Subtotal Features		Total	
	#	%	#	%	#	%	#	%	#	%	#	%	#	%	#	%	#	%	#	%	#	%
Longitudinal Knife			2	22.2			2	22.2	4	44.4			2	22.2			1	11.1	7	77.9	9	100
Unifacial Scraper	1	3.8	5	19.2	3	11.5	9	34.6	10	38.6	1	3.8	2	7.7			4	15.4	17	65.4	26	100
Bifacial Scraper	3	20	2	13.3			5	33.3	3	20	1	6.7					6	40	10	66.7	15	100
Drill			2	15.4	2	15.4	4	30.8	2	15.4			3	23.1	1	7.7	3	23.1	9	69.2	13	100
Mano Abrading Stone	1	33.3					1	33.3	1	33.3	1	33.3							2	66.7	13	100
Plano-Convex Adze									1	50	1	50							2	100	2	100
Chopper															1	100			1	100	1	100
Pitted Anvilstone			3	25	1	8.4	4	33.3	6	50	1	8.3					1	8.4	8	66.6	12	100
N	5	6.2	14	17.3	6	7.4	25	30.9	27	33.3	5	6.2	7	8.6	2	2.5	15	18.5	56	69.1	81	100

15-20% increase in efficiency for an atlatl and indicates that the use of decorative techniques to embellish the weight may have implied its importance.

Artifacts of Processing

Those artifacts functionally grouped under the heading processing, include knife scrapers, scrapers, adzes, mano abrading stones, pitted stones, and choppers. These artifacts generally relate either to processing food and by-products of subsistence activity, or to acting upon other materials, perhaps in order to modify them for short-term use (Table 4.15). An example of this would be the use of the adze for woodworking. Heavy distribution of these artifacts is seen in features, 69%, with the largest single occurrences in rock heaps, 33%, and composite features, 19% (Table 4.13). Table 4.13 also shows a concentration of processing artifacts in features, 69.1%, with the majority of this figure clustered in rock heaps, 33.3%. The next highest grouping is the 18.5% found in the house. These figures may suggest the relative importance of processing, a possible processing activity area, and a house within which some processing is ordinarily implied.

Longitudinal Knife Scrapers (Pl. 6*i-r*)

Nine longitudinal knife scrapers were recovered. These asymmetrical blanks appear to be discards from the manufacture sequence (Fig. 1.2). The common attribute of all these artifacts is an excurvate working edge, often appearing as a saw-toothed denticulate edge (Table A.10*b*, App. A) created by rough percussion flaking and often modified by wear, appearing as tertiary use scars. Seven of the longitudinal knife scrapers exhibit stepped flaking on the edge opposing the working edge, as if one edge of the blade had been for hand use. One scraper shows a vertical fracture face which does effectively blunt the blade edge. All of the knife scrapers show thick cross sections.

Almost 50% of the sample, four, occur in rock heaps and may have been utilized in activities related to that of the rock heap – hearth feature complex at the western edge of the site (Table 4.15).

Since the longitudinal knife scraper is a utilized discard, these artifacts may have been used and then immediately discarded once wear had dulled the utilized edges. Only one gives evidence of retouching on one edge. This appears on the opposing edge, while the former working edge was blunted by removal of the major portion of the working surface (seen as a steep vertical removal scar). The type generally conforms to that described by Ritchie (1969:Pl. 64, no. 1) as the "ovate knife."

Unifacial Scrapers (Pl. 7)

The 26 unifacial scrapers formed on flakes were distributed in the following varieties:

Circumferential-over 85% of the edge used		3
End Scrapers		7
Side Scrapers	Large	6
	Small	6
	Composite	2
Spokeshave		2

The figures for each variety were generally consistent with attribute association in the attribute, "working edge location" (Table A.11*b*, App. A). Few further associations could be determined due to variation in size or degree of preparation (Wobst 1968:212). Two side scrapers show evidence of graver spurs, one displaying two, the other one broad apical spur. Eight, or 31%, displayed ventral flaking, while 14, or 54%, were dorsally flaked (Table A.11*b*, App. A).

Ventral flaking is displayed by removal of used flakes from the unmodified surface of a flake or the flakes's detachment scar. This condition, usually a characteristic of utilized flakes, where no further modification is present has formed a recognizable reused working edge on the flake side scrapers. Ventral flaking may result from a push stroke (ibid.: 214), which ultimately dulls the scraper leading to discard, whereas a pull stroke often results in continued resharpening on forms such as the end scraper. This hints at a division between activities, perhaps the difference between the pull stroke of hide scraping and the push stroke of fish scaling.

The distribution of unifacial scrapers is also instructive. Fifteen, 60%, of these scrapers were located in Sampling Tract 5. Although all varieties were represented, all eight of the scrapers with ventral scars were located here. Ten of the 15 scrapers were feature related, all in rock heaps (Table 4.15). The association in Sampling Tract 5 of uniface scrapers with netsinkers was significant when tested by Fisher's Exact Test, showing that such an association occurs by chance less than one time in 100. A test for association in rock heaps was also significant at a Fisher's Exact probability of .04483. Five unifacial scrapers consisting of two large side scrapers, two composite side scrapers, and a spokeshave were located in the features of Composite Feature 2. Here the distribu-

TABLE 4.16
DISTRIBUTION OF VENTRAL AND DORSAL WEAR FLAKING ON UTILIZED FLAKES

Samp. Tr.	Units Exclusive of Features						Features															
	Ventral		Dorsal		N		Ventral		Dorsal		N		ΣN		Feature Type	Ventral		Dorsal		N		
	#	%	#	%	#	%	#	%	#	%	#	%	#	%		#	%	#	%	#	%	%/N
1	9	30	21	70	30	100							30	4.5	Rock Heap	49	81.7	11	18.3	60	100	21.8
2	4	33.3	8	66.7	12	100							12	1.8								
3	76	51	73	49	149	100	27	39.7	41	60.3	68	100	217	32.2	Hearths	24	47.1	27	52.9	51	100	18.6
4	11	39.3	17	60.7	28	100	14	31.8	30	68.2	44	100	72	10.7								
5	129	87.2	19	12.8	148	100	86	86	14	14	100	100	248	36.9	Storage/ Refuse	3	37.5	5	62.5	8	100	2.9
6	5	45.5	6	54.5	11	100	29	46	34	54	63	100	74	11								
7	1	33.3	2	66.7	3	100							3	0.4	Mfg./Cache	47	46.5	54	53.5	101	100	36.7
8	1	100	0	0	1	100							1	0.1								
9	5	31.2	11	68.8	16	100							16	2.4	Composite	24	43.6	31	56.4	55	100	20
N	241	60.6	157	39.4	398	100	156	56.7	119	43.3	275	100	673	100		147	53.5	128	46.5	275		100
%/ΣN	35.8		23.3		59.1		23.2		17.7		40.9		100									

tion was almost equal to that of the bifacial scrapers with six bifacial to four unifacial. The two scrapers exhibiting graving spurs were also associated with Feature 2.

Utilized flakes may be broadly considered to be unifacial scrapers (Wobst 1968:214). Six-hundred and seventy-three were recovered from the site. The majority, 397 or 59%, showed ventral wear flaking as defined above. Table 4.16 shows the distributions of these attributes by units, features, and feature types. Significantly, Sampling Tract 5 shows greater than 85% flakes with ventral wear flaking in both features (87.2%) and units (86%). A similar distribution occurs in the feature type rock heap (Fig. 4.13), which has 60% of its distribution in Sampling Tract 5 (Table 4.1). We suggested above that ventral flaking may have been related to a push technique (ibid.: 222-24) used in fish processing. The removal of fish scales is accomplished by a push stroke away from the body against the lie of the scales. The scales are lifted and dislodged at their articulation. The relatively even or moderately inverse percentages in the other sampling tracts are strikingly dissimilar from Sampling Tract 5, which displays the highest proportion of netsinkers on the site, 97%. This same situation applies to other feature types (Table 4.16, Fig. 4.13).

Bifacial Scrapers (Pl. 8)

A sample of 15 bifacial scrapers contained the following varieties (as suggested by A. White 1963:5-32).

End Scrapers	Hafted	2
	Trianguloid	4
	Parallel-Lateral edge	5
Side Scrapers	Parallel-Lateral edge	2
Spokeshave		2
Total		15

Tests for association of particular varieties with feature type showed no significant distribution, except that almost 50% of the population, including one hafted end, three trianguloid end, two parallel end, and a parallel side scraper, were all recovered from Sampling Tract 3, six from within Feature 2, with the single exception being a parallel end scraper located outside but adjacent to the feature. Three scrapers, one trianguloid end, one spokeshave, and one parallel end were associated with rock heaps. The spokeshave also gives evidence of fire pocking (Table 4.15).

The scrapers represent a homogeneous group both in material and finish flaking. One scraper is, however, of an extremely dark material

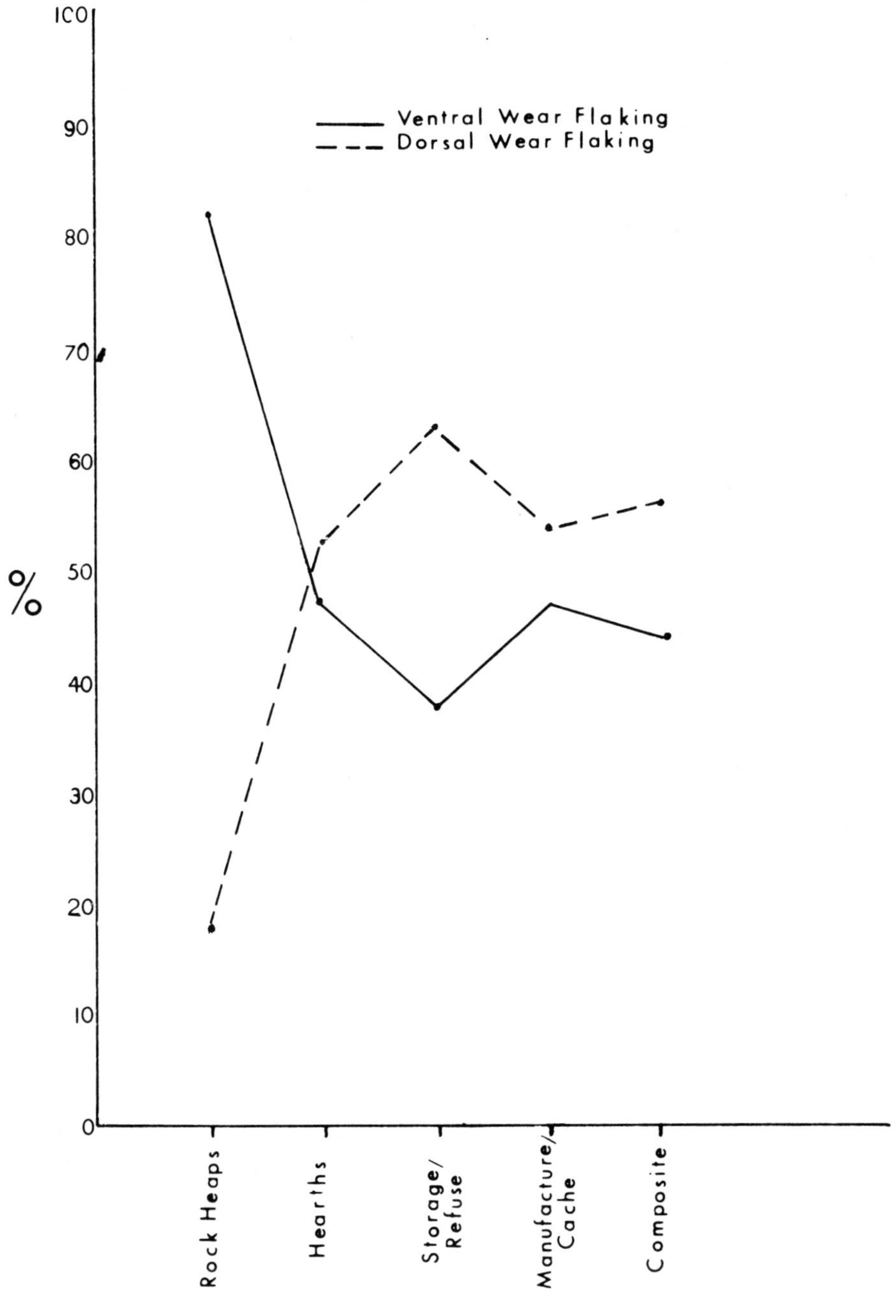

Fig. 4.13 Utilized flakes in feature types.

and may be an exotic chert although such material does overlap with the color range of Onondaga chert. Dorsal flaking, that is, flakes detached from the convex or ridged face characterized all the bifacial scrapers with a steep angle predominating on the majority, 8 or 53%, (Table A.12*b*, App. A).

Attempts to systematize the description of these using scraping edge location, index of utilization, and other attributes, proved to have inconclusive results with so much variation and overlap that the figures were deemed unreliable (Table A.12*b*, App. A). Index of utilization which is computed by dividing the working edge length by the circumference and multiplying by 100, considered separately, suggests that low range scores define end scrapers, while high range scores define side or circumferential scrapers. Spokeshaves are, however, usually lumped with end scrapers by this index.

The hafted end scrapers, one broad-stemmed, the other a reworked sidenotched point, may be separated from the sample purely because of the presence of a haft element. Eleven of the scrapers were made on blanks or blank fragments with various degrees of reworking. The trianguloid end scrapers used fragmentary tips of blanks and parallel lateral edge scrapers used the basal portions of whole blanks. Comparison of the percent of trianguloids to tips versus the percent of parallels to bases of quaternary blanks revealed close percentages of 9 and 12%. Those scrapers formed on whole blanks—a parallel end, and a parallel side scraper—revealed a similar rate of selection of 12% when compared to whole quaternary blanks. Generally the selection of tips, bases, or even whole quaternary blanks was quite low, perhaps due to a high production and fragmentation rate of blanks and lack of need for bifacial scrapers.

Drills (Pl. 6*a-g*)

The drills at Sinking Ponds show a diversity of form. The variety includes the expanded base and the T-form (Ritchie 1969:Pl. 64). Three of the seven have expanded bases, while four display basal and edge retouch. Fifty-four percent of the sample, 13, showed a shank width between 11 and 15 mm, and a maximum length of 26 mm (Table A.13*b*, App. A). One drill shows clear derivation by reworking from a quaternary blank. The base shows no further modification from the nibbled retouch of tertiary flaking on the quaternary blank base, but the lateral edges of the shank show step-fracture and steep alternating scars to create a shank from the medial portion of the blank.

The greatest occurrence of drills, 8 or 68%, was within the compacted floor and features of the composite feature or house in Sampling

Tract 3 (Table 4.15). A similar percentage of fragmentation, 8 or 68%, indicates a heavy utilization of this tool type. The close distribution within the house pattern of the drill coupled with the heavy fragmentation suggests an activity either related to the house construction or use during daily living in which drills were broken through heavy use.

Mano Abrading Stones (Pl. 9*f-g*)

Three "mano"-type pebble abraders were recovered. Two were recovered from features and one from the surface (Table 4.15). Two of the manos displayed one worn flat surface where striations perpendicular to the longitudinal axis of the pebble could be seen microscopically. One mano found on the surface was of orthoclase feldspar. The other was of sandstone and located in Feature 19, a hearth.

In Feature 20, a large biconvex pebble had a shallow depression worn in one surface. Striations indicated that this pebble had been used in a forward–backward motion, as well as a circular fashion. Such manos or mullers were common during the Late Archaic (Ritchie 1969:31-201).

Celts or Adzes (Pl. 10*a-c*)

Two plano-convex celts made from dolomitic rock were recovered. Both were broken on the bit edge. The one found in Feature 24 was complete except for a large flake broken from the bit. It was of a light gray dolomite and finely ground, although not polished, and its length was 128 mm, its width 47 mm, and its thickness 26 mm. The other celt found in Feature 7 had no trace of the cutting edge remaining (Table 4.15). Heavily fragmented, it was of a dark gray-green color and finely polished on the flat ventral surface. The width was 53 mm and the thickness 27 mm. Reconstructed length was 112 mm. Each celt or adze had a rounded poll, and the more fragmented form showed some battering on this end.

It should be noted that at Sinking Ponds these items fall within median ranges for these tools elsewhere. They also are similar to the dimensions noted for the chopper about to be described. Their average width is 3 mm larger and their average thickness 2.5 mm greater than the chopper fragment.

Chopper (Pl. 10*c*)

One chopper fragment was found in Feature 12 (Table 4.15). The artifact was crudely percussion flaked around the lateral edges on both faces, giving a sinuous cutting or utilization edge. It was manufactured from a fine-grained tan sandstone. Although the length was indeterminate due to fragmentation, the width of 61 mm and thickness 29 mm fall within the range of choppers defined at the Lamoka Lake site (Ritchie 1969:Pl. 17, Nos. 3-6). It is possible that the chopper is Stage I in the preparation of a "blank" to be later ground into an adze or celt. The rough subconvex to convex outline in cross section suggests this possibility. Although the finely grained sandstone contrasts with the dolomitic material of two celts recovered at Sinking Ponds, sandstone was used for celts at Riverhaven 2.

Pitted Anvilstones (Pl. 9*a-b*; 10*d*)

A sample of 12 pitted anvilstones was recovered, four in units and eight in features. Six of these artifacts, or 50%, were clustered in the rock heaps (Table 4.15), while the others were randomly distributed horizontally over the site. Three occurred in Level I.

Most of these stones had a depression pecked in one surface. These pits ranged from 50 mm to 15 mm in width, with a depth no greater than 9 mm. Two of the anvilstones found in Level I give evidence of having been used as hammerstones with the presence of light edge battering. The others conform to Ritchie's definition of an anvilstone (1929:8-9), i.e., lacking edge battering and having only a single pit. Generally, these anvilstones, none of which were fragmentary, and which comprise 75% of the total sample, seem to be discards. All six from rock heaps were fragmentary, hinting that after use they were as available as any other pebble for heat fracture and use in the rock heap.

Artifacts of Manufacture

The direct manufacturing process of flint artifacts is represented by four stages of blanks: primary, secondary, tertiary, and quaternary as defined in Chapter 1 (Fig. 1.2). Also included in the articles relating to the manufacture of lithic tools are hammerstones.

Grooved abrading stones represent the best evidence from the site for an active bone industry. A well-developed industry of this type was seen at Lamoka Lake (Ritchie 1969:67-69), and bone working has been recorded in more detail for the Riverhaven 2 site, discussed below. The abrading stone appears to be a primary implement for the shaping of bone tools, especially pointed varieties such as awls (ibid.).

The distribution of artifacts of manufacturing is random over the site with the lowest frequencies recorded for storage and composite features (Table 4.17), whereas rock heaps and manufacture pits produced concentrations of such materials (Table 4.17). The presence of

TABLE 4.17
DISTRIBUTION OF ARTIFACTS OF MANUFACTURE

	Surface		Level I		Level II		Non-Feature Subtotal Units		Rock Heap		Hearth		Mfg./ Cache		Storage/ Refuse		Composite		Subtotal Features		Total	
	#	%	#	%	#	%	#	%	#	%	#	%	#	%	#	%	#	%	#	%	#	%
Primary Blank			2	16.7			2	16.7	3	25	2	16.7	3	25	1	8.3	1	8.3	10	83.3	12	100
Secondary Blank	1	5	8	40	1	5	10	50	3	15	2	10	1	5	1	5	3	15	10	50	20	100
Tertiary Blank	5	8.2	11	18			16	26.2	8	13.1	6	9.9	11	18	8	13.1	12	19.7	45	73.8	61	100
Quaternary Blank	11	10.5	23	21.9	5	4.8	39	37.1	16	15.2	12	11.4	21	20	8	7.6	9	8.6	66	62.9	105	100
Hammerstn.			4	21.1			4	21.1	13	68.4	1	5.3	1	5.3					15	78.9	19	100
Grooved Abrd. Stn.			2	25			2	25	2	25	1	12.5	2	25			1	12.5	6	75	8	100
N	17	7.6	50	22.2	6	2.7	73	32.4	45	20	24	10.7	39	17.3	18	8	26	11.6	152	67.5	25	100

TABLE 4.18
DISTRIBUTION OF BLANK FRAGMENTATION

Blanks		Rock Heaps #	Hearths #	Storage Refuse #	Mfg./ Cache #	Compo-site #	Non-Feature Units #	N #	N %	%N %
Primary	Whole	0	0	0	0	0	0	0	0	0
	Fragment	3	2	1	3	1	2	12	100	6.1
	N	3	2	1	3	1	2	12	100	6.2
Secondary	Whole	0	0	0	0	2	0	2	10	1
	Fragment	3	2	1	1	1	10	18	90	9.1
	N	3	2	1	1	3	10	20	100	10.1
Tertiary	Whole	1	0	1	1	1	2	6	9.8	3
	Fragment	7	6	7	10	11	14	55	90.2	27.8
	N	8	6	8	11	12	16	61	100	30.8
Quaternary	Whole	4	6	0	3	0	4	17	16.2	8.6
	Fragment	12	6	8	18	9	35	88	83.8	44.4
	N	16	12	8	21	9	39	105	100	53
Total N		30	22	18	36	25	67	198		100

	Rock Heaps #	Rock Heaps %	Hearths #	Hearths %	Storage Refuse #	Storage Refuse %	Mfg./Cache #	Mfg./Cache %	Composite #	Composite %	Non-Feature Units #	Non-Feature Units %	N #	N %
Whole	5	16.7	6	27.3	1	5.6	4	11.1	3	12	6	9	25	12.6
Fragment	25	83.3	16	72.7	17	94.4	32	88.9	22	88	61	91	173	87.4
N	30	100	22	100	18	100	36	100	25	100	67	100	198	100
%/N Whole		20		24		4		16		12		24		100
%/N Fragment		14.5		9.2		9.8		18.5		12.7		35.3		100

high frequencies of flint detritus characterizes the manufacture pits, however.

Using all the blanks the ratio of whole blanks to fragments is 25:173 (Table 4.18), suggesting a high casualty rate, shown by a nearly 90% frequency of breakage in the various stages. This skewed distribution could also have been the result of removal of the complete blanks.

Primary Blanks (Pl. 5*a*)

Twelve fragmentary blanks representing the primary stages of manufacture were found. Ten, or 83%, were discovered in features (Table 4.17). However, no particular feature type showed a preponderant number (Table 4.17). Rock heaps and manufacture pits showed the greatest frequency, with three in each feature type. Cores, 442, which also represent the primary manufacture stage showed an inverse distribution of 359, 81%, occurring as detritus outside features. The cores were all fragmentary as well. When this distribution of cores was tested by chi-square a nonrandom distribution was found to have occurred by chance less than one time in 1000, showing that cores were not retained in caches for further work. Other highly significant distributions occurred when cores were tested against flint pebbles at the .001 level of significance for occurrence in features or units. One hundred percent of the 25 pebbles were found in features. Primary blanks were tested against flint pebbles by feature type. This nonrandom occurrence was found to have a Fisher's Exact Probability of .00168. These distributions suggest that cores were immediately considered detritus, as were fragmentary blanks. The stock of pebbles of raw material was retained in manufacture pits for further use, but anything which was a by-product of manufacture or fragmentation was discarded. Raw material does not appear to have been converted to manufactured forms for storage or retention in caches at Sinking Ponds.

The primary blank is a generally thick unifacial flake retaining a detachment scar on the ventral surface and a proximal striking platform. It appears to be generally trianguloid in shape, plano-convex in cross section, and displays only large deep primary flake scars (Table A.14*b*, App. A; Ch. 1, Fig. 1-2).

Secondary Blanks (Pl. 5*b-c*)

The distribution of the 20 secondary blanks at Sinking Ponds was random (Table 4.17) with ten in units and ten in features. Two, or 10%, were whole although flawed by fossil inclusion in one case and a large chunk of unworkable matrix in the other. Both of these were located in the composite feature, Feature 2 (Table 4.18).

The large number that were fragmented, 18, or 90%, indicates a situation like that of the primary blanks, where broken secondary blanks were either considered detritus or were worked into other tools. All workable secondary blanks were apparently modified in subsequent stages of manufacture.

The attribute data for secondary blanks are summarized in Table A.15*b*, Appendix A. All were of local flint with 15, or 75%, retaining the generally trianguloid shape of the primary blank as well as the plano-convex cross section. Sixteen, or 80%, were 11-20 mm in thickness. These secondary blanks were shaped by lateral directed primary flaking with some secondary percussion flaking, and all retain the striking platform on the proximal end, although modified by initial shaping of the base.

Tertiary Blanks (Pl. 5*d-e*)

Tertiary blanks represent the stage of manufacture where a change from directed primary percussion flaking to lateral pressure flaking took place and where the blank assumes the general shape of the finished quaternary blank or blade (Ch. 1, Fig. 1.2). Generally the base retained a portion of the striking platform and is convex. The lateral edges are more irregular and excurvate than the quaternary blank and there is a lack of continuous tertiary edge flaking. Length, width, and thickness are approximately one third greater than the next stage. Attributes for tertiary blanks are summarized in Tables A.7*b*, A.8*b* and A.9*b*, Appendix A.

The tertiary blanks show the same percentage of broken to whole as the secondary blanks, 90% (Table 4.18), indicating that the manufacture process once begun is generally carried through to completion or at least to the quaternary level. Whole tertiary blanks show a random distribution as do the fragments (Table 4.17). A 4:7 ratio of tips to bases may indicate that some tips were reused as bifacial trianguloid end scrapers, and retention of a larger number of tips than bases in a 3:2 ratio in the manufacture pits and a ratio of 7:4 in composite Feature 2, suggests that this may well have been the case (Table 4.18). As seen in the diagram of manufacture process (Fig. 1.2) the use of tertiary stage by-products could normally be expected to rise upon the degree of completion of the bifacial tool at this stage. Fragmentation at this stage would leave the by-products available for subsequent modification into tool types not originally intended. Blanks between the secondary and tertiary stages of manufacture where thickness of the medial ridge or presence of unworkable inclusions such as fossils precluded further refinement, appear to have been modified into longitudinal knife scrapers. Bifacially worked scrapers on fragments appear to have been secondary by-products of the manufacture process beginning with the tertiary stage.

Quaternary Blanks (Pl. 5*f-m*)

The sample of "cache blades" or quaternary blanks at Sinking Ponds was quite large, 105. Seventeen or 16.2% whole blanks were found, with the largest concentration (13) in features (Table 4.18). Fragments were more evenly distributed (Tables 4.17 and 4.18) except in manufacture pits where a concentration of 18 was noted. Ten whole blanks clustered in rock heaps and hearths. Four of the six whole blanks in hearths exhibit some fire pocking.

This blank type appears to have been the final stage of modification prior to the addition of a hafting element, in this case side notches, and as such seems to have represented a generalized commodity. Presence of a greater number of these blanks, 17 or 68% of 25 whole secondary, tertiary and quaternary blanks suggests that at this stage the blanks were held as a reserve supply to be modified into other tools or projectile points as needed. Ceremonial or trade involvement also seems to be present at this level of manufacture, since the small observed population of quaternary blanks, projectile points, and expanded base drills does not seem to be directly correlated with the large amount of flint detritus on the site.

Generally these quaternary blades conform to the description of "mortuary blade" given by Ritchie to this class of artifact (1955:57-60). These blanks are thin with an ovate or trianguloid shape and subconvex base. No portion of the striking platform remains at the proximal end. Flat expanding pressure flaking obscures the deeper primary flakes. Fine secondary pressure flaking with some tertiary nibble flaking has been applied laterally and basally. Attribute frequencies for 20 variables are summarized in Tables A.4*b*, A.5*b*, and A.6*b*, Appendix A and compared to other Meadowood "cache blade" samples.

Hammerstones (not illustrated)

This artifact type consisted entirely of pebble hammerstones which displayed end or edge battering, but no evidence of further modification. The variation in size and weight among the hammerstones was great, although for the most part they were sufficiently small to be used by one hand. Indurated sandstone was the material predominantly utilized (Table A.17*b*, App. A), although three were of granite or other igneous material.

Nineteen were found, with the largest number, 12 or 70%, located in rock heaps, apparently as discards (Table 4.17). Fragmentation in this group was great due to heat fracture. In only one case, in Feature 36, was an endbattered hammer found in direct association with chert material. Here, the hammerstone lay close to decortication flakes, cores, and other detritus.

The most prominent feature of the hammerstones was that they apparently were not prepared as tools. Convenient pebbles were selected, utilized, and finally discarded, most probably due to the abundance of local materials. A further observation is suggested. The hammerstone, necessary during the initial stages of manufacture, Stages I and II, becomes unimportant in the latter stages III, IV and V. Once the initial modification of the blank was completed, the lithic hammer was apparently replaced by another tool more applicable for pressure flaking, such as a bone or antler tool. There seemed to have been a lack of interest in long-term use of particular hammerstones.

Grooved Abrading Stone (Pl. 10*e-f*)

Eight grooved abrading stones were found. This artifact type has been described as a sinewstone or specialized abrader (Ritchie 1969: Pl. 53:9, Pl. 60:17). Although assigning a specific function to this tool type is hazardous, it has been placed among tools of manufacture because it was observed at Riverhaven 2 in association with a large worked bone and antler assemblage. Presence of wide or narrow grooves on a sandstone pebble perpendicular to the longitudinal axis argue for its use as a sharpening or shaping tool in the manufacture of bone or antler needles, awls or projectile points. However, absence of bone preservation at Sinking Ponds makes direct observation of this relationship impossible.

A specific variety of this tool type can be defined at Sinking Ponds. A contracting ovoid teardrop-shaped abrader is the most common form (Table A.18*b*, App. A). The abrading groove is present at the broadest portion of the tool on one or both surfaces and is usually perpendicular to the longitudinal axis. The contracting end was evidently utilized as a handle. There appears to be a specific selection for this shape pebble, and where it was too thick, the pebble was split longitudinally to provide a thinner cross section. This longitudinal fracture was present on two cases.

Lengths of grooved abrading stones range between 70 and 111 mm and their width between 45 and 61 mm. Thickness clusters at 31-33 mm. The distribution of these abrading stones is concentrated heavily in features, 96 or 75%, although it is random within feature types (Table 4.17).

TABLE 4.19
DISTRIBUTION OF CEREMONIAL AND STORAGE ARTIFACTS

		Rock Heap		Storage/ Refuse		Composite		Totals		Nonfeature Units	
		#	%	#	%	#	%	#	%		
Ceremonial	Gorget	1	50	1	50			2	100	0	0
	Bead (Slate)			1	100			1	100	0	0
	Pipe (Stone)					1	100	1	100	0	0
	N=	1	25	2	50	1	25	4	100	0	0
Storage	Steatite Vessel	2	100					2	100	0	0
	Pottery Vessel	1	33.3			2	66.7	3	100	0	0
	N=	3	60			2	40	5	100	0	0

Storage Artifacts

The distribution of storage artifacts, vessels of pottery or steatite, is concentrated in two feature types. Pottery vessels were related to composite features with 66.7% of the vessels occurring there, while 100% of the steatite vessels occurred in the rock heaps (Table 4.19). Their frequency was too small to test by a nonparametric statistic.

Steatite Vessels (Pl. 12*a-d*)

Steatite sherd fragments were restricted in distribution to Sampling Tract 5. Fifty-seven sherds, 58.8%, were assigned to features, while 40, 41.2%, were found in units. Ninety-seven sherds were recovered, 7 of which were rims. The 90 body sherds were separated on the basis of thickness into basal and body sherds yielding the following distribution:

Rim sherds 7 7.3%
Basal sherds (thickness 25-35mm) 24 24.7%
Body sherds (thickness 15-25mm) 66 68%

Analysis of the fragments showed that there were two varieties of steatite present. One was a more hardy variety with less inclusion and less pocking from leaching out of soluble impurities. This variety was represented by three rims, four body sherds, and one body sherd reworked by drilling. Several of these fitted together giving a portion of a small shallow bowl or dish with smooth interior and exterior, possibly reworked from a larger piece of steatite. The remaining 89 sherds clearly seemed to be from the same vessel. They were uniformly leach-pocked and represented rim, body and base of a large ovoid vessel. No lugs were detected. The exterior surface of most of the sherds large enough to analyze, 49, displayed horizontal channelling (Ritchie 1969:162). Interiors were smooth. The rim sherd uniformly displayed a cross rim incision or nick spaced approximately 5 mm apart on a rim approximately 1 cm thick at the lip. The lip was slightly rounded. A large basal sherd showed evidence of having secondary reworking which hollowed out a small depression. This reworking was interrupted when a large, hard mineral inclusion was found in the center of the depression.

Two vessel types are represented by these sherds. One shows the characteristics of exterior channelling that Ritchie described for Frost Island steatite vessels from Christiana Co., Pennsylvania (ibid.). The other is more similar to his proposed Orient style that is completely smooth inside and out (ibid.). Neither one is represented by an adequate number of large fragments to form a complete vessel. Ritchie remarks on the practice of inland groups of reworking fragments of steatite vessels into gorgets, beads or pendants (1969: 159). The drilled sherd of one vessel and the hollowed portion of the other argue persuasively for this reuse of steatite, which appears to have been a scarce item.

Clay Pottery (Pl. 12*e-j*)

The clay pottery was an essentially homogeneous sample of 587 body sherds and five rim sherds. An examination of the variations among these sherds showed that they represented a continuum; therefore a single description and classification fits the group. The system of descriptive categories used by Ritchie and MacNeish (1949) and slightly modified by Lopez (1971) and Kinsey (1972) has generally been followed.

I. Paste

- A. Temper — very large grit
- B. Texture — contorted, no clear coil breaks were recognized
- C. Color — paste ranged from medium grey to red (reduced to oxidized) with the majority of those examined in the reds or browns
- D. Hardness — approximately 2.0-2.5 Mohs Scale
- E. Thickness — bodies 10-15 mm
rims 9-11 mm

II. Surface Finish

Exterior — interior cordmarking of varying size and depth. Two body sherds show smoothed-over cord interior conforming to the Modified Vinette I type defined by Lopez (1971:231-33) and Kinsey (1972:453-55). Some sherds had surface finish generally obscured by abrasion.

III. Decoration — none

IV. Form

A. Rims — straight, undistinguished from the neck.

B. Lips — rounded or slightly rolled

C. Necks — indeterminate

D. Body — indeterminate

E. Base — indeterminate

V. Condition of sherds — abraded and worn, extremely crumbly and incapable of being washed in water without loss of surface

The pottery, based upon the above description, falls within the type defined by Ritchie and MacNeish as Vinette I (1949:100) although the two interior smoothed sherds suggest that there was a modified form of Vinette I present as well. Marion E. White has pointed out the same phenomenon, but in reverse, within a group of sherds which would ordinarily be classified as Wickham Punctate (1966:8). In the Delaware River Valley and on the coast of New York, Lopez (1971:231-33) and Kinsey (1972:455) indicated that the smoothed variant is differentiated only by its smooth interior, and on at least one site Faucette is temporarily earlier than the "classic" Vinette I. He terms this an "early series" (ibid.: 453) encompassing a possible development from steatite tempered wares, such as Marcy Creek Plain (Kinsey 1972: 360).

The distribution of pottery was restricted, with 488 or 84.7% of the body sherds occurring in Feature 2, 87 or 14.8% in Feature 3 which is part of Feature 2, and two or 0.3% in Feature 27. All of the rim sherds occurred in Feature 2. In Feature 2, 323 or 55% of the body sherds were classified as mini-sherds less than 20 mm square, while in Feature 3, 39 or 6.6% were so classified.

Analysis of sherd exteriors and interiors, sherd size, and rim form suggest that at a maximum two vessel types are represented in Sampling Tract 3, Features 2-3, and one in Sampling Tract 5. For the purpose of further analysis the pottery will be classified as three artifacts instead of 592, a disproportionate figure which tends to obscure more meaningful intrasite relationships.

Ceremonial Artifacts

The distribution of the artifacts is shown in Table 4.19. This distribution appears to be random except that all of the items were found in features. Since all except the bead are fragmentary it is not unexpected that 50% of the category were found in features containing refuse.

Gorgets (Pl. 11*d-e*)

Two fragmentary artifacts which may be assigned to the category gorgets were recovered from Features 3 and 24. The latter was a blank or partially worked slab of indurated shale. On one edge this blank was ground with multiple striations, indicating a forward-backward motion on an abrading stone or other abrasive implement. The assignment of this incompletely worked item rests upon a similar form seen at Riverhaven 2 (Ritchie 1969:Pl. 64, no. 17), on which the edges show wear striations but on which the faces show little alteration beyond initial shaping. This blank was 81 mm long, 35 mm in width, and 12 mm thick. It was unmodified except for wear on a single edge. Both ends had been broken, with the step fracture on 90° planes characteristic of shale.

The gorget fragment exhibited one hole and a portion of another (Fig. 17) and was found in Feature 3. Its dimensions are 6 mm uniform thickness throughout, 51 mm in width, 18.5 mm between holes, and a reconstructed length of 80 mm. It is a light tan indurated shale with dark gray-brown striations (Fig. 4.12). It is ovoid rather than rectangular and bears little resemblance to any pictured by Ritchie (1944, 1955, 1969) for the Meadowood phase. Three-hole gorgets are rare in Woodland phases, with most holes numbering more than the usual two being pairs of mend holes. Variation in the shape of gorgets has been noted in many early Woodland ties (Ritchie 1944: Pl. 60, nos. 15, 9; 1955: Pl. 64, no. 17; 1969: Pl. 69, no. 1, 3, 4).

Bead (Fig. 4.12; Pl. 11*c*)

This was a unique artifact whose identity went unrecognized in the field. Found in Feature 3, it was made from green indurated shale, striated with black bands. Its dimensions are 16 mm in height, 10 mm in width, and 3 mm in thickness. No relationships with other Meadowood sites are obvious, with the possible exception of a Middlesex pendant from Vine Valley, which is much larger (Ritchie 1965:Pl. 72, no. 7). Although there is the possibility that it served as a separator in a string of bone or shell beads, nothing else was preserved.

Pipe (Pl. 11*a*)

The pipe fragment (Fig. 4.12), found on the floor of Feature 2 is of red fire-pocked sandstone with a deeply scored bowl slightly constricted toward one end. Interior scoring is indicated by deep vertical scars on the inside of the bowl. Near the constricted end, a small patch of blackened material suggests charring from smoking and this in turn implies that the pipe was not broken during manufacture. The entire fragment appears fire-cracked with some exterior pitting. A hypothetical reconstruction of this tube-shaped pipe may be seen in Figure 4.12. Riverhaven 2 showed some tubular pipe fragments of pottery (Ritchie 1969: Pl. 68, no. 4) as did Morrow (ibid.: Pl. 69, no. 5) and Oberlander 2 (ibid.: Pl. 60, no. 13).

NATURAL RESOURCES

The resources of the Sinking Ponds area during the occupation of the Meadowood people were probably quite abundant. Those resources selected for use by occupants of the Sinking Ponds site may be divided into those which were used in manufacturing artifacts and those directly related to subsistence activities, either as products of such activities or in processing the products. It will be possible to discuss with some assurance the inorganic evidence (Table 4.20) but the evidence of organic resources has been dissipated by poor preservation. It is interesting to note that the very condition which provided for the unusually undisturbed condition of the living floor was the primary cause of the total absence of organic remains. The leaching, erosion, and low humus formation on the ridge tips made the area unsuitable for agriculture in historic times but destroyed all traces of bone. The processes even destroyed the collagenic content of charcoal, leaving only tiny charred flecks in the hearths.

Floral and faunal resources must be discussed in a somewhat more inferential way consistent with clues to utilization gleaned from the artifactual and inorganic nonartifactual inventory of the site.

Chert

The material of 301 artifacts and all of the flint detritus at the Sinking Ponds site is blue-gray Onondaga Chert. This chert or flint has

TABLE 4.20
MATERIAL OF LITHIC ARTIFACTS COMPARED TO LOCAL LITHIC PEBBLE AVAILABILITY AT SINKING PONDS SITE

	Kame Above Waterwork		Sinking Ponds 60S 100W		Lithic Artifacts	
Rock	#	%	#	%	#	%
Shale	67	29.4	26	43	4	0.9
Limestone	29	12.8	7.5	12.5	4	0.9
Dolomite	29	12.8	7.5	12.5	1	0.2
Sandstone	34	15	12	20	120	27.2
Siltstone	30	13.5	2	3	0	0
Chert	16	7.1	3	5	301	67.5
Igneous	15	6.3	1	2	1	0.2
Quartzite	7	3.1	1	2	14	3.1
Total	277	100	60	100	444	100

a color variation from light to dark gray and may have large inclusions of indurated limestone and fossiliferous materials. Three chert artifacts give quite detailed portraits of Ordovician brachiapods and crinoids. The primary source of Onondaga chert is the exposed portion of the Onondaga Escarpment stretching from Fort Erie, Ontario to Akron, New York, and its nearest point to the site is 24-29 km (15-18 mi). The quality of the Sinking Ponds varieties differs significantly from the high grade chert available in the Onondaga escarpment. The Sinking Ponds varieties contain massive inclusions of indurated limestone matrix. Generally the artifacts display an inclusion of 20-60% of the matrix material. The inclusion may have affected the durability of the artifact but in all likelihood did not substantially affect manufacture since the matrix was only slightly less hard (Moh's Scale: 8.5) than the chert (Moh's Scale: 9).

The source of chert for the manufacture of artifacts at the Sinking Ponds site seems to have been pebbles gathered in the immediate area rather than from high grade quarry blocks from the escarpment to the north. Features 4 and 32 show caches of chert pebbles, 8 and 17 respectively, both whole and fragmented. A particularly large pebble, weighing 1.04 kg (2.3 lb), from Feature 4 demonstrated the following inclusions of fossils and indurated limestone when broken open:

Chert	65%
Indurated Limestone	25%
Fossils	10%

This composition is within the normal range of most of the Sinking Ponds chert artifacts, higher and lower levels of inclusion depending upon the particular pebble. Pebble utilization may also account for the relative infrequency of primary blanks on the site. The selection of flint pebbles is considered to be the result of conscious effort rather than fortuitous circumstance. The distance from the major source, the Onondaga Escarpment, while not great, is inconvenient and while pebbles of chert are not common, they are locally available. Transportation of roughed out primary and secondary blanks for finishing on the site cannot, however, be entirely precluded.

Indurated Shale

Four artifacts made from indurated shale are of colors varying from tan to light green to dark green and black. Shale is abundant in the local area and while no precise stratigraphic association has been made for the indurated varieties, the colors coincide fairly well with what is available in proximity to the site. Dark green indurated shale is represented strikingly in an outcrop near Lewiston on the Niagara Escarpment about 36 miles from the site (personal inspection). Numerous outcroppings of black shale occur in the steep walls of Cazenovia Creek within 1.6-3.2 km (1-2 mi) of the site.

Igneous Rocks

Igneous rock is represented by only one artifact on the Sinking Ponds site. This is an abrading stone of the mano type made of striated light green orthoclase feldspar which is locally available in pebble form.

Dolomite

This hard, Moh's Scale 6.5 sedimentary rock was confined to two artifacts, both plano-convex adzes, indicating an obvious preference for this dense, hard rock as a material for impact cutting tools. Dolomite represents approximately 12.5% of the local pebble counts and these adzes appear to conform well to the general color range, light gray, and purity, only 5-10% inclusion, of unworked dolomite pebbles coming from the site.

Limestone

Acid conditions in the site area contributed to the very poor preservation of limestone. Underrepresentation in the artifact inventory is not, however, seen as a function of poor preservation. Where limestone pebbles were present, they were soft and powdery but recognizable. Four netsinkers were made of limestone; all were very soft and poorly preserved.

Sandstone

Several varieties of this rock, from fine-grained to coarse-grained and hard to soft, were of particular interest to the aboriginal occupants at Sinking Ponds. In pebble counts on and off the site ridge, sandstone represents 15-20%, mean 17.5%, of the unworked pebble population. However, in two features where counts were conducted, heat fractured pebbles comprised:

Feature 15	80%
Feature 16	71%
Mean	75.5%

When the means 75.5% and 17.5% are compared a striking selectivity which can only be the result of cultural behavior appears. Although inflated somewhat by fragmentation, the figure of 75.5% leads one to conclude that sandstone has some property, even as unworked pebbles, that commended its use to people on the site. We believe that this property is its tendency to fragment quickly and easily under heat combined with the heat retentive capability of the igneous sand grains of which it is composed. Heated sandstone pebbles were being used to create a bed of hot rocks. Such a bed of fragmented pebbles with numerous faceted surfaces would provide even heat convection over the entire surface of the bed, rather than the vertical columnar convection typical of round rocks. (University of Louisville Physics Department 1973: personal communication).

Sandstone pebbles also played an important role in artifact production, with 121 being made of this material. These are distributed among the following categories:

Netsinkers	88
Abrading Stones	10
Anvilstones	9
Hammerstones	13
Pipe	1
Total	121

The fine-grained red to brown varieties were used in artifact production. In all cases these were locally available. The precise selective processes for properties of shape, size, and other attributes are discussed under each artifact category above. However, the percentage of available pebbles, 12.5%, is less than half that of percentages of artifacts of this material in the inventory, 27.2% (Table 4.20).

Quartzite

Quartzite was also selected beyond its percentage of natural occurrence 2-3.1%, mean 2.5%, and, as represented in Table 4.20, its distribution percentage as unworked pebbles in cultural context was 17-19.5%, mean 18.3%. Because it is a metamorphic rock and a relative of the sedimentary rock, sandstone, its popularity was probably conditioned by the same factors as sandstone. The most frequent color was tan slightly reddened by heat. Naturally occurring pebbles were light to dark tan in color.

Artifacts of quartzite were roughly equal to the percentage available, 3.1% (Table 4.20). Although selection again seems to have been based upon size, perhaps an additional factor, hardness, Moh's Scale 7, was considered. Impact tools account for the majority of quartzite artifacts in the following distribution:

Hammerstones	6
Anvilstones	3
Netsinkers	5
Total	14

Other Local Lithic Resources

Although not reflected in the pebble counts, features, or artifact inventory several other potentially useful rocks were available to the site's occupants. Although two quartz crystals, one hematite pebble, and one limonite chunk, were present on the site as unworked pebbles, these occurred in no cultural context but were available to people who in other situations had made use of such materials.

Exotic or Imported Lithic Resources: Steatite

No discussion of lithic raw material would be complete without a discussion of the origin of the steatite sherds which were found on the site ridge. Steatite, a variety of talc, is not a local material; its nearest occurrences are on the Atlantic coast approximately 486 km (300 mi) away. Although no identification of a particular source has been made, the closest natural outcrop is the Christiana County, Pennsylvania area 424 km (265 mi) to the southeast.

The steatite found on the site exhibits the action of the acid soil conditions. This is seen in numerous pock marks caused by dissolution of carbonate and sulfate inclusions in the steatite (University of Louisville Geology Department 1973: personal communications). Ninety-three sherds were found. The rarity of steatite is confirmed by a partially reworked large basal sherd which was hollowed out and abandoned. Since steatite is generally regarded as having spread in the form of vessels rather than being manufactured in sites, this probably represents an inability to deal with the material.

Eight steatite sherds from Sampling Tract 5 were submitted during 1974 to neutron activation analysis at University of Virginia. The Lanthanide rare earth series was used to produce identity curves; however, these curves do not match exactly any known quarry sample (Alvin Luckenbach: personal communication). The reporter did, however, see a general similarity to east coast sources (ibid.).

INTRASITE ACTIVITIES AND CHRONOLOGY

Intrasite Activities

Excavation at Sinking Ponds has provided information on several subsistence and maintenance activities. We have examined above the location, excavations, features, artifacts and natural resources. The structure of the site reveals particular expressions of the activities of procurement, processing, storage, ceremony and residence. The examination of three lines of evidence should allow us to suggest the form each activity took at the Sinking Ponds site. This evidence is artifactual, nonartifactual and structural. As remarked above, preservation, or the lack of it, has clouded some of the information in natural resources, especially faunal and floral materials. With reservations, however, it is possible to infer that some tools may express a particular resource without direct evidence of that resource being present.

Features on the Sinking Pond Site have been spatially arranged, with distances between them plotted in Figure 4.14. Here a cluster of rock heaps and hearths can be seen at the head of a ravine which drops from a 280.6 m (920 ft) contour and extends down to the 274.5 m (900 ft) contour in a westerly direction. This ravine leads to a marsh, formerly a lake (Map 4.2.) The site's location between two of these extinct shallow lakes has a great significance in understanding the spatial distribution of features on the site.

We have noted above that the site was covered by a thin mantle of midden through which, in many cases, features protruded. It seems possible to suggest that the thinness of this midden mantle denoted recurrent but short-term occupation in the absence of disturbance. Certainly erosion has created a discontinuity between the actually

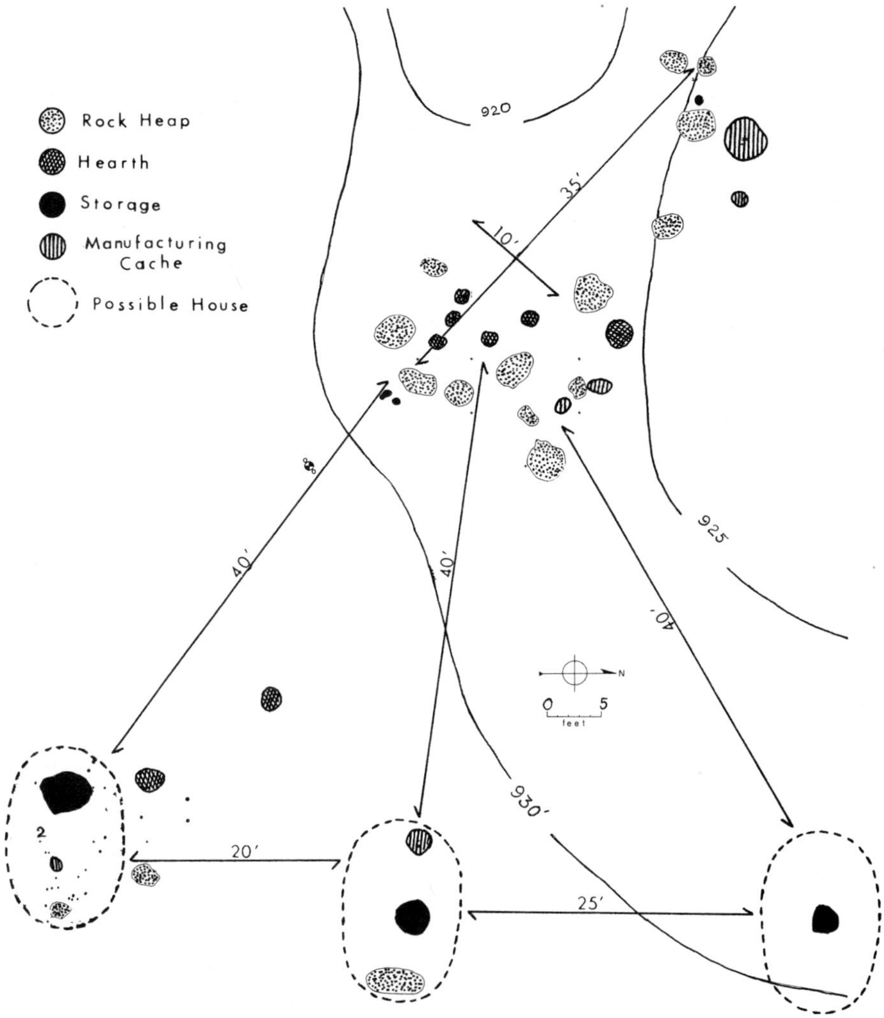

Fig. 4.14 Feature relationships at Sinking Ponds site.

deposited and the recently observed depth, but the areas of the site displaying the most features and other artifactual evidence are the least eroded.

The biotic resources available to the inhabitants of Sinking Ponds were varied. Beech and sugar maple trees, which prefer a hydric situation, were present, as was the more xerically related oak, although in lesser frequency (Zenkert 1934:305). Berries such as chokeberry, raspberry, elderberry, gooseberry, black currant, and serviceberry were available in summer as well as other herbaceous plants like wild onion, leek, *Chenopodium* (goosefoot), and several edible wild forms of cabbage, ferns, and rushes (ibid.).

Mammals available in this area of shallow lakes included bear, deer, moose, cottontail rabbit, raccoon, muskrat, and beaver. Other animals such as several varieties of turtle, frogs, and birds such as grouse, bobwhite, turkey, and ducks were also present (App. C).

It appears that the shallow lake was an ideal place for obtaining fish. Populous shallow water species such as catfish, sheepshead, burbot, several types of sucker, pike, muskellunge, bass, and perch were all available. Shellfish such as the freshwater mussel would, however, be unavailable. The Sinking Ponds site represented an abundance of biotic resources in the summer. In the winter the low frequency of the best mast producer, oak, would make the area less hospitable to animals which exploited this as food, and ice would drive fish to the deepest portions of the shallow lake. Suckers and sheepshead are not well adapted to through-ice line fishing (Rostlund 1952:113-26). The Sinking Ponds site was situated in a productive subsistence area, but especially during the spring and midsummer months.

Procurement Activities (Table 4.21)

Structural evidence pertaining to procurement of nearby resources is generally unavailable beyond the site. We have noted that inorganic resources such as chert were procured locally with the possibility of additional forays of some distance to obtain higher grade materials than those locally available as pebbles.

Exploitation of biotic resources involves a more tenuous inference due to the lack of floral or faunal remains. The ratio of projectile points to netsinkers seems to form an instructive index, 40-94 or 30-70% of the procurement assemblage (Table 4.21). Based strictly on single items this indicates a 2:1 emphasis on fishing. Another important feature is a cache of 17 netsinkers in Feature 25. This feature is surrounded by intense podzolic deposit of the type that forms around a loose organic deposit; this may have been created by a net with attached sinkers

TABLE 4.21
DISTRIBUTION OF CULTURAL MATERIALS
RELATED TO PROCUREMENT

Artifactual Materials	Sampling Tract										
	1	2	3	4	5	6	7	8	9	10	11
Sidenotched Projectile Point	0	0	5	1	9	3	1	0	2	0	0
Cornernotched Projectile Point	0	0	2	0	8	0	0	0	0	0	0
Stemmed Projectile Point	1	0	2	0	2	2	0	0	3	0	0
Netsinkers	0	0	2	1	94	0	0	0	0	0	0
Birdstone	0	0	0	0	1	0	0	0	0	0	0
Total (N = 139)	0	0	11	2	114	5	1	0	5	0	0
%	0.7	0	8	1.5	82.6	3.6	0.7	0	3.6	0	0

NOTE: No assignable or available evidence was found for structural or non-artifactual materials.

which was left in situ (U.S. Soil Conservation Service 1968: personal communication).

The distribution of artifacts of procurement shows 114 or 83% of the total in Sampling Tract 5 at the head of the ravine mentioned above and 11% in the areas close to what may be houses (Table 4.21). Supporting the apparent emphasis on fishing is the fact that 98% of the netsinkers appear in the group of rock heaps close to the ravine.

Taggart notes that small slender points may represent waterfowling practices (1967:162), but the nine slender points with unfinished stem bases noted here may, on the other hand, denote points inset into reeds for fish spears or leisters as Brennan et al. suggest (1970:16). Such speculation cannot, however, be positively documented at present.

Rostlund remarks that weirs constructed of nets and poles cannot be successfully utilized in deep water; rather they are used in shallow water where movement of fish can be induced (1952:101). These weirs operate on two principles, obstruction and impoundment, both of which are possible in the embayments to either side of the largest perpendicular ridge at Sinking Ponds (ibid.). We have remarked that the flat netsinkers may act as mud anchors to hold a net close to the bottom. Combining these with emplaced nets to form a barrier across the narrow embayments speaks for the highly strategic placement of the site.

Processing Activities (Table 4.22)

Activities of processing are suggested by all three forms of evidence. The artifacts are many; knives, scrapers, abrading stone, manos, pitted stones, drills, celts, choppers, and vessels indicate cooking. Structrual evidence is exhibited by rock heaps, hearths, and even houses, in which processing of food for meals may have been carried out. Such nonartifac-

TABLE 4.22
DISTRIBUTION OF CULTURAL MATERIALS RELATED TO PROCESSING

Materials	Sampling Tract										
	1	2	3	4	5	6	7	8	9	10	11
Artifactual:											
Longitudinal Knives	0	1	2	0	5	1	0	0	0	0	0
Unifacial Scrapers	0	1	6	0	15	2	0	0	2	0	0
Bifacial Scrapers	0	0	8	0	4	0	0	0	3	0	0
Abrading Stone	0	0	3	1	6	0	0	0	1	0	0
Pitted Anvilstone	0	0	2	0	10	0	0	0	0	0	0
Drill	0	0	7	0	4	2	0	0	0	0	0
Celt	0	0	1	0	1	0	0	0	0	0	0
Chopper	0	0	0	0	0	0	1	0	0	0	0
Steatite Vessels	0	0	0	0	1	0	0	0	0	0	0
Pottery Vessels	0	0	6	0	1	0	0	0	0	0	0
Structural:											
Hearths	0	0	1	1	6	1	0	0	0	0	0
Rock Heaps	0	0	2	1	9	2	0	0	0	0	0
Houses	0	0	1	1?	0	0	1?	0	0	0	0
Nonartifactual:											
Utilized Flakes	30	12	217	72	248	74	3	1	16	0	0
Fire-cracked Rock	(0)	(0)	(26)	(44)	(420)	(40)	(6)	(7)	(0)	(0)	(0)
Total (N = 796)	30	14	257	77	314	83	6	2	23	0	0
%	3.5	1.5	32.2	9.5	39.2	10.4	0.7	0.3	2.8	0	0

tual evidence, as the 673 utilized flakes and 246.3 kg (543 lb) of the fire-cracked rock, also suggests a great intensity of processing activities at Sinking Ponds.

Scrapers are an important indicator of processing. Taggert has offered the notion that the use of bifacial scrapers was evidence of bone and hide working (1967:164) and unifacial scrapers indicated fish scaling, woodworking, or plant processing tools (ibid.). We prefer the fish scaling of fish accomplished by a push stroke (Table 4.22). On utilized flakes, ventral flaking dominated dorsal, shown by this ratio, 397:276 or 59%:41%. Taggart remarked that on the site he was investigating unifaces dominated bifaces and fish was a dominant item in the faunal inventory (1967: 165). At Sinking Ponds unifacial scrapers, including utilized flakes (Wobst 1968:209), form the following ratio with bifacial scraping or cutting tools: 699:24 or 97%:3% (Table 4.22). The greatest clusterings of these unifacial tools occur in the area close to the ravine, 263, and in the area outlined by post molds of the possible house, 223, where the greatest number of pottery vessels also occurred (Table 4.16).

The area close to the gully produced the most distinctive feature, the 13 rock heaps. It has been suggested above that the rock heap was a form of radiant heat oven, used for the drying of fish. Rostlund relates that drying of fish is an ethnographically ubiquitous activity but that smoking is often coincidental (1952:138). We suggest that rock was heated in hearths removed and subsequently piled in these rock heaps which were formed in a double reversed J-shape (Fig. 4.14). It may also be noted that this area is 40 ft away from the clusters of features suggested as houses. Celt, choppers, manos, and drills also suggest a well developed woodworking activity in these areas.

Manufacture Activity (Table 4.23)

Several features at Sinking Ponds have been suggested as manufacture cache pits. Two, Features 36 and 10, are quite clearly related to this function and contained great quantities of manufacture debris (Table 4.23).

Since manufacture detritus was present over much of the site, however, it is difficult to separate specific areas of activity. The presence of cache pits in two possible houses indicates manufacture may have been an in-house preoccupation as well as peripherally associated with processing activities near the ravine (Fig. 4.14).

The great amount of manufacture detritus also suggests that formation of projectile points was not the only concern. Figure 1.2 illustrated a developmental sequence for Meadowood chert tools. Possibly other forms such as the quaternary blank or cache blade were sought. In

TABLE 4.23
DISTRIBUTION OF CULTURAL MATERIALS RELATED TO MANUFACTURE

Materials	Sampling Tract										
	1	2	3	4	5	6	7	8	9	10	11
Artifactual:											
Hammerstones	0	0	0	2	16	1	0	0	0	0	0
Primary Blank	0	0	3	1	4	4	0	0	0	0	0
Secondary Blank	0	0	7	0	11	1	0	0	1	0	0
Quaternary Blank, Whole	3	0	3	3	5	1	0	0	2	0	0
Quaternary Blank, Base	3	2	11	5	6	8	2	0	4	0	0
Quaternary Blank, Tip	2	0	15	8	7	9	2	0	4	0	0
Tertiary Blank, Whole	0	0	3	1	2	0	0	0		0	0
Tertiary Blank, Base	0	0	6	4	4	2	0	0	3	0	0
Tertiary Blank, Tip	1	1	12	4	9	6	0	0	2	0	0
Abrading Stone, Grooved	0	0	3	1	4	0	0	0	0	0	0
Structural:											
Mfg. Caches	0	0	1	1	2	2	0	0	0	0	0
Nonartifactual:											
Cores	0	21	67	31	257	54	12	0	0	0	0
Nonutilized Flake	3	2	6	5	8	6	13	2	66	0	0
Chips	7	6	14	6	8	7	21	2	77	0	0
Flint Pebbles	0	0	8	0	0	17	0	0	0	0	0
Total (N = 956)	19	32	159	72	343	118	50	4	159	0	0
%	2	3.5	16.6	7.5	35.9	12.3	5.2	0.4	16.6	0	0

any case, fragmentation was quite high at all stages, at over 83%, the total sample of blanks showing 87% breakage.

The manufacture activity on this site has been called a localized industry for three reasons: first, the presence in caches such as Feature 4, of large selected flint pebbles; second, the high degree of matrix inclusion in flint artifacts on the site with a mean of 60%; and third, the 24-29 km (15-18 mi) distance to outcrops of good chert. Evidence scaling idea, since ventral wear on the utilized flakes seems to suggest suggesting the local tool manufacturing may be seen in Table 4.20 where lithic artifacts are compared to lithic availability both on the site at 60S 100W and on the glacial kame near the East Aurora Waterworks. We note that 67.5% of the artifacts were chosen from chert which occurs as 5% of the pebbles on the site and 7.1% in the vicinity, and 27.2% of the artifacts were chosen from sandstone which was 15% and 20% of the local pebbles (Table 4.20). Although bone was not preserved on the site, the eight grooved abrading stones argue for a limited bone industry.

Storage Activity (Table 4.24)

Several features related to the refuse aspect of storage activity contain fragments of tools whose further modification would have been superfluous: the pipe, gorget, chopper, birdstone, and celt. These items occurred in shallow basin-shaped pits with a variety of debris from chippage and pottery sherds. Three of these large shallow pits occured in a context which suggests residence; therefore, they may not always have had a pure refuse function but rather may have functioned for in-house storage as well. The shallowness of such pits indicates a distinct lack of permanence. Several small deep pits, Features 13 and 14, also contained refuse but may have acted as incidental storage near the ravine processing area (Fig. 4.14). They do not appear to have been postmolds.

Ceremonial Activity (Table 4.25)

Little can be said about ceremony at Sinking Ponds, although several items such as the gorget and bead indicate that ceremony involved personal ornamentation. The birdstone, remarked upon as a possible atlatl weight or hook may also represent either a form of waterfowl propitiation or a corporate group symbol. (Ritchie 1969:191). Closer analysis by experimentation might reveal that light feathered darts of reed were projected at waterfowl. (Taggart 1967:162), but in the absence of bone preservation we do not know how much emphasis the inhabitants placed on this particular subsistence source. The pipe also

TABLE 4.24
DISTRIBUTION OF CULTURAL MATERIALS RELATED TO STORAGE

Materials	Sampling Tract										
	1	2	3	4	5	6	7	8	9	10	11
Artifactual:											
Pottery Vessel	0	0	6	0	1	0	0	0	0	0	0
Steatite Vessel	0	0	0	0	1	0	0	0	0	0	0
Quat. Blade Base	3	2	11	5	6	8	2	0	4	0	0
Quat. Blade Tip	2	0	15	8	7	9	2	0	4	0	0
Tert. Blade Base	1	0	6	4	4	2	0	0	3	0	0
Tert. Blade Tip	1	1	12	4	9	6	0	0	2	0	0
Celt	0	0	1	0	0	0	0	0	0	0	0
Gorget	0	0	1	0	1	0	0	0	0	0	0
Pipe	0	0	1	0	0	0	0	0	0	0	0
Chopper	0	0	0	0	0	0	1	0	0	0	0
Birdstone	0	0	0	0	1	0	0	0	0	0	0
Structural:											
Shallow Basin Pits	0	0	1	1	0	0	1	0	0	0	0
Small Deep Pits	0	0	0	0	2	0	0	0	0	0	0
Cache (Net)	0	0	0	0	1	0	0	0	0	0	0
Nonartifactual:											
Flint Pebbles	0	0	8	0	0	17	0	0	0	0	0
Total (N = 188)	7	3	62	22	33	42	6	0	13	0	0
%	3.5	1.5	31.1	11.1	16.6	26.6	3.1	0	6.5	0	0

TABLE 4.25
DISTRIBUTION OF CULTURAL MATERIALS
RELATED TO CEREMONIAL ACTIVITIES

Materials	Sampling Tract										
	1	2	3	4	5	6	7	8	9	10	11
Artifactual:											
Gorget	0	0	1	0	1	0	0	0	0	0	0
Beads	0	0	1	0	0	0	0	0	0	0	0
Pipes	0	0	1	0	0	0	0	0	0	0	0
Birdstone	0	0	0	0	1	0	0	0	0	0	0
Total (N = 5)	0	0	3	0	2	0	0	0	0	0	0
%	0	0	60	0	40	0	0	0	0	0	0

NOTE: No assignable or available evidence for structural or non-artifactual materials was found.

suggests individual emphasis on ceremony. All the ceremonial items were fragmentary and appear to have been discards. The distribution of these artifacts was random.

Habitation Activity (Table 4.26)

Residence activity is normally demonstrated by houses (Taggart 1967:153). At Sinking Ponds only one possible house, Feature 2, can be clearly demonstrated as the association of a patterned group of postholes and features. Two further houses may be suggested by the juxtaposition of features (Fig. 4.14). These "houses" have an assemblage of storage, manufacture and processing artifacts, representing all normal activities performed at, near, or in a house (Table 4.26). The house itself may have been a simple affair, possibly shaped by bent saplings and covered with reeds, marsh grass, or perhaps bark. The arc of postmolds

TABLE 4.26
DISTRIBUTION OF CULTURAL MATERIALS
RELATED TO HABITATION ACTIVITIES

Materials	Sampling Tract										
	1	2	3	4	5	6	7	8	9	10	11
Artifactual:											
In-House Assem. (Artifacts & Ut. Flk.)	0	0	141	67	0	6	0	0	0	0	0
Trade Artifacts	3	0	9	3	7	1	0	0	2	0	0
Structural:											
House	0	0	1	1?	0	1?	0	0	0	0	0
Nonartifactual:											
Localized Refuse	0	0	1	1	1	1	1	0	0	0	0
Total	3	0	152	72	8	9	1	0	2	0	0
%	1.2	0	61.6	29.2	3.2	3.6	.4	0	.8	0	0

at Feature 2 also implies that the house may have been made in the form of an open front shelter. Whatever aspect the houses took, they were small, approximately 4.6 m (15 ft) long and 3.7 m (12 ft) wide, and probably adequate to support a nuclear family of about four. The houses were spaced about 6.1-7.6 m (20-25 ft) apart.

Residence is also suggested by the distribution of refuse, localized in or near houses. In the area which we assign to houses, the midden in depressed areas close to the houses was up to two-tenths deeper than elsewhere. Also, fire-cracked rock was localized in the houses and the house area. Feature 2 shows a hearth near several larger postmolds which may form some type of screen or rack (Fig. 4.10). Rock heaps in the house appear more flatly and diffusely composed than those in the processing area, while Feature 10, the large manufacture pit in the central house, and Feature 36 are the only deep straight-sided pits on the site. The last house is only very tenuously suggested by a shallow storage pit. With the addition of two or three more houses the space on the main parallel ridge at the base of the perpendicular ridge in which the houses are situated would be wholly consumed. A very loosely calculated population figure for six houses or six families would be approximately 30 people, probably a high figure (Lee and De Vore 1968:245-48).

In summarizing the intrasite activities, we note that the majority of the features on the site are concerned with processing. Contrasting the internal distribution of structures related to processing with structures related to storage or manufacture shows that the latter activities are peripheral to processing. There are in two cases linear associations of features which suggest residence, and in one case postmolds are present. Spatially these associated features and artifact groupings are located 40 ft from the largest group of processing-oriented structures and 20-25 ft apart. In substantiation of the hypothesis that these areas were houses, we found the majority of pottery in one. This pottery was a major storage item and was not readily transportable.

The processing area seems to be located at the head of a ravine leading down to a marsh, formerly a shallow lake. Here we see a semicircular formation. Many netsinkers were associated with the rock heaps and along with other artifacts suggest that fishing and fish processing were primary activities here and on the site, while manufacture of chert tools appears to be a secondary activity associated both with the living and processing areas.

Chronology

Two charcoal samples derived from the Sinking Ponds site were submitted to Gakushuin University, Japan, for radiocarbon assay. These dates GAK 2049 (0 ± 150 B.P.) and GAK 2050 (800 ± 800 B.P.) were so divergent from the estimated temporal position of the site that the only possible explanation is:

> Large probable errors are due to the scarcity of carbon in the samples. Owing to the scarcity of the amount of samples 3(2049) and 4(2050) we could not remove possible modern rootlet by chemical processing. (Kigoshi 1967:personal communication)

Thus, the chronology of the Sinking Ponds site rests upon typological grounds or sharing traits with other dated sites of Meadowood cultures. According to Ritchie's postulated material inventory for Meadowood (1969:180-200) the trait sharing in the subsistence category is 16 traits out of 29 with three categories accounting for an additional 11 traits. Comparison on this level alone allows a 16:18 ratio or the significant percentage association of 88%. Ornamental, trade, or other items cannot provide a significant measure of association with sites which are burial or ceremonially oriented. Gorgets, birdstones, "cache" blades, steatite, pipes, and beads defined as having Meadowood traits, are however, also associated with site. Much more important is the fact that the Sinking Ponds site shares many environmental associations with its presumed contemporaries. Location near embayed shallow fossil or existing lakes is significant for many Meadowood sites although not necessarily for all. Obviously activities in each site are determined by the selective processes that led the people to choose that particular location. Artifact and feature associations both at this site and others represent the only clear and unassailable measure of activities and affiliations. We have discussed the location of the Sinking Ponds site and these activities above and have seen that fishing in the spring and summer may have conditioned the selection of this particular location strategically emplcaced between two embayments in what was then a shallow lake. We noted above that similar perpendicular ridge locations characterized other Meadowood habitation sites as well.

Sinking Ponds does not resemble the Riverhaven 2 or the Scaccia site nor does it resemble a burial station such as the Morrow site. On the contrary, it may provide another dimension of this culture, exploitation of a particular subsistence resource. This aspect can only be understood as a portion of the complete subsistence–settlement pattern for Meadowood culture, and therefore its activities and location should not be expected to correlate perfectly with other sites which may represent another portion of that settlement pattern.

There are those who maintain that projectile points which look like "Lamokas" and which occur in the assemblage with "Meadowood" points mean the site was mixed or that the presence of steatite means the site was early (Funk 1972:personal communication). Obviously in the absence of uncontaminated charcoal samples which can be radiocarbon assayed these arguments cannot be wholly laid to rest. The chronological position of the Sinking Ponds site based upon its artifact inventory is 1000 B.C.–500 B.C., the dates proposed by Ritchie for the Meadowood phase (1969:181). Until more substantive dating can be obtained by chemical or physical means, the measure of age must rest upon affiliation by the number of physiographic associations which are similar and the number of activities demonstrated which can be replicated at sites presumed to be local and coeval.

Sinking Ponds represents a settlement type associated with the spring–summer dispersal of a band or group into small exploitive or extractive groups whose activites are oriented toward a particular resource or set of resources. We believe that this type of camp is quite common in the vicinity of the Sinking Ponds site and further that evidence of a winter base camp exists nearby. It has not yet been found and may have been destroyed by urban construction but we do not accept the proposition that it did not exist.

Riverhaven 2 and related loci within what we call the Riverhaven complex give us a more complete picture of the settlement pattern with its attendant types. Within this complex the Spicer Creek sites 1-2 are, we believe, typologically equivalent to Sinking Ponds, (Riverhaven 2 appears to be a base settlement) and we will examine this group of sites contemporary with Sinking Ponds site in the next chapter.

CHAPTER V

THE RIVERHAVEN COMPLEX

INTRODUCTION

History of Investigations

Investigation of the Riverhaven Complex began in 1958 when Edward Kochan, a nonprofessional archaeologist, commenced an intensive examination of the northeast portion of Grand Island. Kochan reported finding numerous loci of occupational debris (1959*a*, 1961, n.d.). These so-called sites could be assigned to cultures ranging from Archaic to Iroquois and to the remnant of the nineteenth century Whitehaven Village. From surface indications several occupation areas revealed close formal associations to the Meadowood phase or Point Peninsula I phase (Map 5.1). Kochan tested one area, Location 2, in 1959 by an exploratory trench (Kochan 1959). Here he found numerous artifacts: Vinette I pottery and thin blades associated with a midden deposit. Kochan tested Riverhaven 2 (Twa 3-3, UB193) again in 1961 (Kochan 1961), and carried out excavations from 1961 to 1963. In 1964 he turned over the site, collection, and notes to the State University of New York at Buffalo Anthropology Department because he was transferred to another state. During Kochan's excavation, Marian E. White advised him and visited the site frequently. William A. Ritchie also visited the site (Ritchie 1969:190). Limits on time and the number of crew allowed Kochen to open only small areas, 1.2 x 1.2 m (4 x 4 ft) units, of the site at any one time, leading to problems in interpretation of the complex stratigraphy of the midden deposit at the base of the riverine terrace (Kochan n.d.*c*:11). In an attempt to clarify the stratigraphy, further exploration and mapping of the site was undertaken in 1967 by the author and D. W. Taggart. Subsequent excavations in 1971 were used to verify both Kochan's work and Taggart and Granger's 1967 mapping of the extent of excavations and profiles. During the 1971 field season features were observed in both horizontal and vertical profile, establishing the presence of pits below the terrace.

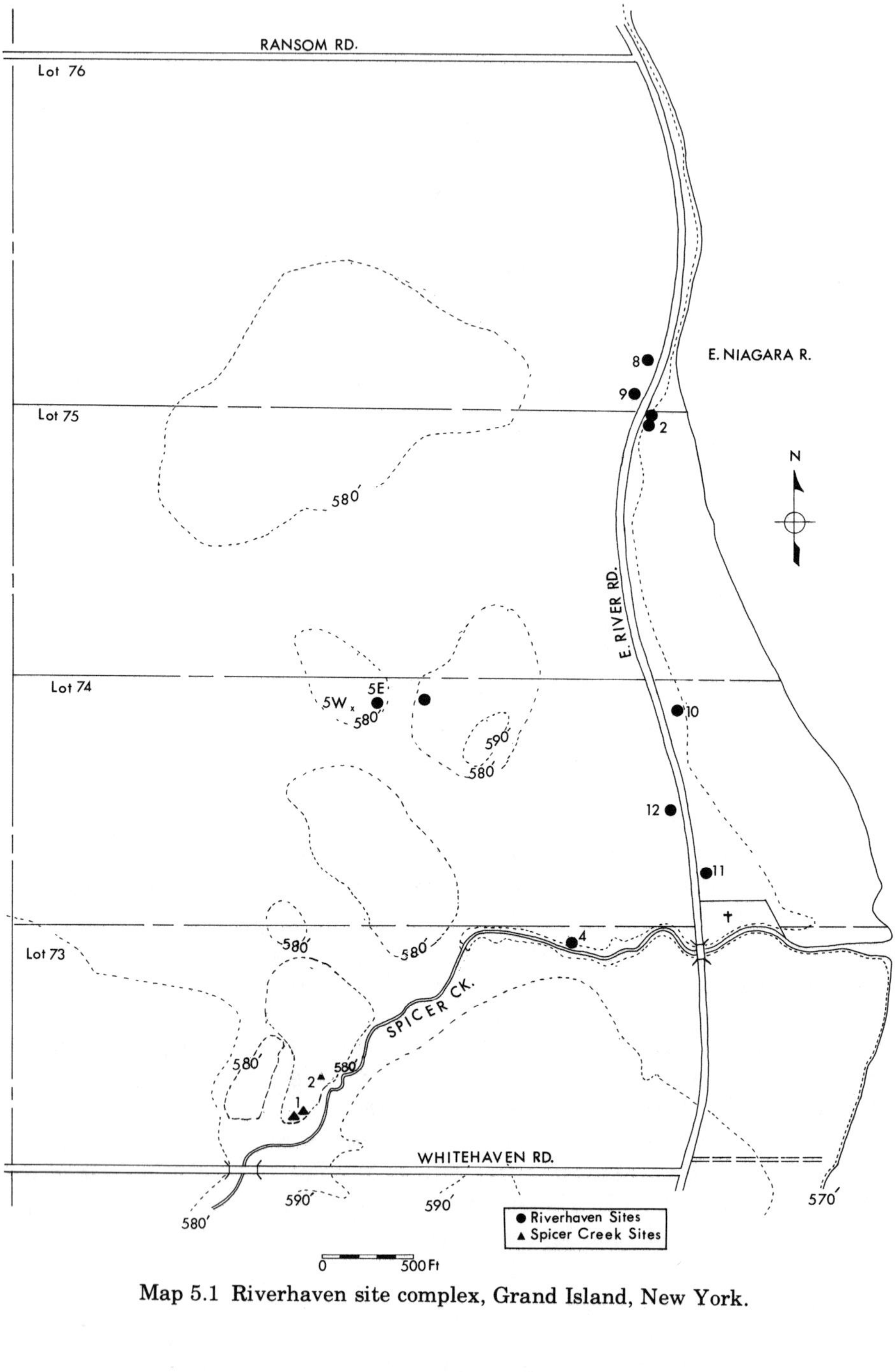

Map 5.1 Riverhaven site complex, Grand Island, New York.

Some of the structural reexaminations have been used here; however, the cultural materials of 1967 and 1971 are still under analysis. These materials do not appear to contradict in any way those from Kochan's excavations; however, they do alter his conclusions somewhat.

The Kochan collection, consisting of 1889 artifacts and other remains, provides the study sample used here. All classes of data were examined, but the unworked faunal remains and flint detritus lack precise level assignment and therefore complicate interpretation.

Between 1961 and 1963, Kochan explored inland areas as well as locations north and south along the Niagara River. He was frustrated by the lack of settlement data on the terrace above the Riverhaven 2 bench or in the areas immediately beyond the East River Road (Map 5.1). It was apparent that sites showing similar flint debris and associated artifacts were clustered on several knolls west of East River Road and along the banks of Spicer Creek (Map 5.1). In this area Granger and Taggart tested Riverhaven 4 in 1967. Construction of a golf course associated with a new development called River Oaks laid bare several more of these loci: Riverhaven 5 East, 5 West, 7 and 12, and Spicer Creek 1 and 2. These loci were investigated during 1970 by Jack Schock, Gordon Schmahl, Karen Noonan, and the author.

Salvage operations funded in part by the developer were conducted in 1970. Only at Spicer Creek 1 and 2 were structural features with associated artifacts noted. All recognized cultural features were excavated as they were disclosed and provenience was noted for all artifacts in undisturbed context. Fortunately, when the stripping and filling were completed, a portion of Spicer Creek 2 and Riverhaven 7 remained intact for future exploration. The fragmentary nature of the salvage information is clear from the subsequent *Report on Spicer Creek 1* (Donahue n.d.:2, 32).

In this chapter we will first examine the data from Spicer Creek 1 and 2, and next the materials from Riverhaven 2.

PHYSIOGRAPHY AND GEOLOGY

The Riverhaven Complex (Twa 3-3, UB-193 and the associated loci UB851 and 852) is situated on Lots 73-76 of Grand Island Township located on Grand Island, New York. Excavations and related manifestations are located on Map 5.1. Maps 5.2 and 5.3 show in greater detail the physiographic associations and extent of excavations on Riverhaven 2 and Spicer Creek 1 and 2. These excavations are on three separate loci but two, Spicer Creek 1 and 2, will be considered as a single entity due to

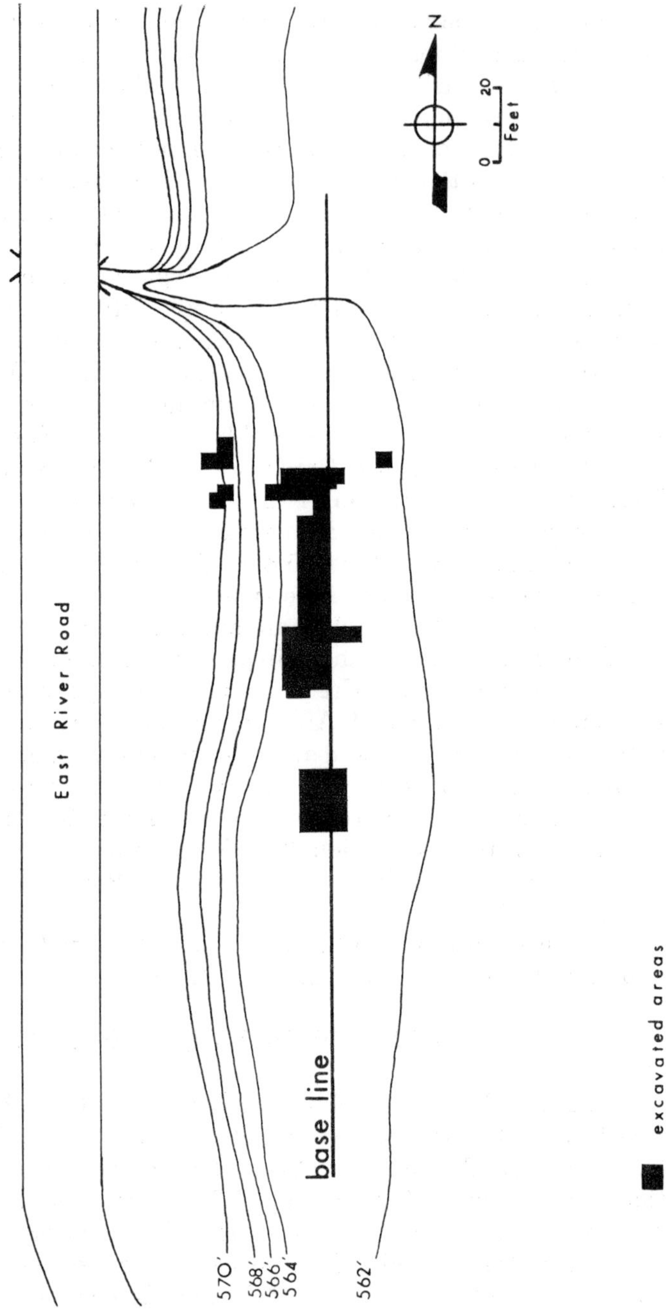

Map 5.2 Kochan excavation at Riverhaven 2.

Map 5.3 Spicer Creek sites 1 and 2.

their close proximity. The main site loci are separated by 1.6 km, almost 1 mile. Riverhaven 2 is close to the East Channel of the Niagara River (Lot 75) and the Spicer Creek sites are located inland on high ground between Spicer Creek and the Gun Creek Marsh (Lot 73). A total of ten additional loci are known to have produced affiliated materials. Five of these are located within 305 m (1000 ft) of the river while another four are inland, close to either Spicer Creek or Gun Creek Marsh. Thus, known loci are evenly divided; six riverine associated and six inland creek or marsh associated. Sampling error may have obscured the picture since only limited testing or exposure during construction has been accomplished in the areas immediate to Gun Creek Marsh. To the south, the Spicer Creek drainage remains essentially untested.

Physiography

The physiography of the area is an extremely complex result of glaciation, lacustrine sedimentation, and riverine activity. The most prominent topographic feature of the area is the Falls of the Niagara River, located approximately 1.6 km (1 river mile) north of Grand Island (Grabau 1901). Grand Island is a teardrop shaped island approximately 12.8 km (8 mi) long and 9.6 km (6 mi) wide (Zenkert 1934:24), with the Niagara River divided into east and west channels around it. Its 69.9 km^2 (27 sq mi) make it the largest of the nine Upper Niagara River islands. Topographically, it is essentially flat with a vertical rise of less than 15.3 m (50 ft) (Kindle and Taylor 1913:21). There are 36.8 km (23 mi) of shoreline, approximately one-third of which have extensive marsh development from alluviation. The marsh developments cluster extensively at the northern end and less at the southern tip of the island.

The northern area of the island is the widest and most diverse in elevation and contains the sites or loci of the Riverhaven Complex. This portion of the island has also seen the most riverine activity and retains broad marshes as testimony to alterations in river channel. To the south 6.1 m (20 ft) knolls composed of glacial till constitute the highest ground on the island (Kochan 1963:3).

The Spicer Creek sites (Map 5.3) are located on a low knoll between the Gun Creek Marsh to the north and west and Spicer Creek to the south and east. This knoll is one of several peripheral areas of high ground, with an elevation of 176.9 m (580 ft) on the east edge of the marsh. These knolls are low, humpbacked and generally of .25-1.5 ha (1-3a) in extent. They constitute the only dry, well drained ground during most of the year on the unaltered land surface. Soil associations at the Spicer Creek locality show an Odessa-Schoharie underlayer of fine grained gray to red silty clays (Cline 1970:17). Overlying this is a brown forest soil with a neutral topsoil and slightly acid B horizon. No podzolic development was noted, but the highest portions of the knolls did exhibit a reduced humic zone and a much stronger acid condition in the B horizon.

Spicer Creek meanders across a small stream valley. The stream runs generally northeast but within 610 m (2000 ft) of the Spicer Creek sites alters course directly to the east and joins the Niagara River. The mouth of the creek is a deltaic marsh which extends northward past the Riverhaven 2 site, where the silt load of Spicer Creek is swept northward by the current of the Niagara River and deposited.

The Riverhaven 2 site occupies portions of the 173.9 m (570 ft) terrace and a bench at 171.4 m (562 ft) which rests at the foot of the terrace (Map 5.2). From the site to the river is the northward portion of the Spicer Creek deltaic marsh. Photographs taken in 1907 show the marsh to be watered and treeless (Reed Collection). Today a second growth of hawthorn, maple and poplar with numerous bushes and wild grape vines cover this marsh with a small belt of rushes bordering the river which is quite shallow and silty close to shore (Zenkert 1934:303-05).

The soil associations at Riverhaven 2 are a brown forest soil which overlays an Odessa-Schoharie fine grained gray to red lacustrine clay with a glacial till admixture (Cline 1970:17). The topsoil on the half terrace closest to the river shows a pH of neutral to slightly alkaline, 7.2-8.2, while the top of the first terrace at an elevation 173.9 m (570 ft) shows neutral to slightly acid soil (7.2-6.8) where a well drained B horizon exists. The red clay-till admixture is slightly acid. Between the red clay-till admixture and the normal brown Niagara silt-loam forest soil buildup lies a zone of light gray Canadaigua sandy silt-loam (U. S. Soil Conservation Service, East Aurora, N.Y., 1974:personal communication). This zone underlying the humic soils was of neutral pH. The upper portion of this soil was stained with organic materials which constituted the main living floor at the site.

Water levels in the area of the Riverhaven 2 site preclude occupation of the half terrace when spring melts begin. The area becomes dry in late summer and remains so until the early spring rains. The terrace is dry year-round.

At Spicer Creek 1 and 2 the locations of the sites are dry year-round but surrounding areas are wet except in exceptionally dry years. Spicer Creek is a large perennial stream, although in dry years it slows to a trickle. The usual depth is 30-62 cm (1-2 ft) and the width is approximately 3.1 m (10 ft) along this portion of its course.

Geology

The geology of the Riverhaven Complex area is characterized by formation of the present Niagara River channel during the late Pleistocene (D'Agostino n.d.). The Niagara River scoured its channel through a gravelly clay deposit formed by the infiltration of a lacustrine clay into a glacial till base and reached an indurated limestone "basal level." Although this rock formation is relatively impervious to wear, softer portions wore away in the vicinity of the southern tip of Grand Island, allowing the river to form an east and west channel (Kindle and Taylor 1913:27-29; D'Agostino n.d.:65).

The east bank of "East River" was abraded away while the west bank on the inside curve of this river channel is aggraded. It appears that it did so for an extended period, gradually filling the north end of

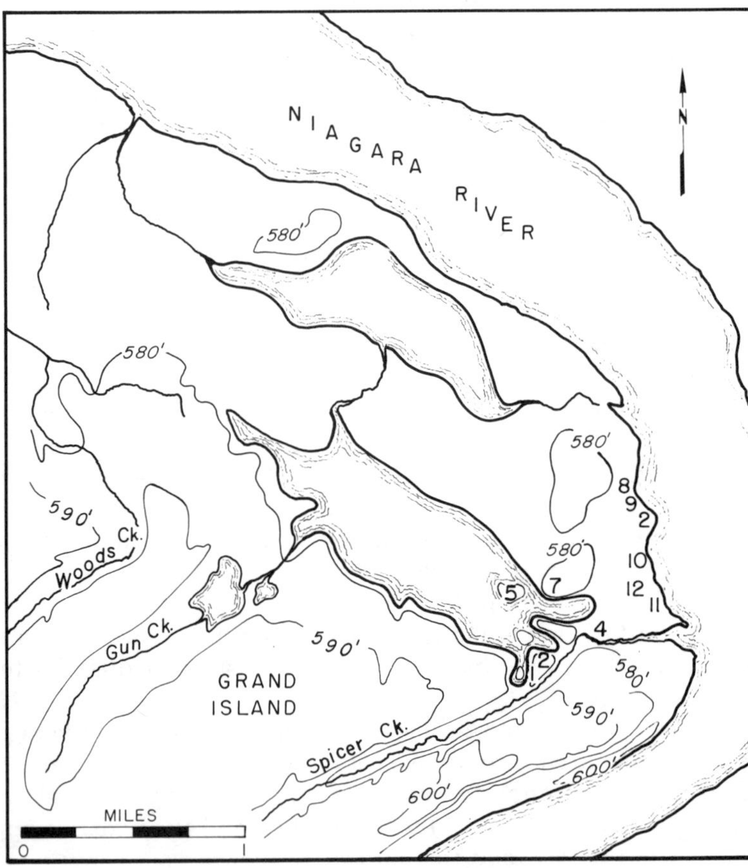

Map 5.4 Original water features on northeast Grand Island.

the island below the 176.9 m (580 ft) contour with fluvial sediments over glacial tills and lacustrine deposits (Kindle and Taylor 1913:31).

The constricted channel of the Niagara River precluded formation of meanders and thereby oxbow lakes; however, aggradation levees did form. These levees trapped water which, when cut off by further aggradational deposition, become shallow lakes and finally marshes such as the Gun Creek Marsh (Map 5.4). Burnt Ship Swamp is a recent example of this type of feature. These levee structures are archaeologically noted as the knolls and ridges below the 176.9 m (580 ft) contour which supported Early Woodland and Archaic populations (Map 5.1). Grand Island north of the 176.9 (580 ft) contour developed from riverine deposition.

The Spicer Creek sites represent loci along with Riverhaven 4, 5E, 5W, and 7 in close proximity not to the river but to its aggradation lines and former channels, now observed as arc-shaped marshes.

Riverhaven 2, 8, 9, 10, 11, and 12 are positioned with reference to another geomorphic phenomenon, the river bank, as it was when Early Woodland and Archaic people occupied the area. Recent excavations of the Riverhaven 2 site (1971) disclosed a beach line in a gray sandy-clay which presumably was the river channel just below the 171.4 m (562 ft) contour. Subsequently the deltaic marsh of Spicer Creek continued to build up, extending northward past the sites due to the velocity of the river and forming an incomplete aggradation levee. The 173.9 m (570 ft) contour represents the most recent complete levee.

SPICER CREEK 1, 2 AND RIVERHAVEN 4 SITES

Excavations

The Spicer Creek excavations of 1970 were emergency archaeological work conducted under adverse and hasty conditions, and the surface of most of the area was disturbed by bulldozer stripping of vegetation and sod to a depth of 15 cm (0.5 ft) (Map 5.5). At Spicer Creek 1, a large area was shovel skimmed and fourteen features were recorded and excavated. Disturbance at Spicer Creek 2 was less severe and the original surface extant. A skimmed trench was cut close to the original surface and excavated to a depth of 20 cm (0.65 ft), where subsoil was encountered. Five features but only one artifact were recorded.

Riverhaven 4, a site further to the east, on the north bank of Spicer Creek, was included in this group of sites. This location had been excavated by Granger and Taggart in their resurvey of the Riverhaven area in 1967. One feature, a rock heap, was revealed. A single artifact was found here.

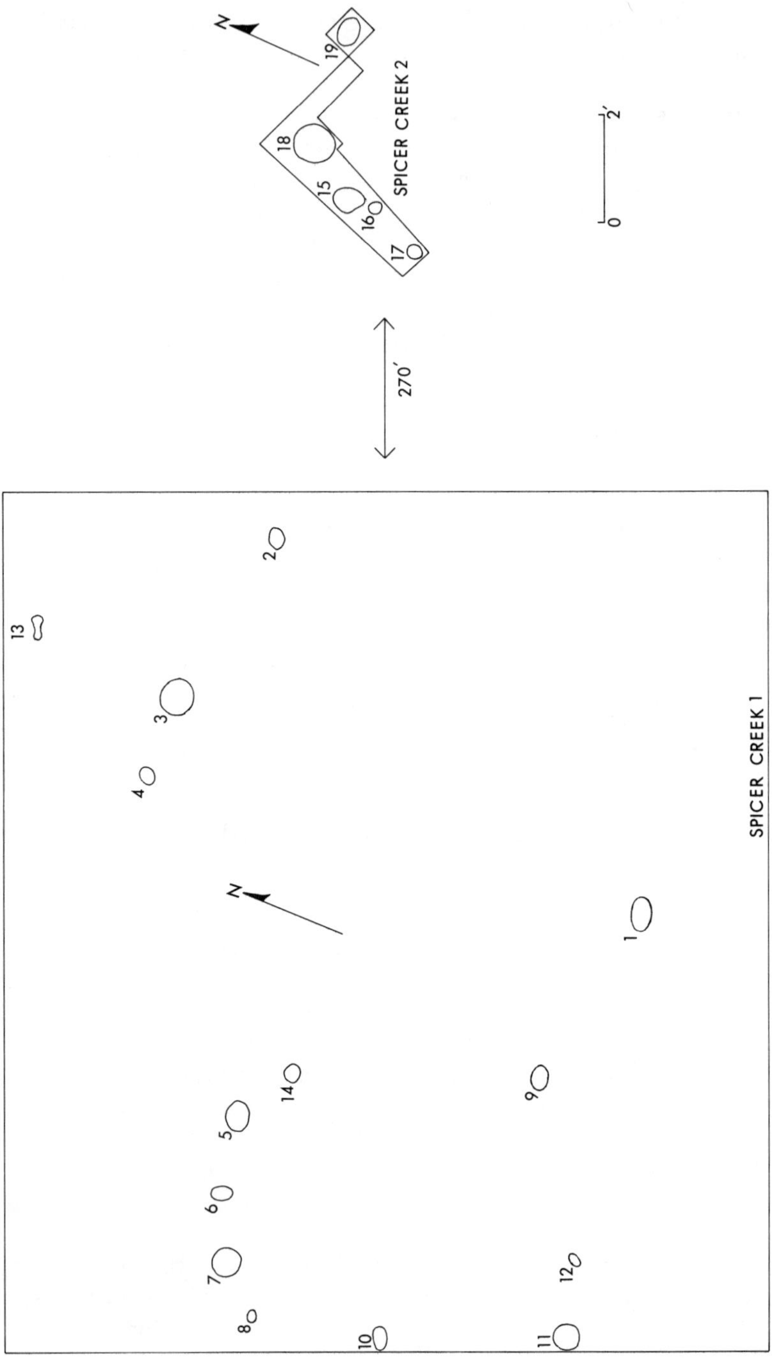

Map 5.5 Spicer Creek excavation areas.

The Spicer Creek area was quite productive of flint detritus but the figures represent sampling error of unknown dimensions. It is likely, however, that Spicer Creek 1-2 represent one site with two areas of differential function, indicated by the artifact and flint detritus distributions. Riverhaven 4 may represent another such site.

Excavation data for these three locations is presented in Table 5.1. The area investigated is used to account for surface observations after stripping. Feature frequency correlates well with area excavated as do artifacts and flint detritus. These associated distributions demonstrate the magnitude of sampling error.

Features

Feature plans and profiles were obtained from notes and floor plan drawings made during the salvage operation (Donahue n.d.), and were numbered sequentially beginning with Spicer Creek 1. Features 1-14 were found at Spicer Creek 1 and 15-19 at Spicer Creek 2, one feature, 20, was recorded by Granger and Taggart at Riverhaven 4. The defined features fell generally into categories previously observed at Sinking Ponds (Chapter 4): rock heaps, hearths, and manufacture pits. Storage features, with the generalized assemblage of artifact types usual to such features, appeared to be absent. The distribution of feature types is shown in Table 5.2. The rock heaps closely conformed to those defined at Sinking Ponds (Chapter 4). The depth or height range of rock heaps was between 18 cm (0.6 ft) and 30 cm (1.0 ft); the two features, 19 and 20, are both 30 cm (1.0 ft) in cross section (Fig. 5.2). Ten hearths comprised 50% of the features found, and their major distribution clustered with the seven rock heaps, 35% (Fig. 5.1). The depth of the hearths ranged between 15 cm (0.5 ft) and 30 cm (1.0 ft); however, nine or 90% had a depth less than 29 cm (0.95 ft) and five or 50% were less than 18 cm (0.6 ft) deep. Hearths duplicated the stone-lined hearths seen at Sinking Ponds (Fig. 5.2). Although the manufacture pits did not display caches of raw materials, the vast quantity of flakes and chips combined with blanks and blank fragments argued for this functional interpretation. These were the largest and deepest of the features, with a depth range of 18 cm-64 cm (0.6-2.1 ft). They were isolated with the exception of an extraordinary large rock heap, Feature 18 (Fig. 5.1). The artifact distribution in feature types was, rock heaps 13 or 16.7%, manufacture pits 61 or 78.2%, and hearths 4 or 5.1%.

The nonartifactual sample of flint detritus was broadly analyzed into flakes, chips and cores by Donahue (n.d.) (Table 5.3). No breakdown of utilized flakes or other types was noted. The Spicer Creek localities

TABLE 5.1
SPICER CREEK 1-2 AND RIVERHAVEN 4,
SQUARE FEET INVESTIGATED,
FEATURES, ARTIFACTS,
FLINT DETRITUS AND FIRE CRACKED ROCK

	Spicer Creek 1		Spicer Creek 2		Riverhaven 4		N	
	#	%	#	%	#	%	#	%
Square Feet Investigated	22,400	97.6	450	1.9	75	0.5	22,925	100
Features	14	70	5	25	1	5	20	100
Artifacts	188	98.9	1	.1	1	0.05	190	100
Flint Detritus	5,382	98.5	84	1.5	0	0	5,466	100
Fire-Cracked Rock	147		Not Counted		58			

were the only ones for which data on flint detritus other than frequency could be elicited. Distribution by functional type of feature shows the highest figure in all categories in manufacture pits (Table 5.3). Chips were the most frequent class in all features (Table 5.3), while manufacture appears to have been as ubiquitous at the Spicer Creek site as at Sinking Ponds.

Hasty record keeping due to bulldozer activity on the Spicer Creek site, Localities l and 2, resulted in fire-cracked rock being counted only in Feature 3. It produced 66.7 kg (147 lb). Fifty-eight pounds (26.3 kg) of fire-cracked rock were recorded from Riverhaven 4.

The frequencies of artifacts and flint detritus are most heavily represented in the manufacture pits. Hearths and rock heaps have a generally low content in both (Tables 5.3 and 5.4). Artifact types are shown in Table 5.4. Blanks of various stages dominate the feature assemblage, with 72 or 93.5% of the total artifacts. The three unifacial scrapers represent the only nonmanufactured items associated with features.

Hearths

Feature 2. Was a small Feature 107 cm (3.5 ft) long by 76 cm (2.5 ft) wide. It was excavated to a depth of 55 cm (1.8 ft). A partial liner of a small amount of fire-cracked rock was present at the bottom.

Feature 4. A small circular hearth approximately 61 cm (2 ft) in diameter and 21 cm (0.7 ft) in depth. Some burnt stone was present on the sides and bottom, and there was a very small amount of charcoal in the fill.

Feature 6. Was a shallow oval hearth 61 cm (2 ft) by 107 cm (3.5 ft) and less than 15 cm (5 ft) in depth. Small fire-cracked rocks lined the

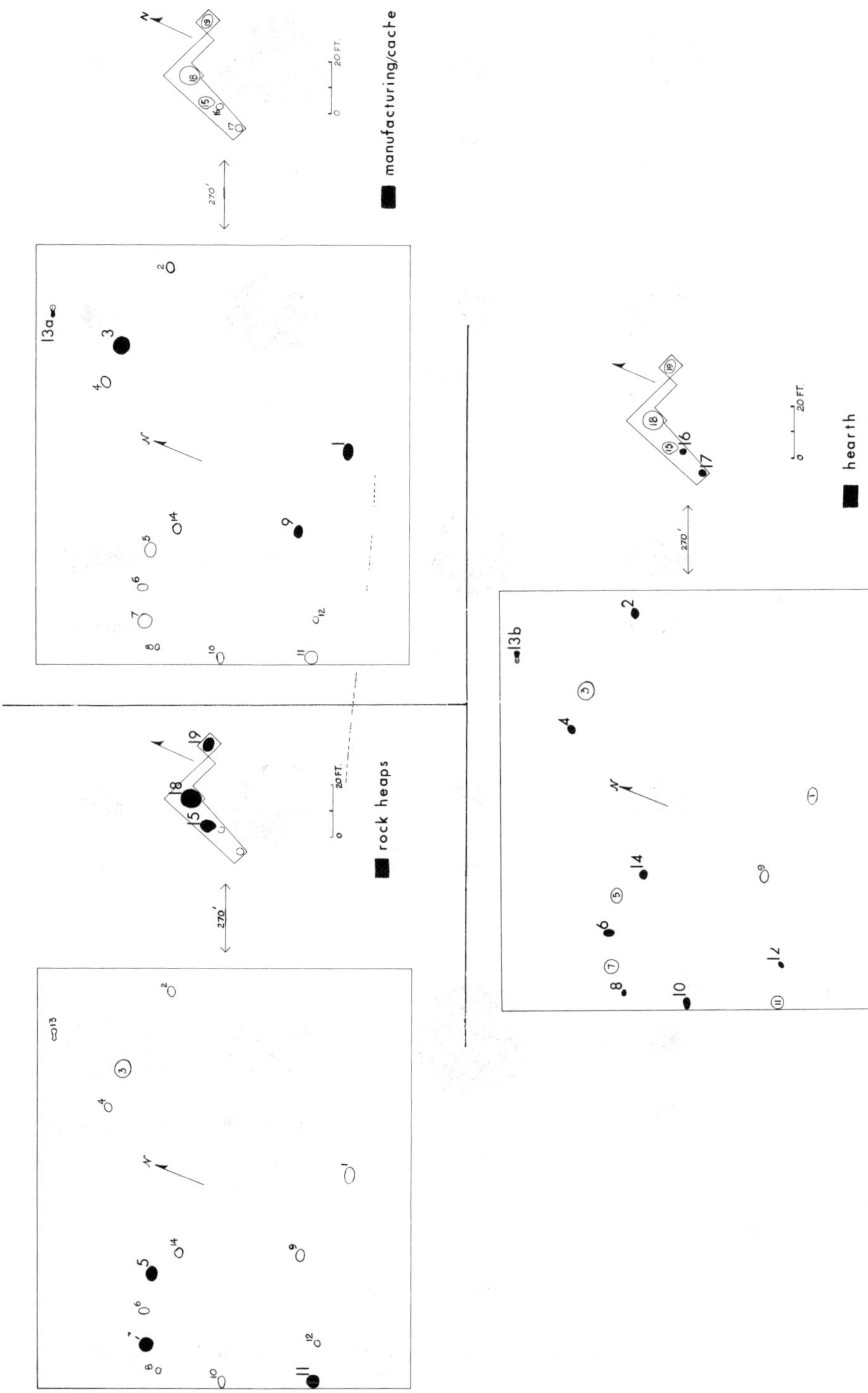

Fig. 5.1 Feature type distribution at Spicer Creek sites 1 and 2.

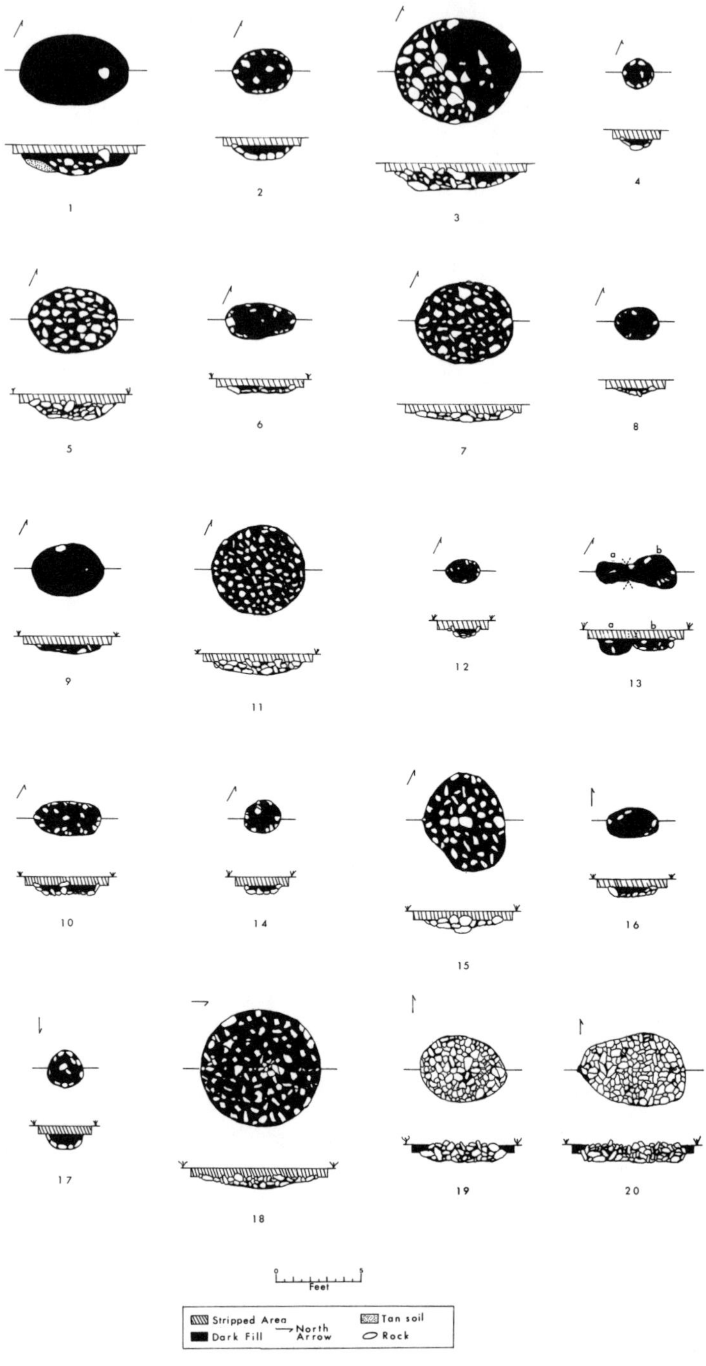

Fig. 5.2 Feature plans and profiles at Spicer Creek 1, 2 and Riverhaven 4.

TABLE 5.2
FEATURES AT SPICER CREEK 1-2 AND RIVERHAVEN 4

Feature Type	Spicer Creek 1		Spicer Creek 2		Riverhaven 4		N	
Rock Heap	3	42.9	3	429	1	14.2	7	100
Manufacture/Cache	3	100	0	0	0	0	3	100
Hearth	8	80	2	20	0	0	10	100
Total	14	70	5	25	1	5	20	100

TABLE 5.3
SPICER CREEK 1 AND 2 FLINT DETRITUS BY FEATURE TYPES

		Manufacture Pit #	Hearths #	Rock Heaps #	N #
Spicer Creek 2	Flakes	103	10	29	143
	Chips	1,885	68	224	2,177
	Cores	2	0	0	2
	N	1,990	78	253	2,322
Spicer Creek 1	Flakes	0	0	16	16
	Chips	0	0	58	58
	Cores	0	0	0	0
	N	0	0	74	74
	ΣN	1,990	78	327	2,396

TABLE 5.4
SPICER CREEK 1, 2 AND RIVERHAVEN 4
FEATURE DISTRIBUTION OF ARTIFACT TYPES

Artifact Type	Spicer Creek 1							Spicer Creek 2	River-Haven 4	N
	1	2	3	7	9	11	13	15	20	
Quaternary Blank										
Whole	1	1	23	3	3	1		1		33
Base	2		9	2			1			14
Tip	3	1	6	2	3	1	1			17
Tertiary Blank										
Tip			4							4
Secondary Blank	1		2	1						4
Unifacial Scraper	1			1	1					3
Grooved Abrading Stn.									1	1
Hammerstone	1									1
N	9	2	44	9	7	2	2	1	1	77

sides and bottom of the hearth which had a few charcoal flecks in the central portion.

Feature 8. Was a shallow, 18 cm (0.6 ft) circular, 61 cm (2 ft) in diameter hearth which had a lining of small fire-broken stones. Some charcoal flecks were present as were several flakes and chips.

Feature 10. Was a shallow, oval, 61 x 122 cm (2 x 4 ft) hearth which contained in its approximately 15 cm (.5 ft) depth a regular lining of broken rock on the bottom and sides. Charcoal flecks were observed in the dark fill, but no flint debris was found.

Feature 12. Was a small oval hearth, 46 x 61 cm (1.5 x 2 ft), and 15 cm (0.5 ft) in depth. Several flakes and chips were recovered from the dark organic fill, in which some charcoal traces were also present. Fired rock fragments lined the side and bottom of this feature.

Feature 13. Consisted of two small oval pits which infringed upon each other. Pit A was a deep pit, 64 cm (2.1 ft), which contained several flakes and numerous chips. The dimensions of this feature were 40 x 64 cm (1.3 x 2.1 ft). The fill contained a large amount of charcoal but few fire-cracked rocks. Pit B was 58 x 92 cm (1.9 x 3.0 ft) in plan and 24 cm (0.8 ft) deep. Fire-cracked rock was present although in no great quantity. Charcoal was scattered throughout the fill but a small concentration was noted in conjunction with a fire-reddened rock.

Feature 14. Was a circular hearth 61 cm (2 ft) in diameter with a fired stone liner. The depth was 15 cm (0.5 ft). This liner was complete except for gaps between the rocks which were reddened, cracked, and broken. Charcoal flecks occurred close to the rock but *not* in the fill. No flint detritus was recovered.

Feature 16. Was an oval hearth 92 x 55 cm (3 x 1.8 ft). The pit was 21 cm (0.7 ft) deep with a grouping of fire-cracked rock on the bottom.

Feature 17. Was a circular hearth 61 cm (2 ft) in diameter, with a depth of nearly 30 cm (1 ft). A cracked and reddened rock liner covered the bottom of the pit but was only partially present on the walls.

Manufacture Pits

Feature 1. Was a large bowl-shaped oval pit, 128 x 195 cm (4.2 x 6.4 ft) and 40 cm (1.3 ft) deep. The pit fill was dark organic soil with the exception of a stained tan portion near the bottom. This feature showed some layering with a layer of fire-cracked rock over several unbroken pebbles close to the bottom of the central portion of the feature. The artifact inventory was taken almost completely from the zone between rock layers, except for a hammerstone found among the unbroken stone. The feature contained a moderately large amount of fire-cracked rock along with a large amount of flint detritus, 287 items, in which chips predominate at 254. A single core is recorded. This feature was isolated from the circular cluster of features on Spicer Creek 1 (Fig. 5.1).

Feature 3. Was a very large, roughly circular basin-shaped pit 198 cm (6.5 ft) in diameter and 30 cm (1 ft) in depth. The most remarkable aspect of this feature was a large cluster of fire-broken and reddened rock in the southwest quadrant, which extended in a crescentic formation to the east. The 66.7 kg (147 lb) of rock were counted and analyzed for material. The 972 items of flint detritus were dominated by chips at 948. Only a single core fragment was recovered. Twenty-three whole or essentially complete quaternary blanks were found. These were cached in the northeast portion of the feature, clustering at a depth of 24 cm (0.8 ft). Little fired rock was encountered here. Elsewhere, scattered throughout the feature, fragments of 15 quaternary blanks, 4 tertiary blanks, and 2 secondary bifaces were disclosed (Table 5.4). This feature was generally isolated from the largest cluster of features at Locality 1 (Fig. 5.1). It was surrounded on three sides by hearths 2, 4, and 13(Fig. 5.1). It was indicated above that Feature 13A might be a manufacture/cache pit. Feature 3 differed from 13A by its lack of charcoal.

Feature 9. Had an oval outline 95 x 143 cm (3.1 x 4.7 ft) but was less deep, 18 cm (0.6 ft) than either Feature 1 or 3, although the bowl-like shape was similar (Fig. 5.2). Little rock was encountered other than two large unbroken pebbles. The fill was of dark organic soil. Most of the flint detritus clustered in the central portion of the feature near a large rock (Fig. 5.2). Chips again predominated, 466 items out of 491. A unifacial scraper was found in association with a large rock near the surface (Fig. 5.2). This feature was closer to the main feature cluster but still appears to be more distant from other features in that circular formation (Fig. 5.1).

Rock Heaps

Feature 5. Was a 30 cm (1 ft) deep bowl-shaped oval pit 122 x 162 cm (4.0 x 5.3 ft) filled with fire-reddened and fire-cracked pebbles. Fifteen items of flint detritus were recovered. Feature 5 formed one of a circular cluster of rock heaps and hearths and was situated between the two hearths, Feature 6 and Feature 14(Fig. 5.1).

Feature 7. Was a shallow, 18 cm (0.6 ft), circular basin 153 cm (5 ft) in diameter filled with fire-cracked and broken rocks, several of which were quite large. This rock heap contained the majority of artifacts found in such features, 9. The count of flint detritus was low with chips being the most numerous category, 66 out of 75. The position of this rock heap was between the hearths, Features 8 and 6 (Fig. 5.1).

Feature 11. Duplicated the basinlike profile and circular plan of Feature 7, 153 cm (5 ft) in diameter. The depth was 24 cm (0.8 ft). This feature yielded more flint detritus than the other rock heaps, 162 items. Here, as elsewhere, chips were most frequent, at 148 items. The flint detritus clustered in the southern hemisphere of the feature where several large glacial cobbles were found. Two broken quaternary blanks were found associated with these cobbles. This feature lay between Features 10 and 12, both hearths (Fig. 5.1). Here the pattern of hearth–rock heap–hearth was broken, there being no rock heap between Features 8 and 10 (Fig. 5.1).

Feature 15. Was an irregular oval rock heap, 134 x 177 cm (4.4 x 5.8 ft), containing several large pebbles and much fire-cracked rock. A single quaternary blank was recovered near some cobbles at the bottom of the feature. There were some charcoal flecks recorded in the fill. This feature together with Feature 18 appeared from indications on the disturbed surface to form a floor "paved" with fire-cracked rock at Spicer Creek 2. Upon excavation this floor was resolved into two features. This feature was quite shallow except for some large pebbles in the center at 21 cm (0.7 ft).

Feature 18. Was an extraordinarily large circular feature, approximately 214 cm (7 ft) in diameter. The excavators record the finding of "some" flakes, an unrecorded number of chips and charcoal interspersed with the fire-cracked rock which was spread like a "floor" in a shallow depression 24 cm (0.8 ft) deep at Spicer Creek 2. The rock was mostly sandstone broken into many jagged-edged, reddened pieces.

Feature 19. Was first indicated on an undisturbed surface as a tight cluster of stones protruding above the soil at Spicer Creek 2. When excavated an oval pile of rocks 122 x 153 cm (4 x 5 ft) was revealed. Many of the stones were water-worn pebbles, heat-reddened but unbroken, interspersed with rock fragments. The depth or height of the pile was approximately 30 cm (1 ft).

Riverhaven 4 Features (Fig. 5.2)

Feature 20. Was a rock heap excavated during a survey in 1967 by Granger and Taggart and its significance was not realized until other similar features had been defined. The flint detritus was field counted at 78 items but on return from the site was dropped and lost. Fortunately the 26.3 kg (58 lb) of fire-cracked rock it contained were retained and analyzed. The frequencies of pebbles and fragments showed that 82 or 62% were sandstone, 29 or 22% dolomite with limestone, with granite and quartzite occurring in lesser numbers. The feature was roughly oval

192 x 104 cm (6.3 x 3.4 ft) and extended to a depth of 30 cm (1 ft) below the surface. The floor was flat so that the feature looked like a straight-sided pan (Fig. 5.2).

Artifacts

Although the Spicer Creek assemblage is discussed here, it has not been as thoroughly studied as that from Riverhaven 2. Categorical decisions were made in association with Spicer Creek's reporter, James C. Donahue, but attribute studies were curtailed by time restrictions and the size of the Riverhaven assemblage being studied at the same time (1970). Therefore, we have included categories of artifacts but little description of the Spicer Creek site's inventory.

Spicer Creek 1, 2 and Riverhaven 4 yielded a total of 190 artifacts, 77 or 40.6% of which come from features, the remaining 113 or 59.4% were surface finds without provenience. The majority, 79%, of the artifacts found in features were found in manufacturing cache pits, with 14% in rock heaps and 7% in the hearths. These artifacts have been divided into functional categories of procurement, 1, processing, 22, and manufacturing, 167 (Table 5.5). Figure 5.3 shows the artifact distribution within each functional group. The low frequencies of artifacts of

TABLE 5.5
DISTRIBUTION OF ARTIFACT TYPES
IN FUNCTIONAL CATEGORIES AT
SPICER CREEK 1 AND 2 AND RIVERHAVEN 4

Artifact	N	% of Total N	% of Subtotal N's	
Projectile Point Sidenotched	1	1	100	Procurement
Subtotal	1	1	100	
Unifacial Scraper	15	8	68.2	
Bifacial Scraper	6	3	27.3	Processing
Abrading Stone, Mano	1	1	4.5	
Subtotal	22	12	100	
Secondary blade	12	6	7	
Tertiary blade	54	27	32	
Quaternary blade	99	52	59	Manufacture
Hammerstone	1	1	1	
Abrading Stone, Grooved	1	1	1	
Subtotal	167	88	100	
Total	190	100	100	

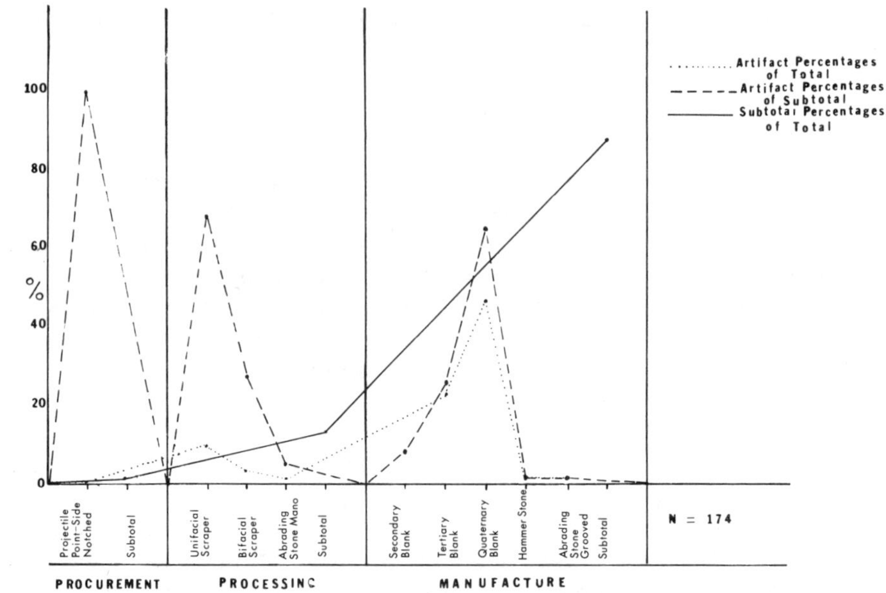

Fig. 5.3 Spicer Creek artifact—category relationships.

procurement (only one) and processing make the curves less than reliable. However, in the manufacture category, it is possible to see the relative frequencies of the blank stages. This curve duplicates that seen at Sinking Ponds and shows progressively more of each of the latter stages with less of the earlier stages. In this case, Stage 1 raw material and primary blanks are entirely missing. Frequencies in all categories were, however, too small to use Fisher's Exact Test for association.

Spicer Creek 1 was the most productive in terms of artifacts since all artifacts were found here, with the exception of two, a quaternary blank on Spicer Creek 2 and a mano-type abrader found on Riverhaven 4.

The artifact distribution is further broken down to associate functional groups with various structures or levels on the sites (Table 5.6). While little can be said about procurement, processing artifacts do appear to cluster on the surface while manufacture is slightly more heavily represented on the surface, 55.6%, than in the next highest concentration, 35.5%, in manufacture pits.

Artifacts of Procurement

The Spicer Creek sites yielded only one representative of this group, a fragmentary side-notched projectile found at Spicer Creek 1

(Table 5.5). It is a surface find without provenience. This category of artifacts, then, reflects only 1% of the total number found at Spicer Creek.

Artifacts of Processing (Table 5.7)

The class of artifacts associated with the processing of food and other goods is represented at the Spicer Creek sites by unifacial scrapers, bifacial scrapers, an abrading stone, and a mano, for a total of 22 in this category. Three or 13% of the total were in the manufacturing pits (Table 5.7). The rest of the artifacts of processing were located on the surface and were without provenience.

Artifacts of Manufacture (Table 5.8)

For the Spicer Creek sites, this category includes secondary blanks, tertiary blanks, quaternary blanks, hammerstones, and a grooved abrading stone. Of the 167 artifacts in this category, 55.6% or 94 belonged to the surface material, and 44.4% or 73 were associated with features. Of these artifacts in features, the majority, 58, were in manufacturing pits, with only 10 and 5 in rock heaps and hearths respectively (Table 5.8). Blank breakage showed a rather low percentage of fragments (58 or 59%) to whole (41 or 41%) (Table 5.9). This percentage was reversed in the manufacture pits. The only figure which approximated the distribution seen at Sinking Ponds was the surface sample, 77% fragments to 23% whole blanks.

In the next sections we will examine the Riverhaven 2 site. This site and its assemblage represent a more intense occupation than that of Spicer Creek 1, 2, and Riverhaven 4. Tests on the sites Riverhaven 5E and 7 yielded artifact assemblages with low frequencies and less intense occupation, much like Spicer Creek 1, 2, and Riverhaven 4. The cultural materials from these sites are as yet unanalyzed. None of these sites resembles the site structure or frequency of artifacts seen at Riverhaven 2.

RIVERHAVEN 2 SITE

Excavations

Excavation of the Riverhaven Complex was carried out from 1960 to 1973, sporadically and on several sites. Unlike other sites discussed here, the excavations at Riverhaven 2 were not done under emergency conditions. The site was first extensively explored by Edward Kochan, of the Ondiara Chapter of the Buffalo and Erie County Historical Soci-

TABLE 5.6
DISTRIBUTION OF FUNCTIONAL CATEGORIES OF ARTIFACTS AT SPICER CREEK 1 AND 2 AND RIVERHAVEN 4

	Surface		Subtotal: Surface		Rock Heap		Hearth Features		Manufact. Pits		Subtotal: Features		Total	
	#	%	#	%	#	%	#	%	#	%	#	%	#	%
Procurement	1	100	1	100	0	0	0	0	0	0	0	0	1	100
Processing	18	86.9	18	86.9	1	4.3	0	0	3	8.6	4	13.1	22	100
Manufacturing	94	55.6	94	55.6	10	5.9	5	2.9	58	35.5	73	44.4	167	100
N	113	59.6	113	55.6	11	5.7	5	2.5	61	32.1	77	40.4	190	100

TABLE 5.7
DISTRIBUTION OF ARTIFACTS OF PROCESSING AT SPICER CREEK 1, 2 AND RIVERHAVEN 4

	Surface		Subtotal		Rock Heap		Hearth		Mfg./ Cache		Feature Subtotal		Total	
	#	%	#	%	#	%	#	%	#	%	#	%	#	%
Unifacial Scraper	12	80	12	80	0	0	0	0	3	20	3	20	15	100
Bifacial Scraper	6	100	6	100	0	0	0	0	0	0	0	0	6	100
Abrading Stone, Mano	0	0	0	0	1	100	0	0	0	0	1	100	1	100
N	18	82	18	82	1	5	0	0	3	13	4	18	22	100

TABLE 5.8
DISTRIBUTION OF ARTIFACTS OF MANUFACTURE FROM SPICER CREEK 1 AND 2

	Surface		Subtotal		Rock Heap		Hearth		Mfg./ Cache		Subtotal: Feature Type		Total	
	#	%	#	%	#	%	#	%	#	%	#	%	#	%
Secondary Blank	8	66.6	8	66.7	1	8.3	0	0	3	25	4	33.3	12	100
Tertiary Blank	50	92.6	50	92.6	0	0	0	0	4	77.4	4	7.4	54	100
Quaternary Blank	35	35	35	35	9	9	5	5	50	51	64	65	99	100
Hammerstone	0	0	0	0	0	0	0	0	1	0	1	100	1	100
Abrading Stone, Grooved	1	100	1	100	0	0	0	0	0	0	0	0	1	100
N	94	56	94	56	10	6	5	3	46	28	73	44	167	100

TABLE 5.9
DISTRIBUTION OF QUATERNARY BLANKS AND FRAGMENTS FROM SPICER CREEK 1 AND 2

	Surface		Rock Heap		Mfg./ Cache		Hearths		Composite		N	
	#	%	#	%	#	%	#	%	#	%	#	%
Whole	8	23	4	44	27	54	2	67	0	0	41	41
Fragment	27	77	5	56	23	46	1	33	2	100	58	59
N	35	100	9	100	50	100	3	100	2	100	99	100

ety, who established the present datum point and baseline at the foot of the 173.9 m (570 ft) terrace of the Niagara River. The north-south baseline was located wholly on the 171.4 m (562 ft) contour (Pl. 13) and most of Kochan's work was accomplished here (Map 5.2). Tests were extended up to the 173.9 m (570 ft) contour. Depths of cultural materials on the 171.4 m (562) contour reached 61 cm (2 ft) Greater depths were recorded but occurred irregularly (Kochan n.d.*b*:8). These greater depths for cultural materials reached approximately 91 cm (36 in) (Kochan n.d.*b*:7).

After opening a 1.2 x 6.1 m (4 x 20 ft) exploratory trench in 1960, Kochan imposed a grid system consisting of 1.2 x 1.2 m (4 x 4 ft) squares upon the site in 1961 (Kochan n.d.*b*:7). During the 1961 field season Kochan was in touch with Marian E. White, who assisted in the preparation of profiles and floor plans. Work continued on the site through the 1963 season.

Excavations were concentrated in two loci (Map 5.6). One was north and the other south of the datum point and several tests elsewhere were made in 1962 (Map 5.6). Kochan completed work on 78.5 m^2 (844 sq ft) but only reported upon 58 m^2 (624 sq ft) (Kochan n.d.*b*:6). An additional 3.7 m^2 (40 sq ft) was excavated during 1967 by Granger and Taggart as part of the resurvey of the Riverhaven site for stratigraphic information. Traces of excavations in all previous units were carefully replotted in 1971 when an additional 201.4 m^2 (2166 sq ft) were excavated. These excavations were conducted to examine as many of Kochan's profiles as possible and determine stratigraphic relationships of his data with new evidence from excavations hastened by an emergency threatening the site.

Kochan catalogued 975 artifacts, 39 of which, upon subsequent examinations by the author, were rejected as surface intrusions, unmodified pebbles, and naturally occurring phenomena such as recent deer antler. An additional 953 artifacts were unearthed but recorded as being either from the exploratory trench (Kochan n.d.*c*) or in various unidentifiable and uncatalogued stages of manufacture (Kochan n.d.*b*:6). Later, after analysis, these artifacts were assigned to each of Kochan's loci but it was not possible to determine further provenience.

We will use Kochan's designations of Locus 1 and Locus 2 but add a third locus for his tests on the 173.9 m (570 ft) terrace which was extended by the 1967 excavations. We will further designate a single unit to the northeast of Locus 1 as Test 1. The 1971 excavations will not be reported here, but the profiles made during that year will be integrated with those from previous excavations. These divisions were appropriate for sampling the terrain because horizontally the Riverhaven 2 site was easily delineated into three particular areas, the 173.9 m

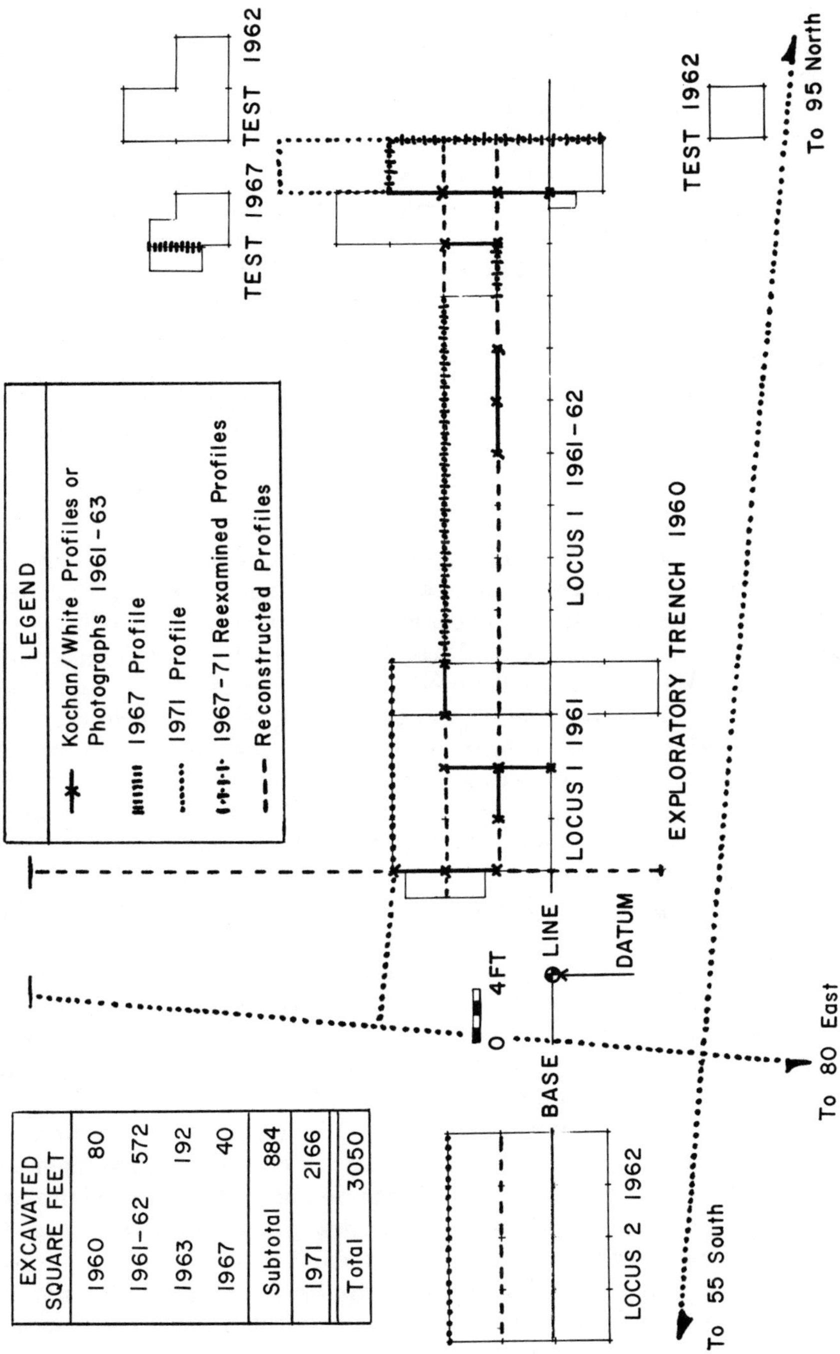

Map 5.6 Riverhaven 2 excavations and profiles.

(570 ft) terrace, the 171.4 m (562 ft) contour where the main excavation was concentrated, and the sterile wet marsh where relatively little excavation was carried out.

Kochan's excavated sample included 1889 artifacts and 959 items of flint detritus distributed as seen in Table 5.10. Here we are able to see clearly that the concentration of artifacts, flint detritus, and excavated area coincide well. Although Kochan was uncertain whether the greater depth of certain artifacts indicated natural depressions or features, laboratory analysis of notes, together with profiles done in 1967 and 1971, have yielded 18 possible features. The distribution of these features coincides almost perfectly with that of the artifacts excavated at greater depth (Table 5.10).

Before dealing further with the excavated areas' stratigraphy, we must look carefully at the location and significance of the features.

Features

We believe that there are approximately 18 features at Riverhaven 2. In Map 5.6, we have indicated profiles made by Kochan or White during excavations. It is suggested that their profiles or photographs showed either wholly or partially eight features, numbers 1, 2, 3, 4, 5, 9, 10, and 11 (Map 5.6). An additional four were described by floor plans or textual references, numbers 8, 12, 13, and 14. (Kochan's Notes, SUNY at Buffalo Department of Anthropology file). Subsequent examination of profiles resulted in the direct observation of eight features including three of those referred to by Kochan, numbers 1, 4, and 11. The features whose remnants were regular but which earlier excavaters classified as either natural *or* man-made were Features 6, 7, 15, 16, and 18. Feature 17 was found during 1967 tests. We have concluded that all were cultural.

We will describe each feature and present, where possible, substantiation for its existence. In our analysis, we found that the possible candidates for features fit fairly well the categories of feature recognized at Sinking Ponds and at the Spicer Creek loci. We will, therefore, use the following categories:

Deep pits with dimensions of 92-153 cm (3-5 ft), oval in form, and from 30.5-45.75 cm (1-1.5 ft) in depth and which have walls steeper than a 70° angle going down to a flat or rounded bottom are called probable *storage pits*. They are usually associated with a generalized refuse fill. The depth range of these pits was 46-95 cm (1.5-3.1 ft) with six, or 67%, larger than 62 cm (2 ft). Mean depth was 79 cm (2.6 ft). A *manufacture pit*, Feature 3, is distinguished from a storage pit only by the presence of a cache of chert preforms.

TABLE 5.10
RIVERHAVEN 2 EXCAVATED AREAS, SQUARE FEET EXCAVATED, FEATURES, ARTIFACTS, AND FLINT DETRITUS

	Locus 1		Locus 2		Locus 3		Test 1		N	
	#	%	#	%	#	%	#	%	#	%
Square Feet Excavated	600	68	192	22	76	9	16	2	884	100
Possible Features	12	67	5	28	1	7	0	0	18	100
Artifacts	1,559	82.5	315	16.7	15	0.8	0	0	1,889	100
Flint Detritus	7,775	85.8	906	10	320	3.5	58	0.7	9,050	100

The possible *rock heaps* and *hearths* generally conform well with those recognized at Sinking Ponds, Spicer Creek 1, 2, and Riverhaven 4. Hearths at Riverhaven 2 appeared to have a depth range of 34-52 cm (1.1-1.7 ft) with a mean of 43 cm (1.4 ft). The shape of these features was similar to the deep refuse filled pits but the depths were strikingly dissimilar (Fig. 5.4).

Possible Rock Heaps (Fig. 5.4, nos. 6, 12, 17)

Feature 6. Was a small oval rock heap in the reopened wall profile of Locus 1 at a depth of 15 cm (0.5 ft). It was 98 cm (3.2 ft) by 119 cm (3.9 ft) and extended to a depth of 70 cm (2.3 ft) below the surface. The pit surface was 15 cm (0.5 ft) below ground level. Rock seen in the profile consisted of large cracked pebbles and fragments of fire-broken stones. No accurate count of fire-cracked rock was made. Four quaternary blank fragments, one tertiary blank and a fragment, three bifacial end scrapers, and a celt were assigned to this feature.

Feature 12. Was described by Kochan as a group of fire-broken stones. Its probable dimensions disclosed by his floor plan were a diameter of 76 cm (2.5 ft) and a depth (from Kochan's note on stratigraphy of Locus 2) of 24 cm (0.8 ft) for the surface of the feature and 64 cm (2.0 ft) for the bottom. He also notes the presence of burned bone, some flint chips, and a quaternary blank fragment in this area.

Feature 17. Was located on the edge of the 173.9 cm (570 ft) terrace. This feature was excavated by Granger and Taggart in the site during 1967. It was discovered at 8 cm (0.25 ft) and extended to a depth of 38 cm (1.25 ft). Its diameter was approximately 92 cm (3 ft). The feature consisted of several large cobbles and numerous fired rock fragments. Eighty-four fragments of rock were counted, weighing 48.1 kg (106 lb). Sixty-one pieces or 72.6% of the rock were sandstone with lesser amounts of dolomite, limestone, and granite. Flint detritus consisted of 13 flakes and 25 chips. Five basal fragments of quaternary blanks were found and a whole one was recovered at the base of a large rock in the central portion.

Probable Hearths (Fig. 5.4, nos. 7, 13, 15, 18)

Feature 7. Was observed in the 1971 profile of the west wall of Locus 1. It commenced at a depth of 27 cm (0.9 ft) below the surface and extended to 79 cm (2.6 ft). It appeared to be roughly circular with a diameter of approximately 150 cm (4.9 ft). A large number of fire-cracked rocks were seen at the bottom and two large pebbles were close to the surface of the feature which was composed of gray-brown soil. Kochan records charcoal from this area at a depth of 75 cm (2.5 ft).

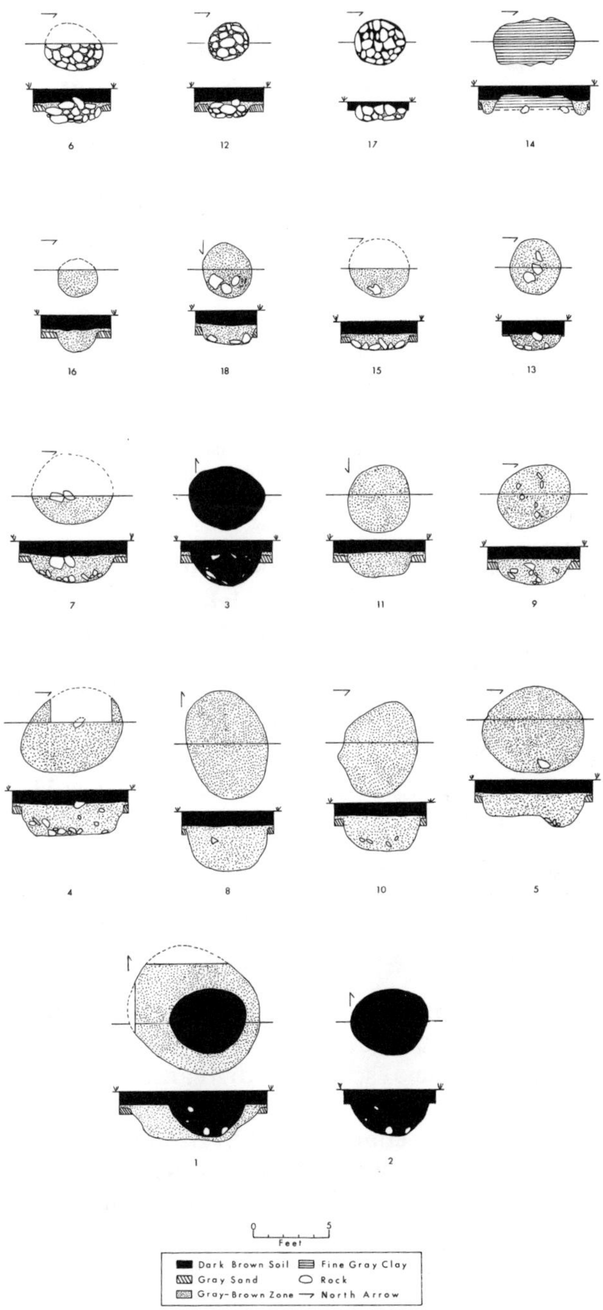

Fig. 5.4 Plans and profiles of features at Riverhaven 2.

Artifacts assigned to Feature 7 were a quaternary blank, tertiary blank fragment, bifacial triangular end scraper, grooved abrading stone, Vinette 1 pottery, a rim and 2 body sherds, three antler flaking tools and a cut antler fragment. Kochan stated that some flint chips and bone were also present.

Feature 13. This feature in Locus 2 was apparently recognized by Kochan after he wrote the 1963 excavation report (n.d.*b*). He describes a roughly circular, 101 x 113 cm (3.3 x 3.7 ft), midden feature 33 cm (13 in) in depth, actually from 27-67 cm (0.9-2.2 ft) (Kochan: Notes, Locus 2). He further describes the pit:

> The matrix [fill] in the pit was composed of a grayish sedimentary type sandy soil flecked throughout with traces of charcoal [and the] surrounding soil was burnt dark red . . . Fire burnt stones were found but not in any definitely large amount . . . Though ash was difficult to determine, there were traces of it. Several fine pot sherds [two of Vinette 1 type] were found in the pit as were several other artifacts [unifacial scraper, birdstone fragment]. A large stone was found and its removal tore up some of the feature. Several clam shells [2] [freshwater mussels], a small quantity of bone [7 items], and flint chips [detritus] in fair quantity were also found. (Kochan: Notes, Locus 2)

The birdstone fragment, which Kochan did not assign to the feature but which occurred at a depth of 30 cm (1 ft), exactly over the feature and adjacent to the stone, was probably disturbed by the process of removing the rock. This feature described by Kochan was photographed and drawn in a floor plan. The amount of burning and presence of stone in the bottom portions suggests it functioned as a hearth.

Feature 15. Was another pit described by Kochan in his Locus 2 notes. He states that the "circular midden feature" was 112 cm (44 in) in diameter and 36 cm (14 in) deep (approximately 24-61 cm or 0.8-2.0 ft).

> Midden Matrix [fill] is a homogeneous mass of charcoal gray clay-like soil with brownish-like sedimentary soil. Charcoal, . . . fire burnt and broken stones are in evidence [and] flint chips [detritus] are fairly prevalent. A very small quantity of animal bone was found as was a trace of clam [freshwater mussel] shells. (Kochan:Notes, Locus 2)

The artifact inventory plotted in the feature was one quaternary blank and three fragments, a tertiary blank and three fragments, two longitudinal knives, a unifacial scraper, a drill and one potsherd of Vinette 1.

The presence of rock, charcoal and fire-reddening at the bottom of the feature argues for the description as a hearth.

Feature 18. Was partially rediscovered in a profile reopening of 1967 and a portion of this feature was recovered from the wall. It was a large, deep, almost circular hearth approximately 104 cm (3.4 ft) in diemeter beginning at 29 cm (0.95 ft) and extending to 69 cm (2.25 ft). Like Features 7, 13, and 15, it contained dark gray-brown sandy clay with numerous charcoal flecks and some fire-reddened clay around rocks. These excavations revealed a large flint flake and 6.3 kg (14 lb) of fire-cracked and reddened rock forming a partial floor (Fig. 5.4). Exact provenience showed that three artifacts were excavated from the feature, a quaternary blank and two fragments.

Probable Manufacture Pit (Fig. 5.4, no. 3)

Feature 3 (Pl. 14). Was defined from photographs taken by Kochan and White. These photographs showed an oval feature filled with a dark brown organic fill, 125 cm (4.1 ft) wide and approximately 146 cm (4.8 ft) long. The depth was 85 cm (2.8 ft) from the surface, measured from the central datum, but no demarcation between humus and the feature's surface could be determined. Artifact association commenced at approximately 24 cm (0.8 ft). Fragments of fire-cracked rock were illustrated in the photographs forming a "circular" pattern around the central portion of the feature. In this central area of the pit, Kochan discerned:

> 21 asymetric shape crude percussion chipped quarry blanks. They lay in no definite pattern or formation and several of them showed secondary chipping . . . A broad trianguloid shape knife [tertiary blank] was found on the perimeter of the cache. The blanks were all fine specimens of blue gray, mottled with tan Onondaga flint. (Kochan n.d.*b*:11)

Analysis of the "cache" showed: nine primary blanks, five secondary blanks, two tertiary blanks, and five core/spalls (unretouched). Elsewhere in the feature were found a fragmented quaternary blank, five unifacial scrapers, three of which were large flakes, and a drill. Kochan notes a heavy concentration of "flint chips," detritus, in this excavated square (Kochan: Notes, Locus 1:1R14).

Clay Heap (Fig. 5.4, no. 14)

Feature 14. Was an unusual formation of irregular outline as seen in Kochan's floor plan of Locus 2. This feature, 162 cm (5.3 ft) long and 92 cm (3 ft) wide, extending in depth from 15 cm (0.5 ft) to 58 cm (1.9 ft) was described as an "intrusive mound of red clay subsoil" (Kochan: Notes, Locus 2). The importance of the red clay was that it contained only two "fire burnt" stones, both at the base of the "mound". An irregular depression 12 cm (0.4 ft) in depth encompassed the periphery of the "mound", like a moat, and was filled with general midden soil (ibid.). Kochan seems to have assigned the artifacts associated with Feature 14 to this depression. These were two quaternary blanks and two fragments, as well as two Vinette I pottery body sherds. Kochan further notes flint debris and a small amount of bone and clam or freshwater mussel shell (ibid.).

The lack of gravel inclusion in the red clay of the "mound" suggests that this feature was a store of clay processed by gravel removal and then deposited for use, perhaps in pottery making.

Possible Storage Pits (Fig. 5.4, nos. 1, 2, 4, 5, 8, 9, 10, 11, 16)

Features 1 and 2. Were first illustrated in a profile drawn by Marian E. White of squares 1L14, 2L14, and 3L15. An extremely complex stratigraphic profile resulted, with lensing intrusions and out-of-place soil members such as red clay above brown midden soil. This reversed stratigraphy was clarified by the 1971 profile reopening, showing it to be confined to an area 272 x 256 cm (8.9 x 8.4 ft) at the north end of Locus 1. The disturbed area in question began at 27 cm (0.9 ft) and continued to a depth of 98 cm (3.2 ft). Although opinion may still be divided on whether this is the result of river action or intentionally dug pits, the profile is interpreted here as two features: one–Feature 2–within another–Feature 1. The productivity of the double feature was great, for 102 artifacts and only those with exact provenience or clear unit or level association which precluded inclusion in Feature 2 were assigned to it. The artifact distribution, then, was 71 in Feature 1 and 31 in Feature 2.

Feature 1. Was large, oval and diverse in fill with apparent "loading" of various soil types. The diverse nature of the soil deposits indicates that the feature may not have been completely filled at any one time and that Feature 2 intruded during a late stage of incomplete filling.

The artifact inventory included two Meadowood projectile points, three quaternary blanks, and 24 fragments; five tertiary blanks and 13 fragments, a bifacial trianguloid end scraper, a primary and a secondary blank, a celt, three bone awls and 17 pottery body sherds of Vinette I type. Kochan notes that this area contained "numerous flint chips."

Feature 2. Was a roughly circular area of dark brown soil 150 cm (4.9 ft) by 120 cm (4.2 ft). Although no surface outline could be isolated, artifacts were disclosed beginning at 23 cm (0.7 ft). The artifacts occurred to a depth of 89 cm (2.9 ft). Kochan appears to have recognized this feature. He states:

> The pit deposit consisted of a black clayish mixture speckled with charcoal and intermixed with various size stones and pebbles. Mixed throughout were flint chips [detritus] and assorted artifacts. Clam shells were found as well as were bone fragments. A typical midden refuse conglomeration. (Kochan: Notes, Locus 1)

The feature contained one sidenotched Meadowood point and one cornernotched projectile point, a quaternary blank and three fragments, three broken tertiary blanks, a secondary blank, two bifacial scrapers, and a grooved abrading stone. Many flint chips were noted. Twelve pottery sherds of Vinette 1 ware were found, two of which were rims. The fairly large sample of bone recovered from the feature contained four bone awls and two split and cut mammal long bones. Since the inventory of Feature 1 and Feature 2 was so similar, no temporal differentiation was possible.

Feature 4. Was identified by the 1971 profile excavations as a depression of dark gray-brown soil with fire-cracked rock commencing at 26 cm (0.85 ft) and reaching the floor at 85 cm (2.8 ft). This large oval feature, 168 x 195 cm (5.5 x 6.4 ft), subsequently reconstructed from Kochan's notes, floor plans, and partial profiles, had steep walls and a flat bottom. There was a moderate amount of fire-cracked rock in the lower portions but no definite concentration. Fifteen artifacts were assigned to this feature: a sidenotched Meadowood point, two whole and six broken quaternary blanks, two portions of tertiary blanks, a secondary blank and three Vinette 1 pottery sherds. No determination of flint debris and faunal materials could be made. Charcoal in light amounts flecked the profile.

Feature 5. Was recognized when an incomplete profile by Kochan (Notes, Locus 1) showed a significantly greater depth in a corner of one of his squares, 1L1N. The plan showed a partial outline encompassing the expression noted in the profile which Kochan assumed was merely a depression in the floor. However, the steep wall of the depression seen in the profile was suspicious, and distribution of artifacts with provenience over the area suggested by the plan showed a concentration at maximum depth of 76-92 cm (2.5-3 ft) by extending lines seen in Kochan's profile and plans. Feature dimensions of 174-201 cm (5.7-6.6 ft) and 70 cm (2.3 ft) depth were developed. The artifact zone appeared to commence at 26 cm (0.85 ft) at this point, and this was assumed to be the pit surface. The feature had steep walls and a flat floor with the exception of a small depression which extended to 95 cm (3.1 ft).

The feature contained five quaternary blanks and nine fragments, four broken tertiary blanks, a secondary blank, a unifacial scraper, two drills, two grooved abrading stones, and 18 Vinette 1 body sherds. No bone sample was recorded but the artifact assemblage included three bone awls, two antler flakers, and a cut and partially worked antler.

Feature 8. First appeared as a cluster of 47 artifacts which occurred below 46 cm (1.5 ft) in the area assigned to this feature. A search of the notes was conducted and it was found that Kochan records the presence of a "unique condition" in the immediate area:

> which was excavated to a depth of 41 inches [3.42 feet; 104 cm] (and) was the deepest square excavated. Due to the depth, the fine sedimentary level (gray-brown sandy-

> clay) was unusually wet and deep. At an average depth of 38 inches [3.17 feet; 97 cm] there were found thin layers or strata of brown colored material that was probably decayed bone. Because of its condition it was impossible to identify the material as bone by shape or form. A fine large sample of antler was found just above this formation in a slightly drier strata. (Kochan: Notes, Locus 1 and n.d.*b*:11)

The feature was drawn, extending a floor plan of Kochan's and encompassing the deepest artifacts. Final reconstructed dimensions were 162 cm (5.3 ft) by 214 cm (7 ft) with a depth of 104 cm (3.42 ft). The pit surface probably was at 24 cm (0.8 ft).

The artifacts assigned to the feature were three sidenotched Meadowood projectile points, a quaternary blank and 11 segments, a tertiary blank and six segments, a secondary blank, two bifacial and one unifacial scraper, five drills, a netsinker, and 13 pottery sherds, Vinette 1. Although the bone sample could not be recovered (Kochan n.d.*b*:11) two bone awls were recorded from the upper, drier portions of the feature (ibid.).

Feature 9. Was recorded by Kochan as:

> A pit-like depression . . . Pit composition consisted of brownish colored sand intermixed with pebbles and various broken stones. It contained specks of charcoal, flint chips [detritus] several artifacts and bone fragments. (Kochan:Notes, Locus 1)

The profile and fragmentary plan he recorded show approximately one quarter of the pit's outline. This was reconstructed symmetrically, and the dimensions were 113 x 150 cm (3.7 x 4.9 ft) with a maximum depth of 76 cm (2.5 ft). The pit surface was 24 cm (0.8 ft). The feature had steep walls but was bowl-shaped. It contained a quaternary blank and two broken portions, two fragments of tertiary blanks, and two secondary blanks.

Feature 10. Was observed by Kochan when:

> . . . the red clay level dropped off sharply, this [depression] was filled with a black clay-like soil mixed with sand and pebbles. Flint chips [detritus] were fairly abundant and several artifacts were found. (Kochan: Notes, Locus 1)

A two-way profile (Map 5.6) and a portion of Kochan's floor plan were used to reconstruct a storage pit 146 cm (4.8 ft) wide and 192 cm (6.3 ft) long extending from 24 cm (0.8 ft) to a depth of 95 cm (3.1 ft). The artifacts recorded from the feature were one stemmed and one corner-notched projectile point, three quaternary blanks and seven fragments, two tertiary blanks and 15 fragments, two secondary blanks, six scrapers (three bifacial trianguloid and three unifacial, two of which were the end variety), a drill, and five pottery Vinette 1 body sherds. No bone or shell was recorded but charcoal flecks were present.

Feature 11. Was described by Kochan:

> It [the pit] was difficult to locate and contained flint chips [although scarce], specks of charcoal and several artifacts. It contained no stones to speak of and no gravel. (Notes, Locus 1)

The feature was not a substantial one from the above record. It was clarified, however, by the discovery of half the feature left in the south wall of Locus 1 during 1967 and 1971 excavation (Map 5.6). It was subsequently excavated and although artifactually sterile, produced 3 kg (6.5 lb) of fire-cracked rock, seven flint flakes, and 21 chips. Artifacts assigned to this feature are a quaternary blank and two segments and three tertiary blank fragments. The pit was almost circular with a 122 cm (4 ft) diameter and had a minimum depth of 24 cm (0.8 ft) and a maximum depth of 73 cm (2.4 ft). It was steep-sided and had a flat floor.

Feature 16. Was recorded by Kochan as "a small pit filled with midden refuse" (Notes, Locus 2). A plan shows it to be 76 cm (2.5 ft) in diameter and the notes also indicate that it occurred between 27 cm (0.9 ft) and 73 cm (2.4 ft). It was steep-walled and bowl-shaped. This feature was also recorded in 1971 when the unexcavated portions were removed and found to be sterile. No artifacts were recorded within this feature which was quite regular in form.

We have discussed above (see also Map 5.6) the location of excavations and profiles which were used to recognize features both in the field and the laboratory. Under each feature we have supplied the evidence for its recognition and its strength and weaknesses. All of the intrusions described here as features were recognized in the field by Kochan or one of the excavators either wholly or partially. In the analysis we have correlated evidence and classified the features. Distribution of feature classes is shown in Figure 5.5. The largest frequency of features recognized was in Locus 1 where a group of seven deep basin pits were found and related to a storage function based upon content and suggested analogies (Ritchie 1969:188-89). Other features are distributed more randomly.

Below we will discuss the vertical distribution of cultural materials, before continuing with an interpretation of the stratigraphy of the Riverhaven 2 site.

Vertical Distribution of Artifactual Materials

The primary field problem at Riverhaven 2 was the question of whether the varying depths of artifacts were the result of feature intrusion or deposition on an uneven surface. We discussed above the evidence for recognizing features. We will summarize here the distribution of artifacts as evidence in support of our feature assignments. Two propositions were advanced to account for the variable artifact depth,

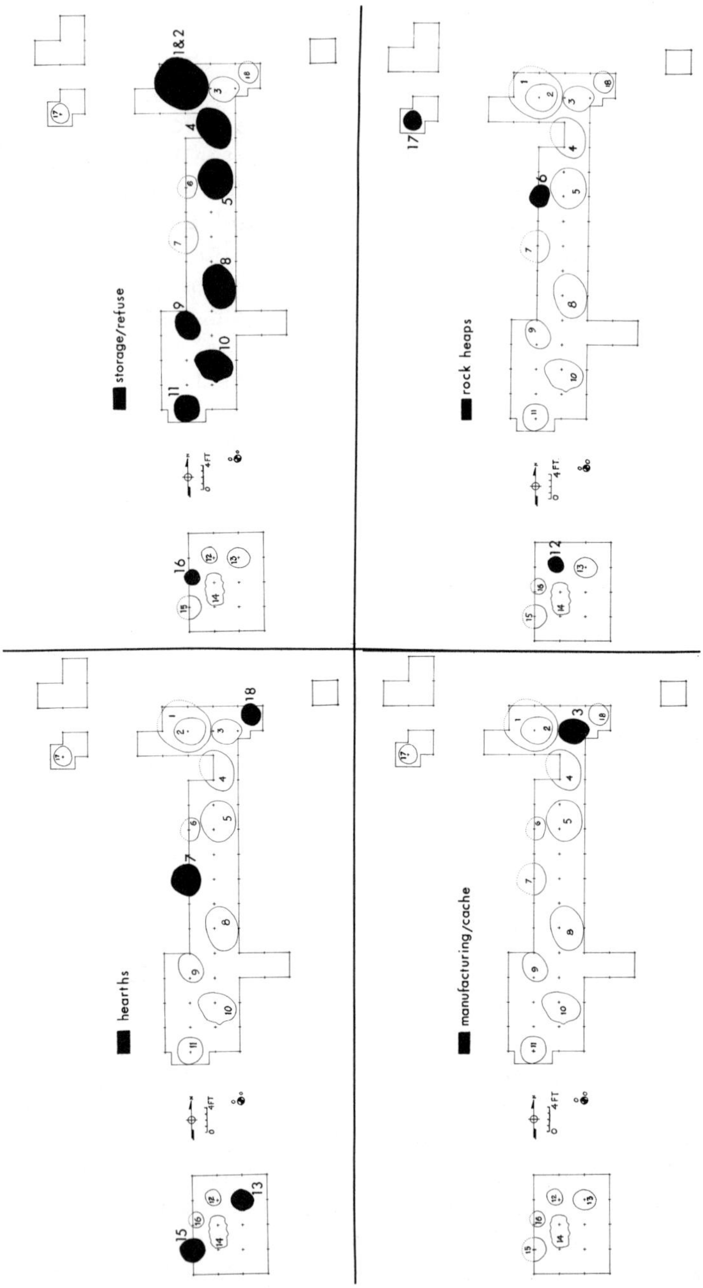

Fig. 5.5 Distribution of feature types at Riverhaven 2.

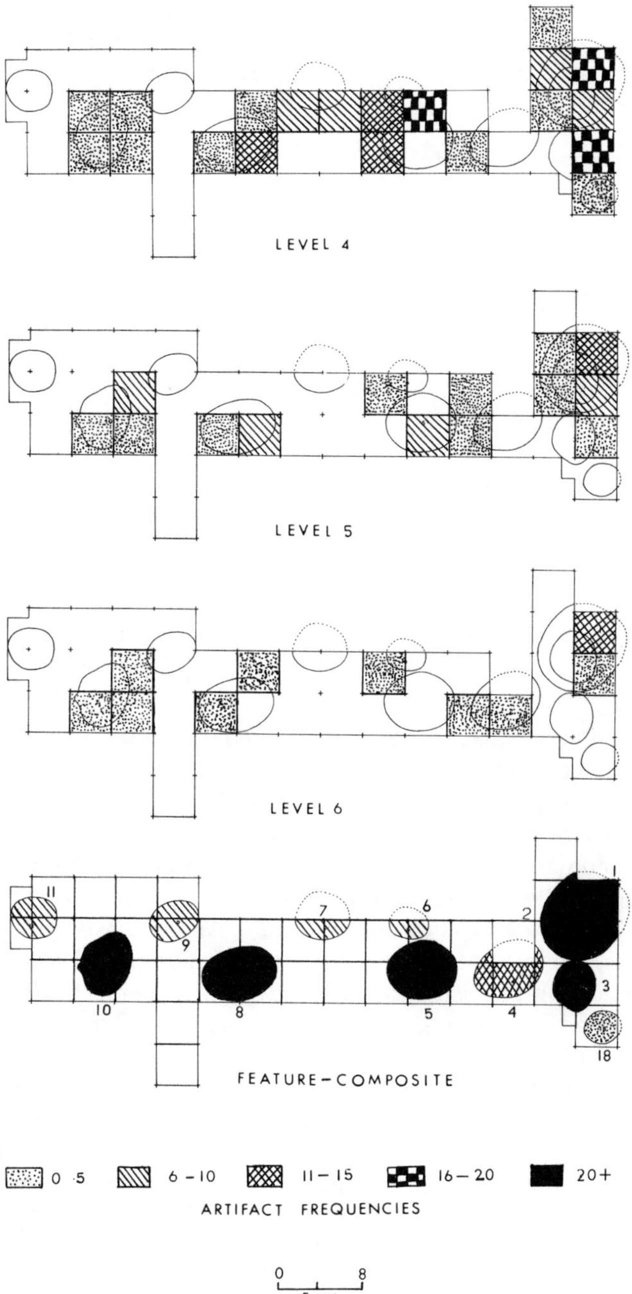

Fig. 5.6 Riverhaven 2 artifact frequency distribution in features of Locus 1.

TABLE 5.11
RIVERHAVEN 2 VERTICAL DISTRIBUTION OF ARTIFACTUAL MATERIALS BY THOSE ASSIGNED TO FEATURES AND THOSE EXCLUSIVE OF FEATURES

	Locus 1		Locus 2		Locus 3		N		% of Category
	#	%	#	%	#	%	#	%	N
Level 2									
Exclusive of Features	177	43	220	55	7	2	404	100	68
Features	25	69	5	17	6	14	36	100	10
Subtotal	202	46	225	51	13	3	440	100	
Level 3									
Exclusive of Features	118	64	63	34	2	1	183	100	30.3
Features	19	50	19	50	0	0	38	100	11
Subtotal	137	62	82	37	2	1	221	100	
Level 4									
Exclusive of Features	8	100	0	0	0	0	8	100	
Features	163	100	0	0	0	0	163	100	47
Subtotal	171	100	0	0	0	0	171	100	
Level 5									
Exclusive of Features	1	100	0	0	0	0	1	100	0.7
Features	74	99	1	1	0	0	75	100	22
Subtotal	75	99	1	1	0	0	76	100	
Level 6									
Features	34	100	0	0	0	0	34	0	10
Subtotal	34	100	0	0	0	0	34	100	
N Exclusive of Features	304	51	283	48	9	1	596	100	100
N Features	315	91	25	7	6	2	346	100	100
Σ N	619		308		15		942		

(1) an undifferentiated midden deposited on an uneven surface, or (2) the likelihood of a midden area with feature intrusions into an essentially even surface, with regular natural stratigraphy.

No convincing evidence that there were successive occupations or major typological differences in the sample was derived from the previous studies of the artifact assemblage (Ritchie 1969:190; Taggart 1966, 1967, 1969: personal communications). As discussed above, profiles, floor plans, photographs and notes strongly suggested certain features, and distribution of artifacts assigned some to these features. Artifact distributions in Locus 1, composed into "suggested features" are shown in Figure 5.6.

The vertical distribution of artifacts is shown in Table 5.11. Nine hundred and forty-seven artifacts had no provenience and have not been included, nor has Level 1, .0 to 15 cm (0.5 ft), since it was sterile of artifactual materials. We have plotted the materials by arbitrary level in Figure 5.7. The highest percentage of area exclusive of features occurs in Levels 2-3, with the highest feature association in Level 4 and lesser amounts in Levels 5-6. When Levels 2-3 and 4-5-6 were tested against feature or non-feature association by chi-square in a 2 x 2 cell table, the probability was less than one case out of 1000 that such a

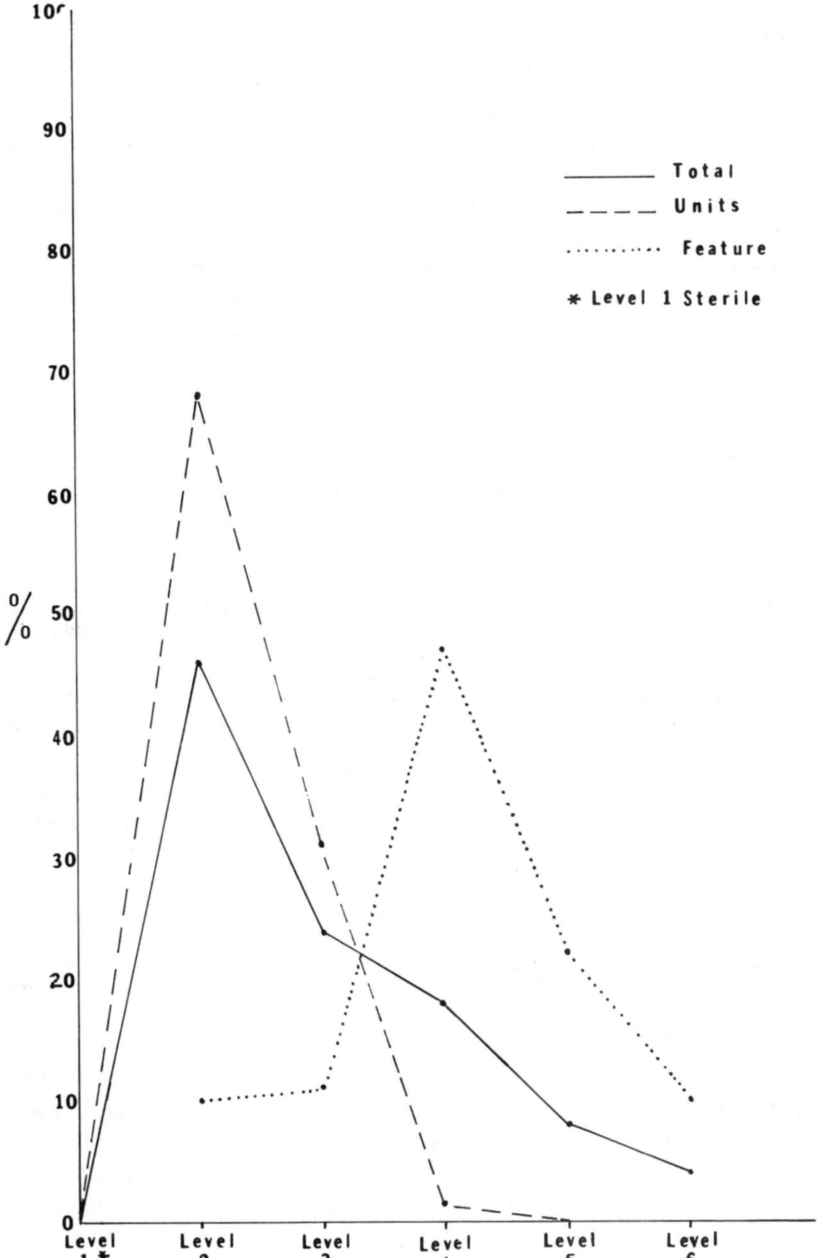

Fig. 5.7 Artifacts by 0.5 foot arbitrary levels.

distribution was caused by chance. Similar tests were accomplished after integrating the distribution study of Level 3 and assignment of those artifacts clustered over a feature to the suggested feature. This produced a probability of chance occurrence of two cases out of 100. We suspect, based upon such studies, that the main living floor occurred at a depth of approximately 30 cm (1 ft).

Since many of Kochan's profiles were short and adjacent sections were not opened, immediately subsequent profiles made in 1967 and 1971 were studied to determine if there were any regular natural occurrence which might account for the clustering of artifacts, exclusive of features. No such occurrence was defined. To the contrary five deep basin-shaped pits were noted during the 1971 excavations. We shall discuss the natural stratigraphy in the next section.

Stratigraphy

Another complex problem at Riverhaven 2 was stratigraphy, natural and cultural. Kochan (n.d.*b*:8) summarized the stratigraphy on the 171.4 m (562 ft) contour as occurring in several levels which he described as:

Level 1. Surface soil, which is heavily rooted black sandy humus, ranges in depth from 1 inch at the crest of the ridge to 8 inches at the base. It may be considered sterile, as it is totally devoid of artifacts or artifactual debris.

Level 2. The second or artifact level is composed of black sandy humus-like soil, containing minute quantities of clay and large amounts of flint debris. This is intermixed with clam shells, bone refuse, gravel pebbles, a large quantity of burnt limestone and lesser amount of fire broken stones.

Level 3. The third level, when encountered in the central area of the site, is a sickly grey colored clay which is considered to be subsoil. In the northern and southern portions of the site, it is composed of a light fine sandy sedimentary soil, ranging to a depth of 12 inches. This level is also devoid of artifacts, although minute traces of charcoal and bone were found in it.

Level 4. The fourth level, which is only encountered beneath the light sandy sedimentary soil and does not exceed a depth of three inches, is composed of a coarser light colored sand intermixed with gravel, pebbles and artifactual debris. Artifacts were found in this level, as were minute traces of charcoal.

Level 5. The fifth level is of a hard stony red clay composition and may be considered to be subsoil.

Four 0.76 x 0.76 m^2 (2.5 x 2.5 sq ft) tests east of the 171.4 m (562 ft) contour were made in 1967; they showed a regular natural sequence of deposition in the marsh between the 171.4 m (562 ft) bench and the river. The culturally sterile natural soil sequence was:

I.	Humic-peat	0-34 cm (0-1.1 ft)
II.	Medium gray compacted clay	34-79 cm (1.1-2.6 ft)
III.	Red compacted till (clay)	79-? cm (2.6-? ft)

The juncture between each soil member was clearly demarcated with little or no transition zone. The significant observations here were that

TABLE 5.12
RIVERHAVEN 2 NATURAL STRATIGRAPHY OF THE 562 FOOT (171.4 METER) CONTOUR BENCH

Stratum	Description of Natural Soil Zones	Depth in Feet and Tenths	Remarks and Correlation
A	Humus, sand admixture, roots, black-dark brown	0-0.8 ft (0-24 cm)	Sterile, corresponds to Kochan's Level 1 and Marsh I
B	Humus-subsoil transition, charcoal, fired clay, medium brown-gray	0.8-1.3 ft (varies 0.2 ft) (24-40 cm, varies 6 cm)	Numerous artifacts and occupation debris, corresponds to Kochan's Levels 2 and 3
C	Sandy clay subsoil, white sand lenses, yellow	0.8 ft (24 cm)-occurs below D on bench to 2.0 feet (61 cm)	Sterile, pinches out at the foot of the 570′ (173.9 m) terrace by A, B, & D on bench
D	Sandy clay with sand dominant, light gray	1.3-1.7 ft (varies 0.2 ft) (40-52 cm varies 6 cm)	Some artifacts, bone, charcoal flecks, flint detritus; corresponds to Kochan's Level 4 and Marsh II. Clay is dominant in marsh
D_1	Extension of D at the edge of the 562 foot bench	1.7-1.6 ft (52-70 cm)	Bone debris found at 2.35 feet (72 cm) in 1971 at edge of bench
E	Compacted clay glacial till, pebbles, red-pink	1.7-? and in the marsh 2.6-? (52-100 cm)	Sterile, corresponds to Kochan's Level 5 and Marsh III

the marsh lacked the gray sandy clay zone seen by Kochan and that the natural sequence of deposition appeared to be regular.

The excavations of 1971 were partially conducted to recover older profiles in the 1960-1961 excavation area. When the older profiles were correlated with profiles made during additional excavations, it was observed that these were sections of the site with cultural materials that had regular sequences of natural deposition without disturbance. These excavations also revealed several large intrusive pits just west of the datum point and directly adjacent to Loci 1 and 2.

It was found that cultural materials were distributed throughout in an almost 61 cm (2 ft) vertical zone over most of the site and that there were certain soil zones which were sterile. The distribution of cultural materials is correlated with the natural deposition sequence and presented in Table 5.12.

Two interpretations were possible for the observed phenomenon. (1) There was a deep midden deposit with the living debris having its source on the top of the terrace. This debris was either thrown over the bank intentionally or carried over the bank by natural agency, or both. During and after deposition it was undisturbed where it had been deposited in hollows and depressions left by natural agency. (2) The deposit was the result of habitation activities below the terrace. During and after deposition it was disturbed by subsequent cultural activities.

Above, we discussed the evidence suggesting features. Therefore, it is considered that alternative (2) is the more likely interpretation. In order to examine this interpretation we used all extant profiles, photographs, and notes to reconstruct long profiles.

A 240-ft long elevation map from East River Road to the Niagara River through Kochan's datum point was used in conjunction with a profile made in 1971 from 40 west to 80 east, to lengthen a profile made by Kochan on the south wall of Locus 1 (Map 5.6). This extended profile is shown in Figure 5.8. It shows a regularity of deposit, except in the feature disturbance. This situation was also revealed in two long profiles executed to lengthen and correct profiles made from 1961-71 (Fig. 5.9).

The cultural stratigraphy, according to Kochan, began at approximately 8 in (20 cm) and continued to 39 in (99 cm) in "spots" (ibid.:8). The main occupation level appears to begin at 23-24 cm (0.75-0.8 ft), or arbitrary Level 2 in the 15 cm (0.5 ft) level, or Stratum B (Table 4.6), and continue to the top of or just into Stratum D, 40-43 cm (1.3-1.4 ft), or arbitrary Level 3 (Figs. 5.8 and 5.9). Commencing with arbitrary Level 4, 46 cm (1.5 ft), cultural deposits appear to be contained in features which displayed confusing admixtures of soils, possibly from relaid fill or slope wash. The feature fill was the gray-brown sandy clay organic

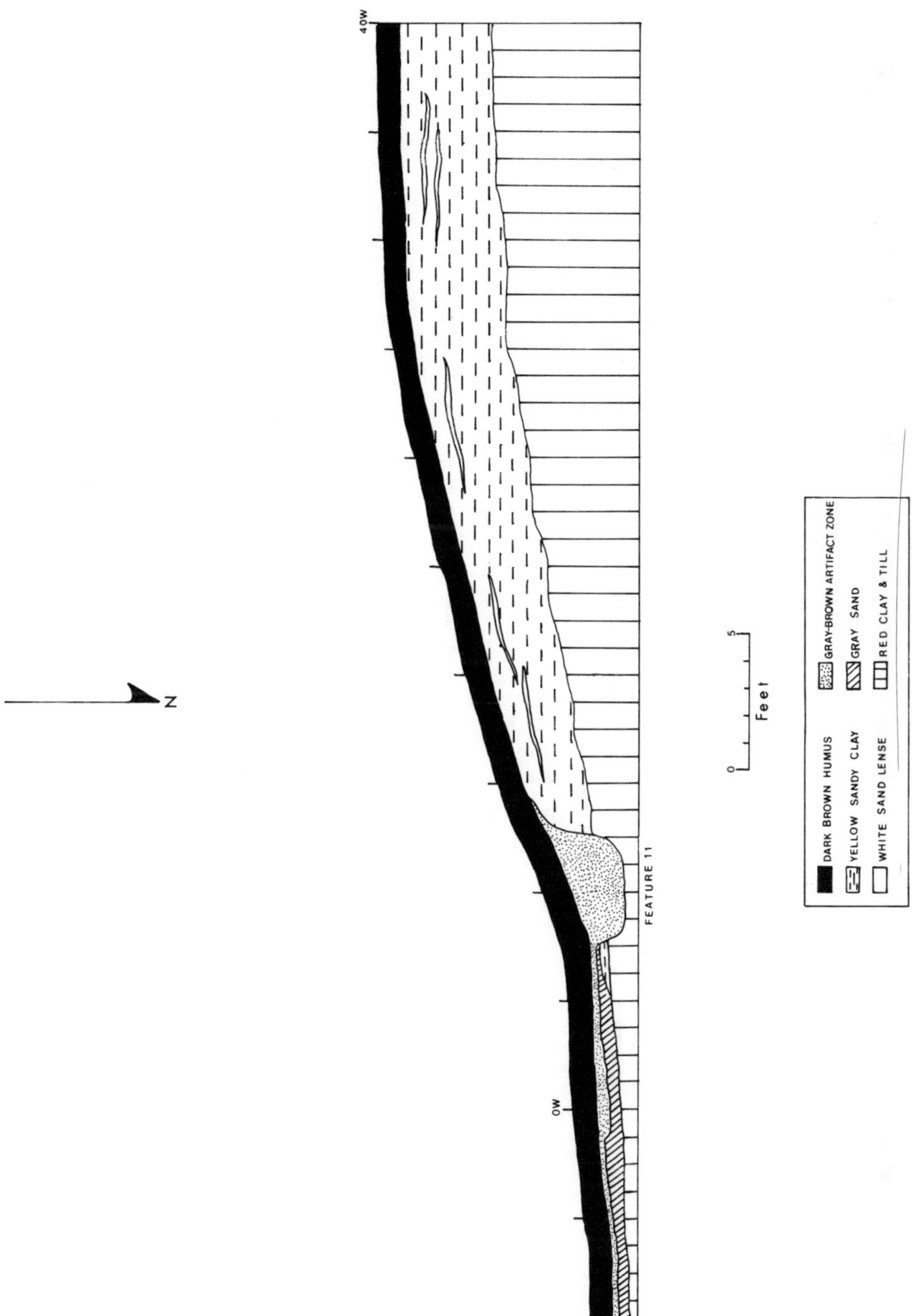

Fig. 5.8 Riverhaven 2 reconstructed profile at 8 North.

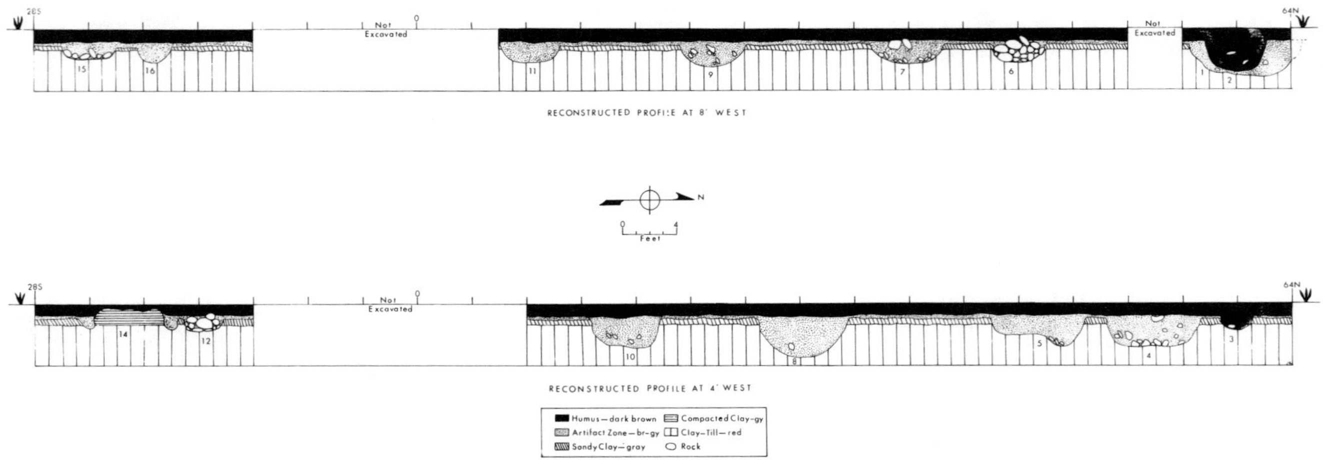

Fig. 5.9 Riverhaven 2 reconstructed profiles at 4 West and 8 West.

TABLE 5.13
FLINT DETRITUS BY AREA INVESTIGATED

Type	Locus 1 #	Locus 1 %	Locus 2 #	Locus 2 %	Locus 3 #	Locus 3 %	Test 1 #	Test 1 %	N #	N %
Utilized Flakes	107	2.2	19	2.1	9	2.8	0	0	135	1.5
Nonutilized Flakes	2,241	28.4	284	31.3	73	22.8	16	26.6	2,614	28.9
Chips	4,962	63.4	547	60.4	231	72.2	41	70.7	5,781	63.8
Cores/Spalls	465	6	56	6.2	7	2.2	1	1.7	529	5.8
N	7,775	100	906	100	320	100	58	100	9,059	100
% of N	7,775	85.8	906	10	320	3.5	58	.7	9,059	100

transition zone soil (Figs. 5.8 and 5.9). This composition of features was observed in 1971.

Areas Investigated

Four areas were investigated at Riverhaven 2. These include Locus 1, Locus 2, Locus 3, and Test 1 (Maps 5.6 and 5.7). Figure 5.10 shows the concentration of artifactual materials in each locus. No artifacts were recovered from Test 1. This graph coincides well with the concentration of excavation in Locus 1 and this ratio seems to fall close to the artifacts versus square feet excavated in each of the other two loci.

Flint detritus proved to be difficult to interpret, or even locate. Although in several units Kochan had saved *all* flint or chert refuse, it was not identified by level. The flint sample from Locus 2 was simply referred to as a flint refuse. It was found that the lack of provenience for substantial portions of the large sample made further distribution analysis fruitless, beyond preparation of a breakdown by locus (Table 5.13). The flint detritus frequency, 85.8% in Locus 1, closely paralleled the artifact distribution, 83% in Locus 1 (Table 5.13).

The typological categories of detritus do, however, show remarkable similarities in each locus and test, especially between nonutilized flakes and chips (Table 5.13). Where present, utilized flakes represented less than 2.8% of the sample (Table 5.13).

Locus 1

This area was centered on the 174 m (562 ft) half-terrace or bench (Map 5.7). Most of Kochan's excavations were conducted in this area north of the datum with 55.8 m^2 (600 sq ft) or 68% of the total excavation located here. The tract encompassed the initial exploratory trench located along the 20 north line (Map 5.6).

Twelve features were identified in this locus and 1558 artifacts or fragments (distributed 315 to features and 1243 to units exclusive of features) were analyzed. The ratio of artifacts to excavated area was 2.6:1. The features thus suggested seem to be primarily large, deep, probable storage pits with a rock heap, manufacture pit, and two hearths (Map 5.7).

The largest number of utilized flakes were derived from this locus, 107 items, constituting 2.2% of the flint detritus. Other flint detritus was collected, but level attribution was so uneven that overall distributions were not possible. A large sample of 465 cores or spalls was used to examine the early stages and by-products of the manufacture process. Kochan mentions in his notes that moderate to large amounts of fire-

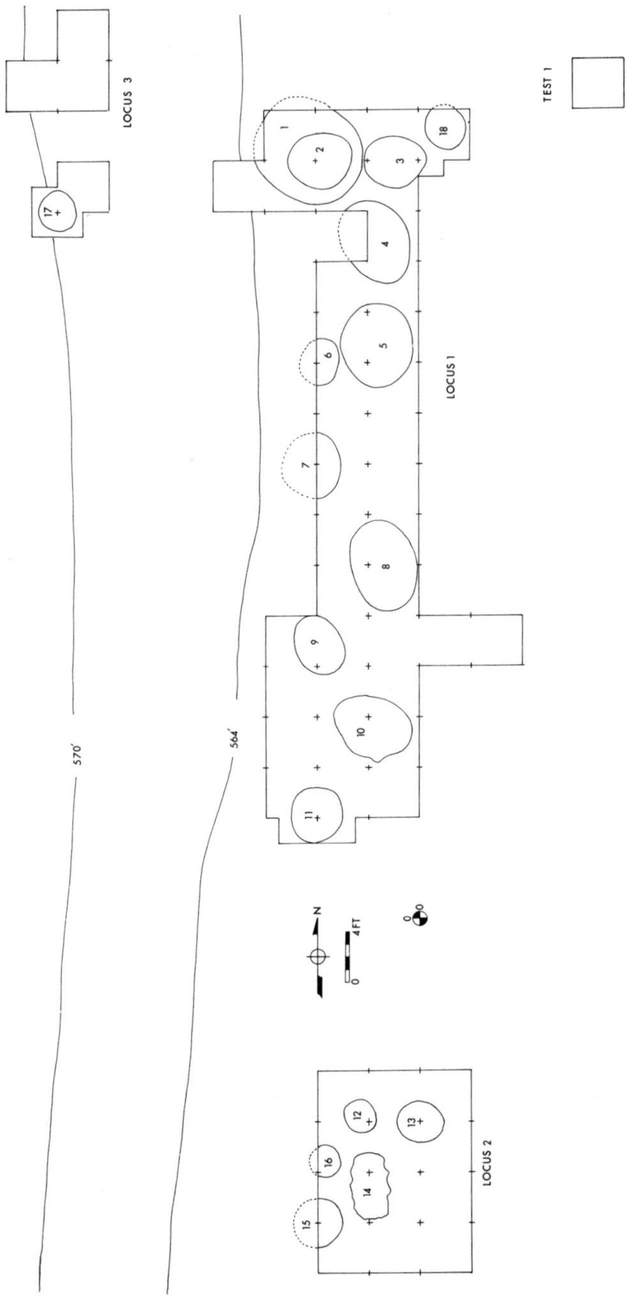

Map 5.7 Riverhaven 2 areas investigated.

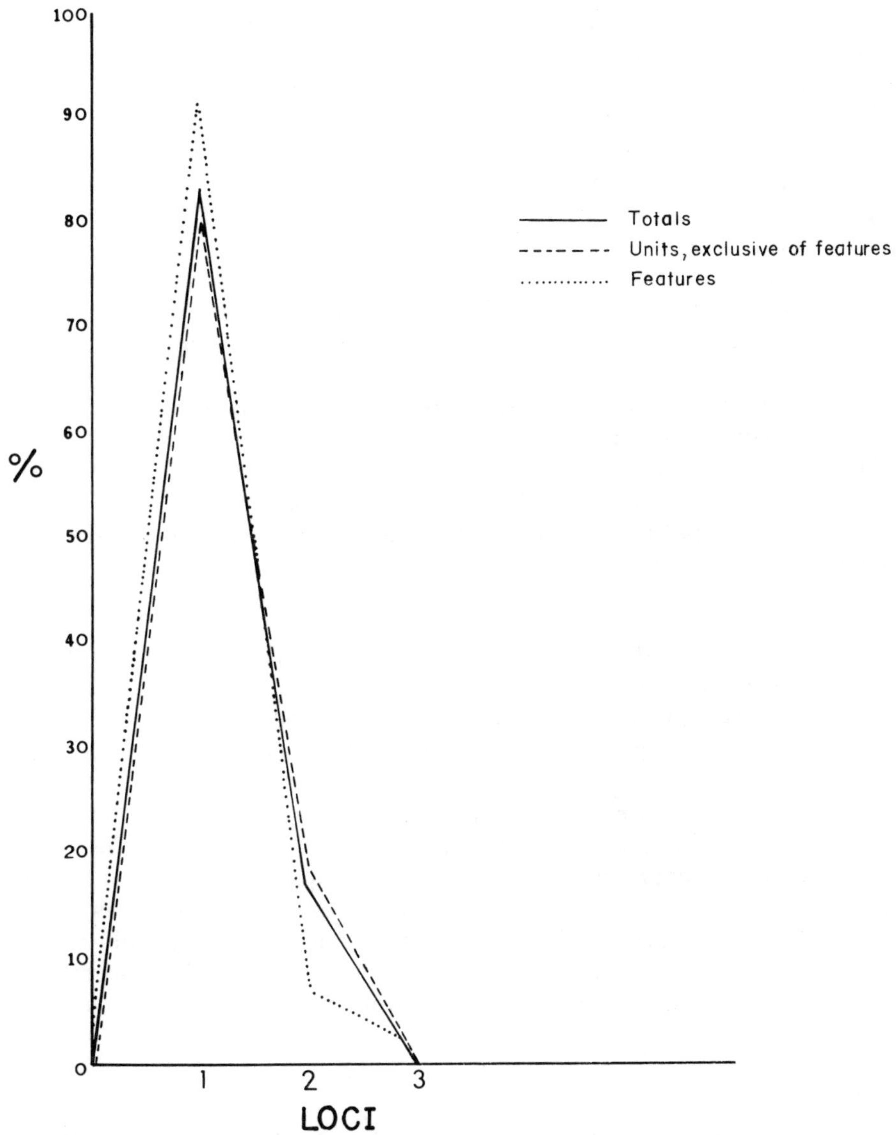

Fig. 5.10 Distribution of artifact percentages of N for units exclusive of features, features, and totals in each locus.

cracked rock did occur in northerly units on the 8 west line. It was in this area that a rock heap, Feature 6, was located during the 1971 profile reexamination.

Locus 2

This locus was essentially a southward extension of Locus 1 occurring south of the datum and 6.1 m (20 ft) from the other tract. This tract was the last cohesive section opened by Kochan and was represented by several plans and profiles which showed features or at least indicated that the floors and walls gave evidence of soil changes. Four small concentrations of artifacts were identified and the field notes indicated that a "heap of clay" constituted a fifth manifestation called by Kochan "pit tailings." The features which were identified on a floor plan made by Kochan clearly organized the data retrieved from notes (Map 5.7). Two features, 16 and 15, incompletely excavated by Kochan, were later seen in wall profile in 1971. Besides the clay heap, a rock heap, a shallow storage pit, and two hearths (Features 15 and 13) were recorded in plan or elsewhere.

The artifact frequency was somewhat less than in Locus 1. Here the ratio of artifacts to excavated portion was 1.6:1 (Table 5.10). The utilized flakes comprised about the same percentage as in Locus 1, 2.1%. The types of flint detritus were also quite similar to Locus 1 (Table 5.13). Kochan notes that the amount of fire-cracked rock excavated here was moderate.

Locus 3

This area tested the side and top of the 183.9 m (570 ft) terrace. Kochan excavated 4.5 m² (48 sq ft) and later, in 1967, Granger and Taggart excavated 2.6 m² (28 sq ft), discovering one feature, Number 17. This was a rock heap, and amount and weight of fire-cracked rock was recorded for the feature.

The artifact distribution was 60-40% both in units exclusive of features and in features, but the sample of 15 was quite small. The ratio of artifacts to excavated area was 2:1. The frequency of utilized flakes was highest here, 2.8%, otherwise, the types of flint detritus were distributed in a manner which duplicated Loci 1 and 2 (Table 5.13). Kochan records that further tests closer to East River Road were not accomplished because of the legal consequences of impinging upon the road right of way.

Test 1

This test square was only one 1.2 x 1.2 m (4 x 4 ft) pit placed close to the edge of the 171.4 m (562 ft) bench. No artifacts or features were discovered. The distribution of the types of flint detritus present was approximately the same as that recorded elsewhere on the site (Table 5.13). Kochan recorded that he believed that this unit portrayed the northern extent of the main occupation area; however, excavations of 1971 showed that cultural materials extended further.

Artifacts

The artifact assemblage at Riverhaven 2 consisted of 1889 items. Many of these are represented in the Kochan Catalog (Kochan n.d.*c*) available at the State University of New York at Buffalo, but as the full catalog of items shows, there were substantial numbers of artifacts which did not have specific provenience (Kochan n.d.*b*:12-27). Correlations between catalogs and excavation notes enabled us to place several items, but generally those artifacts which went unrecognized as such by Kochan were consigned either to the "Miscellaneous Rocks" or "Flint Debris" categories in his catalog. Locations could only be assigned by loci or tests because exact provenience was not recorded.

The distribution of the artifacts in the catalog which could be directly assigned to possible features was:

Rock Heaps	17	(4.9%)
Hearths	31	(9.0%)
Storage/Refuse	268	(77.5%)
Manufacture/Cache	24	(6.9%)
Clay Heap	6	(1.7%)
Total	346	(100.0%)

This distribution is presented graphically in Figure 5.11. There is a large disparity in the frequency of artifacts in the features assumed to have been used for storage or refuse, for artifacts from these features showed no clear concentration of function and appeared to be general refuse. Table 5.14 shows the distribution of artifact types in features. Only in Feature 3 does an emphasis on a particular function occur; in this case it is manufacture products and end products (Table 5.13) (Kochan n.d.*b*:11).

Table 5.15 distributes artifact types by functional category. Here 67% of artifacts can be observed to be for manufacture with 17% for processing, 11% for storage and 5% for procurement. These distributions are shown graphically in Figure 5.12. Within the procurement category, sidenotched Meadowood points are most frequently followed by netsinkers at less than 50% of the frequency of the points. Unifacial and bifacial scrapers dominate the processing category while quaternary blanks do so in the manufacture category. Ceremonial and storage

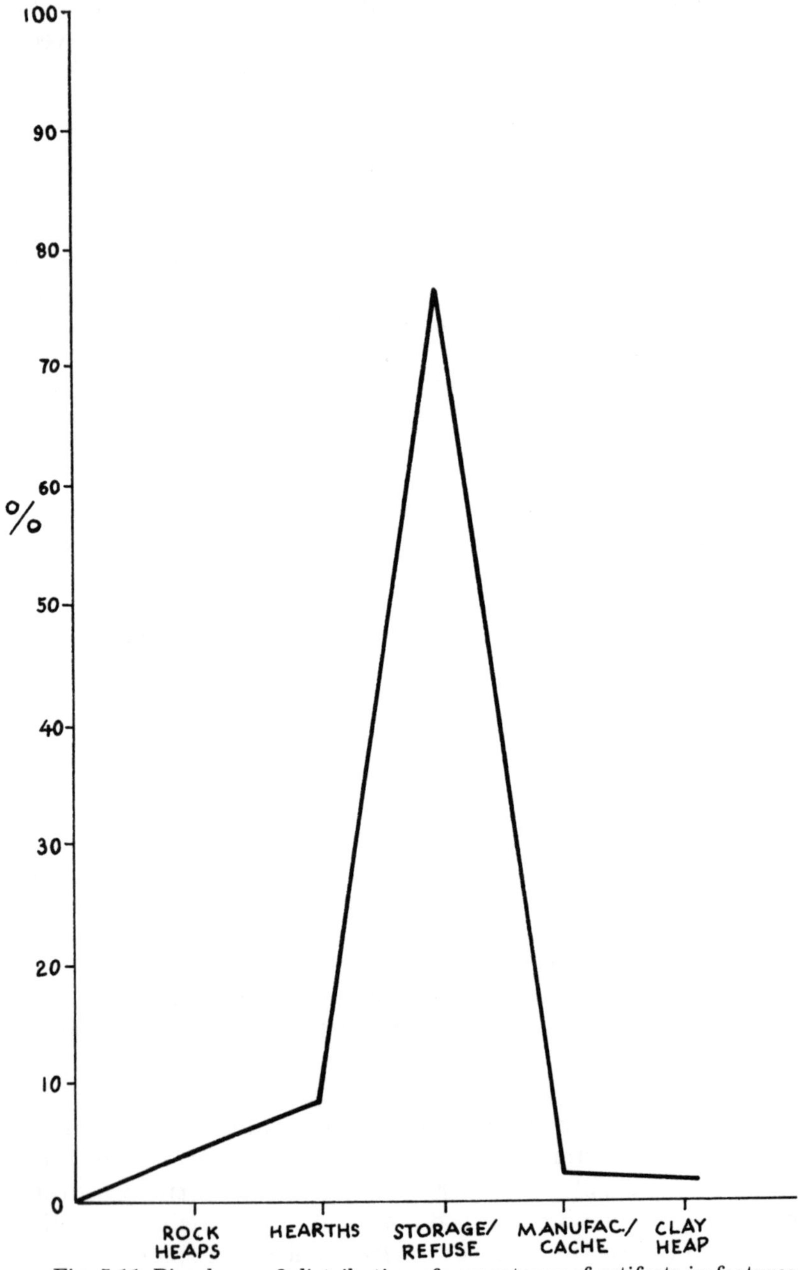

Fig. 5.11 Riverhaven 2 distribution of percentages of artifacts in features.

TABLE 5.14
FEATURE ASSOCIATIONS OF ARTIFACT TYPES, RIVERHAVEN 2

Artifact Types	1	2	3	4	5	6	7	8	9	10	11	12	13	14	15	16	17	18	N
Sidenotched Proj. Pt.	2	1		1				3											7
Lateral Basal Proj. Pt.		1								1									2
Cornernotched Proj. Pt.										1									1
Quat. Blades, Whole	3	1		2	5	2	1	1	1	3	1				1		1	1	23
Quat. Blades, Base	6	1	1	3	7	2		7	1	3	1			2	2		5	2	43
Quat. Blades, Tip	18	2		3	2			4	1	4	1	1		2	1				39
Tert. Blades, Whole	5		3			1		1		2					1				13
Tert. Blades, Base	8			1	3		1	5	1	4					1				24
Tert. Blades, Tip	5	3		1	1	1		1	1	11	3				2				29
Longitudinal Knives															2				2
Bifacial Scrapers	1	2				3	1	2		3									12
Unifacial Scrapers			5		1			1		3			1		1				12
Primary Blanks	1		9																10
Secondary Blanks	1	1	5	1	1			1	2	2									14
Netsinkers								1											1
Grooved Abrading Stone		1			2		1												4
Drills			1		2			5		1					1				10
Celts	1					1													2
Birdstone													1						1
Pottery Rim Sherds		2					1												3
Pottery Body Sherds	17	10		3	18		2	13		5			2	2	1				73
Bone Awls	3	4			3			2											12
Antler Flakers					2		3												5
Other Worked Bones		2			1		1												4
Total	71	31	24	15	48	10	11	47	7	43	6	1	4	6	13	0	6	3	346

TABLE 5.15
DISTRIBUTION OF ARTIFACT TYPES
IN FUNCTIONAL CATEGORIES,
RIVERHAVEN 2

Artifact	N	% of Sub-Total N	% of Total N	
Projectile Points:				
Sidenotched	52	55	3	
Cornernotched	5	5	0.002	
Stemmed	1	1	0.0005	
Indeterminate or absent	4	4	0.002	Procurement
Lateral Basal	6	6	0.003	
Netsinkers	25	27	1	
Birdstone	1	1	0.0005	
Subtotal	94	100	5	
Longitudinal Knives	30	9	2	
Unifacial Scrapers	92	29	5	
Bifacial Scrapers	104	33	6	
Drills	49	15	3	
Mano Abrading Stone	7	2	0.003	Processing
Pitted Anvilstone	8	3	0.004	
Celts	6	2	0.003	
Beveled Adze	1	.001	0.0005	
Bone Awls	20	6	0.01	
Subtotal	317	100	17	
Primary Blanks	46	4	2	
Secondary Blanks	114	9	6	
Tertiary Blades	353	28	19	
Quaternary Blades	705	55	37	Manufacture
Hammerstone	10	1	0.005	
Grooved Abrading Stone	18	1	0.009	
Antler Flakers	9	1	0.004	
Cores	8	1	0.004	
Worked bone and stone	11	1	0.005	
Subtotal	1,274	100	67	
Pipe	1	50	0.0005	
Gorget	1	50	0.0005	Ceremonial
Subtotal	2	100	0.001	
Pottery Rim Sherds	5	2	0.002	
Pottery Body Sherds	197	98	10	Storage
Subtotal	202	100	11	
Total N	1,889	100	100	

artifact types were not sufficiently variable to assess the distributions. Artifacts of manufacture dominate the assemblage out of all proportion and would imply that the site was a workshop. Examination of the curve of other products of manufacture shows an emphasis on the last stages of manufacture due primarily to breakage and a lack of reuse.

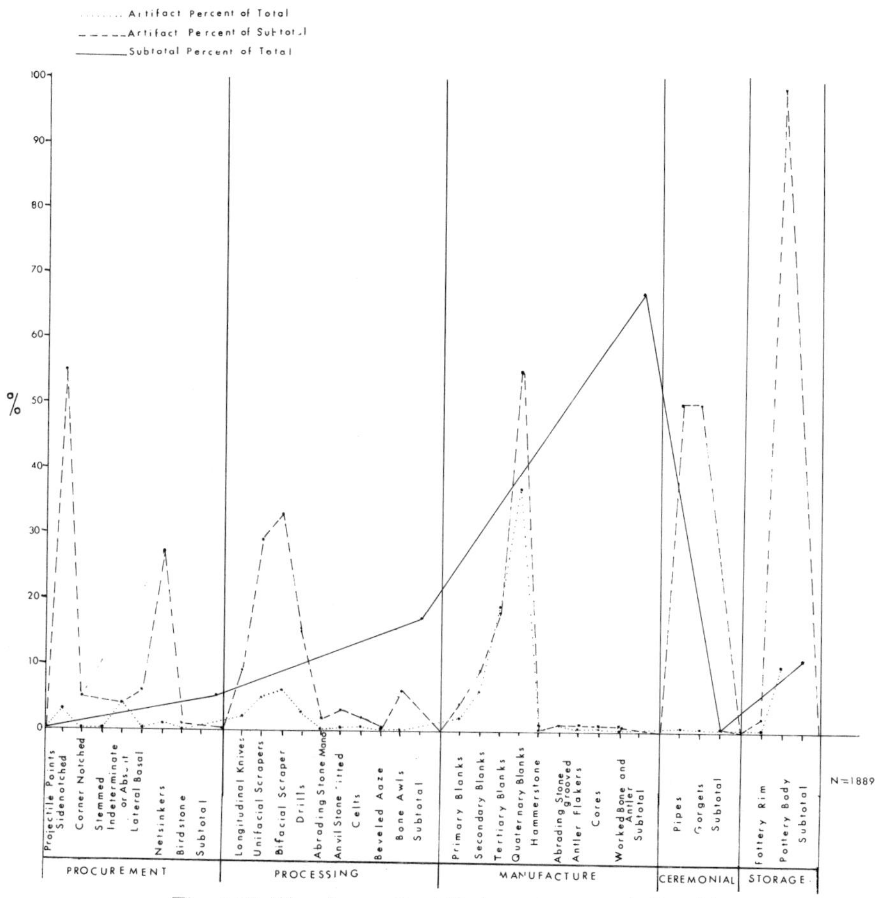

Fig. 5.12 Riverhaven 2 artifact—category relationships.

Artifacts of Procurement

The artifacts of procurement at Riverhaven 2 include the projectile points, netsinkers, and birdstones (Table 5.16). These are functionally related to the procurement of food. The 68 projectile points are 73% of this assemblage of 85 artifacts, which includes an additional birdstone not found in situ. Four projectile points were so fragmented as to be unassignable to type but were recognizable by the presence of a haft element. The projectile points are divided:

Sidenotch	52	(76.4%)
Stemmed	1	(1.4%)
Cornernotch	5	(7.5%)

TABLE 5.16
DISTRIBUTION OF ARTIFACTS OF PROCUREMENT, RIVERHAVEN 2

	No Prov.		Level 1		Level 2		Level 3		Level 4		Subtotal	
	#	%	#	%	#	%	#	%	#	%	#	%
Projectile Points:												
Sidenotched	24	46	Sterile		9	17	11	21	1	2	45	87
Cornernotched	2	40			2	40					4	80
Lateral Basal	4	67									4	67
Stemmed	1	100									1	100
Indeterminate or absent	4	100									4	100
Netsinkers	15	60			9	36					24	96
Birdstone											0	
N	50	53			20	21	11	12	1	1	82	87

	Hearth		Storage		Subtotal		Total	
	#	%	#	%	#	%	#	%
Projectile Points:								
Sidenotched			7	13	7	13	52	100
Cornernotched			1	20	1	20	5	100
Lateral Basal			2	33	2	33	6	100
Stemmed			0		0		1	100
Indeterminate or absent			0		0		4	100
Netsinkers			1	4	1	4	25	100
Birdstone	1	100			1	100	1	100
N	1	1	11	12	12	13	94	100

Corner Removed	6	(8.9%)
Indeterminate	4	(5.8%)
Total	68	(100.0%)

Twenty-five netsinkers form 26% of the procurement artifacts and birdstones, 1%.

The majority of the feature-associated artifacts of this group appear in the suggested storage pits, 11 or 92% (Table 5.16). Level-associated artifacts cluster in Level 2, 20 or 62.5%.

Projectile Points, Sidenotched (Kochan n.d.*b*:12; Ritchie 1971:Pl. 64, nos. 12-16, Ritchie 1961:Pl. 17) (Table 5.16; App. A, Table A.1*a* and A.1*b*, Pls. 15, 16, 17*a-d*). A sample of 52 Meadowood projectile points was recovered. This sample showed a high degree of variation in size and shape. Although criteria by which to separate the groups were difficult to make, some rough criteria were established. The groups are:

A.	"Typical" Broad, Sub-convex "Rocker" Base (Ritchie 1961:Pl. 17, nos. 3-8, 13; Ritchie 1969:Pl. 64, nos. 13, 16)	21	(40.4%)
B.	Typical, Broad, Convex Base (Ritchie 1961:Pl. 17, no. 9)	10	(19.2%)
C.	Narrow, Sidenotched 10 mm above Base (ibid.: Pl. 17, no. 11; Ritchie 1969:Pl. 64, no. 12)	5	(9.6%)
D.	Short Blade Element, Convex Base (Ritchie 1961:Pl. 17, no. 2; Ritchie 1969:Pl. 64, no. 14)	10	(19.2%)
E.	Reworked, Blade Element Lateral Edges Sub-concave (Ritchie 1969:Pl. 64, no. 15)	6	(11.5%)
	Total	52	(99.9%)

The attributes, morphological and metrical, are presented in Table A.1*b*, and compared with other sites. Broadness was defined at 50% of the length (see Chapter 4, Projectile Points: Sidenotched). In all cases the attribute of thickness clustered at a mean of 5 mm. Fragmentation was seen on 34 or 65.4% of the sample.

The distribution of these projectile points did not indicate vertical or horizontal separation of any of the categories noted above. Often, however, members of at least three subgroups were associated. Almost 50% or 24 of the projectile points of this group were given no vertical provenience in Locus 1. All seven feature-associated points were located in the probable storage features, 1, 2, 4, and 8, in this tract and ten were located in the occupation zone, Levels 2-4. In Locus 2, eleven were noted in Levels 2-3.

Projectile Point, Stemmed (Kochan n.d.*b*:12; Ritchie 1961:Pl.14) (Table 5.16; Pl. 17*i-o*; App. A, Tables A.2*a*, A.2*b*). A single point of this type was found at Riverhaven 2 and it was given no vertical location in Locus 1. In almost all respects it coincides with the Lamoka B—Dustin projectile point illustrated by Ritchie (1971: Pl. 17, no. 22). The length was 63 mm, width 19 mm, and thickness 7 mm. Stem width was 10 mm.

Projectile Points, Cornernotched (Table 5.16; App. A, Tables A.3*a*, A.3*b*; Pl. 17*h*). Five cornernotched projectile points were found in the Riverhaven 2 assemblage. These points appear to cluster within the defined range of what is referred to in Michigan as the "Feheeley" projectile point type (Fitting 1970:Fig. 27). Bases are generally convex to sub-convex with deep notches forming an expanded stem having a "dovetail" appearance. The distal point of juncture with a moderately wide blade is a right angle. These points had a mean length of 34 mm, mean width of 18 mm, and mean thickness of 7 mm.

Two points were found in the exploratory trench of Locus 1 and one in the occupation zone. In Tract 2 another was found in this same zone. One point was found at the very bottom of a storage feature (Table 5.16).

For many years this type point has been lumped with other cornernotched types, more specifically the Brewerton cornernotched type; however, evidence is increasing that it forms a specific type associated with the Terminal Archaic (ibid.). Unfortunately the sample in the Riverhaven assemblage is neither large enough nor in such a condition, as all points are fragmented, to permit definition of this group of points as a type.

Projectile Points, Corner-Removed (Lateral-Basal) (Kochan n.d.*b*:13-14; Ritchie 1951) (Table 5.16; Pl. 17*e-o*). This category at Riverhaven 2 contained six points of various origin and type. The corner-removed shape implies a form which is stemmed with the basal edge symmetry defining the stem. A perfect example of this type is a Christmas Tree shape. This form of juncture defines two possible Genesee points (Ritchie 1961:Pl. 10, no. 3), both crudely made on Onondaga chert and fragmented. One has a blade unmodified by tertiary flaking. No dimensions were noted beyond the width, mean 27 mm, and stem width, mean 15 mm. Both of these fragments were found in the deep storage pits. All four other points of this category had no vertical provenience on the site and were located in the exploratory trench or elsewhere in Locus 1.

The other types represented in this grouping are two points which conform to the Brewerton Eared Notch type (ibid.:Pl. 5, no. 4), one of Onondaga chert, the other of a yellow tinted chalcedony (Kochan n.d.*b*:13). Kochan describes a thick stemmed point formed on black Heldeberg chert as a Bare Island point. The author, however, prefers an untyped assignment because of the material. It does, however, conform well to the shape and thickness characteristics of the Bare Island (Ritchie 1971:14-15). The last of the points was a fragment of a small thick Brewerton Sidenotched variety (ibid.:Pl. 7, no. 8). This fragment did show that the point was formed on a side-struck flake.

Netsinkers (Kochan n.d.*b*:19) (Table 5.16; App. A, Tables A.16*a*, A.16*b*; Pl. 31). Twenty-five large sidenotched netsinkers were recovered from the site. Twenty-two were on large flat pebbles, six of which had been edge modified by percussion flaking with two also showing crude bifacial flaking (ibid.). Nineteen, 76%, cluster within the weight range of 200-600 g, well above that observed at Sinking Ponds (see Chapter 4, Netsinkers). This heavier netsinker weight suggests some exploitation of areas where the Niagara River's swift current would disturb nets held by smaller weights. Length ranged between 50 and 175 mm, width between 50 and 125 mm and thickness between 13 and 35 mm, except for one, which was a rounded pebble of 49 mm thickness.

Fifteen of the netsinkers had no exact provenience but do appear to have clustered in the exploratory trench of Locus 1. Three were found in the occupation level, Level 2, of Locus 2; an additional nine are from the same level in Locus 1, where one was also associated with a possible storage feature.

Birdstone (Table 5.16; Pl. 32*a-b*). A single birdstone fragment was found in situ at Riverhaven 2 in Feature 13, a hearth. This fragment was 62 mm long, 23 mm wide at the base, 28 mm high, and the head was missing. The head appeared to have been broken off by firing since the scar of detachment appeared to be fire marked. Two angled holes of 2 mm bore, biconically drilled, slope from the front and rear to the base at angles of 45 degrees. The material of manufacture appeared to be a banded slate foreign to the immediate area which was of a medium dark-greenish hue. There was no upstanding tail, rather a step was indented 2 mm above the base and the rear swept up to a height level with the medial dorsal ridge. Some battering had taken place at the tail. This precise type of body shape has not been illustrated elsewhere for Meadowood phase, although fragmentation may have taken place before the dorsal ridge was further modified (Ritchie 1969:Pl. 69, no. 6).

Another birdstone fragment was discovered in the Mark Reed Collection at the Buffalo Museum of Science. Since Reed had located the find precisely on the 173.9 m (570 ft) terrace at Riverhaven 2, we will include this artifact. The fragment was of a popeyed detached head with a taper to the beak which was missing. The head was 46 mm long, 22 mm wide at the neck, and 10 mm thick, also at the neck. Circular eyes 15 mm in diameter projected approximately 5 mm to each side. The scar of detachment of the head was 40 degrees to the body but the beak was broken at right angles to the sloping forehead. This form was of a light green banded slate also not seen in the immediate area. Although Reed remarked in his notes that this fragment had been associated with a "fireplace" this could not be determined positively.

Artifacts of Processing (Table 5.17)

The artifacts grouped under processing are a mixed tool kit. The bone tools, awls, may have been used to process faunal materials such as hides or fiber products. These are 6% of the sample.

The ground stone tools, celts or adzes, mano-type abrading stones and anvilstones may be indicative of processing floral materials such as wood, seeds and nuts. These represent 7% of the processing artifacts. The greatest percentage of the tools used in processing materials are chert tools such as longitudinal knives, unifacial and bifacial scrapers, and drills. These are 87% of the processing assemblage (Table 5.17).

In the features the majority of processing tools occur in the storage features as discards. In fact, the random distribution of most of the tools throughout the occupation zone indicates high consumption of such implements.

Longitudinal Knife-scrapers (Kochan n.d.*b*:15) (Table 5.17; App. A, Tables A.10*a*, A.10*b*; Pl. 22). This category of tool is represented by 30 forms at Riverhaven 2. The size of the tool ranges from the large "ovate" knife illustrated by Ritchie (1969:Pl. 64, no. 1; Kochan n.d.*b*:15) to smaller forms well below the mean length of the tertiary blank. Most of the knife-scrapers, 90% or 27, appear to have been intensively used, since tertiary wear chipping is evident on lateral edges of what appears to be a stage intermediate between the secondary and tertiary blank (Fig. 1.2). All of the forms illustrate at least one quite excurvate lateral edge. This edge displays the greatest amount of wear. On 23 of the forms, or 77%, this edge was quite dull, leading to the speculation that these were discards. Attributes of this tool type are presented in Table A.10*b*, Appendix A.

The distribution of the knife-scraper was not instructive, due to a lack of vertical provenience for 20. Horizontally, the artifact is apportioned with 21 in Locus 1, four in the occupation levels, and seven in Locus 2, also with four in the same levels. Two occur in the possible

TABLE 5.17
DISTRIBUTION OF ARTIFACTS OF PROCESSING, RIVERHAVEN 2

Artifacts	No Prov. #	No Prov. %	Level 1 #	Level 1 %	Level 2 #	Level 2 %	Level 3 #	Level 3 %	Level 4 #	Level 4 %	Subtotal #	Subtotal %		
Longitudinal Knives	20	67	Sterile		6	21	2	7			28	93		
Unifacial Scrapers	47	51			23	29	10	11			80	86		
Bifacial Scrapers	70	67			15	16	7	7			92	88		
Drills	17	35			15	38	7	14			39	80		
Mano Abrading Stone	2	29			3	43	2	29			7	100		
Beveled Adze											1	100		
Anvilstone	6	75			2	25					8	100		
Celts	4	67									4	67		
Bone Awls	4	20					3	15	1	5	8	40		
N	170	54			65	24	31	10	1	0.003	267	84		
	Rock Heaps #	**Rock Heaps %**	**Hearth #**	**Hearth %**	**Mfg./Cache #**	**Mfg./Cache %**	**Storage/ Refuse #**	**Storage/ Refuse %**	**Clay Heap #**	**Clay Heap %**	**Subtotal #**	**Subtotal %**	**Total #**	**Total %**
Longitudinal Knives			2	7							2	7	30	100
Unifacial Scrapers			2	2	5	5	5	5			12	13	92	100
Bifacial Scrapers	3	3	1	1			8	8			12	12	104	100
Drills			1	2	1	2	8	16			10	20	49	100
Mano Abrading Stone											0	0	7	100
Beveled Adze											0	0	1	100
Anvilstone											0	0	8	100
Celts	1	17					1	17			2	33	6	100
Bone Awls							12	60			12	60	20	100
N	4	1	6	2	6	2	34	11	0	0	50	16	315	100

hearth, Feature 15, and show evidence of fire pocking. An additional three show firing as well.

Bifacial Scrapers (Kochan n.d.*b*:16) (Tables 5.17, 5.18; App. A, Tables A.12*a*, A.12*b*; Pls. 23, 24, 25). The bifacial scraper sample at Riverhaven 2 of 104 was quite close to the sample of 92 unifacial scrapers. Two broad categories, those formed on distal tips and those formed on proximal bases, show an almost even distribution, 47:57 or 45% to 55%. Other categories are based upon working edge placement. These are shown in Table 5.18, where they have been defined after Anta White (1963:5-18). A chi-square test of the occurrence of end scrapers as opposed to all other types, yielded a probability of .001 that such a distribution did not occur by chance. Thus, although fragments were selected almost equally, it was for specialized functions. Distal portions formed the characteristic Meadowood triangular end scraper (Ritchie 1969:Pl. 60, no. 1; Ritchie 1955:Pls. 23, no. 1, 7, 8), while proximal portions formed other scrapers, especially those having lateral edges such as side and circumferential scrapers.

TABLE 5.18
BIFACIAL SCRAPERS, RIVERHAVEN 2

	Distal		Proximal		N	
Variety	#	%	#	%	#	%
End Scrapers (Apex, Transverse)	44	93.6	7	12.3	51	49.1
Side Scrapers (Lateral)	0		30	52.6	30	28.8
Circumferential	2	4.3	16	28.1	18	17.3
Spokeshaves (Concave)	1	2.1	4	7	5	4.3
N	47	100	57	100	104	100
% ΣN	45.2		54.8			

Four scrapers of this bifacial type show ventral modification on the scraping edge. On two, this appears to have been accidentally caused during utilization which created step fracture on the cutting edge. Steep dorsal flaking above characterized all of the end scrapers while dorsal flaking of less than 45 degrees was displayed on the rest of the sample.

Seventy scrapers had no vertical provenience. All these were found in Locus 1. There were eight scrapers, two end and six side, in the storage features 1, 2, 8, and 10. One large fire-marked circumferential scraper was located in a probable hearth and three end scrapers were disclosed in a rock heap, two fire pocked. Ten of the remaining scrapers occurred randomly in the occupation zone or Locus 1, and 12 occurred in Locus 2 (Table 5.17).

Unifacial Scrapers (Kochan n.d.*b*:16) (Table 5.17; App. A, Tables A.11*a*, A.11*b*; Pl. 26). Ninety-two unifacial scrapers were recovered from Riverhaven 2. These artifacts were quite variable in shape and size but were distributed in the following varieties by edge utilization location (White 1963:5-18):

End Scrapers (apex or transverse)	45	(49.0%)
Side Scrapers (unilateral or bilateral)	25	(27.1%)
Circumferential	18	(19.5%)
Spokeshave (concave)	4	(4.3%)

The form of flaking was significant in the 27 or 29.3% which showed flat dorsal flaking less than 45 degrees on the utilization edge, 62 or 67.4% showed steep dorsal flaking, 45 to 90 degrees, and only three side scrapers, 3.3%, showed ventral flaking. Dorsal flaking was preferred in 96.7% of the sample. Thirty-four scrapers (16 end, 8 side, 6 circumferential and all 4 spokeshaves) display graving spurs, perhaps reflecting a burgeoning bone industry. However, no tool type was specifically classified as a graver.

The distribution of the unifacial scrapers is fortuitous throughout the excavated portions, except in features. Two large end scrapers occurred in probable hearths, Features 13 and 15, while five side scrapers occurred in Feature 3. An additional five side scrapers occurred in suggested storage features 5, 8, and 10. The end scrapers were the most variably dispersed of all; 36 had no vertical provenience in Locus 1 and an additional four were found within the living zone. Side scrapers in this area showed a distribution of five in Levels 2-3 and three had no vertical location. Four spokeshaves and 18 circumferential scrapers were located in this area's occupation zone. The rest of the scrapers were distributed in the occupation zone, Level 2-3 or Locus 2, eight with no vertical location.

The sample of 135 utilized flakes analyzed for Riverhaven 2 was quite small and may reflect sampling error. The largest cluster of such flakes was 107 in Locus 1, falling off significantly to 19 in Locus 2, and nine in Locus 3.

These flakes all displayed wear flaking spaced indiscriminately on the lateral edges of an otherwise unmodified flake. As at Sinking Ponds, two basic forms of chip removal demonstrated wear, both dorsal, with flakes removed from the external flake surface and ventral, with flakes removed from the interior surface.

This distribution was:

	Dorsal	Ventral
Locus 1 (107)	86 (80.4%)	21 (19.6%)
Locus 2 (19)	16 (84.2%)	3 (15.8%)
Locus 3 (9)	9 (100%)	0 (0%)
Total (135)	111 (82.2%)	24 (17.8%)

The low percentage of ventral wear, 17.8%, compared with that evidenced by the more refined unifacial scrapers, 3.3%, suggests that the processing of fish may not have been a significant activity on the site. We have remarked above (see Chapter 4, Unifacial Scrapers) on the possible association of ventral flaking on unifaces with fish scale removal (Fitting 1969:367).

Drills (Kochan n.d.*b*:16-17; Ritchie 1969:Pl. 64, nos. 2-6) (Table 5.17; App. A, Tables A.13*a*, A.13*b*; Pl. 27). The Riverhaven 2 drills exhibit three general categories (Ritchie 1969:Pl. 64, nos. 2-6). These are identified by basal form and are:

Expanded (ibid.:2, 3)	31	(64%)
T (ibid.:4)	4	(8%
Hafted (ibid.:5, 6)	7	(14%)
Indeterminate Fragments	7	(14%)
Total	49	(100%)

The expanded base forms show 18 convex and 13 straight bases and range in length from 28-67 mm and in width from 9-31 mm. Measurable shank length covaried with maximum width. This form was distributed randomly with no provenience within Locus 1 on five drills, three in the exploratory trench, and 13 in the occupation level. One, a large, crudely worked form, was located in a manufacture related pit and eight were in the Locus 2 occupation zone. One was in the living zone in Locus 3.

The T form appears to be reworked from a quaternary blank, as the mean base height of 4 mm and mean maximum width 28 mm fall well within the median range of such blanks. The shanks on all but one of these forms were close to 30 mm in length. The four T forms were not randomly distributed. All occurred in storage features 5, 8, and 10. The hafted forms were obviously reworked projectile points of the sidenotched type. The bases, sidenotches and shank areas all exhibited alteration. All T drills showed extensive wear. The maximum length was close to the low end of the range for such projectile points, ca 30 mm, at 34 to 36 mm. In Locus 1 these drills were distributed in one feature, four in a refuse filled storage pit, and in Locus 2, two were found in the occupation zone and one in a hearth.

Celts (Adzes) and Beveled Adze (Kochan n.d.*b*:21) (Table 5.17; Pl. 28). Six celts were obtained during excavations on the site. However, four have no provenience, having been discovered among fragments of fired rock or elsewhere but unrecorded. These four were fragmentary bases, generally of a plano-convex form with basal widths clustering around 35 mm and thicknesses ranging from 25-30 mm. Another fragment of a blunt cutting edged plano-convex form was found associated with a rock heap. This light gray granite form was 55 mm wide on the cutting edge and 27 mm thick. The only complete celt or adze was a dark gray banded felsite one, which had been chipped along one lateral edge. It was found associated with general refuse fill in the largest basin pit, and this flat, ovoid, celt was 75 mm long, 45 mm wide and 15 mm thick.

A single fragment of a beveled adze of light tan granitic rock was discovered in situ in Level 2. The poll end of the adze was 31 mm wide with each of the bevel surfaces running to the rounded butt, approximately 10 mm wide. Its thickness was 27 mm. This type of adze is generally considered to be a diagnostic trait for Lamoka phase, but no other such connection to Lamoka was established at Riverhaven 2 with the possible exception of the stemmed point mentioned above (Ritchie 1969:Pl. 11, nos. 49, 50).

Anvil or Pitted Stones (Kochan n.d.*b*:21) (Table 5.17; App. A, Tables A.17*a*, A.17*b*; Pl. 30*a-b*). The distribution in the site of the eight pebbles with one or more depressions pecked into their surfaces was not clear, since Kochan records only one with provenience and classifies another as a miscellaneous stone. One of these was from Locus 1 and the other from Locus 2. Three from the exploratory trench are only briefly noted (Kochan, n.d.*c*) and are disregarded elsewhere; an additional three were wholly uncatalogued.

Four, or 50%, show depressions on both faces while the rest are pitted on only one side. All eight conform to Ritchie's definition of anvilstones (1929:8-9). Size and shape were variable but none exceeded 89 mm in length or 70 mm in width. All appear to have been formed on casually acquired pebbles. Two show wear in the pit depression, suggesting some form of grinding had occurred. Functionally, these stones appear to have depressions deliberately made so they could serve as small mortars, perhaps for grinding small seeds, nuts, or pigments.

Abrading Stone–Mano (Table 5.17; App. A, Tables A.18*a*, A.18*b*). Seven abrading tools, hand size pebbles with abrasion striations, occurred at Riverhaven 2. Five, three from Locus 1 and two from Locus 2, were recovered from the occupation levels. An additional two were uncatalogued but assigned to Locus 2. The pebble size and shape were variable.

Wear striations on the pebbles are longitudinal on two pebbles and perpendicular to the long axis on five. Four were of sandstone and three of an igneous granitic composition.

Bone Awls (Kochan n.d.*b*:24) (Table 5.17; Pl. 33*a*, *d-e*, *g-i*, *m-l*). Twenty bone or antler awls were discovered at Riverhaven 2 (Ritchie 1969:Pl. 65, nos. 4-6). All but one, a catfish *(Ictalurus)* spine, were fragmented. The distribution of animal bone or antler used was:

TABLE 5.19
DISTRIBUTION OF ARTIFACTS OF MANUFACTURE, RIVERHAVEN 2

	No Prov.		Level 1		Level 2		Level 3		Level 4		Subtotal	
	#	%	#	%	#	%	#	%	#	%	#	%
Primary Blanks	16	35	Sterile		15	33	5	11			36	78
Secondary Blanks	63	53			27	24	10	9			100	88
Tertiary Blades	184	52			77	22	26	7			387	81
Quaternary Blades	383	54			156	22	58	8	3	.004	600	85
Hammerstone	7	70			3	3					10	100
Grooved Abrading Stone	7	39			1	6	6	33			14	78
Antler Flakers					1	11	3	33			4	44
Cores	3	38			5	63					8	100
Worked Bone	3	27			1	9	2	18	1	9.000	7	64
N =	666	53			286	23	110	9	4	.008	1166	84

	Rock Heap		Hearth		Mfg/ Cache		Storage/ Ref.		Clay Heap		Subtotal		Total	
	#	%	#	%	#	%	#	%	#	%	#	%	#	%
Primary Blanks					9	20.000	1	2			18	22	46	100
Secondary Blanks					5	4.000	9	8			14	12	114	100
Tertiary Blades	2	1	5	1	3	1.000	56	16			16	19	303	100
Quaternary Blades	11	2	8	1	1	.001	81	11	4	.003	105	15	705	100
Hammerstone											0	0	10	100
Grooved Abrading Stone			1	6			3	17			4	22	18	100
Antler Flakers			3	33			2	22			5	56	9	100
Cores											0	0	8	100
Worked Bone			1	9			3	27			4	36	11	100
N =	13	1	18	1	18	1.000	155	12	4	.003	208	16	1284	100

Fish spine	1	(5%)
Bird long bone	2	(10%)
Mammal ulna	2	(10%)
Mammal antler	5	(25%)
Mammal long bone	10	(50%)
Total	20	(100%)

The range of awl or needle fragments was:

Tips	5	(25%)
Basal portion	6	(30%)
Medial portion	9	(45%)
Total	20	(100%)

Length, width and other measurements were quite variable. The distribution of bone awls was essentially nonrandom with 12 or 60% of the sample being found in the large basin-shaped pits of Locus 1, while four were discovered in the occupation level of that area. Four additional items had no horizontal provenience (Table 5.17).

Artifacts of Manufacture (Table 5.19; Pls. 18, 19, 20, 21)

Artifacts of manufacture are those artifacts involved with the production of tools at Riverhaven 2. All stages of the development of chert tools as shown in Figure 1.2 are represented, except for stage 1A. The favored raw material was Onondaga chert. In more than 50% of the sample there was no indurated limestone matrix inclusion. Stage 1A, the flint pebble, was not represented at Riverhaven 2 but 1B, the tabular core, appears. It seems that raw material was transported to the site in this form and later modified through the various steps to finish tools.

Fracture during the process of manufacture was high (Table 5.20). The 182 whole forms contrasted with 1036 fragments showed the rate of fracture to be 85%. Thus a high breakage rate characterizes the formation of the extremely thin Meadowood blade and further products even with the use of a good quality chert.

Selection of fragments for modification into scrapers or other tools appears to have been uniformly concentrated on both basal and tip fragments. The virtual absence of medial portions of blanks suggests that the longer or wider forms of distal or proximal fragments were so selected.

This category also includes the hammerstone which was not well represented, suggesting the possible use of an alternative soft hammer percussive technique.

Grooved abrading stones, characteristic of bone working, are also described in this section (Ritchie 1969:193), as are the samples of antler flakers and worked bone. The distribution of manufacture was basically random over the excavated portions of the site except for a cluster of stage products in Feature 3, assigned as a manufacture/cache pit. Unfortunately the sample of flint detritus from this feature could not be isolated.

The primary products of chert tool manufacture, cores, primary and secondary blanks, and the primary products of bone tool manufacture, the worked bone, together equal 14.1% of the tools of manufacture. The secondary products of chert tool manufacture, the tertiary and quaternary blanks, equal 83%, but tools of production, hammerstones, antler flakers and grooved abrading stones, represent 2.9% of the manufacture assemblage.

Cores–Tabular (Table 5.19). The tabular core block appears to be the basic raw material from which the flint tools at Riverhaven 2 were made. These blocks were found wholly to the exclusion of flint pebbles of sufficient size to form tools (Chapter 4). Figure 1.2 illustrates to scale a tabular core from Riverhaven 2. These cores may have been quarried from local chert sources and shaped to size. This size range is between 95 and 138 mm long, 83 to 90 mm wide, and 29 to 51 mm in thickness. Long longitudinal flakes have been detached to shape the core.

Eight cores were found but they were not regarded as tools (Kochan n.d.*b*). Provenience in Locus 1 and occupation level was recorded for three of them. Two of these three were located over Feature 3, in which a cache of manufacture stage products was located. Three more found in this locus are unrecorded by level. In Locus 2, two were found in situ.

Primary Blanks (Table 5.17; App. A, Tables A.14*a*, A.14*b*; Pl. 18). There were 46 primary blanks of Onondaga chert represented in the Riverhaven 2 sample (Fig. 1.2). One was recognized from a possible storage pit, Feature 1, and nine were found associated in a cache in Feature 3. Eleven were uncatalogued by level in Locus 1 and five more were found in the exploratory trench. However, five were found in Level 3, in the living zone. In Locus 2, 14 were disclosed in Level 2, in the occupation zone, and one was found in this same level in Locus 3.

One form of this blank is pictured in Figure 1.2 and is a representative type of crudely worked percussion flaked blank. Scars of detachment are deep and a remnant striking platform is usually at the base or proximal end. Wide variation in shape is characteristic but length clusters near 70 mm and width between 38 and 49 mm. Thickness ranges between 16 and 27 mm (App. A, Table A.14*b*). Eighty-nine percent of these blanks were fragmented discards (Table 5.19), but in Feature 3 an almost even distribution, four whole to five fragmented, was observed. On the site, the manufacture activity was apparently carried through to virtual completion, eliminating almost all whole primary blanks.

Secondary Blanks (Table 5.19; App. A, Tables A.15*a*, A.15*b*; Pl. 19). The sample of 114 secondary blanks was distributed with 74 in Locus 1, 63 with no vertical provenience, and 11 in the occupation levels. In these levels of Locus 2, 26 were recorded. Fourteen were feature associated, with nine in the large deep features, seven of which showed evidence of firing. Five were located in Feature 3, associated with primary and tertiary blanks and unretouched core spalls. Seventy-four or 65% of the blanks were fragmented (Table 5.20), but in Feature 3, all were whole. The figure 65% indicates that although these blanks were quite prevalent as discards, many unmodified forms also remained, awaiting further work. It is the lowest such fragmentation figure and is 18% below the nearest percentage, 83% fragmentation for tertiary blanks. This phenomenon cannot be readily explained except that at this stage a decision may have been made regarding the size required to continue the manufacture process. At least 27 or 24% of these blanks were more than 10 mm below the mean length. A further suggestion is that whole secondary blanks were being retained for modification into longitudinal knife-scrapers (Fig. 1.2). The collection of five of these blanks cached with 9 whole primaries and three whole tertiaries exhibits a clear manufacture sequence. One of these is illustrated in Figure 1.2.

The attributes of these blanks are presented in Table A.15*b*, Appendix A. Fifty-seven percent were excurvate-ovate in shape with a mean length of 62 mm and mean width of 39 mm. Mean thickness was 18 mm. Of those 99 forms with a proximal portion remaining, 61-60% had a portion of the striking platform remaining. The secondary blank shows some edge retouch by soft hammer percussion to a more refined and symmetrical shape. In this blank some of the pronounced ridges formed by scars on the primary blank are removed by low angle flake removal.

Tertiary Blanks (Kochan n.d.*b*:13-15) (Table 5.20; App. A, Tables A.7*a*, A.7*b*, A.8*a*, A.8*b*, A.9*a*, A.9*b*; Pl. 20). The stage of manufacture represented by the tertiary blank was plentiful at Riverhaven 2, with 353 items recorded. Attributes for these blanks are recorded in Tables A.7*b*, A.8*b*, and A.9*b*, Appendix A. In these forms the blank is further resolved by shaping with primary and secondary pressure flaking (Fig. 1.2). Generally the blank is one-fifth to one-third larger than the next succeeding stage and one-quarter smaller than the previous stage.

TABLE 5.20
DISTRIBUTION OF BLANKS AND FRAGMENTS AT RIVERHAVEN 2

Blanks		Rock Heaps #	Hearths #	Storage #	Mfg./ Cache #	Clay Heap #	Non-Feature Units #	N #	N %	%N %
Primary	Whole	0	0	0	4	0	1	5	11	.004
	Fragment	0	0	1	5	0	35	41	89	3
	N =	0	0	1	9	0	36	46	100	4
Secondary	Whole	0	0	5	5	0	30	40	35	3
	Fragment	0	0	4	0	0	70	74	65	6
	N =	0	0	9	5	0	100	114	100	9
Tertiary	Whole	1	1	8	3	0	48	61	17	5
	Fragment	1	4	48	0	0	239	292	83	24
	N =	2	5	56	3	0	287	353	100	29
Quaternary	Whole	3	3	17	0	0	53	76	11	6
	Fragment	8	5	64	1	4	547	629	89	52
	N =	11	8	81	1	4	600	705	100	58
	N =	13	13	147	18	4	1023	1218		100

	Rock Heaps #	%	Hearths #	%	Storage #	%	Mfg./ Cache #	%	Clay Heap #	%	Non-Feature Units #	%	N #	%
Whole	4	31	4	31	30	21	12	68	0	0	132	13	182	15
Fragment	9	69	9	69	116	79	6	33	4	100	891	87	1036	85
N =	13	100	13	100	147	100	18	100	4	100	1023	100	1218	100
%N Whole		2		2		16		7		0		73		100
%N Fragment		1		1		11		1		.003		86		100

The ratio of fragmentary blanks to whole is high, 89% to 11%, showing that discards dominate the sample (Table 5.20). When the ratio of 170 tips to 122 bases (58% to 42%) is investigated, the suggestion that one particular fragment of this blank was being utilized for other tools does not hold up substantively. Three large whole blanks are represented in the cache in Feature 3. Elsewhere the whole forms are smaller and more finely flaked (ibid.:9-10). The distribution of the tertiary blank in features is concentrated in the large deep pits with eight whole and 48 fragments. In other features and units, these production varieties are distributed more equally in the occupation levels 2 and 3. The five tertiary blanks found in hearths all give evidence of fire pocking as do 19 of those found in the deep large refuse-filled pits and ten in the occupation levels. All these blanks are of natural varieties of Onondaga chert. The mean length is 44 mm, mean width 29 mm, and mean thickness 11 mm. None of the forms classified as tertiary blanks show edge wear or modification by tertiary type flaking.

Quaternary Blanks (Kochan n.d.*b*:13-15; Ritchie 1969:Pl. 64, nos. 7, 11) (Table 5.20; App. A, Tables A.4*a*, A.4*b*, A.5*a*, A.5*b*, A.6*a*, A.6*b*; Pl. 21). The sample of 705 cache blades evidenced in the assemblage at Riverhaven 2 was very extensive. The whole blanks were quite homogeneous and well defined by secondary and tertiary flaking on the lateral and basal edges. The mean length was 41 mm, the mean width 26 mm, and the mean thickness 5 mm. Other attributes are compared in Tables A.4*b*, A.5*b*, and A.6*b*. All display a convex to sub-convex base and a generally ovate form (Ritchie 1969:Pl. 64, nos. 7, 11). This blank or blade was the last stage of manufacture before addition of haft elements and additional lateral resolution by tertiary nibble-flaking. The size of the cache blade usually differs only in width from the sidenotched projectile point. At this stage all traces of proximal striking platform are removed.

Ten of the whole blanks and 31 of the bases show evidence of firing; all eight of those associated with hearths show pockmarking as do three assigned to a rock heap and 24 with provenience in refuse filled probable storage features. Vertical and feature distributions for these artifacts are shown in Table 5.19. Distribution was essentially random. Locus 1 had 505, 346 with no vertical provenience; the other 159 clustered in Levels 2 and 3. Ninety-two were found in Locus 2, 55 in Levels 2-4, and three in Level 2 of Locus 3.

Curiously, only one quaternary blank fragment was found in the manufacture pit, Feature 3. The possible storage features contained 81, rock heaps 11, hearths eight, and the depression surrounding the clay heap held four.

Eighty-nine percent fragmentation tends to maintain the trend observed in primary and tertiary blanks. Those in storage features show a similar ratio, 79%-21% (Table 5.20). The ratio of bases and tip shows *no* differential selectivity of one or the other for further modification, i.e., tips into triangular end scrapers. The sample of 529 fragments shows fracture due to inclusions in the chert in only 23 cases, supporting the observation that better than 50% of the quaternary blanks showed *no* matrix inclusion, a characteristic of the high grade chert found in the Onondaga Escarpment. The most common form of fracture seen on 532 was misapplied pressure, causing a modified hinge fracture in 84.5% of the cases.

The very frequency of the quaternary blank, 58% of the sample, shows that this form was an end product of manufacture activities, and the increasing numbers of fracture discards along the sequence attests to the difficulties of producing the well-made finished product.

Abrading Stones–Grooved (Kochan, n.d.*b*:19-20) (Table 5.19; App. A, Tables A.18*a*, A.18*b*; Pl. 29). Eighteen grooved abrading stones, variously classified by Kochan as "sinew-stones" or "whetstones," occurred in the sample excavated (n.d.*b*:19-20; Ritchie 1969:Pl. 60, no. 17). Five of these tools were uncataloged, and two were from the exploratory trench of Locus 1, where an additional seven occur in the zone of living debris. One is recorded from Locus 2, another, fire-cracked, from a hearth, and three from storage related features.

Nine of the sample were of the contracting ovoid or tear drop shape, common at Sinking Ponds and occurring at Spicer Creek 1. This group showed a heavy emphasis on broad grooves of 10 mm on seven, with two of the narrow groove variety. All six parallel ovoid forms also showed broad grooves as did one ovoid expanding form. Wide grooves were seen on 14 or 17.8%, while narrow grooves appear to characterize 4 or 22.2%. All pebbles were essentially less thick than they were wide, the range of thickness 12-28 mm and the width range 46-79 mm, with three unmeasurable due to fragmentation.

The preferred material for these tools seems to be indurated sandstone since 15 are formed from it and only three are formed of dolomitic pebbles. In all cases the wear grooves were perpendicular or oblique to the long axis of the pebble.

Hammer stones (Tables 5.19; App. A, Tables A.17*a*, A.17*b*; Pl. 30*c-g*). Ten hammerstones were recognized in the assemblage. These were about the size of an orange, and material varied with four of igneous rock, three of sandstone, and three of chert. All of these types of pebbles were naturally available in the area to the south and west, away from the Niagara River.

These artifacts were isolated from a large number of such pebbles retained by Kochan for study, by the presence of end or edge battering which was fairly restricted in extent. Thus, if a pebble was battered randomly over much of its surface it was excluded. In the case of the flint hammers, step fracture characterized the impact areas. These flint hammers were the only hammerstones to have full provenience. They occurred in Level 2 of Locus 1. The seven others (Kochan n.d.*b*:19) had no provenience other than the fact that they occurred in Locus 1.

Antler Flakers (Kochan n.d.*b*:23-24; Fitting 1972:Fig. 73*a-d*; Ritchie 1969:Pl. 65, nos. 8-12) (Table 5.19; Pl. 34*a-h*). Nine of these modified antlers, described by some sources as flakers, were in the Riverhaven 2 assemblage. In order to determine that these tools were indeed flakers, a limited microscopic analysis was performed on the six "broad heads" showing skull articulations which were smoothed by abrasion. The surface of the "head" was repeatedly indented and the further end showed breakage on four or battering on two. Diameter of the "heads" ranged between 19 and 22 mm and the shafts ranged between 13 and 20 mm in diameter. The two complete forms had nearly identical lengths of 85 and 92 mm. Two narrow end fragments were also found, as was a medial portion.

Functionally these tools appear to be associated with production of bone tools (Ritchie 1969:193). The great frequency of the wide groove at Riverhaven 2 may be associated with the large sample of worked antler tools which clustered at a diameter of approximately 10-20 mm.

The two complete forms were found in Feature 5, a deep large pit, while three fragmentary forms were disclosed in a hearth, Feature 7. Three of the others were distributed in the occupation level of Locus 1 with another in Locus 2.

Worked Antler and Teeth (Kochan n.d.*b*:24-25; Ritchie 1969:Pl. 65, nos. 1, 2, 7) (Table 5.19; Pl. 33*w-bb*, 34*i-n*). Six fragments of antler and three modified teeth were represented. The three teeth, two canines of a dog and a bear and a beaver incisor, were modified only by abrasion. The antler sample showed a variety of cut marks (Ritchie 1969:Pl. 65, nos. 1-2), one fragment showing a deep, 2 mm incision around the shaft of what may have been a flaking tool preform. Another was a basally fractured tine abraded to a point (Ritchie 1969:Pl. 65, no. 3), but which displayed no further modification. An object of some curiosity was a worked antler fragment which Ritchie has called a uni-barbed bone point (Ritchie 1969:Pl. 65, no. 3). The tip of this fragment, found in a refuse-filled feature, 5, had been abraded to a dullness inconsistent with use as a point, and the barb was a ridge 5 mm in width projecting perpendicular to the shaft. Noting these contradictions, it must be mentioned that although this may have been a point in the process of being manufactured, it is not a functional point per se.

The worked faunal items were randomly distributed; three antler fragments occurred in storage features, while the remaining five were in Locus 1 occupation debris and two were in Locus 2.

Storage Artifacts: Pottery Rims and Body Sherds (Kochan n.d.*b*:26-27) (Plate 35).

Five pottery rims and 197 body sherds were found at Riverhaven. The distribution of the sherds with exact provenience shows that two broad clusters were found in the occupation levels, Levels 2-4, one in Locus 1, consisting of one rim and 91 body sherds, the other in Locus 2 with one rim and 31 body sherds. In Locus 1, three rim sherds and 65 body sherds also occurred in the pit fill of the deep bowllike storage features 1, 2, 4, 5, 8, and 10, and three body sherds occurred in the hearth, Feature 7. In Locus 2, the hearths, Features 13 and 15, yielded three body sherds while the peripheral depression around the clay heap contained two body sherds.

Analysis of the pottery showed that the 197 body sherds ranged in thickness from 15 to 23 mm and were all interior-exterior cordmarked. These displayed the characteristic horizontal interior cord impressions and variable-direction exterior cord marks (Ritchie 1969:Pl. 68, nos. 1-3, 5-8). The rim sherds showed a rounded lip generally 9 mm in width with the cord impressions running up to and onto the lip. No essential differences in rim or body form were noted between those sherds in Loci 1 and 2 or elsewhere in the sample and therefore no approximation of vessel number could be determined other than the fact that at least one vessel is represented and we speculate that a maximum of three could be present. The wide disproportion between rims, five or 2%, and bodies, 197 or 98%, suggests that the lower figure of one vessel is more likely. In several cases on sherds derived from the living floor, the cord impressions appear to have been obscured by post-firing abrasion (Kochan n.d.*b*:27; Ritchie 1969:Pl. 68, no. 6). The pottery type conforms to the description of Vinette I offered in Chapter 4 (Ritchie and MacNeish 1949:100; Lopez 1971; Kinsey 1972).

Ceremonial Artifacts: Pipe and Gorget (Kochan n.d.*b*:21-22, 27) (Pl. 32*c-d*)

There were only two artifacts at Riverhaven 2 which could be equated with any ceremonial function. Both were found in the general occupation level unassociated with any feature.

The pipe was a clay, tubular variety which was broken off approximately 3.2 mm from the proximal, mouthpiece, end. The diameter of the opening at the proximal end was 9 mm and increased to 11 mm at the distal fracture (Ritchie 1969:Pl. 68, no. 4). The tube tapered from a diameter of 26 mm to 19 mm in a distance of 32 mm. This artifact was found in Locus 1, close to Feature 4.

The gray slate gorget was roughly rectangular—143 mm in length, 26 mm in width, tapering to approximately 20 mm at each end and 9 mm in thickness (Ritchie 1969:Pl. 64, no. 17). Two holes with a bore diameter of 3 mm, were situated 10 mm from each end. One was biconically drilled and other was drilled only from one face (Kochan n.d.*b*:122). The gorget is a quite unusual bar shape, not common in the literature on Meadowood phase. A similar but fragmentary form was, however, present in the Kuster Collection from the Allen site.

NATURAL RESOURCES OF THE RIVERHAVEN COMPLEX

Above, we have pointed out the diversity of the environment and physiography of the area encompassed by the Riverhaven Complex. The natural resources of this area were extremely varied. The biota of the area was probably quite diverse with marsh and upland flora and fauna. The well drained southern portion of the island supported upland floral populations of oak, maple and hickory while the marshy northern sector had hemlock, maple, beech, and numerous varities of wetland flora (Zenkert 1934:303-05). A varied faunal sample from the Riverhaven 2 site was collected and the analysis is presented below.

Inorganic resources, such as clay for pottery manufacture, were also immediately available and were utilized by the inhabitants. Chert supplies were, however, only available at a distance. Pebbles of various rock types, which were used as hammerstones, anvilstones, and abrading stones, could have been extracted from the basal clay-till but were probably introduced from the southern end of the island where exposures of glacial till provided numerous pebbles of all sizes. Flat, river-abraded pebbles ideal for netsinkers were available at the lower southern point of the island where they were deposited from the river load in the slower currents in backwaters and eddies.

Faunal Analysis

Kochan's midden excavations made a faunal sample of 1607 bone fragments and shells available for analysis. Provenience on much of the material was not kept with the exception of several pieces which had been altered into artifacts; thus assignment of much of the bone could be no more precise than the broad locations Locus 1, Locus 2, and refuse bone.

The Kochan sample may, however, be regarded as a representative sample of all excavations (as above, Chapter 3) on the site, since he continuously notes that bone was being found associated with the artifact bearing levels and that all bones and shells identifiable as such were saved. In 1961, he submitted a sample of bone fragments large enough to be identified to John Guilday for analysis (Kochan n.d.*b*:25). This sample consisted mostly of the worked bone (ibid.:23-25).

Often the quantity of bone was deceiving. For example, most of the fish bone was found in a compact mass of light gray sandy clay resembling ash. When this was broken down in the laboratory few actual fish bones remained.

Preliminary analysis of the entire bone sample was accomplished in 1963 by Barbara Butler and subsequently by D. W. Taggart in 1966, and by Earl Casler in 1967. Each of these investigators developed a special line of inquiry. Butler attempted separation by minimum number of individuals and gross generic or specific identification of fragments large enough for assignment, while Taggart used the whole collection to extract as much additional identification as possible. He also tried to classify those bones that were previously designated unidentifiable by species or genus. Casler was interested in the birds, fish, reptiles and shellfish and under Taggart's direction examined, enumerated, and identified these fauna. The results of their work are shown in Table 5.21. Subsequent excavations (1971) have further enlarged the sample which has been submitted for reanalysis (Chapter 3).

When all analyses of the Kochan bone sample were compiled they displayed 314 or 19.5% bone fragments identifiable as to genus and/or species and 1293 or 80.5% fragments which were unassignable except to broad categories. The categories — large mammal, small mammal, bird, reptile, fish and shellfish — all display similar curves for unidentified, identified, and total sample with the exception of fish and shellfish which, once thoroughly studied, showed a high rate of identification (Table 5.21, Fig. 5.13). Percentage occurrence in the total sample was as follows:

Large mammal	52.4%
Small mammal	29.3%
Bird	10.0%
Shellfish	4.9%
Fish	3.2%
Reptile	0.3%

In the sample identified by individual, shellfish outnumber birds at 13.7% and fish display a higher percentage, 11.5%, than in their occurrence in total sample. Thus, the sample of identified individuals might

TABLE 5.21
COMPILED FAUNAL ANALYSIS, RIVERHAVEN 2

Common Name	Genus-Species	Sample #	Sample % of N	Minimum Individuals #	Minimum Individuals % of N	Usable Meat #	Usable Meat % of N
MAMMAL	Unidentifiable	1122	69.8				
Whitetail Deer	***Odocoileus virginianus***	105	6.50	12	14.8	1200.00	54.30
Elk	*Cervis canadensis*	1	0.10	1	1.2	350.00	15.80
Black Bear	*Ursus americanus*	19	1.20	2	2.5	420.00	19.00
Dog or Wolf	***Canis* (sp.)**	4	0.30	1	1.2	30.00	1.40
Red Fox	*Vulpes fulva*	1	0.10	1	1.2	4.00	0.18
Beaver	*Castor canadensis*	3	0.25	1	1.2	38.5	1.70
Raccoon	*Procyon lotor*	41		8	9.9	72.00	3.30
Muskrat	*Ondatra zibethicus*	14	0.90	4	4.9	8.00	0.36
Gray Squirrel	Sciurus carolinensis	3	0.25	1	1.2	0.25	0.01
Subtotal		1313	81.7	31	38.3	2122.75	96.00
BIRD	Unidentifiable	119	7.40				
Wild Turkey	*Meleagris gallopavo*	16	1.00	4	4.9	34.00	1.5
Duck	***Anas* (sp.)**	17	1.10	5	6.2	8.75	0.4
Canada Goose	*Branta canadensis*	9	0.65	2	2.5	11.20	0.5
Subtotal		161	10.00	11	13.6	53.95	2.4
REPTILE	Unidentifiable	2	0.15				
Snapping Turtle	*Chelydra serpentina*	2	0.15	1	1.2	3.00	0.14
Subtotal		4	0.3	1	1.2	3.00	0.14
FISH	Unidentifiable	14	0.90				
Catfish	*Amiurus* (sp.)	11	0.70	4	4.9	12.00	0.54
Drumfish	*Aplodinotus grunniens*	7	0.40	2	2.5	4.00	0.18
Bullhead	*Ictalurus nebulosus*	13	0.80	5	6.2	10.00	0.45
Sucker	*Catostomus* (sp.)	5	0.35	2	2.5	4.00	0.18
Subtotal		50	3.10	13	16.0	30.00	1.36
SHELLFISH	Unidentifiable	36	2.20				
Freshwater Mussel	*Alasmidonta* (sp.)	19	1.20	9	11.1	.25	.01
Common Mussel	*Elliptio* (sp.)	24	1.50	16	19.8	.50	.02
Subtotal		79	4.90	25	30.9	.75	.03
Total		1607	100.00	81	100.0	2210.45	100.00

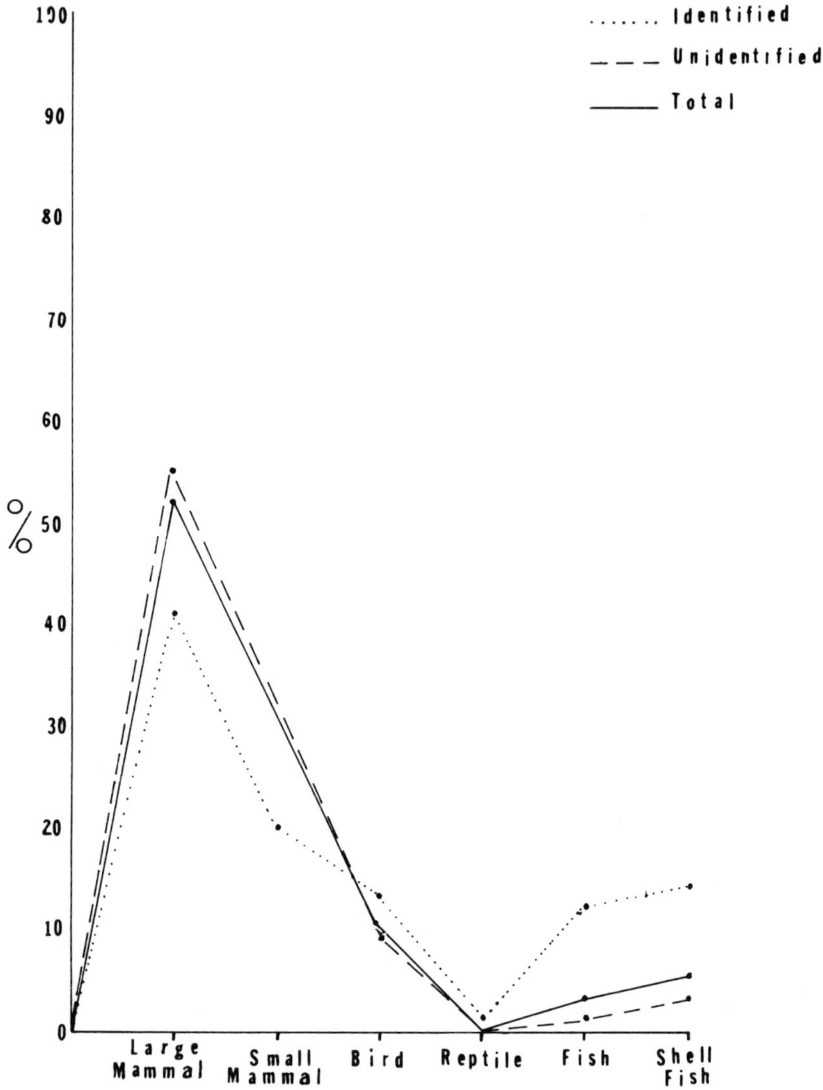

Fig. 5.13 Riverhaven 2 faunal sample.

be misleading if considered in isolation especially with regard to fish and shellfish frequency (Fig. 5.13).

The analysis into minimum number of individuals clarifies the situation somewhat. Shellfish, with 30.9% of the individuals, represent only 0.03% of the usable meat. Fish, with 16% of the individuals, represent only 1.36% of the usable meat (Table 5.21). Mammals clearly represent the maximum proportion of usuable meat at 96%, but this

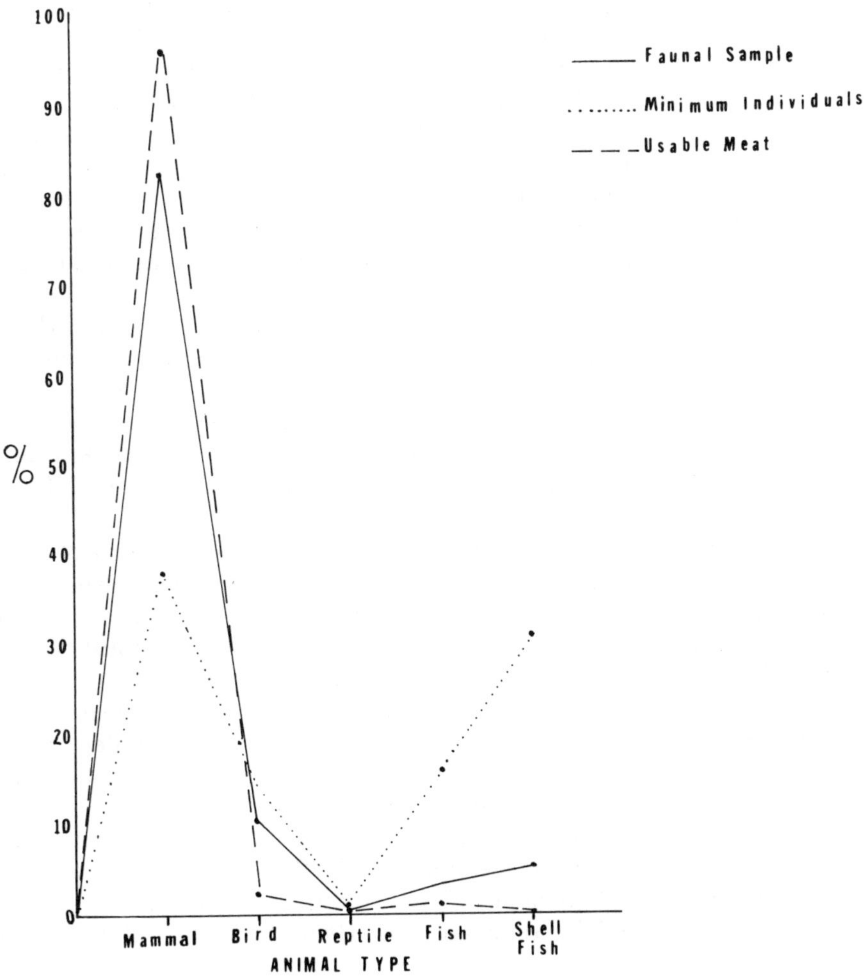

Fig. 5.14 Riverhaven 2 comparison of faunal sample, minimum individuals and usable meat.

discrepancy is less obvious in the frequency of individuals, which is 38.5% (Fig. 5.14).

The single largest meat producing animal was the whitetail deer at 54.3% of the total amount. Many of the bone fragments show marks of butchering, 43 or 41% of the 105 identified fragments indicating disarticulation cuts for on-site processing.

Division of the sample into broad habitat associations of shoreline and upland (Burt 1957; Burt and Grossenweiler 1964; Cleland 1966:109-44; Taggart:personal communication) appears to offer a significant breakdown of the faunal material at Riverhaven 2 (Table 5.22). It suggests that upland hunting yielded 92.2% of the usable meat from only 22.2% of the individuals. Chi-square tests of this distribution show that the probability is less than one case out of 1000, that it is a chance occurrence. Shoreline hunting or fishing appear to have been productive only of supplemental foods, when available (Table 5.22). Many of the shoreline species such as shellfish yield very small amounts of meat per individual and others like ducks and snapping turtle, are available only seasonally. Upland species, deer, bear, and turkey are year-round residents but are most easily procured in late fall and in winter when foliage is at a minimum, especially in forested areas with open clearings (Burt 1957:151-53). In the division in Table 5.22, a clear concentration on herbivorous mammals is noticed, 72.2% of the total sample. If all mammals are included, a 96% preference is noted. If the preferences for categories other than mammals are used, upland birds like turkey, and fish especially of genus *Ictalurus* are dominant at 1.5% and 1.4% of usable meat.

In order to determine whether choices were made exclusive of meat poundage per animal the percentages of meat in the Riverhaven 2 sample were plotted against a standard curve which consists of one individual's usable meat expressed as a percentage of the total (White 1953:397-98). Only those species represented at Riverhaven 2 were used. The result showed no deviation greater than 4% with the majority of variations under 2% (Fig. 5.15). Clearly the programmatic decision to select the available animals with the most meat operated most consistently (Grayson 1974:127; Cleland 1966:42-45).

The role of fishing as a procurement industry on the Riverhaven 2 site is underscored when the frequency of the 25 netsinkers is compared to the frequency of fish bones. The netsinkers represent 1% of the artifact inventory and fish represent slightly more than 1% of the usable meat.

The meat producing animals utilized at Riverhaven 2 raise the question of whether the site was positioned adjacent to the Niagara River for purposes of acquiring water-associated animals (Ritchie 1969:181). While fishing was evidenced at the site, it does not appear to be a major activity. The inland stands of oak and hickory on Grand Island provided a mast production ideal for sustaining large populations of deer and turkey in a restricted hunting area bounded by water. The Riverhaven 2 faunal sample suggests an inland rather than a riverine subsistence economy.

TABLE 5.22
RIVERHAVEN 2 FAUNA BY SHORELINE OR UPLAND ASSOCIATION

Category	Habitat	Animal	Individuals		Usable Meat			
			#	% ΣN	#	%SHORE ΣN	%UP ΣN	% ΣN
Herbivorous Mammals	Shoreline	Beaver	1	1.0	38.5	22.4		1.7
		Muskrat	4	4.0	8.0	4.6		0.4
		Subtotal	5	5.1	46.5	27.0		2.1
	Upland	Elk	1	1.0	350.0		17.2	15.8
		White Tail Deer	12	12.2	1200.0		58.9	54.3
		Squirrel	1	1.0	0.25		0+	0+
		Subtotal	14	14.2	1550.25		76.0	70.1
	N =		19	19.2	1596.75			72.2
Carnivorous Mammals	Upland	Dog or Wolf	1	1.0	30.00		1.5	1.4
		Fox	1	1.0	4		0.2	0.2
	N =		2	2.0	34		1.7	1.5
Omnivorous Mammals	Shoreline	Raccoon	8	8.2	72	41.9		3.3
	Upland	Bear	2	2.0	420		20.6	19.0
	N =		10	10.1	492			22.3
	Sum of N	MAMMALS	31	31.3	2122.75			96.0
Birds	Shoreline	Canada Goose	2	2.0	11.2	6.5		0.5
		Duck (sp.)	5	5.1	8.75	5.1		0.4
		Subtotal	7	7.1	19.95	11.6		0.9
	Upland	Turkey	4	4.0	34		1.6	1.5
	N =		11	11.1	43.95			2.0
Reptile	Shoreline	Snapping Turtle	1	1.0	3	1.7		0.1
	N =		1	1.0	3	1.7		0.1

TABLE 5.22 (Continued)

Category	Habitat	Animal	Individuals		Usable Meat			
			#	% Σ N	#	%SHORE Σ N	%UP Σ N	% Σ N
		Catfish	4	4.0	12	7.0		0.51
		Bullhead	5	5.1	10	5.8		0.5
Fish	Shoreline	Sucker	2	2.0	4	2.3		0.2
		Drum	2	2.0	4	2.3		0.2
	N =		13	13.2	30.00	17.4		1.4
Shellfish	Shoreline	Mussel	19	19.2	0.25	0.1		0+
		Common Mussel	24	24.2	0.5	0.3		0+
	N =		43	43.4	0.75	0.4		0+
	Sum of N for Shoreline		77	77.8	172.2	100.0	8.4	7.8
	Sum of N for Upland		22	22.2	2038.25		100.0	92.2
	SUM OF TOTAL N =		99	100.0	2210.45			100.0

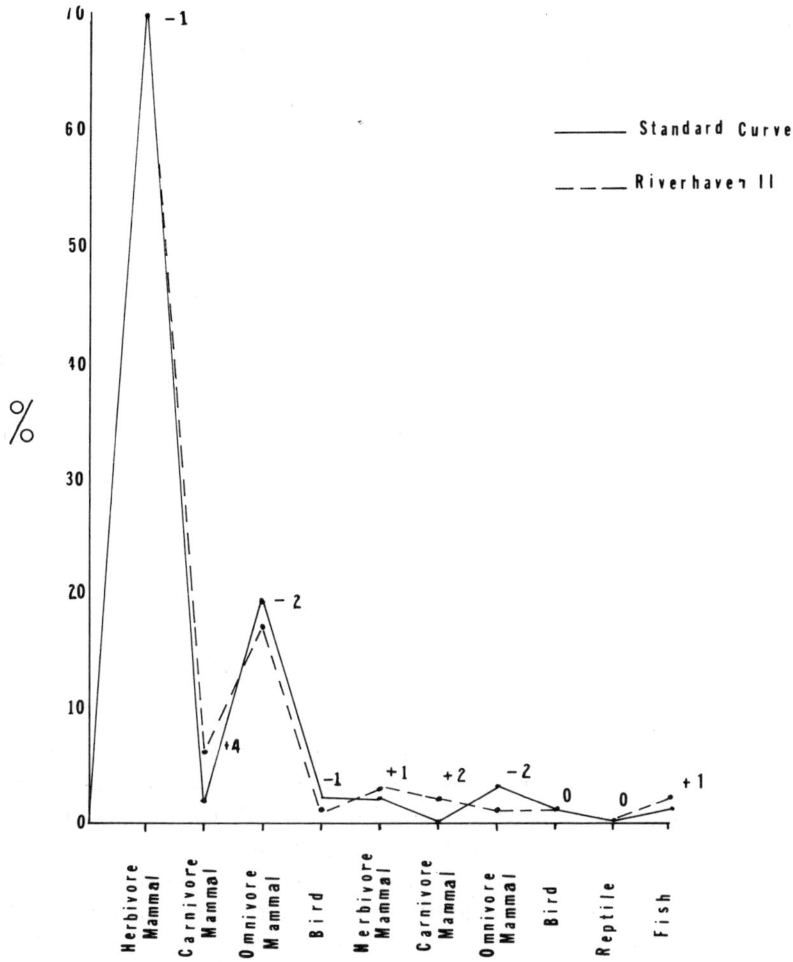

Fig. 5.15 Riverhaven 2 faunal sample compared to standard usable meat curve.

Chert

The most prevalent material for artifact manufacture at Riverhaven 2 was Onondaga chert, and 1552 or 95.4% of the lithic artifact sample was formed of its natural varieties. (Table 5.23). The color variations ranged from light gray to dark blue-gray which was the most common. The darker varieties were also determined to have less than 40% inclusion of indurated limestone. Several authors have commented upon the high grade nature of chert used at Riverhaven 2 (Kochan n.d.*a*; Ritchie 1969:191). The closest principal sources for such chert of the

TABLE 5.23
SUMMARY OF LITHIC MATERIALS, RIVERHAVEN 2

Type	Material	#	Artifacts % of N	% of N
Chert	Onondaga	1552	99.8	95.2
	Flint Ridge	1	0.1	0.1
	Jasper	1	0.1	0.1
	Subtotal	1154	100.0	95.4
Igneous	Granitic	14	82.4	0.8
	Felsitic	3	17.6	0.2
	Subtotal	17	100.0	1.0
Sedimentary	Sandstone	39	67.2	2.4
	Limestone	6	10.4	0.4
	Dolomite (Indurated Limestone)	10	17.2	0.6
	Indurated Shale	3	5.2	0.2
	Subtotal	58	100.0	3.6
	% of N	1629		100.0

particular dark blue-gray color are all located on the Onondaga Escarpment, the closest occurrence of which is 9.6-12.8 km (6-8 mi). Since these major source outcrops occur within 32 km (20 mi), there appears to be some validity to the suggestion made above.

The small number of decortication flakes in the samples of flint detritus collected by Kochan lends support to the proposition that high quality chert was used. In a selected sample of Locus 2 flint refuse, a breakdown as follows was noted:

Decortication flakes	38	4.3%
Flakes	246	27.7%
Chips	547	61.7%
Core fragments	56	6.3%
Total	887	100%

Here decortication flakes were 13% of the sample of 284 flakes, while at Sinking Ponds such flakes comprised approximately 33.3% of the very large nonutilized flake inventory of 10,357 items. Although flint pebbles were available from the glacial till on Grand Island, they were infrequently used as raw material for chert artifacts at Riverhaven 2. Three hammerstones of chert show that the chert pebbles had considerably more matrix inclusion than did the general population of chert materials. Transportation of chert raw material to the Riverhaven 2 site probably took place in the form of rough tabular blocks as indicated by the presence of primary blanks, spalls, and numerous tabular core fragments. Complete utilization in the manufacture process was clearly high due to the low frequency of primary blanks which formed only 4% of all blanks on the site.

Exotic cherts were present but in an extremely minor capacity. Red-brown jasper of the Pennsylvania type represented by one artifact and one flake, and Flint Ridge White variety with yellow tints were the principal exotics (Table 5.23). Although Kochan reported a Heldeberg chert projectile point, it could not be distinguished from the dark blue-gray Onondaga chert and was so classified (Kochan n.d.*b*:13).

Igneous Rocks (Granite and Felsite) (Table 5.23)

Igneous rocks are infrequent in the Niagara Quadrangle outside of glacial till (Grabau 1901:327) where pebbles of igneous origin are deposited. There was some selection of this material for tools of impact and grinding. Generally the coarser grained granite was preferred, with a frequency of 82% compared to 17.6% fine-grained felsite which occurs plentifully in the red clay till at the base of the Riverhaven 2 deposits.

Artifact distribution was as follows:

	Granite	Felsite
Netsinkers	1	1
Hammerstones	3	1
Anvilstones	2	0
Abrading stones (mano)	3	0
Celts	4	1
Beveled adze	1	0
Total	14 (82.4%)	3 (17.6%)

Sandstone (Table 5.23)

The third member of the triumvirate of common rocks in the Niagara Frontier is sandstone. It is found in all forms from soft and crumbling to very hard, dense varieties. The harder dense sandstone was uniformly selected over the soft types. All of the artifacts of this material were formed on hard sandstone pebbles. These were again locally available and quite common in the glacially deposited red clay till of the base of the Riverhaven 2 deposits. The common red-brown and dark tan varieties were equally present in the sample of sandstone artifacts which was the dominant sedimentary rock, 67.2%, and the second most frequent material of manufacture after chert, 2.4%. Distribution of sandstone artifacts was:

	Red	Tan
Netsinkers	5	7
Hammerstones	1	2
Anvilstones	4	1
Abrading stones (mano)	2	2
Grooved abrading stones	7	8
Total	19 (49.8%)	20 (50.2%)

Although no overall count of fire-cracked rock was made at Riverhaven 2 in the early excavations, subsequent examinations of excavation spoil areas and fire-split rocks derived from features and other test excavations have suggested that the popularity of sandstone for heat convection observed at Sinking Ponds, 75%, is duplicated in the Riverhaven Complex. Three rock heap features were delineated at Riverhaven 2, one at Riverhaven 4, and six at Spicer Creek 1 and 2. One feature from each site was analyzed for material (Table 5.24). Here we see that selection was above 60% for sandstone, and the difference between sandstone and the next most heavily selected category, dolomite, is a mean of 58% (Table 5.24).

TABLE 5.24
ROCK MATERIAL FREQUENCIES IN FEATURES AT RIVERHAVEN 2, 4 AND SPICER CREEK 1, 2

Rock Type	Riverhaven 2 Feature 17		Riverhaven 4 Feature 20		Spicer Creek 1, 2 Feature 3		Total	
Sandstone	61	72.6	82	61.7	176	85.8	319	75.7
Dolomite	13	15.4	29	21.8	21	10.2	63	14.9
Limestone	8	9.5	16	12.0	0	0.0	24	5.7
Granite	2	2.5	5	3.7	8	4.0	15	3.5
Quartzite	0	0.0	1	0.8	0	0.0	1	.2
Total	84	100.0	133	100.0	205	100.0	422	100.0

Limestone and Dolomite (Indurated Limestone) (Table 5.23)

The most common rock in the area outside of shale is the local limestone which appears in almost every outcrop on the Niagara Frontier. Dolomite is a denser, more compact and harder, or indurated, form of limestone. It was generally preferred when the two were equally available, especially for impact tools. This preference may be seen below:

	Limestone	Dolomite
Netsinkers	6	5
Anvilstones	0	1
Grooved abrading stones	0	3
Celts	0	1
Total	6 (41.2%)	10 (58.8%)

The dolomite observed on the Riverhaven 2 site was the light tan to light gray local form found most commonly as pebbles in the local glacial tills. Flat limestone and dolomite pebbles are quite common around the southern tip of Grand Island where they are deposited in the sluggish current between Strawberry, Motorboat, and Beaver Islands.

One artifact at Spicer Creek 1-2, a grooved abrading stone, was of dolomite.

Indurated Shale (Table 5.23)

Indurated shale is a variety of shale which has been formed by metamorphic processes into a compact stone less easily fractured than the soft varieties of shale which are so numerous in the Niagara Quadrangle (Grabau 1901:324-26). This form of shale, or its precisely defined metamorphic derivative slate, occur in local deposits. Usual colors are black to dark green. These colors are represented by two of the three artifacts of this material, a gorget and birdstone fragment. Although varieties of the black and dark green indurated shale or slate occur in eastern New York, Ohio, and elsewhere, there is no reason to suspect that local sources were not utilized. Indeed, the material of the dark green Riverhaven birdstone fragment and that of the Sinking Ponds birdstone fragment are quite similar and probably local. Another fragmented birdstone, a head in the Reed Collection presumed to have come from Riverhaven 2, displays a light green color indicative of eastern argillaceous shale (Zumberge 1957:13-19).

Bone, Antler and Teeth

The local fauna provided material for 40 artifacts. In a sample of 20 bone awls, 16 were formed on mammal bone while three were of bird, turkey, and one was a catfish spine. Nine flaking tools and seven other worked fragments were made of deer antler while other worked material included a worked portion of bear mandible and teeth as follows: a canid canine, a beaver incisor, and a bear canine.

Bone, antler, and teeth were apparently used indiscriminately for specialized artifacts. Concentration on by-products of the deer probably reflects the popularity of the animal in the subsistence economy. Artifacts on faunal material are summarized:

Beaver	1	2.5%
Miscellaneous small mammal	5	12.5%
Whitetail deer	27	67.5%
Bear	2	5.0%
Bird (Turkey)	3	7.5%
Canid	1	2.5%
Fish	1	2.5%
Total	40	100%

Clay

The silty clays deposited by Spicer Creek and the Niagara River at Riverhaven 2 formed a resource material for pottery making. Tests by students at the University of Buffalo Anthropology Department on the pottery specific properties of clays gathered at the Martin site on the south end of the island were quite successful (Gordon Schmahl 1969:personal communication). This red clay found in abundance admixed with a glacial pebble till was apparently recognized by the Meadowood inhabitants of Riverhaven 2 who may have deposited a heap consisting almost entirely of red clay minus rocks. This clay heap is described by Kochan and assigned the designation of Feature 14 (Kochan: Notes, Locus 2). The uniformity and lack of artifactual inclusions in the clay imply its presence as a stockpile of necessary material. While we cannot be sure that the red clay was being gathered and preliminarily processed by removing pebbles, the presence of the heap of clay without pebbles close to two hearths is quite suggestive.

RIVERHAVEN COMPLEX: INTRASITE ACTIVITIES

Spicer Creek 1-2 and Riverhaven 4 are described above as an integral part of the Riverhaven Complex and so we will discuss the activities it has been possible to recognize on these sites before proceeding to discuss activities at Riverhaven 2.

Spicer Creek 1-2 and Riverhaven 4 Activities

These sites are located inland on Grand Island west of the Niagara River on several islandlike humps of high ground near the extensive Gun Creek Marsh, an extinct levee cutoff or oxbow lake. In Gun Creek Marsh the flora and fauna are hydric. During the summer months, shallow water fish would have been available as well as deer and smaller marsh-related mammalian game. Reptiles, frogs, and waterfowl were all present although during the summer the fowl would be likely to be heron and marsh hen. During winter, deer would retreat to the higher south end of the island on the glacial ridges to consume the mast of the extensive oak forests in this well-drained area. Freshwater mussel was probably available in the broad, sluggish flow area of the confluence of Spicer Creek and the Niagara River.

Procurement activity was represented by one fragmentary projectile point at Spicer Creek 1 and no ceremonial storage or residence activity could be determined.

Processing Activities

Artifacts of the functional class processing represent 12% of the total sample and the 15 unifacial scrapers represent 68% of the total of 22. Six bifacial scrapers and a single mano make up the rest of the assemblage. The feature distribution is more instructive. Rock heaps similar to those discussed at Sinking Ponds were noted, as were hearths. At the Spicer Creek 1 loci, the distribution of these features, eight hearths and three rock heaps, displayed a circular pattern, with a rock heap partially between two hearths (Fig. 5.1). This arrangement is similar to that observed at Sinking Ponds where hearths clustered inside a semicircular pattern of three rock heaps and two hearths were noted. These appear to be small hearths for heating rocks grouped near, between, or within the arrangements of rock heaps (Fig. 5.1). Riverhaven 4 was a single rock heap located on the north bank of Spicer Creek.

Manufacture Activities (Table 5.25)

As at Sinking Ponds, manufacture artifacts show a ubiquitous distribution. Only at Spicer Creek 1 was there structural evidence for this form of activity. All stages of manufacture, except primary blanks and raw material, were present and a progression in frequency of the latter stages of manufacture can be noted (Table 5.25). At Spicer Creek 1, the fragments of the last production stage, quaternary blank, were only slightly more numerous, 59%, than the whole blanks, 41%, some of which were clustered in features. A hammerstone and grooved abrader completed the assemblage. The distribution of features which display large amounts of flint detritus, fragments of worked stages, and several

TABLE 5.25
DISTRIBUTION OF CULTURAL MATERIALS RELATED TO MANUFACTURE, SPICER CREEK 1, 2, RIVERHAVEN 4

Materials	Spicer Creek 1	Spicer Creek 2	Riverhaven 4
Artifactual:			
Hammerstones	1	0	0
Secondary Blank	12	0	0
Quaternary Blank Width	40	1	0
Quaternary Blank Base	30	0	0
Quaternary Blank Tip	28	0	0
Tertiary Blank Base	27	0	0
Tertiary Blank Tip	27	0	0
Grooved Abrading Stone	1	0	0
Structural:			
Manufacturing Caches	3	0	0
Nonartifactual:			
Cores	30	0	0
Flakes	444	26	0
Chips	4908	58	0
Total (N=5636)	5551	85	0
%	98	2	0

complete blanks again show a peripheral placement around the rock heap area but not of it. Around one such large deep feature, Feature 3, three hearths were spaced (Fig. 5.1). Other features of this type, Features 1 and 9, were isolated.

Summarizing Spicer Creek 1-2 and Riverhaven 4, we believe that a processing area exists in a marsh-oriented situation, in this case, less than 1000 yards from a more extensive coeval site. Little or no evidence for procurement, storage, ceremony or residence is available, perhaps due to sampling error. Manufacture activity appears to be extensive over the Spicer Creek 1 loci, and where concentrations do exist they are peripheral to the processing area.

Riverhaven 2 Activities

The activities at the Riverhaven 2 site contrast significantly with those evidenced at Spicer Creek 1-2. Occupation of Riverhaven 2 was intense with approximately 18-24 cm (.6-.8 ft) of living debris in the main excavation areas. Artifactual evidence from the site reveals the probable presence of procurement, processing, manufacture, storage and ceremonial activities. Structural data show that processing, storage, manufacture and habitation activities were carried out. These features have been plotted in Figure 5.16. Deep basin-shaped pits seem

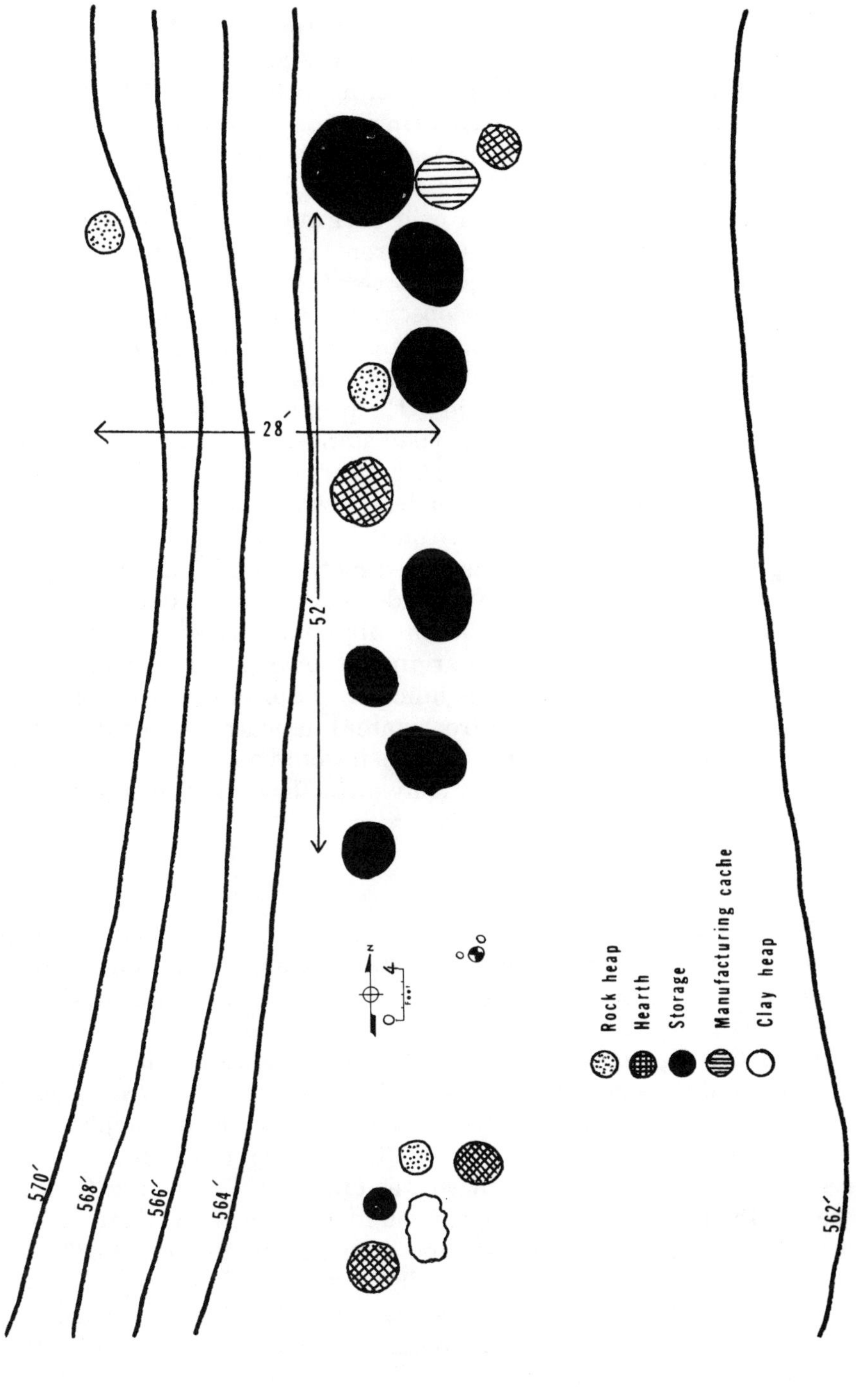

Fig. 5.16 Riverhaven 2 feature relationships.

to be located in an arc on a low bench at the bottom of the 173.9 m (570 ft) terrace off the Niagara River. Seen in this grouping are several hearths and two rock heaps (Fig. 5.16). The river now lies 36.6 m (120 ft) to the east, although during the period of principle occupation it was probably much closer to the 171.4 m (562 ft) bench. We have noted above that the midden on the 171.4 m (562 ft) bench was deep and extensive and extended along the riverfront for over 38.1 m (125 ft). The very depth and size of the midden suggests recurrent and long-term occupation. Very little erosion has taken place over the site. Conversely, little vertical buildup from siltation is observed. Leaf mold and humic buildup have continued almost uninterrupted to form a highly organic humus zone of almost one foot over the occupation level.

The biotic resources available to the peoples of Riverhaven 2 were extensive. To the southwest large open stands of xerically conditioned white oak occurred while to the west a large marsh or shallow lake occurred, Gun Creek Marsh, an oxbow form in a levee cutoff area. During the winter, deer and elk could be found "yarding" in forest clearings, exploiting the mast produced by the oaks. Bear, in hibernation, might also be available in their dens. Many nuts and fruits were available to the site occupants, as the abundance of wild grape today attests. Along the slower water margins of the Niagara River and in the estuarine situation caused by the juncture of Spicer Creek on the slow water side of the Niagara River freshwater mussels could be taken. The drumfish, bullhead, burbot, and whitefish would all be available in the Niagara River, although its relatively swift flow and depth would reduce ability to take them.

Procurement Activities (Table 5.26)

Riverhaven 2 had an excellent faunal assemblage which has been discussed above. Taggart suggested (1967:154) use of a shoreline index. Application of this index to the Riverhaven 2 site is surprising in view of its riverine location. The shoreline index is 171, quite low when compared to the figures exhibited by shoreline adapted sites such as Feheeley and Schmidt, 667 and 400 (ibid.). When the percentages of animals utilized as meat are calculated, they show a heavy emphasis on upland mammals, deer, bear, and elk (Table 5.21). Burt notes that the deer and elk are best taken in winter (1954:149-53), while Cleland observes that the bear is taken year round but is most available in late autumn and early spring, before and after hibernation (1966:163).

The ratio of projectile points to other items of procurement substantiates the taking of large game. This ratio, excluding the stemmed point, is 67:26 or 71:29%. Although emphasis was placed upon upland mam-

TABLE 5.26
DISTRIBUTION OF CULTURAL MATERIALS
RELATED TO PROCUREMENT, RIVERHAVEN 2

Materials	Loci		
	1	2	3
Artifactual:			
Projectile Point, Sidenotched	41	11	0
Projectile Point, Cornernotched	4	1	0
Projectile Point, Stemmed	1	0	0
Projectile Point, Lateral Basal	5	1	0
Projectile Point, Indeterminate	4	0	0
Netsinkers	22	3	0
Birdstone	0	1	0
Structural:			
N.A.E.			
Nonartifactual:			
N.A.E.			
Total (N = 94)	77	17	0
%	80	20	0

N.A.E. = No assignable or available evidence for structural or nonartifactual materials.

mals, shellfish and fish were also obtained. The 25 netsinkers were 27% of the sample. The size and weight of these objects imply that limited weir net fishing in the Niagara River was carried on at Riverhaven 2.

Processing Activity (Table 5.27)

When the structural evidence of processing is considered a similar situation to that discussed above is presented. There was evidence of two rock heaps on the bench, one located at some distance from the storage area, the other located within the arc circumscribed by the large deep features (Fig. 5.16). Three hearths were also distributed outside the storage area, two close to a rock heap, Feature 12. This distribution of features related to processing suggests that such activity was peripheral and unimportant, if as we have previously stated the rock heap–hearth association may be connected with fish processing.

The ratio of bifacial processing tools to unifaces is indicative of hide preparation or bone alteration. The bifacial tools, longitudinal knife-scrapers, scrapers of various shape and drills contrasted with unifacial tools, scrapers and utilized flakes yields the following ratio: 183:135 or 58:42% (Table 5.27). When wear or abrasion on the uniface tools is noted, the ratio is much more heavily in favor of dorsal abrasion than ventral–111:24 or 82:18%. The pull stroke evidenced by the bifacial scrapers' steep or flat dorsal flaking is repeated by the unifacial tools. This stroke is suggestive of hide working or bone tool preparation

TABLE 5.27
DISTRIBUTION OF CULTURAL MATERIALS RELATED TO PROCESSING, RIVERHAVEN 2

Materials	Loci		
	1	2	3
Artifactual:			
Longitudinal Knives	21	9	0
Scrapers, Unifacial	72	20	0
Scrapers, Bifacial	92	12	0
Abrading Stone, Mano	3	4	0
Anvilstone, Pitted	6	1	0
Drills	37	11	1
Celts	6	0	0
Pottery Vessels	4	1	1
Structural:			
Hearths	2	2	0
Rock Heaps	1	1	1
Nonartifactual:			
Utilized Flakes	107	19	9
Total (N = 443)	351	80	12
%	80	20	.02

TABLE 5.28
DISTRIBUTION OF CULTURAL MATERIALS RELATED TO MANUFACTURE, RIVERHAVEN 2

Materials	Loci			
	1	2	3	Test
Artifactual:				
Hammerstones	10	1	0	0
Primary Blank	31	14	1	0
Secondary Blank	88	26	0	0
Quaternary Blank Width	55	20	1	0
Quaternary Blank Base	272	46	6	0
Quaternary Blank Tip	260	33	2	0
Tertiary Blank Width	50	11	0	0
Tertiary Blank Base	104	18	0	0
Tertiary Blank Tip	144	24	2	0
Grooved Abrading Stone	17	1	0	0
Structural:				
Manufacturing Caches	1	0	0	0
Nonartifactual:				
Cores/Spalls	465	56	7	1
Nonutilized Flakes	2241	284	73	16
Chips	4962	547	231	41
Total (N = 10,162)	8700	1081	323	58
%	90	10	.03	.005

(Taggart 1967:164; Wobst 1968:214). The bone awls present us with substantive demonstration of not only bone tool preparation but hide working as well.

Manos and pitted stones demonstrate that grinding and processing of vegetable foods was also practiced, but the relatively low frequency–5%–of the processing tools is not informative as to the importance of floral resources (Table 5.27). Celts and adzes also imply work with fibrous materials and suggest active woodworking (Table 5.27).

The clay heap, Feature 14, represents an enigma but it may legitimately be thought of as related to processing and preparation of clay for pottery making. This activity may account for the hearth–rock heap complex at the south end of the site as a production area for pottery, even though the greatest frequency of sherds was in the storage area.

Manufacture Activity (Table 5.28)

The artifactual evidence for manufacture is quite large and varied. The frequency of evidence is so great, in fact, that Kochan refers to the site as a workshop. He states:

> The large accumulation of chipping debris in the hollow was either the result of the erosion of a bank-side midden, or the location of the area in which the actual chipping took place. Our opinion leans toward the latter hypothesis, as it seems incredible to believe that flint in such various forms and large quantities was hauled from the habitation area to be dumped over the bank as midden refuse. Also it is unreasonable to believe that quarry blanks, large spalls, etc. whose source was several miles away were so abundant that they could be discarded so indiscriminately and in such quantities. (n.d.*b*:4)

We agree with his hypothesis although for differing reasons. The manufacture detritus was randomly distributed, except in one instance, a manufacture cache located in Feature 3. Here was a cache involving all stages of manufacture (Fig. 1-2; Pls. 18, 19, 20, 21) except large tabular cores which were, however, located nearby, outside the feature. Nevertheless, when fragmentation is examined (Table 5.20), we note a ratio of 1036 fragments to 136 whole forms or 85:15%. A high breakage rate characterizes this industry. It was remarked elsewhere that selection of fragments for scrapers or other tools was relatively even for distal and proximal portions. However, the rate of increase of fracture in stages is as follows:

$$\frac{\text{Stage } N_2 - \text{Stage } N_1}{N}$$

Number	Percent
Stage 1A - 2 - 38	3
Stage 2 - 3 - 68	6

Stage 3 - 4 - 239	20
Stage 4 - 5 - 352	20
Stage 5 - End - 649	53

The rate shows a progressive trend toward full utilization of raw materials transported to the site. Discards were not indiscriminate but rather the result of increasing casualty in production of end products, be they quaternary blanks or projectile points. It is more reasonable to expect that workshop activity was necessitated by a demand for quaternary blanks or "cache blades" and projectile points. We do, however, have no reason to suspect a concentration of activity at base of the terrace, unless this area saw processing of meat for storage and other various activities coincident with hunting.

Manufacture of chert tools at Riverhaven 2 was not localized in that it involved active procurement of chert from outside the site. Although more properly a procurement activity, returning to the site with tabular cores of chert from one of the local outcrops forms the basis for the manufacture activity. We hold that the low frequency of tabular cores is due in part to the nonlocal nature of the industry (Table 5.28).

We stated above that the grooved abrading stones were good evidence for manufacture of two forms of bone or antler tool: narrow grooved for pointed tools and broad grooved for antler flakers. The worked antler assemblage also indicates that antlers were cut into desired lengths by banding a piece with a deep groove and then snapping the excess length off the portion to be used. Manufacture of bone tools was random in the central area of Locus 1.

Storage Activity (Table 5.29)

Storage activities at Riverhaven 2 are suggested by the large number of storage refuse features that have been described above, Features 1, 2, 4, 5, 8-11, and 16. These features form an open arc at the base of the terrace. The depth of 30-61 cm (1-2 ft), straight walls and size of approximately 122 cm (4 ft) in diameter, except for Feature 1 which is 229 cm (7.5 ft) in diameter, is quite consistent.

We are not sure of the form of storage represented by those pits. Excavation of a pit into the hard red clay and till level implies a purposeful intent. We suggest that during the dry fall months and the cold winter months the pits which would ordinarily be wet during other times of the year could have been used as dry storage. Van Stone (1965:39-46), Bock (1966:42-51) and Rogers (1962:C50) suggest a possible analogy: frozen storage. Rogers also remarks that:

> Moose and caribou meat are preserved for the future in one of two ways. The most common is to freeze it. This, of course, is not possible in warm weather, but very few

TABLE 5.29
DISTRIBUTION OF CULTURAL MATERIALS RELATED TO STORAGE, RIVERHAVEN 2

Materials	Loci		
	1	2	3
Artifactual:			
Pottery Vessels	4	1	1
Quaternary Blade Base	272	46	6
Quaternary Blade Tip	268	35	2
Tertiary Blade Base	104	18	0
Tertiary Blade Tip	144	24	2
Celt	6	0	0
Gorget	1	0	0
Pipe	1	0	0
Birdstone	0	1	0
Structural:			
Small Deep Pits	0	1	0
Large Deep Pits	8	0	0
Nonartifactual:			
N.A.E.			
Total (N = 945)	808	126	11
%	90	10	.01

N.A.E. = No assignable or available evidence for nonartifactual materials.

> moose are killed then and those that are are immediately distributed to a majority of the members of the village and soon consumed. (ibid.:C50-1)

Meat was also dried on racks over fires or hot stones, packed in hides or in the modern situation, cardboard boxes, and placed in houses or elsewhere in the camp; pit-caches were however, no longer used at the time of Rogers' study (ibid.).

The use of the bench has been commented upon by Kochan (n.d.*b*), who described periodic inundation. However, during the late autumn to spring, it is quite dry. Use of the large pits, possibly to store meat in cool storage, cannot be documented, but it does seem reasonable in the light of the high frequency of scrapers and processing tools found in and around these features.

The refuse function is demonstrated by the fragmentary discards found within them. For example, the celt fragments were all quite small, and the pipe was broken beyond any repair. The gorget also shows an incomplete finish. Much manufacture debris was also pitched into the refuse accumulation.

The presence of the large number of deep, steep sidewall storage pits argues persuasively for recurrent occupation. The effort expended in digging into the subsoil is great. To consistently excavate such large pits demonstrates a long difficult process and a clear conception of their functional utility. We have shown above that there was a concentration on hunting meat producing upland mammals, most likely during winter. Unless immediately consumed, storage was probably necessary.

Ceremonial Activity

There are only some very slight indications of this form of activity. Obviously the birdstone implies some aesthetic as well as functional context; the gorget, individual ornamentation; and the pipe form, some type of activity, perhaps curing, analogous to the False Face Society smoke blowing. However, we really can only conjecture about ceremonial activity at Riverhaven 2, since the evidence is so scant.

Habitation Activity

We agree, with Kochan when he states:

> The area of habitation was above the ridge, which was probably overgrown with large oaks such as were found here in the early nineteenth century. (n.d.*b*:7)

However, there is a dearth of information on the distribution of any habitation structures. A tantalizing clue is offered in the rock heap, Feature 17, excavated on the top of the 173.9 m (570 ft) terrace. Whether this represents a portion of a house and what type it is, are open questions at this time. Subsequent excavations in 1971 have shown that this tenuous inference is quite possibly justified although to what degree awaits further analysis.

At this time a further inference will be advanced. If each storage feature represented the storage area for one nuclear family, a population of 45 to 50 persons might have occupied the site, probably a low figure since the entire area at the base of the terrace was not fully excavated by Kochan. In 1971 an additional five to seven storage features were located but remain unanalyzed.

The Riverhaven 2 site is an intensively occupied seasonal site located in a riverine situation but with a decided inland exploitive orientation in its faunal materials. Further, it appears that the faunal assemblage gives the site a late autumn–winter–early spring seasonal assignment. Its assemblage shows a grouping of features which relate to storage clustering at the base of the first terrace off the Niagara River. The artifacts show that processing and manufacture activity was great in this same area. Pottery manufacture on the site is suggested by the clay heap and its constellation of features. Chert tool manufacture on the site appears to be nonlocalized and reflects the closeness of major sources of good chert.

The proximity to the Spicer Creek loci which have a distinctly different structure does, however, raise certain questions as to the chronological relationship between the sites of what we call the Riverhaven Complex.

RIVERHAVEN COMPLEX: CHRONOLOGY

Three charcoal samples from the excavations by Kochan were submitted for radiocarbon assay. An initial sample processed by Geochron, GX-0113, from the basal levels of the midden yielded a date of 1380 ± 135 (570 A.D.); however, resubmission of a further portion of this sample to Gakushuin University (GAK-2048) resulted in a significantly older date of 3460 ± 160 (1510 B.C.). The sample was obtained "from an area close to the water level of the Niagara River. It has probably been under water at various unknown times" (White 1966:personal communication). Although this second date appears to be quite old, at two sigma it falls within the temporal range for Meadowood, established in the Susquehanna River Valley at approximately 1200 B.C., 1230 ± 95, (I-6740) from the Fortin 2 component (Funk and Rippeteau 1973:16). A further date from the same depth but a different unit, 1730 ± 210 (GAK-2048) at 220 A.D. suggests that the water-soaked samples are unreliable, not because of repeated inundation, but probably due to contamination by the chemical or organic pollution in the Niagara River.

Thus the chronological placement of Riverhaven 2 must be inferred from the artifact inventory. Ritchie assigned the assemblage to Meadowood phase (1969:190-91). Its association with other sites of the complex must be judged from the relationship between artifactually similar but undated loci. Ritchie further stated that test pits dug in the field west of East River Road, six feet above the bench, produced chipping refuse and artifacts which unequivocally tied the loci together (ibid.). Those materials were not confined to this field but occur up to three quarters of a mile inland, distributed on knolls rising 5-10 ft above the surrounding marshy areas (Map 5.1). Spicer Creek 1 and 2 and Riverhaven 4 are such loci. They are an integral portion of the subsistence–settlement pattern that characterizes Meadowood habitation on this portion of Grand Island. However, their temporal association with Riverhaven 2 is based on typological inference.

In this chapter we have attempted to compile what is known of the sites in the Riverhaven Complex. Several sites such as Riverhaven 7 and 5E await analysis as do the extensive excavations conducted in 1971 on Riverhaven 2. Other sites, Riverhaven 8, 9, 10, 11, and 12 await more complete excavation. The large data collection that was available has been analyzed, and we feel that it has been possible to identify and separate various activities carried out on each site. Unfortunately, we cannot reexamine Spicer Creek 1 or Riverhaven 4 which are now wholly destroyed and only a small, inaccessable portion of Spicer Creek 2 remains behind a golf course green. There may be other, undiscovered loci of the Meadowood phase along Spicer Creek, but this too awaits future investigation.

In the next chapter, we will compare and contrast the Sinking Ponds site with Riverhaven 2 and the other loci of the Riverhaven Complex and attempt to describe from these data the settlement system of which these sites form a part while remaining separable settlement types.

CHAPTER VI

SINKING PONDS, RIVERHAVEN 2 AND AFFILIATED SITES AS SETTLEMENT TYPES

Meadowood phase in New York State was examined in the hope that it could be organized into a form which could be used to help us determine this culture's distribution over the landscape, especially in the Niagara Frontier. Chapters 4 and 5 intensively described the two sites, Sinking Ponds and Riverhaven 2, and in the latter case, subsidiary loci and the primary data for defining the activity areas on each site were presented. The activity area was described as that portion of a site which can be differentiated by a tool and structural assemblage which together with nonartifactual by-products is related to some specific function which delineates an activity, such as processing of food. The separate activities present at Riverhaven 2, Spicer Creek 1-2, and Sinking Ponds were worked out with as much precision as possible in order to elucidate their structures as settlement types, a concept we have equated with particular kinds of sites. The settlement type is a category of site delimited by an aggregate of activities directed toward a specific function; thus a campsite or burial site are each a different settlement type (Ritchie and Funk 1973:5).

Riverhaven 2 and Sinking Ponds sites represent two different Niagara Frontier settlement types. Each settlement type complements the other in some way although, perhaps, not in the same locality. First we will explain this difference and then we will present the settlement pattern of Meadowood phase in the Niagara Frontier, by suggesting settlement types, their localities, and the reasons for their arrangement.

SINKING PONDS AND ASSOCIATED LOCI AS SETTLEMENT TYPES

The relationship of the Sinking Ponds site to its location is of primary importance to the definition of its internal structure and seasonal utilization as a settlement type. The site lay close to a marsh, formerly a shallow lake formed in a region of glacial moraine and

Map 6.1 Aerial photograph of Sinking Ponds and vicinity.

kettle-holes. Using an aerial photograph, locations of other probable sites have been plotted along with that of Sinking Ponds and a similar site, Allen, which is as yet unexcavated (Map 6.1). Recently a large collection from the Allen site consisting of 109 artifacts was made available for analysis. Although the study is as yet incomplete the degree of correspondence between its morphology and frequency of artifact categories is remarkable. Statistical tests conducted to this date have all supported the null hypothesis that there was no difference in relative frequencies of artifact categories represented.

These "probable site loci" are areas from which collections were derived before modern land alterations (Kuster:personal communication). Each of these locations was examined by the author in 1970, as were collections from each, which are in the hands of the East Aurora Historical Society, Mr. Robert Kelly, Mr. Walter Sowyrda, the Aurora Country Club, and Mr. James O'Conner, East Aurora Village Engineer. At each locus on the map, at least one diagnostic Meadowood artifact from a projectile point or quaternary blank fragment was found. At Location A, at least 15 netsinkers were found by Sowyrda. These collections, (with the exception of Allen's) most of which were extant, were analyzed only to determine their affiliation. They are similar both in artifact types and frequencies of artifact occurrence to both Sinking Ponds and Allen. All of these sites are located or were located on the contours overlooking the shallow fossil lake at 274.5 m (900 ft) above sea level. However, many of the original contours have been obscured by modern land alterations which have destroyed loci C, D, E, and F. Location B is on a golf course and is inaccessible to excavation. Only Location A shows any promise of availability for excavation. The loss of locations C and D is particularly unfortunate in that they lie opposite each other across Pond Creek where it leaves the marsh. Sinking Ponds, Allen, and the cluster of six other loci, which could be attributed to Meadowood phase, seem to be placed strategically on projecting ridges in proximity to embayments. These were situated above optimum locations for establishing fish traps or weirs for cutting off egress of fish to the main body of water, as discussed above (see Chapter 4, Intrasite Activities). A clearer conception of these constrictions and embayments may be seen in Map 6.2 on which the complete reconstructed marsh or lake is shown. The placement of a camp above the embayments may have allowed easy access down to the shallow lakes from above rather than access around the marshy border. As fish became scarce in one embayment, the camp or camps might be moved to another portion of the lake or to another such lake.

The Sinking Ponds site and associated loci were only a few of the contemporary manifestations of Meadowood culture situated close to constrictions and embayments in shallow lakes. Elsewhere in the region a similar situation is seen at the Petrie Site (Map 6.2). Petrie has similar artifact types but is as yet generally unexplored, except for surface indications. Larkin, another site, has an inventory resembling Sinking Ponds, Allen and Petrie, yet it does not conform to the pattern adduced above (Map 6.2). There is some reason to expect that this site will *not* resemble the configuration of activities at Sinking Ponds. A. W.

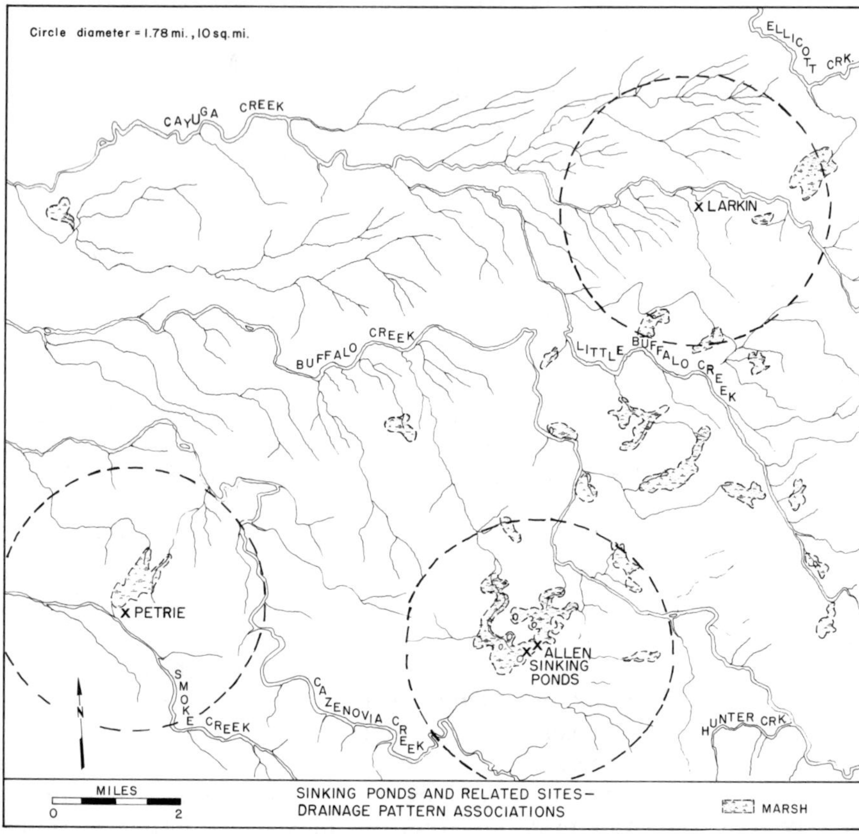

Map 6.2 Sinking Ponds and related sites in the East Aurora area—drainage pattern association.

Abbey's notes reflect a quite dissimilar situation, with Larkin located high above a small tributary of Cayuga Creek close to the confluence with the major stream (Map 6.2). Inspection of the site showed a fairly large, flat area of approximately 0.5 ha (1 a) close to Cayuga Creek from which occupation debris was derived. With the exception of one Meadowood projectile point, a bifacial trianguloid scraper, and a birdstone fragment, no further collection was made.

All of the sites or locations discussed above are small in extent, with the exception of Larkin, which is approximately 0.5 ha (1 a) in extent (A. W. Abbey:collection notes). Most cover less than half a hectare and often less than one quarter hectare or half an acre. The size of Sinking Ponds equals roughly 0.15 ha (0.35 a), as does the Allen site.

The prehistoric potential for floral and faunal subsistence resources in this section of the Niagara Frontier region, based upon site locations, was probably greatest during the spring and summer months. It seems that the area, like most of the Niagara Frontier, is dominated by the maple–beech–hemlock floral association (Shelford 1963:64). Zenkert's reconstructions of flora in the Cazenovia Creek valley coincide with Shelford's assessment (1934:276-78). In summer, numerous fruits and vegetable foods are found close to and on the margins of the wetland areas of the Cazenovia Creek valley (ibid.:276-77). The high sand ridges here offered little, beyond some berries, in the way of nuts or productive plant foods, but the stream, marsh, or lake borders were quite the opposite and were highly productive of floral subsistence items (ibid.:275-77; Shelford 1963:46). Since we have no faunal samples from Sinking Ponds, the suggestion offered in Chapter 4 that fishing was a dominant form of subsistence activity, rests with the artifact and structural inventory and with Rostlund's postulate that shallow lakes formed an excellent fishery (1952:45). Above we have described the processing area at Sinking Ponds, which we believe is associated with fishing, as well as the netsinker frequency and presence of stemmed points which were possibly sockets hafted to serve as leisters or fish darts (see Chapter 4). We suggest that these argue quite favorably, at least for Sinking Ponds, for a fish extractive camp. Other species of animal available in the Niagara Frontier region were quite numerous here (Shelford 1963:47). More than 100 deer, more than 10,000 squirrels, 5 bear, more than 200 turkey, 3000 cottontail rabbits, 1200 raccoon and 1000 woodchucks were postulated by Shelford to have inhabited a 25.9 km^2 (10 sq mi) area, and these could have been exploited, although possibly differentially by season. Beaver, muskrat and other water-related species are not included here nor are waterfowl, whose presence in spring and early fall was prodigious, but for which no records older than fifty years could be located. During winter, however, fish would go deep and deer and mast-oriented herbivores would yard in the broader stream valleys away from the steeply dissected areas around Sinking Ponds, Allen, or Petrie. If we draw a 10 sq mi circle around these sites we see that *each* circle includes a broad stream valley and a shallow lake or marsh (Map 6.2).

Geologically, all of the site loci are well drained and located on glacial gravels, with soils which are podzolic and highly acidic. No particular source of inorganic material appears to have conditioned selection of the location for Sinking Ponds site or the other manifestations of this period in the area; rather, as demonstrated at Sinking Ponds, pebbles of chert existed in sufficient quantity to form the basis of a fairly well developed industrial activity in the manufacture of chert tools. In this sense Sinking Ponds represents a seasonal settlement with a supply of chert which was more than adequate to meet the needs of its inhabitants.

The small size of the Sinking Ponds, Allen, Petrie, and the other six loci suggests that these were not occupied by a large number of persons. We estimated 30 as probably a large figure for Sinking Ponds, based upon the number of possible houses. The thinness of the midden also argues for lack of permanence or intensity of occupation, although a condition of low humic formation may have caused some distortion in this observation.

There is no present candidate for a fall-winter-spring site, occupied for a long period of the year in this area, unless Larkin proves to be such a settlement type. This settlement type would contrast with Sinking Ponds, for its range of activities leads us to propose that it is only an extractive settlement. A site occupied for a longer period by a large number of people would be a base settlement close to the meaning of Winters' term "settlement" (1969:131), but minus burials and with many projectile points. We suspect that such a site exists or did exist quite close to the Sinking Ponds area; it may possibly have been destroyed by the village of East Aurora as some evidence now indicates. This observation results from the unidirectional emphasis on exploitation of a particular resource, fish, evidenced at Sinking Ponds. This limited focus does not seem to conform to what we have discovered about the full range Meadowood subsistence practice. We cannot speculate as to whether such a site will be discovered, but such a subsistence system probably did exist, one portion of which Sinking Ponds, the six loci, and Allen represent. This segment of a yearly cycle was most likely the late spring and summer, and perhaps extended to early autumn. The occupation of each site was transitory and perhaps recurrent, and several may have been utilized at one time, in adjacent lakes or marshes. Sinking Ponds is only one of many similar contemporary settlements in the area.

THE RIVERHAVEN COMPLEX SITES AS SETTLEMENT TYPES

Twenty-three miles to the northwest of Sinking Ponds lies the contemporary Riverhaven Complex on the northeast lobe of Grand Island in the Niagara River. Here information on the distribution of sites is more complete than at Sinking Ponds, because more sites were extant and because much more intensive survey, testing, and excavation were accomplished due primarily to salvage activities. Four loci, including Spicer Creek 1-2, Riverhaven 4, 5E, and 7, cluster around the margin of what is believed to be a shallow levee-trapped water feature now evidenced by Gun Creek Marsh (Map 6-3). These sites are located on small sand knolls which describe embayments in the marsh and are each less than .25 ha (0.5 a) in extent, and these generally exhibit a depth of occupational debris less than 15 cm (0.5 in), exclusive of features. Other loci in Gun Creek Marsh are known, but the material is inconclusive in demonstrating affiliation with those listed above.

Spread along the river bank are six loci, five of which are located on the 173.9 m (570 ft) contour and a 171.4 m (562 ft) bench nearer the river. During flooding in the early spring this bench is inaccessible due to water cover to the base of the 173.9 m (570 ft) terrace. The sites are situated close together along the shore and may overlap to some degree. Although these six locations on the riverbank have not been fully explored, each of the occupations does exhibit greater thickness of occupational materials, 0-21 cm (0-0.7 ft), than those situated further inland.

The faunal and floral resources of Grand Island have been outlined above (Chapter 5, Natural Resources). This reconstruction has been based upon a faunal sample available from the Riverhaven 2 site and on Zenkert's work (1934:303-05). Shelford's 25.9 km^2 (10 sq mi) indices for a floral and faunal community are also applicable; however the faunal sample of Riverhaven 2 makes it easier to reconstruct the faunal exploitation pattern. Revealed in this material is a heavy emphasis on the hunting of mast-eating herbivores such as deer and elk, with bear also exploited. Taylor (1956:136-39) notes that oak forests like those thought to have been so extensively present in the inland upland areas (above 176.9 m or 580 ft) of Grand Island have forest openings which made excellent deer yarding areas during the winter. It has been suggested that deer are most easily

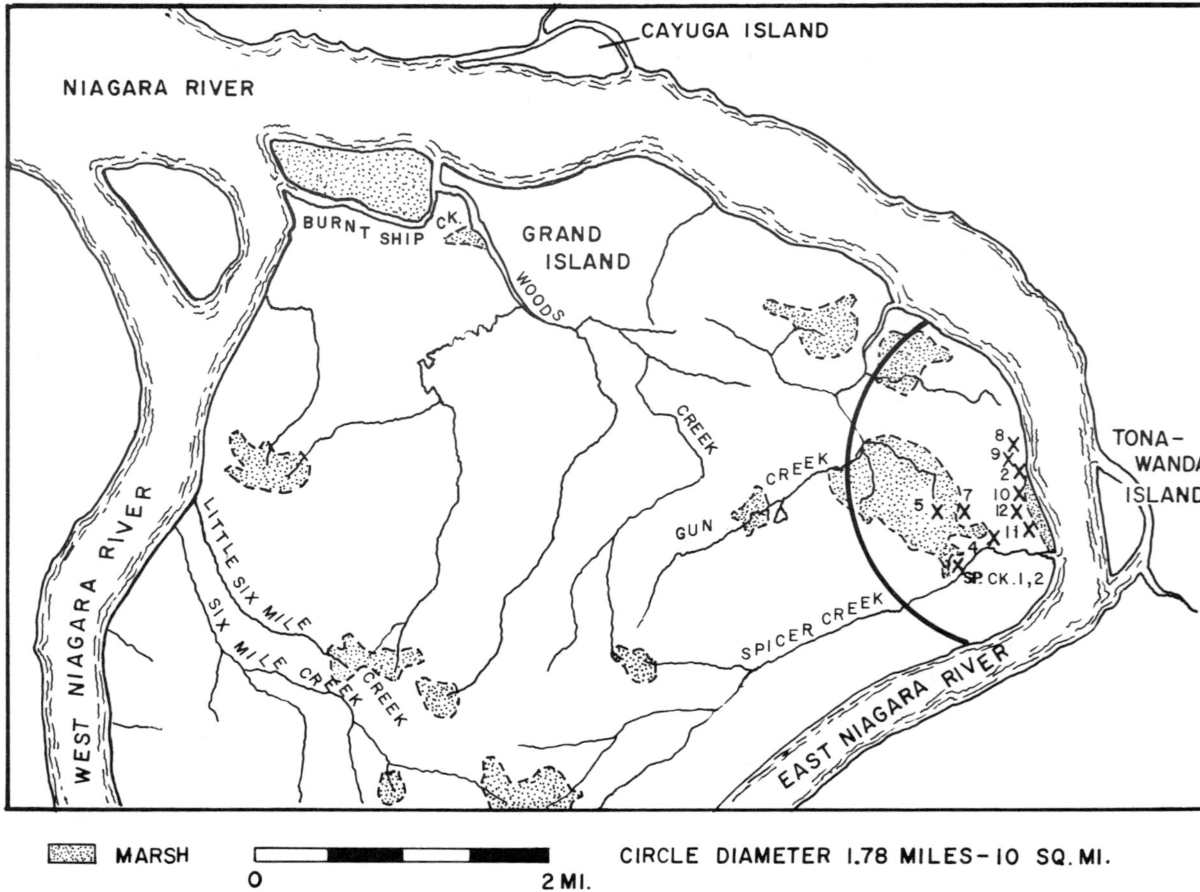

Map 6.3 Riverhaven site complex—Grand Island area—drainage pattern association.

acquired during the late fall and winter (Taylor 1956:10; Hamilton 1943:404; Cahalane 1947:30). At Riverhaven 2, less well represented in terms of available meat are the shoreline species of mammal, fish, reptile, birds, and shellfish.

The cultural inventory, with its low frequencies of netsinkers, utilized flakes, and rock heaps and its high frequencies of projectile points, bifacial scrapers, bone and antler tools, and the abrading stones used to manufacture them, seems to support the assumption that the inhabitants focused on hunting.

We do not have any information on faunal materials from the other loci; however, Spicer Creek 1-2 shows a pattern of features and location similar to Sinking Ponds (Chapter 4) (Map 6.3), which in turn implies an extractive orientation toward fishing, possibly in the shallow lake, now Gun Creek Marsh.

Using the indices developed by Taggart (1967:154) for shoreline utilization we note that Riverhaven 2 has an index of 171, quite low.

Riverhaven 2, in conjunction with loci 8-12, appears to represent intense occupation of approximately .8 km (.5 mi) of river terrace heavily forested during prehistoric times by mast producing trees. Riverhaven 2 shows a heavy occupation midden on the 171.4 m (562 ft) bench, and the material inventory is quite extensive as well. It has been suggested above that a cluster of deep basin-shaped pits may be related to storage. The intensity of occupation evidenced by the deep midden zone and heavy artifact yield suggest that Riverhaven 2 is a base settlement. Within 25.9 km (10 sq mi) (Map 6.3), the inland loci cluster above a shallow lake or marsh and the implication from their location is that they were so situated in order to utilize the embayments or fingerlike extensions of what was once a shallow lake. It should be noted here that the term "inland" is actually confusing since the contention is that these are sites more related to the shoreline exploitation pattern which we believe characterizes Sinking Ponds and sites like it. Their small size and proximity to Riverhaven 2 suggest that the population did not move far to exploit a different set of resources and indeed the richness of the flora and fauna may have imposed a loose form of sedentarization around which the yearly subsistence round was accomplished.

Nowhere on any of the loci in the Riverhaven Complex was chert available (Chapter 5). This raw material appears to have been imported in the form of tabular cores from chert sources, the nearest of which was on the Onondaga escarpment, six miles eastward across the Niagara River. We may postulate that one form of settlement type allied with the Riverhaven complex is the chert resource site from which raw material is extracted, although no specific contemporary site is now known beyond the Fort Erie flint quarry which was used extensively throughout the prehistoric period. The picture presented by the Ríverhaven Complex shows that differing resources were exploited seasonally.

Thus one settlement type is the large late autumn, winter and early spring base settlement partially represented by Riverhaven 2. This site, covering approximately 1 ha (2 a), was arranged lineally along the river, and from it large herbivorous mammals were hunted. A second type is the small extractive camp, like Spicer Creek 1-2, occupied during the spring and summer and located inland in a marsh-lake micro-environment suitable for fishing or water fowling. A third settlement type is the chert resource site, which provided raw material for the intensive manufacture activities which appear to be ubiquitous in all settlement types in the complex. It also appears that these settlement types were spatially arranged so that a minimum of effort was required to shift residence from a settlement related to one exploitive form to another.

SUMMARY OF SETTLEMENT TYPES

In this chapter we have attempted to show certain trends in the distribution of sites which we have loosely classified by function as habitation sites. There was no simple division from other sites such as burial loci, by location, although it was noted that some of our habitation sites clustered above 600 ft in elevation and on perpendicular ridges near either streams or shallow lakes. On the other hand some habitation sites were near major rivers or deep lakes and were located on terraces or parallel ridges. These sites with large deep midden deposits did not conform to the usual pattern of elevation and stream and/or lake association. Of the reported sites, Vinette, Nahrwold 2, Scaccia, and Riverhaven 2 fit this situation most readily. They were different from many of the other habitation sites in terms of size, depth of occupation zone, and most of all, location. All were located on or close to major streams and generally situated on terraces. Tests conducted between Scaccia, Riverhaven 2, and Lamoka Lake on the amounts of meat utilized all show a similar focus on the meat of upland herbivores. It does not seem fortuitous that Lamoka Lake, a large possibly year-round site now dated at circa 2500 B.C., also fits the same location pattern (Ritchie and Funk 1973:338), situated on a parallel ridge at the mouth of a deep extant lake. All of these sites had large deep pits, some used for storage, others for a less securely known function.

The division between the two forms of habitation sites suggested that if the requisite amount of data were present in a region, one might look for some distribution of functional settlement types within Meadowood phase. There is a seasonal basis for dividing sites into functional types based upon the activities represented upon each.

The data from Sinking Ponds and Riverhaven 2 show that it is based upon a different exploitive strategy. Shallow lakes were excellent fisheries and had numerous herbaceous plants available during the spring and summer months, whereas the riverine terrace area contained well-watered places near a large stand of oak, and the exploiters of mast, deer and other larger mammals, were usually hunted during the fall and winter months. The Sinking Ponds site gave evidence of being a small, lightly occupied camp whose inhabitants were concerned with fishing in the shallow lake and processing their catches. The manufacture of tools was carried out here from locally available materials, but storage and ceremonial activities appeared to be lacking. Habitation was light, probably less than 30 persons. Riverhaven 2 gave evidence of long-term, recurrent occupation, especially in the depth of the midden. Processing activities seemed most concerned with herbivorous mammals which were heavily represented in the faunal sample. Some smaller sites, Spicer Creek 1-2 and Riverhaven 4, located near Riverhaven 2 did, on the other hand, appear to be more similar in processing activity to Sinking Ponds. We feel sure that the large deep pits that are present at Riverhaven 2 function primarily as storage areas and secondarily as receptacles for refuse. The complete structure of the habitation activity at Riverhaven 2 has yet to be determined. Ceremony is, however, clearly absent on this site as well as on the smaller ones in what we have called the Riverhaven Complex. Manufacture at Riverhaven 2 was performed on high grade chert derived from sources up to six miles from the site and off Grand Island. Thus, we propose that the chert resource site is part of the complex, for materials were quarried and carried back in the form of tabular blocks for further modification.

We conclude from our examination that Sinking Ponds and associated loci, Spicer Creek 1-2 and Riverhaven 4, were probably occupied by a portion of a band in the early spring, summer and perhaps early autumn. During this time fishing was the dominant form of subsistence, supplemented by the hunting of waterfowl and gathering of vegetable foods found in proximity to shallow lakes. Riverhaven 2, Larkin, and sites like it were occupied during autumn, winter, and early spring. During the autumn some fishing and gathering of shellfish were carried out as well as intensive deer hunting which lasted for the whole winter. Nuts may have been the dominant form of floral resource, although we have no direct evidence from these sites of this being the case. This site and adjacent loci on the river terrace were probably occupied by a band of up to 150 members. It is most likely that a site of this type existed and is yet to be discovered in the Sinking Ponds area.

Perhaps during autumn or early spring when people were on the move, ceremonial activities were carried out at a central location with local bands combining to form the loose aggregate known as the regional band. At this time trade, exchange of women in marriage, and other social activities could have been carried out; however, we have no direct evidence of this being the case in the Niagara Frontier.

CHAPTER VII

THE SYSTEMICS OF MEADOWOOD PHASE SETTLEMENT PATTERN: INTERPRETATION AND SPECULATION

In this chapter we will discuss the systemics of the settlement pattern of Meadowood culture in the Niagara Frontier and present comparative data from elsewhere in New York State and the Lake Forest region. We have presented the Sinking Ponds site and the Riverhaven 2 site as settlement types in Chapter 4.

Our method for associating the above sites with one another has been based upon their relation to nearby resources and the evidence of activities which demonstrate their utilization of these resources. In the general analysis of Meadowood site location in Chapter 3, it was noted that there seemed to be a distinction between fluvial locations and marsh locations. The more specific data from Sinking Ponds and Riverhaven 2 show that this association is based upon a different exploitive strategy. Munsen, Parmallee, and Yarnell have suggested a model for analyzing exploitive strategy (1971:413-15). Basing their subsistence potentials upon the concepts of Shelford (1963), they suggest a radius of 1.78 mi from a site or an area of 10 sq mi, be used to examine potentials available to the population of that site. We have used that model above in order to give some territorial parameters for populations at Sinking Ponds and Riverhaven. Locations in juxtaposition to certain resources conditioned in a systematic way the scheduling and the taking of those resources. Shallow lakes were excellent fisheries and had numerous herbaceous plants available during the spring and summer months, whereas the riverine terrace areas contained well-watered places near large stands of oak, and the exploiters of the abundant mast, deer and other larger mammals, were usually hunted during the fall and winter months.

Winters (1959) has suggested that:

> From the data available at present, one might hazard a guess that bands tended to return to sites year after year, covering the same area repeatedly. It is possible that a band would cover some 400 square miles in zones of maximum natural food resources. For zones less favorably supplied, the area would naturally be considerably

> larger. Various bands might, of course, have had overlapping territories, and there would certainly have been shifting of areas from time to time. (Winters 1959:12)

He has also indicated that only half the area may have really been intensively exploited (Winters 1969:110). We have modified Winters' proposition, suggesting that a local band utilizing a region might exploit it in an effective way by moving occupation loci only if the year-round cycle failed to produce requisite resources within a relatively small portion of it, perhaps 10 sq mi, as Munsen et al. suggest, or a somewhat larger area if Winters' proposition is correct. However, it may be that control was exerted over more extensive resources than were actually being used at any one moment; therefore the figure of 400 sq mi or a diameter of 22.58 mi which delineates a local band exploitation area will be retained. Over-exploitation in one areal segment could cause the carrying capacity to be reduced in and around a band's base settlement and subsidiary extractive camps. The base settlement might then have been moved to another location which showed the same favorable juxtaposition of subsistence resources within an area over which that local band could have effective resource control.

Ritchie and Funk have hypothesized that Meadowood groups were strongly oriented toward riverine and/or lacustrine locations and resources (1973:348). Further, they suggest that "back country" sites were not utilized and that this signifies the lack of a seasonal round. Investigation of data for all Meadowood habitation sites generally supports the first proposition, but the statement needs refinement. For example, water does not always equal fish, for much depends upon the form of its disposition, i.e., deep rivers, shallow streams, deep lakes without embayment, or shallow glacial relicts with numerous coves.

As stated above control of a resource area similarly does not always mean constant use of all parts of it simultaneously or consecutively. Indeed Ritchie and Funk have said that "these groups remained on or near major waterways in all seasons, perhaps camping within a special microenvironment" (1973:348). Our contention is, however, that there is no "back country", but only areal segments that may not have the optimum juxtaposition of micro-environmental niches sought by Meadowood peoples. The ten square mile paradigm suggested above appeared to fit the association of resources and sites in both of the areas we studied intensively. It seems logical to assume that as one segment of an area became over exploited, movement would take place to another favorable combination of resources within the immediate area, or more specifically in the case of our model, within an approximately 400 square mile area. At first glance, the general distribution of settlement types remains unchanged, but one complete yearly subsistance acquisition area has been substituted for another, in almost precisely the same fashion as has been documented for later cultures (White 1963). Ritchie and Funk remark that:

> The question of cultivation of corn by Meadowood people remains unanswered. But it is difficult to explain the apparent shift in settlement pattern and the elaboration of mortuary ceremonialism without invoking some degree of change in the subsistence base. (1973:348)

We believe that the system of subsistence aquisition need not have radically changed, rather the selection and scheduling of resource production areas was probably more restricted and efficient giving the impression of semisedentary character (ibid.) but leaving the systemic network of settlement relatively unchanged from that of the Late Archaic (Table 2.5).

In order to understand the proposed exploitation pattern and settlement system, it is necessary to review some considerations on the nature of band composition and size. This question has been debated at length and will not be debated again here. We shall follow Steward's extremely basic, open definition:

> The only useful heuristic, diagnostic and delimiting criteria of bands are that these societies shall have, first, a fairly wide-ranging nomadism (which may or may not involve territoriality) and, second, permanent membership, even though the society fragments into smaller groups during certain portions of the year. These delimitations would make the concept of bands include many though by no means all, hunters and gatherers. (1969:187)

Band population is another controversial subject, although majority opinion in a discussion of band size clusters at the "magic numbers" of 500 for regionally cohesive bands and 25 for the segments (Lee and DeVore 1968:245-48). However, Helm has designated the tripartite division: "task group," "local band" and "regional band" within a "band society." After setting aside the regional band, she defines the "local band" and "task group" as:

> . . . segments of the total population—sets of nuclear families enduring in co-settlement for at least a few years—which I call local bands . . . I further distinguish the foregoing kinds of groups from those seasonal groupings at the fishery, or on the trapline or on hunt I have called task groups . . . In the more enduring groups sharing some form of socio-territorial identity, I have looked for some kind of patterning. (1969:214-15)

Using this hierarchy of organization of information we suggest some limits. A discussion of size in ethnographically known groups produced the following consensus on size, although not on definition of segments (Damas 1969:209-11):

Task Group: 15-35 persons.
Local Band: 100-150 persons.
Regional Band: 250-500 persons.

This population division is probably as close to a general consensus on the nature of the band size as can be gleaned from the literature and the concept has some utility in understanding the situation such as that presented by this distribution of Meadowood social groups which must have had some form of integrative system. Obviously there is a limit to the imposition of an ethnographic model on prehistoric groups, but in the literature surveyed (Damas 1969; Lee and DeVore 1968; Steward 1955) only those groups with similar adaptive strategies are used to select the figures used above. These groups are North American, sub-artic hunters and gatherers, and also, where possible, we have used prehistoric reconstructions (Binford, response to query in Lee and DeVore 1968:248). The degree of consistency of this paradigm with the data derived from excavation is significant. The task group is equated with the extractive camp; the local band with the base settlement and the regional band with the conjunction of two or more local bands.

We have chosen to apply the tri-level classification offered by Helm within Winters' suggested territorial limits of 400 sq mi for the Niagara Frontier region. Although we are unable to define precisely the number of local bands, we can show what we believe are two: the *"Grand Island" Local Band* consisting of Riverhaven 2 and associated loci, and the *"East Aurora" Local Band,* composed of Sinking Ponds and associated or postulated loci. Possibly a third might be a *South Erie County Band* containing Winters' site and associated loci, if any (Map 7.1).

Although the data are now fragmentary and in some areas quite weak, we believe that it is possible to define a logically consistent settlement system for Meadowood, which associates the known facts and illustrates culture process. To do this we will again use the functional categories procurement, processing, manufacture, storage, ceremony and habitation and will try to demonstrate their systemic nature not merely as activities within sites but as parts of the system which produces the distinctive form of Meadowood settlement pattern (Fig. 1.1).

THE SYSTEM OF PROCUREMENT

We discussed above the locations of the Niagara Frontier sites, their interrelationships within their localities and their possible interactions with the environment. The evidence for such interaction is the basis of subsistence activity or procurement of food. We have distributed the evidence for procurement in Table 7.1. The artifacts relating to that activity may actually separate sites into different

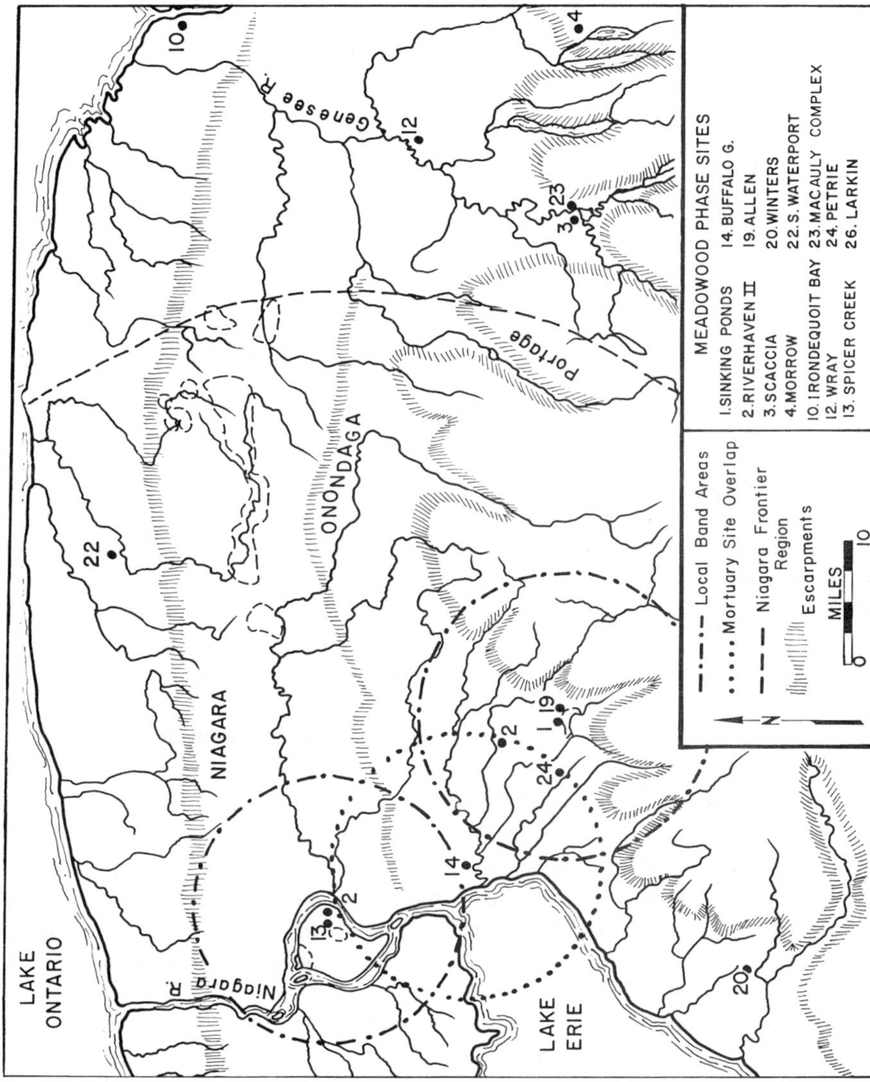

Map 7.1 Niagara Frontier local band areas.

TABLE 7.1
DISTRIBUTION OF CULTURAL MATERIALS
RELATED TO PROCUREMENT BY SITE

Materials	Sinking Ponds	River-haven 2	Spicer Creek
Artifactual:			
Projectile Point, Sidenotched	21	52	1
Projectile Point, Cornernotched	10	5	
Projectile Point, Stemmed	10	1	
Projectile Point, Lateral Basal		6	
Projectile Point, Indeterminable		4	
Netsinkers	97	25	
Birdstone	1	1	
Total (N = 234)	139	94	1
%	59	40	1

N.A.E. = No assignable or available evidence for structural or nonartifactual materials.

settlement types by illustrating emphases on different means of procurement. Using the distribution of netsinkers versus projectile points at Sinking Ponds and Riverhaven 2 (Table 7.1), a chi-square test was performed and yielded a significance level of 1 case out of 1000 that this was not a random occurrence. Spicer Creek 1-2 showed a sample too low to be tested. The Vinette site, when tested against Sinking Ponds using the same distribution of netsinkers and projectile points, also showed a nonrandom occurrence at the .001 level. On the other hand, no significant difference with Riverhaven 2 was developed using the same test. The separation of the two forms of habitation sites as differing settlement types is evidenced by the appropriation of materials relating to faunal procurement.

Faunal material at Riverhaven 2 seems to support the contention that a fall–winter–spring occupation is indicated by hunting, but only indirectly by artifact and activity were we able to sustain the hypothesis that Sinking Ponds was a spring–summer fishing station. This hypothesis had been earlier demonstrated only by analogy with present day resources (Ritchie and Funk 1973:347).

Outside the Niagara Frontier, the Scaccia site provides some interesting insights to the Meadowood procurement system. Ritchie and Funk regard it as the first component where hunting instead of fishing was the primary procurement activity (1973:347). The nut and vegetable materials found in pits bolster the hunting assignment by indicating the presence of abundant mast in the biomass. The bulk of the assemblage points toward a fall–winter–spring occupation but the presence of some woodchuck, geese, ducks, turtles,

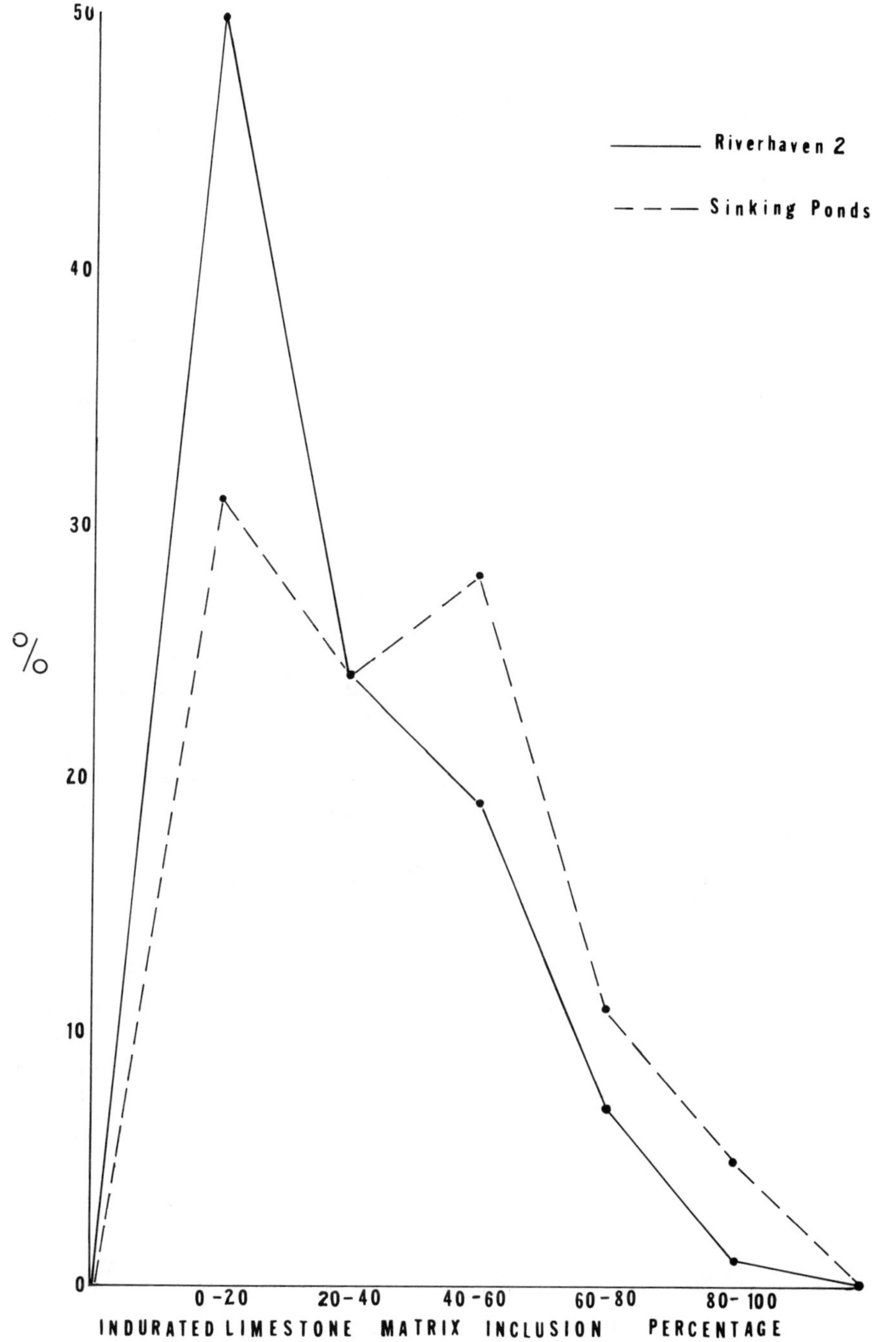

Fig. 7.1 Chert inclusion comparison.

frogs, and fishes does not indicate to us that a summer occupation was sustained.

The location of the site might argue for its assignment as a summer extractive camp, yet its size, probable population, and available evidence indicate that it is a base settlement. Fishing, a late spring activity, may however, have been carried out near the site in the creek and open water portions of the marsh. Although no netsinkers were recovered, stemmed points were found in association with Meadowood sidenotched points in pits and with fish bone of species such as suckers, most available to spear or leister capture (App. C, Table C.4). Although the investigator argues that these points indicate a distinct earlier occupation, there seems to be no further substantiation for it beyond two beveled adze fragments found on the surface. Both of these elements have also been found on other Meadowood sites and the stemmed point is almost ubiquitous as a minority type on most Meadowood sites. The functional assignment of such a point for fishing or fowling darts would imply that it was retained long beyond its major distribution in the Lamoka phase, especially in derivative cultural expressions like that of Meadowood phase.

Procurement of chert raw material suggests that when chert was not readily available, an intermediate form of transitory settlement type was necessitated, the chert resource site. We suspect that the primary chert resource site in the Niagara Frontier was located at the Onondaga Escarpment, possibly where Ellicott Creek intersects it, or to the west. Riverhaven 2, a base settlement type of site, is located directly across the river from Ellicott Creek. In order to determine whether the Riverhaven 2 chert utilization did in fact benefit from proximity to high grade sources, the chert artifacts of Sinking Ponds and Riverhaven 2 were examined for matrix or indurated limestone inclusion, were tabulated by percent inclusion, and then were cumulatively graphed (Fig. 7.1). The Riverhaven 2 curve was high at the 0-20% level but steadily declined at higher levels of inclusion whereas the Sinking Ponds curve was sustained through the 40-60% levels. A chi-square test was made in a 2x2 table by site on the categories 0-20% and 40-60%. The distribution showing higher grade chert at Riverhaven 2 was supported at the .01 level, providing some substantiation for earlier impressions.

THE SYSTEM OF PROCESSING

Evidence for functional interrelationship between examples of settlement types generated within this category is primarily structural and is shown in Table 7.2. Although the numbers of features are too

TABLE 7.2
DISTRIBUTION OF CULTURAL MATERIALS
RELATED TO PROCESSING BY SITE

Materials	Sinking Ponds	River-haven 2	Spicer Creek
Artifactual:			
Longitudinal Knives	9	30	
Scrapers, Unifacial	26	92	18
Scrapers, Bifacial	15	104	6
Abrading Stone, Mano	11	7	1
Anvilstone, Pitted	12	7	
Drills	13	49	
Celts	2	6	
Chopper	1		
Steatite Vessel	1		
Pottery Vessel	7	6	
Structural:			
Hearths	9	4	10
Rock Heaps	14	3	9
Houses	1		
Nonartifactual			
Utilized Flakes	673	135	
Fire-cracked Rock	543		
Total (N = 1824)	1337	443	44
%	73	24	3
Vessel Measurement	100+		
Fxd. Rock 1 Present	100 0-absent	1 each present +	100

small and too skewed to give an accurate probability statistic, we note a coincident distribution of hearths and rock heaps at Sinking Ponds and Spicer Creek 1-2, whereas both structures are quite infrequent at Riverhaven 2 (Table 7.2). We mentioned above that the rock heap was probably related to the drying and/or smoking of fish. Cursory examination of the Scaccia features shows the ratio of rock heaps to storage features to be roughly 1 to 3 or about the same as that present at Riverhaven 2, 3 to 8, suggesting fish processing was relatively unimportant at both sites.

Another index of function is the relationship of unifaces to bifaces (Fitting 1969:367; Taggart 1967:164). The index $\frac{\text{Unifaces}}{\text{Bifaces}}$ x 100 has been devised as a means of demonstrating the frequency of unifaces which might imply fish related processing, at any one station, an index of over 100 (Wobst 1968; Fitting et al. 1969). The Riverhaven 2 distribution of bifaces to unifaces yields a uniface index of 15.5. The distribution of unifaces to bifaces at Sinking Ponds is an index of 282.2. The juxtaposition of 16:282 again leads to the conclusion that if unifaces imply fish association as Wobst, Fitting and others have suggested, and bifaces imply bone or hide working on hunting stations, then Riverhaven 2 and Sinking Ponds contrast significantly. Although the sample is so low as to be statistically unreliable, the index calculated for Spicer Creek 1-2 is 300.

Mano abrading stones at Sinking Ponds and Riverhaven 2 show a 2:1 ratio, perhaps indicating processing vegetable materials was more pronounced at Sinking Ponds, but sampling error is possible here as it is in the number of celts which imply woodworking, in reverse trend, as being important at Riverhaven 2. At Scaccia several milling stones and the presence of acorns and hickory nuts as well as *Chenopodium* and *Polygonum* demonstrate clearly the heavy reliance upon processed vegetable foods. This activity is tied closely to that of storage, because nuts and seeds were stored before or after processing (Ritchie and Funk 1973:348). This site represents the best evidence for processing of vegetal material and its prior or subsequent storage.

THE SYSTEM OF MANUFACTURE

In the manufacture of chert tools the only division between the Niagara Frontier sites is the frequency of occurrence of artifactual materials, which also show almost the same proportions of whole blank to fragment (Table 7.3). It is not possible to compare meaningfully the flint detritus from the sites because of differential sampling. However, we may note that at Sinking Ponds flakes make up 38% of the detritus, while chips are 62% (Table 7.3). At Riverhaven 2 flakes were 26% and chips 74%, while at Spicer Creek 1-2 flakes were 8% and chips comprised 92% of the sample.

It has been noted on all habitation sites of the Meadowood phase that the working of chert was a subsidiary or even dominant form of activity. Similarity with the pattern of manufacture at Riverhaven 2 has been noted at Nahrwold 2 where "quarry blanks" or tabular blocks were brought from local sources for on-site modification. This is substantiated by the high frequency of artifacts made from the local Deepskill chert. Local manufacture is also seen at Dennis where Normanskill chert is used for 50% of the projectile point sample (Ritchie and Funk 1973:116).

Much discussion of Meadowood phase has centered on the distribution and/or function of the characteristic leaf-shaped cache blades or mortuary blanks. We examined samples of cache blades from 13 sites either in whole or in part and developed 20 variables with some 92 values (App. A, Table A.4*b*). A matrix was prepared to illustrate the coefficients of correlation between cache blade samples. These coeffi-

TABLE 7.3
DISTRIBUTION OF CULTURAL MATERIALS RELATED TO MANUFACTURE BY SITE

Materials	Sinking Ponds	River-haven 2	Spicer Creek
Artifactual:			
Hammerstones	19	11	1
Primary Blank	12	46	
Secondary Blank	20	114	12
Quaternary Blank Width	17	76	41
Quaternary Blank Base	41	324	30
Quaternary Blank Tip	47	295	28
Tertiary Blank Width	6	61	
Tertiary Blank Base	19	122	27
Tertiary Blank Tip	35	170	27
Abrading Stone, Grooved	8	18	1
Structural:			
Manufacturing Caches	6	1	3
Nonartifactual:			
Cores/Spalls	442	529	3
Chips	16,168	5781	4966
Flint pebbles	25		
Flakes	10,357	2614	470
Total (N = 42,993)	27,222	10,162	5609
%	63	24	13

cients are presented in Table 7.4. In this table it may be noted that the least correlation below 0.5, when 1.0 is perfect correlation, is between those sites where local chert sources are used, i.e., Deepskill chert. Onondaga chert accounted for 85% of the total sample of nearly 500 items, and it is obvious that a great degree of similarity of morphology and metrics is apparent on all sites of Meadowood phase, burial sites included, and that such homogeneity may be due to some process unrelated to manufacture, such as exchange. Once the manufacture process is understood (Fig. 1.2) the process of exchange of raw material and finished products can be investigated, but products at parallel stages must be compared, i.e., quaternary blanks or cache blades with quaternary blanks. This obviates the impressions of "crudity" and "degree of skillfulness" in manufacture which tend to obscure more meaningful comparisons (Ritchie and Funk 1973:115). Projectile points of the sidenotched Meadowood type display much more variation than the cache blades referred to above. It appears that modification of a blank to a projectile point with a haft element was more individualized and idiosyncratic on separate sites and may even have bypassed the quater-

TABLE 7.4
CORRELATION COEFFICIENTS FOR "CACHE BLADE" ATTRIBUTES AT MEADOWOOD SITES

	Sinking Ponds	Riverhaven 2	Scaccia	Morrow	Oberlander 2 WCH 2	Oberlander 2 WBR16	Buffalo G	Muskalonge Lake	Hunter	Nahrwold 2	Vinette	Irondequoit Bay	Rene Menard 2
Sinking Ponds	1.0000	.7689	.8059	.7700	.8244	.8492	.7507	.3918	.6166	.6054	.8301	.5945	.6938
Riverhaven 2	.7689	1.0000	.8707	.6727	.7090	.7799	.6451	.4456	.5814	.6269	.7632	.5708	.6718
Scaccia	.8059	.8707	1.0000	.6606	.6612	.7690	.6187	.3894	.5471	.6140	.7440	.5662	.6303
Morrow	.7700	.6728	.6606	1.0000	.8497	.8807	.7155	.6550	.8694	.5648	.5641	.6085	.7410
Oberlander 2 WCH 2	.8244	.7090	.6612	.8497	1.0000	.9023	.8252	.5388	.7532	.5937	.7280	.6822	.7564
Oberlander 2 WBR16	.8492	.7799	.7690	.8807	.9023	1.0000	.8389	.5894	.7941	.6608	.7222	.7376	.8175
Buffalo G	.7507	.6451	.6187	.7155	.8252	.8389	1.0000	.5339	.6843	.6573	.7208	.7691	.7793
Muskalonge Lake	.3918	.4456	.3894	.6550	.5388	.5894	.5339	1.0000	.8572	.2918	.3471	.4717	.5147
Hunter	.6166	.5814	.5471	.8694	.7532	.7941	.6843	.8572	1.0000	.4431	.4575	.4971	.6732
Nahrwold 2	.6054	.6269	.6140	.5648	.5937	.6608	.6573	.2918	.4431	1.0000	.5312	.5904	.7174
Vinette	.8301	.7632	.7440	.5641	.7280	.7222	.7208	.3471	.4575	.5312	1.0000	.6199	.5609
Irondequoit Bay	.5945	.5708	.5662	.6085	.6821	.7376	.7691	.4717	.4971	.5904	.6199	1.0000	.8224
Rene Menard 2	.6938	.6718	.6303	.7410	.7564	.8175	.7793	.5147	.6732	.7174	.5609	.8224	1.0000

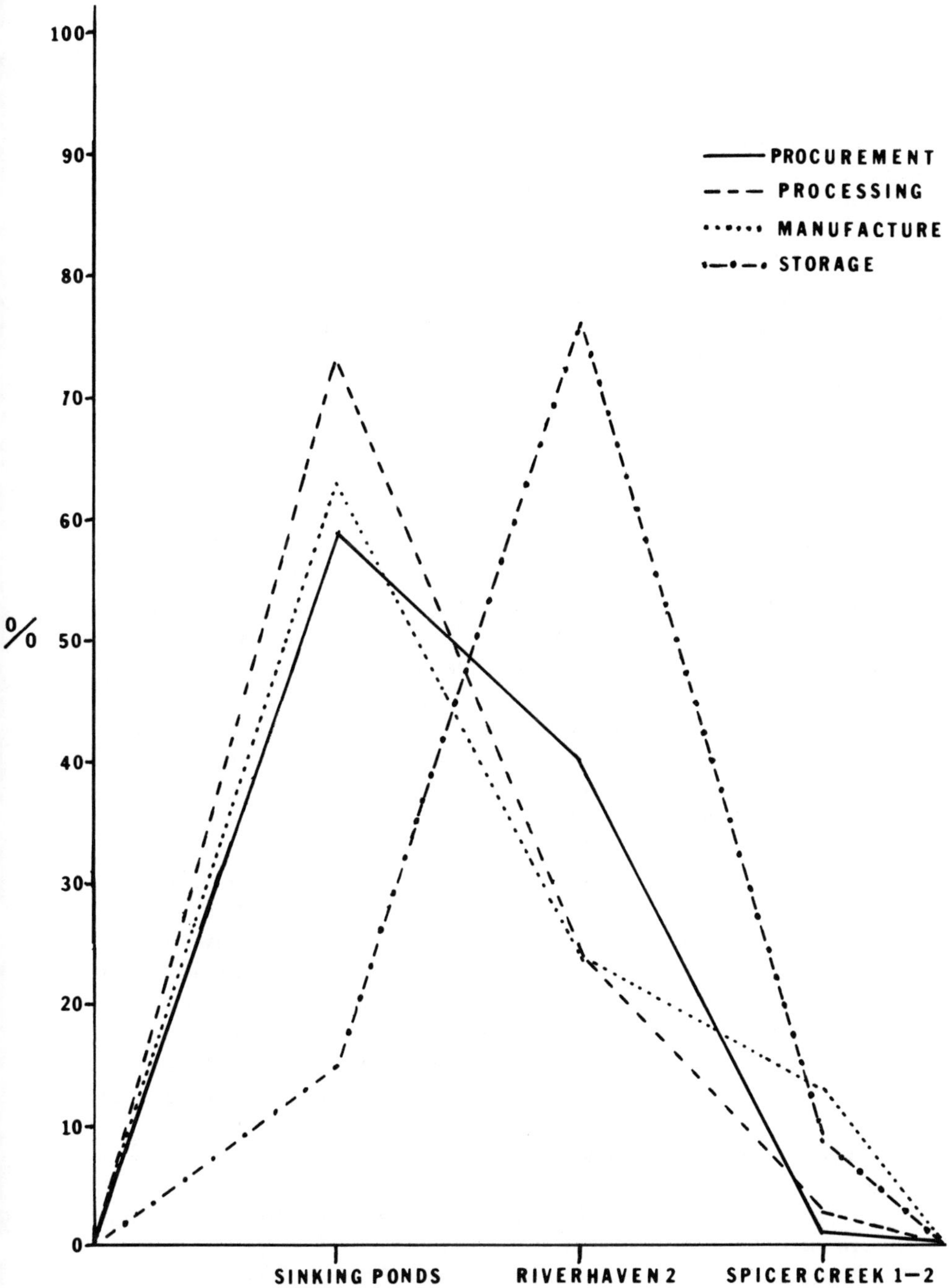

Fig. 7.2 Comparison of activities at Sinking Ponds, Riverhaven 2 and Spicer Creek 1-2.

nary blank stage accounting for a deviation in thickness such as that seen at Scaccia (ibid.).

The production of bone and antler tools appears to be more prevalent at Riverhaven 2 and Scaccia due to the high ratios of grooved abrading stones and the large samples of bone awls and worked bone and antler. This also substantiates the hunting orientation previously delineated for both sites.

Manufacture/cache pits appear to have been more frequent at the task-oriented fishing stations, possibly implying that materials were harder to come by at these stations or at least it was not necessary to continue to provide material from distant sources for chert production while the occupants were engaged in the procurement of summer subsistence resources.

THE SYSTEM OF STORAGE

Storage or refuse functions at Sinking Ponds appear to be intimately connected with three possible houses and to be of a transitory nature, as evidenced by shallow pits and a shallow midden. At the Dennis site, a series of small camp loci, the same situation appears to be present with small hearths and other features, none of which alter its transitory nature (Ritchie and Funk 1973:348). Like Dennis, Spicer Creek 1-2 had little evidence of storage yet had a high degree of similarity to other activities represented at Sinking Ponds. At Riverhaven 2, a deep accumulation of refuse is accompanied by several large deep pits which relate to some form of storage as did the large basin-shaped pits which formed a majority of the 128 features excavated at Scaccia (ibid.:347). These storage pits were prominent due to their size and depth and to their characteristic structure, straight walled, with a relatively flat floor (Table 7.5). They were differentiated by the frequency of artifacts representing debris. As at both Riverhaven 2 and Scaccia much the same artifact percentages occur in the shallow pits at Sinking Ponds (Table 7.5). Spicer Creek had no evidence of storage. The inference drawn from the diversity of storage structures represented by features associated with shelter at one site and with a probable storage or concentrated refuse area at others is clear. The one is not as intensively occupied for as long a period as the other, nor is the population as large.

At Scaccia direct evidence shows that some of the storage pits held nuts, principally acorns and that these pits are strikingly similar in size, structure, and content to many found at Lamoka Lake and at the Cole Gravel Pit (ibid.:348). It is quite likely that these pits did, as others

TABLE 7.5
DISTRIBUTION OF CULTURAL MATERIALS RELATED TO STORAGE BY SITE

Materials	Sinking Ponds	River-haven 2	Spicer Creek
Artifactual:			
Pottery Vessels	7	6	
Steatite Vessels	1		
Quaternary Blade Base	41	324	30
Quaternary Blade Tip	47	305	28
Tertiary Blade Base	20	122	27
Tertiary Blade Tip	35	170	27
Celt	1	6	
Gorget	2	1	
Pipe	1	1	
Chopper	1		
Birdstone	1	1	
Structural:			
Shallow Basin Pits	3		
Small Deep Pits	2	1	
Large Deep Pits		8	
Cache (Net)	1		
Nonartifactual			
Flint Pebbles	25		
Total (N = 1245)	188	945	112
%	15	76	9

have pointed out, function to store food over the winter. The emphasis here is that this was their primary function on a fall–winter–early spring base settlement. Overlap and intersection of storage features at Scaccia furthers the suggestion that occupation was repeated. Similar overlap was also seen in features excavated at Riverhaven 2 in 1971 but is not reported here.

It is on the basis of this intensity of occupation and occurence of storage as a major activity that great homogeneity is seen between the Riverhaven 2 site and the Scaccia site and that they are seen as the best defined base settlements of Meadowood phase. Concentration of population and storage differs little from Lamoka Lake, where the deep storage pits are found in arc formations (Ritchie 1969:72-73) and in a much more pronounced form at the Cole Gravel Pit or Farrell Farm (Hayes 1966:170; 1969:2-3). The form and content are obviously the same, and when a more extensive analysis of Riverhaven 2, Scaccia, Lamoka Lake, and Cole are undertaken it is quite likely that there will be *storage feature clusters,* generally arc-shaped and possibly relating to one kin group. Certainly combination of storage features and houses, where present at these Late Archaic–Early Woodland sites offers us our best clue to the social structure. The presence of the large deep storage pits unequivocally associated with sites, demonstrating along with other evidence the greater size, density, and recurrence of occupation, is the most definite indication that Meadowood populations were organized into large stable camp sites approaching village size during a significant portion of the year.

THE CEREMONY AND EXCHANGE SYSTEM

Neither the Sinking Ponds site nor the Riverhaven 2 site can be associated with group ceremonialism based upon the assemblages from them, but this is also true of the other Meadowood habitation components outside of the Niagara Frontier (Ritchie and Funk 1973:348). The only evidence at all from these sites is several fragmentary artifacts and from Scaccia, several casual interments. However, this lack of data caused a search for some meaningful association of Sinking Ponds and Riverhaven 2 with ceremonial or burial sites. One such site, Buffalo G, known to have existed on Buffalo Creek, produced at least one burial with red ochre, cache blades, and several other objects. Little is known about the site other than its location, which is now completely altered by urban activities. Several areas near the site have also given evidence of some Meadowood materials but with no clear structural relationship. It is speculated that local bands in the Niagara Frontier may have utilized a common sacred precinct convenient along major waterways, such as the Niagara River. The Riverhaven 2 site is located on this major east–west communication route and the Sinking Ponds site is close to a major tributary. Comparative evidence which supports such a conclusion is the patterning of burial clusters at Morrow Site (White n.d.). It has been theorized that this patterning may have been a result of lineage groups or other kin-based corporate groups utilizing slightly differing locations within a burial site (ibid.). Most burial sites contain from 1 to 30 individuals and no real indication of habitation, although 22 "storage pits" were noted at Oberlander 2 (Ritchie and Funk 1973:348). The burial pits had generally the same structure as the storage pits, which also may have resulted from kin-based clustering in habitation sites. Evidence of separation between the Vinette site and the Oberlander 2 burial station supports the above proposition, and at Muskelonge Lake and Hunter sites, Ritchie notices separable loci of crematoria and burial pits (1944:152, 160; 1955:61-65). He also states that:

> The separated burial loci suggest the periodic performance of mortuary ritualism at a "sacred" area by a group resident elsewhere in the region for the habitation traces on both sites are too limited to account for more than a brief sojourning while cremation and inhumation of the dead were accomplished. (1955:61)

The crematoria present at these Indian River sites also appear to have a functional correlation with rock heaps utilized possibly as radiant heat ovens, which have been found at summer fishing stations, and the same association is present with crematoria in the coastal Orient phase (Ritchie 1955:66-70).

It would seem a likely proposition that the settlement type known as the *mortuary activity site* represents a unifying factor in a region, binding the various local bands into a cohesive regional band through performance of ritual activity over the dead on some territorially neutral ground. The mortuary activity site is the settlement type represented by the two Indian River sites, Hunter and Muskalonge Lake as well as by Oberlander 2. Morrow and in the Niagara Frontier by Buffalo G. In these sites human inhumation or cremation followed by secondary disposal is the most prevalent and obvious form of activity represented archaeologically. When Map 7.1 is consulted, we see that the Buffalo G locus lies almost midway between the Riverhaven 2 and Sinking Ponds sites.

Although we recognize that only one site, Buffalo G, is weak evidence to suggest as a unifying concept for joining two local bands into a regional band, this proposition seems to account for the data observed elsewhere in the Meadowood phase distribution, especially where evidence is strong, as at Vinette and Oberlander.

Most of the grave goods accompanying cremations are artifacts present on all habitation sites. These utilitarian objects are, however, often present in a frequency which transcends simple utilitarianism. Exotic goods are also present, but in most cases do not represent major frequencies in the grave lots. Often these exotic elements are also present as minority types on habitation sites as well. Ritchie has stated consistently that cremation and grave good inclusions represent social stratification, personal prestige, and cultic concepts (Ritchie 1955:59-61, 1969:196-200; Ritchie and Funk 1973:349). While this is obviously true to some extent, there appear to be more factors at work than social status. No Meadowood burial stations are known from eastern or southern New York yet the "mortuary cache blade" is known from New England to the Delaware and Susquehanna Rivers. An exchange network systematically passing goods in and out of central and western New York is the most logical explanation. Ritchie (1969:161) suggests that some of the exotic items which enter Meadowood phase are:

ITEM	SOURCE
Marine Shell Beads	Atlantic Coast
Chalcedony	Quebec
Jasper	Eastern Pennsylvania
Steatite	Eastern Pennsylvania
Copper Tools	Upper Great Lakes
Striped Slate Gorgets and Birdstones	Upper Great Lakes
Hornstone	Indiana

Another suggestion was that this was a peaceful trade within a system of "trading partners" and that:

> The location of Meadowood sites on rivers and lakes, all part of an extensive system of inter-linked waterways, doubtless facilitated this inter-communication, possibly . . . by canoe travel, as in earlier times, rather than by overland forest trails. (ibid.:196)

One of the most consistent elements, however, of the Meadowood ceremonial system is the presence of cache blades in varying quantities in inhumations, cremated or otherwise. Ritchie has suggested that these distinctive thin sub-triangular blanks were especially made for this purpose (1969:196). Papworth agrees but infers that while these tools imply status or other indications of social role, they also were "raw materials for the production of finished utilitarian points" and may have represented fulfillment of a presumed need in the "afterlife" (Papworth 1967:232; Ritchie 1969:197-99, 1955:64). What is most clear is that this practice was shared over a wide, common environment, the Lake Forest area.

Analysis of the system of Meadowood manufacture activity has shown that there is a well developed sequence of production (see Fig. 1.2) from raw material to finished products (Papworth 1967:107-10; White, Binford, and Papworth 1963). Further analysis showed that at each stage subsidiary tools were derived from the sequence; for example, drills, two forms of bifacial end scrapers, and projectile points could all be made from quaternary blanks. The main chert quarries for Onondaga chert are all within the area of most intensive Meadowood settlement and were convenient to most sites along major waterways. Not coincidentally, it can also be demonstrated that the *major* utilized outcrops of Onondaga chert occur west of the Genessee River.

From analysis of manufacture, we find that wherever it was possible quaternary blanks were being produced in excess on high grade chert derived from sources prevalent in the vicinity of some Meadowood sites and that these blanks are, at least in one instance, available in the same territory where ceremonial activities may have taken place. Where needs and production correlated more directly, as at Sinking Ponds, an extractive camp, local pebbles were used; however, where excess production occurred high grade imported chert was consistently the raw material.

If blanks were produced primarily for inhumation, we would expect to see in the Niagara Frontier a high correlation between those produced within local bands only at Buffalo G. However, when the correlation matrix seen in Table 7.4 was produced for 92 values of 20 attributes in a sample of 487 quaternary blanks or "cache blades" at Meadowood sites, high positive values were produced over all sites compared, with one exception, Nahrwold 2. For example, the highest correlation for Sinking Ponds was with Oberlander 2, Burial 16 and for Riverhaven 2, Scaccia, suggesting a leveling agent at work over the entire principal distribution area of Meadowood phase. Correlations between sites to the west and sites in the central portion of this distribution cluster, as do correlations between sites in the center and the east. The exception, Nahrwold 2, was located close to outcrops of Deepskill chert. If exchange passing Onondaga chert in the form of cache blades within and between the regional bands is considered to be the leveling process, such a series of correlations becomes likely. Obviously the properties of Onondaga chert caused it to be actively sought from the major sources located in the westerly portion of the Meadowood distribution area. It is probable that major communication developed via the acquisition of chert by regional bands less favored by the presence of usable outcrops. General reciprocity in chert, marriageable women, and exotic trade goods may have knit Meadowood regional bands into a cohesive whole. (Sahlins 1972:191-204, 222-30). It may also have established a form of "peace fare" conducive to active exchange (G. Wright 1974:49-30).

The diversity of trade items which entered the Meadowood hearth area has been mentioned above, but few specific data are available on their precise source (Ritchie 1969:196-200). Neutron activation analyses of reworked steatite fragments from Sinking Ponds site done by Alvin H. Luckenbach of the University of Virginia have provided inconclusive results in finding the precise quarry from which they were derived. They do not match particularly well samples from seven eastern Pennsylvania quarries (Luckenbach:personal communication).

Nevertheless, it seems possible to account for the spread of cache blades of Onondaga chert outside the hearth area (Table 7.6). Considering the sequence of manufacture again and the implications of excess production of quaternary blanks or cache blades, the distribution of cache blades and subsidiary tools outside the area of intensive Meadowood occupation is instructive. Kinsey states that on sites in the Upper Delaware Valley, "the lack of a significant accumulation of occupational debris and features and the paucity of spalls of Onondaga chert are reason to infer that Meadowood occupation was brief and in

TABLE 7.6
DISTRIBUTION OF QUATERNARY BLANKS AND SUBSIDIARY PRODUCTS OUTSIDE PRINCIPAL AREA OF MEADOWOOD PHASE OCCUPATION

Area	Sites	Materials of Onondaga Chert
Upper Delaware River Valley (Pennsylvania, New Jersey)	Faucette, Zimmerman, Van Campen Woods	Quaternary Blanks, Sidenotched Projectile Points, Triangular Bifacial End Scrapers, Some Onondaga Chert Spalls (Kinsey 1969:32)
Susquehanna River Valley (New York, Pennsylvania)	Fortin 2, Oscar Leibhart	Quaternary Blanks, Sidenotched Projectile Points (Funk et al. 1973; Kinsey 1969)
Long Island (New York)	Orient Phase Sites	Quaternary Blanks (Ritchie 1959:55)
Southern New England Coast (Massachusetts)	Hawes Group Sites	Quaternary Blanks, Sidenotched Projectile Points, Triangular Bifacial End Scrapers (Dincauze 1968:87-88)
St. Lawrence River Valley	Batiscan	Quaternary Blanks, Sidenotched Projectile Points, Triangular Bifacial End Scrapers, Strike-a-Lites (Levesque 1964:20-22)
Southwestern Ontario	Saugeen Culture Sites	Quaternary Blanks, Sidenotched Projectile Points, Triangular Bifacial End Scrapers, Drills, and a Wide Range of Other Chert Tools (J.V. Wright 1972:40-42)
Saginaw Valley (Michigan)	Late Archaic – Early Woodland Sites	Bayport chert used. Few Blanks, Projectile Points or Scrapers of Onondaga Chert (Fitting 1970:68-95)

essence migratory" (1969:362). However, Meadowood cache blades, projectile points, and bifacial end scrapers were all present as were secondary flakes of Onondaga chert (ibid.). The same situation occurs contemporaneously in the Susquehanna River Valley (Table 7.6) (ibid.; Funk et al. 1973), the St. Lawrence River Valley (Levesque 1964), along the New England coast (Dincauze 1968:87-88), and on some sites in southwestern Ontario (J. Wright 1972*b*:42-37; Hurley and Kenyon 1970). In Michigan, where locally available Bayport chert was chiefly used, the distribution of Onondaga chert cache blades falters (Fitting 1970:68-95).

Quaternary blanks of Onondaga chert probably were manufactured initially for trade. They were small and easily transportable in large numbers to areas without chert resources or to groups desirous of acquiring high grade Onondaga chert. Furthermore, they could be used as raw material to produce subsidiary tools (Figure 1.2). G. A. Wright remarks that uneven distribution of raw materials in closely spaced biotic zones is common to trade and communication spheres (1974:49-51). Given this proposition, Meadowood peoples would have been interacting and communicating widely in an exchange network where their position with respect to Onondaga chert allowed some control over its distribution (Winters 1968:219). Friendly relations via balanced reciprocity with neighboring groups probably reinforced this favorable trade situation (ibid.; Ritchie 1969:196; Sahlins 1972:221; G. Wright 1974:49-51). Communication on major waterways in accordance with already established patterns fostered the continuance of both friendly relations and disposal of an excess resource (Ceci n.d.:4-7; G. Wright 1974:49-51).

Sahlins' model equating the various forms of reciprocity with kinship distance characterized interarea exchange at the band level as balanced reciprocity with negative overtones; he deems it essentially an attempt to get a little more than is given. Such a situation would in effect place a negative value on surplus, that which cannot be exchanged within one area or outside of it. Thus it seems most logical to suggest that in order to retire a surplus created at an individual producer's death, his blanks or his kin group's surplus blanks would be interred at periodic intervals during socially integrative ceremonies. This would account for the extremely wide frequency variance of from 10-1500 quaternary blanks found in interments and for the apparent lack of social significance of blanks in terms of status goods, which has been noted by some investigators (Ritchie 1969:196-200; Papworth 1967:231-32). It might also explain why trade items were "ritually killed," since a demand for such goods would presumably reinforce the trade network (Winters 1969:216-19).

THE HABITATION SYSTEM AND SETTLEMENT PATTERN

Detailed structural evidence of residence in the Niagara Frontier is available only from Sinking Ponds, in the form of three possible houses. These houses, 15 x 11 ft, are similar in form and size to one disclosed at Scaccia site (Ritchie and Funk 1973:107). That house was 16 x 12 ft with a roughly east-west orientation, like the houses at Sinking Ponds, and had postmolds of a similar size as well. Funk noticed five features within the house, two fireplaces, two storage pits, and a rock heap, but considered them not to be associated with the house (ibid.). There is an interesting correlation in house pattern between those which may exist on Meadowood sites, the houses outlined at Lamoka Lake (Ritchie 1969:73-74) which fall perfectly within the size range of the one most completely defined house at Sinking Ponds, 4.48 x 3.20 m (14.7 x 10.8 ft), and the Scaccia house. However, we must note that the number of intrusive pits at Lamoka Lake precluded any definition of internal structures in the houses.

Houses of the later Canoe Point phase at the Donaldson and Kipp Island sites were also quite close in size and structure to those of Meadowood phase and Lamoka phase (Ritchie and Funk 1973:350). There seems to have been little change in house form and, by extension, the use of houses by nuclear families or quite restricted extended families. It is possible that population concentration came from accretion of family household units in the base settlements.

Habitation on any Meadowood site cannot be understood in isolation from the other activities. Therefore, in Figure 7.2 we have compared in graphic form the activities on the Sinking Ponds, the Riverhaven 2, and the Spicer Creek loci. Here the division between the sites is expressed as percentages in the activities: procurement processing, manufacture, and storage. The division between Sinking Ponds and Riverhaven 2 is most clearly based upon storage, 76% at Riverhaven 2 (Table 7.5), and processing, 73% at Sinking Ponds (Table 7.2). Procurement appears to be closer, 50% at Sinking Ponds, and 40% at Riverhaven 2 (Table 7.1). The manufacture curve was skewed by retention of the total detritus sample at Sinking Ponds while only a portion of it was retained at Riverhaven 2 (Table 7.3). The figures for the Spicer Creek loci reflect those of Sinking Ponds, but seem too small to be considered (Figure 7.2). With the above frequencies in mind, the differences in density of habitation are easily portrayed. Greater density in population is directly proportional to the maintenance activity: major storage.

We suggested that the population which occupied the Sinking Ponds site was a miximum of 30 persons living in approximately six nuclear family dwellings. This figure would seem to correlate well with

Helm's "task group" (1969:214). At Riverhaven 2, if the nine possible storage or refuse features actually indicated one per family, a population of between 45 and 50 persons would have occupied this site. If we project this figure to the loci 8, 9, 10, 11, and 12, all located within a half mile and concentrated in a linear arrangement, we could have a total resident population of between 225 and 250, which is well above the figure for the local band of 150 persons. The accumulated error could certainly be close to 50-75 persons. Discussants of band population agree, however, that aboriginal bands were probably larger than those post-contact groups observed ethnographically (Damas 1969:210-11).

It was proposed above that the local band exploited intensively a 10 sq mi area which contained at least two juxtaposed microenvironments, a shallow lake shore and a riverine–open forest zone. An area of 400 square miles with a diameter of 22.58 miles was suggested as a band controlled exploitation territory. Winters indicated that people moved to exploit recurrently this size area. We believe that the Riverhaven sites represent one such complex of settlement types, controlling and exploiting the Grand Island local band area. Conceivably another site could be a focus for another constellation of settlement types that utilized the East Aurora local band area (Map 7.1).

In the Niagara Frontier Region we recognize that there were many more than two band areas and that perhaps only a very small number of extant sites are known to us. Study of the Riverhaven Complex is especially revealing, however, since it is a restricted context with associated micro-zones that are quite obvious. Here all major settlement types were associated even more closely than the geographic restrictions made necessary. In East Aurora, the same situation prevailed even more in contravention of geographic limitation. These clusters of settlement types are most easily understood as responses to subsistence needs. Resource sites and especially mortuary sites appear to be the links and foci binding together the social system, and both within and without the Niagara Frontier they function to join habitation areas on major communication routes. As befits their integrative function, they were probably utilized at times of greatest disjunction, perhaps during population fission or segmentation, or in movement from one form of settlement type to another (such as base to extractive camp or vice versa in the spring or fall).

Figure 7.3 portrays schematically the habitation system and settlement pattern we believe to have been operating in the Niagara Frontier and elsewhere in central and western New York during Meadowood phase. The relationships between the elements are outlined as follows:

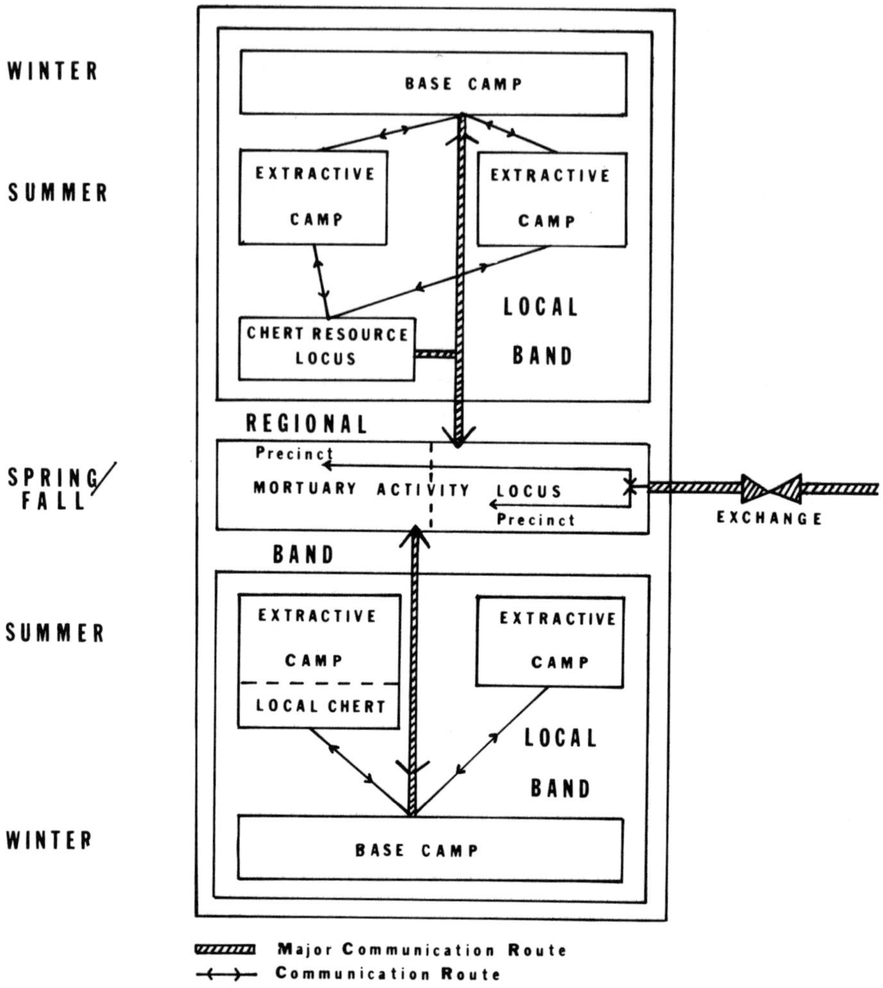

Fig. 7.3 Meadowood settlement pattern in the Niagara Frontier.

I. A Regional Band:

A. Occupies the Niagara Frontier

B. Consists of two or more local bands

C. Has a population of approximately 500 persons

D. Is integrated by group ritual at a *Mortuary Activity Site* utilized by two or more bands at periods of disjunction during segmentation in spring or fall

E. May be connected with other regional bands through exchange or ceremonialism in an area of similar economic adaptions (Lake Forest area)

II. A Local Band:

A. Occupies or controls subsistence resources in a territory approximating 400 sq mi

B. Utilizes the following settlement types:

1. *Base settlement* is occupied during autumn, winter and early spring and gives evidence of the hunting of large herbivores in riverine–open forest zones, gathering of large quantities of storable mast, processing of hides and bone, intensive storage activity, and periodic movement to a similar adaptive situation. Manufacture of chert tools is a constant subsidiary activity

2. *Extractive settlement* represents population fission into seasonal task groups for fish exploitation and flora resource gathering during the mid-spring to late summer and which occupies knolls and ridges in proximity to the shores of shallow lakes where net and weir fishing is done. Processing of fish is accomplished on the site by no more than 25-30 people, probably a kin group. There is no limit beyond local band size for the number of these camps

3. *Chert resource site* is utilized for raw material by individuals from all settlement types, especially if none is locally available at extractive settlements

C. Shares with other local bands a *Mortuary Activity Site* where rituals concerning the dead are carried out, probably in distinct corporate group areas. Cremation and inhumation are practiced

D. Has a population of approximately 150 persons

III. Task Group:

A. Represents a seasonal segment of the local band which occupies an *extractive settlement,* which with a *base settlement* exploits a 10 sq mi area containing several microenvironments until a decrease in carrying capacity or other event causes a move within the local group territory. Manufacture of chert tools is carried on continuously

B. Has a population of 25-50 persons

C. Is probably a kin group such as an extended family or lineage segment

FIGURE 7.4

DISTRIBUTION AND RELATIONSHIPS OF MEADOWOOD COMPONENTS AS SETTLEMENT TYPES

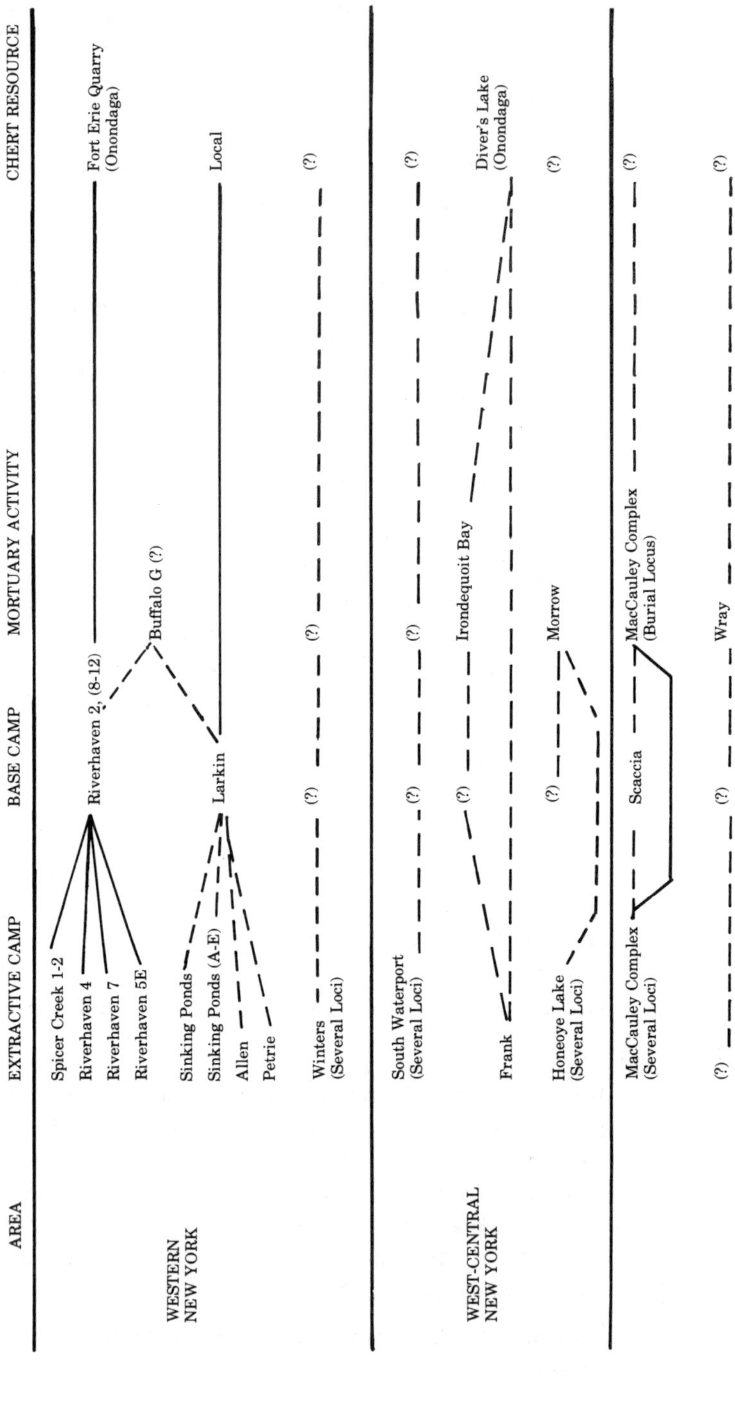

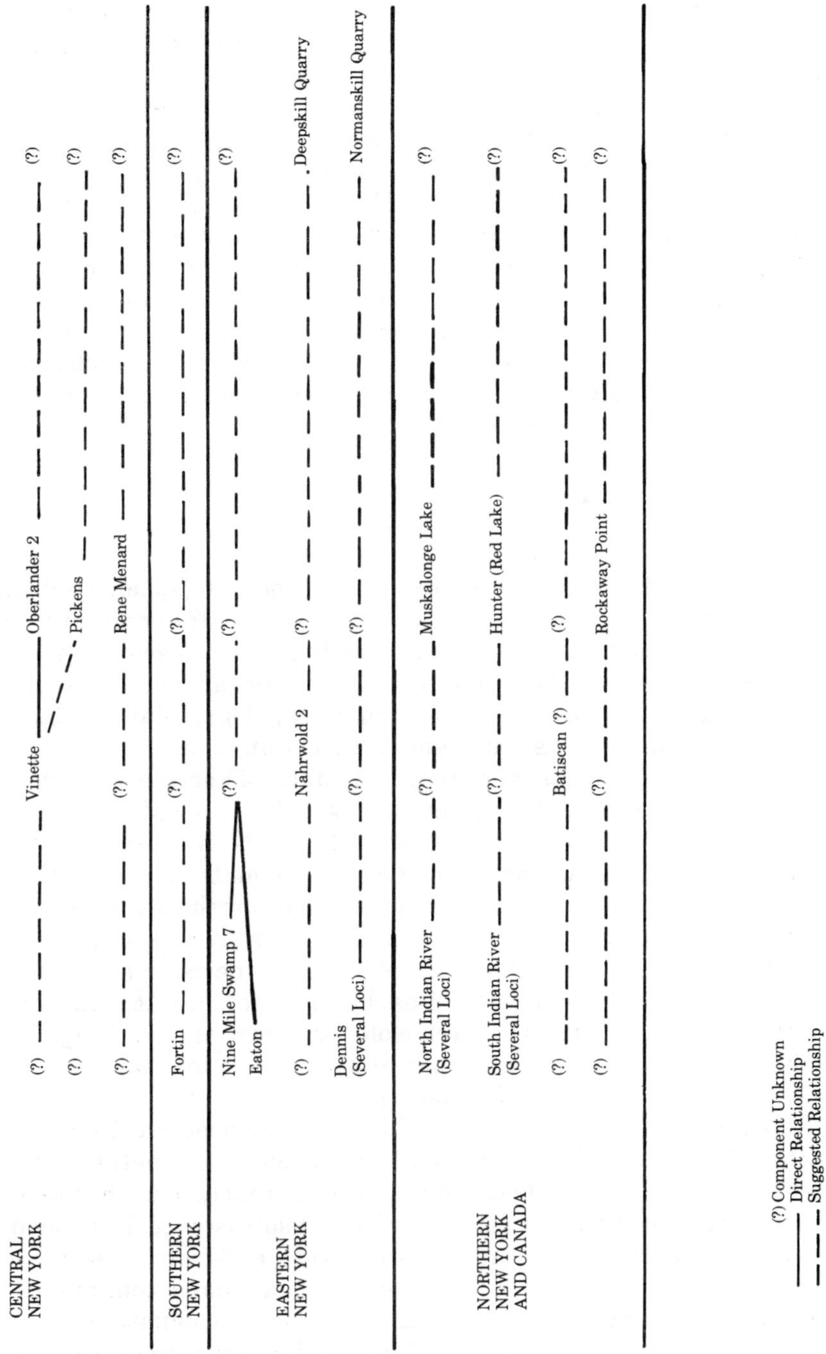
CENTRAL NEW YORK
(?)
Vinette
Oberlander 2
(?)
(?)
Pickens
(?)
(?)
(?)
Rene Menard
(?)
SOUTHERN NEW YORK
Fortin
(?)
(?)
(?)
EASTERN NEW YORK
Nine Mile Swamp 7
Eaton
(?)
(?)
(?)
(?)
Nahrwold 2
(?)
Deepskill Quarry
Dennis (Several Loci)
(?)
(?)
Normanskill Quarry
NORTHERN NEW YORK AND CANADA
North Indian River (Several Loci)
(?)
Muskalonge Lake
(?)
South Indian River (Several Loci)
(?)
Hunter (Red Lake)
(?)
(?)
Batiscan (?)
(?)
(?)
(?)
(?)
Rockaway Point
(?)
(?) Component Unknown
Direct Relationship
Suggested Relationship

We have attempted to present the known components of Meadowood phase, distributed according to our definition of settlement types, in Figure 7.4. Although our assignments are based on very small amounts of evidence in some cases, it is gratifying when a new component is discovered which was predicted by the model proposed. The Frank site, located near a marsh in Genessee County is such a site. It gives evidence of having a small Meadowood component with some mixing of Late Archaic materials from an earlier occupation (Wicks 1973:6-13). It falls close to an area possibly served by the Irondequoit Bay mortuary locus and is in an area where several environmental micro-zones are juxtaposed. Tonawanda Creek is the major communication route situated near the site. The chert is high grade Onondaga chert from the nearby Divers Lake Quarry. As with so many of the sites and areas, more intensive investigation is needed to define all parts of the settlement pattern.

SUMMARY

In this work we have presented what is known of Meadowood phase settlement in order to commence an explanation of the configuration or patterning of its distribution. The work began with excavation of two sites which were clearly single component sites and clearly affiliated with Meadowood phase through artifact typology. While seeking to describe the fundamental differences in location of these sites, features and artifact frequencies were noted. As analysis proceeded it became obvious that the terms "camp" or "workshop" or "burial site" were too general to account for the data observed and the regularity of its distribution. It was found that as increasing amounts of information became available, there was little reinforcement for the models which up until 1969 were valid. There was a need for a fresh appraisal of the situation. Coincidently, others made the same decision at almost the same moment. Fortunately the sites chosen were those at which important new data awaited the archaeologists involved. Sinking Ponds, Nahrwold 2, Scaccia, and Riverhaven 2 have been instrumental in our understanding of the Meadowood phase.

Explicit in all examinations of Meadowood phase site distributions is the relationship of such sites with water features, whether streams, lakes, or marshes. This leads to one general conclusion, that fish and their procurement were a dominant form of subsistence. Furthermore, the impression of social interactions on a wider and more intensive scale is reinforced by postulation of water routes as major communication channels. On a more restricted scale, however, explanations of social relations based only upon traits obscured the differences between settlement types. If only obvious variations such as those sites with or without burials were considered, a whole range of diversity could be missed in large or small sites, especially the subtle distinctions between the forms of habitation sites. This study intensively examined a large habitation site and a small habitation site. The suggestion that different activities were being carried out on these sites and that they conditioned artifact types and frequency was investigated. Gaps in the data often led to false starts and erroneous inferences, but gradually the data proved amenable to analysis under the broad categories of procurement, processing, storage, manufacture, habitation, and ceremony. Once such divisions were made, each activity could be cross-correlated at each site, taking into account the sampling involved.

Analysis of procurement activity showed that there were definite seasonal distinctions in exploitation when various resources became available but that the different resources exploited were closely juxtaposed. The scheduling of the taking of those resources apparently did not cause major population dislocations or shifts but rather task-regulated segmentation along family or lineal points of cleavage within a local band, which were probably organized by patrilineal descent and patrilocal residence. Procurement became the basis for small camps primarily concerned with fishing during the summer and for larger base settlements whose subsistence needs during the autumn and winter were supplied by exploitation of mast and mast-eating herbivores.

Analysis of the location of Meadowood habitation sites showed that there was a close association of smaller sites with shallow lakes or fossil lakes, now marshes, where weir-net and leister fishing were quite profitable. In contrast, the larger sites were located on larger streams or deep lakes and usually associated with areas of high mast production. Quite coincidentally, it was noted that these areas were spatially very close to each other as were many of the components such as those in the Riverhaven Complex and the McCauley Complex.

Chert resources were exploited heavily and high grade Onondaga chert was quarried from loci probably available along navigable streams at points where they intersected with the Onondaga Escarpment. Occasionally chert was derived from pebbles found in the local glacial tills, but this usage formed only a minor and rather localized procurement pattern possibly only related to extractive camps where primary emphasis was upon subsistence activities rather than manufacture.

On the smaller components, processing of fish was accomplished coincident with procurement. The fish were dried over beds of stone heated in nearby hearths. Milling and pitted or "nutting" stones found on all habitation sites demonstrate a pronounced processing activity related to exploitation of vegetable materials, especially acorns, hickory nuts, goosefoot, smartweed, and grape seeds. Evidence gathered from several sites shows that the processed items, whether floral or faunal, were passed on into the storage activity which allowed larger populations to pass the winter in large base camps.

Storage was once only inferred for Meadowood phase and the deep pits so characteristic of Lamoka phase were only rarely seen on Meadowood sites. Scaccia and Riverhaven 2 have produced the hard evidence for storage areas. Additionally, the patterned arrangements of such pits may illustrate kin group affiliations when spatially tested against house patterns. The evidence also suggests differential types of storage: cold dry storage of meats in pits sunk in impermeable clays and vegetable material storage in pits of similar structure located in well drained soils. Intensive examination of the nature and association of storage structures is still needed, and we suspect that this activity will give important insights into not only subsistence practices but also into the social structure.

Manufacture activities produced a wide range of chert tools on all Meadowood habitation components. There was, however, a systematic economy to the process, whereby blanks were produced from the raw material. By-products, fortuitous or otherwise, were reutilized as derived tool types; however the manufacture of quaternary blanks, or "cache blades", appeared to be the desired end product. These blanks were being produced far in excess of the need for modification to projectile points, as the high frequency of unreworked fragments attests. This end product could be modified into a projectile point, knife, or drill and may have represented an alteration of high grade raw material into an easily transportable form for introduction into an exchange network. Both control by occupation of the resource area and the ubiquitous nature of manufacture seem to point in this direction.

This work has touched only briefly upon the Meadowood mortuary sites once so important to definition of the phase. These sites need reexamination urgently, principally because data on social structure may be present, not in the individual cremations or interments, but in the arrangement or clustering of burial groupings. The uniform location of these sites on arteries of easy access by water but *not* in close association with any single base settlement (except in the case of Vinette and Oberlander) implies that groups had to make deliberate pilgrimages to the loci to perform ceremonies over the dead. At these centralized locations, accessible from two or more local band areas, socially integrating activities such as exchange of women and goods, retirement of disruptive surpluses by "killing" and burial as status objects and, most important, face to face interactions probably created the loosely knit aggregate known as the regional band. This may have occured at the points of stress in the yearly subsistence cycle, as people moved to or from base or extractive camps in the spring and/or autumn. Inter-regional band exchange has been suggested and is evidenced by exotic goods from places far outside the Meadowood hearth area and the intrusion of characteristic Meadowood "cache blades" and derivative tools in several of those areas. Numerous studies are now clarifying the nature of resource control and exchange networks at this time period in the Northeast and will probably have an important bearing on future statements about Meadowood phase.

Perhaps the most intriguing problem yet to be resolved is the association of Meadowood phase with phases earlier and later in time. We have suggested that there was great similarity in adaptation, artifacts, and settlement pattern throughout the Lake Forest area during the time period 1000-500 B.C. This similarity was conditioned by the rich and varied flora and fauna in this environmental zone. If adaptation and subsistence practice is used as the basis of explanations of cultural change, then there is little difference between Meadowood phase and Lamoka phase in either technology or settlement. Use of the projectile points of these two phases as rigid cultural markers obscures the differing functions they may have represented. We agree with those who correlate technologic traditions in projectile point manufacture with adaptive function in subsistence, with frequency changes occurring only when the subsistence emphasis alters. Only in cultures with focal economies such as the Paleo-Indian big-game hunting adaptation would one projectile point type necessarily represent a discrete cultural entity. It seems quite likely that the Meadowood phase subsistence settlement system denotes only a minor shift from heavy emphasis on fishing toward hunting. Floral resource exploitation probably was more or less constant. More noticeable social, artifactual, and subsistence practice shifts appear to occur in the succeeding Canoe Point phase. These changes (larger residence structures, altered ceremonialism, year-round settlements and proliferation of new pottery types) may be the significant demarcation between Archaic cultures and those of the Woodland period in New York State. Meadowood phase shows greater affinity to the Archaic period and may be the terminal expression of that period in central and western New York State. Future work will probably clarify both the nature of the phase and its chronological relationships. This study has been a small step in that direction.

APPENDIX A: ARTIFACT ATTRIBUTES

This appendix has been compiled from a descriptive analysis of materials from several sites of the Meadowood culture. All individual artifacts were initially coded by qualitative observation, with quantitative data being entered as directly observed. Qualitative data on the flint artifacts was organized for coding by using a modified version of Binford's *Proposed Attribute List for the Description and Classification of Projectile Points* (1963*c*), which was modified only in the selection of variables and their values. The terms, definitions, and general order of presentation were retained. Other definitions for attributes of tools not included in the original classificatory scheme were derived from Binford (1963*a* and 1963*b*) and A. White (1963).

The rationale for using this terminology was twofold. First, the similarity of the materials for which the classification was designed to those artifacts under study (Binford 1963*a* and 1963*b*; Papworth 1963), or the generality of the tool, made any systematic morphological classificatory arrangement applicable. Secondly, we believe that flint tools of the Meadowood culture were products of a unified process (see discussion in Chapter 2), and we hoped that by attempting to describe as much of the flint cultural material as possible, comparative studies could be facilitated. Thus, we grouped artifact categories into types of data, Type One (TONE) covering exclusively certain flint artifacts which share variables (i.e., blade shape) and variable categories (i.e., blade element), and Type Two (TTWO), a more heterogeneous grouping of artifact types, including flint and non-flint for which more discrete variables and variable categories were necessary. The distribution (with table assignments) is as follows:

	TABLE
Projectile Points, Sidenotched	(A.1*a*, *b*)
Projectile Points, Cornernotched	(A.2*a*, *b*)
Projectile Points, Stemmed	(A.3*a*, *b*)
Quaternary Blanks, Whole	(A.4*a*, *b*)

Type One (TONE)	Quaternary Blanks, Bases	(A.5*a*, *b*)
	Quaternary Blanks, Tips	(A.6*a*, *b*)
	Tertiary Blanks, Whole	(A.7*a*, *b*)
	Tertiary Blanks, Bases	(A.8*a*, *b*)
	Tertiary Blanks, Tips	(A.9*a*, *b*)
	Longitudinal Knives	(A.10*a*, *b*)
	Scrapers, Unifacial	(A.11*a*, *b*)
	Scrapers, Bifacial	(A.12*a*, *b*)
Flint	Drills	(A.13*a*, *b*)
	Primary Blanks	(A.14*a*, *b*)
	Secondary Blanks	(A.15*a*, *b*)
Type Two (TTWO)		
	Netsinkers	(A.16*a*, *b*)
Non-flint	Hammer-Anvil Stones	(A.17*a*, *b*)
	Abrading Stones	(A.18*a*, *b*)

The raw data IBM cards containing both nominal and ordinal observations were fully nominalized by testing the quantitative attributes for significant intervals and recording. In all cases, except where noted, interval data are presented in millimeters. Frequencies and percentage figures were used in subsequent correlations. Two tables were prepared for each artifact class, the first (A) showing variables where variation occurs and those which are constant (95% or more of the observation), the second (B) comparing variables in each type by site.

TABLE A.1*a*
SIDENOTCHED PROJECTILE POINT ATTRIBUTES

Variation	Constant (+95%)
Material	Blade Primary Flake Type (unifacial)
% Matrix Inclusion	Blade Secondary Flake Type (expanding)
Blade Outline	Blade Secondary Flake Placement (bifacial—bilateral)
Blade Length (mm)	Blade Tertiary Flake Type (nibbled)
Blade Width (mm)	Haft Juncture Type (lateral—lateral)
Blade Width Tip—2cm (mm)	
Blade Transverse Section	
Blade Longitudinal Section	
Blade Secondary Flake Pattern	
Blade Lateral Edge	
Base Outline	
Base Width (mm)	
Base Height (mm)	
Base Preparation	
Haft Width (mm)	
Haft Length (mm)	
Haft Preparation	
Maximum Thickness (mm)	
Overall Length (mm)	

TABLE A.1*b*
SIDENOTCHED PROJECTILE POINTS — TABLE OF VARIABLE ATTRIBUTE FREQUENCY

	Sinking Ponds		Riverhaven 2		Scaccia		Morrow		Oberlander		Muskalonge Lake		Hunter		Nahrwold 2		Vinette		Buffalo G		Totals		
	#	%	#	%	#	%	#	%	#	%	#	%	#	%	#	%	#	%	#	%	#	%	
Onondaga Chert	19	90.5	43	82.7	23	82.1	8	80	5	55.6	3	27.3	4	100	1	20	11	91.7	2	50	119	76.3	Material
Onon. Chert Fired	2	9.5	9	17.3	4	14.3	2	20	4	44.4	0	0	0	0	0	0	0	0	0	0	21	13.5	
Onon. Chert Pigm.	0	0	0	0	0	0	0	0	0	0	7	63.6	0	0	0	0	0	0	2	50	9	5.8	
Deepskill Ch.	0	0	0	0	0	0	0	0	0	0	0	0	0	0	4	80	0	0	0	0	4	2.6	
Ryolite	0	0	0	0	1	3.6	0	0	0	0	1	9.1	0	0	0	0	1	8.3	0	0	3	1.9	
N=	21	100	52	100	28	100	10	100	9	100	11	100	4	100	5	100	12	100	4	100	156	100	
Indeter-minate	1	4.8	0	0	1	3.6	0	0	0	0	0	0	0	0	0	0	1	8.3	0	0	3	1.9	Indurated Lime-stone Matrix Inclusion
0-20	12	57.1	25	48.1	15	53.6	4	40	3	33.3	2	18.2	1	25	3	60	9	75.1	3	75	77	49.4	
20-40	4	19	14	26.9	5	17.9	2	20	3	33.3	4	36.4	2	50	1	20	0	0	1	25	36	23.1	
40-60	2	9.5	8	15.4	3	10.7	2	20	2	22.2	3	27.3	0	0	0	0	1	8.3	0	0	21	13.5	
60-80	2	9.5	5	9.6	2	7.1	1	10	1	11.1	1	9.1	0	0	1	20	1	8.3	0	0	14	9.0	
80-100	0	0	0	0	2	7.1	0	0	0	0	1	9.1	1	25	0	0	0	0	0	0	4	2.6	
M+5 Pock	0	0	0	0	0	0	1	10	0	0	0	0	0	0	0	0	0	0	0	0	1	0.6	
N=	21	100	52	100	28	100	10	100	9	100	11	100	4	100	5	100	12	100	4	100	156	100	
Indeter-minate	8	38.1	9	17.3	2	7.1	1	10	0	0	1	9.1	1	25	1	20	0	0	0	0	23	14.7	Blade Outline
Triangular	1	4.8	8	15.4	4	14.3	1	10	2	22.2	1	9.1	0	0	2	40	3	25	0	0	22	14.1	
Excurvate	0	0	5	9.6	6	21.4	0	0	0	0	1	9.1	0	0	0	0	0	0	0	0	12	7.7	
Ovate	12	57.1	29	55.8	12	42.9	8	80	7	77.8	8	72.7	3	75	2	40	9	75	4	100	94	60.3	
In-excurvate Opp.	0	0	0	0	1	3.6	0	0	0	0	0	0	0	0	0	0	0	0	0	0	1	0.6	
Parallel Ovate	0	0	1	1.9	3	10.7	0	0	0	0	0	0	0	0	0	0	0	0	0	0	4	2.6	
N=	21	100	52	100	28	100	10	100	9	100	11	100	4	100	5	100	12	100	4	100	156	100	

TABLE A.1*b* (Continued)

	Sinking Ponds		Riverhaven 2		Scaccia		Morrow		Oberlander 2		Muskalonge Lake		Hunter		Nahrwold 2		Vinette		Buffalo G		Totals		
	#	%	#	%	#	%	#	%	#	%	#	%	#	%	#	%	#	%	#	%	#	%	
Indeterminate	9	42.9	9	17.3	5	17.9	2	20	0	0	1	9.1	1	25	2	40	0	0	0	0	29	18.6	Blade Length
10-20	0	0	3	5.8	1	3.6	0	0	0	0	0	0	0	0	0	0	0	0	0	0	4	2.6	
21-30	0	0	10	19.2	5	17.9	0	0	0	0	1	9.1	0	0	1	20	1	8.3	0	0	18	11.5	
31-40	7	33.3	25	48.1	10	35.7	2	20	3	33.3	3	27.3	1	25	1	20	4	33.3	2	50	58	37.2	
41-50	3	14.3	4	7.7	3	10.7	2	20	2	22.2	3	27.3	2	50	1	20	6	50	0	0	26	16.7	
51-60	2	9.5	1	1.9	4	14.3	2	20	2	22.2	0	0	0	0	0	0	1	8.3	1	25	13	8.3	
61-70	0	0	0	0	0	0	1	10	2	22.2	3	27.3	0	0	0	0	0	0	1	25	7	4.5	
71-80	0	0	0	0	0	0	1	10	0	0	0	0	0	0	0	0	0	0	0	0	1		
N=	21	100	52	100	28	100	10	100	9	100	11	100	4	100	5	100	12	100	4	100	156	100	
Indeterminate	1	4.8	1	1.9	0	0	0	0	0	0	0	0	0	0	0	0	0	0	0	0	2	1.3	Blade Width
15-20	4	19	15	28.8	8	28.6	1	10	0	0	1	9.1	0	0	2	40	6	50	0	0	37	23.7	
21-25	12	52.1	34	65.4	16	57.1	5	50	6	66.7	6	54.5	3	75	2	40	6	50	2	50	92	59	
26-30	4	19	2	3.8	4	14.3	3	30	3	33.3	4	36.4	1	25	1	20	0	0	2	50	24	15.4	
31-35	0	0	0	0	0	0	1	10	0	0	0	0	0	0	0	0	0	0	0	0	1	0.6	
N=	21	100	52	100	28	100	10	100	9	100	11	100	4	100	5	100	12	100	4	100	156	100	
Indeterminate	9	42.9	10	19.2	5	17.9	1	10	0	0	1	9.1	1	25	2	40	0	0	0	0	29	18.6	Blade Width 2 Cm.
5-10	0	0	0	0	0	0	0	0	0	0	1	9.1	0	0	0	0	0	0	0	0	1	0.6	
11-15	4	19	17	32.7	6	21.4	4	40	6	66.7	6	54.5	0	0	2	40	9	75	0	0	54	34.6	
16-20	8	38.1	25	48.1	17	60.7	5	50	3	33.3	3	27.3	3	75	1	20	3	25	4	100	72	46.2	
N=	21	100	52	100	28	100	10	100	9	100	11	100	4	100	5	100	12	100	4	100	156	100	
Plano-Convex	6	28.6	12	23.1	10	35.7	1	10	2	22.2	2	18.2	1	25	2	40	5	41.7	1	25	42	26.9	Blade Transverse Section
Bi-Plano	5	23.8	4	7.7	3	10.7	5	50	0	0	3	27.3	3	75	2	40	0	0	1	25	26	16.7	
Bi-Convex	10	47.6	34	65.4	15	53.6	4	40	7	77.8	6	54.5	0	0	1	20	5	41.7	2	50	84	53.8	
Asymet Bi-Convex	0	0	2	3.8	0	0	0	0	0	0	0	0	0	0	0	0	2	16.7	0	0	4	2.6	
N=	21	100	52	100	28	100	10	100	9	100	11	100	4	100	5	100	12	100	4	100	156	100	

TABLE A.1*b* (Continued)

	Sinking Ponds		Riverhaven 2		Scaccia		Morrow		Oberlander 2		Muskalonge Lake		Hunter		Nahrwold 2		Vinette		Buffalo G		Totals		
	#	%	#	%	#	%	#	%	#	%	#	%	#	%	#	%	#	%	#	%	#	%	
Plano-Convex	11	52.4	12	23.1	9	32.1	1	10	0	0	5	45.4	1	25	2	40	4	33.3	1	25	46	29.5	Blade Longitudinal Section
Bi-Plano	4	19	14	26.9	3	10.7	6	60	2	22.2	3	27.3	3	75	2	40	3	25	1	25	41	26.3	
Bi-Convex	5	23.8	25	48.1	15	53.6	3	30	3	33.3	3	27.3	0	0	1	20	3	25	2	50	60	38.5	
Asymet Bi-Convex	0	0	1	1.9	0	0	0	0	0	0	0	0	0	0	0	0	0	0	0	0	1	0.6	
Concavo-Convex	0	0	0	0	1	3.6	0	0	4	44.5	0	0	0	0	0	0	0	0	0	0	5	32.2	
Asymet Excurvate	0	0	0	0	0	0	0	0	0	0	0	0	0	0	0	0	2	16.7	0	0	2	1.3	
Asymet Concave Convex	1	4.8	0	0	0	0	0	0	0	0	0	0	0	0	0	0	0	0	0	0	1	0.6	
N=	21	100	52	100	28	100	10	100	9	100	11	100	4	100	5	100	12	100	4	100	156	100	
Indeterminate	14	9.5	0	0	0	0	0	0	0	0	0	0	0	0	0	0	0	0	0	0	4	2.6	Blade Second Flake
Continuous	16	85.7	50	96.2	25	89.3	10	100	9	100	11	100	4	100	4	80	11	91.7	4	100	144	92.3	
Discontinuous	1	4.8	2	3.8	3	10.7	0	0	0	0	0	0	0	0	1	20	1	8.3	0	0	8	5.1	
N=	21	100	52	100	28	100	10	100	9	100	11	100	4	100	5	100	12	100	4	100	156	100	
Indeterminate	2	9.5	0	0	0	0	0	0	0	0	0	0	0	0	0	0	0	0	0	0	2	1.3	Blade Lateral Edge
Serration	1	4.8	0	0	0	0	1	10	1	11.1	0	0	0	0	0	0	0	0	0	0	3	1.9	
Even	16	76.2	50	96.2	25	89.3	9	90	8	88.9	10	90.9	4	100	5	100	12	100	4	100	143	91.7	
Irregular	2	9.5	2	3.8	3	10.7	0	0	0	0	0	0	0	0	0	0	0	0	0	0	7	4.5	
Reworked	0	0	0	0	0	0	0	0	0	0	1	9.1	0	0	0	0	0	0	0	0	1	0.6	
N=	21	100	52	100	28	100	10	100	9	100	11	100	4	100	5	100	12	100	4	100	156	100	
Indeterminate	1	4.8	7	13.5	1	3.6	4	40	0	0	1	9.1	0	0	0	0	0	0	1	25	15	9.6	Base Outline
Straight	4	19	5	9.6	4	14.3	0	0	2	22.2	0	0	0	0	1	20	1	8.3	1	25	18	11.5	
Sub-convex	14	66.7	22	42.3	21	75	5	50	7	77.8	9	81.8	2	50	3	60	9	75	2	50	94	60.3	
Convex	2	9.5	18	34.6	2	7.1	1	10	0	0	1	9.1	2	50	1	20	2	16.7	0	0	29	18.6	
N=	21	100	52	100	28	100	10	100	9	100	11	100	4	100	5	100	12	100	4	100	156	100	

TABLE A.1*b* (Continued)

	Sinking Ponds		Riverhaven 2		Scaccia		Morrow		Oberlander 2		Muskalonge Lake		Hunter		Nahrwold 2		Vinette		Buffalo G		Totals		
	#	%	#	%	#	%	#	%	#	%	#	%	#	%	#	%	#	%	#	%	#	%	
Indeterminate	1	4.8	2	3.8	2	7.1	4	40	0	0	0	0	0	0	0	0	0	0	2	50	11	7.1	Base Width
11-15	0	0	0	0	2	7.1	0	0	0	0	0	0	0	0	0	0	0	0	0	0	2	1.3	
15-20	3	14.3	15	28.8	11	39.3	0	0	0	0	3	27.3	0	0	2	40	6	50	1	25	41	26.3	
21-25	11	52.4	26	50	10	35.7	2	20	4	44.4	7	63.6	2	50	2	40	4	33.3	0	0	68	43.6	
25-30	6	28.6	9	17.3	3	10.7	3	30	4	44.4	0	0	2	50	1	20	2	16.7	1	25	31	19.9	
31-35	0	0	0	0	0	0	1	10	1	11.2	1	9.1	0	0	0	0	0	0	0	0	3	1.9	
N=	21	100	52	100	28	100	10	100	9	100	11	100	4	100	5	100	12	100	4	100	156	100	
Blank	1	4.8	0	0	0	0	0	0	0	0	0	0	0	0	0	0	0	0	1	25	2	1.3	Base Height
0-3	0	0	9	17.3	2	7.1	6	60	0	0	1	9.1	1	25	0	0	2	16.7	1	25	22	14.1	
3-6	17	81	26	50	23	82.1	1	10	6	66.7	7	63.6	1	25	4	80	9	75	1	25	95	60.9	
7-9	3	14.3	17	32.7	3	10.7	3	30	3	33.3	3	27.3	2	50	1	20	1	8.3	1	25	37	23.7	
N=	21	100	52	100	28	100	10	100	9	100	11	100	4	100	5	100	12	100	4	100	156	100	
Indeterminate	2	9.5	8	15.4	1	3.6	4	40	0	0	1	9.1	0	0	0	0	1	8.3	1	25	18	11.5	Base Preparation
Striking platformouly	0	0	0	0	2	7.1	0	0	0	0	1	9.1	0	0	1	20	0	0	0	0	4	2.6	
Primary Thinning	1	4.8	0	0	0	0	1	10	0	0	0	0	0	0	0	0	0	0	0	0	2	1.3	
Secondary Thinning	8	38.1	8	15.4	10	35.7	1	10	2	22.2	5	45.5	2	50	2	40	4	33.3	1	25	43	27.6	
Tertiary Thinning	9	42.9	36	69.2	13	46.4	3	30	7	77.8	4	36.4	2	50	2	40	7	58.3	2	50	85	54.5	
Grinding Pri.	0	0	0	0	0	0	1	10	0	0	0	0	0	0	0	0	0	0	0	0	1	0.6	
Grinding Sec.	1	4.8	0	0	2	7.1	0	0	0	0	0	0	0	0	0	0	0	0	0	0	3	1.9	
N=	21	100	52	100	28	100	10	100	9	100	11	100	4	100	5	100	12	100	4	100	156	100	

TABLE A.1*b* (Continued)

	Sinking Ponds		Riverhaven 2		Scaccia		Morrow		Oberlander 2		Muskalonge Lake		Hunter		Nahrwold 2		Vinette		Buffalo G		Totals		
	#	%	#	%	#	%	#	%	#	%	#	%	#	%	#	%	#	%	#	%	#	%	
Indeterminate	0	0	1	1.9	1	3.6	1	10	0	0	0	0	0	0	0	0	0	0	1	25	4	2.6	Haft Width
5-10	0	0	0	0	1	3.6	0	0	0	0	0	0	0	0	0	0	0	0	0	0	1	0.6	
11-15	3	14.3	13	25	8	28.6	4	40	2	22.2	3	27.3	1	25	1	20	6	50	1	25	42	26.9	
16-20	16	76.2	34	65.4	15	53.6	4	40	3	33.3	7	63.6	3	75	4	80	4	41.7	1	25	92	59	
21-25	1	4.8	4	7.7	3	10.7	1	10	3	33.3	1	9.1	0	0	0	0	1	8.3	1	25	15	9.6	
26-30	1	4.8	0	0	0	0	0	0	1	11.2	0	0	0	0	0	0	0	0	0	0	2	1.3	
N=	21	100	52	100	28	100	10	100	9	100	11	100	4	100	5	100	11	100	4	100	156	100	
Indeterminate	1	4.8	1	1.9	1	3.6	1	10	0	0	0	0	0	0	0	0	0	0	0	0	4	2.6	Haft Length
1-3	2	9.5	27	57.9	9	32.1	2	20	3	33.3	3	27.3	0	0	2	40	0	0	2	50	50	32.1	
4-6	18	85.7	23	44.2	17	60.7	5	50	5	55.6	8	72.7	4	100	3	60	7	58.3	1	25	91	58.3	
7-9	0	0	1	1.9	1	3.6	1	10	1	11.1	0	0	0	0	0	0	4	33.3	1	25	9	5.8	
10-12	0	0	0	0	0	0	0	0	0	0	0	0	0	0	0	0	1	8.3	0	0	1	0.6	
16-18	0	0	0	0	0	0	1	10	0	0	0	0	0	0	0	0	0	0	0	0	1	0.6	
N=	21	100	52	100	28	100	10	100	9	100	11	100	4	100	5	100	12	100	4	100	156	100	
Indeterminate	0	0	1	1.9	0	0	0	0	0	0	0	0	0	0	0	0	0	0	0	0	1	0.6	Haft Preparation
Primary	0	0	0	0	0	0	0	0	0	0	1	9.1	0	0	0	0	0	0	0	0	1	0.6	
Secondary	16	76.2	44	84.6	12	42.9	6	60	6	66.7	9	81.8	2	50	3	60	10	83.3	0	0	108	69.2	
Tertiary	4	19	7	13.5	14	50	4	40	3	33.3	1	9.1	2	50	2	40	2	16.7	2	50	41	26.3	
Grinding	1	4.8	0	0	2	7.1	0	0	0	0	0	0	0	0	0	0	0	0	2	50	5	3.2	
N=	21	100	52	100	28	100	10	100	9	100	11	100	4	100	5	100	12	100	4	100	156	100	
4-6	20	95.2	48	0	25	0	9	90	7	77.8	7	63.6	4	100	4	80	8	66.7	3	75	135	86.5	Maximum Thickness
7-9	1	4.8	4	92.3	3	89.3	1	10	2	22.2	4	36.4	0	0	1	20	2	16.7	1	25	19	12.5	
10-12	0	0	0	7.7	0	10.7	0	0	0	0	0	0	0	0	0	0	1	8.3	0	0	1	0.6	
13-15	0	0	0	0	0	0	0	0	0	0	0	0	0	0	0	0	1	8.3	0	0	1	0.6	
N=	21	100	52	100	28	100	10	100	9	100	11	100	4	100	5	100	12	100	4	100	156	100	

TABLE A.1*b* (Continued)

	Sinking Ponds		Riverhaven 2		Scaccia		Morrow		Oberlander 2		Muskalonge Lake		Hunter		Nahrwold 2		Vinette		Buffalo G		Totals		
	#	%	#	%	#	%	#	%	#	%	#	%	#	%	#	%	#	%	#	%	#	%	
Indeterminate	9	42.9	11	21.2	6	21.4	6	60	0	0	2	18.2	1	25	2	40	0	0	1	25	38	24.4	Overall Length
21-30	0	0	2	3.8	2	7.1	0	0	0	0	0	0	0	0	0	0	0	0	0	0	4	2.6	
31-40	0	0	13	25	5	17.9	0	0	0	0	1	9.1	0	0	2	40	2	16.7	0	0	23	14.7	
41-50	6	28.6	22	42.3	9	32.1	2	20	2	22.2	3	27.3	0	0	1	20	2	16.7	1	25	48	30.8	
51-60	4	19	3	5.8	2	7.1	0	0	3	33.3	2	18.2	2	50	0	0	5	41.7	1	25	22	14.1	
61-70	2	9.5	1	1.9	4	14.3	1	10	2	22.2	1	9.1	1	25	0	0	3	25	0	0	15	9.6	
71-80	0	0	0	0	0	0	1	10	2	22.2	2	18.2	0	0	0	0	0	0	0	0	5	3.2	
81-90	0	0	0	0	0	0	0	0	0	0	0	0	0	0	0	0	0	0	1	25	1	0.6	
N=	21	100	52	100	28	100	10	100	9	100	11	100	4	100	5	100	12	100	4	100	156	100	

TABLE A.2*a*
CORNERNOTCHED PROJECTILE POINT ATTRIBUTES

Variation	Constant (+95%)
Material	Blade Secondary Flake Type (expanding)
% Matrix Inclusion	
Blade Outline	
Blade Length (mm)	
Blade Width (mm)	
Blade Width Tip—2 cm (mm)	
Blade Transverse Section	
Blade Longitudinal Section	
Blade Primary Flake Type	
Blade Secondary Flake Placement	
Blade Secondary Flake Pattern	
Blade Tertiary Flake Type	
Blade Lateral Edge	
Base Outline	
Base Width (mm)	
Base Height (mm)	
Base Preparation	
Haft Juncture Type	
Haft Width (mm)	
Haft Length (mm)	
Haft Preparation	
Maximum Thickness (mm)	
Overall Length (mm)	

TABLE A.2*b*
CORNERNOTCHED PROJECTILE POINTS—TABLE OF VARIABLE ATTRIBUTE FREQUENCY

	Sinking Ponds		Riverhaven 2		Scaccia		Totals		
	#	%	#	%	#	%	#	%	
Onondaga Chert	9	100	2	40.0	11	84.6	22	81.5	Material
Onon. Chert, Fired	0	0	3	60.0	2	15.4	5	18.5	
N=	9	100	5	100	13	100	27	100	
0-20	3	33.3	2	40.0	7	53.8	12	44.4	% Matrix Inclusion
20-40	3	33.3	2	40.0	3	23.1	8	29.6	
40-60	2	22.2	1	20.0	2	15.4	5	18.5	
80-100	1	11.1	0	0	1	7.7	2	7.4	
N=	9	100	5	100	13	100	27	100	
Indeterminate	2	22.2	1	20.0	3	23.1	6	22.2	Blade Outline
Triangular	1	11.1	1	20.0	0	0	2	7.4	
Excurvate	3	33.3	2	40.0	2	15.4	7	25.9	
Ovate	1	11.1	1	20.0	6	46.2	8	29.6	
Excur.-Incur.	0	0	0	0	1	7.7	1	3.7	
Opposing-Lateral Parallel Ovate	2	22.2	0	0	1	7.7	3	11.1	
N=	9	100	5	100	13	100	27	100	

TABLE A.2*b* (Continued)

	Sinking Ponds		Riverhaven 2		Scaccia		Totals		
	#	%	#	%	#	%	#	%	
Blank or Zero	3	33.3	1	20.0	7	53.8	11	40.7	Blade Length (mm)
10-20	1	11.1	0	0	0	0	1	3.7	
21-30	0	0	4	80.0	2	15.4	6	22.2	
31-40	2	22.2	0	0	2	15.4	4	14.8	
41-50	1	11.1	0	0	2	15.4	3	11.1	
51-60	2	22.2	0	0	0	0	2	7.4	
N=	9	100	5	100	13	100	27	100	
15-20	2	22.2	3	60.0	1	7.7	6	22.2	Blade Width (mm)
21-25	5	55.6	2	40.0	8	61.5	15	56.6	
26-30	0	0	0	0	3	23.1	3	11.1	
31-35	2	22.2	0	0	1	7.7	3	11.1	
N=	9	100	5	100	13	100	27	100	
Blank or Zero	4	44.4	1	20.0	7	53.8	12	44.4	Blade Width Tip (mm)
11-15	2	22.2	2	40.0	1	7.7	5	18.5	
16-20	1	11.1	2	40.0	5	38.5	8	29.6	
21-25	2	22.2	0	0	0	0	2	7.4	
N=	9	100	5	100	13	100	27	100	
Plano-Convex	0	0	2	40.0	5	38.5	7	25.9	Blade Transverse Section
Bi-Plano	0	0	0	0	2	15.4	2	7.4	
Bi-Convex	7	77.8	3	60.0	6	46.2	16	59.3	
Asymmetrically Bi-Convex	2	22.2	0	0	0	0	2	7.4	
N=	9	100	5	100	13	100	27	100	
Plano-Convex	3	33.3	3	60.0	5	38.5	11	40.7	Blade Longitudinal Sect.
Bi-Plano	2	22.2	0	0	2	15.4	4	14.8	
Bi-Convex	3	33.3	2	40.0	6	46.2	11	40.7	
Asymmetrically Bi-Convex	1	11.1	0	0	0	0	1	3.7	
N=	9	100	5	100	13	100	27	100	
Unifacial	7	77.8	3	60.0	12	92.3	22	81.5	Blade Primary Flake Tp.
Bifacial Expanding	0	0	1	20.0	1	7.7	2	7.4	
External Face Expanding	1	11.1	0	0	0	0	1	3.7	
Internal Face Expanding	1	11.1	1	20.0	0	0	2	7.4	
N=	9	100	5	100	13	100	27	100	
Indeterminate	1	11.1	0	0	0	0	1	3.7	Blade Sec. Flake Pl.
Bifacial-Bilateral	6	66.7	3	60.0	12	92.3	21	77.8	
Unifacial-Bilateral	2	22.2	1	20.0	0	0	3	11.1	
Bilateral	0	0	1	20.0	1	7.7	2	7.4	
	9	100	5	100	13	100	27	100	
Indeterminate	2	22.2	0	0	0	0	2	7.4	Blade Sec. Flk. Pt.
Continuous	7	77.8	3	60.0	8	61.5	18	66.7	
Discontinuous	0	0	2	40.0	5	38.5	7	25.9	
	9	100	5	100	13	100	27	100	

TABLE A.2*b* (Continued)

	Sinking Ponds		Riverhaven 2		Scaccia		Totals		
	#	%	#	%	#	%	#	%	
Indeterminate	4	44.4	1	20.0	2	15.4	7	25.9	Blade Tert. Flk. Tp.
Crushed	1	11.1	0	0	0	0	1	3.7	
Nibbled	4	44.4	4	80.0	7	53.8	15	55.6	
Grinding	0	0	0	0	4	30.8	4	14.8	
N=	9	100	5	100	13	100	27	100	
Indeterminate	2	22.2	0	0	0	0	2	7.4	Blade Lateral Edge
Bevel-Serration	7	77.8	4	80.0	9	69.2	20	74.1	
Bevel-Even	0	0	0	0	1	7.7	1	3.7	
Irregular	0	0	1	20.0	2	15.4	3	11.1	
Reworked	0	0	0	0	1	7.7	1	3.7	
N=	9	100	5	100	13	100	27	100	
Indeterminate	1	11.1	0	0	0	0	1	3.7	Base Outline
Straight	3	33.3	2	40.0	2	15.4	7	25.9	
Subconvex	0	0	2	40.0	9	69.2	11	40.7	
Convex	0	0	1	20.0	2	15.4	3	11.1	
Subconcave	5	55.6	0	0	0	0	5	18.5	
N=	9	100	5	100	13	100	27	100	
Blank or Zero	1	11.1	0	0	0	0	1	3.7	Base Width (mm)
11-15	0	0	2	40.0	0	0	2	7.4	
15-20	2	22.2	3	60.0	5	38.5	10	37.0	
21-25	5	55.6	0	0	6	46.2	11	40.7	
25-30	1	11.1	0	0	1	7.7	2	7.4	
31-35	0	0	0	0	1	7.7	1	3.7	
N=	9	100	5	100	13	100	27	100	
Blank only	8	88.9	0	0	0	0	8	29.6	Base Height (mm)
0-3	0	0	2	40.0	1	7.7	3	11.1	
3-6	1	11.1	3	60.0	10	76.9	14	51.9	
7-9	0	0	0	0	2	15.4	2	7.4	
N=	9	100	5	100	13	100	27	100	
Striking Platform only	0	0	1	20.0	2	15.4	3	11.1	Base Prepar-ation
Secondary Thinning	7	77.8	3	60.0	7	53.8	17	63.0	
Tertiary Thinning	1	11.1	1	20.0	1	7.7	3	11.1	
Grinding Secondary	1	11.1	0	0	3	23.1	4	14.8	
N=	9	100	5	100	13	100	27	100	
Lateral-lateral	1	11.1	0	0	0	0	1	3.7	Haft Juncture Type
Lateral-Basal	2	22.2	0	0	0	0	2	7.4	
Lateral-Coincidental	6	66.7	5	100	12	92.3	23	85.2	
Coincidental-Basal	0	0	0	0	1	7.7	1	3.7	
N=	9	100	5	100	13	100	27	100	
11-15	3	33.3	5	100	2	15.4	10	37.0	Haft Width (mm)
16-20	6	66.7	0	0	9	69.2	15	55.6	
21-25	0	0	0	0	2	15.4	2	7.4	
N=	9	100	5	100	13	100	27	100	

TABLE A.2*b* (Continued)

	Sinking Ponds #	Sinking Ponds %	Riverhaven 2 #	Riverhaven 2 %	Scaccia #	Scaccia %	Totals #	Totals %	
1-3	0	0	2	40.0	3	23.1	5	18.5	Haft Length (mm)
4-6	1	11.1	1	20.0	10	76.9	12	44.4	
7-9	0	0	2	40.0	0	0	2	7.4	
10-12	5	55.6	0	0	0	0	5	18.5	
13-15	3	33.3	0	0	0	0	3	11.1	
N=	9	100	5	100	13	100	27	100	
Secondary	8	88.9	5	100	8	61.5	21	77.8	Haft Prep.
Tertiary	0	0	0	0	1	7.7	1	3.7	
Grinding	1	11.1	0	0	4	30.8	5	18.5	
N=	9	100	5	100	13	100	27	100	
4-6	3	33.3	2	40.0	9	69.2	14	51.9	Max. Thi. (mm)
7-9	6	66.7	3	60.0	4	30.8	13	48.1	
N=	9	100	5	100	13	100	27	100	
Blank or Zero	3	33.3	1	20.0	7	53.8	11	40.7	Overall Length (mm)
21-30	1	11.1	0	0	1	7.7	2	7.4	
31-40	0	0	4	80.0	1	7.7	5	18.5	
41-50	2	22.2	0	0	3	23.1	5	18.5	
51-60	1	11.1	0	0	1	7.7	2	7.4	
61-70	2	22.2	0	0	0	0	2	7.4	
N=	9	100	5	100	13	100	27	100	

TABLE A.3*a*
STEMMED PROJECTILE POINT ATTRIBUTES

Variation	Constant (+95%)
Material	Blade Primary Flake Type (unifacial)
% Matrix Inclusion	Blade Secondary Flake Type (expanding)
Blade Outline (mm)	Haft Juncture Type (lateral base defining)
Blade Length (mm)	
Blade Width (mm)	
Blade Width Tip—2cm (mm)	
Blade Transverse Section	
Blade Longitudinal Section	
Blade Secondary Flake Placement	
Blade Secondary Flake Pattern	
Blake Tertiary Flake Type	
Blade Lateral Edge	
Base Outline	
Base Width (mm)	
Base Height (mm)	
Base Preparation	
Haft Width (mm)	
Haft Length (mm)	
Haft Preparation	
Maximum Thickness (mm)	
Overall Length (mm)	

TABLE A.3*b*
STEMMED PROJECTILE POINTS—TABLE OF VARIABLE ATTRIBUTE FREQUENCY

	Sinking Ponds		Riverhaven 2		Scaccia		Muskalonge Lake		Hunter		Nahrwold 2		Buffalo G		Totals		
	#	%	#	%	#	%	#	%	#	%	#	%	#	%	#	%	
Onon. Chert	5	50.0	0	0	26	92.2	1	100	2	66.7	0	0	1	50.0	35	72.9	Material
Onon. Chert, Fired	5	50.0	0	0	2	7.1	0	0	0	0	0	0	0	0	7	14.2	
Deepskill Flint	0	0	0	0	0	0	0	0	1	33.3	3	100	0	0	4	8.3	
Flint Ridge Chert	0	0	0	0	0	0	0	0	0	0	0	0	1	50.0	1	2.1	
Jasper, Pa.	0	0	1	100	0	0	0	0	0	0	0	0	0	0	1	2.1	
N=	10	100	1	100	28	100	1	100	3	100	3	100	2	100	48	100	
Indeterminate	0	0	1	100	0	0	0	0	1	33.3	0	0	1	50.0	3	6.3	% Matrix Inc.
0-20	3	30.0	0	0	20	71.4	1	100	2	66.7	3	100	1	50.0	30	62.5	
20-40	4	40.0	0	0	2	7.1	0	0	0	0	0	0	0	0	6	12.5	
40-60	2	20.0	0	0	4	14.3	0	0	0	0	0	0	0	0	6	12.5	
60-80	1	10.0	0	0	1	3.6	0	0	0	0	0	0	0	0	2	4.2	
80-100	0	0	0	0	1	3.6	0	0	0	0	0	0	0	0	1	2.1	
N=	10	100	1	100	28	100	1	100	3	100	3	100	2	100	48	100	
Indeterminate	1	10.0	1	100	1	3.6	0	0	0	0	0	0	1	50.0	4	8.3	Blade Outline
Triangular	4	40.0	0	0	6	21.4	0	0	0	0	0	0	0	0	10	20.8	
Excurvate	0	0	0	0	8	28.6	1	100	0	0	0	0	1	50.0	10	20.8	
Ovate	4	40.0	0	0	9	32.1	0	0	3	100	3	100	0	0	19	39.6	
Excur.-Incur.	1	10.0	0	0	3	10.7	0	0	0	0	0	0	0	0	4	8.3	
Opposing Lateral Parallel Ovate	0	0	0	0	1	3.6	0	0	0	0	0	0	0	0	1	2.1	
N=	10	100	1	100	28	100	1	100	3	100	3	100	2	100	48	100	
Blank or Zero	1	10.0	1	100	3	10.7	0	0	0	0	0	0	1	50.0	6	12.5	Blade Length (mm)
10-20	0	0	0	0	1	3.6	0	0	0	0	0	0	0	0	1	2.1	
21-30	3	30.0	0	0	17	60.7	0	0	2	66.7	1	33.3	0	0	23	47.9	
31-40	6	60.0	0	0	3	10.7	0	0	1	33.3	1	33.3	1	50.0	12	25.0	
	0	0	0	0	4	14.3	1	100	0	0	1	33.3	0	0	6	12.5	
N=	10	100	1	100	28	100	1	100	3	100	3	100	2	100	48	100	

TABLE A.3*b* (Continued)

	Sinking Ponds		Riverhaven 2		Scaccia		Muskalonge Lake		Hunter		Nahrwold 2		Buffalo G		Totals		
	#	%	#	%	#	%	#	%	#	%	#	%	#	%	#	%	
Blank or Zero	0	0	1	100	3	10.7	0	0	1	33.3	0	0	0	0	5	10.4	Blade Width (mm)
15-20	8	80.0	0	0	19	67.9	0	0	0	0	0	0	2	100	29	60.4	
21-25	2	20.0	0	0	3	10.7	0	0	2	66.7	2	66.7	0	0	9	18.8	
26-30	0	0	0	0	3	10.7	1	100	0	0	1	33.3	0	0	5	10.4	
N=	10	100	1	100	28	100	1	100	3	100	3	100	2	100	48	100	
Plano-convex	3	30.0	0	0	11	39.3	0	0	0	0	0	0	1	50.0	15	31.3	Blade Tran. Section
Bi-plano	0	0	0	0	1	3.6	0	0	1	33.3	1	33.3	0	0	3	6.3	
Bi-convex	6	60.0	1	100	16	57.1	1	100	2	66.7	2	66.7	1	50.0	29	60.4	
Asymmetrically Bi-convex	1	10.0	0	0	0	0	0	0	0	0	0	0	0	0	1	3.1	
N=	10	100	1	100	28	100	1	100	3	100	3	100	2	100	48	100	
Plano-convex	3	30.0	1	100	11	39.3	0	0	0	0	0	0	1	50.0	16	33.3	Blade Long. Section
Bi-plano	0	0	0	0	0	0	0	0	1	33.3	1	33.3	0	0	2	4.2	
Bi-convex	6	60.0	0	0	15	53.6	1	100	2	66.7	2	66.7	2	50.0	27	56.3	
Concavo-convex	0	0	0	0	2	7.0	0	0	0	0	0	0	0	0	2	4.2	
Asymmetrically Concavo-convex	1	10.0	0	0	0	0	0	0	0	0	0	0	0	0	1	2.1	
N=	10	100	1	100	28	100	1	100	3	100	3	100	2	100	48	100	
Bifacial-Bilateral	9	90.0	1	100	28	100	1	100	2	66.7	3	100	1	50.0	45	93.8	Blade Sec. Flk. Place
Bifacial-Unifacial	0	0	0	0	0	0	0	0	0	0	0	0	1	50.0	1	2.1	
Unifacial-Bilateral	1	10.0	0	0	0	0	0	0	1	33.3	0	0	0	0	2	4.2	
N=	10	100	1	100	28	100	1	100	3	100	3	100	2	100	48	100	
Continuous	10	100	1	100	17	60.7	1	100	2	66.7	2	66.7	1	50.0	33	70.8	Blade Sec. Flk. Pattern
Discontinuous	0	0	0	0	11	39.3	0	0	0	0	1	33.3	1	50.0	13	27.1	
Patterned Clusters	0	0	0	0	0	0	0	0	1	33.3	0	0	0	0	1	2.1	
N=	10	100	1	100	28	100	1	100	3	100	3	100	2	100	48	100	

TABLE A.3*b* (Continued)

	Sinking Ponds		Riverhaven 2		Scaccia		Muskalonge Lake		Hunter		Nahrwold 2		Buffalo G		Totals		
	#	%	#	%	#	%	#	%	#	%	#	%	#	%	#	%	
Indeterminate	1	10.0	0	0	0	0	0	0	2	66.7	0	0	1	50.0	4	8.3	Blade Tert. Flk. Type
Crushed	9	90.0	0	0	0	0	0	0	0	0	0	0	0	0	9	18.8	
Nibbled	0	0	1	100	28	100	1	100	1	33.3	3	100	1	50.0	35	72.9	
N=	10	100	1	100	28	100	1	100	3	100	3	100	2	100	48	100	
Even	8	80.0	1	100	26	92.9	1	100	2	66.7	3	100	1	50.0	42	87.5	Blade Lateral Edge
Irregular	1	10.0	0	0	2	7.1	0	0	1	33.3	0	0	1	50.0	5	10.4	
Reworked	1	10.0	0	0	0	0	0	0	0	0	0	0	0	0	1	2.1	
N=	10	100	1	100	28	100	1	100	3	100	3	100	2	100	48	100	
Not Applicable	10	100	0	0	27	96.4	1	100	3	100	2	66.7	2	100	45	93.8	Base Outline
Subconvex	0	0	0	0	0	0	0	0	0	0	1	33.3	0	0	1	2.1	
Convex	0	0	0	0	1	3.6	0	0	0	0	0	0	0	0	1	2.1	
Subconcave	0	0	1	100	0	0	0	0	0	0	0	0	0	0	1	2.1	
N=	10	100	1	100	28	100	1	100	3	100	3	100	2	100	48	100	
Blank or Zero	2	20.0	0	0	0	0	1	100	3	100	0	0	0	0	6	12.5	Base Width (mm)
5-10	3	30.0	0	0	7	25.0	0	0	0	0	0	0	0	0	10	20.8	
11-15	5	50.0	0	0	14	50.0	0	0	0	0	0	0	1	50.0	20	41.7	
15-20	0	0	1	100	4	14.3	0	0	0	0	2	66.7	1	50.0	8	16.7	
21-25	0	0	0	0	3	10.7	0	0	0	0	1	33.3	0	0	4	8.3	
N=	10	100	1	100	28	100	1	100	3	100	3	100	2	100	48	100	
Blank only	1	10.0	0	0	0	0	0	0	0	0	0	0	0	0	1	2.1	Base Height (mm)
0-3	2	20.0	1	100	20	71.4	1	100	3	100	2	66.7	0	0	29	60.4	
3-6	5	50.0	0	0	2	7.1	0	0	0	0	0	0	1	50.0	8	16.7	
7-9	2	20.0	0	0	6	21.4	0	0	0	0	1	33.3	1	50.0	10	20.8	
N=	10	100	1	100	28	100	1	100	3	100	3	100	2	100	48	100	
Indeterminate	2	20.0	0	0	0	0	0	0	0	0	0	0	0	0	2	4.2	Base Preparation
Striking Platform	7	70.0	0	0	10	35.7	0	0	0	0	1	33.3	1	50.0	19	39.6	
Sec. Thinning	1	10.0	0	0	18	64.3	0	0	3	100	2	66.7	1	50.0	25	52.1	
Tert. Thinning	0	0	1	100	0	0	0	0	0	0	0	0	0	0	1	2.1	
Grinding Sec.	0	0	0	0	0	0	1	100	0	0	0	0	0	0	1	2.1	
N=	10	100	1	100	28	100	1	100	3	100	3	100	2	100	48	100	

TABLE A.3*b* (Continued)

	Sinking Ponds #	Sinking Ponds %	Riverhaven 2 #	Riverhaven 2 %	Scaccia #	Scaccia %	Muskalonge Lake #	Muskalonge Lake %	Hunter #	Hunter %	Nahrwold 2 #	Nahrwold 2 %	Buffalo G #	Buffalo G %	Totals #	Totals %	
Blank or Zero	0	0	0	0	0	0	0	0	0	0	0	0	1	50.0	1	2.1	Haft Width (mm)
5-10	7	70.0	0	0	15	53.6	1	100	1	33.3	0	0	1	50.0	25	52.1	
11-15	3	30.0	1	100	12	42.9	0	0	2	66.7	2	66.7	0	0	20	41.7	
16-20	0	0	0	0	1	3.6	0	0	0	0	1	33.3	0	0	2	4.2	
N=	10	100	1	100	28	100	1	100	3	100	3	100	2	100	48	100	
Blank or Zero	2	20.0	0	0	0	0	0	0	0	0	0	0	0	0	2	4.2	Haft Length (mm)
4-6	4	40.0	0	0	1	3.6	0	0	0	0	0	0	2	100	7	14.6	
7-9	2	20.0	1	100	7	25.0	0	0	1	33.3	1	33.3	0	0	12	25.0	
10-12	2	20.0	0	0	17	60.7	1	100	2	66.7	1	33.3	0	0	23	47.9	
13-15	0	0	0	0	2	7.1	0	0	0	0	0	0	0	0	2	4.2	
16-18	0	0	0	0	1	3.6	0	0	0	0	1	33.3	0	0	2	4.2	
N=	10	100	1	100	28	100	1	100	3	100	3	100	2	100	48	100	
Indeterminate	1	10.0	0	0	2	7.1	0	0	0	0	0	0	0	0	3	6.3	Haft Prepar-ation
Secondary	9	90.0	0	0	26	92.9	0	0	2	66.7	3	100	1	50.0	41	85.4	
Tertiary	0	0	1	100	0	0	0	0	1	33.3	0	0	1	50.0	3	6.3	
Grinding	0	0	0	0	0	0	1	100	0	0	0	0	0	0	1	2.1	
N=	10	100	1	100	28	100	1	100	3	100	3	100	2	100	48	100	
4-6	7	70.0	1	100	17	60.7	0	0	1	33.3	0	0	0	0	26	54.2	Max. Thick (mm)
7-9	3	30.0	0	0	11	39.3	1	100	2	66.7	3	100	2	100	22	45.8	
N=	10	100	1	100	28	100	1	100	3	100	3	100	2	100	48	100	
Blank or Zero	2	20.0	1	100	3	10.7	0	0	0	0	0	0	1	50.0	7	14.6	Overall Length (mm)
21-30	1	10.0	0	0	2	7.1	0	0	0	0	0	0	0	0	3	6.3	
31-40	0	0	0	0	15	53.6	0	0	1	33.3	1	33.3	0	0	17	35.4	
41-50	6	60.0	0	0	4	14.3	0	0	2	66.7	1	33.3	1	50.0	14	29.2	
51-60	1	10.0	0	0	3	10.7	1	100	0	0	0	0	0	0	5	10.4	
61-70	0	0	0	0	1	3.6	0	0	0	0	1	33.3	0	0	2	4.2	
N=	10	100	1	100	28	100	1	100	3	100	3	100	2	100	48	100	

TABLE A.4*a*
QUATERNARY BLADE ATTRIBUTES

Variation	Constant (+95%)
Material	Blade Primary Flake Type (unifacial)
% Matrix Inclusion	Blade Secondary Flake Type (expanding)
Blade Outline	Blade Secondary Flake Placement (bifacial—bilateral)
Blade Length (mm)	Blade Tertiary Flake Type (nibbled)
Blade Width (mm)	
Blade Width Tip—2cm (mm)	
Blade Transverse Section	
Blade Longitudinal Section	
Blade Secondary Flake Pattern	
Blade Lateral Edge	
Base Outline	
Base Width (mm)	
Base Height (mm)	
Base Preparation	
Maximum Thickness (mm)	
Overall Length (mm)	

TABLE A.4*b*
QUATERNARY BLADES — TABLE OF ATTRIBUTES

	Sinking Ponds		Riverhaven II		Scaccia		Morrow		Oberlander II WCH 11		Oberlander II WBR 16		Buffalo G		
	#	%	#	%	#	%	#	%	#	%	#	%	#	%	
Onondaga Chert	17	100	66	86.8	9	100	42	100	27	96.4	36	81.8	0	0	Material
Onon. Chert Fired	0	0	10	13.2	0	0	0	0	1	3.6	8	18.2	0	0	
Deepskill Flint	0	0	0	0	0	0	0	0	0	0	0	- 0	0	0	
Onon. Chert Pigmentation Added	0	0	0	0	0	0	0	0	0	0	0	0	18	100	
N=	17	100	76	100	9	100	42	100	28	100	44	100	18	100	
Indeterminate	0	0	0	0	0	0	42	100	0	0	0	0	0	0	% Matrix Inc.
0-20	5	29.4	45	59.2	5	55.6	0	0	7	20	18	40.9	6	33.3	
20-40	3	17.6	18	23.7	3	33.3	0	0	1	3.6	16	36.4	4	22.2	
40-60	3	17.6	11	14.5	0	0	0	0	0	0	5	11.4	6	33.3	
60-80	3	17.6	2	2.6	1	11.1	0	0	0	0	4	9.1	2	11.1	
80-100	3	17.6	0	0	0	0	0	0	0	0	1	2.3	0	0	
Matrix pocking, plus 50%	0	0	0	0	0	0	0	0	20	71.4	0	0	0	0	
N=	17	100	76	100	9	100	42	100	28	100	44	100	18	100	
Indeterminate	2	11.8	0	0	0	0	0	0	0	0	0	0	0	0	Blade Outline
Triangular	3	17.6	21	27.6	1	11.1	0	0	2	7.1	7	15.9	0	0	
Excurvate	1	5.9	22	28.9	2	22.2	4	9.5	2	7.1	3	6.8	2	11.1	
Ovate	11	64.7	29	38.2	3	33.3	38	90.5	22	78.6	31	70.5	15	83.3	
Excurvate-incurvate															
Opposing lateral	0	0	3	3.9	2	22.2	0	0	0	0	0	0	0	0	
Parallel-ovate	0	0	1	1.3	1	11.1	0	0	2	7.1	3	6.8	0	0	
Contracting ovate	0	0	0	0	0	0	0	0	0	0	0	0	0	0	
Excurvate-ovate	0	0	0	0	0	0	0	0	0	0	0	0	1	5.6	
N=	17	100	76	100	9	100	42	100	28	100	44	100	18	100	

TABLE A.4*b* (Continued)

	Muskalonge Lake		Hunter		Nahrwold II		Vinette		Irondequoit Bay		Rene Menard		Totals		
	#	%	#	%	#	%	#	%	#	%	#	%	#	%	
Onondaga Chert	55	42.3	39	81.3	0	0	12	100	0	0	1	3	304	62.4	Material
Onon. Chert Fired	34	26	9	18.8	0	0	0	0	0	0	0	0	62	12.7	
Deepskill Flint	0	0	0	0	7	100	0	0	0	0	0	0	7	1.4	
Onondaga Chert Pigmentation Added	42	32.1	0	0	0	0	0	0	22	100	32	97	114	23.4	
N=	131	100	48	100	7	100	12	100	22	100	33	100	487	100	
Indeterminate	131	100	48	100	0	0	0	0	0	0	0	0	221	45.4	% Matrix Inclusion
0-20	0	0	0	0	6	85.7	8	66.7	19	86.4	27	81.8	146	30	
20-40	0	0	0	0	1	14.3	2	16.7	3	13.6	6	18.2	57	11.7	
40-60	0	0	0	0	0	0	1	8.3	0	0	0	0	20	5.3	
60-80	0	0	0	0	0	0	1	8.3	0	0	0	0	13	2.7	
80-100	0	0	0	0	0	0	0	0	0	0	0	0	4	0.8	
Matrix Pocking plus 50%	0	0	0	0	0	0	0	0	0	0	0	0	20	4.1	
N=	131	100	48	100	7	100	12	100	22	100	33	100	487	100	
Indeterminate	0	0	0	0	0	0	0	0	0	0	0	0	2	0.4	Blade Outline
Triangular	2	1.5	0	0	2	28.6	1	8.3	1	4.5	9	27.3	49	10.1	
Excurvate	27	20.6	2	4.2	1	14.3	0	0	2	9.1	0	0	68	14	
Ovate	56	42.7	46	95.8	2	28.6	6	50	7	31.8	23	69.7	289	59.3	
Excurvate-incurvate Opposing lateral	0	0	0	0	1	14.3	1	8.3	2	9.1	0	0	9	1.8	
Parallel-ovate	11	8.4	0	0	1	14.3	4	33.3	10	45.5	1	3	34	7	
Contracting ovate	35	26.7	0	0	0	0	0	0	0	0	0	0	35	7.2	
Excurvate-ovate	0	0	0	0	0	0	0	0	0	0	0	0	1	0.2	
N=	131	100	48	100	7	100	12	100	22	100	33	100	487	100	

TABLE A.4*b* (Continued)

	Sinking Ponds		Riverhaven II		Scaccia		Morrow		Oberlander II WHC 11		Oberlander II WBR 16		Buffalo G		
	#	%	#	%	#	%	#	%	#	%	#	%	#	%	
Blank	2	11.8	0	0	2	22.2	0	0	0	0	1	2.3	0	0	Blade Length
10-20	0	0	0	0	0	0	0	0	0	0	0	0	0	0	
21-30	0	0	14	18.4	0	0	0	0	0	0	0	0	0	0	
31-40	0	0	40	52.6	2	22.2	1	2.4	1	3.6	4	9.1	0	0	
41-50	6	35.3	20	26.3	4	44.4	21	50	5	17.9	16	36.4	1	5.6	
51-60	7	41.2	2	2.6	1	11.1	18	42.9	16	57.1	14	31.8	11	61.1	
61-70	2	11.8	0	0	0	0	2	4.8	6	21.4	7	15.9	6	33.3	
71-80	0	0	0	0	0	0	0	0	0	0	2	4.5	0	0	
81-90	0	0	0	0	0	0	0	0	0	0	0	0	0	0	
91-100	0	0	0	0	0	0	0	0	0	0	0	0	0	0	
N=	17	100	76	100	9	100	42	100	28	100	44	100	18	100	
Blank	0	0	0	0	0	0	0	0	0	0	0	0	0	0	Blade Width mm
15-20	0	0	14	18.4	1	11.1	0	0	0	0	1	2.3	1	5.6	
21-25	11	64.7	41	53.9	6	66.7	11	26.2	9	32.1	11	25	7	38.9	
26-30	5	29.4	20	26.3	2	22.2	26	61.9	17	60.7	25	59.1	10	55.6	
31-35	1	5.9	1	1.3	0	0	4	9.5	2	7.1	6	13.6	0	0	
36-40	0	0	0	0	0	0	0	0	0	0	0	0	0	0	
51-60	0	0	0	0	0	0	0	0	0	0	0	0	0	0	
N=	17	100	76	100	9	100	42	100	28	100	44	100	18	100	
Blank	2	11.8	0	0	1	11.1	0	0	0	0	1	2.3	0	0	Blade Width Tip
5-10	0	0	2	2.6	0	0	0	0	0	0	0	0	0	0	
11-15	8	47.1	29	38.2	2	22.2	12	28.6	8	28.6	11	25	0	0	
16-20	7	41.2	44	57.9	5	55.6	30	71.4	20	71.4	30	68.2	18	100	
21-25	0	0	1	1.3	1	11.1	0	0	0	0	2	4.5	0	0	
26-30	0	0	0	0	0	0	0	0	0	0	0	0	0	0	
N=	17	100	76	100	9	100	42	100	28	100	44	100	18	100	

TABLE A.4*b* (Continued)

	Muskalonge Lake		Hunter		Nahrwold II		Vinette		Irondequoit Bay		Rene Menard		Totals		
	#	%	#	%	#	%	#	%	#	%	#	%	#	%	
Blank	42	32.1	0	0	0	0	1	8.3	0	0	0	0	48	9.9	Blade Length (mm)
10-20	1	0.8	0	0	0	0	0	0	0	0	0	0	1	0.2	
21-30	0	0	0	0	0	0	0	0	0	0	0	0	14	2.9	
31-40	0	0	1	2.1	2	28.6	2	16.7	0	0	1	3	54	11.1	
41-50	3	2.3	21	43.8	3	42.9	1	8.3	0	0	20	60.6	121	24.8	
51-60	20	15.3	21	43.8	2	28.6	3	25	5	22.7	11	33.3	131	26.9	
61-70	33	25.2	4	8.3	0	0	4	33.3	11	50	1	3	76	15.6	
71-80	24	18.3	1	2.1	0	0	1	8.3	6	27.3	0	0	34	7	
81-90	7	5.3	0	0	0	0	0	0	0	0	0	0	7	1.4	
91-100	1	0.8	0	0	0	0	0	0	0	0	0	0	1	0.2	
N=	131	100	48	100	7	100	12	100	22	100	33	100	487	100	
Blank	2	1.5	0	0	0	0	0	0	0	0	0	0	2	0.4	Blade Width (mm)
15-20	0	0	0	0	0	0	2	16.7	0	0	0	0	19	3.9	
21-25	3	2.3	4	8.3	3	42.9	9	75	9	40.9	11	33.3	135	27.7	
26-30	64	48.9	34	70.8	3	42.9	0	0	13	59.1	21	63.6	241	49.5	
31-35	62	47.3	10	20.8	1	14.3	0	0	0	0	1	3	88	18.1	
36-40	0	0	0	0	0	0	1	8.3	0	0	0	0	1	0.2	
51-60	0	0	0	0	0	0	0	0	0	0	0	0	1	0.2	
N=	131	100	48	100	7	100	12	100	22	100	33	100	487	100	
Blank	21	16	0	0	0	0	1	8.3	0	0	0	0	26	5.3	Blade Width (TP)
5-10	0	0	0	0	0	0	0	0	0	0	0	0	2	0.4	
11-15	3	2.3	4	8.3	1	14.3	5	41.7	8	36.4	8	24.2	99	20.3	
16-20	90	68.7	41	85.4	5	71.4	6	50	14	63.6	25	75.8	335	68.8	
21-25	17	13	2	4.2	1	14.3	0	0	0	0	0	0	24	4.9	
26-30	0	0	1	2.1	0	0	0	0	0	0	0	0	1	0.2	
	131	100	48	100	7	100	12	100	22	100	33	100	487	100	

TABLE A.4*b* (Continued)

	Sinking Ponds		Riverhaven II		Scaccia		Morrow		Oberlander II WHC 11		Oberlander II WBR 16		Buffalo G		
	#	%	#	%	#	%	#	%	#	%	#	%	#	%	
Plano-convex	6	35.3	28	36.8	3	33.3	26	61.9	13	46.4	23	52.3	6	33.3	Blade Trans. Section
Bi-plano	4	23.5	2	2.6	0	0	2	4.8	3	10.7	5	11.4	0	0	
Bi-convex	6	35.3	45	59.2	6	66.7	14	33.3	12	42.9	16	36.4	10	55.6	
Asymmetrically Bi-convex	1	5.9	1	1.3	0	0	0	0	0	0	0	0	2	11.1	
N=	17	100	76	100	9	100	42	100	28	100	44	100	18	100	
Plano-convex	6	35.3	19	25	3	33.3	20	47.6	7	25	18	40.9	6	33.3	Blade Long. Section
Bi-plano	3	17.6	7	9.2	0	0	8	19	13	46.4	14	31.8	7	38.9	
Bi-convex	4	23.5	41	53.9	6	66.7	14	33.3	7	25	5	11.4	5	27.8	
Asymmetrically Bi-convex	0	0	0	0	0	0	0	0	0	0	0	0	0	0	
Concavo-convex	0	0	9	11.8	0	0	0	0	1	3.6	7	15.9	0	0	
Asymmetrically Concavo convex	4	23.5	0	0	0	0	0	0	0	0	0	0	0	0	
N=	17	100	76	100	9	100	42	100	28	100	44	100	18	100	
Continuous	16	94.1	62	81.6	6	66.7	42	100	26	92.9	41	93.2	17	94.5	Bld. Sec. Flk. Pat.
Discontinuous	1	5.9	14	18.4	3	33.3	0	0	2	7.1	3	6.8	1	5.6	
N=	17	100	76	100	9	100	42	100	28	100	44	100	18	100	
Serration	0	0	1	1.3	0	0	0	0	0	0	0	0	0	0	Blade Lateral Edge
Even	14	82.4	56	73.7	6	66.7	42	100	28	100	43	97.7	18	100	
Bevel-even	1	5.9	0	0	0	0	0	0	0	0	0	0	0	0	
Irregular	2	11.8	19	25	2	22.2	0	0	0	0	1	2.3	0	0	
Reworked	0	0	0	0	1	11.1	0	0	0	0	0	0	0	0	
N=	17	100	76	100	9	100	42	100	28	100	44	100	18	100	
Indeterminate	0	0	0	0	0	0	0	0	0	0	0	0	1	5.6	Base Outline
Straight	4	23.5	3	3.9	4	44.4	0	0	0	0	8	18.2	2	11.1	
Subconvex	13	76.5	44	57.9	3	33.3	42	100	27	96.4	30	68.2	12	66.7	
Convex	0	0	29	38.2	2	22.2	0	0	1	3.6	6	13.6	3	16.7	
Subconcave	0	0	0	0	0	0	0	0	0	0	0	0	0	0	
N=	17	100	76	100	9	100	42	100	28	100	44	100	18	100	

TABLE A.4*b* (Continued)

	Muskalonge Lake		Hunter		Nahrwold II		Vinette		Irondequoit Bay		Rene Menard		Totals		
	#	%	#	%	#	%	#	%	#	%	#	%	#	%	
Plano-convex	82	62.6	29	60.4	3	42.9	3	25	8	36.4	16	48.5	246	50.5	Blade Trans. Section
Bi-plano	8	6.1	5	10.4	1	14.3	1	8.3	0	0	1	3	32	6.6	
Bi-convex	41	31.3	14	29.2	2	28.6	8	66.4	14	63.6	16	48.5	204	41.9	
Asymmetrically Bi-convex	0	0	0	0	1	14.3	0	0	0	0	0	0	5	1.0	
N=	131	100	48	100	7	100	12	100	22	100	33	100	487	100	
Plano-convex	62	47.3	24	50	2	28.6	1	8.3	8	36.4	14	42.4	190	39	Blade Long. Section
Bi-plano	34	26	11	22.9	1	14.3	9	75	7	31.8	3	9.1	117	24	
Bi-convex	35	26.7	13	27.1	2	28.6	2	16.7	5	22.7	12	36.4	151	31	
Asymmetrically Bi-convex	0	0	0	0	2	28.6	0	0	0	0	0	0	2	0.4	
Concavo-convex	0	0	0	0	0	0	0	0	2	9.1	4	12.1	23	4.7	
Asymmetrically Concavo-convex	0	0	0	0	0	0	0	0	0	0	0	0	4	0.8	
N=	131	100	48	100	7	100	12	100	22	100	33	100	487	100	
Continuous	116	88.5	48	100	4	57.1	12	100	20	90.9	30	90.9	440	90.3	Bld. Sec. Flk. Pat.
Discontinuous	15	11.5	0	0	3	42.9	0	0	2	9.1	3	9.1	47	9.7	
N=	131	100	48	100	7	100	12	100	22	100	33	100	487	100	
Serration	0	0	0	0	0	0	0	0	0	0	0	0	1	0.2	Blade Lateral Edge
Even	131	100	48	100	5	71.4	12	100	22	100	33	100	458	94	
Bevel-even	0	0	0	0	0	0	0	0	0	0	0	0	1	0.2	
Irregular	0	0	0	0	1	14.3	0	0	0	0	0	0	25	5.1	
Reworked	0	0	0	0	1	14.3	0	0	0	0	0	0	2	0.4	
N=	131	100	48	100	7	100	12	100	22	100	33	100	487	100	
Indeterminate	2	1.5	0	0	0	0	0	0	0	0	0	0	3	0.6	Base Outline
Straight	1	0.8	0	0	0	0	3	25	7	31.8	0	0	32	6.6	
Subconvex	4	3.1	9	18.8	6	85.7	8	66.7	15	68.2	28	84.8	241	49.5	
Convex	123	93.9	39	81.3	1	14.3	1	8.3	0	0	5	15.2	210	43.1	
Subconcave	1	0.8	0	0	0	0	0	0	0	0	0	0	1	0.2	
N=	131	100	48	100	7	100	12	100	22	100	33	100	487	100	

TABLE A.4*b* (Continued)

	Sinking Ponds #	Sinking Ponds %	Riverhaven II #	Riverhaven II %	Scaccia #	Scaccia %	Morrow #	Morrow %	Oberlander II WCH 11 #	Oberlander II WCH 11 %	Oberlander II WBR 16 #	Oberlander II WBR 16 %	Buffalo G #	Buffalo G %	
Blank	0	0	0	0	0	0	0	0	0	0	0	0	0	0	Base Width
15-20	0	0	21	27.6	1	11.1	0	0	1	3.6	1	2.3	1	5.6	
21-25	12	70.6	37	48.7	5	55.6	11	26.2	8	28.6	12	27.3	7	38.9	
25-30	4	23.5	17	22.4	2	22.2	26	61.9	17	60.7	25	56.8	10	55.6	
31-35	1	5.9	1	1.3	1	11.1	4	9.5	2	7.1	6	13.6	0	0	
36-40	0	0	0	0	0	0	0	0	0	0	0	0	0	0	
46-50	0	0	0	0	0	0	1	2.4	0	0	0	0	0	0	
N=	17	100	76	100	9	100	42	100	28	100	44	100	18	100	
0-3	10	58.8	33	43.4	6	66.7	25	59.5	12	42.9	28	63.6	12	66.7	Base Height
3-6	7	41.2	33	43.3	2	22.2	17	40.5	15	53.6	12	27.5	5	27.8	
7-9	0	0	10	13.2	1	11.1	0	0	1	3.6	4	9.1	1	5.6	
N=	17	100	76	100	9	100	42	100	28	100	44	100	18	100	
Indeterminate	0	0	0	0	0	0	0	0	0	0	0	0	1	5.6	Base Preparation
Striking Platform Only	0	0	6	7.9	1	11.1	0	0	2	7.1	3	6.8	1	5.6	
Secondary Thinning	10	58.8	33	43.4	4	44.4	0	0	9	32.1	11	25	10	55.6	
Tertiary Thinning	6	35.3	37	48.7	4	44.4	42	100	17	60.7	30	68.2	6	33.3	
Grinding Pri.	1	5.9	0	0	0	0	0	0	0	0	0	0	0	0	
Grinding Sec.	0	0	0	0	0	0	0	0	0	0	0	0	0	0	
N=	17	100	76	100	9	100	42	100	28	100	44	100	18	100	
4-6	11	64.7	53	69.7	6	66.7	42	100	27	96.4	42	95.5	15	83.3	Max. Thick-ness
7-9	6	35.3	23	30.3	2	22.2	0	0	1	3.6	2	4.5	3	16.7	
10-12	0	0	0	0	1	11.1	0	0	0	0	0	0	0	0	
N=	17	100	76	100	9	100	42	100	28	100	44	100	18	100	

TABLE A.4*b* (Continued)

	Sinking Ponds		Riverhaven II		Scaccia		Morrow		Oberlander II WCH 11		Oberlander II WBR 16		Buffalo G		
	#	%	#	%	#	%	#	%	#	%	#	%	#	%	
Blank	2	11.8	0	0	1	11.1	0	0	0	0	1	2.3	0	0	Overall Length
21-30	0	0	1	1.3	0	0	0	0	0	0	0	0	0	0	
31-40	0	0	41	53.9	1	11.1	0	0	1	3.6	0	0	0	0	
41-50	2	11.8	30	39.5	4	44.4	16	38.1	2	7.1	14	31.8	0	0	
51-60	10	58.8	4	5.3	3	33.3	22	52.4	11	39.3	17	38.6	6	33.3	
61-70	3	17.6	0	0	0	0	4	9.5	13	46.4	99	20.5	10	55.6	
71-80	0	0	0	0	0	0	0	0	1	3.6	2	4.5	2	11.1	
81-90	0	0	0	0	0	0	0	0	0	0	1	2.3	0	0	
91-100	0	0	0	0	0	0	0	0	0	0	0	0	0	0	
N=	17	100	76	100	9	100	42	100	28	100	44	100	18	100	

TABLE A.4*b* (Continued)

	Muskalonge Lake		Hunter		Nahrwold II		Vinette		Irondequoit Bay		Rene Menard		Totals		
	#	%	#	%	#	%	#	%	#	%	#	%	#	%	
Blank	1	0.8	0	0	0	0	0	0	0	0	0	0	1	0.2	Base Width
15-20	0	0	0	0	0	0	3	25	0	0	0	0	28	5.7	
21-25	3	2.3	4	8.3	3	42.9	8	66.7	9	40.9	11	33.3	130	26.7	
25-30	65	49.6	34	70.8	3	42.9	0	0	13	59.1	21	63.6	237	48.7	
31-35	62	47.3	10	20.8	1	14.3	0	0	0	0	1	3	89	18.3	
36-40	0	0	0	0	0	0	1	8.3	0	0	0	0	1	0.2	
46-50	0	0	0	0	0	0	0	0	0	0	0	0	1	0.2	
N=	131	100	48	100	7	100	12	100	22	100	33	100	487	100	
0-3	6	4.6	4	8.3	4	57.1	7	58.3	19	86.4	11	33.3	177	36.3	Base Height
3-6	50	38.2	22	45.8	3	42.9	5	41.7	3	13.6	20	60.6	194	39.8	
7-9	75	57.3	22	45.8	0	0	0	0	0	0	2	6.1	116	23.8	
N=	131	100	48	100	7	100	12	100	22	100	33	100	487	100	

TABLE A.4*b* (Continued)

	Muskalonge Lake		Hunter		Nahrwold II		Vinette		Irondequoit Bay		Rene Menard		Totals		
	#	%	#	%	#	%	#	%	#	%	#	%	#	%	
Indeterminate	2	1.5	0	0	0	0	0	0	0	0	0	0	3	0.6	Base Preparation
Striking Platform Only	14	10.7	0	0	1	14.3	0	0	2	9.1	3	9.1	33	6.8	
Secondary Thinning	23	17.6	9	18.8	3	42.9	12	100	2	9.1	8	24.2	134	27.5	
Tertiary Thinning	85	64.9	39	81.3	3	42.9	0	0	18	81.8	22	66.7	309	63.4	
Grinding Pri.	0	0	0	0	0	0	0	0	0	0	0	0	1	0.2	
Grinding Sec.	7	5.3	0	0	0	0	0	0	0	0	0	0	7	1.4	
N=	131	100	48	100	7	100	12	100	22	100	33	100	487	100	
4-6	90	68.7	47	97.9	3	42.9	9	75	19	86.4	31	93.9	395	81.1	Max. Thick-ness
7-9	41	31.3	1	2.1	2	28.6	3	25	3	13.6	2	6.1	89	18.3	
10-12	0	0	0	0	2	28.6	0	0	0	0	0	0	3	0.6	
N=	131	100	48	100	7	100	12	100	22	100	33	100	487	100	
Blank	42	32.1	0	0	0	0	1	8.3	0	0	0	0	47	9.7	Overall Length
21-30	1	0.8	0	0	0	0	0	0	0	0	0	0	2	0.4	
31-40	0	0	0	0	0	0	1	8.3	0	0	0	0	44	9	
41-50	0	0	6	12.5	3	42.9	2	16.7	0	0	9	27.3	88	18.1	
51-60	7	5.3	28	58.3	3	42.9	1	8.3	2	9.1	19	57.6	133	27.3	
61-70	25	19.1	12	25	1	14.3	5	41.7	14	63.6	5	15.2	101	20.7	
71-80	36	27.5	1	2.1	0	0	2	16.7	5	22.7	0	0	49	10.1	
81-90	17	13	1	2.1	0	0	0	0	1	4.5	0	0	20	4.1	
91-100	3	2.3	0	0	0	0	0	0	0	0	0	0	3	0.6	
N=	131	100	48	100	7	100	12	100	22	100	33	100	487	100	

TABLE A.5*a*
QUATERNARY BLADE BASE ATTRIBUTES

Variation	Constant (+95%)
Material	Blade Secondary Flake Type (expanding)
% Matrix Inclusion	Blade Secondary Flake Pattern (continuous)
Blade Width (mm)	Blade Tertiary Flake Type (nibbled)
Blade Transverse Section	Blade Lateral Edge (even)
Blade Primary Flake Type	
Blade Secondary Flake Placement	
Base Outline	
Base Width (mm)	
Base Height (mm)	
Base Preparation	
Maximum Thickness (mm)	

TABLE A.5*b*
QUATERNARY BLADE BASE FRAGMENTS — TABLE OF ATTRIBUTES

	Sinking Ponds		Riverhaven II		Buffalo G		Totals		
	#	%	#	%	#	%	#	%	
Indeterminate	1	2.4	0	0	0	0	1	0.3	Material
Onondaga Chert	40	97.6	292	90.1	1	50	333	90.7	
Onondaga Chert, Fired	0	0	31	9.6	1	50	32	8.7	
Flint ridge chert	0	0	1	0.3	0	0	1	0.3	
N=	41	100	324	100	2	100	367	100	
Indeterminate	0	0	19	5.9	0	0	19	5.2	% Matrix Inclusion
0-20	12	29.3	182	56.2	1	50	195	53.1	
20-40	15	36.6	59	18.2	1	50	75	20.4	
40-60	9	22	43	13.3	0	0	52	14.2	
60-80	5	12.2	20	6.2	0	0	25	6.8	
80-100	0	0	1	0.3	0	0	1	0.3	
N=	41	100	324	100	2	100	367	100	
Blank	41	100	0	0	0	0	41	11.2	Blade Width
15-20	0	0	14	4.3	0	0	14	3.8	
21-25	0	0	100	30.9	2	100	102	27.8	
26-30	0	0	133	41	0	0	133	36.2	
31-35	0	0	64	19.8	0	0	64	17.4	
36-40	0	0	12	3.7	0	0	12	3.3	
41-45	0	0	1	0.3	0	0	1	0.3	
N=	41	100	324	100	2	100	367	100	
Plano-convex	14	34.1	107	33	0	0	121	33	Blade Trans. Section
Bi-plano	8	19.5	10	3.1	0	0	18	4.9	
Bi-convex	17	41.5	191	59	2	100	210	57.2	
Asymmetrically Bi-convex	2	4.9	13	4	0	0	15	4.1	
Asymmetrically Triangular	0	0	2	0.6	0	0	2	0.5	
Convexo-Triangular	0	0	1	0.3	0	0	1	0.3	
N=	41	100	324	100	2	100	367	100	

TABLE A.5*b* (Continued)

	Sinking Ponds		Riverhaven II		Buffalo G		Totals		
	#	%	#	%	#	%	#	%	
Unifacial	41	100	304	93.8	2	100	347	94.6	Blade Primary Flake
Bi-facial expanding	0	0	3	0.9	0	0	3	0.8	
External Face-expanding	0	0	11	3.4	0	0	11	3	
Internal Face-expanding	0	0	4	1.2	0	0	4	1.1	
External Face Lamellar	0	0	2	0.6	0	0	2	0.5	
N=	41	100	324	100	2	100	367	100	
Bi-facial - Bi-lateral	41	100	303	93.5	2	100	346	94.3	Blade Section Placement
Bi-facial - Unilateral	0	0	1	0.3	0	0	1	0.3	
Unifacial - Bi-lateral	0	0	14	4.3	0	0	14	3.8	
Unifacial - Unilateral	0	0	3	0.9	0	0	3	0.8	
Bi-facial	0	0	3	0.9	0	0	3	0.8	
N=	41	100	324	100	2	100	367	100	
Indeterminate	8	19.5	6	1.9	0	0	14	3.8	Base Outline
Straight	6	14.6	40	12.3	0	0	46	12.5	
Subconvex	21	51.2	220	67.9	1	50	242	65.9	
Convex	6	14.6	57	17.6	1	50	64	17.1	
Subconcave	0	0	1	0.3	0	0	1	0.3	
N=	41	100	324	100	2	100	367	100	
11-15	0	0	2	0.6	0	0	2	0.5	Base Width
15-20	3	7.3	28	8.6	0	0	31	8.4	
21-25	10	24.4	111	34.3	2	100	123	33.5	
25-30	23	56.1	130	40.1	0	0	153	41.7	
31-35	5	12.2	48	14.8	0	0	53	14.4	
36-40	0	0	5	1.5	0	0	5	1.4	
N=	41	100	324	100	2	100	367	100	
Blank	41	100	0	0	0	0	41	11.2	Base Height
0-3	0	0	152	46.9	1	50	153	41.7	
3-6	0	0	123	38	0	0	123	33.5	
7-9	0	0	49	15.1	1	50	50	13.6	
N=	41	100	324	100	2	100	367	100	
Striking Platform Only	0	0	23	7.1	0	0	23	6.3	Blade Prepara-tion
Primary Thinning	1	2.4	0	0	0	0	1	0.3	
Secondary Thinning	40	97.6	176	54.3	2	100	218	59.4	
Tertiary Thinning	0	0	125	38.6	0	0	125	34.1	
N=	41	100	324	100	2	100	367	100	
4-6	29	70.7	243	75	2	100	274	74.7	Max. Thick-ness
7-9	11	26.8	80	24.7	0	0	91	24.8	
10-12	1	2.4	1	0.3	0	0	2	0.5	
N=	41	100	324	100	2	100	367	100	

TABLE A.6*a*
QUATERNARY BLADE TIP ATTRIBUTES

Variation	Constant (+95%)
% Matrix Inclusion Blade Width 2cm (mm) Blade Transverse Section Blade Primary Flake Type Blade Secondary Flake Placement Blade Secondary Flake Pattern Blade Lateral Edge Maximum Thickness (mm)	Material (Onondaga Chert-natural varieties) Blade Secondary Flake Type (expanding) Blade Tertiary Flake Type (nibbled)

TABLE A.6*b*
QUATERNARY BLADE TIP FRAGMENTS — TABLE OF ATTRIBUTES

	Sinking Ponds		Riverhaven II		Buffalo G		Totals		
	#	%	#	%	#	%	#	%	
Indeterminate	0	0	51	16.7	0	0	51	14.4	% Matrix Inclusion
0-20	16	34	129	42.3	1	50	146	41.2	
20-40	8	17	55	18	1	50	64	18.1	
40-60	18	38.3	44	14.4	0	0	62	17.5	
60-80	4	8.5	20	6.6	0	0	24	6.8	
80-100	1	2.1	6	2	0	0	7	2	
N=	47	100	305	100	2	100	354	100	
Blank	5	10.6	2	0.7	0	0	7	2	Blade Width
15-20	1	2.1	1	0.3	0	0	2	0.6	
21-25	6	12.8	28	9.2	0	0	34	9.6	
26-30	20	42.6	166	54.4	1	50	187	52.8	
31-35	12	25.5	92	30.2	1	50	105	29.7	
36-40	3	6.4	15	4.9	0	0	18	5.1	
41-45	0	0	1	0.3	0	0	1	0.3	
N=	47	100	305	100	2	100	354	100	
Indeterminate	7	14.9	0	0	0	0	7	2	Blade Transverse Section
Plano-convex	12	25.5	118	38.7	1	50	131	37	
Plano-Triangular	0	0	1	0.3	0	0	1	0.3	
Bi-plano	1	2.1	25	8.2	1	50	27	7.6	
Bi-convex	21	44.7	143	46.9	0	0	164	46.3	
Bi-Triangular	0	0	1	0.3	0	0	1	0.3	
Asymmetrically Bi-convex	6	12.8	12	3.9	0	0	18	5.1	
Asymmetrically Triangular	0	0	5	1.6	0	0	5	1.4	
N=	47	100	305	100	2	100	354	100	

TABLE A.6b (Continued)

	Sinking Ponds #	Sinking Ponds %	Riverhaven II #	Riverhaven II %	Buffalo G #	Buffalo G %	Totals #	Totals %	
Unifacial	47	100	283	92.8	2	100	332	93.8	Blade Primary Flk.
Bi-facial expanding	0	0	12	3.9	0	0	12	3.4	
External Face expanding	0	0	5	1.6	0	0	5	1.4	
Internal Face expanding	0	0	3	1.0	0	0	3	0.8	
Internal Face Conchoidal	0	0	1	0.3	0	0	1	0.3	
External Face Lamellar	0	0	1	0.3	0	0	1	0.3	
N=	47	100	305	100	2	100	354	100	
Bi-facial - Bi-lateral	47	100	283	92.8	2	100	332	93.8	Blade Sec. Flk. Placement
Unifacial - Bi-lateral	0	0	9	3	0	0	9	2.5	
Unifacial - Unilateral	0	0	1	0.3	0	0	1	0.3	
Bi-lateral	0	0	10	3.3	0	0	10	2.8	
Unilateral	0	0	2	0.7	0	0	2	0.6	
N=	47	100	305	100	2	100	354	100	
Continuous	47	100	285	93.1	1	50	332	93.8	Blade Sec. Flk. Pattern
Discontinuous	0	0	1	6.9	1	50	22	6.2	
N=	47	100	305	100	2	100	354	100	
Even	44	93.6	285	93.4	1	50	330	93.2	Blade Lateral Edge
Bevel-Even	0	0	1	0.3	0	0	1	0.3	
Irregular	0	0	1	6.2	1	50	20	5.6	
Reworked	3	6.4	0	0	0	0	3	0.8	
N=	47	100	305	100	2	100	354	100	
4-6	36	76.6	240	78.7	2	100	278	78.5	Max. Thick-ness
7-9	11	23.4	62	20.3	0	0	73	20.6	
10-12	0	0	3	1.0	0	0	3	0.8	
N=	47	100	305	100	2	100	354	100	

TABLE A.7a
TERTIARY BLADE ATTRIBUTES

Variation	Constant (+95%)
Material	Blade Secondary Flake Type (Expanding)
% Matrix Inclusion	
Blade Outline	
Blade Length (mm)	
Blade Width (mm)	
Blade Width Tip—2cm (mm)	
Blade Transverse Section	
Blade Longitudinal Section	
Blade Primary Flake Type	
Blade Secondary Flake Placement	
Blade Secondary Flake Pattern	
Blade Tertiary Flake Type	
Blade Lateral Edge	
Base Outline	
Base Width (mm)	
Base Height (mm)	
Base Preparation	
Maximum Thickness	
Overall Length (mm)	

TABLE A.7*b*
TERTIARY BLADE WIDTH — TABLE OF ATTRIBUTES

	Sinking Ponds #	Sinking Ponds %	Riverhaven II #	Riverhaven II %	Buffalo G #	Buffalo G %	Totals #	Totals %	
Onondaga Chert	6	100	54	88.5	0	0	60	88.2	Material
Onondaga Chert-fired	0	0	7	11.5	0	0	7	10.3	
Onondaga-Pigmentation Added	0	0	0	0	1	100	1	1.5	
N=	6	100	61	100	1	100	68	100	
0-20	1	16.7	28	45.9	0	0	29	42.6	% Matrix Inclusion
20-40	2	33.3	15	24.6	1	100	18	26.5	
40-60	0	0	12	19.7	0	0	12	17.6	
60-80	1	16.7	5	8.2	0	0	6	8.8	
80-100	2	33.3	1	1.6	0	0	3	4.4	
N=	6	100	61	100	1	100	68	100	
Triangular	2	33.3	6	9.8	0	0	8	11.8	Blade Outline
Excurvate	1	16.7	35	57.4	1	100	37	54.4	
Ovate	2	33.3	15	24.6	0	0	17	25	
Excurvate-incurvate Opposing Lateral	0	0	2	3.3	0	0	2	2.9	
Parallel Ovate	0	0	2	3.3	0	0	2	2.9	
Excurvate-ovate	1	16.7	1	1.6	0	0	2	2.9	
N=	6	100	61	100	1	100	68	100	
21-30	0	0	4	6.6	0	0	4	5.9	Blade Length
31-40	0	0	24	39.3	0	0	24	35.3	
41-50	0	0	15	24.6	0	0	15	22.1	
51-60	1	16.7	13	21.3	0	0	14	20.6	
61-70	3	50	2	3.3	1	100	6	8.8	
71-80	2	33.3	1	1.6	0	0	3	4.4	
81-90	0	0	2	3.3	0	0	2	2.9	
N=	6	100	61	100	1	100	68	100	
15-20	0	0	2	3.3	0	0	2	2.9	Blade Width
21-25	0	0	18	29.5	0	0	18	26.5	
26-30	2	33.3	15	24.6	0	0	17	25	
31-35	1	16.7	16	26.2	0	0	17	25	
36-40	2	33.3	7	11.5	0	0	9	13.2	
41-45	1	16.7	1	1.6	1	100	3	4.4	
46-50	0	0	2	3.3	0	0	2	2.9	
N=	6	100	61	100	1	100	68	100	
16-20	2	33.3	27	44.3	0	0	29	42.6	Blade Width Tip - 2 cm.
21-25	3	50	22	36.1	0	0	25	36.8	
26-30	1	16.7	11	18	0	0	12	17.6	
36-40	0	0	1	1.6	1	100	2	2.9	
N=	6	100	61	100	1	100	68	100	
Plano Convex	2	33.3	7	11.5	1	100	10	14.7	Blade Trans. Sect.
Plano-Triangular	1	16.7	0	0	0	0	1	1.5	
Bi-convex	1	16.7	35	57.4	0	0	36	52.9	
Asymmetrically Bi-convex	2	33.3	17	27.9	0	0	19	27.9	
Convexo-Triangular	0	0	2	2.3	0	0	2	2.9	
N=	6	100	61	100	1	100	68	100	

TABLE A.6*b* (Continued)

	Sinking Ponds #	Sinking Ponds %	Riverhaven II #	Riverhaven II %	Buffalo G #	Buffalo G %	Totals #	Totals %	
Plano-Convex	4	66.7	6	9.8	1	100	11	16.2	Blade Long. Sect.
Bi-plano	0	0	1	1.6	0	0	1	1.5	
Bi-convex	1	16.7	35	57.4	0	0	36	52.9	
Asymmetrically Bi-convex	0	0	12	19.7	0	0	12	17.6	
Concavo-convex	0	0	7	11.5	0	0	7	10.3	
Asymmetrically Concavo-convex	1	16.7	0	0	0	0	1	1.5	
N=	6	100	61	100	1	100	68	100	
Unifacial	2	33.3	0	0	1	100	2	2.9	Blade Pri. FlK - Type
Bi-facial expanding	4	66.7	46	75.4	0	0	51	75	
External face expanding	0	0	14	23	0	0	14	20.6	
Internal face expanding	0	0	1	1.6	0	0	1	1.5	
N=	6	100	61	100	1	100	68	100	
Bifacial-Bilateral	1	16.7	0	0	1	100	1	1.5	Blade Sec. FLK Placement
Unifacial-Bilateral	2	33.3	15	24.6	0	0	17	25	
Bilateral	1	16.7	46	75.4	0	0	48	70.6	
Unilateral	2	33.3	0	0	0	0	2	2.9	
N=	6	100	61	100	1	100	68	100	
Continuous	0	0	17	27.9	0	0	17	25	Blade Sec. FLK Pattern
Discontinuous	2	33.3	44	72.1	1	100	47	69.1	
Fortuituous cluster	4	66.7	0	0	0	0	4	5.9	
N=	6	100	61	100	1	100	68	100	
Indeterminate	2	33.3	60	98.4	1	100	63	92.6	Blade Tertiary FLK Type
Nibble-crush	4	66.7	0	0	0	0	4	5.9	
N=	6	100	61	100	1	100	68	100	
Even	0	0	17	27.9	0	0	17	25	Blade Lateral Edge
Irregular	6	100	44	72.1	1	100	51	75	
N=	6	100	61	100	1	100	68	100	
Straight	2	33.3	4	6.6	0	0	6	8.8	Base Outline
Subconvex	2	33.3	31	50.8	0	0	33	48.5	
Convex	2	33.3	26	42.6	1	100	29	42.6	
N=	6	100	61	100	1	100	68	100	
15-20	0	0	4	6.6	0	0	4	5.9	Base Width
21-25	1	16.7	17	27.9	0	0	18	26.5	
25-30	2	33.3	22	36.1	0	0	24	35.3	
31-35	0	0	12	19.7	0	0	12	17.6	
36-40	2	33.3	5	8.2	0	0	7	10.3	
41-45	1	16.7	1	1.6	1	100	3	4.4	
N=	6	100	61	100	1	100	68	100	
Blank	2	33.3	0	0	0	0	2	2.9	Base Height
0-3	2	33.3	22	36.1	1	100	25	36.8	
3-6	2	33.3	23	37.7	0	0	25	36.8	
7-9	0	0	16	21.3	0	0	16	23.5	
N=	6	100	61	100	1	100	68	100	

TABLE A.6*b* (Continued)

	Sinking Ponds #	Sinking Ponds %	Riverhaven II #	Riverhaven II %	Buffalo G #	Buffalo G %	Totals #	Totals %	
Striking Platform	2	33.3	5	8.2	1	100	8	11.8	Base Prepara-tion
Primary Thinning	0	0	2	3.3	0	0	2	2.9	
Secondary Thinning	4	66.7	54	88.5	0	0	58	85.3	
N=	6	100	61	100	1	100	68	100	
7-9	1	16.7	18	29.5	0	0	19	27.9	Maximum Thickness
10-12	2	33.3	27	44.3	1	100	30	44.1	
13-15	2	33.3	8	13.1	0	0	10	14.7	
16-18	0	0	6	9.8	0	0	6	8.8	
19-21	1	16.7	2	33.3	0	0	3	4.4	
N=	6	100	61	100	1	100	68	100	
31-40	0	0	7	11.5	0	0	7	10.3	Overall Length
41-50	0	0	32	52.5	0	0	32	47.1	
51-60	1	16.7	12	19.7	0	0	13	19.1	
61-70	1	16.7	6	9.8	0	0	7	10.3	
71-80	3	50	1	1.6	1	100	5	7.4	
81-90	1	16.7	2	3.3	0	0	3	4.4	
91-100	0	0	1	1.6	0	0	1	1.5	
N=	6	100	61	100	1	100	68	100	

TABLE A.8*a*
TERTIARY BLADE BASE ATTRIBUTES

Variation	Constant (+95%)
Material	Blade Secondary Flake Type (expanding)
% Matrix Inclusion	
Blade Width (mm)	
Blade Transverse Section	
Blade Primary Flake Type	
Blade Secondary Flake Placement	
Blade Secondary Flake Pattern	
Blade Tertiary Flake Type	
Blade Lateral Edge	
Base Outline	
Base Width (mm)	
Base Height (mm)	
Base Preparation	
Maximum Thickness (mm)	

TABLE A.8*b*
TERTIARY BLADE BASE FRAGMENTS

	Sinking Ponds		Riverhaven II		Buffalo G		Totals		
	#	%	#	%	#	%	#	%	
Onondaga Chert, natural varieties	17	85.0	106	86.9	3	100	126	86.8	Material
Onondage Chert, Fired	2	10.0	16	13.1	0	0	18	12.4	
Deepskill Flint	1	5.0	0	0	0	0	1	0.7	
N=	20	100	122	100	3	100	145	100	
Indeterminate	0	0	1	0.8	0	0	1	0.7	% Matrix
0-20	5	25	45	36.9	1	33.3	51	35.2	
20-40	3	15	36	29.5	2	66.7	41	28.3	
40-60	8	40	27	22.1	0	0	35	24.1	
60-80	1	5	10	8.2	0	0	11	7.6	
80-100	3	15	3	2.5	0	0	6	4.1	
N=	20	100	122	100	3	100	145	100	
Blank or Zero	20	100	1	0.8	0	0	21	14.5	Blade Width
15-20	0	0	7	5.7	0	0	7	4.8	
21-25	0	0	11	9	0	0	11	7.6	
26-30	0	0	28	23.0	0	0	28	19.3	
31-35	0	0	35	28.7	0	0	35	24.1	
36-40	0	0	22	18	1	33.3	23	5.9	
41-45	0	0	15	12.3	1	33.3	16	11	
46-50	0	0	1	0.8	1	33.3	2	1.4	
51-60	0	0	2	1.6	0	0	2	1.4	
N=	20	100	122	100	3	100	145	100	
Plano-convex	9	45	14	11.5	1	33.3	24	16.6	Blade Trans. Sect.
Bi-convex	9	45	81	66.4	2	66.7	92	63.4	
Asymmetrically Bi-convex	2	10	27	22.1	0	0	29	20	
N=	20	100	122	100	3	100	145	100	
Bi-facial expanding	20	100	73	59.8	3	100	96	66.2	Blade Sec. Platform
External face expanding	0	0	37	20.3	0	0	37	25.5	
Internal face expanding	0	0	12	9.8	0	0	12	8.3	
N=	20	100	122	100	3	100	145	100	
Indeterminate	2	10	0	0	0	0	2	1.4	Blade Sec. Flk. Placement
Bifacial-Bilateral	18	90	0	0	0	0	18	12.4	
Unifacial-Bilateral	0	0	49	40.2	0	0	49	33.8	
Unifacial-Unilateral	0	0	1	0.8	0	0	1	0.7	
Bilateral	0	0	72	59	3	100	75	51.7	
N=	20	100	122	100	3	100	145	100	
Indeterminate	2	10	0	0	0	0	2	1.4	Blade Plcm. Flake
Continuous	18	90	62	50.8	0	0	80	55.2	
Discontinuous	0	0	60	49.2	3	100	63	43.4	
N=	20	100	122	100	3	100	145	100	

TABLE A.8*b* (Continued)

	Sinking Ponds		Riverhaven 2		Buffalo G		Totals		
	#	%	#	%	#	%	#	%	
Indeterminate	11	55	121	99.2	3	100	135	93.1	Bld. Ter. Type
Nibbled	9	45	1	0.8	0	0	10	6.9	
N=	20	100	122	100	3	100	145	100	
Indeterminate	1	5	0	0	0	0	1	0.7	Blade Lateral Edge
Even	12	60	62	50.8	0	0	75	51	
Irregular	0	0	0	0	3	100	63	43.4	
Reworked	7	35	60	49.2	0	0	7	4.8	
N=	20	100	122	100	3	100	145	100	
Indeterminate	15	75	2	1.6	0	0	17	11.7	Base Outline
Straight	1	5	16	13.1	0	0	17	11.7	
Subconvex	3	15	59	48.4	1	33.3	63	43.4	
Convex	1	5	44	36.1	2	66.7	47	32.4	
Subconcave	0	0	1	0.8	0	0	1	0.7	
N=	20	100	122	100	3	100	145	100	
Blank or Zero	0	0	1	0.8	0	0	1	0.7	Base Width
21-25	0	0	1	0.8	0	0	1	0.7	
26-30	0	0	6	4.9	0	0	6	4.1	
31-35	2	10	28	23	0	0	30	20.7	
36-40	9	45	48	32.8	0	0	49	33.8	
41-45	1	5	29	23.8	0	0	30	20.7	
46-50	6	30	12	9.8	1	33.3	19	13.1	
51-60	1	5	4	3.3	1	33.3	6	4.1	
61 plus	1	5	1	0.8	1	33.3	3	8.1	
N=	20	100	122	100	3	100	145	100	
Blank Only	20	100	0	0	0	0	20	13.8	Base Height
0-5	0	0	72	59	3	100	75	51.7	
3-6	0	0	38	31.1	0	0	38	26.2	
7-9	0	0	12	9.8	0	0	12	8.3	
N=	20	100	122	100	3	100	145	100	
Indeterminate	0	0	2	1.6	0	0	2	1.4	Base Preparation
Unprepared	0	0	1	0.8	0	0	1	0.7	
Striking Platform Only	3	15	15	12.3	1	33.3	19	13.1	
Primary Thinning	8	40	1	0.8	0	0	9	6.2	
Secondary Thinning	9	45	103	84.4	2	66.7	114	78.6	
N=	20	100	122	100	3	100	145	100	
4-6	0	0	4	3.3	0	0	4	2.8	Max. Thickness
7-9	11	55	69	56.6	1	33.3	81	55.9	
10-12	8	40	38	31.1	2	66.7	48	33.1	
13-15	1	5	9	7.4	0	0	10	6.9	
16-18	0	0	2	1.6	0	0	2	1.4	
N=	20	100	122	100	3	100	145	100	

TABLE A.9*a*
TERTIARY BLADE TIP ATTRIBUTES

Variation	Constant (+95%)
Material % Matrix Inclusion Blade Width Tip—2cm (mm) Blade Transverse Section Blade Primary Flake Type Blade Secondary Flake Placement Blade Secondary Flake Pattern Blade Tertiary Flake Type Blade Lateral Edge Maximum Thickness (mm)	Blade Secondary Flake Type (expanding)

TABLE A.9*b*
TERTIARY BLADE (TIPS) — TABLE OF ATTRIBUTES

	Sinking Ponds		Riverhaven II		Buffalo G		Totals		
	#	%	#	%	#	%	#	%	Attribute
Onondaga Chert	34	97.1	147	86.5	4	100	185	88.5	Mater-ial
Onondaga Chert, Fired	1	2.9	23	13.5	0	0	24	11.5	
N=	35	100	170	100	4	100	209	100	
Indeterminate	0	0	28	16.5	3	75.0	28	13.4	% Matrix Inc.
0-20	7	20.0	62	36.5	0	0	72	34.4	
20-40	8	22.9	37	21.8	0	0	45	21.5	
40-60	12	34.3	30	17.6	0	0	42	20.1	
60-80	7	20.0	12	7.1	1	25.0	20	9.6	
80-100	1	2.9	1	.6	0	0	2	1.0	
N=	35	100	170	100	4	100	209	100	
Blank or Zero	2	5.7	0	0	0	0	2	1.0	Blade Width (mm)
21-25	0	0	8	4.7	1	25.0	9	4.3	
26-30	5	14.3	59	34.7	0	0	64	30.6	
31-35	14	40.0	84	49.4	1	25.0	99	47.4	
36-40	11	31.4	17	10.0	1	25.0	29	13.9	
41-45	3	8.6	1	.6	1	25.0	5	2.4	
46-50	0	0	1	.6	0	0	1	.5	
N=	35	100	170	100	4	100	209	100	
Indeterminate	1	2.9	0	0	0	0	1	.5	Blade Trans-verse Section
Plano-convex	12	34.3	21	12.4	3	75.0	36	17.2	
Bi-plano	2	5.7	0	0	0	0	2	1.0	
Bi-convex	10	28.6	116	68.2	1	25.0	127	60.8	
Asymmetrically Bi-convex	10	28.6	32	18.8	0	0	42	20.1	
Asymmetrically Triangular	0	0	1	.6	0	0	1	.5	
N=	35	100	170	100	4	100	209	100	

TABLE A.9*b* (Continued)

	Sinking Ponds #	%	Riverhaven II #	%	Buffalo G #	%	Totals #	%	
Bifacial Expanding	34	97.1	139	81.8	4	100	177	84.7	Blade Pri. Flake
External Face-Expanding	0	0	16	9.4	0	0	16	7.7	
Internal Face-Expanding	0	0	15	8.8	0	0	15	7.2	
Bifacial-Conchoidal	1	2.9	0	0	0	0	1	.5	
N=	35	100	170	100	4	100	209	100	
Indeterminate	0	0	2	1.2	0	0	2	1.0	Blade Sec. Flake Placement
Bifacial-Bilateral	23	65.7	1	.6	0	0	24	11.5	
Unifacial-Bilateral	5	14.3	31	18.2	0	0	36	17.2	
Unifacial-Unilateral	1	2.9	3	1.8	0	0	4	1.9	
Bilateral	5	14.3	122	71.8	4	100	131	62.7	
Unilateral	1	2.9	11	6.5	0	0	12	5.7	
N=	35	100	170	100	4	100	209	100	
Indeterminate	0	0	3	1.8	0	0	3	1.4	Blade Sec. Fl. Pat.
Continuous	25	71.4	73	42.9	0	0	98	46.9	
Discontinuous	10	28.6	94	55.3	4	100	108	51.7	
N=	35	100	170	100	4	100	209	100	
Indeterminate	19	54.3	170	100	4	100	193	92.3	Blade Tert. Flk.
Nibbled	16	45.7	0	0	0	0	16	7.7	
	35	100	170	100	4	100	209	100	
Indeterminate	0	0	3	1.8	0	0	3	1.4	Blade Lat. Edge
Even	24	68.6	82	48.2	0	0	106	50.7	
Irregular	11	31.4	85	50.0	4	100	100	47.8	
N=	35	100	170	100	4	100	209	100	
4-6	1	2.9	14	8.2	0	0	15	7.2	Maximum Thickness (mm)
7-9	18	51.4	105	61.8	1	25.0	124	59.3	
10-12	11	31.4	40	23.5	3	75.0	54	25.8	
13-15	5	14.3	7	4.1	0	0	12	5.7	
16-18	0	0	4	2.4	0	0	4	1.9	
N=	35	100	170	100	4	100	209	100	

TABLE A.10*a*
LONGITUDINAL KNIFE ATTRIBUTES

Variation		Constant (+95%)
Material	(None)	(None)
% Matrix Inclusion		
Blade Outline		
Blade Length (mm)		
Blade Width (mm)		
Blade Width Tip—2cm (mm)		
Blade Transverse Section		
Blade Longitudinal Section		
Blade Primary Flake Type		
Blade Secondary Flake Type		

TABLE A.10*a* (Continued)

Variation	Constant (+95%)
Blade Secondary Flake Placement	
Blade Secondary Flake Pattern	
Blade Tertiary Flake Type	
Blade Lateral Edge	
Base Outline (mm)	
Base Width (mm)	
Base Height (mm)	
Base Preparation	
Maximum Thickness	
Overall Length (mm)	

TABLE A.10*b*
LONGITUDINAL KNIVES — TABLE OF ATTRIBUTES

	Sinking Ponds		Riverhaven II		Buffalo G		Totals		
	#	%	#	%	#	%	#	%	
Onondaga Chert	9	100	25	83.3	2	100	36	87.8	Mater-ial
Onondaga Chert, Fired	0	0	5	16.7	0	0	5	12.2	
N=	9	100	30	100	2	100	41	100	
Indeterminate	2	22.2	0	0	0	0	2	4.9	% Matrix Inclusion
0-20	3	33.3	8	26.7	1	50	12	29.3	
20-40	1	11.1	13	43.3	0	0	14	34.1	
40-60	3	33.3	8	26.7	1	50	12	29.3	
60-80	0	0	1	3.3	0	0	1	2.4	
N=	9	100	30	100	2	100	41	100	
Excurvate	1	11.1	1	3.3	0	0	2	4.9	Blade Outline
Ovate	0	0	6	20	0	0	6	14.6	
Excurvate-Incurvate									
Opposing Parallel	4	44.4	4	13.3	2	100	10	24.4	
Excurvate-Ovate	4	44.4	19	63.3	0	0	23	56.1	
N=	9	100	30	100	2	100	41	100	
Blank	0	0	1	3.3	0	0	1	2.4	Blade Length
21-30	0	0	1	3.3	0	0	1	2.4	
31-40	0	0	19	63.3	0	0	19	46.3	
41-50	1	11.1	6	20	1	50	8	19.5	
51-60	8	88.9	3	10	1	50	12	29.3	
N=	9	100	30	100	2	100	41	100	
Blank	0	0	1	3.3	0	0	1	2.4	Blade Width
15-20	0	0	4	13.3	2	100	6	14.6	
21-25	2	22.2	12	40	0	0	14	34.1	
26-30	6	66.7	12	40	0	0	18	43.9	
31-35	0	0	1	3.3	0	0	1	2.4	
36-40	1	11.1	0	0	0	0	1	2.4	
N=	9	100	30	100	2	100	41	100	

TABLE A.10*b* (Continued)

	Sinking Ponds #	Sinking Ponds %	Riverhaven II #	Riverhaven II %	Buffalo G #	Buffalo G %	Totals #	Totals %	
11-15	0	0	5	16.7	2	100	7	17.1	Blade Width 2Cm- Tip
16-20	5	55.6	19	63.3	0	0	27	58.5	
21-25	3	33.3	6	20	0	0	9	22	
31-35	1	11.1	0	0	0	0	1	2.4	
N=	9	100	30	100	2	100	41	100	
Plano-convex	4	44.4	7	23.3	0	0	11	26.8	Blade Trans. Section
Bi-plano	1	11.1	1	3.3	0	0	2	4.9	
Bi-convex	2	22.2	15	50	0	0	17	41.5	
Asymmetrically Bi-convex	2	22.2	5	16.7	2	100	9	22	
Asymmetrically Triangular	0	0	2	6.7	0	0	2	4.9	
N=	9	100	30	100	2	100	41	100	
Plano-convex	2	22.2	4	13.3	0	0	6	14.6	Blade Long. Section
Bi-plano	1	11.1	1	3.3	0	0	2	4.9	
Bi-convex	2	22.2	15	50	0	0	17	41.5	
Asymmetrically Bi-convex	0	0	5	16.7	0	0	5	12.2	
Concavo-convex	0	0	5	16.7	2	100	7	17.1	
Asymmetrically concavo-convex	4	44.4	0	0	0	0	4	9.8	
N=	9	100	30	100	2	100	41	100	
Unifacial	3	33.3	6	20	2	100	11	26.8	Blade Primary Flk. Type
Bi-facial expanding	3	33.3	9	30	0	0	12	29.3	
External Face expanding	2	22.2	13	43.3	0	0	15	36.6	
Internal Face expanding	0	0	1	3.3	0	0	1	2.4	
External Face lamellar	1	11.1	1	3.3	0	0	2	4.9	
N=	9	100	30	100	2	100	41	100	
Stepped Lamellar	5	55.6	0	0	0	0	5	12.2	Bld. Sec. Flk. Plcm.
Expanding	4	44.4	30	100	2	100	36	87.8	
N=	9	100	30	100	2	100	41	100	

TABLE A.10*b* (Continued)

	Sinking Ponds		Riverhaven II		Buffalo G		Totals		
	#	%	#	%	#	%	#	%	
Bi-facial - Bi-lateral	3	33.3	5	16.7	2	100	10	24.4	Blade Secondary Flk. Placement
Bi-facial - Unilateral	2	22.2	1	3.3	0	0	3	7.3	
Unifacial - Bi-lateral	0	0	12	40	0	0	12	29.3	
Unifacial - Unilateral	1	11.1	3	10	0	0	4	9.8	
Alternating Bi-lateral	0	0	1	3.3	0	0	1	2.4	
Bi-lateral	3	33.3	4	13.3	0	0	7	17.1	
Unilateral	0	0	4	13.3	0	0	4	9.8	
N=	9	100	30	100	2	100	41	100	
Continuous	1	11.1	9	30	2	100	12	29.3	Blade Sec. Flk. Pattern
Discontinuous	1	11.1	0	0	0	0	1	2.4	
Patterned clusters	7	77.8	16	53.3	0	0	23	56.1	
Fortuituous	0	0	5	16.7	0	0	5	12.2	
N=	9	100	30	100	2	100	41	100	
Indeterminate	0	0	1	3.3	0	0	1	2.4	Blade Tertiary Flk. Type
Crushed	3	33.3	11	36.7	0	0	14	34.1	
Nibbled	0	0	2	6.7	2	100	4	9.8	
Grinding	0	0	2	6.7	0	0	2	4.9	
Grind-crush	0	0	1	3.3	0	0	1	2.4	
Nibble-crush	6	66.7	12	40	0	0	18	43.9	
Nibble-grind-crush	0	0	1	3.3	0	0	1	2.4	
N=	9	100	30	100	2	100	41	100	
Even	0	0	0	0	2	100	2	4.9	Blade Lateral Edge
Irregular	1	11.1	0	0	0	0	1	2.4	
Reworked	8	88.9	30	100	0	0	38	92.7	
N=	9	100	30	100	2	100	41	100	
Indeterminate	1	11.1	1	3.3	0	0	2	4.9	Base Outline
Straight	2	22.2	1	3.3	0	0	3	7.3	
Subconvex	2	22.2	9	30	1	50	12	29.3	
Convex	4	44.4	19	63.3	1	50	24	58.5	
N=	9	100	30	100	2	100	41	100	
Blank	0	0	2	6.7	0	0	2	4.9	Base Width
15-20	3	33.3	6	20	2	100	11	26.8	
21-25	2	22.2	14	46.7	0	0	16	39	
25-30	3	33.3	7	23.3	0	0	10	24.4	
31-35	1	11.1	1	3.3	0	0	2	4.9	
N=	9	100	30	100	2	100	41	100	
Blank	1	11.1	0	0	0	0	1	2.4	Base Height
0-3	4	44.4	12	40	0	0	16	39	
3-6	3	33.3	4	13.3	1	50	8	19.5	
7-9	1	11.1	14	46.7	1	50	16	39	
N=	9	100	30	100	2	100	41	100	
Indeterminate	0	0	1	3.3	0	0	1	2.4	Base Preparation
Striking Platform Only	2	22.2	2	6.7	0	0	4	9.8	
Primary Thinning	0	0	4	13.3	0	0	4	9.8	
Secondary Thinning	7	77.8	20	66.7	1	50	28	68.3	
Tertiary Thinning	0	0	2	6.7	1	50	3	7.3	
Grinding-Secondary	0	0	1	3.3	0	0	1	2.4	
N=	9	100	30	100	2	100	41	100	

TABLE A.10*b* (Continued)

	Sinking Ponds #	Sinking Ponds %	Riverhaven II #	Riverhaven II %	Buffalo G #	Buffalo G %	Totals #	Totals %	
4-6	1	11.1	3	10	0	0	4	9.8	Maximum Thickness
7-9	2	22.2	14	46.7	2	100	18	43.9	
10-12	4	44.4	8	26.7	0	0	12	29.3	
13-15	2	22.2	4	13.3	0	0	6	14.6	
16-18	0	0	1	3.3	0	0	1	2.4	
N=	9	100	30	100	2	100	41	100	
Blank	0	0	1	3.3	0	0	1	2.4	Overall Length
31-40	0	0	7	23.3	0	0	7	17.1	
41-50	0	0	17	56.7	0	0	17	41.5	
51-60	0	0	3	10	2	100	11	26.8	
61-70	3	33.3	2	6.7	0	0	5	12.2	
N=	9	100	30	100	2	100	41	100	

TABLE A.11*a*
UNIFACIAL SCRAPER ATTRIBUTES

Variation	Constant (+95%)
Material	Flint Tool Type (scraper)
Scraper Utilization Edge Length (mm)	
Scraper Flaking & Shape Type	
Scraper Utilization Edge Retouch Type	
Scraper Basal Form Type	
Scraper Working Edge Location	
Scraper Index of Utilization	
Maximum Thickness (mm)	
Maximum Length (mm)	
Maximum Width (mm)	
Fragmentation	

TABLE A.11*b*
UNIFACIAL SCRAPERS — TABLE OF VARIABLE ATTRIBUTE FREQUENCY

	Sinking Ponds #	Sinking Ponds %	Riverhaven 2 #	Riverhaven 2 %	Totals #	Totals %	
Onondaga Chert	22	84	89	97	110	94	Mater- ial
Onondaga Chert, Fired	4	16	3	3	7	6	
	26	100	92	100	117	100	
1-20	3	12	14	15	17	14	Scraper Util. Edge Length
21-40	13	50	23	25	36	31	
41-60	3	12	19	21	22	19	
61-80	6	23	22	24	28	24	
81-100	0	0	10	11	10	8	
101-120	1	4	1	1	2	2	
121-140	0	0	3	3	3	3	
	26	100	92	100	118	100	

TABLE A.11*b* (Continued)

	Sinking Ponds		Riverhaven 2		Totals		
	#	%	#	%	#	%	
Unifacial, Trianguloid	5	19	27	29	32	27	Scraper Flaking & Shape Type
Unifacial, Discoid	3	12	10	11	13	11	
Unifacial, Rectanguloid	0	0	8	9	8	7	
Unifacial, Ovoid	1	4	21	23	22	19	
Unifacial, Asymmetrical	17	65	26	28	43	36	
N=	26	100	92	100	118	100	
Cont. Dorsal Flat (45)	1	4	24	26	25	21	Scraper Util. Edge Retouch Type
Cont. Dorsal Steep (45)	14	54	54	59	68	58	
Discon. Dor. Flat	1	4	3	3	4	3	
Discon. Dor. Steep	0	0	8	9	8	7	
Cont. Ventral Flat	2	8	3	3	5	4	
Discon. Ventral Flat	8	31	0	0	8	7	
N=	26	100	92	100	118	100	
Not applicable	21	81	73	79	94	80	Scraper Basal Form
Contracting-Convex	2	8	8	9	10	8	
Contracting-Straight	2	8	6	7	8	7	
Missing	1	4	5	5	6	5	
N=	26	100	92	100	118	100	
Apex	7	27.0	0	0	7	6.0	Scraper Working Edge Location
Apex-Lateral	1	4.0	7	7.6	8	7.0	
Transverse	0	0	19	20.7	19	16.5	
Transverse-Lateral	3	12.0	6	6.5	9	8.0	
Oblique Transverse	0	0	6	6.5	6	5.0	
Bi-oblique Trans.	0	0	7	7.6	7	6.0	
Unilateral	6	23.0	15	16.3	21	17.0	
Bilateral	3	12.0	10	10.9	13	11.0	
Circumferential	3	12.0	18	19.5	21	17.0	
Lateral-Concave	3	12.0	4	4.4	7	6.0	
N=	26	100	92	100	118	100	
0-15	1	4.0	2	2.0	3	3.0	Index of Utilization
16-25	3	12.0	14	15.0	17	14.0	
26-35	9	35.0	19	21.0	28	24.0	
36-50	8	31.0	25	27.0	33	28.0	
51-70	2	8.0	18	20.0	20	17.0	
71-100	3	12.0	14	15.0	17	14.0	
N=	26	100	92	100	118	100	
0-10	20	77.0	69	75.0	89	75.0	Max. Thick.
11-20	5	19.0	23	25.0	28	24.0	
21-30	1	4.0	0	0	1	1.0	
N=	26	100	92	100	118	100	
Blank or Zero	6	23.0	7	8.0	13	11.0	Max. Length
1-25	0	0	2	2.0	2	2.0	
26-50	14	54.0	62	67.0	76	64.0	
51-75	6	23.0	21	23.0	27	23.0	
N=	26	100	92	100	118	100	

TABLE A.11*b* (Continued)

	Sinking Ponds #	Sinking Ponds %	Riverhaven 2 #	Riverhaven 2 %	Totals #	Totals %	
Blank or Zero	1	4.0	2	2.0	3	3.0	Maximum Width
1-20	3	12.0	10	11.0	13	11.0	
21-30	14	54.0	45	49.0	59	50.0	
31-40	4	15.0	27	29.0	31	26.0	
41-50	3	12.0	7	8.0	10	8.0	
51-60	1	4.0	1	1.0	2	2.0	
N=	26	100	92	100	118	100	
Fragmentary	3	12.0	14	15.0	17	14.0	Frag.
Non-Frag.	23	88.0	78	85.0	101	86.0	
N=	26	100	92	100	118	100	

TABLE A.12*a*
BIFACIAL SCRAPER ATTRIBUTES

Variation	Constant (+95%)
Material	Flint Tool Type (scraper)
Scraper Utilization Edge Length (mm)	
Scraper Flaking & Shape Type	
Scraper Utilization Edge Retouch Type	
Scraper Basal Form Type	
Scraper Working Edge Location	
Scraper Index of Utilization	
Maximum Thickness (mm)	
Maximum Length (mm)	
Maximum Width (mm)	
Fragmentation	

TABLE A.12*b*
BIFACIAL SCRAPERS — TABLE OF ATTRIBUTES

	Sinking Ponds #	Sinking Ponds %	Riverhaven II #	Riverhaven II %	Buffalo G #	Buffalo G %	Totals #	Totals %	
Onondaga Chert	14	93	99	95	0	0	113	94	Mater-ial
Onondaga Chert, Fired	1	7	5	5	1	100	7	6	
N=	15	100	104	100	1	100	120	100	
1-20	1	7	16	15	0	0	179	14	Scraper Utili-zation Edge Length
21-40	10	67	32	31	1	100	43	36	
41-60	3	20	17	16	0	0	20	17	
61-80	0	0	15	14	0	0	15	13	
81-100	1	7	12	12	0	0	13	11	
101-120	0	0	9	9	0	0	9	7	
121-140	0	0	2	2	0	0	2	2	
141-160	0	0	1	1	0	0	1	1	
N=	15	100	104	100	1	100	120	100	

TABLE A.12*b* (Continued)

	Sinking Ponds		River. II		Buffalo G		Totals		
	#	%	#	%	#	%	#	%	
Bifacial, Trianguloid	9	60	42	40	1	100	52	43	Scraper Flaking & Shape Type
Bifacial, Discoid	1	7	8	8	0	0	9	7	
Bifacial, Ovoid	0	0	16	15	0	0	16	13	
Bifacial, Rectanguloid	1	7	25	24	0	0	26	22	
Bifacial, Asymmetrical	4	27	13	13	0	0	17	14	
N=	15	100	104	100	1	100	120	100	
Continuous Dorsal Flat (-45°)	5	33	19	18	0	0	24	20	Scraper Utilization Edge Retouch Type
Continuous Dorsal Steep (+45°)	8	53	49	47	1	100	58	48	
Continuous Dorsal Tertiary Only	1	7	1	1	0	0	2	2	
Discontinuous Dorsal Flat	0	0	14	13	0	0	14	12	
Discontinuous Dorsal Steep	1	7	17	16	0	0	18	15	
Continuous Ventral Flat	0	0	2	2	0	0	2	2	
Discontinuous Ventral Flat	0	0	2	2	0	0	2	2	
N=	15	100	104	100	1	100	120	100	
Not applicable	4	27	67	64	0	0	71	59	Scraper Basal Form Type
Contracting-apex	4	27	23	22	1	100	28	23	
Contracting convex	1	7	5	5	0	0	6	5	
Contracting straight	1	7	5	5	0	0	6	5	
Parallel Convex	0	0	1	1	0	0	1	1	
Parallel Straight	0	0	2	2	0	0	2	2	
Haft Element Side Notch	1	7	0	0	0	0	1	1	
Haft Element Stem	1	7	0	0	0	0	1	1	
Missing	3	20	1	1	0	0	4	3	
N=	15	100	104	100	1	100	120	100	
Apex Lateral	0	0	3	3	0	0	3	2	Scraper Working Edge Location
Transverse	8	53	7	7	1	100	16	13	
Transverse-Lateral	4	27	29	28	0	0	33	27	
Oblique Transverse	1	7	6	6	0	0	7	6	
Bi-obliqye Transverse	0	0	6	6	0	0	6	5	
Unilateral	2	13	13	13	0	0	15	13	
Bilateral	0	0	17	16	0	0	17	14	
Circumferential	0	0	18	17	0	0	18	15	
Lateral, Concave	0	0	5	5	0	0	5	4	
N=	15	100	104	100	1	100	120	100	
0-15	0	0	5	5	0	0	5	4	Scraper Index of Utilization
16-25	3	20	21	20	1	100	25	21	
26-35	5	33	21	20	0	0	26	22	
36-50	6	40	20	19	0	0	26	22	
51-70	0	0	20	19	0	0	20	17	
71-100	1	7	17	16	0	0	18	15	
N=	15	100	104	100	1	100	120	100	

TABLE A.12*b* (Continued)

	Sinking Ponds #	Sinking Ponds %	River. II #	River. II %	Buffalo G #	Buffalo G %	Totals #	Totals %	
0-10	14	93	68	65	1	100	83	69	Max. Thick.
11-20	1	7	36	35	0	0	37	31	
N=	15	100	104	100	1	100	120	100	
Blank or Zero	4	27	6	6	0	0	10	8	Max. Length
1-25	0	0	1	1	0	0	1	1	
26-50	11	73	79	76	1	100	91	76	
51-75	0	0	18	17	0	0	18	15	
N=	15	100	104	100	1	100	120	100	
1-20	4	27	6	6	0	0	10	8	Max. Width
21-30	10	67	55	53	1	100	66	55	
31-40	1	7	29	28	0	0	30	25	
41-50	0	0	14	13	0	0	14	12	
N=	15	100	104	100	1	100	120	100	
Fragmentary	5	22	23	22	0	0	28	24	Frag.
Non-fragmentary	10	78	81	78	0	0	92	76	
N=	15	100	104	100	0	0	120	100	

TABLE A.13*a*
DRILL ATTRIBUTES

Variation	Constant (+95%)
Material Flint Tool Base Type Drill Basal Form Type Drill Shank Length (mm) Drill Shank Width (mm) Maximum Length (mm) Maximum Width (mm) Drill Base Height (mm)	Flint Tool Type (drill) Maximum Thickness (mm) (0-10 mm)

TABLE A.13*b*
DRILLS

	Sinking Ponds #	Sinking Ponds %	Riverhaven II #	Riverhaven II %	Totals #	Totals %	
Onon. Chert, Nat. varieties	9	69	44	90	53	85	Mat-erial
Onon. Chert, Fired	4	31	5	10	9	15	
N=	13	100	49	100	62	100	
Flake (Blank)	13	100	1	2	14	23	Fl. Tool Bs. Typ
Reworked bi-facial	0	0	48	98	48	77	
N=	13	100	49	100	62	100	

TABLE A.13*b* (Continued)

	Sinking Ponds #	Sinking Ponds %	Riverhaven II #	Riverhaven II %	Totals #	Totals %	
Indeterminate	6	46	7	14	13	21	Drill Basal Form Type
Tee-convex	0	0	4	8	4	6	
Tee-straight	1	8	0	0	1	2	
Expanded convex	3	23	18	37	21	34	
Expanded straight	3	23	13	27	16	26	
Haft element side-notch	0	0	7	14	7	11	
N=	13	100	49	100	62	100	
Blank or zero	6	46	11	22	17	27	Drill Shank Length (mm)
5-15	2	15	2	4	4	6	
16-25	2	15	17	35	19	31	
26-35	1	8	17	35	18	29	
36-45	2	15	2	4	4	6	
N=	13	100	49	100	62	100	
0-10	5	38	19	39	24	39	Drill Shank Width (mm)
11-15	7	54	24	49	31	50	
16-20	1	8	6	12	7	11	
N=	13	100	49	100	62	100	
Blank or zero	0	0	18	37	18	29	Maximum Length (mm)
1-25	3	23	0	0	3	5	
26-50	7	54	29	59	36	58	
51-75	3	23	1	2	4	6	
76-100	0	0	1	2	1	2	
N=	13	100	49	100	62	100	
Blank or zero	4	31	7	14	11	18	Drill Base Height (mm)
1-20	5	38	18	37	23	37	
21-30	4	31	22	45	26	42	
31-40	0	0	2	4	2	3	
N=	13	100	49	100	62	100	
Blank or zero	6	46	7	14	13	21	Max. Width (mm)
1-10	2	15	11	22	13	21	
11-15	2	15	17	35	19	31	
16-20	1	8	6	12	7	11	
21-25	0	0	3	6	3	5	
26-30	0	0	3	6	3	5	
31-35	1	8	2	4	3	5	
36-40	1	8	0	0	1	2	
N=	13	100	49	100	62	100	

TABLE A.14*a*
PRIMARY BLANK ATTRIBUTES

Variation	Constant (+95%)
Flint Tool Type	Material
Biface Blade Outline	Flint Tool Base Type
Biface Base Outline	Core & Core Tool Flake Type
Biface Transverse Section	
Biface Longitudinal Section	
Biface Flake Type	
Maximum Thickness (mm)	
Maximum Length (mm)	
Maximum Width (mm)	

TABLE A.14*b*
PRIMARY BLANKS

	Sinking Ponds		Riverhaven II		Totals		
	#	%	#	%	#	%	
Indeterminate	9	75	0	0	9	16	Flint Tool Typ.
Biface (Indeterminate)	3	25	46	100	49	84	
N=	12	100	46	100	58	100	
Trianguloid	9	75	4	9	13	22	Biface Blade Outline
Excurvate	0	0	4	9	4	7	
Asymmetrical Excurvate	0	0	6	13	6	10	
Excurvate-Incurvate Lateral	1	8	1	2	2	3	
Ovate	0	0	5	11	5	9	
Asymmetrical Ovate	0	0	13	28	13	22	
Rectanguloid	0	0	2	4	2	3	
Ovoid	2	17	11	24	13	22	
N=	12	100	46	100	58	100	
Indeterminate	6	50	2	4	8	14	Biface Base Outline
Convex	6	50	29	63	35	60	
Concave	0	0	2	4	2	3	
Straight	0	0	9	20	9	16	
Binectorial	0	0	4	9	4	7	
N=	12	100	46	100	58	100	
Plano-Convex	2	17	15	33	17	29	Biface Trans. Section
Plano-Triangular	3	25	2	4	5	9	
Biplano	1	8	4	9	5	9	
Biconvex	0	0	12	26	12	21	
Asymmetrically Biconvex	3	25	12	26	15	26	
Convexo-Triangular	1	8	1	2	2	3	
Plano-Trapezoidal	2	17	0	0	2	3	
N=	12	100	46	100	58	100	

TABLE A.14*b* (Continued)

	Sinking Ponds #	Sinking Ponds %	Riverhaven II #	Riverhaven II %	Totals #	Totals %	
Plano-Convex	8	67	14	30	22	38	Biface Long. Section
Biplano	0	0	4	9	4	7	
Biconvex	0	0	11	24	11	19	
Asymmetrically Biconvex	2	17	13	28	15	26	
Concavo-Convex	0	0	3	7	3	5	
Asymmetrically Excurvate	0	0	1	2	1	2	
Asymmetrically Concavo-Convex	2	17	0	0	2	3	
N=	12	100	46	100	58	100	
Primary only	12	100	40	87	52	90	Bifac. Flk. Sec.
Pri: Sec. Lateral	0	0	6	13	6	10	
N=	12	100	46	100	58	100	
0-10	1	8	0	0	1	2	Maximum Thickness (mm)
11-20	5	42	23	50	28	48	
21-30	6	50	21	46	27	47	
31-40	0	0	2	4	2	3	
N=	12	100	46	100	58	100	
Blank or zero	6	50	2	4	8	14	Maximum Length (mm)
26-50	0	0	1	2	1	2	
51-75	6	50	38	83	44	76	
76-100	0	0	5	11	5	9	
N=	12	100	46	100	58	100	
Blank or zero	1	8	2	4	3	5	Maximum Width (mm)
21-30	1	8	4	9	5	9	
31-40	3	25	18	39	21	36	
41-50	6	50	20	43	26	45	
51-60	1	8	2	4	3	5	
N=	12	100	46	100	58	100	

TABLE A.15*a*
SECONDARY BLANK ATTRIBUTES

Variation	Constant (+95%)
Material	Flint Tool Base Type
Flint Tool Type	Core & Core Tool Flake Type
Biface Blade Outline	
Biface Base Outline	
Biface Transverse Section	
Biface Longitudinal Section	
Biface Flake Type	
Maximum Thickness (mm)	
Maximum Length (mm)	
Maximum Width (mm)	

TABLE A.15*b*
SECONDARY BLANKS

	Sinking Ponds #	Sinking Ponds %	Riverhaven II #	Riverhaven II %	Buffalo G #	Buffalo G %	Totals #	Totals %	
Onondaga Chert	20	100	107	94	1	50	128	94	Material
Onondaga Chert, fired	0	0	7	6	1	50	8	6	
N=	20	100	114	100	2	100	136	100	
Indeterminate	14	70	0	0	0	0	14	10	Flint Tool Type
Biface-Indeterminate	6	30	114	100	2	100	122	90	
N=	20	100	114	100	2	100	136	100	
Trianguloid	15	75	18	16	0	0	33	24	Biface Blade Outline
Asymmet. Trianguloid	0	0	1	1	0	0	1	1	
Excurvate	1	5	65	57	0	0	66	49	
Asymmet. Excurvate	1	5	5	4	0	0	6	4	
Excurvate-Incur.-Lateral	1	5	3	3	0	0	4	3	
Ovate	1	5	10	9	2	100	13	10	
Asymmet. Ovate	0	0	1	1	0	0	1	1	
Rectanguloid	0	0	1	1	0	0	1	1	
Ovoid	1	5	10	9	0	0	11	8	
N=	20	100	114	100	2	100	136	100	
Indeterminate	8	40	15	13	2	100	25	18	Biface Base Outline
Convex	5	25	73	64	0	0	78	57	
Subconvex	5	25	20	18	0	0	25	18	
Concave	1	5	1	1	0	0	2	1	
Straight	1	5	1	1	0	0	2	1	
Binectorial	0	0	4	4	0	0	4	3	
N=	20	100	114	100	2	100	136	100	
Plano-Convex	13	65	10	9	0	0	25	17	Biface Trans. Section
Plano-Triangular	0	0	2	2	0	0	2	1	
Biplano	0	0	1	1	0	0	1	1	
Biconvex	3	15	52	46	0	0	55	40	
Bitriangular	0	0	1	1	0	0	1	1	
Asymmet. Biconvex	3	15	36	32	0	0	39	29	
Asymmet. Bitriangular	0	0	1	1	1	50	2	1	
Convexo-Triangular	1	5	5	4	0	0	6	4	
Plano-Trapezoidal	0	0	6	5	1	50	7	5	
N=	20	100	114	100	2	100	136	100	
Plano-Convex	15	75	5	4	1	50	21	15	Biface Long. Section
Bi-plano	0	0	3	3	0	0	3	2	
Bi-convex	3	15	53	46	0	0	56	41	
Asymmet. Bi-convex	0	0	42	37	1	50	43	32	
Concavo-convex	0	0	9	8	0	0	9	7	
Ovate or trianguloid	0	0	2	2	0	0	2	1	
Asymmet. Concavo-convex	2	10	0	0	0	0	2	1	
N=	20	100	114	100	2	100	136	100	

TABLE A.15*b* (Continued)

	Sinking Ponds #	Sinking Ponds %	Riverhaven II #	Riverhaven II %	Buffalo G #	Buffalo G %	Totals #	Totals %	
Indeterminate	8	40	0	0	0	0	8	6	Biface Flake Type
Primary only	8	40	97	85	2	100	107	79	
Pri. Sec. Lateral	4	20	17	15	0	0	21	15	
N=	20	100	114	100	2	100	136	100	
0-10	2	10	0	0	0	0	2	1	Max. Thick. (mm)
11-20	16	80	101	89	2	100	119	88	
21-30	2	10	13	11	0	0	15	11	
N=	20	100	114	100	2	100	136	100	
Blank or zero	14	70	34	30	2	100	50	37	Maximum Length (mm)
26-50	0	0	27	24	0	0	27	20	
51-75	6	30	51	45	0	0	57	42	
76-100	0	0	2	2	0	0	2	1	
N=	20	100	114	100	2	100	136	100	
Blank or zero	14	70	11	10	2	100	27	20	Maximum Width (mm)
21-30	0	0	11	10	0	0	11	8	
31-40	3	15	59	52	0	0	62	46	
41-50	3	15	29	25	0	0	32	24	
51-60	0	0	4	4	0	0	4	3	
N=	20	100	114	100	2	100	136	100	

TABLE A.16*a*
NETSINKER ATTRIBUTES

Variation	Constant (+95%)
Material Non-flint Tool Base Type Non-flint Tool weight (gm) Maximum Thickness (mm) Maximum Length (mm) Maximum Width (mm) Netsinkers Notch Width (mm)	Non-flint Tool Type (Netsinkers, notched)

TABLE A.16*b*
NETSINKERS — TABLE OF ATTRIBUTES

	Sinking Ponds #	Sinking Ponds %	Riverhaven II #	Riverhaven II %	Totals #	Totals %	
Deepskill Flint	1	1	0	0	1	1	Maximum Thickness
Igneous, Unidentified	0	0	2	8	2	2	
Sandstone	96	99	12	48	108	89	
Limestone	0	0	11	44	11	9	
N=	97	100	25	100	122	100	
Pebble, Bi-plano	73	75	22	88	95	78	Non-Flint Tool Weight (gm)
Pebble, Bi-convex	3	3	2	8	5	9	
Pebble, Bi-concave	4	4	1	4	4	3	
Pebble-Plano-Convex	17	18	0	0	18	15	
N=	97	100	25	100	122	100	
1-100	67	69	2	8	69	57	Non-Flint Tool-Base Type
101-200	30	31	4	16	34	28	
201-300	0	0	8	32	8	7	
301-400	0	0	4	16	4	3	
401-500	0	0	5	20	5	4	
501-600	0	0	2	8	2	2	
N=	97	100	25	100	122	100	
0-10	12	12	0	0	12	10	Material
11-20	63	65	8	32	71	58	
21-30	21	22	13	52	34	28	
31-40	0	0	3	12	3	3	
41-50	0	0	1	4	1	1	
51-70	1	1	0	0	1	1	
N=	97	100	25	100	122	100	
26-50	5	5	0	0	5	4	Maximum length (mm)
51-75	33	34	3	12	36	30	
76-100	52	54	6	24	58	48	
101-125	6	6	10	40	16	13	
126-150	1	1	4	16	5	4	
151-175	0	0	2	8	2	2	
N=	97	100	25	100	122	100	
Blank or Zero	1	1	2	8	3	2	Maximum Width (mm)
1-20	1	1	0	0	1	1	
21-30	2	2	0	0	2	2	
31-40	4	4	0	0	4	3	
41-50	14	14	0	0	14	11	
51-60	34	35	1	1	35	29	
61-70	30	31	3	12	33	27	
71-90	11	11	7	28	18	15	
91-120	0	0	10	40	10	8	
120 plus	0	0	2	8	2	2	
N=	97	100	25	100	122	100	
Blank or Zero	96	99	5	20	101	83	Notch Width (mm)
10-70	0	0	8	32	8	7	
71-100	1	1	12	48	13	11	
N=	97	100	25	100	122	100	

TABLE A.17*a*
HAMMER-ANVILSTONE ATTRIBUTES

Variation	Constant (+95%)
Material	(None)
Non-flint Tool Base Type	
Non-flint Tool Type	
Non-flint Tool weight (gm)	
Maximum Thickness (mm)	
Maximum Length (mm)	
Maximum Width (mm)	
Fragmentation	

TABLE A.17*b*
HAMMER/ANVILSTONE — TABLE OF ATTRIBUTES

	Sinking Ponds		Riverhaven II		Buffalo G		Totals		
	#	%	#	%	#	%	#	%	
Onon. Chert, Nat. varieties	0	0	3	17	0	0	3	6	Mater.
Igneous, unidentified	5	16	6	33	0	0	11	22	
Sandstone	26	84	8	44	1	100	35	70	
Limestone	0	0	1	6	0	0	1	2	
N=	31	100	18	100	1	100	50	100	
Indeterminate	1	3	0	0	0	0	1	2	Non-flint Tool Base Type
Pebble Biplane	11	35	1	6	0	0	12	24	
Pebble Biconvex	6	19	17	94	1	100	24	48	
Pebble Biconcave	1	3	0	0	0	0	1	2	
Pebble Plano-concave	12	39	0	0	0	0	12	24	
N=	31	100	18	100	1	100	50	100	
Indeterminate	0	0	1	6	0	0	1	2	Non-fl. Tool Type
Hammerstone	19	61	11	61	0	0	30	60	
Anvilstone, Pitted	12	39	2	11	1	100	15	30	
Anvilstone, Polypitted	0	0	4	22	0	0	4	8	
N=	31	100	18	100	1	100	50	100	
1-20	5	16	2	11	0	0	7	14	Non-flint Tool Weight (gm)
21-40	8	26	5	28	0	0	13	26	
41-60	4	13	3	17	0	0	7	14	
60-80	4	13	2	11	1	100	7	14	
81-100	4	13	2	11	0	0	6	12	
101-120	4	13	0	0	0	0	4	8	
121-140	1	3	2	11	0	0	3	6	
141-160	0	0	2	11	0	0	2	4	
160 plus-	1	3	0	0	0	0	1	2	
N=	31	100	18	100	1	100	50	100	
11-20	3	10	0	0	0	0	3	6	Max. Thickness (mm)
21-30	2	6	3	17	0	0	5	10	
31-40	7	23	4	22	1	100	12	24	
41-50	10	32	8	44	0	0	18	36	
51-70	8	26	2	11	0	0	10	20	
71-90	1	3	1	6	0	0	2	4	
N=	31	100	18	100	1	100	50	100	

TABLE A.17*b* (Continued)

	Sinking Ponds #	%	Riverhaven II #	%	Buffalo G #	%	Totals #	%	
21-30	0	0	2	11	0	0	2	4	Max. Length (mm)
31-40	13	42	7	39	0	0	20	40	
41-50	10	32	5	28	1	100	16	32	
51-60	6	19	2	11	0	0	8	16	
61-70	1	3	1	6	0	0	2	4	
71-90	1	3	1	6	0	0	2	4	
N=	31	100	18	100	1	100	50	100	
Blank or zero	0	0	1	6	0	0	1	2	Maximum Width (mm)
21-30	0	0	1	6	0	0	1	2	
31-40	1	3	1	6	0	0	2	4	
41-50	5	16	4	22	0	0	9	18	
51-60	7	23	3	17	0	0	10	20	
61-70	6	19	2	11	1	100	9	18	
71-90	9	29	3	17	0	0	12	24	
90-100	3	10	2	11	0	0	5	10	
120 plus-	0	0	1	6	0	0	1	2	
N=	31	100	18	100	1	100	50	100	
Fragmentary	9	30	0	0	0	0	9	30	Frag.
Non-fragmentary	22	70	0	0	0	0	22	70	
N=	31	100	0	0	0	0	31	100	

TABLE A.18*a*
ABRADING STONE ATTRIBUTES

Variation	Constant (+95%)
Material	(None)
Non-flint Tool Base Type	
Non-flint Tool Type	
Non-flint Tool weight (gm)	
Maximum Thickness (mm)	
Maximum Length (mm)	
Maximum Width (mm)	
Fragmentation	
Abrading stone Shape Type	

TABLE A.18*b*
ABRADING STONES — TABLE OF ATTRIBUTES

	Sinking Ponds #	Sinking Ponds %	Riverhaven II #	Riverhaven II %	Totals #	Totals %	
Metamorphic, unidentified	0	0	15	63	15	43	Material
Igneous, unidentified	2	18	2	8	4	11	
Sandstone	9	22	5	21	14	40	
Limestone	0	0	2	8	2	6	
N=	11	100	24	100	35	100	
Indeterminate	5	45	0	0	5	14	Non-flint Tool Base Type
Pebble Biplane	1	9	7	29	8	23	
Pebble Biconvex	3	27	13	54	16	46	
Pebble Plano-convex	1	9	4	17	5	14	
Pebble Plano-concave	1	0	0	0	1	3	
N=	11	100	24	100	35	100	
Indeterminate	0	0	2	8	2	6	Non-flint Tool Type
Abradingstone (Mano)	3	27	6	25	9	26	
Abradingstone Grooved, Narrow	4	36	2	8	6	17	
Abradingstone Groved, Wide	4	36	14	58	18	51	
N=	11	100	24	100	35	100	
Blank or Zero	0	0	19	79	19	34	Non-flint Tool Weight
1-20	2	18	0	0	2	6	
21-40	5	45	2	8	7	20	
41-60	3	27	0	0	3	9	
61-80	0	0	3	13	3	9	
121-140	1	9	0	0	1	3	
N=	11	100	24	100	35	100	
11-20	1	9	6	25	7	20	Max. Thickness (mm)
21-30	2	18	18	75	20	57	
31-40	6	55	0	0	6	17	
41-50	1	9	0	0	1	3	
51-70	1	9	0	0	1	3	
N=	11	100	24	100	35	100	

TABLE A.18*b* (Continued)

	Sinking Ponds #	Sinking Ponds %	Riverhaven II #	Riverhaven II %	Totals #	Totals %	
Blank or zero	0	0	18	75	18	51	Maximum Length (mm)
1-20	1	9	0	0	1	3	
31-40	5	45	0	0	5	14	
41-50	2	18	3	13	5	14	
51-60	3	27	2	18	5	14	
61-70	0	0	1	4	1	3	
N=	11	100	24	100	35	100	
Blank or zero	0	0	3	13	3	9	Maximum Width (mm)
31-40	1	9	0	0	1	3	
41-50	4	36	1	4	5	14	
51-60	5	45	12	50	17	49	
61-70	0	0	6	25	6	17	
71-90	0	0	2	8	2	6	
91-120	1	9	0	0	1	3	
N=	11	100	24	100	35	100	
Fragmentaries	6	55	19	79	25	71	Frag- menta- tion
Non-fragmentary	5	45	4	17	9	26	
Reconstructed	0	0	1	4	1	3	
N=	11	100	24	100	35	100	
Indeterminate	1	9	2	8	3	9	Abrading Stone Shape Type
Ovoid	2	18	2	8	4	11	
Ovoid parallel	1	9	6	25	7	20	
Ovoid Contracties	6	55	12	50	18	51	
Ovoid Expanding	0	0	2	8	2	6	
Discoid	1	9	0	0	1	3	
N=	11	100	24	100	35	100	

APPENDIX B: FLINT DETRITUS ANALYSIS

This appendix is a morphological and metrical analysis of a sample of flint detritus derived from wholly unprovenienced materials from Riverhaven 2. A selective process was applied to separate flakes and chips according to a purposefully gross definition. An exterior flaking angle of 90° or better was initially used to define flakes as opposed to 90° or less characterizing chips. At the first stage, size was not considered.

When the entire sample of 1538 items of nonprovenienced flint detritus was divided it was found that there were 74 cores, 769 flakes, 654 chips and 41 utilized items. Thirty of the unfractured flakes and 30 chips were then chosen for further analysis by the author and David W. Taggart. The bulb of percussion, striking platform, lipping, and bulbar scar were examined qualitatively. Quantitatively, the length, width, thickness, weight, platform width, and platform index $\frac{\text{Platform Width}}{\text{Width}}$ X 100, were calculated.

Table B.1 and Figure B.1 compare the qualitative attributes which were tested comparatively in a 3 x 3 table. The null hypothesis that there was no qualitative difference between flakes and chips was rejected at the .001 level. When bulb of percussion, striking platform, lipping and bulbar scar were tested separately, it was seen that each attribute value in Table B.1 was almost mutually exclusive in separating flakes and chips. These distributions show a cruciform cumulative graph when the descriptive attributes are plotted.

Quantitatively little was noted except that flakes were indeed larger in thickness, weight and platform width (Table B.2, Fig. B.2). The platform index showed little utility as a selective device other than a general trend to higher indices on flakes and lower on chips. When sample means are compared for attributes plotted in Figure B.2, it can be noted that flakes are consistently higher by almost 50%. The standard deviations for flakes also show that the sample is more variable in all attributes (Table B.2).

Throughout this work the following attributes were used to distinguish flakes from chips:

Flakes	Chips
Exterior flaking angle +90°	Exterior flaking angle −90°
Conspicuous bulb of percussion	Inconspicuous bulb of percussion
Single facet striking platform	Multi-faceted striking platform
Lipping absent	Lipping present
Bulbar scar present	Bulbar scar absent

As a test, the unprovenienced flint detritus sample was again divided; however this time attributes derived from this study were used. The following distribution was seen:

	Number	Percent
Cores	74	5
Utilized items	41	3
Flakes	825	53
Chips	598	39
TOTAL	1538	100

Flakes were grossly larger, thicker, and more variable in size with larger platform widths. Checks made throughout the analysis of the detritus from all sites appeared to maintain trends noted in this analysis.

TABLE B.1

QUALITATIVE ATTRIBUTES OF THE SELECTED SAMPLE OF FLINT DETRITUS

	Bulb of Percussion			Striking Platform				Lipping			Bulbar Scar		
	Conspicuous (Large)	Inconspicuous (Small	Total	Single Facet	Double Facet	Multi-Facet	Total	Present	Absent	Total	Present	Absent	Total
Number of Flakes	29	1	30	23	7	0	30	2	28	30	21	9	30
Percent of N (30)	97	3	100	77	23	0	100	7	93	100	70	30	100
Number of Chips	3	27	30	7	5	18	30	23	7	30	1	29	30
Percent of N (30)	10	90	100	23	17	60	100	77	23	100	3	97	100

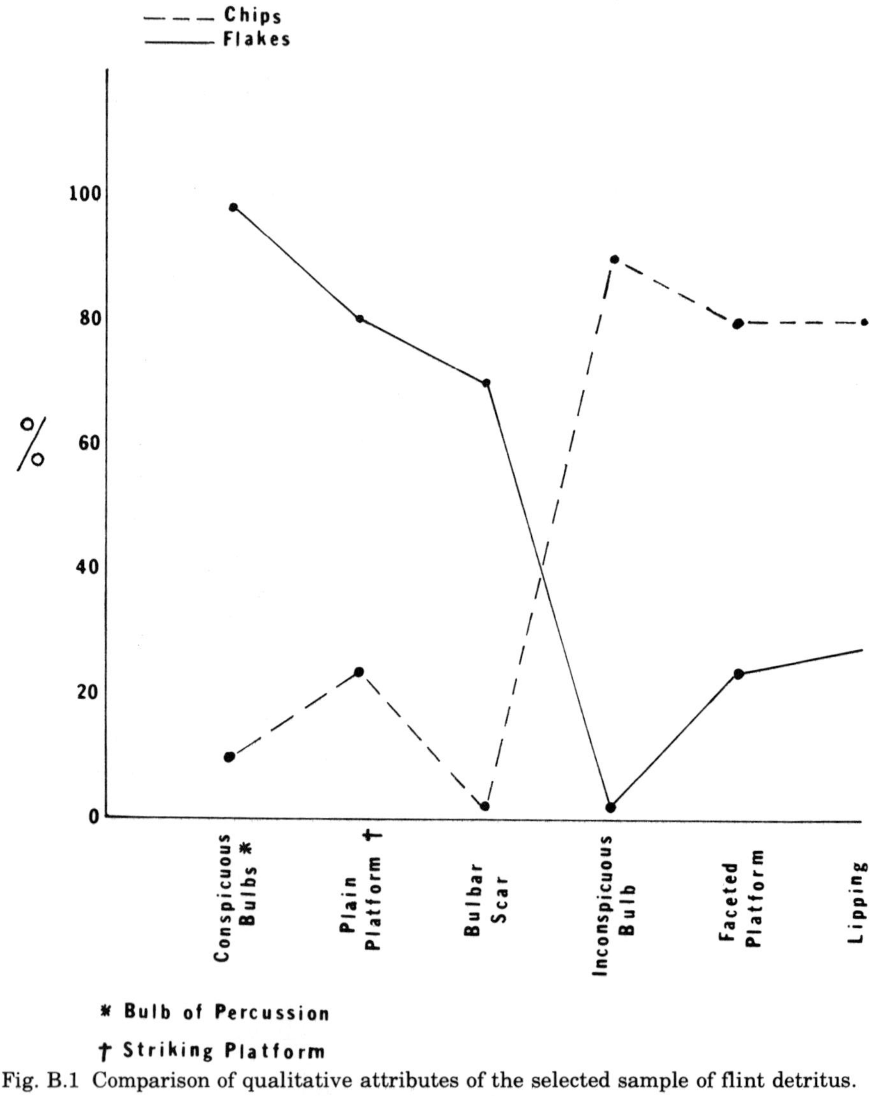

Fig. B.1 Comparison of qualitative attributes of the selected sample of flint detritus.

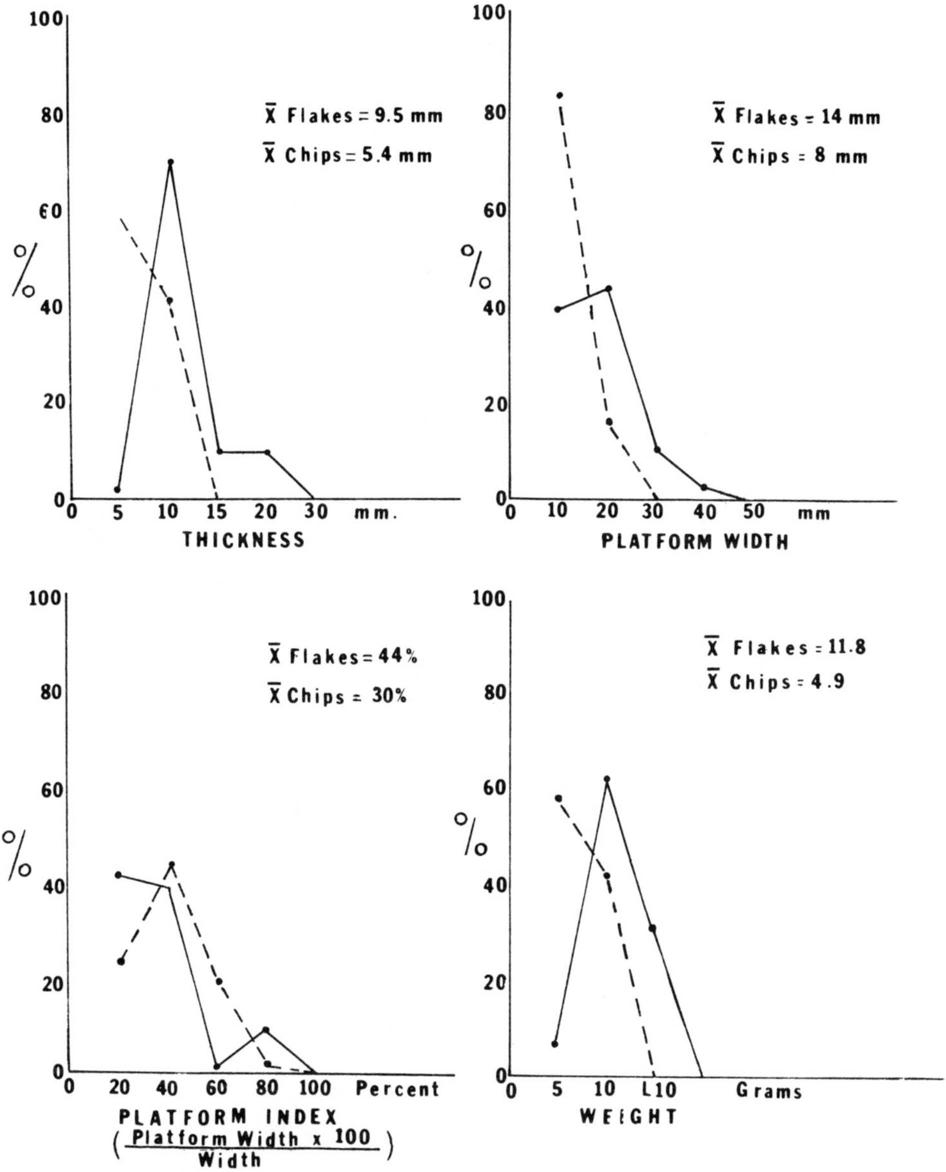

Fig. B.2 Distributions of ranges of quantitative attributes of the selected sample of flint detritus.

TABLE B.2
QUANTITATIVE ATTRIBUTES OF THE SELECTED SAMPLE OF FLINT DETRITUS

	Length (mm)		Width (mm)		Thickness (mm)		Weight (grams)		Platform Width (mm)		Platform Index (#)	
#	Flakes	Chips	Flakes	Chips	Flakes	Chips	Flakes	Chips	Flakes	Chips	Flakes	Chips
1	40	45	59	23	18	4	48	4	22	8	38	35
2	70	33	45	26	16	6	51	4	35	5	78	19
3	49	42	25	28	9	4	11	6	12	9	48	32
4	45	38	35	29	7	5	7	4	10	5	29	17
5	35	45	40	24	7	6	10	4	16	6	40	25
6	30	42	33	32	7	7	5	6	11	3	33	9
7	36	39	27	26	10	7	6	5	8	5	30	19
8	41	40	32	31	12	3	11	3	19	7	59	23
9	24	53	41	32	10	4	10	6	9	8	22	25
10	45	41	27	27	8	8	7	6	6	14	22	52
11	44	40	29	27	7	6	7	6	14	7	48	6
12	53	44	28	23	16	6	23	5	16	8	57	35
13	64	43	21	31	7	6	6	6	6	6	29	19
14	26	34	31	25	8	3	7	3	15	5	48	20
15	41	39	35	22	7	5	7	4	6	10	24	45
16	32	36	33	31	8	7	10	7	8	17	24	55
17	30	41	36	30	7	5	6	5	8	5	22	17
18	43	37	33	29	5	4	9	4	14	4	42	14
19	47	44	34	28	14	7	16	8	10	14	29	50
20	42	56	32	24	7	4	6	5	10	6	31	25
21	32	34	34	35	11	9	9	8	29	10	85	29
22	45	51	17	19	8	6	6	5	7	9	41	47
23	57	46	39	23	17	5	28	5	18	7	46	30
24	36	44	34	26	11	5	10	7	14	8	41	31
25	43	36	20	24	7	6	5	4	11	14	55	58
26	37	45	36	29	10	5	10	6	20	8	56	28
27	30	36	29	21	6	4	3	2	24	7	83	33
28	47	37	25	18	6	5	7	3	20	7	80	39
29	45	42	30	26	9	5	11	4	9	5	30	19
30	41	46	17	9	8	5	4	4	14	7	82	78
N	30	30	30	30	30	30	30	30	30	30	30	30
ΣX	1250	1249	947	778	285	162	356	149	421	234	—	—
$\bar{X}$	41.7	41.7	31.6	25.9	9.5	5.4	11.9	5.0	14.0	7.8	44%	30%
ΣX^2	3783	879.5	2093	764.2	357	57.2	3843	54	1421	273.1	—	—
S	11.2	5.42	8.35	5.05	3.45	1.38	11.3	1.34	6.88	3.02	—	—

APPENDIX C: FAUNAL RELATIONSHIPS

Appendix C is a compilation of data from many sources on animals and their associations in the Niagara Frontier Region. We have attempted to compile this data into usable form in Tables C.1-C.5. Generally the tables are arranged by habitat, habits, food, density and mode of capture. In Figure C.1, mammals are arranged by form of food, density and usable meat into a dendrogram for the Niagara Frontier Region.

The sources used are:

Mammals:

De Vos (1964)
Collins (1959)
Cleland (1966)
Burt (1957)
Burt and Grossenweiler (1964)
Kendeigh (1961)
Hamilton (1943)
Taylor (1969)
Cahalane (1947)
Stewart (1961)
Shelford (1963)

Birds:

Cleland (1966)
Collins (1959)
Reilly and Parks (1960)
Axtell (1958)
Linduska (1964)

Reptiles and Amphibians:

Cleland (1966)
Collins (1959)

Fishes:

Cleland (1966)
Collins (1959)
Bean (1903)
N.Y. Conservation Department (1929)
N.Y. Conservation Department (1940)
Hawkinson (1924)
Robins and Deubler (1955)
Buffalo Society of Natural Sciences, Proceedings (1969)
Rugir and Hartman (1973)
Witt (1960)

Shellfish:

Clark and Berg (1959)

TABLE C.1
HABITAT, HABITS, DENSITY, AND MEAT VALUE OF NIAGARA FRONTIER MAMMALS

MAMMALS	HABITAT												HABITS							
	Canadian	Carolinian	Coniferous Forest	Deciduous Forest	Open	Dense	Swamp	Lake or Pond	Stream	Margins of Water	Upland	Lowland	Nocturnal	Diurnal	**Terrestrial Shelters**	**Arboreal Shelters**	Solitary	Social	Stores Food	Seasonal Grouping
Elk	x	x		x	x															
White Tail											x	x		x	x		x	x		x
Deer	x	x		x	x		x				x	x		x	x		x	x		x
Moose	x	x	x		x					x		x		x	x		x	x		x
Snowshoe Hare	x		x			x	x			x		x	x		x		x	x		
Cottontail	x	x		x	x		x			x		x	x		x			x		x
Black Bear	x	x	x	x	x	x	x			x	x	x		x	x		x			
Wolf	x	x		x	x						x	x		x	x			x	x	
Coyote	x	x	x	x	x						x	x	x		x			x	x	
Red Fox	x			x		x	x			x		x	x		x			x	x	
Gray Fox	x	x		x		x	x			x		x	x		x			x	x	
Mountain Lion	x	x		x	x		x			x	x			x	x		x			
Bobcat	x		x	x		x	x			x		x	x		x		x			
Lynx	x		x			x	x			x	x		x		x		x			
Marten	x	x	x			x					x			x		x	x		x	
Fisher	x		x			x	x			x		x	x			x	x			
Weasel	x	x		x	x		x			x	x		x		x		x		x	
Mink	x	x		x	x		x			x	x	x	x		x		x		x	
Porcupine	x	x	x	x	x						x		x		x		x	x		x
Woodchuck	x	x		x	x					x	x			x	x		x			
Opossum	x			x	x		x			x		x	x			x	x			
Striped Skunk	x	x	x	x	x					x	x		x		x			x		
Raccoon	x	x		x	x		x			x		x		x		x		x		
Muskrat	x	x		x			x	x	x	x		x	x		x			x		
Otter	x	x						x	x	x		x		x	x		x			
Beaver	x	x						x	x	x		x		x				x	x	x
Red Squirrel	x	x	x	x	x						x		x	x	x	x		x		
Gray Squirrel	x	x		x	x						x			x		x	x	x	x	x
East Fox Squirrel	x	x	x	x		x	x			x		x		x́	x		x		x	
Chipmunk	x	x		x	x						x			x	x		x		x	
TOTAL	29	23	12	22	18	9	16	3	3	20	16	19	14	15	23	6	20	15	12	7

+75%
Canadian
Carolinian
Deciduous Forests
Terrestrial Shelter

+50%
Low Density
Open Cover
Swamp
Margin Water
Upland-Lowland

Diurnal
Solitary-Social

TABLE C.1 (Continued)

MAMMALS	HABITS: Primary-Herbivorous	Primary-Omnivorous	Primary-Carnivorous	Hibernates	False Hibernation	High Density/10+ 100 Sq. miles	Low Density/10 100 Sq. miles	Usable meat high/ +50 lbs.	Usable meat Moderate 10-50 lbs.	Usable Meat Low 0-10 lbs.
Elk	x					x		x		
White Tail Deer	x					x		x		
Moose	x						x	x		
Snowshoe Hare	x					x				x
Cottontail	x					x				x
Black Bear		x		x			x	x		
Wolf			x				x		x	
Coyote			x				x		x	
Red Fox			x				x			x
Gray Fox			x				x			x
Mountain Lion			x				x	x		
Bobcat			x				x		x	
Lynx			x				x		x	
Marten			x				x			x
Fisher			x				x			x
Weasel			x			x				x
Mink			x			x				x
Porcupine	x				x		x			x
Woodchuck	x			x		x				x
Opossum		x			x		x			x
Striped Skunk		x			x		x			x
Raccoon		x			x		x		x	
Muskrat	x					x				x
Otter			x				x		x	
Beaver	x				x		x		x	
Red Squirrel	x				x	x				x
Gray Squirrel	x				x	x				x
East Fox Squirrel	x				x	x				x
Chipmunk		x		x		x				
TOTAL	12	5	12	3	8	12	17	5	7	11

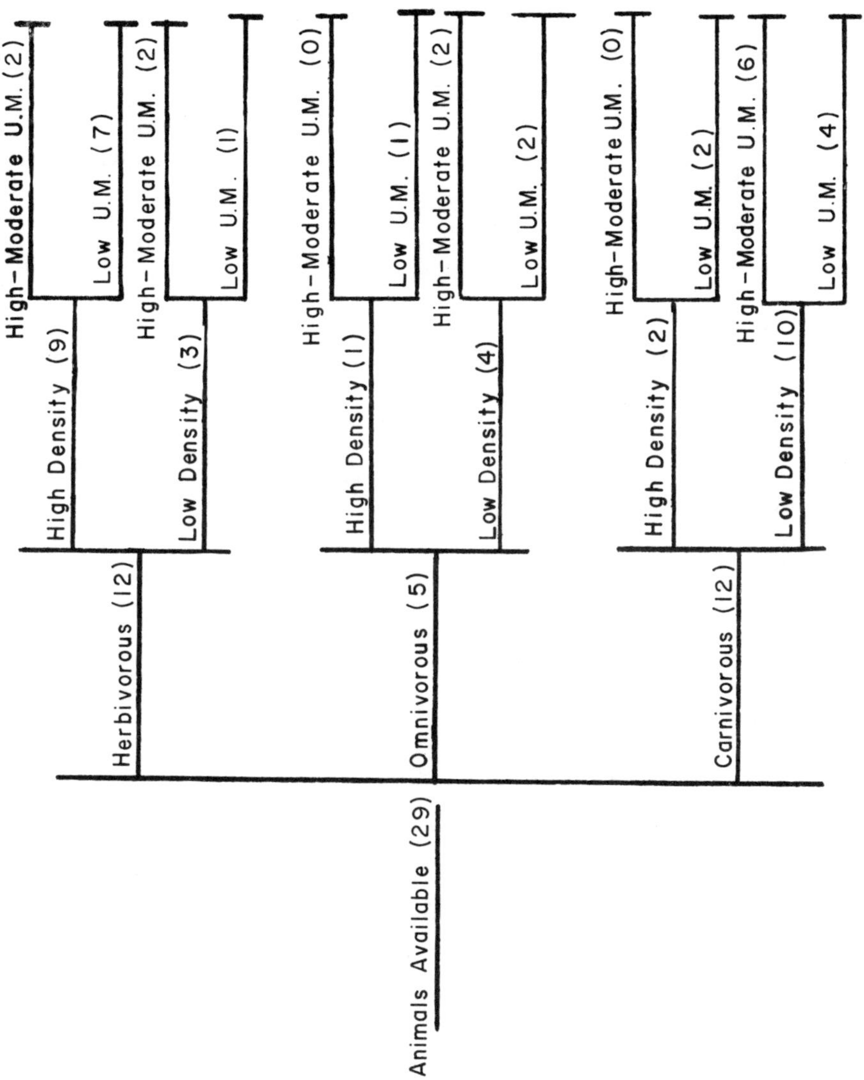

Fig. C.1 Mammals by eating habits, density, and usable meat.

TABLE C.2
HABITAT, HABITS, AND FOOD OF NIAGARA FRONTIER BIRDS

LAND BIRDS	HABITAT			HABITS											FOOD					
	Dense Woodland	Open Woodland	Fields/Brush	Runs	Freezes	Low Flyer	High Flyer	Large Flock	Small Flock	Solitary	Feeds on Ground	Feeds off Ground	Nests on Ground	Nests in Trees	Berries	Seeds	Green Plants	Nuts	Insects	Seasonal Migration
Bob White	x		x		x	x			x		x		x		x	x	x		x	
Ruffed Grouse	x				x	x			x		x		x		x	x	x		x	
Turkey		x		x		x			x		x			x	x	x		x	x	
Passenger Pigeon*		x				x		x			x			x	x	x				x
Mourning Dove*		x				x		x			x			x	x	x				x
TOTAL (5)	2	3	1	1	2	5	0	2	3	0	5	0	2	3	5	5	2	1	3	2

ALL	Low Flyer Feed On Ground Berries Seeds
+50%	Open Woodland Small Flock Insects Nest in Trees

* Pigeon and Dove = chicken-like birds.

TABLE C.3
HABITAT, HABITS, AND FOOD OF NIAGARA FRONTIER AQUATIC BIRDS

AQUATIC BIRDS	HABITAT											HABITS						
	Shallow Marsh (S)	Shallow Marsh (F)	Shallow Lake (F)	Shallow Bay (S)	Shallow River (F)	Deep Lake (F)	Deep River (F)	Deep Bay (S)	Surface Fields	Nest near Water	Nest away from Water (1 mi.)	Feeds on Shore	Feeds Surface	Feeds Deep (Diver)	Large Flock	Small Flock	Solitary Pairs	Seasonal Migration Spring/Autumn
Common Loon						x				x			x				x	
Red Neck Grebe	x	x								x			x				x	x
Horned Grebe	x	x								x				x			x	x
Pied-Bill Grebe	x	x								x				x			x	x
Canada Goose		x	x		x	x	x		x			x			x			x
Mallard	x	x	x	x	x	x	x	x		x			x		x			x
Black Duck	x	x	x	x	x	x	x	x		x			x		x			x
Pintail	x	x	x	x	x						x		x		x			x
Green Wing Teal	x	x	x	x	x						x	x	x		x			x
Blue Wing Teal		x	x		x						x	x	x		x			x
Amer. Widgeon		x	x		x	x	x				x				x			x
Shoveler	x	x	x	x						x			x		x			x
Wood Duck		x	x		x						x		x			x		
Red Neck Duck	x	x	x	x	x	x	x	x		x				x		x		x
Canvasback						x	x	x	x	x				x	x			x
Lesser Scaup						x	x			x				x	x			x
Comm. Golden Eye						x	x	x		x				x	x			x
Bufflehead						x	x	x		x				x		x		x
Old Squaw						x	x	x		x				x		x		x
W.W. Scoter						x	x	x		x				x	x			x
Ruddy Duck						x	x	x		x				x	x			x
Hooded Merganser		x	x		x					x				x			x	x
Comm. Merganser		x	x		x					x				x			x	x
Amer. Coot	x	x	x	x	x					x		x	x	x			x	
Gr. Blue Heron	x	x	x	x	x					x		x	x				x	
Gr. Green Heron	x	x	x	x	x					x		x	x				x	
Blk. Cr. Night Heron	x	x	x	x	x					x		x	x				x	
L. Bittern	x	x								x		x	x				x	
Am. Bittern	x	x								x		x	x				x	
TOTAL (29)	15	21	16	10	15	13	12	9	2	23	5	9	15	13	13	3	13	21

TABLE C.3 (Continued)
HABITAT, HABITS, AND FOOD OF NIAGARA FRONTIER AQUATIC BIRDS

AQUATIC BIRDS	FOOD										
	Small Mammals	Insects	Crustacean	Mollusks	Amphibians	Seeds	Aquatic Plants	Nuts	Roots & Tubers	Fish	Grass
Common Loon							x				
Red Neck Grebe							x				
Horned Grebe							x				
Pied-Bill Grebe							x				
Canada Goose						x	x				x
Mallard						x	x				x
Black Duck				x		x	x				
Pintail				x		x					
Green Wing Teal			x	x			x				
Blue Wing Teal			x	x		x	x				
Amer. Widgeon							x				
Shoveler		x	x	x		x	x				
Wood Duck						x	x	x			
Red Neck Duck						x	x				
Canvasback				x			x		x		
Lesser Scaup		x		x	x		x				
Comm. Golden Eye		x		x	x		x				
Bufflehead		x	x	x						x	
Old Squaw		x	x	x						x	
W. W. Scoter			x	x			x				
Ruddy Duck		x	x	x			x				
Hooded Merganser		x	x	x	x					x	
Comm. Merganser			x		x					x	
Amer. Coot						x	x				x
Gr. Blue Heron		x	x	x	x		x			x	
Gr. Green Heron		x	x	x	x		x			x	
Blk. Cr. Night Heron	x	x	x	x	x		x			x	
L. Bittern	x	x			x					x	
Am. Bittern	x	x			x					x	
TOTAL (29)	3	12	12	16	9	9	22	1	1	9	3
		+75%	Nest near water Aquatic plants Shallow marsh (F) Seasonal migration			+50%	Shallow Marsh (s)				

TABLE C.4
HABITAT, HABITS, FOOD, AND CAPTURE METHODS OF NIAGARA FRONTIER FISHES

FISH	HABITAT																			HABITS					
	Salt-Fresh	Fresh Only	Deep Water	Shallow Water	Clear Water	Silty Water	Vegetation Water	Cold Water	Warm Water	Fast Flow	Sluggish	Lake	Stream	Ocean	Spawn Shallow	Spawn Deep	Fast Stream	Slow Stream	Lake	Spawn Spring/Summer	Spawn Summer/Autumn	Spawn Autumn/Winter	Ess. Solitary	Schools	Seasonal Runs (Spawn)
Silver Lamprey		x	x		x			x				x	x		x		x			x			x		
Sea Lamprey	x		x		x			x				x	x	x		x	x			x					x
Lake Sturgeon		x	x		x			x		x		x	x		x		x			x					x
Bowfin		x		x		x			x		x	x	x		x			x		x			x		
Shortnose Gar		x		x			x		x			x	x		x				x	x			x		
Longnose Gar		x		x			x		x			x	x		x				x	x			x		
Mooneye		x	x		x			x		x		x	x		x		x			x					x
Rainbow Trout		x	x		x			x		x		x	x		x		x			x					x
Atlantic Salmon	x		x		x			x		x		x	x	x	x		x			x					x
Lake Trout		x	x		x			x				x				x			x			x	x		
Whitefish		x	x		x			x		x		x	x		x				x			x		x	
Lake Whitefish		x		x	x			x		x		x	x		x			x				x		x	
White Sucker		x		x		x			x		x	x	x		x			x		x			x		
Longnose Sucker		x	x		x				x			x			x		x			x			x		
Northern Sucker		x		x	x			x		x			x		x		x			x			x		
Redhorse Sucker		x	x		x			x		x			x		x		x			x			x		
Silverhorse Sucker		x	x		x			x		x		x	x		x		x			x			x		
Chubsucker		x	x			x			x		x	x	x		x			x		x			x		
Shorthead Redhorse		x		x	x			x		x		x	x		x		x			x			x		
Carpsucker		x	x			x			x		x		x			x		x		x			x		
Creek Chup		x		x	x			x		x			x		x			x		x			x		
Channel Cat		x	x			x			x		x	x	x			x			x		x			x	
Catfish		x		x		x	x		x		x	x	x		x				x		x			x	
Stone Cat		x		x			x		x			x	x		x				x	x				x	
SUBTOTAL A	2	22	14	10	15	6	4	14	10	11	6	20	22	2	20	4	11	6	7	19	2	3	14	5	5

TABLE C.4 (Continued)

FISH	HABITAT: Salt-Fresh	Fresh Only	Deep Water	Shallow Water	Clear Water	Silty Water	Vegetation Water	Cold Water	Warm Water	Fast Flow	Sluggish	Lake	Stream	Ocean	Spawn Shallow	Spawn Deep	Fast Stream	Slow Stream	Lake	HABITS: Spawn Spring/Summer	Spawn Summer/Autumn	Spawn Autumn/Winter	Ess. Solitary	Schools	Seasonal Runs (Spawn)
Sand Pike		x		x		x			x		x	x	x		x				x	x			x		
Walleye Pike		x	x		x			x		x		x	x		x				x	x			x		
Redfin Pike		x		x		x	x	x			x	x	x		x				x	x			x		
Northern Pike		x		x		x	x		x		x	x	x		x				x	x			x		
Muskellunge		x		x			x		x		x	x	x		x				x			x	x		
Amer. Eel	x			x	x	x			x		x	x	x	x		x					x				x
Amer. Burbot		x	x		x			x				x				x			x			x		x	
White Bass		x	x		x	x		x				x			x				x	x				x	
Smallmouth Bass		x	x		x			x				x				x			x	x			x		
Largemouth Bass		x			x			x				x				x			x	x			x		
Rock Bass		x		x	x			x		x		x	x			x			x	x				x	
Yellow Perch		x	x		x		x	x		x		x	x			x			x	x				x	
Bluegill Sunfish		x		x		x	x		x			x			x				x		x		x		
Crappie		x		x		x	x		x		x	x			x				x		x			x	
Warmouth Sunfish		x		x		x	x		x		x	x	x		x				x		x		x		
Freshwater Drum		x		x		x	x		x		x	x	x		x			x		x					x
Trout Perch		x	x		x			x				x			x				x	x			x		
SUBTOTAL B	1	16	6	10	9	9	8	9	8	3	8	17	10	1	11	6	0	1	15	11	4	2	10	5	2
TOTAL A & B	3	38	20	20	24	15	12	23	18	14	14	37	32	3	31	10	11	7	22	30	6	5	24	10	7

TABLE C.4 (Continued)

FISH	FOOD								CAPTURE								
	Insects & Plankton	Crustaceans	Mollusks	Vegetation	Fish	Worm	Amphibians	Parasitic	Capture-Nets	Weirs	Hooks & Gorge	Spear & Leister	Poison		High Food Utilization	Moderate Food Utiliz.	Poor Food Utilization
Silver Lamprey								x	x	x					x		
Sea Lamprey								x	x	x					x		
Lake Sturgeon	x	x	x	x	x				x	x		x			x		
Bowfin		x			x				x			x				x	
Shortnose Gar					x				x			x				x	
Longnose Gar					x				x			x				x	
Mooneye	x	x	x		x				x	x		x					x
Rainbow Trout		x	x		x		x		x	x		x			x		
Atlantic Salmon		x	x		x		x		x	x		x			x		
Lake Trout		x	x		x		x		x		x				x		
Whitefish	x					x			x	x					x		
Lake Whitefish	x					x			x	x					x		
White Sucker	x		x	x		x			x	x					x		
Longnose Sucker	x		x	x		x			x	x					x		
Northernsucker	x			x					x	x					x		
Redhorse Sucker	x		x						x	x					x		
Silverhorse Sucker	x		x						x	x					x		
Chubsucker	x		x						x	x					x		
Shorthead Redhorse	x		x						x	x					x		
Carpsucker				x					x	x					x		
Creek Chup	x	x	x	x	x				x		x						x
Channel Cat	x	x	x	x	x	x	x		x	x	x	x	x		x		
Catfish	x	x	x	x	x	x	x		x	x	x	x	x		x		
Stone Cat	x	x	x	x	x	x	x		x	x	x	x	x		x		
SUBTOTAL 1	15	10	15	9	12	7	6	2	24	19	5	10	3	0	19	3	2

TABLE C.4 (Continued)

FISH	FOOD: Insects & Plankton	FOOD: Crustaceans	FOOD: Mollusks	FOOD: Vegetation	FOOD: Fish	FOOD: Worm	FOOD: Amphibians	FOOD: Parasitic	CAPTURE: Capture-Nets	CAPTURE: Weirs	CAPTURE: Hooks & Gorge	CAPTURE: Spear & Leister	CAPTURE: Poison		High Food Utilization	Moderate Food Utiliz.	Poor Food Utilization
Sand Pike					x						x	x					x
Walleye Pike		x			x						x	x					x
Redfin Pike					x		x				x	x					x
Northern Pike					x		x				x	x					x
Muskellunge					x		x				x	x					x
Amer. Eel		x	x		x	x				x		x	x		x		
Amer. Burbot	x				x				x	x		x			x		
White Bass	x	x			x				x	x	x					x	
Smallmouth Bass					x				x	x	x					x	
Largemouth Bass	x	x			x		x		x	x	x					x	
Rock bass	x	x			x				x	x	x					x	
Yellow Perch	x	x			x				x	x	x				x		
Bluegill Sunfish	x	x			x				x	x		x				x	
Crappie	x				x				x	x		x				x	
Warmouth Sunfish	x	x			x				x	x		x				x	
Freshwater Drum		x	x	x						x					x		
Trout Perch	x	x							x								
SUBTOTAL 2	9	10	2	1	15	1	4	0	10	11	10	10	1	0	4	7	6
TOTAL 1 & 2	24	20	17	10	27	8	10	2	34	30	15	20	4	0	23	10	8

ca. 75%
Fresh water
Lake
Streams
Spawn Shallow
Spawn Spring
Nets
Weirs

ca. 50%
Deep — Shallow
Clear — Others
Cold — Warm
Insects
Crustaceans
Mollusks
Fish
Lake Spawn
Spear Leister
High Utilization
Essentially Solitary

TABLE C.5
HABITAT, HABITS, FOOD OF NIAGARA FRONTIER TURTLES AND FROGS

TURTLES & FROGS	HABITAT				HABITS														FOOD						
	Aquatic Only	Aquatic-Terrestrial	Terr. Moist	Terr. Dry	Groups	Solitary	Timid	Diurnal	Nocturnal	Swims	Basks	Burrows	Feeds Bottom	Feeds Surface	Migrates at times	Hatch Spring/Sum.	Hatch Sum./Fall	Hibernates Winter/ Fall	Crustaceans	Mollusks	Fish Carrion	Insects	Other Invert.	Aquatic Plants	Terr. Plants	Vertebrates
Wood Turtle		x				x		x		x				x			x	x			x	x		x		
Spotted Turtle	x				x			x		x	x		x			x		x				x	x			
Blandings Turtle		x				x	x	x		x	x		x				x	x	x			x				
Painted Turtle	x				x		x	x		x	x		x		x	x		x	x	x	x	x	x	x		
Map Turtle	x					x	x	x		x	x		x	x			x	x	x	x	x	x	x	x		
Box Turtle			x			x		x				x					x	x	x	x					x	
Spiny Soft Shell Turtle	x					x		x		x	x	x	x				x	x	x	x	x	x	x	x		x
Snapping Turtle	x					x		x		x		x	x				x	x	x	x	x	x	x	x		x
Stinkpot Turtle	x					x		x		x		x	x				x	x	x	x	x	x	x			x
Bullfrog	x					x			x	x		x		x			x	x			x	x	x			x
Leopard Frog		x				x		x		x							x	x				x	x			
Wood Frog			x			x		x									x	x				x	x			
Green Frog	x					x		x		x		x	x				x	x				x	x			
TOTALS	8	3	2	0	2	11	3	12	1	11	5	6	8	3	1	2	11	13	7	6	7	12	10	5	1	4

+75%: Solitary, Diurnal, Swims, Hatch Sum./Fall, Hibernate, Insects, Other Invert.

+50%: Aquatic, Feed on Bottom, Crustaceans, Fish Carrion

REFERENCES CITED

Axtell, Harold H.
1956 The geese at Oak Orchard Swamp. Hobbies 37:(4)1-4.

Bean, Tarleton H.
1903 The fishes of New York. Albany: New York State University.

Beardsley, Richard K., Preston Holder, Alex D. Krieger, Betty J. Meggers, and John B. Rinaldo.
1956 Functional and evolutionary implications of community patterning. Society for American Archaeology, Memoir 2:131-57.

Binford, Lewis R.
1962 Archaeology as anthropology. American Antiquity 28:217-25.
1963*a* A proposed attribute list for the description and classification of projectile points. In: Miscellaneous studies in typology and classification, by Anta M. White, Lewis R. Binford, and Mark L. Papworth. Museum of Anthropology, University of Michigan, Anthropological Papers 19:193-221.
1963*b* The Hodges site. A Late Archaic burial station. In: Miscellaneous studies in typology and classification, by Anta M. White, Lewis R. Binford, and Mark L. Papworth. Museum of Anthropology, University of Michigan, Anthropological Papers 19:124-48.
1963*c* The Pomranky Site. A Late Archaic burial station. In: Miscellaneous studies in typology and classification, by Anta M. White, Lewis R. Binford, and Mark L. Papworth. Museum of Anthropology, University of Michigan, Ann Arbor, Anthropological Papers 19:149-92.
1963*d* "Red ochre" caches from the Michigan area: A possible case of cultural drift. Southwestern Journal of Anthropology 19:89-108.
1964 A consideration of archaeological research design. American Antiquity 29:425-41.
1965 Archaeological systematics and the study of culture process. American Antiquity 31:203-10.
1967 Comments on major aspects of the interrelationship of archaeology and ethnology by K.C. Chang. Current Anthropology 8:234-35.
1968*a* Methodological considerations of the archeological use of ethnographic data. In: Man the hunter, edited by Richard B. Lee and Irven DeVore. Chicago: Aldine.
1968*b* Archeological perspectives. In: New perspectives in archeology, edited by Sally R. Binford and Lewis R. Binford. Chicago: Aldine.
1972 An archeological perspective. New York: Seminar Press.

Binford, Lewis R. and Mark L. Papworth
1963 The Eastport site, Antrim County, Michigan. In: Miscellaneous studies in typology and classification, by Anta M. White, Lewis R. Binford, and Mark L. Papworth. Museum of Anthropology, University of Michigan, Anthropological Papers 19:71-123.

Binford, Sally R. and Lewis R. Binford, eds.
1968 New perspectives in archeology. Chicago: Aldine.

Blackmon, Paul D.
n.d. Glacial geology of the East. Unpublished 1956 MA Thesis. State University of New York at Buffalo.

Bock, Philip K.
1966 The Micmac Indians of Restigouche: historic and contemporary. Ottawa: National Museum of Canada.

Braun, S. Lucy
1950 Deciduous forests of eastern North America. Philadelphia: The Blackiston Company.

Brennan, Louis A., Charles W. Merritt, Roberta Wingerson, Carolyn Merritt, and Karyn Landauer.
1970 The Twombly Landing Site II. The New York State Archeological Association Bulletin 49:13-29.

Brown, Christa, J. Kelley, J. Penman, and J. Sparling
1973 Faunal analysis of the Cole Quarry Archaic site. New York State Archeological Association Bulletin 58.

Buhler, E.J. and I.H. Tesmer
1963 Geology of Erie County. Buffalo Society of Natural Sciences Bulletin 21:3.

Boughton, J.G., D.W. Fisher, Y.W. Isachsen, and L.V. Rickard.
1966 Geology of New York. Albany: New York State Museum Educational Leaflet 20.

Burt, William H.
1957 Mammals of the Great Lakes region. Ann Arbor: The University of Michigan Press.

Burt, William H. and Richard P. Grosenweiler
1964 A field guide to the mammals. Boston: Houghton-Mifflin.

Butzer, Karl W.
1971 Environment and archaeology. 2nd ed. Chicago: Aldine-Atherton.

Byers, Douglas S.
1959 The Eastern Archaic: some problems and hypotheses. American Antiquity 24:233-56.

Cahalane, Victor H.
1947 Mammals of North America. New York: Macmillan.

Caldwell, Joseph R.
1958 Trend and tradition in the prehistory of the eastern United States. American Anthropological Association Memoir 58.

Ceci, Lynn
n.d. Archaic band mobility and Long Island archaeology. Paper read at 1972 meeting of the Northeast Anthropological Society.

Chang, K.C.
1968 Settlement archaeology. Palo Alto: National Press Books.

Clarke, Arthur H. and Clifford D. Berg
1959 The freshwater mussels of central New York. Ithaca: New York State Agricultural Experiment Station Memoir 367.

Cleland, Charles E.
1966 The prehistoric animal ecology and ethnozoology of the upper Great Lakes region. Museum of Anthropology, University of Michigan, Anthropological Papers 29.

Cline, Marlin G.
1970 Soils and soil associations of New York State. Ithaca: New York State College of Agriculture.

Collins, Henry H.
1959 Complete field guide to American wildlife. New York: Harper and Row.

Cox, Donald D.
1959 Some postglacial forests in central and eastern New York State as determined by the method of pollen analysis. Albany: New York State Museum and Science Service Bulletin 377.

Cox, Donald D. and Donald M. Lewis
1965 Pollen studies in the Crusoe Lake area of prehistoric Indian occupation. Albany: New York State Museum Bulletin 397.

Crumley, Carole S.
1973 The Kantzler site (20 by 30): A multi-component site in Bay County, Michigan. Michigan Archaeologist 19(3-4):183-291.

Cunningham, Wilbur M.
1948 A study of the Glacial Kame culture in Michigan, Ohio, and Indiana. Museum of Anthropology, University of Michigan, Occasional Contributions 12.

D'Agostino, J.P.
n.d. Lake Tonawanda history and development. Unpublished 1958 MA Thesis. State University of New York at Buffalo.

Damas, David, ed.
1969 Contributions to anthropology: band societies. Ottawa: National Museum of Canada.

Day, Gordon M.
1953 The Indian as an ecological factor. Ecology 34:329-46.

Deetz, James F.
1968 Cultural patterning of behavior as reflected by archaeological materials. In: Settlement archaeology, edited by K.C. Chang. Palo Alto: National Press.

Deevey, Edward S.
1958 Bogs. Scientific American 199(4):141-47.

Deevey, Edward S. and Richard F. Flint
1957 Postglacial hypsithermal interval. Science 125:182-84.

De Vos, Antoon
1964 Range changes of mammals in the Great Lakes region. The American Midland Naturalist 71:210-31.

Dice, Lee R.
1943 The biotic provinces of North America. Ann Arbor: University of Michigan Press.

Dincauze, Dena F.
1968 Cremation cemeteries in eastern Massachusetts. Papers of the Peabody Museum of Archaeology and Ethnology, Harvard University, 59:1.

Donahue, James C.
n.d. Spider Creek, number one. Manuscript on file, State University of New York at Buffalo.

Dragoo, Don W.
1959 Archaic hunters of the upper Ohio Valley. Pittsburgh: Carnegie Museum.
1963 Mounds for the dead: an analysis of the Adena culture. Pittsburgh: Carnegie Museum.

Fairchilde, Harold L.
1932 The closing stage of New York glacial history. Geological Society of America Bulletin 43:603-26.

Fenneman, Nevin M.
1938 Physiography of eastern United States. New York and London: McGraw-Hill Book Company.

Fitting, James E.
1968 Environmental potential and the postglacial readaptation in eastern North America. American Antiquity 33:441-45.
1969 Settlement analysis in the Great Lakes region. Southwestern Journal of Anthropology 25:360-77.
1970 The archaeology of Michigan. Garden City: The Natural History Press.

Fitting, James E., ed. and comp.
1972 The Schultz site at Green Point. Memoirs of The Museum of Anthropology, The University of Michigan 4.

Fitting, James E. and David S. Brose
1970 The northern periphery of Adena. In: Adena: The seeking of an identity, edited by B.K. Swartz. Muncie: Ball State University.

Fitting, James E., David S. Brose, Henry T. Wright, and James Dinerstein
1969 The Goodwin-Gresham site, 20 IS 8, Iosco County, Michigan. The Wisconsin Archeologist 50:3.

Fitting, James E. and Susan Sasse
1969 The Hodges site, 20 SA 130, Saginaw County, Michigan. The Michigan Archeologist 15(3):57-77.

Flint, Richard F.
1971 Glacial and Pleistocene geology. New York: John Wiley & Sons, Inc.

Funk, Robert E.
1965 The Archaic of the Hudson Valley—new evidence and new interpretations. Pennsylvania Archaeologist, 25(3-4):139-60.
n.d. The Scaccia site (Cda-17-3). Unpublished (1969) manuscript on file. New York State Museum, Albany.

Funk, Robert E., B.E. Rippeteau, and R.M. Houck
1973 A preliminary cultural framework for the upper Susquehanna Valley. New York State Archeological Association Bulletin 57:11-27.

Grabau, A.W.
1901 Guide to the geology and paleontology of Niagara Falls and vicinity. Albany: New York State Museum Bulletin 45.

Granger, Joseph E.
n.d. A preliminary description and analysis of the Sinking Ponds site. Unpublished (1966) Masters Project Paper Department of Anthropology, State University of New York at Buffalo.

Grayson, Donald K.
1974 The Riverhaven 2 vertebrate fauna: Comments on methods in faunal analysis and subsistence potential in prehistoric New York. Man in the Northeast 8.

Griffin, James B.
1961 Post-glacial ecology and culture changes in the Great Lakes area of North America. Great Lakes Resources Division, Institute Science and Technology, University of Michigan Publication 7:147-55.
1965 Late quaternary prehistory in the Northeastern Woodlands. In: The quaternary of the United States, edited by H.E. Wright and D.C. Frey. Princeton: Princeton University Press.
1967 Eastern North American archaeology: A summary. Science 156:175-91.

Griffin, James B., ed.
1952 Archeology of eastern United States. Chicago: The University of Chicago Press.

Hamilton, William J.
1943 The mammals of eastern United States. Ithaca: Comstock.

Hawkinson, Thomas L.
1924 A preliminary report on a fish survey in western New York. Buffalo Society of Natural Science Bulletin 13(3):57-87.

Hayes, Charles F. III
1963 Point Peninsula burial. Museum Service, Bulletin of Rochester Museum of Arts and Sciences 36:6-7.
1966*a* The archaeology of New York State by William A. Ritchie (Review). Museum Service, Bulletin of the Rochester Museum of Arts and Sciences 39:27-29.
1966*b* Pits of the Archaic stage salvaged from the Farrell Farm. Museum Service, Bulletin of the Rochester Museum of Arts and Sciences 39:167-75.
1969 A progress report on an Archaic site on the Farrell Farm: The Cole Gravel Pit 1966-68. New York State Archeological Association Bulletin 47:1-11.

Helm, June
1969 Remarks on the methodology of band composition analysis. In: Band Societies, edited by D. Damas. Ottawa: National Museum of Canada.

Heubsch, Carole
1967 How the great glaciers changed the Niagara Frontier. Hobbies 38(3):1-11.

Hole, Frank and Robert F. Heizer
1973 An introduction to prehistoric archeology. New York: Holt, Reinhart and Winston, Inc.

Hough, Jack L.
1958 Geology of the Great Lakes. Urbana: University of Illinois Press.
1963 The prehistoric Great Lakes of North America. American Scientist 51(1):84-109.

Houghton, Frederick
1915 The geology of Erie Co. Buffalo Society of Natural Sciences Bulletin 31:1.

Hurley, William M. and I.T. Kenyon
1970 Algonkian Park archaeology: 1970. Department of Anthropology, University of Toronto.

Jennings, J.D.
1968 Prehistory of North America. New York: McGraw-Hill Book Company.

Jennings, J.D. and Edward Norbeck, eds.
1964 Prehistoric man in the New World. Chicago: The University of Chicago Press.

Johnston, Richard B.
1968 The archaeology of the Serpent Mounds site. Art and Archaeology Division, Royal Ontario Museum, Occasional Paper 10.

Kendleigh, S.C.
1961 Animal ecology. Englewood Cliffs, N.J.: Prentice-Hall.

Kenyon, Walter
1957 The Inverhuron site. Art and Archaeology Division, The Royal Ontario Museum, Occasional Paper 1.

Kenyon, Walter and Nancy S. Cameron
1961 The Brock Street burial. Art & Archaeology Division, Royal Ontario Museum, Occasional Paper 3.

Kindle, E.M. and F.B. Tyler
1913 Description of the Niagara Quadrangle. Washington: U.S. Geological Survey, Atlas, Folio:190.

Kinsey, W. Fred
1973 Archaeology in the Upper Delaware Valley. Harrisburg: Pennsylvania Historical and Museum Commission.
1974 Faucett and Byram sites: Chronology and settlement in the Delaware. Pennsylvania Archaeologist 45:1-104.

Kochan, Edward
1959 Riverhaven Sites #1 and #2, Grand Island, N.Y. The New York State Archeological Association Bulletin 22.
1962 Riverhaven #1 (Twa 4-3) Site, Grand Island, N.Y. The New York State Archeological Association Bulletin 26.
n.d.*a* A possible mortuary blade factory site. Unpublished manuscript on File. Anthropology Department, State University of New York at Buffalo.
n.d.*b* Riverhaven #2 Site, (Twa 3-3) Grand Island, N.Y.; Report 2. Unpublished manuscript on file. Anthropology Department, State University of New York at Buffalo.
n.d.*c* Riverhaven #2 (Twa 3-3) Artifact catalog. Unpublished manuscript on file. Anthropology Department, State University of New York at Buffalo.

Lee, Richard B. and Irven DeVore
1968 Man the hunter. Chicago: Aldine.

Leet, L. Don and Sheldon Judson
1971 Physical geology. Englewood Cliffs, N.J.: Prentice-Hall, Inc.

Levesque, Rene
1964 Le gisement de batiscan. Etudes Anthropolgiques, Musée National du Canada, 6.

Linduska, Joseph P., ed.
1964 Waterfowl tomorrow. Washington: U.S. Government Printing Office.

Lopez, Julius
Interior cordmarked pottery from coastal New York. In: Foundations of Pennsylvania prehistory, edited by Barry C. Kent, et al. Harrisburg: Pennsylvania Historical and Museum Commission.

McCarthy, Richard L. and Harrison Newman
1961 Prehistoric people of western New York. Buffalo and Erie County Historical Society.

MacNeish, Richard S.
1952 The archaeology of the northeastern United States. In: The archaeology of the eastern United States, edited by J.B. Griffin. Chicago: University of Chicago Press.

Mau, Clayton
1963 Experiments with the spearthrower. New York State Archeological Association Bulletin 29:1-13.

Mayer-Oakes, William J.
1955 Prehistory of the upper Ohio Valley: An introductory archeological study. Pittsburgh: Carnegie Museum.

Mitchell, Barry M.
1963 Occurrence of overall corded pottery in the upper Ottawa Valley, Canada. American Antiquity 39:114-15.

Munsen, Patrick J., Paul W. Parmalee and Richard A. Yarnell
1971 Subsistence ecology of Scovill, a Terminal Middle Woodland village. American Antiquity 36:410-31.

New York Conservation Department
1929 A biological survey of the Erie-Niagara system. Albany: J.B. Lyon.
1940 A biological survey of the Lake Ontario watershale. Albany: J.B. Lyon.

Odum, Eugene P.
1971 Fundamentals of ecology. Philadelphia: W.B. Saunders.

Ogden, J. Gordon, III
1969 Correlation of contemporary and Late Pleistocene pollen records in the reconstruction of postglacial environments in northeastern North America. Mitteilungen Internationale Vereinigung für Theoretische und Angewandte Limnologie 17:64-77.

Papworth, M.L.
1967 Cultural traditions in the Lake Forest region during the late high water stages of the post glacial Great Lakes. Unpublished Ph.D. dissertation. The University of Michigan, Ann Arbor.

Parker, Arthur C.
1922 The archaeological history of New York: Part I. Albany: New York State Museum Bulletin 235.

Plog, Fred and James N. Hill
1971 Explaining variability in the distribution of sites. In: The distribution of prehistoric population aggregates, edited by G.K. Gumerman. Prescott: Prescott College.

Potzger, J.E.
1946 Phytosociology of the primeval forest in central-northern Wisconsin and upper Michigan, and a brief post-glacial history of the Lake Forest Formation. Ecological Monographs 16:211-250.

Regier, H.A. and W.L. Hardman
1973 Lake Erie's fish community: 150 years of cultural stress. Science 180:1248-55.

Reilly, E.M. and K.C. Parkes
1959 Preliminary annotated checklist of New York State birds. Albany: New York State Museum.

Rhodes, Wendall R.
n.d. The MacCauley complex. Manuscript on file, Department of Anthropology, State University College, Geneseo, New York.

Ritchie, William
1929 Hammerstones, anvils and certain pitted stones. Researches and Transactions of the New York Archeological Association 7:2.
1932*a* The Algonkin sequence in New York. American Anthropologist 34:406-15.
1932*b* The Lamoka Lake site, the type station of the Archaic Algonkin period in New York. Researches and Transactions of the New York State Archeological Association, Lewis H. Morgan Chapter, Rochester.
1936 New evidence relating to the Archaic occupation of New York. Researches and Transactions of the New York State Archeological Association. Lewis H. Morgan Chapter, Rochester.
1944 The Pre-Iroquoian occupations of New York State. Rochester Museum of Arts and Sciences.
1949 An archaeological survey of the Trent Waterway in Ontario Canada and its significance for New York State prehistory. Researches and Transactions of The New York State Archeological Association. Rochester.
1951 A current synthesis of New York prehistory. American Antiquity 17:130-36.
1953 Point Peninsula ceremonialism in the light of recent discoveries. Eastern States Archaeological Federation Bulletin 11:7-8.
1955*a* Recent discoveries suggesting an Early Woodland burial cult in the northeast. New York State Museum and Science Service Circular 40. Albany: The University of the State of New York.
1955*b* The Northeastern Archaic — a review. New York State Museum and Science Service.

1956 Prehistoric settlement patterns in northeastern North America. In: Prehistoric settlement patterns in the New World, edited by G.R. Willey. New York: Viking Fund Publication 23.

1959 The Stony Brook site and its relation to Archaic and Transitional cultures on Long Island. New York State Museum Bulletin 372.

1962 The antiquity of pottery in the northeast. American Antiquity 27:583-84.

1965 The archaeology of New York State. Garden City: The Natural History Press.

1969 The archaeology of New York State. 2nd ed. The Natural History Press, Garden City.

1971 A typology and nomenclature for New York projectile points. Rev. ed. New York State Museum and Science Service Bulletin 384. Albany: The University of the State of New York.

1972 The Archaic in New York. New York State Archaeological Association Bulletin 52:1-12.

Ritchie, William A. and Don W. Dragoo

1960 The eastern dispersal of Adena. New York State Museum and Science Service Bulletin 379. Albany: The University of the State of New York.

Ritchie, W.A. and R.E. Funk

1973 Aboriginal settlement patterns in the northeast. New York State Museum Memoir 20.

Ritchie, William A. and Richard S. MacNeish

1949 The Pre-Iroquoian pottery of New York State. American Antiquity 15:97-124.

Robins, C.R. and E.E. Deubler

1955 The life history and systematic status of the Burbot in the Susquehanna River system. New York State Museum Circular 30.

Robbins, Maurice

1968 An Archaic ceremonial complex at Assawompsett. Attleboro: The Massachusetts Archaeological Society, Inc.

Rogers, Edward S.

1962 The Round Lake Ojibwa. Toronto: Ontario Department of Lands and Forests.

Rootenberg, S.

1964 Archaeological field sampling. American Antiquity 30:181-88.

Rostlund, Erhard

1952 Freshwater fish and fishing in native North America. Berkeley: University of California Press.

Rouse, Irving

1972 Introduction to prehistory. New York: McGraw-Hill.

Sahlins, Marshall

1972 Stone age economics. Chicago: Aldine-Atherton Inc.

Schiffer, M.B.

1972 Archaeological context and systemic context. American Antiquity 37:156-65.

Sears, William H.

1961 The study of social and religious systems in North American archaeology. Current Anthropology 2:223-46.

Shantz, H.L. and R. Zon

1924 Natural vegetation of the United States. Washington, D.C.: U.S. Government Printing Office.

Shelford, Victor E.

1963 The ecology of North America. Urbana: University of Illinois Press.

Smith, Carlyle S.
1950 The archaeology of coastal New York. Anthropological Papers of the American Museum of Natural History 43(Pt.2).

Smith, Phillip W.
1965 Recent adjustments in animal ranges. In: The quaternary of the United States, edited by H. Wright and D. Frey. Princeton: Princeton University Press.

Steward, Julian H.
1955 Theory of culture change. Urbana: University of Illinois Press.

Stewart, Margaret M., ed.
1961 Biology of the Allegheny Indian reservation and vicinity. New York State Museum Bulletin 383.

Struever, S.
1968*a* Problems, methods and organization: A disparity in the growth of archaeology. In: Anthropological archeology in the Americas, edited by Washington: The Anthropological Society of Washington.
1968*b* Woodland subsistence-settlement systems in the lower Illinois Valley In: New perspectives in archaeology, edited by Sally R. Binford and Lewis R. Binford. Chicago: Aldine.
1971 Comments on archaeological data requirements and research strategy. American Antiquity 36:9-19.

Taylor, Walter P., ed.
1956 The deer of North America. Harrisburg: Stackpole.

Trigger, Bruce G.
1968 The determinants of settlement patterns. In: settlement archaeology, edited by K.C. Chang, Palo Alto: National Press.

Taggart, David W.
1967 Seasonal patterns in settlement, subsistence and industries in the Saginaw Late Archaic. Michigan Archaeologist 13:153-70.

Thornbury, William D.
1965 Regional geomorphology of the United States. New York: John Wiley and Sons, Inc.

Tuck, James A.
1970 An Archaic Indian cemetery in Newfoundland. Scientific American 222(6):112-21.

Vonderlaan, Stanley
1966 The Waterport South site Ood 3-3. Morgan Chapter Newsletter 6:8-12.

Van Stone, James W.
1965 The changing culture of the Snowdrift Chipewayan. Ottawa: National Museum of Canada.

Von Engeln, O.D.
1961 The Finger Lakes region. Ithaca: Cornell University Press.

Wallace, Anthony F.C.
1966 Religion, an anthropological view. New York: Random House.

Watson, Patty J., S.A. LeBlanc, and C.L. Redman
1971 Explanation in archaeology. New York: Columbia University Press.

White, A.M.
1963 Analytic description of the chipped-stone industry from Snyders site, Calhoun County, Illinois. In: Miscellaneous studies in typology and classification, by Anta M. White, Mark L. Papworth and Lewis R. Binford. Museum of Anthropology, University of Michigan, Anthropological Papers 19.

White, Marian E.

1957 A salvage dig at Honeoye Lake, Museum Service 30(2):24-25.

1963 Settlement pattern change and the development of horticulture in the New York-Ontario area. Pennsylvania Archaeologist 33(1-2):1-12.

1964 The 1963 excavations on Grand Island's East River. Science on the March 44(3):48-53.

1966 The Orchid site. Ossuary, Fort Erie, Ontario. New York State Archaeologist Association Bulletin 38:1-35.

n.d. The Morrow site. Untitled and unpublished manuscript on file, Department of Anthropology, State University of New York at Buffalo.

White, Theodore A.

1953 A method of calculating the dietary percentage of various food animals utilized by aboriginal peoples. American Antiquity 18:396-18.

Whitney, Theodore

1967 A small blade cache. Chenango Chapter Newsletter, N.Y.S.A.A. 9(1):1-10.

1970 Nine Mile Swamp site #7 (Sgf-2-N). Chenango Chapter Newsletter, N.Y.S.A.A. 11(2):1-12.

Wicks, Norman J.

1973 The Frank site: A preliminary report on a Late Archaic-Early Woodland site in Genesee County. New York State Archeological Association Bulletin 59:6-13.

Willey, Gordon R., ed.

1956 Prehistoric settlement patterns in the New World. New York: Viking Fund Publications in Anthropology.

Willey, G.R. and Philip Phillips

1958 Method and theory in American archaeology. Chicago: The University of Chicago Press.

Winters, Howard C.

1959 The Archaic period. In: Illinois archaeology, edited by E. Bluhm. Urbana: Illinois Archaeological Survey.

1969 The Riverton culture. Illinois State Museum, Monograph No. 1.

Witt, Arthur Jr.

1960 Length and weight of ancient freshwater drum, *Aplodinotus grunniens*, calculated from otoliths found in Indian middens. Copeia 3:181-85.

Wobst, H. Martin

1968 The Butterfield site. In: Contributions to Michigan archaeology, by James E. Fitting, John R. Halsey, and H. Martin Wobst. Museum of Anthropology, The University of Michigan, Anthropological Papers No. 32.

Wray, Charles F.

1965 Scaccia site (Cda-17-3): An Early Woodland site near Cuylerville, New York. Morgan Chapter Newsletter 5(Summer):3-7.

Wright, H.E., Jr. and David G. Frey, eds.

1965 The quaternary of the United States. Princeton: Princeton University Press.

Wright, Gary A.

1974 Archaeology and trade. New York: Addison Wesley Publishing Co.

Wright, Henry T.

1964 A transitional Archaic campsite at Green Point. Michigan Archaeologist 10(1):17-22.

Wright, J.V.

1972*a* The Knechtel I site, Bruce County, Ontario. Archaeological Survey of Canada Paper 4.

1972*b* Ontario prehistory. Ottawa: National Museum of Canada.

Wright, J.V. and J.E. Anderson
1963 The Donaldson site. Ottawa: National Museum of Canada.

Yarnell, Richard A.
1964 Aboriginal relationships between culture and plant life in the Upper Great Lakes region. Museum of Anthropology, The University of Michigan, Anthropological Papers No. 23.

Zenkert, Charles A.
1934 Flora of the Niagara Frontier region, Buffalo Society of Natural Sciences Bulletin 16.

Zumbarge, J.H.
1957 A manual for physical geology. Dubuque: W.C. Brown.

Plate 1. Sinking Ponds site: overall site view. The primary perpendicular ridge extends to the west toward the fossil lake, one remnant of which is visible in the background. To the right of the area shown is the swale leading down from the ridge to another embayment.

Plate 2. Sinking Ponds site: Feature 2. The feature is outlined by the small stakes within the excavated area. The feature and associated subfeatures are shown by the darker compact floor.

Plate 3. Sinking Ponds site: Meadowood sidenotched projectile points.

Plate 4. Sinking Ponds site: *a-g*, cornernotched and *h-n*, stemmed projectile points.

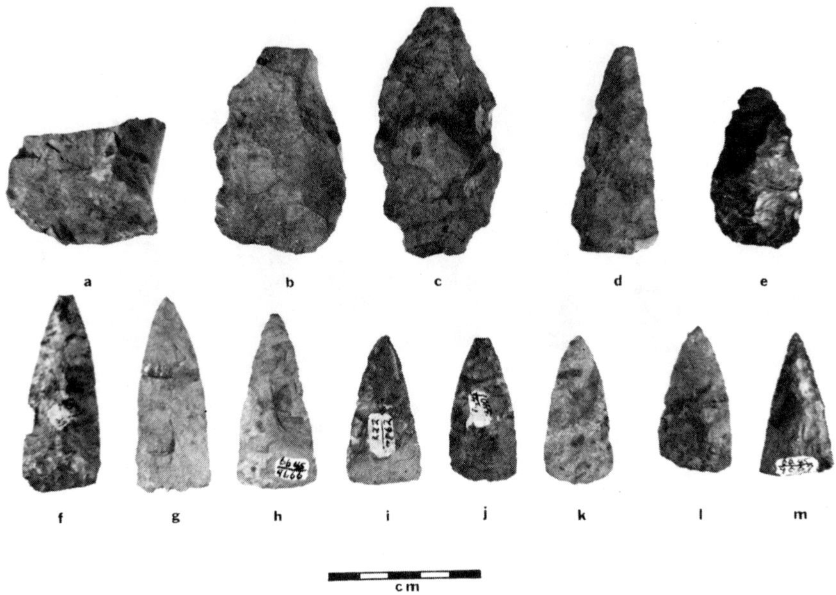

Plate 5. Sinking Ponds site: blanks. *a*, primary blank fragment; *b-c*, secondary blanks; *d-3*, tertiary blanks; *f-m*, quaternary blanks.

Plate 6. Sinking Ponds site: drills and longitudinal knife/scrapers. *a*, T-shaped drill; *b-g*, expanding base drills; *i-r*, longitudinal knife/scrapers.

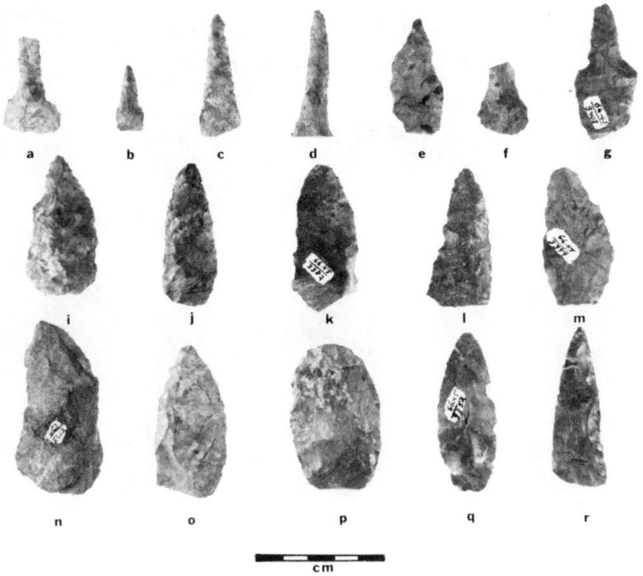

Plate 7. Sinking Ponds site: uniface scrapers. *a-d*, side scrapers; *e-g*, ovoid circumferential scrapers; *h-i*, apical circumferential scrapers, *j*, end scraper/graver; *k-n*, end scrapers; *o-q*, large circumferential scrapers; *r-s*, circumferential scrapers/gravers.

Plate 8. Sinking Ponds site: biface scrapers. *a-b*, side scrapers; *c-f*, trianguloid end scrapers; *g-1*, end scrapers; *m*, circumferential scraper/graver; *n*, circumferential scraper; *o-p*, hafted end scrapers.

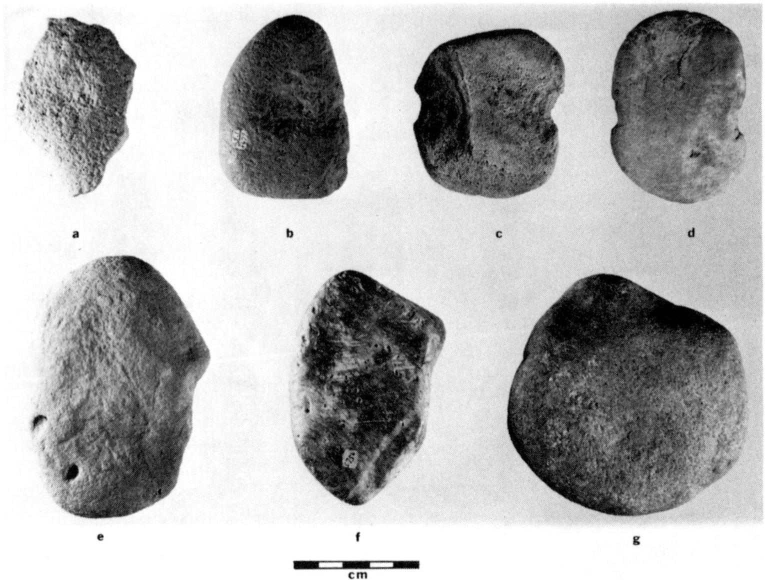

Plate 9. Sinking Ponds site: *a-b*, pitted stones; *c-e* netsinkers, and *f-g* mano abrading stones.

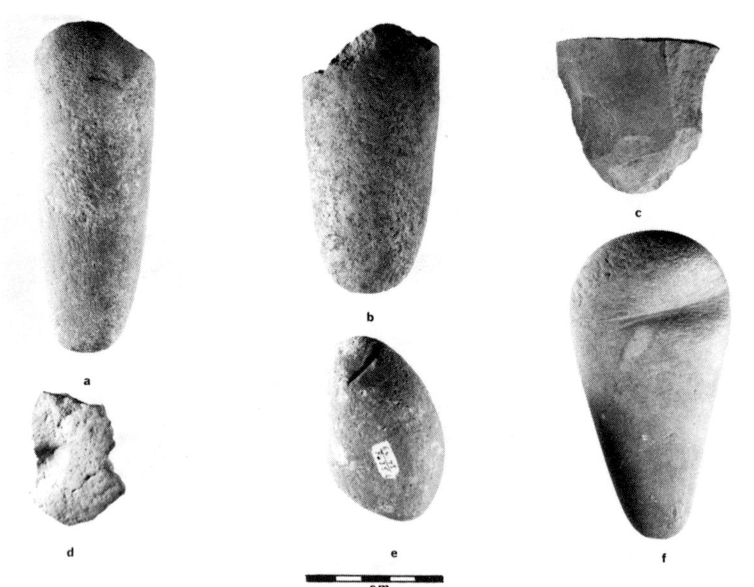

Plate 10. Sinking Ponds site: adzes and abrading stones. *a-b*, plano-convex adzes; *c*, chopper or adze blank; *d*, pitted abrading stone; *e*, narrow grooved abrading stone; *f*, bifacially grooved abrading stone.

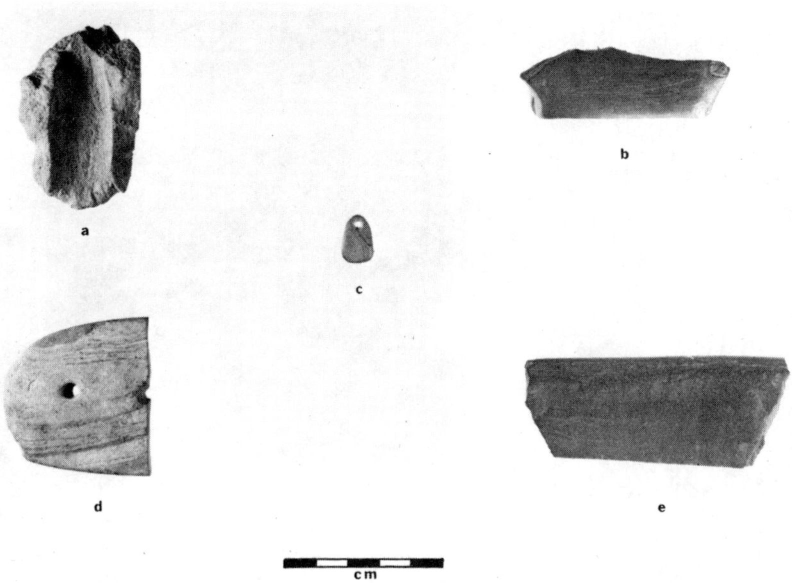

Plate 11. Sinking Ponds site: pipe, bead, birdstone, and gorgets. *a*, pipe fragment; *b*, birdstone fragment, *c*, bead; *d*, gorget fragment; *e*, gorget blank.

Plate 12. Sinking Ponds site: clay and steatite vessels. *a*, rim sherd, smooth vessel; *b-d*, rim sherds, channeled exterior vessel; *f-h*, rim sherds, Vinette I (f-interior); *e, i, j*, body sherds, Vinette I (e-interior).

Plate 13. Riverhaven 2 site: overall view of Kochan's excavations. This view looking toward the northeast shows the excavation units placed by Kochan on the low half-terrace bench. Feature 3 was disclosed in the north wall of the open unit.

Plate 14. Riverhaven 2 site: Feature 3 profile. This is the north wall profile of the manufacture/cache pit. The stone seen in the center of the profile is a hammerstone.

Plate 15. Riverhaven 2 site: Meadowood sidenotched projectile points.

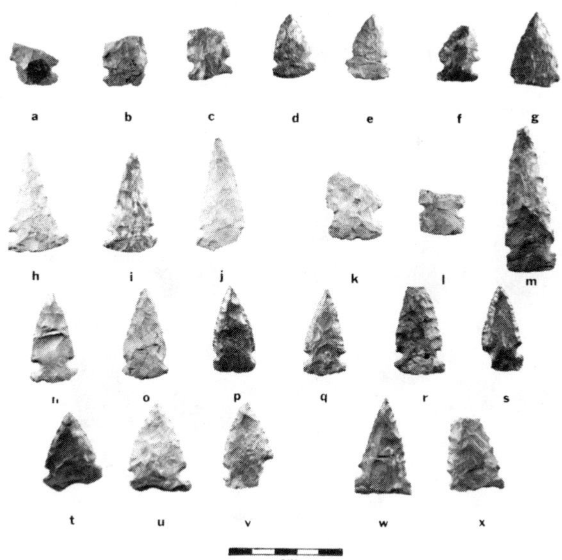

Plate 16. Riverhaven 2 site: sidenotched projectile points (Meadowood Variants). *a-g*, Variant 1; *h-j*, Variant 2; *k-m*, Variant 3; *n-s*, Variant 4; *t-v*, Variant 5; *w-x*, Variant 6.

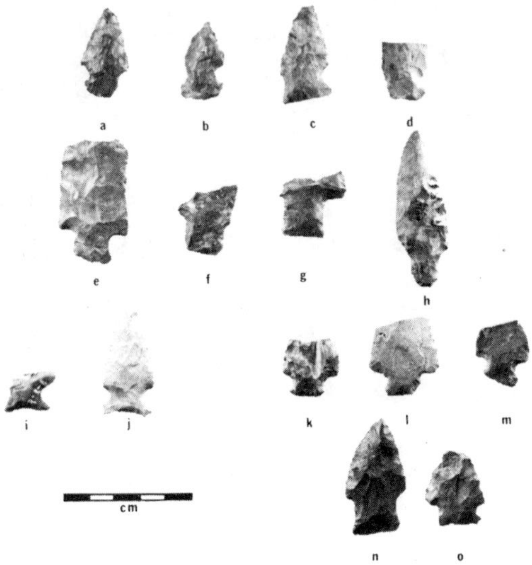

Plate 17. Riverhaven 2 site: miscellaneous projectile points. *a-d,* sidenotched projectile points; *e-h*, stemmed points; *i-o*, cornernotched points.

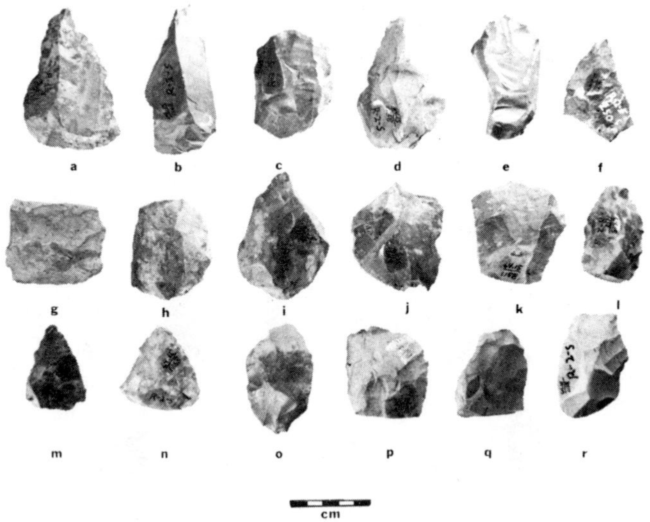

Plate 18. Riverhaven 2 site: primary blanks.

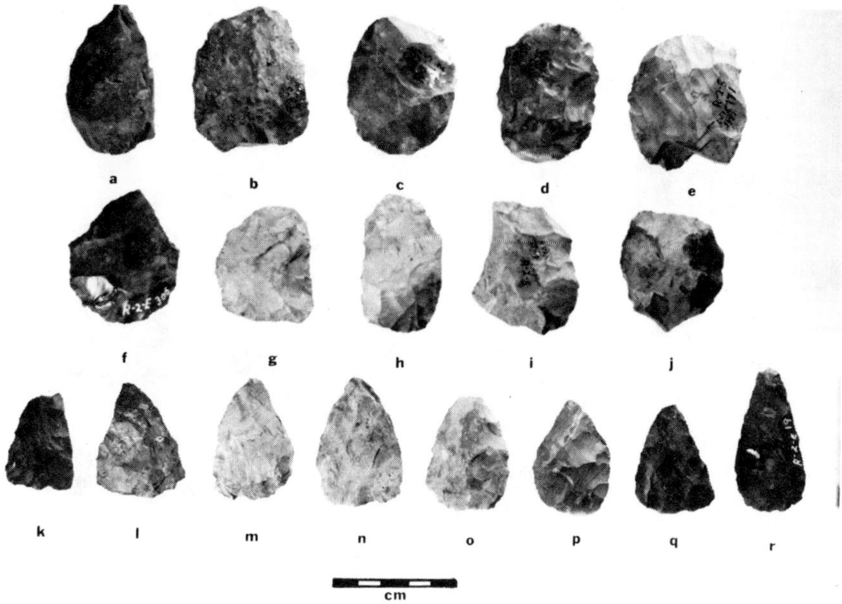

Plate 19. Riverhaven 2 site: secondary blanks.

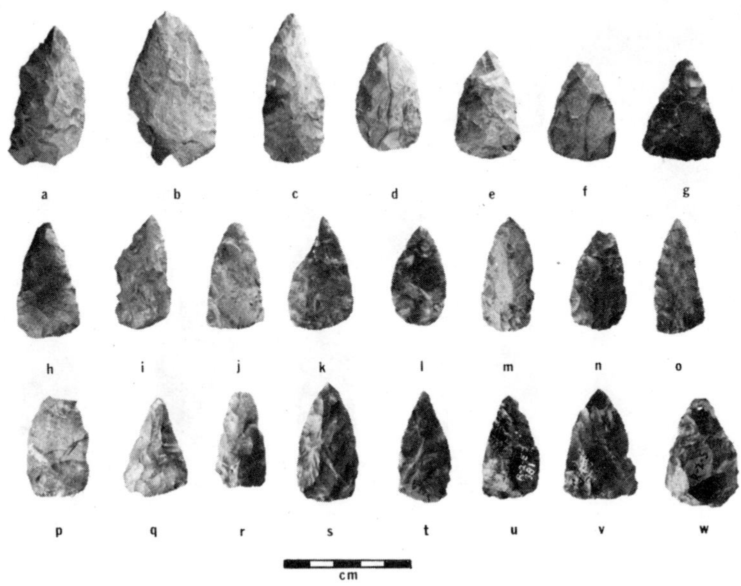

Plate 20. Riverhaven 2 site: tertiary blanks.

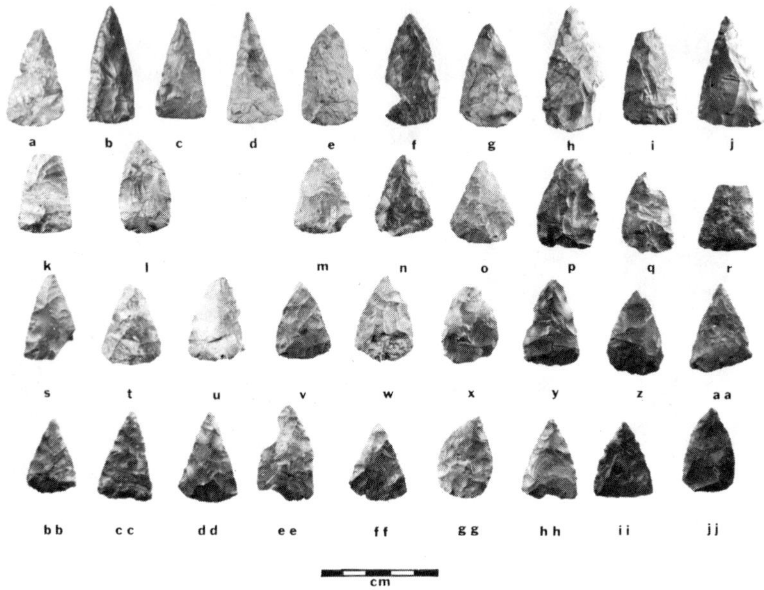

Plate 21. Riverhaven 2 site: quaternary blanks ("Mortuary Cache Blades"). *a-l,* large; *m-jj,* small.

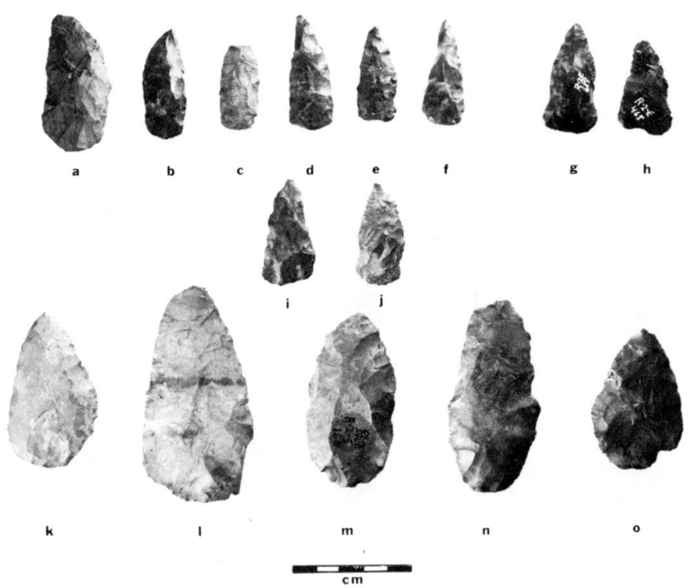

Plate 22. Riverhaven 2 site: longitudinal knife/scrapers. *a-j,* small; *k-o,* large.

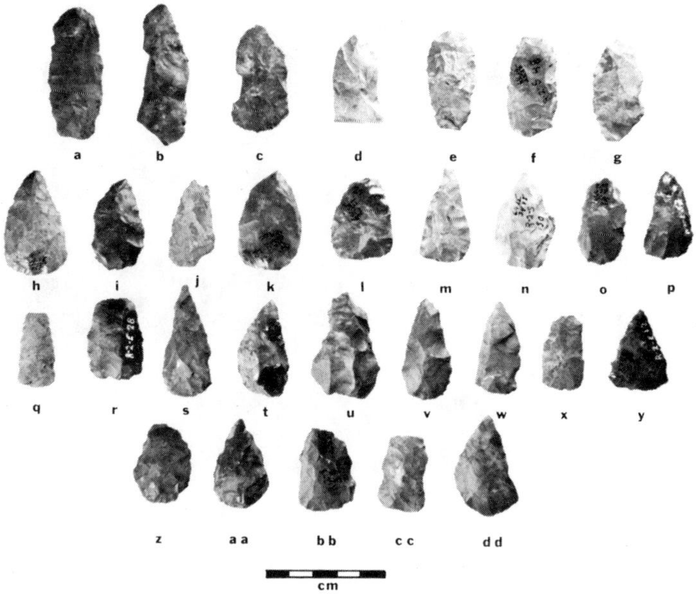

Plate 23. Riverhaven 2 site: biface sidescrapers.

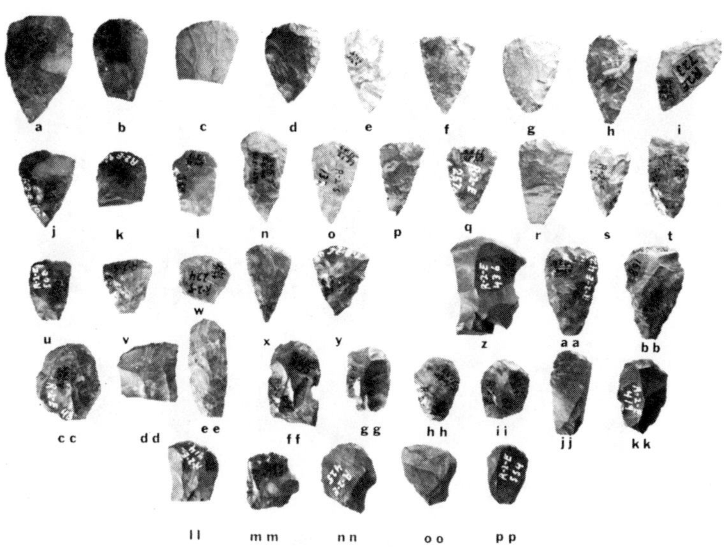

Plate 24. Riverhaven 2 site: end scrapers. *a-y*, biface trianguloid; *z-bb*, longitudinal; *cc-pp*, ovoid.

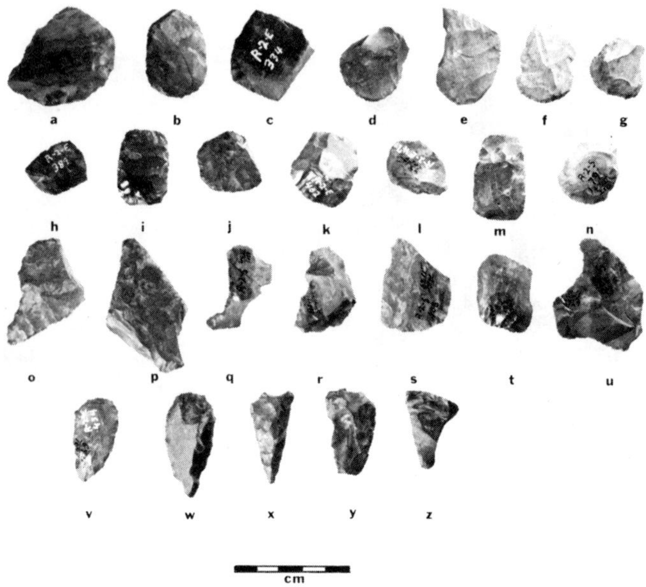

Plate 25. Riverhaven 2 site: circumferential and spokeshave scrapers. *a-n,* ovoid circumferential scrapers; *o-u,* spokeshave scrapers; *v-z,* apical circumferential scrapers.

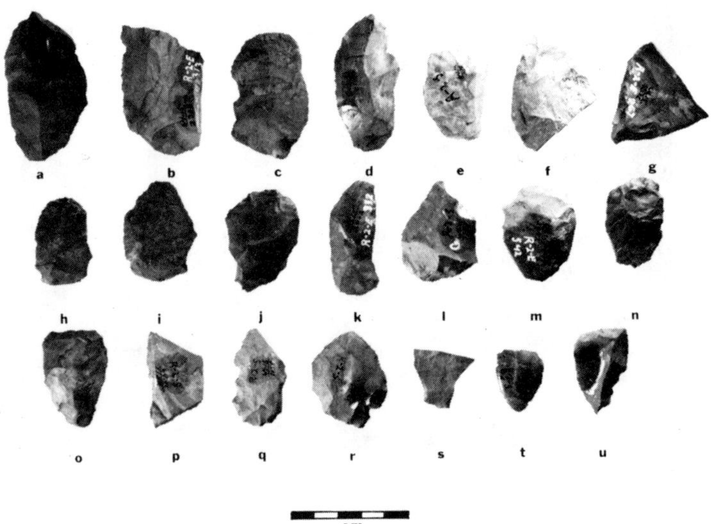

Plate 26. Riverhaven 2 site: uniface side scrapers and utilized flake scrapers. *a-o,* uniface side scrapers; *p-u,* utilized flake scrapers.

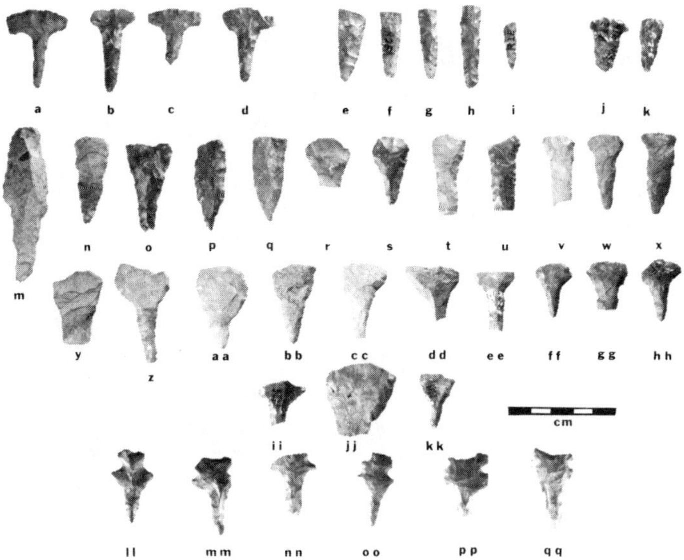

Plate 27. Riverhaven 2 site: drills. *a-d,* T-shaped base; *e-i,* shank fragments; *j-x,* expanded base (narrow); *y-kk,* expanded base (broad); *ll-qq,* hafted (side-notched).

Plate 28. Riverhaven 2 site: adzes. *a-c, e-f,* plano-convex; *d,* beveled.

Plate 29. Riverhaven 2 site: grooved abrading stones. *a, f, g,* narrow groove; *b-e, h,* broad groove.

Plate 30. Riverhaven 2 site: hammerstones and pitted stones (anvilstones). *a-b,* pitted stones (anvilstones); *d, g,* chert hammerstones; *c, e-g,* hammerstones.

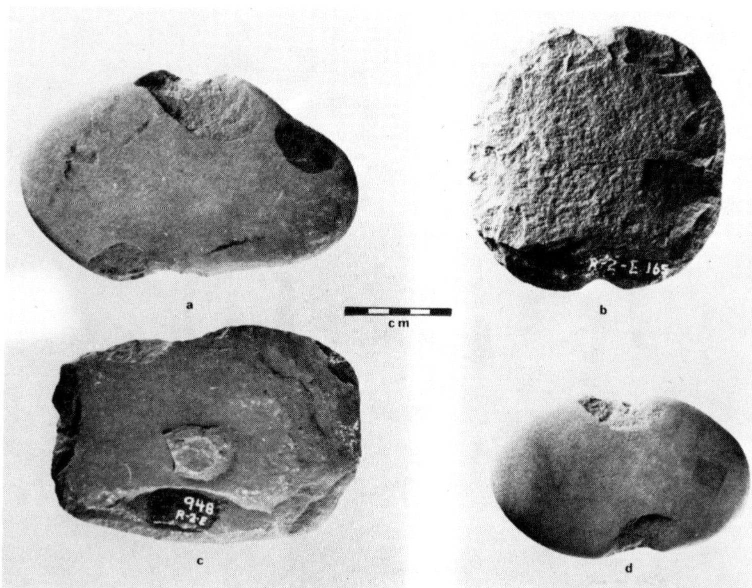

Plate 31. Riverhaven 2 site: netsinkers.

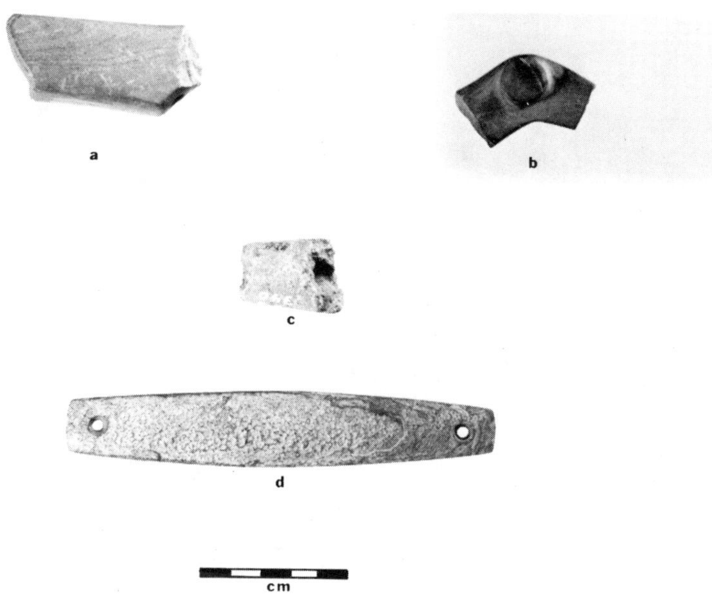

Plate 32. Riverhaven 2 site: birdstones, pipe, and gorget. *a-b,* birdstone fragments; *c,* clay pottery pipe; *d,* gorget.

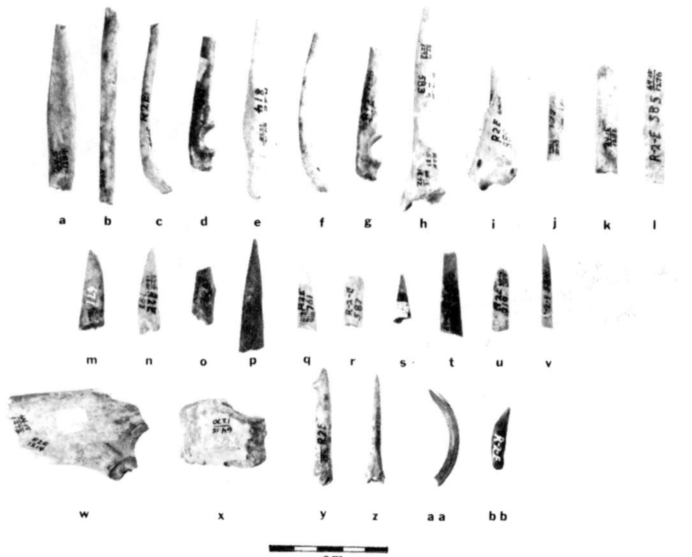

Plate 33. Riverhaven 2 site: bone and tooth artifacts. *a, d, e, g-i, m-l,* bone awls; *b, c, f, j, k, l, v,* bone pins; *w, x,* cut deer tarsal; *y,* bone "harpoon" or hook; *z,* catfish spine awl; *aa,* beaver incisor chisel; *bb,* partially drilled wolf canine.

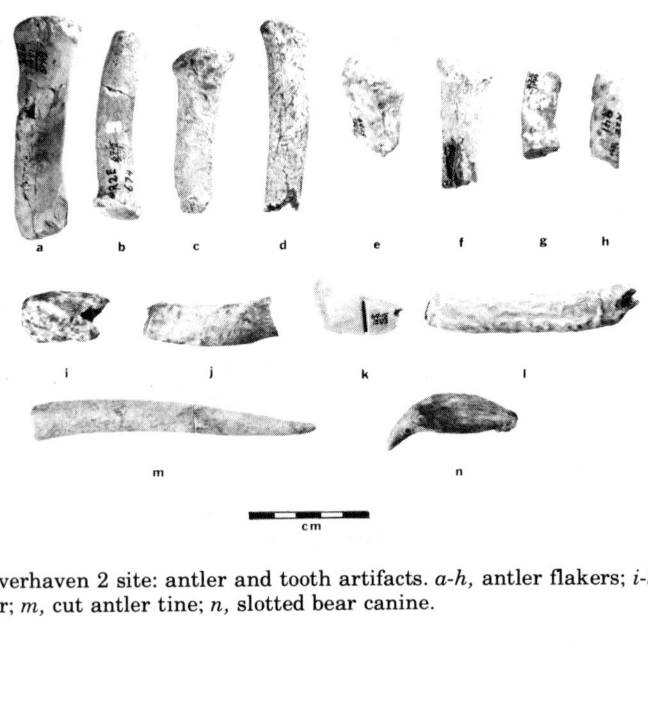

Plate 34. Riverhaven 2 site: antler and tooth artifacts. *a-h,* antler flakers; *i-l,* cut and slotted antler; *m,* cut antler tine; *n,* slotted bear canine.

Plate 35. Riverhaven 2 site: Vinette I clay pottery. *a,* rim sherd, exterior; *b,* rim sherd interior; *c-e,* body sherds, exterior; *f-h,* body sherds, interior.